ANTI-ZIONISM ON CAMPUS

D1739226

STUDIES IN ANTISEMITISM

Alvin H. Rosenfeld, *Editor*

ANTI-ZIONISM

ON CAMPUS

THE UNIVERSITY, FREE SPEECH, AND BDS

CAMPUS

Edited by
ANDREW PESSIN and DORON S. BEN-ATAR

INDIANA UNIVERSITY PRESS

This book is a publication of

Indiana University Press
Office of Scholarly Publishing
Herman B Wells Library 350
1320 East 10th Street
Bloomington, Indiana 47405 USA

iupress.indiana.edu

Library of Congress Cataloging-in-Publication Data

Names: Pessin, Andrew, editor. | Ben-Atar, Doron S., editor.
Title: Anti-Zionism on campus : the university, free speech, and BDS / edited
    by Andrew Pessin and Doron S. Ben-Atar.
Description: Bloomington, Indiana : Indiana University Press, [2018] |
    Series: Studies in antisemitism | Includes bibliographical references and
    index.
Identifiers: LCCN 2018000247 (print) | LCCN 2017060899 (ebook) | ISBN
    9780253034083 (e-book) | ISBN 9780253034076 (hardback : alk. paper) | ISBN
    9780253034069 (pbk. : alk. paper)
Subjects: LCSH: Zionism—United States—Public opinion. | Zionism—Public
    opinion. | Public opinion—United States. | Education, Higher—Political
    aspects—United States. | Boycott Divestment and Sanctions (Movement) |
    Israel—Politics and government—Foreign public opinion, American. |
    Propaganda, Anti-Israeli.
Classification: LCC DS149.5.U6 (print) | LCC DS149.5.U6 A58 2018 (ebook) |
    DDC 320.540956940973—dc23
LC record available at https://lccn.loc.gov/2018000247

1 2 3 4 5   23 22 21 20 19 18

ובמקום שאין אנשים השתדל להיות איש

In a place where there are no persons of integrity, try to be one.

—Pirke Avot 2.5

Contents

III. Concluding Thoughts

Acknowledgments

WE GRATEFULLY ACKNOWLEDGE the generous support of the Academic Engagement Network in the production of this volume. We are also grateful to Fordham University for its Marketing and Book Publishing Award in support of this volume.

ANTI-ZIONISM ON CAMPUS

Introduction and Overview: The Silencing

Andrew Pessin and Doron S. Ben-Atar

> If someone dared to publish among us books that openly favored Judaism, we would punish the author, the publisher, the book dealer. That arrangement is a convenient and sure way to always be right. It is easy to refute people who do not dare speak ... [when] conversing with Jews.... The unfortunates feel themselves at our mercy. The tyranny practiced against them makes them fearful.... I will never believe that I have rightly heard the Jews' reasoning as long as they do not have a free state, schools, universities where they might speak and argue without risk.
>
> Jean-Jacques Rousseau, *Emile*, Book IV (1762)

The Campus Situation

Change the word *Judaism* to *Israel* and *Jews* to *Zionists* and Rousseau's eighteenth-century observation is disturbingly applicable to today's campuses, two and a half centuries later. Those in the academy who support Israel, or who merely don't despise Israel, are finding it increasingly difficult to speak up without risking verbal attack, social and professional ostracization, setbacks to their careers, and sometimes even physical threats. As a result, the Israel-friendly (or merely non-anti-Israel) voice on campuses around the world and in the global "republic of letters" is rapidly being *silenced*. The implications of this phenomenon, not only for Jews but also, we believe, for free speech, for the academy, and for Western values in general, are chilling.

Where some might see in Israel a prosperous (if flawed) liberal democracy, or the only modern example of an indigenous people reclaiming lost sovereignty over its homeland, the new campus orthodoxy sees only an apartheid regime founded on racism, genocide, ethnic cleansing, and colonialist imperialism. Zionism, it believes, can be neither defended nor corrected, because the very idea of a Jewish state in that region depends on the dispossession of others and because the concept of Jewish democracy is an offensive oxymoron that can only perpetuate the unjust and discriminatory status quo. Israel and Zionism are thus cast as illegitimate, incorrigible *abominations*.

Those believing this are welcome to their opinion, of course, and should be free to advocate for it appropriately on campus and elsewhere. Indeed, freedom of speech requires tolerance of anti-Israel and even antisemitic hate speech, and we oppose efforts, however well intentioned, to spare universities this toxic scourge by denying advocacy groups a foothold on campuses.[1] The much bigger problem is that anti-Israel activists themselves are generally not interested in genuine open and honest debate. They don't want to hear what the other side says, nor let anyone else hear it, because to them there simply is no other side; they seek to delegitimize Israel and Zionism as part of a long-term strategy of destroying the lone Jewish state in the world. Painting it as an abomination is a crucial part of that strategy. In pursuing that strategy, they exchange the mantle of scholarship for activism, or use the mantle of scholarship as a cover *for* activism. The current volume will show that these thinking-class activists sacrifice the appropriate norms of scholarship and freedom of speech (including respect for truth); they violate basic community standards of civility, decency, and respectful discourse; and they regularly harass and bully Israel-friendly individuals.

The problems raised by campus hostility to Israel were already serious a decade ago when Manfred Gerstenfeld published *Academics against Israel and the Jews*.[2] Its chapters document disturbing incidents on major American campuses (such as Columbia, Harvard, and the University of California at Irvine and Santa Cruz), Canadian campuses, and campuses in Europe and Australia. As its title suggests, many of the essays are keenly aware of the blurry distinction between anti-Israelism and antisemitism.[3] However one draws that distinction, nearly every one of its chapters also attests to the fact—since empirically verified by several studies—that wherever there is a strong anti-Israel campus atmosphere, many Jewish students, staff, and faculty feel uncomfortable and often outright unwelcome.[4] Many in the anti-Israel movement deny the connection to antisemitism and sometimes even officially denounce it, but the fact remains to this day: many campus Jews experience most anti-Israel activism as a form of ethnic-based hostility. And the problems have only grown in the past decade, in both frequency and intensity.

As far as we know, there has not yet been *serious* physical harm against Jewish members of campus communities. Rather, there have been scuffles and some troubling isolated incidents, and the overall trend is worrisome. There has been plenty of physical vandalism directed toward Jews—particularly, but not only, toward those who openly support Israel—including slashed tires, broken windows, and smashed-up dorm spaces.[5] There has been an abundance of antisemitic graffiti: calls for another Holocaust,[6] "Zionists to the gas chamber,"[7] "Jews out of CUNY!,"[8] "Gas Jews Die,"[9] and swastikas appearing on dozens of campuses just in the past year alone.[10] There is increasingly intimidating verbal abuse directed toward Jews on campus, who are called "racists," "colonialists," "white supremacists," "religious supremacists," "murderers," and more. Protests and disruptions confront not only Israel-related campus events but also Jewish events, including talks by famous people about their Jewish heritage, campus Shabbat dinners, and Hillel student meetings. Jewish students receive mock eviction notices, endure week-long "Israeli Apartheid" events, confront enormous "Apartheid walls" decorated with propaganda and slogans endorsing violence, and walk the gauntlet through mock checkpoints and die-ins blaming Israel for the worst atrocities, including genocide, while angry mobs shout the violent slogan "Intifada! Intifada! Long live the Intifada!" Dozens of academic lectures, either by Israelis or about Israel, have been disrupted or invaded, often with loud chants endorsing violence, as have numerous cultural events and performances.[11] Jewish and Israel-related events are often held either secretly or under increased security, with campus and sometimes local police at hand.[12] More and more, individuals are being targeted, smeared, falsely accused of saying or doing objectionable things, shamed, singled out for public condemnation and rage, and subjected to hateful and threatening messages.

In a May 2016 incident discussed in chapter 10 of the current volume, more than fifty anti-Israel protesters stormed an Israeli film screening at the University of California at Irvine. The ten or so terrified students watching the film had to hold the doors to the room closed as the mob screamed anti-Israel and antisemitic chants and pounded, trying to get in.[13] According to an official document we obtained, one female student "who had briefly stepped out of the classroom to call her mother was refused re-entry while the mob yelled 'if we can't go in, you can't go in.' The protesters physically blocked [her] from the door, yelled at, and hounded her as she tried to get away. The protesters were so emboldened that they chased [her] into a building where she came across a woman who helped her hide in an unlocked room. [She] hid in terror, crying on her cell phone to her mother who called the police while the protesters searched for [her]." Police finally arrived to remove the protesters and to escort the trapped students out of the screening room.[14] A similar scene occurred in October 2016 at the University College London, when Jews and Israel supporters were trapped in a locked room by screaming protesters until the police could rescue them.[15]

Such incidents are occurring on campuses all over the world. They may start off as political activism but all too often degenerate into hate-filled aggression directed not merely toward Israel and Israeli Jews, but also, despite efforts to disguise it, toward Jews *simpliciter*. It is hard to look at the pattern of incidents over the past few years, many of which are documented in this volume, and not worry that serious physical violence is not too far off in the future. That antisemitic incidents, including violent attacks, continue to be a growing concern in general, particularly in Europe, only increases the sense of foreboding.[16] It is not exactly comforting that UK police recently advised Jewish and pro-Israel students to not publicly announce the locations of their events,[17] nor that the UK government pledged millions to protect every "Jewish school, college, nursery, and synagogue" in the country.[18]

Campus anti-Israel hostility has recently escalated so severely that Jewish and Israel advocacy groups have finally begun kicking into high gear to combat it. Money is being spent, conferences are being held, and legal measures are being pursued on the federal and state levels. Alumni groups are forming to monitor anti-Israel extremism at their alma maters, and Jewish communities are holding workshops to prepare high school students for what they're going to experience in college. The *Algemeiner*, a daily news source focused on Jewish and Israel-related matters, recently created an entire Campus Bureau to document the phenomenon, a bureau of which one of us is editor (Pessin) and in that capacity has come to appreciate the scope of Israel hostility on campuses around the world.

There is some debate about what to call the growing anti-Israel activism. *Anti-Zionism* is the most common term, while some refer to it as the *new antisemitism*. Both are valid terms. New antisemitism connects the singling out of Israel to two millennia of anti-Jewish prejudice and notes that the tropes of anti-Israel arguments often echo traditional antisemitic accusations of Jewish conspiracy, blood libels, Jewish control of media, banks, and politics, and more. Anti-Zionism is fundamentally about denying to Jews territorial self-determination in their ancient homeland, for example by openly calling for the destruction of Israel as a Jewish state. Since most campus hostility in fact directly targets the State of Israel itself—its policies, its practices, its citizens, and its very existence—we ourselves have opted here to use the term *anti-Israelism* and its cognates. Nevertheless, we have kept *anti-Zionism* for the book's title in light of its common use, and we have allowed each contributor to use the terminology he or she considers most appropriate.

With that in mind, the problem, we believe, is not merely a Jewish or Israel one. For as the essays in this volume show, campus anti-Israelism isn't merely an attack on Israel, or on Israel-friendly members of the campus community, or Jews in general. As Stanford University president John Hennessy has warned, the "atmosphere of intimidation or vitriol" generated by campus anti-Israelism "endangers our ability to operate as an intellectual community."[19] Or, in other words, anti-Israelism is an attack on the very norms and values of the university—and with it, some might argue, on the norms and values at the heart of Western civilization.

The Thesis of This Volume

The essays in this volume will show that obsessive anti-Israelism corrodes the academy in nearly every way on nearly every level, undermining its most fundamental values.

It corrodes scholarship, limiting the kinds of questions scholars can ask and leading scholars to violate the most basic academic norms. It corrodes teaching and the classroom, turning what should be learning spaces welcoming diverse points of view into political advocacy forums for the reigning orthodoxy that intimidate and silence divergent voices. It corrodes entire departments and disciplines, diverting them from their academic missions and subject matters. It corrodes academic organizations, causing them also to abandon their professional missions and disciplinary focus.[20] It corrodes student governments, forcing them to divert their attention for months to a foreign policy matter concerning a complicated conflict half a world away rather than spending their scant time and resources on students' most immediate pressing concerns. It corrodes civility, by rejecting it as a tool of oppression while at the same time using its codes to stifle dissent, and with the deterioration of civility comes the corrosion of community. Anti-Israel campaigns are stunningly divisive. They bring out animosities that undermine the collegiality essential to the efficient functioning of the institution. After such campaigns, people stop speaking to colleagues, stop participating in campus events, stop accepting invitations to social gatherings, and stop working together. How could you act collegially, after all, when anti-Israelists have informed you that colleagues who support Jewish self-determination in their ancestral homeland are, in fact, unconditionally racist, genocidal ethnic cleansers?

This volume focuses on the struggles of some in the academy against the rising anti-Israel orthodoxy, providing stories of individuals who have been on the receiving end of anti-Israel intimidation, harassment, and smear campaigns.[21] These battles can and do destroy personal and professional reputations, work environments, and relationships, and subject their targets to emotional and psychological duress, including, in some cases, death threats. We thus aim to put a personal face on the issue to drive home the point that the problem isn't only *intellectual*; it's not about arguments for or against this or that policy or position. It is about people—mostly, but not only, Jewish people—who are in what one would expect to be an enlightened environment but where being enlightened increasingly means being against Israel, against Israeli Jews, and often by extension, against Jews in general. It is about how profoundly uncomfortable it is becoming on campuses for anyone who is not exclusively hostile to Israel, and particularly for Jews.

On this point, it's worth stressing that the individuals who tell their stories here are not all *pro-Israel* in any strong sense of that phrase and certainly not *right wing* in the relevant senses of that phrase. Many self-identify as left wing, sometimes very much so—here meaning that they are highly critical of many Israeli policies (including its ongoing control of territories captured in 1967) and strongly supportive of self-determination and other rights for the Palestinians. Indeed, neither this volume's editors nor its contributors believe that Israel is immune to criticism or that freedom of speech to criticize Israel must be limited or suppressed. Many of its contributors have, in fact, done their share of such criticism. The point of this volume, assuredly, is not to defend Israel, either in general or from any of the specific charges regularly levied against it.

That said, there is something about the specific *manner* in which anti-Israelism manifests on campuses that is deeply disturbing. Its proclamations notwithstanding, it often does not operate like a genuinely academic movement governed by the ordinary norms of the academy, which include both intellectual norms (such as objectivity, rigor, and the pursuit of truth) and moral or social norms (such as civility and respect). An academic movement governed by those norms would favor freedom of speech and welcome the diversity of views. But this is not the case, as campus anti-Israelism refuses even to entertain the possibility that Israel is not entirely evil and that Israeli Jews, being not entirely demonic, have a legitimate claim of their own to self-determination in their ancestral homeland.

No, anti-Israelism seems—in its many corrosive effects on all aspects of the academy and particularly in its invasions, disruptions, and personal attacks on those who do not absolutely hate Israel—to be about something much darker. Not dialogue, debate, and free exchange of ideas; not openness, pluralism, and diversity; not the pursuit of knowledge that ought to characterize the Western university, as well as the civilization of which the university is the heart, but rather:

Silencing.[22]

Boycott, Divestment, and Sanctions (BDS)

BDS is the well-known acronym for the Boycott, Divestment, and Sanctions campaign against Israel, although it is frequently employed as a name for the anti-Israel movement in general. On campuses, it often takes the form of a student government resolution calling on the institution to boycott or divest from Israel. However, anti-Israelism is significant or even dominant on many campuses even when no such resolution is under consideration—at least not yet.

It is not an accident that universities are a primary arena for BDS activists. As one of our contributors, English professor Cary Nelson, puts it: "BDS supporters target universities because faculty and students can become passionate about justice, sometimes without adequate knowledge about the facts and consequences. Like other targeted institutions in civil society, universities also offer the potential for small numbers of BDS activists to leverage institutional status and reputation for a more significant cultural and political impact."[23]

To these points—which will be amply documented in the current volume—we may add three others.

First, it's not merely that the largely progressive humanities and social sciences of the academy are passionate about justice. It's that this otherwise admirable passion for justice can readily serve to mask a deeper, darker agenda. Hostility toward Israel and toward Israeli Jews can conveniently be framed as a passion for justice, for human rights, for diversity, and for equality.[24] Activists can think of themselves as "pro-Palestinian" even while pursuing actions and policies that are often far more accurately labeled as "anti-Israel."[25] Endorsement and dissemination of the most despicable antisemitic tropes—that the blood libels are true; that Jews control the banks, the media, and the world; that Israelis are Nazis and baby-killers; and so on—are justified as being "for the Palestinians" rather than "against the Jews." As such, campus anti-Israelism makes possible a strange alliance between left-wing progressive groups and extremely antiprogressive groups that ordinarily would have nothing to say to each other.[26] Campuses are now places where protolerance, prodiversity, antiracism groups can make common cause with intolerant, antidiversity, straightforwardly antisemitic groups that target Israel in general and Israeli Jews specifically.

Second, the BDS movement is unlikely to move the government of Israel to modify policies, much less convince Israeli Jews (as BDS activists would like) to give up on Zionism and quit the land. As we document below, since the launching of the BDS campaign in Durban the Israeli economy has only grown and BDS activists know it.[27] Their assault in fact is not on the state of Israel but on the community of Israel supporters abroad, in particular on diaspora Jews. BDS, like previous forms of racial antisemitism, thus turns Jewishness itself into a source of shame—an inescapably innate sin and stain.

Third, as Alan Dershowitz and others point out, BDS supporters are in it for the long haul.[28] Their immediate goal is to get universities to pass BDS resolutions. But their long-term goal is to transform the minds of impressionable and passionate young students by bombarding them with the most toxic images of Israel possible. BDS campaigns take over campuses sometimes for months, with anti-Israel lectures, performances, and films; separation walls; and checkpoints, often culminating in a spring Israeli Apartheid Week before turning (perhaps) to days of campus argument for a student government BDS resolution.[29] These events are rarely dry or factual or scholarly but rather emotional, graphic, imagistic, and sloganistic, designed to pair *Israel* with words such as *apartheid, racist, colonial,* and such. On many campuses, students spend an entire academic year repeatedly confronted with these toxic images and word pairings. They may learn little about Israel or the Israeli-Palestinian conflict, but they will come away with *Israeli Apartheid* burned into their brains.

These are the brains of those who, in one or two decades' time, will be the leaders, thinkers, politicians, journalists, and teachers—the opinion-makers— of their generation. They (like all of us) may remember little of the specifics of what they learned in classes or heard in lectures, but those toxic images, the toxic impression, will remain with them.

That is the long-term goal of the BDS movement. And the essays in this volume suggest it is well on its way to achieving this goal.

A Brief History of the BDS Movement

Boycotts against Jews and the Jewish state are hardly new. Featured during various periods and in various European regions, they were also employed by the Arab national movement during the early days of the conflict in Mandatory Palestine. Boycotts against Israel itself began immediately upon its founding, the most famous being the Arab League boycott initiated in 1948 and still officially in place to this day, though only sporadically and ambiguously enforced.[30] The current BDS movement thus continues the long history of boycotting Jews, as the latest iteration in what the late historian Robert Wistrich aptly called "the longest hatred."[31] Whether you think that anti-Israelism and BDS are antisemitic in the traditional sense or not—and at present, we may lack the historical and political perspectives to reach a decisive conclusion about that—a complete understanding of the movement would necessarily place it in that historical context.[32]

That said, many trace the origin of today's BDS movement specifically to the United Nations World Conference against Racism, convened in Durban, South Africa, in the late summer of 2001.[33] Although mandated to address global concerns, the Durban conference, along with its concurrent forum of nongovernmental organizations (NGOs), soon devolved into such obsessive Israel-bashing and blatant antisemitism that it generated walkouts by the United States, Israel, the Jewish Caucus, and others.[34] The Durban NGO forum subsequently produced a declaration that repeatedly smeared Israel with the word *apartheid* and thus unleashed a global campaign of delegitimization against the Jewish state.[35] It launched this anti-Israel campaign (incidentally) precisely as the Second Intifada, with its many deadly suicide bombings murdering hundreds of Israeli civilians, was raging in full force.

Numerous boycott calls followed, borrowing language directly from the Durban NGO declaration. British, French, Italian, and Australian academics called for a scientific and academic boycott in 2002.[36] Activists launched divestment drives at the University of California and then at Columbia, Harvard, Massachusetts Institute of Technology (MIT), Princeton, and elsewhere. BDS soon made its way into nonacademic domains as well. In 2004, the Church of Sweden instituted an economic boycott,[37] while mainline Protestant churches in the US began public condemnations of Israel as early as 2003 and, by 2004, were calling for a phased divestment plan.[38] Trade and labor unions in Canada and the United Kingdom were quick to get in on the action as well, as contributions in the current volume attest.

Palestinian opponents of Jewish self-determination also swung into action. In 2002, a group of Palestinian organizations, including the Palestinian NGO Network, called for a comprehensive boycott of Israel, followed in 2003 by Palestinian academics and intellectuals calling for an academic boycott.[39] In 2004, the official Palestinian Campaign for the Academic and Cultural Boycott of Israel (PACBI) was founded by (among others) Omar Barghouti, who remains a key leader and, for many, the public face of the BDS movement today. A year later, in July 2005, some 170 "Palestinian political parties, organizations, trade unions and movements" endorsed a "Palestinian Civil Society Call for BDS."[40] Subsequently, the BDS National Committee (BNC) formed in 2007 to serve "as the Palestinian coordinating body for the BDS campaign worldwide."[41] In 2009, Palestinian Christians issued the *Kairos Document* to mobilize global Christian support for BDS as well.[42]

The civil society call has since played an important role in the BDS movement—for it allows the activists to answer the regularly posed objection that their single-minded focus on boycotting Israel (among all the far worse human rights violators in the world) smacks of antisemitism. Why focus only on Israel? Answer: "We are just answering Palestinian civil society's call for help."[43] That "the call" actually came after several years of vigorous international boycotting activity is easily overlooked, particularly since the call also provides an important appealing veneer for the BDS movement. The people suffering are calling for help. Surely the right and decent thing to do is to help them. Plus—of course—the mode of help, the boycott, is "nonviolent," at least officially, exactly the kind of mode of activism that decent people pursue.[44]

But when we dig a little, things look somewhat different.

To be sure, the movement is diverse. Many well-intentioned individuals sincerely believe that they are engaged in a nonviolent human rights campaign and that exerting international pressure on Israel in the form of BDS actually serves the overall cause of peace between the two peoples. But these same individuals are perhaps unaware of the organizational structures and sinister agenda that fuel the movement. Studies of the BDS coalitions find broad and deep financial, material, and ideological connections to antisemitic jihadi and terrorist organizations, including the Muslim Brotherhood and the Popular Front for the Liberation of Palestine.[45] Congressional testimony about the involvement of America's Hamas backers in campus BDS campaigns suggests that significant actors in the BDS movement subscribe to that group's antisemitic and eliminationist agenda.[46] To make matters worse, evidence indicates that American tax dollars also go to support the campus activities of these individuals.[47]

Indeed, the picture that emerges upon investigation is that of a central group of hard-core activists, driven by less-than-noble ideals (including that of destroying the lone Jewish state in the world and even murdering Jews), initiating and guiding the campus BDS campaign—and successfully increasing the campaign's appeal to a less well-informed, more nobly motivated coalition of progressive activists by marketing what is actually a hateful attack on the rights and physical safety of Israeli Jews as a peaceful social justice movement responding to a grassroots call by ordinary Palestinians. Through intersectional coalitions with activists for ethnic minorities, for gay and women's rights, and against globalization, these hard-core activists have made the destruction of Israel synonymous with progress and justice.[48] Opposing the movement has become synonymous with being on the wrong side of the historical arc of the "moral universe" that, as Theodore Parker famously declared, "bends toward justice."[49]

That BDS presents itself as a nonviolent, pro-peace, social justice movement is what allows many otherwise well-intentioned, decent people to sign on to it. But what if it is not that at all? What if, instead, it has no interest in peace (between peoples) but seeks the destruction of one people at the hands of the other; has no interest in justice except to deprive one people of all rights for the benefit of the other; and proclaims its peacefulness while working in alignment with parties that openly advocate violence?

What if, in other words, the acclaimed writer Cynthia Ozick gets it right?

> Beneath an ostensibly weaponless crust, [the boycott movement] brings no critical inquiry to the ethos it silently and unblinkingly validates—a predatory ethos that justifies the continued siege and bloody ambush of random civilians, a boy on his bike, a girl asleep in her bed, rabbis at prayer, passengers in a bus, families in cars, celebrants at a Seder, city folk in pubs. It is, besides, an officially sanctioned ethos that lauds teenage stabbers, car-rammings, kidnappings, a school curriculum instilling hatred of Jews from kindergarten on, children's summer camps training for the killing of Jews, proud mothers celebrating their murdering sons as heroes and patriots and servants of God.[50]

In fact, the movement's leaders make no secret of its actual goals—even if they sometimes present them carefully and ambiguously to their Western audiences.[51]

BDS's Rejection of Coexistence

Put simply, the leaders of the BDS movement reject entirely the legitimacy of Jewish self-determination. They, therefore, oppose the two-state solution, which recognizes the Jewish state's legitimacy, at least within the pre-1967 borders. Consider, for example, these statements by Omar Barghouti, reflecting opinions expressed countless times over by BDS leaders and activists:[52]

> If the occupation [of 1967 lands] ends, would that end our call for BDS? No, it wouldn't.[53]

> The Right of Return is something we cannot compromise on.... I clearly do not buy into the two-state solution.... If the refugees were to return, you

would not have a two-state solution. You would have a Palestine next to a Palestine, rather than a Palestine next to Israel.[54]

People fighting for refugee rights, like I am, know that you cannot reconcile the Right of Return for refugees with a two-state solution. That is the big white elephant in the room, and people are ignoring it—a return for refugees would end Israel's existence as a Jewish state. The Right of Return is a basic right that cannot be given away; it's inalienable. A two-state solution was never moral, and it's no longer working.[55]

A Jewish state in Palestine in any shape or form cannot but contravene the basic rights of the indigenous Palestinian ... most definitely we oppose a Jewish state in any part of Palestine.... Ending the occupation doesn't mean anything if it doesn't mean upending the Jewish state itself.[56]

Calls for destroying the Jewish state—which would surely involve the expulsion and perhaps deaths of many Jews—ought to be incompatible with progressive principles that support diversity, tolerance, and equality. You would think—you would hope—that intellectuals, professors, and students would see through the human rights language and understand that this is what, in fact, BDS is calling for.

Apparently not.[57]

The social-justice veneer allows BDS to appeal to a wide range of campus groups. Students for Justice in Palestine (SJP), the primary anti-Israel campus organization, regularly allies with other (genuinely) progressive campus groups, including various ethnic groups (such as Black Lives Matter or Latinx groups); feminist groups; lesbian, gay, bisexual, transgender, questioning, queer (LGBTQ) groups; and so on. Many of these then end up cosponsoring, with SJP, student government BDS resolutions—despite the fact that Israel generally shares their same progressive values, while the Arab and Muslim societies that seek Israel's destruction generally do not. Indeed, if you were to compare how well gays, women, ethnic minorities, religious minorities, and such fare in Israel (for all its many warts) as compared to those in the Palestinian territories or most Arab or Muslim countries, it is quite clear which side these campus groups probably *ought* to be supporting—that is, if human rights is their driving concern. The social-justice veneer of the BDS movement is so effective, then, that it misleads groups into ultimately opposing even their own agendas.

That it is just a veneer, *even on campus*, is clear. In April 2016 at the University of Minnesota, SJP sponsored a student government bill in the name of human rights, calling for divestment from companies that do business with Israel. But when opponents amended the bill so that it would apply not just to Israel but to all alleged human rights violators, and thus no longer singled out Israel, SJP removed its sponsorship.[58] The same month at the University of Chicago, the groups that had advocated for an earlier anti-Israel BDS resolution on the basis of human rights refused to support a similar resolution introduced against China.[59] Instead, they expressed concern about how passing such a resolution might alienate Chinese students on their campuses; they realized that they didn't know all the facts about a complicated foreign situation—concerns that were deemed irrelevant when Israel was the target. At the same university in February 2016, Palestinian human rights activist Bassem Eid was shouted down and confronted with death threats.[60] Why? Because he dedicated his remarks not to Israeli abuses of Palestinian human rights but to such abuses by the Palestinian authorities. These representative cases suggest that BDS activists are less concerned with human rights in general, and even with the human rights of Palestinians, than they are with vilifying Israel.

This point is only reinforced when we take a closer look at SJP.

Students for Justice in Palestine (SJP), Campus Tactics, and Anti-Normalization

Hatem Bazian, then a graduate student at the University of California, Berkeley and now a professor there, founded SJP in 2001. Believing that the Muslim identities of both the General Union of Palestinian Students (GUPS) (founded in Egypt in the 1950s) and the Muslim Student Association (affiliated with the Muslim Brotherhood) limited their potential broader appeal, Bazian cast SJP as a secular human rights organization, albeit one whose agenda was largely indistinguishable from its Islamist root organizations.[61] The strategy has paid off. SJP has grown rapidly over the past decade, with chapters now in some two hundred American universities.[62] As of November 2017, its national Facebook page had thirty-five hundred likes and its Twitter feed had over forty-five hundred followers, numbers generously supplemented by the social media presence of its local chapters. It has now emerged as the primary sponsor of campus anti-Israel activism.[63]

SJP sometimes sponsors bona fide campus lectures by serious credentialed scholars who present serious scholarship—precisely as they should in a university setting committed to a diversity of perspectives engaged in reasonable, civil debate in the mutual pursuit of truth and knowledge. The problem is that SJP also brings to campus speakers who depict Israel as a genocidal monster while peddling variations of the old antisemitic blood-libel trope. And SJP members, calling for Israel's destruction with violence-endorsing slogans, often intimidate fellow students and professors, in some cases even assaulting Jewish students.[64]

Then there are the menacing (and sometimes violent) disruptions of campus Israel-related lectures and events, many of which are documented in this volume.[65] The disruptions take different forms, but they commonly feature a large group of activists standing up and cutting off the speaker, lining up in front of the room and screening the speaker from the crowd, shouting hateful and violent slogans through megaphones, slandering the speaker (calling him or her a murderer or a rapist), and slandering Israel about apartheid and genocide and calling for its destruction. Sometimes they get explicitly violent, including smashed windows and physical confrontations, particularly if audience members resist (as they did at the University of Texas and University of Sydney incidents discussed in this volume). Sometimes the activists manage to shut down the event entirely; at the very least, they delay it and derail it. The experience is deeply disturbing to those who are subjected to it.

The message these episodes convey—these acts of intimidation, these shout-downs, these chants of "Intifada! Intifada!"—is clear: Israeli voices or perspectives, even those critical of the policies of the Israeli government, must not be allowed on campuses.[66]

So proclaims the increasingly popular anti-Israel doctrine of anti-normalization. Although there are local variations in policy and tactics, SJP and its BDS allies oppose any form of normal engagement with Israel, its representatives, or its advocates. The "theory" is simple: Israel and Israeli Jews are such abominations that it is immoral not only to engage them but also to let them function. Any interaction with Israeli entities gives them legitimacy and diverts attention from their evil acts, beliefs, and essence. The same is true for any organization or individual who does not entirely repudiate the Zionist entity. You cannot allow pro-Israel individuals and groups to do *anything* "normal"—sponsor a lecture, have a meal, attend a performance, or even come to the discussion table—for that too would legitimize them and divert attention away from their evilness.

This policy has been encouraged by SJP's national leadership and instituted at important chapters, including the New York City chapter[67] and chapters at campuses such as Columbia and Yale.[68] But it traces directly back to broader elements in the Muslim and Arab world, including PACBI,[69] and indeed reveals the intimate relationship between campus anti-Israelism and the broader BDS movement. Consider, for example, the very idea of the cultural boycott of Israel, which generates regular disruptions of Israeli performances and exhibitions abroad and unleashes massive social media campaigns against any artist or musician who contemplates performing in Israel.[70] Such a boycott can only be construed as part of an antinormalization project since, as our contributor Cary Nelson puts it, "there aren't any symphonies or art museums doing military research";[71] they can't be charged with the "complicity in Israel's crimes" that is often invoked (however flimsily) to justify commercial and academic boycotts.[72]

Nor does the broader antinormalization campaign target *only* Israelis and their advocates. It also targets those who simply want to learn something about Israel or even prefer to stay neutral on the conflict. In recent incidents at the University of California, Los Angeles, for example, non-Jewish students in the student government were harassed by SJP for accepting trips to Israel to learn about the country and its perspective on the conflict. Further, as described in chapter 26 of this volume, the non-Jewish president of the graduate student government there was subjected to months-long harassment by SJP, including an SJP-initiated university investigation that required him to obtain legal counsel, simply because he wanted the student government to adopt a neutrality policy with respect to the conflict.

Antinormalization also targets *Palestinians* who are willing to engage with the evil entity or its advocates.[73] In an April 2016 joint interview, for just one example, BDS leader Omar Barghouti vigorously denounced normalization while his colleague condemned three propeace groups that were working with Palestinians in the Palestinian territories and promoting coexistence.[74] As Syracuse University political scientist Miriam Elman comments, "All three of these organizations have as their stated mission to bring Israelis and Palestinians together in an effort to build trust and create the grassroots infrastructure upon which they believe that peace can be forged.... It may be a fool's errand, but if you care about peace, justice, and human rights then certainly bringing people together to try to promote greater understanding and mutual acceptance is something worthy of support."[75]

In the name of peace, diversity, human rights, and justice, the BDS movement shuns and disrupts the very individuals who genuinely *are* working for peace, diversity, human rights, and justice—for *all*. BDS activists are not only uninterested in dialogue themselves; they oppose *anyone* engaging in dialogue—with Israel, with Israelis, with anyone even minimally sympathetic with the cause of Israeli Jews. They don't want anyone even to *see* or *experience* Israelis, so they harass "Birthright" tables, demand hummus be removed from campus shelves, and shut down cultural performances.

In this climate, disturbing incidents at Brown University in March 2016—discussed in chapter 30 of the current volume—and at London's School of Oriental and African Studies (SOAS) in January 2017 come as no surprise. At Brown, a Hillel-affiliated social justice student group called Moral Voices had cosponsored (with other campus groups such as the Queer Alliance and the LGBTQ center) a campus visit by leading transgender activist Janet Mock. The Brown chapter of SJP launched a campaign to persuade Mock to reject the cosponsorship of Moral Voices, accusing its fellow student group of "pinkwashing"—that is, of trying to distract attention from alleged Israeli crimes by supporting the cause of the LGBTQ community. Due to the controversy, Mock decided to cancel her appearance altogether.[76] Jewish students, by virtue of being affiliated with the Jewish student organization Hillel,[77] were deemed unfit even to cosponsor a gay-rights campus event.

At SOAS, a student government motion was passed in January 2017 placing restrictions on who from outside the university could speak on campus, and it was stated unequivocally, without any objections, that no one who had any affiliation with Zionist ideology could speak on campus *on any topic whatsoever*, even topics unrelated to Israel. Since, according to a prominent blogger who follows campus anti-Israelism in the United Kingdom closely, some 93 percent of British Jews are supportive of Zionism, with this motion the student government essentially "banned British Jews from speaking on campus."[78] It's not about Israelis and Palestinians, in other words. It's about Jews, or more specifically, the wrong kind of Jews.

From the broader global BDS movement to SJP's local campus chapters, from Durban in 2001 to this very day, the message is clear and consistent: see no Israel, hear no Israel, *speak* no Israel. Make no space for the alternative perspective. Make no space for the possibility that Israelis, Israeli Jews, might not be demonic monsters but simply normal human beings. To that end, SJP and BDS activists refuse to participate in dialogue. They fight to prevent *anyone* from participating in any conversation with those who do not share their point of view. Claiming a monopoly over virtue and morality, they undermine the open exchange of ideas at the academy and beyond. They thereby threaten the philosophical foundations of the modern university.

From the top of the movement to its bottom, from its start to today, what they want instead is—again—to silence dissent.

BDS Report Card: Concrete Achievements

So how is the BDS movement actually doing?

The commercial boycott has had some noticeable successes: some companies have ceased doing business with Israel, and some organizations have divested from relevant companies or refused to invest with Israeli companies or banks.[79] The cultural boycott boasts of some cultural figures who endorse the boycott,[80] of successful protests and cancellations of Israeli performances abroad,[81] and of musicians who have canceled Israel visits or refuse to book them in the first place, egged on most famously by former Pink Floyd member Roger Waters. The academic boycott can point to many academics who publicly support BDS[82] (including recent declarations by some two hundred Brazilian academics[83] and some six hundred Chilean academics[84]), a number of cases of boycotts of individuals (including one discussed in chapter 1 of this volume), and several professional academic organizations that have passed BDS resolutions (including the American Studies Association [ASA] and the National Women's Studies Association).[85] Several significant American mainline Protestant churches continue their early support of BDS, most notably (and recently) the Presbyterian Church, in a June 2016 vote.[86] When the Evangelical Lutheran Church in America passed a BDS resolution in August 2016, that marked the ninth religious denomination to do so.[87] Omar Barghouti wrote in January 2016 that the fact that the Israeli Knesset was now discussing ways to respond to BDS indicated.that the movement was working, that Israel was developing a "fear of isolation."[88]

In the sense of actual concrete achievements, however, the report card is less impressive. June 2016 articles published by the Bloomberg financial news service, for example, report how well Israel is doing economically. Its gross domestic product (GDP) has nearly doubled between 2006 (the early days of the BDS movement) and 2015.[89] Foreign investment in Israel has tripled during the same period, with tremendous growth over the past several years even while BDS activity has been feverish.[90] That same article documents not only the growth of Israeli start-ups but also the thriving business specifically of "nine Israeli companies with ties to the settlement and occupation economy." In general, the news is regularly filled with stories of major companies engaging in business with, or investing in, Israel or Israeli businesses; governments sending trade missions to Israel; Israeli achievements in medicine and technology; and Israel's growing economic ties with new major partners such as India and China.[91] The July, 2017 visit to Israel by Indian Prime minister Modi, the first ever such visit, was widely viewed as a great coup by Israel.

And while some musicians are respecting the boycott, other equally major musicians are performing in Israel even after being barraged with anti-Israel social media pressure to cancel. In recent years, these have included Aerosmith, Madonna, Paul Simon, Paul McCartney, the Rolling Stones, Lady Gaga, Justin Timberlake, and Elton John.[92] Performers just in 2016 and 2017 included the Beach Boys' Brian Wilson, Alice Cooper, Barry Manilow, Carlos Santana, Guns N' Roses, Alan Parsons, Radiohead, and Nick Cave, to name a few.[93] There are now growing counter-boycott organizations aiming to bring artists and musicians to Israel, such as Artists4Peace[94] and Creative Community for Peace,[95] which boast of their own successes. Even some of BDS's initial cultural successes have turned into failures. Over the summer of 2016, the mere threat of a BDS protest at Syracuse University led a timid Syracuse professor to disinvite an Israeli filmmaker from an international conference being hosted there. When news of the disinvitation spread through major media outlets, the resulting backlash prompted the university to extend its own invitation to the filmmaker.[96]

In the legal arena, in the United States, as of late 2017, at least twenty-three states had passed various forms of anti-BDS legislation, while many others are in the pipeline.[97] On the federal level, anti-BDS legislation has been introduced into both houses of Congress,[98] which by November 2017 had 50 Senate cosponsors and 268 in the House of Representatives;[99] in December 2016, the Senate passed a bill acknowledging certain forms of anti-Israelism to be antisemitic.[100] A nascent European movement is rejecting BDS as well, with, for example, several previous Spanish boycotts either being declared illegal or shut down from the fear of being illegal,[101] the city of Paris passing an anti-BDS resolution,[102] the

Green Party of Bavaria (Germany) doing the same,[103] and the Austrian National Union of Students condemning BDS as antisemitic.[104] And while some churches are endorsing BDS, other equally important ones are rejecting it—including most recently and notably the United Methodist Church, which in May 2016 not only rejected BDS but urged its affiliates to actively *dis*affiliate with institutions that promote it.[105]

Even in the academic arena, our primary focus, the concrete score for BDS is not impressive overall. Although several professional organizations have passed boycotts, they are widely considered quite minor. Meanwhile, other more significant organizations are rejecting them, such as the Modern Language Association, the American Historical Association, and, as discussed in our volume, the American Anthropological Association (where many believed BDS would easily pass). Even the 2013 BDS endorsement by the ASA was not an unambiguous victory for anti-Israelists. A half-dozen universities promptly withdrew their ASA institutional membership in protest, and dozens of academic organizations and hundreds of universities condemned it.[106] In fact, it is now facing a lawsuit, as several ASA members charged that endorsing the boycott violated the organization's academic mission as spelled out by its charter[107]—a theme that, this volume will show, is quite common, as are the deceptive practices exploited by BDS activists to win the vote, which were exposed during the course of the lawsuit.[108] Meanwhile, a study published in December 2016 shows that academic collaboration between American and Israeli scholars has grown dramatically in recent years.[109]

On campuses, the situation is somewhat complicated. Focusing just on the United States, campus antisemitism watchdog AMCHA Initiative has tracked one hundred twelve BDS votes on campuses primarily between the years 2012 and 2017, of which fifty-nine failed and fifty-three passed.[110] What that does not reflect is the sense of scale: according to one source, there are some 4,700 Title IV–eligible four- or two-year institutions of higher education in the United States, the vast majority of which see no BDS activity.[111] Nor do the raw numbers of resolutions reflect the fact that many campuses have been the site of multiple such votes, partly because BDS advocates are relentless. In November 2017, the student government of the University of Michigan at Ann Arbor finally passed a BDS resolution, for example, at the eleventh such vote since 2002;[112] at its sister campus in Dearborn, there have been five successful BDS votes over the past decade, as subsequent student governments continued to affirm it. More generally, the Israel on Campus Coalition tracks what it calls "detractor" and "supporter" campus events, of which BDS votes are just a small subset. Its most recent report, released in mid-2017, finds some worrisome trends but also notes that pro-Israel activity on American campuses has seen significant growth over the past several years.[113] On the other hand, some anti-Israelists are eager to claim that their side is doing well, with one site commemorating in 2017 what they called the "twelfth anniversary" of BDS with a list of "200 Victories."[114]

But some campus BDS victories were subsequently overturned. At least two graduate student unions passed BDS resolutions only to have their parent unions override them.[115] While Vassar College, a recent campus hotbed of anti-Israelism, surprised no one when its student government endorsed BDS in March 2016, it surprised many when its student body as a whole rejected it in May 2016.[116] A similar pattern occurred at Montreal's McGill University, when a February 2016 student government vote passed BDS[117] only to be followed days later by the student body as a whole failing to ratify it[118]—and then some weeks later, as discussed in chapter 32 of our volume, McGill's Judicial Board found BDS resolutions in general to be in violation of the student government constitution and thus impermissible.[119]

Most important, not one single university as an institution has actually endorsed or openly acted on the BDS resolutions passed by its student governments, and not one dollar has been divested from university endowments (at least publicly). To the contrary, over 400 college or university presidents signed a 2007 anti-BDS statement by Columbia University president Lee Bollinger,[120] and over 250 signed a similar statement again in 2014.[121]

One might reasonably conclude that, overall, the BDS movement is failing— so much so that the hashtag #BDSFail draws thousands of hits on Twitter, and one source, UK Media Watch, has been issuing monthly newsletters for the past two years titled "BDS is Failing: A Continuing Series."[122] But then again, if the movement really is failing, why does UK Media Watch feel the need to keep issuing its reports? And why does Omar Barghouti tell Bloomberg News, in the same article mentioned above about the growth of foreign investment in Israel, that "BDS is not just working, it is working far better and spreading into the mainstream much faster than we had anticipated"?

BDS Report Card: Actual Achievements

Omar Barghouti may partly be posturing, but his remarks are also sincere—and justified. The BDS movement, recall, is in it for the long haul.

And in that respect, it may be succeeding.

When activists lose a particular battle, they are not deterred. They come back again, almost immediately. The successful McGill student government divestment vote was the fourth try after three failures within the previous couple of years. The successful University of Michigan student government divestment vote was the *eleventh* try in fifteen years. The close defeat at the American Anthropological Association brought out the announcement that their battle was not yet over, as was also the case at the Modern Language Association. The picture is the same on campuses all over the Western world.

Why this relentlessness? Because their goal isn't merely to pass resolutions, which they realize have no policy consequences. Rather, the BDS debates and the often months-long campaigns leading up to them aim to change the conversation about Israel and Zionism. To this end, even purely symbolic gestures suffice: the BDS crowd declared a victory in October 2016 when the student government at Portland State University (PSU) endorsed BDS despite knowing that the university does not even have any control over its investments.[123] After years of such campus gestures, always accompanied by the relentless screaming of terrible things about Israel, they *have* changed the conversation quite significantly. It is now permissible to say things about Israelis and Jews, both in mainstream society and particularly on campuses, that not long ago were impermissible.[124] Not only do polls show that millennials are significantly more sympathetic to the Palestinians than their older counterparts are,[125] but some polls of college students report numbers like these, which once would be considered shocking: thirty-four percent aren't sure if Israel has the right to exist, thirty-nine percent believe all Israeli land should be returned to Palestinians, forty-four percent believe Israel is practicing apartheid on Palestinian land, and forty-eight percent trust the Palestinian government more than the Israeli government.[126]

The intimidation and silencing tactics of campus BDS activists have surely contributed to this cultural sea change. As documented throughout our volume and elsewhere,[127] Jewish and pro-Israel faculty and students now hesitate to speak up or out, even just to identify themselves as supportive of Israel, much less directly confront the propaganda and lies. They worry about (and share anecdotal evidence about) being shunned, not being invited to conferences, and having journal submissions rejected or not even reviewed.[128] Many stories abound in this volume and elsewhere of Jewish and pro-Israel individuals privately supporting but refusing to publicly speak out in support of those individuals who do speak out and of graduate students remaining silent so as to preserve their job prospects.[129]

In fact, Jewish students are beginning to shut down their own events, without even waiting for SJP to do its thing. In November 2017, the Princeton University Hillel disinvited Israeli deputy foreign minister Tzipi Hotovely at the last minute, under pressure from a Jewish "progressive social action" student group.[130] In November 2016 at the University of Texas, Austin—where SJP had orchestrated a major disruption a year earlier, as discussed in our volume—Jewish campus groups also rejected at the last minute a scheduled campus lecture by unapologetic pro-Israel American-Israeli journalist Caroline Glick. One student leader, who sits on the board of a group called Texans for Israel, explained, "There are fears she may alienate student groups and minorities we are trying to attract, which have traditionally taken a non-pro-Israel stance."[131] They were worried, in other words, how anti-Israel activists would respond to someone who unapologetically stands up for Israel. It was hardly a surprise when a student SJP leader promptly posted on his Facebook page, "When you don't even have to mobilize to shut shit down. Shout to the Palestine Solidarity Committee and the work we've done over the past few years."

Relentless anti-Israel campaigns inevitably take their toll, not just on pro-Israel students, but on everyone. PSU president Wim Wiewel noted that the "tone and tenor of the BDS movement has made members of our community feel unsafe and unwelcome at PSU, and it is not acceptable to marginalize or scapegoat them. Antisemitism cannot and will not be tolerated on our campus."[132] Similarly, Vassar professor of Russian history Michaela Pohl wrote in March 2016:

> The atmosphere at Vassar College ... is troubled. I am not Jewish, but even I have experienced an increase in hostility and strained silences among students and colleagues.... I have been called a "f--king fascist," "Zionist" and "idiot" for speaking out against Vassar's BDS resolution and speaking up for Israel and for U. S. policy. I have seen Jewish students profiled and singled out at a BDS meeting. I have felt the icy silence that reigns in some departments.... Academics who suggest that Israel is harvesting organs ... earn [approving] tweets and clicks—and deal in hate speech.... It is speech that angers and mobilizes and that relishes its effects but denies that the effect was ever the intention.[133]

As for the long-term effects of such an environment, Pohl pointed to the phenomenon of "students look[ing] down at their desks when I say things about Jewish emancipation [in Russia] or ... embarrassed silences in class while discussing Jewish history."

Embarrassed silence when matters of Jewish interest are discussed in the classroom.

With respect to the campus, then, Barghouti seems to be right.

Overview of the Current Volume

Our book documents the corrosive effect that the anti-Israel movement has on all aspects of the academy, with emphasis on its use of personal attack. The contributions make the case that the anti-Israel movement, as it currently manifests itself, is having a profoundly deleterious impact on the global republic of letters. The movement reintroduces tropes of the oldest hatred into everyday discourse. It replaces respectful dialogue with sanctimonious Manicheanism. It stifles and silences debate. It damages collegiality. And it undermines the trust that is so essential for the working of intellectual institutions.

This grim picture is brought to life through some of the recurring themes in our essays:

(1) *Intimidation, personal attacks, and the singling out of Jews.* As most of our contributors demonstrate, anti-Israelists employ these tactics over and over,

whether by grilling Jewish students about their legitimacy as candidates for student government, targeting Jewish students with eviction notices or harassing Birthright tables, or undertaking malicious and intimidating smear campaigns that use lies and misrepresentations to attack the reputations and threaten the physical safety of Jewish or pro-Israel individuals.

(2) *Antinormalization and the disruption of events.* These, too, appear in nearly every single essay. But while SJP and BDS advocates repeatedly attempt to silence the Jewish and pro-Israel voice in these ways, we regularly find the Jewish and pro-Israel individuals and groups playing nice, attempting dialogue, and offering to co-host panel discussions and other events with their opponents, only to be rebuffed and rejected at every turn. Several of the essayists describe reaching out to anti-Israel opponents only to have their efforts characterized as further manifestations of Zionist racism and colonialism.

(3) *Anticivility.* It's not just that BDS activists often fail to be civil—they often outright *reject* civility as a campus norm. Our contributor Jill Schneiderman describes how the Vassar open forum that put her proposed study trip to Israel-Palestine on trial began with the faculty chair announcing that "cardboard notions of civility" need not restrict the conversation. Cary Nelson quotes University of California, Irvine professor Mark LeVine: "People like Cary Nelson ... get up in arms about BDS. Well, Cary Nelson and the rest of you: F--- you. Call me uncivil, but still, f--- you. F--- all of you who want to make arguments about civility." Indeed, some anti-Israelists consider civility "a pillar of white supremacist imperialism."[134] As University of California, Los Angeles, SJP activist Omar Zahzah explains:

> "Civility," a colonial and racializing concept that privileges tone over content and establishes a rubric for etiquette by creating a contrast with a savage and non-white Other.... "Civility" allows for proponents of an allegedly all-encompassing freedom of speech to conveniently falter in their enthusiasm when the object of criticism is considered off limits—in this case, Palestinian oppression and dispossession, and the entrenchment of Israeli ... racialized state violence, surveillance and white supremacy. "Civility" can magically transform groups of vulnerable black, brown, undocumented, queer and trans students standing up to powerful politicians and soldiers responsible for the implementation of violent and racist policies of military occupation and ethnic cleansing into an "angry mob," and divert what should be righteous indignation at the brutality endured by a colonized population into patronizing *tut-tutting* about the means of protest.[135]

We don't dispute that calls for civility can sometimes serve an unjust status quo.[136] But, in licensing wholesale distortions of truth and the abandonment of other academic norms, the rejection of civility by the BDS movement often appears to aim at eliminating genuine freedom and diversity of opinion by simply shutting down the other side. Many of the essays in the volume document how profoundly uncivil—how filled with hatred, rage, and outrage—the BDS movement is and how its advocates thereby intimidate community members.

(4)   *Not playing by the rules.* As many of our essays attest, anti-Israel activists, and BDS campaigns in particular, often cheat or operate clandestinely:[137]

- BDS resolutions are often sprung with minimal advance notice, affording no time for the opposition to organize.[138]
- Panels and materials are arranged that tell only the anti-Israel side of the story, deliberately ignoring or suppressing alternative voices.[139]
- Anti-Israelists make efforts to stack the deck, so to speak, by getting their people into positions of power and removing opposing voices.[140]
- They call important meetings or votes on or just before the Jewish Sabbath or Jewish holidays to restrict the ability of some or many Jews to participate.[141]
- They call for quick votes before the other side can be heard and limit publicity to decrease participation by opponents.[142]
- They deliberately fail to post minutes of meetings or publish agendas so that opponents don't know when a vote is coming.[143]
- They bring in outsiders to sway opinions when outsiders are not allowed.[144]
- They allow people to vote who aren't franchised to vote, if they will vote for BDS.[145]
- They attempt to vote twice on online polls.[146]
- They hold important elections without the candidates disclosing their relevant positions on BDS.[147]
- They change the texts of resolutions after they are passed.[148]
- They exploit conditions where a small number of activists can sway a vote and thus give the appearance of a broad mandate.[149]
- They bypass ordinary vetting procedures in order to offer extremely biased courses promoting the Palestinian narrative.[150]
- They falsely accuse pro-Israel students of various violations in an effort to shut them down.[151]
- In one instance, a congressional staffer secretly used his or her boss's position to schedule a pro-BDS briefing on Capitol Hill without informing the boss.[152]

When you believe you have a monopoly on truth and virtue and that you have a mandate to eliminate the abominable evil about which you are so profoundly angry, and when you are blind to the humanity of the other side, then you can either flout or exploit ordinary procedural rules to bring about the desired outcome.

(5) *Disinterest in truth or other intellectual norms.* Many of our essays attest that the norms one might expect to govern scholarship—facts, evidence, documentation, careful reasoned argument, and such—often go missing in anti-Israel campaigns and events. In chapter 23, Ernest Sternberg, for example, shows how even the most minimal investigation refutes various claims affirmed by anti-Israel speakers, concluding that such claims must be understood not as ordinary factual ones but as "solidarity-building rituals of execration" instead. In chapter 12, Philip Mendes documents the way some Australian anti-Israelists reject academic conventions. Other contributors examine the widely publicized 2016 incidents involving Rutgers professor Jasbir Puar and Oberlin professor Joy Karega, both of whom made blood-libelous or antisemitic claims against Israel and/or Jews and did so without any regard for evidence.[153]

(6) *Unholy alliances, identity politics, and the exclusion of Jews.* As discussed earlier, the BDS movement exploits the progressive campus environment to make alliances with campus groups that really ought to oppose its agenda. They co-opt others' events, making everything about Israel-Palestine;[154] they get Black Lives Matter proponents, for example, to become rabidly anti-Israel, endorse and promote the claims that Israel is a racist apartheid state committing genocide against Palestinians,[155] and spread wild allegations that Israel is responsible for police shootings of African Americans;[156] and they repeatedly remind Jewish students—even those who may otherwise be very attracted to supporting progressive causes—that they are white, privileged oppressors who are fundamentally unwelcome. Combined with the other themes above, it's no wonder that several of our essays describe Jewish events (and especially pro-Israel events) being held either in secret or under tight security on their campuses.

(7) *Administration incompetence, cowardice, or complicity.* University administrations play key roles in a number of our essays, but generally—with the possible exception of the case of Martin Kramer discussed in chapter 11—they either go along with the anti-Israel campaigns or try to remain above the fray. All too often, they fail to protect the rights of those whose events are disrupted or those individuals who are personally attacked—in some cases, morally equating the disrupters with those who resisted the disruptions, and in other cases, outright supporting the individuals running malicious smear campaigns by defending their free speech. Several contributors (such as Doron S. Ben-Atar and Yaron Raviv) describe Kafkaesque university proceedings, utterly nontransparent and bizarre, of which they (not the miscreants) are the target. Even in cases where the individual who was falsely smeared or accused is exonerated, the damage to his or her personal and professional reputation is already done and the experience leaves the individual battered and scarred. Not only is this devastating to the

individual, but the failure of universities to stand up to the bully tactics of the BDS movement fosters a climate of fear that subdues and intimidates students, faculty, and staff.

The essays that follow, then, depict a toxic social and intellectual atmosphere on campus and beyond. We are not naive enough to think that exposing the corrosive impact of radical anti-Israelism on our educational and cultural institutions will trigger any dramatic about-face. We do hope, however, that the essays in our volume will alert many to the way in which the BDS movement is moving cultural and intellectual discourse toward intolerance and bigotry and, in so doing, undermining the fundamental values of an essential Western institution.

Words, Jewish history teaches us, have consequences.

As does silence.[157]

ANDREW PESSIN is Professor of Philosophy at Connecticut College and Campus Bureau Editor of the *Algemeiner*. Author of many academic articles and books, a philosophy textbook, several philosophical books for the general reader, and two novels, his current research is focused on philosophical matters relevant to both Judaism and Israel.

DORON S. BEN-ATAR is Professor of History at Fordham University and a playwright. In addition to publishing books and articles about early America, he authored, together with his mother, Roma Nutkiewicz Ben-Atar, *What Time and Sadness Spared: Mother and Son Confront the Holocaust*. In recent years, he has turned his attention to the battles over Zionism in the American Jewish community with, among other writings, his satirical play *Peace Warriors*.

Notes

1. Fordham University attempted precisely this in January 2017, when it prohibited the formation of a chapter of Students for Justice in Palestine (SJP) on its campus. SJP responded by filing a lawsuit. See Elizabeth Redden, "Pro-Palestinian Group Banned on Political Grounds," *Inside Higher Ed* (January 27, 2017), https://www.insidehighered.com /news/2017/01/18/fordham-denies-student-palestinian-rights-group-approval-being -too-polarizing.

2. Jerusalem Center for Public Affairs, 2007.

3. Sometimes anti-Israel activity just is *itself* antisemitic in the opinion of many, and sometimes it simply leads to or facilitates distinct antisemitic activity. One interesting case occurred at Toronto's Ryerson University in December 2016, when SJP orchestrated a walkout during a student government vote on a resolution that condemned antisemitism and supported a Holocaust Education Week, in order to lose the quorum and defeat the resolution. The resolution had nothing to do with Israel but was attacked anyway in an

action that many believed was purely antisemitic. See Lea Speyer and Rachel Frommer, "'Blatant Antisemitism' Behind Boycott by Anti-Israel Campus Groups of Vote on Holocaust Education Week at Ryerson U, Jewish Students Say," *The Algemeiner* (December 2, 2016), https://www.algemeiner.com/2016/12/02/walkout-ryerson-university-students-protest -holocaust-education-initiative-blatant-antisemitism-one-step-away-from-holocaust -denial/; "More Details Emerge Of Antisemitism At Ryerson University Meeting," *Israellycool* (December 2, 2016), http://www.israellycool.com/2016/12/02/more-details -emerge-of-antisemitism-at-ryerson-university-meeting/.

4. See both the March 2016 report by campus antisemitism watchdog AMCHA Initiative (http://www.amchainitiative.org/bulletin-first-hard-evidence-antizionism-fuels -antisemitism) and the November 2015 report from the Anti-Defamation League (http://www .adl.org/press-center/press-releases/miscellaneous/adl-report-shows-increase-in-anti -israel-activity-on-us-college-campuses.html). Other recent studies have also found that a majority of Jewish students experienced some antisemitism on their campuses in the past year. See Leonard Saxe, Theodore Sasson, Graham Wright, and Shahar Hecht, "Antisemitism and the College Campus: Perceptions and Realities," Brandeis University Maurice and Marilyn Cohen Center for Modern Jewish Studies (July 2015), http://www.brandeis.edu /cmjs/pdfs/birthright/AntisemitismCampus072715.pdf; and Barry Kosmin and Ariela Keysar, "National Demographic Survey of American Jewish College Students 2014: Antisemitism Report," Trinity College and the Louis D. Brandeis Center for Human Rights Under Law (February 2015), http://digitalrepository.trincoll.edu/cgi/viewcontent.cgi?article=1133&context =facpub. See also these studies documenting a rise in campus antisemitism in 2016: Leonard Saxe, Graham Wright, Shahar Hecht, Michelle Shain, Theodore Sasson, Fern Chertok, "Hotspots of Antisemitism and Anti-Israel Sentiment on US Campuses," Brandeis University Maurice and Marilyn Cohen Center for Modern Jewish Studies (2016), http://www.brandeis. edu/ssri/pdfs/campusstudies/AntisemitismCampuses101316.pdf; and "Report on Antisemitic Activity During the First Half of 2016 At US Colleges and Universities With the Largest Jewish Undergraduate Populations," AMCHA Initiative (2016), http://www.amchainitiative .org/wp-content/uploads/2016/07/Report-on-Antisemitic-Activity-During-the-First-Half -of-2016.pdf (accessed November 13, 2017).

5. "Antisemitism Tracker," AMCHA Initiative, http://www.amchainitiative.org /antisemitism-tracker713 (accessed November 9, 2017); "2015 End of Year Report: Successes and Impact," AMCHA Initiative, http://www.amchainitiative.org/wp-content/uploads /2015/12/AMCHA-Initiative-end-of-year-report-2015.pdf (accessed November 9, 2017). See also Leonard Saxe, Graham Wright, Shahar Hecht, Michelle Shain, Theodore Sasson, Fern Chertok, "Hotspots of Antisemitism and Anti-Israel Sentiment on US Campuses," Brandeis University Maurice and Marilyn Cohen Center for Modern Jewish Studies (2016), http:// www.brandeis.edu/ssri/pdfs/campusstudies/AntisemitismCampuses101316.pdf.

6. "Antisemitic and Homophobic Graffiti Found at Brown University Dorm," *Haaretz* (March 21, 2016), https://www.haaretz.com/jewish/news/1.710117.

7. Tammi Rossman-Benjamin, "Fighting Discrimination and Protecting the First Amendment on Campus, Not a Zero Sum Game," *The Hill* (July 11, 2016), http://thehill.com /blogs/congress-blog/education/287222-fighting-discrimination-and-protecting-the-first -amendment-on.

8. "ZOA Letter to CUNY Leaders About Antisemitic, Violence-Inducing Rallies There," Zionist Organization of America (February 22, 2016), http://zoa.org/2016/02/10315402-letter

-to-cuny-chancellor-and-board-of-trustees-jew-haters-spread-fear-at-cuny-colleges/ (accessed November 13, 2017).

9. William A. Jacobson, "Exclusive: Photo of Antisemitic Note Left at Oberlin College Professor's Porch," *Legal Insurrection* (December 6, 2016), http://legalinsurrection .com/2016/12/exclusive-photo-of-antisemitic-note-left-at-oberlin-college-professors-porch/.

10. The phenomenon is so pervasive that AMCHA Initiative maintains a swastika tracker: http://www.amchainitiative.org/swastika-tracker/ (accessed November 13, 2017).

11. Several such disruptions are documented in the current volume. For lists of disruptions of Jewish and pro-Israel events, see Tammi Rossman-Benjamin, "Antisemitism on Campus Is Not Just Uncivil, It's Intolerant," *Newsweek* (September 28, 2016), http://www .newsweek.com/anti-semitism-campus-not-just-uncivil-its-intolerant-503491; as well as the "Disruption Tracker" kept by AMCHA Initiative, http://www.amchainitiative.org/sjp -disruption-of-jewish-events/ (accessed November 9, 2017).

12. "London Police Warn Pro-Israel Groups Not to Disclose Conference Location," *The Algemeiner* (November 4, 2016), https://www.algemeiner.com/2016/11/04/london-police -warn-pro-israel-groups-not-to-disclose-conference-location/.

13. According to one source, the chants included, "Intifada, Intifada, long live the Intifada!" "Fuck Israel and fuck the police!" "All white people need to die!": Lea Speyer, "Student Protesters at UC Irvine Justify Violent Actions at Pro-Israel Campus Event Where They Shouted 'All White People Need to Die'," *The Algemeiner* (May 27, 2016), http://www .algemeiner.com/2016/05/27/student-protesters-at-uc-irvine-justify-violent-actions-at-pro -israel-campus-event-where-they-shouted-all-white-people-need-to-die/.

14. In an email sent on August 18, 2016, the university announced that its internal investigation had found "that Students for Justice in Palestine (SJP), the group that organized and led the protest, violated Student Conduct Policies regarding disruption.... As a result, SJP was issued a written warning, effective immediately and continuing until March 29, 2017."

15. Rachel Frommer, "Police Called to London University After Protesters Trap Attendees of Israel Event in Room," *The Algemeiner* (October 27, 2016), https://www.algemeiner .com/2016/10/27/police-called-to-london-university-after-protesters-trap-attendees-of -israel-event-in-room/. Some video of the event is available at "Intimidation, Threats and Red Fascism at UCL University," *Beyond the Great Divide* (October 30, 2016), https://www .youtube.com/watch?v=l3JwBxZi44Q.

16. For data on global antisemitism, see: "Antisemitism Worldwide 2016, General Analysis," Kantor Center (2016), http://www.kantorcenter.tau.ac.il/general-analysis-2016 (accessed November 13, 2017). For an analysis of global antisemitism, see Daniel Goldhagen's *The Devil That Never Dies: The Rise and Threat of Global Antisemitism* (Little, Brown and Company, 2013). Data actually show a global decrease in antisemitic physical violence in 2015 compared to 2014, but that is probably attributable to (1) 2014's being exceptionally problematic (due to antisemitic responses to Israel's Operation Protective Edge) and (2) Jews worldwide having dramatically increased their security precautions. Recent FBI statistics show that the majority of hate crimes in the United States are against Jews: Michael Morris, "FBI: 57% of Anti-Religious Hate Crimes Targeted Jews; 16% Targeted Muslims," *CNS News* (December 9, 2015), http://www.cnsnews.com/blog/michael-morris/fbi-us-jews-targeted -57-anti-religious-hate-crimes-muslims-targeted-16. There remains a concerning increase in verbal and visual manifestations of antisemitism, particularly online, and this was

true even before the November 2016 US presidential election—which unleashed plenty more: "ADL Data Shows Antisemitic Incidents Continue Surge in 2017 Compared to 2016," Anti-Defamation League (November 2, 2017), https://www.adl.org/news/press-releases /adl-data-shows-anti-semitic-incidents-continue-surge-in-2017-compared-to-2016 (accessed November 13, 2017).

17. "London Police Warn Pro-Israel Groups Not to Disclose Their Location," *Jewish News Service* (November 3, 2016), http://www.jns.org/news-briefs/2016/11/3/london-police-warn -pro-israel-groups-not-to-disclose-their-location.

18. Christopher Hope, "Amber Rudd Pledges £13.4 Million to Guard Every Jewish School, College, and Nursery and Synagogue in the UK," *The Telegraph* (November 30, 2016), http:// www.telegraph.co.uk/news/2016/11/30/amber-rudd-pledges-134million-guard-every-jewish -school-college.

19. Statement to the Faculty Senate (February 19, 2015), *Stanford News*, http://news .stanford.edu/2015/02/19/hennessy-senate-statement-021915/ (accessed November 13, 2017).

20. That anti-Israel academics deliberately aim to take over such organizations and convert them toward supporting their anti-Israel agenda was exposed during the course of a lawsuit filed against the American Studies Association after it voted to boycott Israel: see "Public Interest Lawsuit Reveals Plot by BDS Activists to Takeover Academic Associations," The Louis D. Brandeis Center for Human Rights Under Law (November 9, 2017), http://brandeiscenter.com/public-interest-lawsuit-reveals-plot-bds-activists-takeover -academic-associations/ (accessed November 13, 2017).

21. There are *many* others whose stories aren't included in this volume, including several individuals who could not contribute because of legal considerations.

22. As one Israeli diplomat put it in 2015, about the United Kingdom, "On Israel, universities are becoming discussion-free zones": Yiftah Curiel, "On Israel, Universities are Becoming Discussion-Free Zones," *Times Higher Education* (February 10, 2015), https://www .timeshighereducation.com/comment/opinion/blog-on-israel-universities-are-becoming -discussion-free-zones/2018449.article.

23. Cary Nelson and Gabriel Brahm, *The Case Against Academic Boycotts of Israel* (MLA Members for Scholars' Rights, 2015), 13.

24. In fact, this has been the case with antisemitism through the ages. As David Nirenberg has shown, anti-Judaism has always been represented as a virtuous cause—a campaign to excise the impure, the formalistic, the legalistic, and the physical from the virtuous soul of the body politic: David Nirenberg, *Anti-Judaism: The Western Tradition* (New York: W.W. Norton, 2014).

25. Indeed, in a belated recognition of this point, a leading BDS group, the "US Campaign to End the Israeli Occupation," changed its anti-Israel-sounding name in late 2016 to the more pro-Palestinian name "US Campaign for Palestinian Rights" (http://uscpr.org/). The name change was unaccompanied by any changes in their anti-Israel activities.

26. Playing an important role in this is the increasingly popular idea of *intersectionality*, that all forms of injustice and oppression are intrinsically connected. That anti-Israelists promote this as a deliberate strategy is documented here: William A. Jacobson, "Exposed: Years-Long Effort to Blame Israel for US Police Shootings of Blacks," *Legal Insurrection* (July 18, 2016), http://legalinsurrection.com/2016/07/exposed-years-long-effort-to-blame-israel -for-u-s-police-shootings-of-blacks/. See also Jon Haber, "The BDS Playbook," *The Algemeiner* (July 10, 2016), http://www.algemeiner.com/2016/07/10/the-bds-playbook/.

27. As City University of New York professor Feisal G. Mohamed admits, "[e]ven the most enthusiastic BDSnik must be aware that the movement is very unlikely to stem this economic tide": Feisal G. Mohamed, "Any and All Available Means," *Dissent* (November 5, 2014), https://www.dissentmagazine.org/online_articles/best-of-intentions-asa-boycott-bds-debate, accessed on November 11, 2017.

28. Dershowitz made this point in his keynote address at the StandWithUs International Conference in Los Angeles, April 10, 2016.

29. Israeli Apartheid Weeks were held in more than 225 cities in the spring of 2016, the largest number ever, at least according to some of its proponents in this Facebook post of May 11, 2016, by "Israeli Apartheid Week": https://www.facebook.com/IsraeliApartheidWeek .IAW/posts/1022822404449475 (accessed November 13, 2017).

30. Martin Weiss, "Arab League Boycott of Israel," Congressional Research Service (August 25, 2017), https://www.fas.org/sgp/crs/mideast/RL33961.pdf (accessed November 13, 2017).

31. Robert S. Wistrich, *Antisemitism: The Longest Hatred* (New York: Pantheon, 1992).

32. For the history of antisemitism in the West, see Wistrich's *Antisemitism: The Longest Hatred* (Pantheon, 1992) and David Nirenberg's *Anti-Judaism: The Western Tradition* (Norton, 2013); for the history and present state of Muslim antisemitism, see also Daniel Goldhagen's *The Devil That Never Dies: The Rise and Threat of Global Antisemitism* (Little, Brown and Company, 2013). For an account that places BDS squarely in the context of the history of boycotting Jews, see William A. Jacobson, "The REAL History of the BDS Movement," *Legal Insurrection* (December 18, 2016), http://legalinsurrection.com/2016/12/the -real-history-of-the-bds-movement/#more-195431.

33. Cornell Law School professor William Jacobson stresses an earlier UN regional conference hosted by Tehran in February 2001, in preparation for the Durban conference, which produced the language about Israeli "apartheid" and "ethnic cleansing" that became the basis for the Durban language: William A. Jacobson, "AP's False History of BDS Movement," *Legal Insurrection* (July 7, 2015), http://legalinsurrection.com/2015/07/aps-false -history-of-bds-movement-aptgoldenberg/.

34. Rachel Swarns, "The Racism Walkout: The Overview; US and Israelis Quit Racism Talks Over Denunciation," *The New York Times* (September 4, 2001), http://www.nytimes .com/2001/09/04/world/racism-walkout-overview-us-israelis-quit-racism-talks-over -denunciation.html.

35. WCAR NGO Forum Declaration (September 3, 2001), http://www.humanrightsvoices .org/assets/attachments/documents/durban_ngo_declaration_2001.pdf (accessed November 13, 2017). See particularly points 420–424, which include such statements as: "Call for an increased awareness of the root causes of Israel's belligerent occupation and systematic human rights violations as a racist, apartheid system," "Call for the establishment of a UN Special Committee on Apartheid and Other Racist Crimes Against Humanity perpetrated by the Israeli Apartheid regime," "Call for the launch of an international anti-Israeli Apartheid movement," "Call upon the international community to impose a policy of complete and total isolation of Israel as an apartheid state."

36. "More Pressure for MidEast Peace," *The Guardian* (April 5, 2002), https://www .theguardian.com/world/2002/apr/06/israel.guardianletters.

37. Lars Grip, "Jewish Council Cuts Ties With Church of Sweden (Boycott of Israel Advocated By Archbishop)," *Free Republic* (May 22, 2004), http://www.freerepublic.com /focus/f-news/1140438/posts.

38. "Israeli/Palestinian Conflict and Divestment from Israel Considered by Various Protestant Churches," Boston College Center for Jewish-Christian Learning, https://www.bc.edu/content/dam/files/research_sites/cjl/texts/cjrelations/topics/Israel_divestment.htm (accessed November 9, 2017).

39. Lisa Taraki, "Boycotting the Israeli Academy," *ZNet* (August 19, 2004), https://zcomm.org/znetarticle/boycotting-the-israeli-academy-by-lisa-taraki/.

40. "Palestinian Civil Society Call For BDS," BDSMovement.Net (July 9, 2005), https://bdsmovement.net/call#.ToDvIrHXDTg (accessed November 9, 2017).

41. "Palestinian BDS National Committee," BDSMovement.Net, https://bdsmovement.net/BNC (accessed November 9, 2017).

42. "Kairos Document," Kairos Palestine, http://www.kairospalestine.ps/index.php/about-us/kairos-palestine-document (accessed November 9, 2017).

43. For example: Alissa Wise and Brant Rosen, "We're Nobody's 'Jew-Washing' Pawns," *The Forward* (August 7, 2012), http://forward.com/opinion/160610/were-nobodys-jew-washing-pawns/.

44. In August 2016, a video surfaced of well-known anti-Israel historian Ilan Pappé acknowledging that the oft-repeated claim that BDS was launched by "The Call"—i.e., initiated by the Palestinians in 2005—is not true: see *Engage Online* (August 28, 2016), https://engageonline.wordpress.com/2016/08/28/ilan-pappe-admits-that-bds-was-not-initiated-by-a-call-from-palestinian-civil-society/. As we have already noted, the modern BDS movement was already well established at least by Durban in 2001, four years before "The Call."

45. See Jonathan Schanzer and Kate Havard, "Boycott, Divestment and Sanctions Movement Attracting Groups With Terrorist Ties," *The Hill* (November 2, 2016), http://thehill.com/blogs/congress-blog/foreign-policy/303970-boycott-divestment-and-sanctions-movement-attracting; and "Boycott-Israel Movement Tainted by Ties to Terrorists, Researchers Find," *The Tower* (November 6, 2016), http://www.thetower.org/4115-boycott-israel-movement-tainted-by-ties-to-terrorists-researchers-find/. For one specific example, the US Campaign for the Academic and Cultural Boycott of Israel acknowledges that its "fiscal sponsor" is a group called Al-Awda, an organization that supports violence against Israel, celebrates terrorist murders of innocent Israeli civilians, denies Jewish history in Jerusalem, etc. (See Max Samarov and Shahar Azani, "Who's Really Behind the Academic Boycott Against Israel?", *The Algemeiner* (January 16, 2017), https://www.algemeiner.com/2017/01/16/whos-really-behind-the-academic-boycott-against-israel/). More generally, in 2012, the Jerusalem Center for Public Affairs (JCPA) published a study of the BDS movement in which it discovered problems with some of the endorsers on "The Call," including that: (1) some of the groups listed as signatories do not seem to exist; (2) the list includes illegal associations, terror organizations, and their affiliates; (3) other endorsers include groups suspected of fundraising and money laundering for the Muslim Brotherhood and organizations whose leaders were reportedly involved in fundraising for Hamas and for other terrorist elements from around the world, including designated al-Qaeda figures (Adam Shay, "Manipulation and Deception: The Anti-Israel 'BDS' Campaign," Jerusalem Center for Public Affairs (March 19, 2012), http://jcpa.org/article/manipulation-and-deception-the-anti-israel-bds-campaign-boycott-divestment-and-sanctions/). An independent report by media watchdog Honest Reporting echoed those observations, adding that "at least 10–15% of the signatories come from organizations outside Israel and the territories, including over 20 organizations from surrounding countries … The potential

[is] that this 'Civil Society' boycott call … reflects a manufactured image of civil society organizations which are actually fronts for terror and other political groups" (see "BDS: An Introduction," Honest Reporting, http://honestreporting.com/wp-content/uploads /2012/07/BDS-an-Introduction.pdf (accessed November 9, 2017)).

46. Terrorism-finance expert Jonathan Schanzer testified to the US House of Representatives Foreign Affairs Committee in April 2016 that a group called American Muslims for Palestine (AMP) is

> a leading driver of the BDS campaign. AMP is arguably the most important sponsor and organizer for Students for Justice in Palestine (SJP), which is the most visible arm of the BDS campaign on campuses in the United States. AMP provides speakers, training, printed materials, a so-called "Apartheid Wall," and grants to SJP activists. AMP even has a campus coordinator on staff whose job is to work directly with SJP and other pro-BDS campus groups across the country. According to an email it sent to subscribers, AMP spent $100,000 on campus activities in 2014 alone. AMP partners with a wide range of BDS organizations, and openly calls for Congress to embrace BDS.

Schanzer documents, then concludes, that "at least seven individuals who work for or on behalf of AMP have worked for or on behalf of organizations previously shut down or held civilly liable in the United States for providing financial support to Hamas" (Jonathan Schanzer, "Israel Imperiled: Threats to the Jewish State," Congressional Testimony, Joint Hearing before House Foreign Affairs Committee (April 19, 2016), http://docs.house.gov /meetings/FA/FA18/20160419/104817/HHRG-114-FA18-Wstate-SchanzerJ-20160419.pdf). See also Dan Diker and Jamie Berk, "Students for Justice in Palestine Unmasked," Jerusalem Center for Public Affairs (2017), http://jcpa.org/wp-content/uploads /2017/11/SJP_Unmasked_Final_edited.pdf (accessed November 13, 2017). Other resources on what one article calls the "opaque funding network" of Students for Justice in Palestine include these: Mitchell Bard, "BDS Money Trail Suggests Opaque Funding Network," *The New York Jewish Week* (October 14, 2015), http://www.thejewishweek.com/news/new-york /bds-money-trail-suggests-opaque-funding-network; "BDS on American Campuses: SJP and its NGO Network," NGO Monitor (November 22, 2015), https://www.ngo-monitor.org /reports/bds_on_american_campuses_sjp_and_its_ngo_network/; and Yona Schiffmiller, "The Rockefeller BDS Empire, the New Israel Fund, and Campus Antisemitism," *Jewish News Service* (November 25, 2016), http://www.jns.org/latest-articles/2016/11/25/the -rockefeller-bds-empire-the-new-israel-fund-and-campus-anti-semitism#. WDmvxcuxXqA=.

47. Jennifer Dekel, "US Taxpayer Dollars Contribute to BDS Activity and Antisemitism on Campuses," *The Weekly Standard* (September 13, 2016), http://www.weeklystandard. com/us-taxpayer-dollars-contribute-to-bds-activity-and-anti-semitism-on-campuses/ article/2004308.

48. For a summary of the many intersectional coalitions made by BDS activists, see William A. Jacobson, "BDS is a Settler Colonial Ideology," *Legal Insurrection* (September 5, 2016), http://legalinsurrection.com/2016/09/bds-is-a-settler-colonial-ideology/. These include Black Lives Matter, LGBTQ advocacy, the international human rights movement, sporting events, environmentalism, water conservation, and indigenous rights activism.

49. For a disturbing account of how Jewish students are increasingly excluded from social justice activism on their campuses, see Seffi Kogen, "How BDS Is Pushing Jewish Students

Out of Social Justice Activism," *The Forward* (September 4, 2016), http://forward.com/opinion/349000/how-bds-is-pushing-jewish-students-out-of-social-justice-activism/?attribution=more-articles-carousel-item-2-headline.

50. Cynthia Ozick, "Names—Like 'America First' or 'Progressive'—Have Histories," *The Wall Street Journal* (August 30, 2016), http://www.wsj.com/articles/nameslike-america-first-or-progressivehave-histories-1472598153.

51. For example, the most commonly cited source documents offer these goals:

   1. Ending [Israel's] occupation and colonization of all Arab lands and dismantling the Wall.
   2. Recognizing the fundamental rights of the Arab-Palestinian citizens of Israel to full equality; and
   3. Respecting, protecting, and promoting the rights of Palestinian refugees to return to their homes and properties as stipulated in UN resolution 194.

(These may be found at the PACBI website tracing back to the "Civil Society Call": "Palestinian Call For Boycott, Divestment, and Sanctions," PACBI, http://pacbi.org/etemplate.php?id=66&key=colonization%20of%20all%20arab%20lands; https://bdsmovement.net/call (accessed November 9, 2017).) There is much here to appeal to the well-intentioned campus activist. But even a cursory analysis of these goals shows they are about destroying the Jewish State—not least by noting that "all Arab lands" includes Israel, and by flooding Israel with millions of alleged Palestinian refugees.

52. See Cary Nelson's essay in the current volume, chapter 14, note 1, where he documents his claim that "Every major BDS spokesperson across the world has been clear in lectures and in print that [eliminating Israel] is their aim."

53. Captured in "Say NO to BDS," StandWithUs (April 15, 2012), https://www.youtube.com/watch?v=ifZLk6Ei9-U (accessed November 9, 2017).

54. Captured in "Say NO to BDS," StandWithUs (April 15, 2012), https://www.youtube.com/watch?v=ifZLk6Ei9-U (accessed November 9, 2017).

55. Ali Mustafa, "'Boycotts Work': An Interview With Omar Barghouti," *The Electronic Intifada* (May 31, 2009), https://electronicintifada.net/content/boycotts-work-interview-omar-barghouti/8263.

56. Dag Hammarskjöld Program, "Omar Barghouti-Strategies for Change," Vimeo, https://vimeo.com/75201955 (accessed November 9, 2017).

57. The alternative is that wide swaths of the academy *are* aware of the not-so-peaceful goals of the BDS movement—and endorse them.

58. Students Supporting Israel Blog, "The True Face of Students for Justice in Palestine," *The Jerusalem Post* (April 21, 2016), http://www.jpost.com/Blogs/Students-Supporting-Israel-SSI-blog/The-True-Face-of-Students-for-Justice-in-Palestine-451706.

59. Paul Soltys, "College Council Candidate Explains China Divestment Resolution," *The Chicago Maroon* (May 2, 2016), http://chicagomaroon.com/2016/05/02/letter-to-the-editor-college-council-candidate-explains-china-divestment-resolution/.

60. Caroline Glick, "Our World: The Lie of Pro-Palestinian Activism," *The Jerusalem Post* (February 22, 2016), http://www.jpost.com/Opinion/Our-World-The-lie-of-pro-Palestinian-activism-445759.

61. Bazian also founded American Muslims for Palestine (AMP). Both he and AMP featured centrally in the congressional testimony discussed above for their role in supporting SJP's anti-Israel campus activities.

62. "Campuses with Chapters of Students for Justice in Palestine (SJP) or Similar Anti-Zionist Group," AMCHA Initiative, http://www.amchainitiative.org/sjp-chapters (accessed November 9, 2017). For more information about SJP, see: "Profile: Students for Justice in Palestine," Anti-Defamation League Report, https://www.adl.org/sites/default/files/documents/assets/pdf /israel-international/sjp-2015-backgrounder.pdf (accessed November 9, 2017); Dan Diker and Jamie Berk, "Students for Justice in Palestine Unmasked," Jerusalem Center for Public Affairs (2017), http://jcpa.org/wp-content/uploads/2017/11/SJP_Unmasked_Final_edited.pdf (accessed November 13, 2017); and Linda Wertheimer, "Students and the Middle East Conflict," *The New York Times* (August 3, 2016), http://www.nytimes.com/2016/08/07/education/edlife/middle-east -conflict-on-campus-anti-semitism.html?rref=collection%2Fsectioncollection%2Feducation &action=click&contentCollection=education&region=rank&module=package&version =highlights&contentPlacement=1&pgtype=sectionfront&_r=0. Campus chapters don't always take the SJP name, sometimes preferring names such as "Palestine Solidarity Committee" or "Students in Solidarity with Palestine," while in Canada, some chapters go by "Students Against Israeli Apartheid" or "Solidarity for Palestinian Human Rights."

63. "Profile: Students for Justice in Palestine," Anti-Defamation League Report, https:// www.adl.org/sites/default/files/documents/assets/pdf/israel-international/sjp -2015-backgrounder.pdf (accessed November 9, 2017).

64. Several episodes are documented in the current volume, but many other examples may be found, with accompanying documentation, at the website of campus watchdog Canary Mission (https://canarymission.org/organizations/sjp/), including incidents where a pro-Israel student was rammed with a shopping cart, a Jewish student was hit in the face and called "kike," Jewish students were harassed at a "Birthright" table, and so on. At Northeastern University in 2013, the entire SJP chapter was suspended for the school year for intimidating students on campus. (Canary Mission has recently come under fire for its blacklist methods of publicly identifying anti-Israel activists, but so far, its basic reliability in reporting facts has not been seriously challenged. See David Greenberg, Rebecca Lesses, Jeffry V. Mallow, Deborah Dash Moore, Sharon Ann Musher, Cary Nelson, Kenneth S. Stern, and Irene Tucker, "The Blacklist in the Coal Mine," *Tablet* (October 26, 2016), http://www.tabletmag.com/scroll/216271/the-blacklist-in-the-coal-mine-canary-missions -fear-mongering-agenda-college-campuses.)

65. As noted earlier, campus disruptions are tracked by AMCHA Initiative at http://www .amchainitiative.org/sjp-disruption-of-jewish-events/ (accessed November 9, 2017). There have been *dozens* in the past several years.

66. Conor Friedersdorf, "How Political Correctness Chills Speech on Campus," *The Atlantic* (September 1, 2016), http://www.theatlantic.com/politics/archive/2016/09/what-it -looks-like-when-political-correctness-chills-speech-on-campus/497387/.

67. Asaf Romirowsky and Alexander Joffe, "The Anti-Israel Movement's 'Anti-Normalization' Campaign," *National Post* (August 3, 2016), http://news.nationalpost .com/full-comment/the-anti-israel-movements-anti-normalization-campaign.

68. "Profile: Students for Justice in Palestine," Anti-Defamation League Report, https:// www.adl.org/sites/default/files/documents/assets/pdf/israel-international/sjp -2015-backgrounder.pdf (accessed November 9, 2017).

69. Khaled Abu Toameh, "The 'Anti-Normalization' Campaign and Israel's Right to Exist," Gatestone Institute (August 8, 2016), https://www.gatestoneinstitute.org/8656/anti -normalization-israel.

70. Two (of many) examples include the 2011 disruption of a London concert by the Israeli Philharmonic Orchestra (John F. Burns, "London Protesters Disrupt Israeli Orchestra's Concert," *The New York Times* (September 2, 2011), http://www.nytimes.com/2011/09/03/world/europe/03london.html?_r=0) and the 2014 Edinburgh protests that forced the cancellation of an Israeli theater group (Mark Brown, "Israeli Theatre Group has Performances Cancelled at Edinburgh Fringe," *The Guardian* (August 1, 2014), https://www.theguardian.com/stage/2014/aug/01/israeli-theatre-group-performances-cancelled-edinburgh-fringe-gaza). The writer Alice Walker, gripped by anti-normalization fever, even refused in 2012 to authorize a Hebrew translation of her novel *The Color Purple*. Israelis are not to be allowed to read her work!

71. Nelson and Brahm, 2015, op. cit., p. 15.

72. Not that this stops anti-Israelists, who in January 2017 charged the Batsheva Dance Company with precisely that offense: "We Call on the Batsheva Dance Company to End its Complicity With Israeli Government Crimes," Adalah-NY (January 19, 2017), http://mondoweiss.net/2017/01/batsheva-complicity-government/. In chapter 20 of the current volume, David Rosen dissects the BDS abuse of the notion of "complicity."

73. Israeli-Palestinian-Arab journalist Khaled Abu Toameh presents several such instances, including incidents where BDS activists broke up Israeli-Palestinian peace conferences and even shut down a Ramallah performance by an Indian dance troupe simply because the troupe had also performed in Tel Aviv ("Palestinians' Anti-Peace Campaign," Gatestone Institute (May 14, 2015), http://www.gatestoneinstitute.org/5750/palestinians-anti-peace). PACBI is also opposed to joint Israeli-Palestinian cultural projects, such as the youth music project "Heartbeat" aimed at fostering mutual understanding ("Heartbeat is a Normalization Project That Violates BDS Guidelines," PACBI (February 23, 2014), http://www.pacbi.org/etemplate.php?id=2383). In a particularly strange twist, even the West-Eastern Divan Orchestra, a musical collaboration between the late Palestinian anti-Israel icon Edward Said and Israeli Daniel Barenboim (who has yet to say something nice about Israel) has generated anti-normalization controversy ("West-Eastern Divan Orchestra: Undermining Palestinian Civil Resistance and Violating Palestinian Cultural Boycott Guidelines," PACBI (March 23, 2010), http://www.pacbi.org/etemplate.php?id=1196).

74. One Voice, Seeds for Peace, and the Peace Alliance. See Miriam Elman, "BDS Leaders Slam Leftist US Peace Groups," *Legal Insurrection* (June 9, 2016), http://legalinsurrection.com/2016/06/bds-leaders-slam-leftist-u-s-peace-groups/.

75. Miriam Elman, "BDS Leaders Slam Leftist US Peace Groups," *Legal Insurrection* (June 9, 2016), http://legalinsurrection.com/2016/06/bds-leaders-slam-leftist-u-s-peace-groups/. Elman also gives more anti-normalization examples, including the violent disruption of the 2015 "Jerusalem Hug."

76. Andrew Pessin, "Transgender Activist Janet Mock Cancels Brown U Talk After Anti-Israel Activists Reject Hillel Co-Sponsorship," *The Algemeiner* (March 18, 2016), https://www.algemeiner.com/2016/03/18/transgender-activist-cancels-brown-u-talk-amid-pinkwashing-controversy-over-hillel-co-sponsorship/.

77. Hillel International, the parent organization, has had a turbulent past few years as a growing chorus of voices demand that it relinquish its current "Standards of Partnership," which prevent campus chapters from working with groups that delegitimize or call for the destruction of Israel. Brown's Hillel itself was in the center of that controversy in the spring of 2016, when it both sponsored a March 2016 lecture by the controversial group Breaking the Silence and then, apparently, permitted its premises to be used for a screening of anti-Israel

films. (See Andrew Pessin, "Hillel Defends Decision to Host Israeli 'Whistleblower' Group 'Breaking the Silence' at Campus Events," *The Algemeiner* (March 19, 2016), http://www .algemeiner.com/2016/03/19/hillel-defends-decision-to-host-israeli-whistleblower-group -breaking-the-silence-at-campus-events/. There is, however, controversy over whether Brown Hillel permitted this: Will Tavlin, "Why We Flouted Hillel Rules To Hold Nakba Event at Brown University," *The Forward* (May 17, 2016), http://forward.com/articles/340840/why -we-flouted-hillel-rules-to-hold-nakba-event-at-brown-university/; Alexandra Markus, "Was Brown U's Hillel Attempting to Cover Up a 'Nakba Day' Event?", *The Algemeiner* (May 13, 2016), http://www.algemeiner.com/2016/05/13/was-brown-us-hillel-attempting-to-cover-up -a-nakba-day-event/.)

78. David Collier, "The Dhimmi Jews of SOAS," *Beyond the Great Divide* (January 26, 2017), http://david-collier.com/soas-antisemitic-dhimmi/.

79. For some examples through June of 2016, see Sangwon Yoon, "The Boycott Israel Movement May Be Failing," Bloomberg (June 1, 2016), http://www.bloomberg.com/news /articles/2016-06-02/israel-boycott-is-failing-when-measured-by-main-economic-gauge.

80. For some recent examples: "Over 100 Writers . . . Call on PEN American Center to Reject Israeli Government Sponsorship," Adalah-NY (April 5, 2016), https://adalahny.org /press-release/1382/over-100-writers-including-pulitzer-winners-junot-d-az-richard-ford -and-alice; "Viet Thanh Nguyen, 2016 Pulitzer Prize Winner, Endorses Academic and Cultural Boycott of Israel," *Mondoweiss* (June 17, 2016), http://mondoweiss.net/2016/06 /endorses-academic-cultural/.

81. For several incidents of Israeli performances being shut down in Scotland (just for one example): David Collier, "Nicola Sturgeon, How Welcome are Jews in Scotland?", *Beyond the Great Divide* (July 25, 2016), http://david-collier.com/?p=2152.

82. For just several examples over the years: "More Pressure for MidEast Peace," *The Guardian* (April 5, 2002), https://www.theguardian.com/world/2002/apr/06/israel .guardianletters "The Call," https://stoptechnionitalia.wordpress.com/the-call/ (accessed November 9, 2017); "Open Letter in Defense of Academic Freedom in Palestine/Israel and in the US," *The Miscellany News* (March 1, 2014), http://miscellanynews.org/2014/03/01/opinions /open-letter-in-defense-of-academic-freedom-in-palestineisrael-and-in-the-united-states/; GSOC-UAW 2110 for BDS Campaign, Faculty Signatories, http://www.nooccupiedpalestine .org/faculty-signatories.html (accessed November 9, 2017).

83. "PACBI Salutes Over 200 Brazilian Intellectuals for Joining the Academic Boycott of Israel," PACBI (January 20, 2016), http://www.pacbi.org/etemplate.php?id=2768.

84. "University of Chile's Law Faculty Students Vote 'Yes' for BDS," BDSMovement.Net (April 27, 2016), https://bdsmovement.net/2016/university-of-chiles-law-faculty-students -vote-yes-for-bds-13967 (accessed November 9, 2013).

85. One list may be found here: "Academic Associations Endorsing Boycott and Resolutions," USACBI, http://www.usacbi.org/academic-associations-endorsing-boycott/ (accessed November 9, 2017).

86. Laurie Goodstein, "Presbyterians Vote to Divest Holdings to Pressure Israel," *The New York Times* (June 20, 2014), http://www.nytimes.com/2014/06/21/us/presbyterians-debating -israeli-occupation-vote-to-divest-holdings.html?_r=0. For other churches: Sean Savage, "Israel Supporters See Successes and Challenges With Protestant Churches on BDS," *Jewish News Service* (May 26, 2016), http://www.jns.org/latest-articles/2016/5/26/israel-supporters -see-successes-and-challenges-with-protestant-churches-on-bds.

87. Source: August 13, 2016, email from the US Campaign to End the Israeli Occupation, listing the Quakers, Mennonite Central Committee, United Methodists, Presbyterians, United Church of Christ, Unitarian Universalists, Catholic Conference of Major Superiors of Men, and the Alliance of Baptists.

88. Omar Barghouti, "Knesset Anti-BDS Meeting Reveals Israeli Fear of Isolation," *Mondoweiss* (January 7, 2016), http://mondoweiss.net/2016/01/knesset-israeli-isolation/.

89. Eli Lake, "Is Israel a Pariah? Not According to Its New Friends," Bloomberg (June 17, 2016), http://www.bloomberg.com/view/articles/2016-06-17/is-israel-a-pariah-not-according -to-its-new-friends.

90. Sangwon Yoon, "The Boycott Israel Movement May be Failing," Bloomberg (June 1, 2016), http://www.bloomberg.com/news/articles/2016-06-02/israel-boycott-is-failing-when -measured-by-main-economic-gauge.

91. For just one example: Yoram Ettinger, "Investment in Israel Defies Global Trend," *Israel Hayom* (October 31, 2016), http://www.israelhayom.com/site/newsletter_opinion .php?id=17537.

92. Binyamin Kagedan, "For Popular Musicians, Performing in Israel Makes a Statement," *The Algemeiner* (May 9, 2013), http://www.algemeiner.com/2013/05/09/for-popular-musicians -performing-in-israel-makes-a-statement/.

93. Adam Levick, "BDS is Failing: A Continuing Series," *UK Media Watch* (May 31, 2016), https://ukmediawatch.org/2016/05/31/bds-is-failing-a-continuing-series-june-2016/; Jessica Steinberg, "Rock N' Roll Bad Boys Guns N' Roses Return to Tel Aviv," *The Times of Israel* (December 5, 2016), http://www.timesofisrael.com/rock-n-roll-bad-boys-guns-n-roses -return-to-tel-aviv/.

94. http://www.artists4israel.org/ (accessed November 13, 2017).

95. https://www.creativecommunityforpeace.com/ (accessed November 13, 2017).

96. Conor Friedersdorf, "How Political Correctness Chills Speech on Campus," *The Atlantic* (September 1, 2016), http://www.theatlantic.com/politics/archive/2016/09/what-it -looks-like-when-political-correctness-chills-speech-on-campus/497387/.

97. For a complete list, see http://www.jewishvirtuallibrary.org/anti-bds-legislation (accessed November 13, 2017).

98. "House Bill Extends Fines to Compliance With BDS, Settlement Boycotts," *Jewish Telegraphic Agency* (November 15, 2016), http://www.jta.org/2016/11/15/news-opinion /politics/house-bill-extends-criminal-penalties-to-compliance-with-bds-settlement -boycotts.

99. Congress.gov on S.720, https://www.congress.gov/bill/115th-congress/senate-bill /720/cosponsors (accessed November 10, 2017); Congress.gov on H.R. 1697, https://www .congress.gov/bill/115th-congress/house-bill/1697 (accessed November 10, 2017).

100. Colleen Flaherty, "Antisemitism Awareness Bill Passes Senate," *Inside Higher Ed* (December 2, 2016), https://www.insidehighered.com/quicktakes/2016/12/02/anti-semitism -awareness-bill-passes-senate. A similar bill was introduced into the House of Representatives shortly thereafter.

101. Adam Levick, "BDS is Failing: A Continuing Series," *UK Media Watch* (July 2016), https://ukmediawatch.org/2016/06/30/bds-is-failing-a-continuing-series-july-2016/; Lidar Gravé-Lazi, "Spanish Israel Lobby Group Deals Triple Blow to BDS Movement in Spain," *The Jerusalem Post* (August 3, 2016), http://www.jpost.com/Arab-Israeli-Conflict/Spanish-Israel -lobby-group-deals-triple-blow-to-BDS-movement-in-Spain-463114.

102. "Jewish Human Rights Organization Lauds Paris for Adopting Anti-BDS Resolutions," *The Algemeiner* (February 18, 2016), https://www.algemeiner.com/2016/02/18/jewish-human-rights-organization-lauds-paris-for-adopting-anti-bds-resolutions/.

103. Benjamin Weinthal, "Bavaria's Green Party: BDS Same As Nazi 'Don't Buy From Jews' Slogan," *The Jerusalem Post* (October 8, 2017), http://www.jpost.com/Diaspora/Bavarias-Green-Party-BDS-same-as-Nazi-Dont-buy-from-Jews-slogan-506976.

104. Shiri Moshe, "Austrian University Students Overwhelmingly Condemn BDS Movement as 'Antisemitic'," *The Algemeiner* (October 16, 2017), https://www.algemeiner.com/2017/10/16/austrian-university-students-overwhelmingly-condemn-bds-movement-as-antisemitic/.

105. Sean Savage, "Israel Supporters See Successes and Challenges with Protestant Churches on BDS," *Jewish News Service* (May 26, 2016), http://www.jns.org/latest-articles/2016/5/26/israel-supporters-see-successes-and-challenges-with-protestant-churches-on-bds.

106. "Organizations and Universities That Have Condemned the American Studies Association's Academic Boycott of Israel," AMCHA Initiative, http://www.amchainitiative.org/organizations-universities-condemned-american-studies-associations-academic-boycott-israel/ (accessed November 10, 2017).

107. Simon Bronner and Michael A. Rockland, "Why We Sued the American Studies Association," *The Hill* (May 8, 2016), http://thehill.com/blogs/congress-blog/foreign-policy/278398-why-we-sued-the-american-studies-association; Elizabeth Redden, "Israel Boycott Battle Heads to Court," *Inside Higher Ed* (April 21, 2016), https://www.insidehighered.com/news/2016/04/21/lawsuit-targets-american-studies-associations-stance-israel-academic-boycott.

108. "Public Interest Lawsuit Reveals Plot by BDS Activists to Takeover Academic Associations," The Louis D. Brandeis Center for Human Rights Under Law (November 9, 2017), http://brandeiscenter.com/public-interest-lawsuit-reveals-plot-bds-activists-takeover-academic-associations/ (accessed November 13, 2017).

109. Jacob Baime, "US – Israel Academic Collaboration Increases Dramatically," *The Times of Israel* (December 6, 2016), http://blogs.timesofisrael.com/u-s-israel-academic-collaboration-increases-dramatically/.

110. "Antisemitic Divestment from Israel Initiatives Scorecard on U.S. Campuses 2012-2017," AMCHA Initiative, http://www.amchainitiative.org/israel-divestment-vote-scorecard/ (accessed November 10, 2017).

111. National Center for Education Statistics, http://nces.ed.gov/programs/digest/d12/tables/dt12_005.asp (accessed November 10, 2017).

112. Martin Slagter, "UM Student Government Passes Resolution to Divest From Israel," *Michigan Live* (November 15, 2017), http://www.mlive.com/news/ann-arbor/index.ssf/2017/11/um_student_government_passes_r.html.

113. Israel On Campus Coalition, "2016-17 Year End Report," https://israelcc.org/wp-content/uploads/2017/09/2016-2017-Year-End-Report.pdf (accessed November 13, 2017).

114. Anna Baltzer, "BDS@12, Two Hundred Victories," US Campaign for Palestinian Rights, https://uscpr.org/bds-turns-12/ (accessed November 10, 2017). As we saw above, BDS actually began before "The Call" in 2005.

115. Mario Vasquez, "UAW Overrules Academic Workers BDS Vote Against Israel Despite Finding Strong Turnout, No Misconduct," *In These Times* (January 6, 2016),

http://inthesetimes.com/working/entry/18731/uaw-university-california-local-2865-boycott
-divestment-sanctions-israel; Danielle Ziri, "NYU Graduate Student Union Repeals Pro-BDS
Resolution," *The Jerusalem Post* (June 23, 2016), http://www.jpost.com/International/NYU
-Graduate-Student-Union-repeals-pro-BDS-resolution-457563.

116. Lea Speyer, "Vassar Alumnus Calls Defeat of BDS Resolution at College a 'Watershed
Moment'," *The Algemeiner* (May 3, 2016), http://www.algemeiner.com/2016/05/03/pro-israel
-alumnus-calls-defeat-of-bds-resolution-at-vassar-a-watershed-moment/.

117. Andrew Pessin, "BDS Motion Passes Easily at Canada's McGill University," *The
Algemeiner* (February 23, 2016), http://www.algemeiner.com/2016/02/23/bds-motion-passes
-easily-at-canadas-mcgill-university/.

118. Andrew Pessin, "McGill University's Student Body Rejects Student Government's BDS
Vote," *The Algemeiner* (February 27, 2016), https://www.algemeiner.com/2016/02/27/mcgill
-universitys-student-body-rejects-student-governments-bds-vote/.

119. Andrew Pessin, "McGill University and How Western Civilization May Have
Just Saved Itself—From Itself," *The Algemeiner* (June 6, 2016), https://www.algemeiner.
com/2016/06/06/mcgill-university-and-how-western-civilization-may-have-just-saved-itself
-from-itself/.

120. "Antisemitism: University Statements Rejecting Academic Boycotts of Israel," Jewish
Virtual Library, https://www.jewishvirtuallibrary.org/jsource/anti-semitism/bdsschools.html
(accessed November 10, 2017). See the statement from Columbia University in particular.

121. William A. Jacobson, "List of Universities Rejecting Academic Boycott of Israel
(Update – 250!)," *Legal Insurrection* (December 22, 2013), http://legalinsurrection.com
/2013/12/list-of-universities-rejecting-academic-boycott-of-israel/.

122. For one recent example: Adam Levick, "BDS is Failing: A Continuing Series
Documenting Israeli Success (Sept. 2017)," UK Media Watch, https://ukmediawatch.org
/2017/09/11/bds-is-failing-a-continuing-series-sept-2017/ (accessed November 10, 2017). In
addition, the advocacy group Scholars for Peace in the Middle East produces a monthly
analysis of all matters BDS, with one recent example here: Alex Joffe, "BDS Monitor
November 2017," SPME, http://spme.org/boycotts-divestments-sanctions-bds/spme
-boycotts-divestments-and-sanctions-bds-monitor/campus-speech-violence-claims-spreads
-state-level-anti-bds-laws-cause-confusion-bds-blames-zionism-weinstein-sex-abuse-center
-jewish-history-cancels-bds-related-tal/24361/ (accessed November 10, 2017).

123. "Israel's 1948 Founding is 'Occupation' in BDS Resolution Approved by Student
Government," *The College Fix* (October 26, 2016), http://www.thecollegefix.com/post/29644/.

124. Best-selling books can resurrect antisemitic memes of Jewish control of world
governments (such as John Mearsheimer and Stephen Walt's *The Israel Lobby and US Foreign
Policy* [Farrar, Straus and Giroux, 2007]); professors can casually resurrect blood libels in
public lectures (Jasbir Puar's February 2016 Vassar lecture) then publish them in books
produced by leading academic presses such as Duke University's (Shiri Moshe, "In Upcoming
Book, Controversial Rutgers Professor Accuses Israel of Sparing Palestinian Lives in Order to
Control Them," *The Algemeiner* (October 22, 2017), https://www.algemeiner.com/2017/10/22/in
-upcoming-book-controversial-rutgers-professor-accuses-israel-of-sparing-palestinian-lives
-in-order-to-control-them/); professors can post outrageous antisemitic claims on Facebook
(Oberlin's Joy Karega, Rutger's Michael Chikindas), while a Stanford student senator can
sincerely suggest that it's "very valid" to discuss whether Jews really do control the world,
the banks, the media, etc. A recent article in *Tablet* shows how far mainstream conversations

can shift, noting that while "Yasser Arafat first fabricated Temple Denial from whole cloth in 2000" the *New York Times* now refers to the "controversy" surrounding Jewish "claims" to the Temple Mount, and that BDS's absurdly false allegations of Israeli "apartheid" and "genocide" have within the past decade "come to dominate discourse among American academics and European parliamentarians" (see Bruce Abramson, Jeff Ballabon, "The End of AIPAC's Israel Monopoly," *Tablet* (July 11, 2016), http://www.tabletmag.com/jewish-news -and-politics/207251/the-end-of-aipacs-israel-monopoly).

125. Uriel Heilman, "Democrats and Young Americans More Sympathetic to Palestinians: Survey," *The Forward* (May 5, 2016), http://forward.com/news/breaking -news/340073/democrats-and-young-americans-more-sympathetic-to-palestinians-survey/.

126. Numbers presented by pollster Frank Luntz to the "Ambassadors Against BDS" conference in New York City on May 31, 2016.

127. Maayan Jaffe, "Despite Limited Practical Impact, BDS Producing Apprehension For Pro-Israel Academics," *Jewish News Service* (March 23, 2014), http://www.jns.org/latest -articles/2014/3/23/despite-limited-practical-impact-bds-producing-apprehension-for-pro -israel-academics.

128. According to research by the International Freedom of Research Center, Israeli academics have begun hiding their nationalities to avoid being boycotted: Judy Maltz, "Survey: Fearing Boycott, One in Six Israeli Academics Hide Their National Identity," *Haaretz* (May 10, 2016), https://www.haaretz.com/israel-news/.premium-1.718964.

129. One graduate student who writes extensively about BDS issues does so under the pseudonym "Occam's Razor" precisely in order to protect his professional future: Occam's Razor, "Israel Boycott Vote at Modern Language Association on January 7," *Legal Insurrection* (December 22, 2016), http://legalinsurrection.com/2016/12/israel-boycott-vote -at-modern-language-association-on-january-7/.

130. Shiri Moshe, "Princeton Hillel Cancels Speech by Top Israeli Diplomat, Drawing Criticism and an Apology," *The Algemeiner* (November 7, 2017), https://www.algemeiner .com/2017/11/07/princeton-hillel-cancels-speech-by-top-israeli-diplomat-drawing-criticism -and-an-apology/.

131. Lea Speyer, Rachel Frommer, "Jewish Students at Texas U Cancel Lecture by Author Caroline Glick for Fear of 'Alienating' Anti-Zionists on Campus," *The Algemeiner* (November 13, 2016), https://www.algemeiner.com/2016/11/13/pro-israel-jewish-groups -university-of-texas-austin-pull-sponsorship-caroline-glick-zionist-speaker-over-fear -alienating-students/.

132. Wim Wiewel, "Divestment Proposal Is Divisive, Ill-Informed," *VOXPREZ* (June 2, 2016), https://voxprez.com/2016/06/02/divestment-proposal-is-divisive-ill-informed/.

133. Andrew Pessin, "Non-Jewish Pro-Israel Vassar Professor Says 'Anti-Jewish Atmosphere' on Campus 'Starting to Have Long-Term Effects'," *The Algemeiner* (March 23, 2016), http://www.algemeiner.com/2016/03/23/non-jewish-pro-israel-vassar-professor-says -anti-jewish-atmosphere-on-campus-starting-to-have-long-term-effects/.

134. Miguel Olvera, "Suggestions of Civility Promote Campus Censorship," *New University: University of California Irvine Official Campus Newspaper* (May 24, 2016), http://www.newuniversity.org/2016/05/opinion/suggestions-of-civility-promote-campus -censorship/.

135. Omar Zazah, "An Escalating Backlash," *Palestine in America* (July 11, 2016), http:// palestineinamerica.com/2016/07/student-activism-repression/.

136. William Chafe documents how calls for civility sought to retard the struggle for civil rights in *Civilities and Civil Rights: Greensboro, North Carolina, and the Black Struggle for Freedom* (New York: Oxford University Press, 1981).

137. One article surveying this behavior is this: Ira Stoll, "'Underhanded Tactics' of BDS Movement Unnerve Jews on College Campuses Worldwide," *The Algemeiner* (December 8, 2016), https://www.algemeiner.com/2016/12/08/underhanded-tactics-of-bds-movement-unnerve-jews-on-college-campuses-worldwide/.

138. Examples include Loyola University Chicago, the Ohio State University, University College London, the University of Chicago, and the University of Toronto: Cara Stern, "Pro-Israel Students Criticize BDS Endorsement," *The Canadian Jewish News* (December 28, 2012), http://www.cjnews.com/living-jewish/jewish-learning/pro-israel-students-criticize-bds-endorsement. The notes to follow will mention just one or two examples of each phenomenon; typically, there are (many) others.

139. The American Anthropological Association.

140. University of Michigan, activists in the American Studies Association.

141. City University of New York and the Ohio State University, among many others.

142. University of Indianapolis.

143. Portland State University in May 2016.

144. McGill University.

145. University of Indianapolis.

146. Stanford University, where "over 90% of those people who tried to vote more than once were voting in support of BDS" (see Harry Elliot, "70% of Stanford Students Oppose BDS, Bringing Into Question Why SJP Seeks Re-Vote," *The Stanford Review*, https://stanfordreview.org/70-of-stanford-students-oppose-bds-bringing-into-question-why-sjp-seeks-re-vote/ (accessed November 10, 2017)).

147. Fordham University, activists in the American Studies Association.

148. Portland State University in May 2016.

149. New York University, Université du Québec à Montréal, and nearly everywhere else. Some particularly notable examples include the University of Edinburgh (where a BDS vote with 36,000 eligible student voters was held in a room holding only 250), University College London (where a BDS resolution passed with the vote of a mere 14 individuals out of 38,500 students), and University of California, Santa Cruz (where BDS passed by a vote of 28 student council representatives on a campus with 16,000 undergraduates).

150. University of California, Berkeley: Lea Speyer, "'Antisemitic Anti-Zionist' Course at UC Berkeley Suspended Following Exposé, Outcry," *The Algemeiner* (September 13, 2016), http://www.algemeiner.com/2016/09/13/antisemitic-anti-zionist-course-at-uc-berkeley-suspended-following-expose-outcry/.

151. University of Washington (see Zion Mike, "Jewish Students At UW Harassed, Israel Display Vandalized," *Israellycool* (February 19, 2017), http://www.israellycool.com/2017/02/19/jewish-students-at-uw-harassed-israel-display-vandalized/).

152. Alina Sharon, "Pro-BDS Briefing on Capitol Hill Cancelled After Backlash," *Jewish News Service* (September 14, 2016), http://www.jns.org/latest-articles/2016/9/14/pro-bds-briefing-on-capitol-hill-cancelled-after-backlash.

153. For one very general and (thanks to the Durban conference) omnipresent example of this sort of phenomenon, slanderers accusing Israel of apartheid are regularly promulgated in academic environments despite what can only be deemed their blatant absurdity. (For a

similar discussion about charges of genocide, ethnic cleansing, and colonialist imperialism, see Andrew Pessin's "Epistemic Antisemitism," *Journal for the Study of Antisemitism* [forthcoming].) One may have legitimate complaints about Israeli policies, but even South African jurist Richard Goldstone, no friend to Israel, has acknowledged the utterly slanderous nature of those charges, concluding, "those who conflate the situations in Israel and the West Bank and liken both to the old South Africa do a disservice to all who hope for justice and peace.... The charge that Israel is an apartheid state is a false and malicious one" (Richard J. Goldstone, "Israel and the Apartheid Slander," *The New York Times* (October 31, 2011), http://www.nytimes.com/2011/11/01/opinion/israel-and-the-apartheid-slander .html?scp=1&sq=richard%20J%20Goldstone&st=cse&_r=0).

154. For just one example, anti-Israel activists made a point of participating in protests held by Native Americans against the building of a pipeline in South Dakota in order to spread by this alliance their own contentious claim that they are the indigenous people of Palestine: William A. Jacobson, "Anti-Israel Activists Continue to Exploit Standing Rock Sioux Pipeline Dispute (#NODAPL)," *Legal Insurrection* (November 6, 2016), http://legalinsurrection.com/2016/11/anti-israel-activists-continue-to-exploit-standing -rock-sioux-pipeline-dispute-nodapl/.

155. Black Lives Matter's controversial platform statement, released in August 2016, may be found at The Movement For Black Lives, https://policy.m4bl.org/ (accessed November 10, 2017).

156. Alan Dershowitz, "Who Do Bigots Blame for Police Shootings in America? Israel, of Course!," Gatestone Institute (July 13, 2016), http://www.gatestoneinstitute.org/8469/police -shootings.

157. We thank Deborah Pollak, Jon Haber, Gabriella Rothman, and audience members at the Columbia, SC, Jewish Community Center, the Merrick Jewish Centre, and Yeshiva University for helpful comments on earlier drafts of this essay.

I. Scholars' Essays

1   BDS and Self-Righteous Moralists

Dan Avnon

Dan Avnon tells of his experience with the BDS movement in Australia. His political work for equality and human rights for all citizens of Israel notwithstanding, he became the target of a very public, if personal, boycott by the director of the University of Sydney's Center for Peace Studies, just because he is an Israeli. This episode demonstrates that the peaceful, social justice declarations of the BDS movement are disingenuous, that BDS targets all Jewish Israelis as part of its program to ultimately end Israel's existence. Avnon highlights how overreaction to the incident by the anti-BDS legal organization Shurat HaDin actually undermined the opposition to BDS and criticizes the self-righteous moralism that has come to dominate the discourse of the Arab-Israeli conflict.

In THE COURSE of the years 2012–2014, I was subject to the actions of the Sydney chapter of the Boycott, Divestment, and Sanctions (BDS) movement, led by a University of Sydney faculty member, Professor Jake Lynch. For Lynch and his associates, I was an embodied representation of Israel, a country whose policies they detest and whose scholars and scientists they boycott.

I had not previously been singled out for boycott merely because of my being a Jewish-Israeli scholar and surely had never been boycotted by the left-wing edges of political activism, whereas ironically, in Israel, I have occasionally been condemned by academic and nonacademic self-anointed Jewish and patriotic zealots. The novelty of this experience—being boycotted due to my national identity and organizational affiliation—is in the backdrop of my reflections.

I will address two aspects of my BDS experiences. First, I'll explain how by subjecting me to their propaganda, leaflets, and demonstrations, the BDS activists enabled me to realize that their actual goal is to end Israel's existence as an independent Jewish state. That's the political aspect. Second, my experiences during the two years of having my image formed and used by various political players provided me with an opportunity to reflect on an attendant dimension of the situation: the morality of protagonists from both pro- and anti-BDS sides of the divide. From this perspective, I'll raise some initial speculations about an overlooked political vice and its harmful effects: self-righteous moralism.[1] I will relate a few episodes that cause or lead me to suggest that self-righteousness may be a particular sensation (of self) that transforms potentially sensitive and sensible people into insensitive and dogmatic champions of absolute justice: self-made, if you will.

The Background

I heard about the faculty exchange fellowship of the Sir Zelman Cowen Universities Fund, which supports exchanges between the University of Sydney and the Hebrew University of Jerusalem, in a chance encounter with a colleague who had been a recipient of this fellowship. It was on a late Thursday afternoon, and the deadline for application was less than a week away. Since I had no prior contacts in Australia, I perused the University of Sydney's website, seeking scholars who would perhaps be interested in sponsoring my application for this grant. I then dashed off a rather hurried email to five unwitting colleagues. Four of them, all senior scholars at the University of Sydney, responded within a couple of hours, agreeing to my using their names on my application form. A fifth, the director of the University of Sydney's Center for Peace and Conflict Studies, Jake Lynch, who, unbeknownst to me, was a zealous supporter of the BDS movement, sent me a surprising response.[2]

Here are the transcripts of my email correspondence with Lynch.[3] The time listed is Israeli local time.

Nov. 16, 2012 02:02

Dear Professor Lynch:

I apologise for dropping into your inbox without an introduction. I am the former Head of the Federmann School of Public Policy and Governance at the Hebrew University, and a political theorist at the Department of Political Science at the Hebrew University of Jerusalem. In my political philosophy niche I specialise in the philosophy of Martin Buber.

I will be on sabbatical leave during the 2013–14 academic year. I would like to spend time in Australia to learn about Australia's civic education policy and curriculum. This is an area of research (and of active, hands-on curriculum development) that has been at the core of my work in the past decade. This work included the writing and implementation of Israel's only (State-sanctioned) program in civics written for joint Jewish-Arab, religious/non-religious high-school kids.

I intend to devote my sabbatical to a comparative study of civic education in societies undergoing demographic (and consequently cultural) changes.

As part of my sabbatical I would like to come to Sydney for two months in 2014 to work on this research. I was alerted today to the possibility of applying to a Hebrew University–University of Sydney fellowship that would fund part of my stay at the University. The application deadline is tomorrow. So, I am working frenetically to get this done on time.

My (embarrassingly urgent) request is: can I mention you as a contact person at your university? I have gone through the list of faculty and schools at the University of Sydney, and you seem to be a colleague whom I would like to meet when I am there. This courtesy will enable me to apply.

Attached are the application forms, partially completed. I attach them so that you can see who I am (academically). No need for you to do anything with or about them.

Thank you for your attention. I hope that you can reply "yes" and this will enable me to complete the application and hope for the best.

Best wishes,

Dan Avnon

Nov. 16, 2012 04:23

Dear Professor Avnon,

Thank you for your email, no apologies necessary.

Indeed, it is I who must apologize to you, for I am bound, by our Center's policy, to decline your request. My apology to you is on a personal level, for neither I nor the Center have anything against you—and your research sounds interesting and worthwhile. However, we are supporters of the campaign of Boycott, Divestment, and Sanctions, and that includes the call for an academic boycott of Israeli universities.

I have attached the letter I wrote to the University Vice Chancellor, after a meeting of my Center's governing Council, and a separate meeting open to the whole university community, when we adopted the policy—along with his response.

Our Center's policy is not the policy of the University, as you will see, but it does foreclose our entering into any such arrangements as you propose.

Yours sincerely, Jake

Associate Professor Jake Lynch
BA, Dip Journalism Studies, PhD
Director, Center for Peace and Conflict Studies

I sent the email late at night (02:02), and Lynch's reply arrived at 04:23, when I was asleep. When I opened my inbox a few hours later, I found his response. Since the response was written in what seemed to be personal terms—"on a personal level, for neither I nor the Center have anything against you"—I naively assumed that this was indeed a personal communication and that a person-to-person response was in order. Hence my reply:

Nov. 16, 2012 11:02

Dear Jake (if I may),

I had no idea that this is your stand, and that the specific fellowship to which I am applying is a symbol of what you oppose!

I hope to have the opportunity to discuss this issue with you. As an opening comment, I find it ironic ... [that for you I am] a symbol of all that you find reprehensible. It is ironic because like myself, many (probably most) [Israeli] intellectuals and scholars in relevant fields are doing our best to effect change in Israeli political culture. We pay prices for going against the institutional grain. And then we turn around and meet such a "blind to the person" policy.

One common tendency that must be changed if we ever want to live sane lives is to debunk categorical and stereotypical thinking when dealing with human beings. I attach an article that I wrote precisely on this issue.[4] You need not read beyond the first two pages. The gist of what I have to say about this is there.

There is so much to be said about this thorny issue (between principle and practice).... Should I have the good fortune of receiving this fellowship and coming to Sydney, perhaps we'll meet (personally) and explore fresh looks at the principled position that you outlined in your letter.

Best personal wishes,

Dan

Lynch never responded to my email. I later learned from University of Sydney colleagues that within a few minutes of sending his reply to me he had sent a copy of my request and his response to a host of recipients, apparently to gain credit for his ability to boycott Israelis. As for me, I filed this correspondence and went on with my life, for a very short while.

In late November 2012, a week after my nondialogical exchange with Lynch, I was contacted by an Australian journalist, Christian Kerr of the *Australian*, who was writing a story about Lynch's decision to boycott me. From the moment of front-page publication of Kerr's report on December 6, 2012, Lynch's decision to publicize my personal request and to trumpet it as his anti-Israel catch of the year created for me a public persona with a life of its own. What attracted attention in Australia and elsewhere was the fact that Lynch had chosen to boycott a scholar whose work proactively promoted civic equality in Israel between majority Jews and minority Palestinian-Israeli Arabs. This curious choice helped anti-BDS activists point to deep contradictions between BDS claims to promote social justice in Israel on the one hand and boycotting someone associated with that very activity on the other hand.

From the distance of my Jerusalem computer, it seemed to me that Lynch's actions had backfired. The dean of the University of Sydney's Faculty of Humanities, Professor Duncan Iveson, stood up for the basic values that underpin scholarly exchange and scientific research.[5] Various items in the Australian press indicated that, by and large, the BDS movement was a marginal, peripheral fringe group. Many Australian citizens, scholars, and a few public figures wrote to me private emails with touching messages of support, expressing their disdain for BDS activism and their objection to the use of university positions as bully pulpits. This sentiment seemed prevalent and prevailed until the ill-advised intervention of Shurat HaDin, an international organization that decided to press legal charges against Lynch. The Shurat HaDin interference led to a reversal in the tide of public sentiment. I'll address this aspect of my experiences shortly.

At this point, I want to present arguments that seem to me sufficient to convince readers that BDS is a dishonest project that may be misleading well-intentioned activists to adopt practices that result in unintended, harmful consequences. Following the presentation of my position regarding the BDS movement, I'll turn to a directly related and troubling issue: the use of this case by nationalistic Israeli activists as an opportunity to attack my work in promoting democratic civic education in Israel and—from a different quarter—to use my case in an ill-advised manner to delegalize Lynch and his BDS ilk. The two parts of my report are linked by my characterizing the actions of leading activists on all sides of the BDS debate as self-righteous moralists. This feature is relevant to a principled study of civic activism, beyond the context of this particular skirmish.

Why I Oppose the BDS Movement: Their Deceptive Goals

There are many reasoned and, at times, passionate discourses against the BDS movement.[6] I won't try to summarize these claims; they are readily available to anyone with access to the internet and to university libraries and databases. I'll highlight my impression that the activities of the academic boycotters are, in fact, part of a broader and deeply troubling agenda to undermine the very existence of Israel.

Let's begin with the BDS movement's declared goals. Without delving into the intricacies of the BDS program, the summary of its goals is as follows: "Ending [Israel's] occupation and colonization of all Arab lands occupied in June 1967 and dismantling the Wall; recognizing the fundamental rights of the Arab-Palestinian citizens of Israel to full equality; and respecting, protecting, and promoting the rights of Palestinian refugees to return to their homes and properties as stipulated in UN Resolution 194."[7]

The goals *seem* to be focused on specific policies or practices. But anyone who knows anything about the circumstances of the founding of Israel knows that the goals are, *in fact*, oriented to ending Israel's existence as a Jewish nation-state. For example, unwitting supporters of BDS read the words "ending the occupation and colonization" and probably think that the 1967 war was a preplanned attempt to colonize areas that in fact were captured as part of a war of self-defense. They hear "dismantling the Wall" (capital *W* in the original wording) and are moved to action by haunting images of the Berlin Wall and Pink Floyd's *Wall*, with their respective bricks and hoped-for downfalls. They read "rights of the Arab-Palestinian citizens of Israel" and are roused to action by the evocative mention of universal civic rights. Finally, they are summoned to support refugees in terms of UN resolution 194, without knowing when and in what context that resolution was adopted. The language is appealing, using catchy metaphors and playing language games with liberal sentiments through references to colonization, international law, and human rights.

This rhetoric obfuscates realities. Let's consider the first goal. Fences and walls separating parts of pre-1967 Israel and the West Bank (also referred to as "the occupied territories" and "Judea and Samaria") were built during the first decade of the twenty-first century. Their purpose was to radically reduce the infiltration of suicide bombers and other forms of terrorism. The purpose was by and large achieved and, on this account, not objectionable. The physical barrier is objectionable, however, when and where it is built on Palestinian land and when it causes illegal, unwarranted, and, at times, outrageous misery to the Palestinian populace. So, there are specific injustices that are due to the wall. But there are also merits to this obstacle to terrorist attacks. The rhetoric of BDS activists, oblivious to the many dimensions of the issue and dedicated to "dismantling the Wall," may be useful for arousing sentiments but is actually insensitive to context and to circumstance.

The second goal, with which I am more intimately involved, implies that all of Israel's Arab-Palestinian citizens are in such a sorry state that they need immediate and urgent international support. This is so far from the truth. As I write these words, the Arab political parties of Israel, which joined forces to run as one alliance in Israel's 2015 parliamentary elections, garnished votes that elected thirteen of their lists' members to the Israeli Knesset. They overcame considerable inner rivalry and factionalism and came together because they realized that political power in Israel's democracy will give them access to resources that can better the lot of their constituencies. That is how democracies work. This political alliance is a sign of positive developments in the status and level of integration of Israel's Arab citizenry.

While BDS activists are focusing on the one Middle Eastern Arab society that is doing relatively well in terms of democratic integration, they overlook Arab societies that are in real and dire need—societies that are just beyond Israel's boundaries. What about the plights of millions of citizens of Syria, Iraq, Yemen, and Sudan? Of women in Saudi Arabia? Of prodemocracy activists in Egypt? I could go on.[8] My point is to put events in proportion: Israeli Arab-Palestinians are fighting an uphill, but in many respects successful, battle for equality. I share that struggle and their aspirations. There are deeply embedded forms of institutional discrimination that must be opposed and removed. I share that goal, too, and have done my best to support Arab colleagues who are actively fighting for and asserting their rights. So, this is a vibrant and major issue in Israel's democracy. With this in mind, one wonders why anyone would launch an international campaign against Israel and its treatment of its Arab citizens while hundreds of thousands of Arabs are being slaughtered and millions dispossessed throughout the Middle East. Why are BDS activists committed to securing rights for a populace that already lives in one of the sole stable and democratic states in the Middle East? There is an aspect of political life called *judgment*, a human capacity that is tempered by a sense of proportion. This is evidently lacking among BDS adherents.

It may be that pro-BDS supporters do not know that Israel is a democracy. Well, it is. Like most democracies, Israel's is imperfect. But that is not uncommon. Democracy is a regime type that actually assumes human and social imperfection and enables processes that endeavor to improve social, economic, and political qualities of life. Like other postcolonial democracies, Israel debates issues of majority-minority relations and questions of discrimination and racial prejudices. Such issues are continually discussed in our public spheres. The debates include those who press for the need to ensure and deepen Arab-Israeli-Palestinian rights, especially in the face of racism and discrimination. In the decades since the founding of the state, there have been advances and retreats on this particular front. Yet this overall positive development of the status and conditions of Israel's Arab-Palestinian citizenry does not matter to BDS activists. For them, the ultimate goal is not to advance rights but rather to weaken Israeli academia as part of the overall goal of weakening Israel as a state of the Jewish people. Otherwise, why would they boycott a scholar who wanted to learn from Australian attempts to develop programs in civic education that address the discriminatory past in order to advance toward greater consolidation of democratic values and practices?

This question has its answer in the BDS movement's third goal. While blatantly partisan, anti-Israel, and lacking in complex perspectives, the aforementioned first and second goals may still be considered as addressing particular policies. Yet the third goal is actually the endgame. To present the goal of BDS as the return of all 1948 refugees and their descendants to their original homes reveals the reasoning and aims of those who fund and support this movement. This goal ignores the sorry and tragic fact that the 1948 war was instigated by the Arab League due to their opposition to the United Nations November 1947

Resolution 181 that established two states, Jewish and Arab, in the territory known as Palestine. Resolution 194—"the rights of Palestinian refugees to return to their homes and properties"—was adopted in December 1948. It was enacted after a ceasefire had been declared between the newly established Jewish State and the various Arab invaders. Resolution 194 did not foresee that the temporary 1949 lines of armistice, later known as the "pre-1967 boundaries," would for all intents and purposes delineate the boundaries of the Jewish State. Regretfully, it did not recommend going ahead with the two-state solution and founding an Arab-Palestinian state on lands originally allotted to the Arab state and not captured by Israel in the course of its 1948 War of Independence. The land not taken by Israel, including the Old City of Jerusalem, became part of the Hashemite Kingdom of Jordan—that is, apart from the Gaza Strip, which eventually came under Egyptian sovereignty.

Let's be clear: the Arab countries could have enabled a Palestinian state in 1948 (in accordance with 181) or established a smaller temporary state in 1949 (after 194), and from that position, they could have negotiated a final settlement of boundaries, refugees, and other issues already determined in 181 but not implemented due to their rejection of the very notion of a Jewish state. They did not do this and opted to freeze the status of the 1949 refugees for an indefinite period of time through the establishment of the United Nations Relief and Works Agency for Palestine Refugees in the Near East (UNRWA).[9] It is now the year 2017. To call in the year 2017 for the return of all refugees and their descendants to the Jewish State of Israel on the basis of resolution 194, while disregarding all that has transpired since December 1948, is not merely a protest against specific policies. It exposes the movement's actual purpose: the destruction of Israel by the "return" of millions of Palestinians. This is tantamount to advocating the dismantling of Sydney—including the grounds on which Lynch teaches "peace and conflict studies"—and returning these lands to their precolonization Aboriginal inhabitants.

I raise these points in this manner because my strong impression from three years of exposure to the rhetoric and actions of anti-Israel BDS activists is that this movement is a cleverly designed tool used in the service of ending the existence of the Jewish State.[10] That is why Lynch and his ilk can boycott Israeli academics without giving a second glance at whom or what they are boycotting. "Are you a Jewish-Israeli scholar who works in an Israeli university?" "Yes." "Aha! Gotcha! A Zionist occupier! Out you go! BDS on you and yours!"

The absurdity of the logic and apparent policy implications of the BDS movement can be exemplified by considering the following facts: In 1834, one of my forefathers, Orthodox Hasidic Rabbi Israel Beck, living in the Ottoman province of Palestine, was granted rights to a plot of land on one of Galilee's highest mountains. The giver was the ruler of the hour, Ottoman Pasha Ibrahim. Beck established an agricultural settlement that was inhabited by over a hundred members of his Hasidic community. In 1839, the ruler was deposed, and a new ruler from a different Ottoman faction ascended to power in Palestine. The shift in power emboldened Beck's Druze neighbors, who gave him and his community twenty-four hours to pack their belongings and leave that land. So off they went, to Jerusalem. According to the logic of BDS, I and the many thousands of Beck's descendants should now march up there and reclaim our land.

These quick comments are enough for me to oppose the BDS movement. I am an Israeli, and I believe in my country's right to exist. I oppose BDS because it is led by self-righteous advocates whose actual goals are to rid the Middle East of a Jewish state. This underlying and overriding goal of the BDS movement explains how it came to be that a Jewish-Israeli scholar such as myself—who has, on occasion, been denigrated for his activities on behalf of Jewish-Palestinian accord within Israel and, in particular, for advancing the declared second goal of the BDS movement ("Recognizing the fundamental rights of the Arab-Palestinian citizens of Israel to full equality")—is subject to boycott by BDS activists. But there is another deceptive element in the BDS campaign that must be highlighted—their use of a South African precedent as a galvanizing frame of reference.

Why I Oppose the BDS Movement: The South African Analogy

Unwitting supporters of BDS do not realize that the anti-Israel BDS movement is grounded in a fundamental, deeply felt rejection of Israel's right to exist. In this respect, the BDS movement is a continuation of the blind folly of the 1948 Arab League's rejection of the very idea of a Jewish State on the lands of partitioned Palestine. This is where the comparison to South Africa is so misleading. Unlike anti-Israel BDS's intention to delegitimize the very foundations of Israel as a nation-state, the original anti-apartheid BDS movement did not seek to abolish the state of South Africa. Rather, it sought merely to rid it of its racist apartheid regime.

In contrast to that example, anti-Israel BDS does not distinguish between Israel's regime (a parliamentary democracy), a particular policy (for example, the two-state solution), or a specific political leadership (right-wing, center, or left-wing). To claim that Israel's parliamentary democracy is indistinguishable from South Africa's apartheid regime is, to say the least, intellectually dishonest. But it is a central element of BDS's propaganda. That is one reason for my being boycotted: if I am a Jewish-Israeli academic, I represent the Israeli state. If I am part of the Israeli state, then I am automatically subject to boycotts and sanctions solely on the basis of my national identity.[11]

Such automatic profiling of individuals and institutions on the basis of their national identity was not the mark of the original South African BDS movement. Quite the contrary. The antiapartheid movement assumed that the state of South Africa was to remain intact. Apartheid was to end, to be replaced by a majoritarian constitutional democracy. South Africa's regime type was to be transformed, not its existence eradicated. To compare the system of institutionalized racial discrimination practiced in South Africa under apartheid to practices in Israel's parliamentary democracy is, therefore, a clever and dishonest rhetorical ploy that enables the goal of ending the existence of Israel to be masked as a campaign for human rights.

My Australian BDS Experience as an Expression of Extreme Self-Righteous Moralism

In my initial correspondence with Lynch, I offered to meet and discuss his anti-Israel stance. He never replied. Instead, a few weeks later, he insinuated in a published commentary that I am not who I seem or claim to be: "Yes, there are academics in Israel who seek to challenge various aspects of their government's policies, and Professor Dan Avnon, whose request to spend his fellowship at my Center I declined, may be one of them. His involvement with the Metzilah Center suggests this aspect of the case may not be as clear-cut as [Sigal Samuel] suggests, which warrants further investigation."[12]

What warrants further investigation? That I am on the academic board of a research and advocacy center (Metzilah) that seeks to generate public debate on controversial issues within Israeli society? Is Lynch implying that policy papers, written by individual scholars associated with a think tank dedicated to deliberating diverse ideas, implicate all who are engaged in that center's committees? Should each such scholar be presumed to share the views of every other individual author who participates in the same research center? Is this how the Center for Peace and Conflict at the University of Sydney is administered? Has Lynch not heard of freedom of thought? Of plurality of ideas? Of think tanks where people actually think, argue, and even disagree?

Instead of simply contacting me and inquiring about my research, opinions, or convictions, Lynch responded to criticism through insinuation and innuendo, conforming with the pattern of his response to my email and his actions thereafter. I and all Israelis are classified according to a very narrow and specific pattern of associations. We are all probably complicit in some heinous, devious activity. If "further investigated, this Zionist, Professor Avnon, will surely be proven to be" whatever is predetermined according to Lynch's categorical preconceptions. This kind of thinking enables Lynch to doubt my integrity and seek evidence in support of his preconception. Damn the person, hail the preconception.

Commenting on the Book of Luke, Bible scholar Mark Allen Powell comments, "The religious leaders in Luke are characters who 'trust in themselves that they are righteous and despise others,'" and then dwells on the characterization of self-righteousness: "Luke characterizes the religious leaders as self-righteous in several ways. The narrator describes one of the leaders as a person who seeks 'to justify (dikaiosai) himself' (10:29) and refers to their representatives as people who 'pretend to be righteous (dikaious)' (20:20). Jesus also describes the leaders as persons who 'justify (dikaiountes) themselves before people' (16:15) and he tells a parable in which one of them proclaims his own righteousness (18:10–12)."[13]

This seems to be a good introduction to the ideal-type behavioral traits of self-righteous moralists. Self-righteousness blinds well-meaning protagonists to facts, to complexity, and to the exercise of morals that in ordinary conduct guide their personal actions. The appearance of zealotry in pursuit of lofty moral goals overshadows the actual—judicious and sensitive—encounter with reality. When self-righteous moralism migrates from the sphere of religious discourse to that of politics, then a common act is to define political opponents as immoral and wrongheaded and the accuser as ethical and pragmatic.

Self-righteous moralism is not limited to Lynch and his supporters, of course. The emphasis in the Australian press on my public record in promoting democratic civic education in Israel made the rounds to Israel. This juicy item was picked up by Israeli right-wing activists. They pounced on the news from Down Under with a mixture of rage and unrestrained glee. In a thundering op-ed titled "Serves Him Right!" one of Israel's prominent publicists, Ben-Dror Yemini, tore into my Israeli public persona. In that hatchet job, he reveled in the fact that I was subject to a dose of BDS activism: "Professor Dan Avnon tried to incite against the Jewish State, and was boycotted because he is Israeli. He suddenly understood that there aren't personal exemptions for an ingratiating academic." He then went on to present a negative portrayal of my advocacy of citizenship studies in Israel. It culminated with the following words: "As part of his academic activities Avnon tried to influence citizenship studies in a very particular direction.... [His publications] clarify that Israeli academia has become the long arm of politics. Primarily the politics of the left and of the radical left."[14]

To claim that I incited against the State of Israel is a blatant lie. I feel strongly about our right to an independent political existence and cannot have been caught claiming otherwise, anytime, anywhere. I am compelled to add that in addition to being a descendant of a relatively longstanding Jewish-Palestinian family (my maternal forefather settled in Ottoman Palestine in 1831), my father's Lithuanian Jewish family was liquidated by the Nazis in the 1941–1944 Ponary forest massacres.[15] So, from both branches of my parents' families, I have inherited cultural and historical contexts that root me firmly in the ancient land and in the modern State of Israel. I know—not merely believe—that as long as the world is divided into nation-states, we too need this nation-state of the Jewish people. I also know that we need this country to be just and humane. My actions have always been commensurate with these convictions and beliefs.

As for the charge that I developed programs in civics that assumed that Israel's citizenry should understand the logic of a democratically constituted polity, I admit the indictment, proudly. I am proud of the fact that I taught quite a number of educators who are doing a great job reforming civics education in Israel. I am also proud of the fact that despite their wide plurality of perspectives, all of my associates—scholars, educators, teachers, and policy makers—fit the democratic mold.[16] Finally, I am proud of the fact that all of the programs that I initiated in schools and in academia included participants from across the spectrum of Israel's society: religious and nonreligious, Jews and non-Jews. In all programs, we have made special efforts to enable socially deprived members to access the education we could offer at or under the auspices of the Hebrew University. So if these activities are considered left or radical, or perhaps both, then I carry this charge too as a badge of honor.

So much for my being castigated by nationalist ultra-patriots in Israel. The public chain of events generated by the ongoing attacks and counterattacks between pro-BDS activists and the many who rallied against them drew the attention of an additional actor. Shurat HaDin, an Israeli organization that specializes in "lawfare" against anti-Israel terrorist organizations,[17] decided to use my incident as an opportunity to stem the rise of BDS activism in Australia and elsewhere. In July 2013, they filed a complaint against Lynch with the Australian Human Rights Commission, under section 46P of the Australian Human Rights Commission Act 1986 (AHRCA), alleging unlawful discrimination under the Racial Discrimination Act 1975. The commission did not accept the complaint. In December 2013, Shurat HaDin moved up the legal ladder and filed a statement of claim against Lynch in the Australian federal court.[18]

The statement of claim included "The Avnon Acts," a series of discriminatory practices to which Professor Dan Avnon had been subjected. Shurat HaDin never contacted me, never consulted with me, nor asked for my permission or advice on this matter, yet decided to file its lawsuit on behalf of apparent victims of BDS activities, using my case as the linchpin. This ill-advised initiative was a turning point in the Australian BDS story and provided the Australian BDS activists an opportunity to regroup and position themselves as victims.

I include in this article reference to the Shurat HaDin case due to their exemplifying what I had already noted when observing Lynch's action. They too seemed to have been acting along lines commensurate with their moralism. Their actions added perspective to my thoughts about the impact of rigidly self-righteous political actors on the quality of their judgment and consequent actions. It seems to me that the various activists who converged around the Australian BDS campaign used my public persona—most of it conjured as reflections of their own interests—as an opportunity to lambast one another's perception of reality, each using his absolute sense of self-righteous moralism to go after the other's equally unqualified sense of rectitude.[19]

The legal case brought by Shurat HaDin against Lynch exemplifies poor judgments that ensue from being guided by self-righteous moralism rather than by clear-headed and well-founded analysis and pursuant political strategies. Shurat HaDin is successful in using legal systems as a means to go after the funders of terrorist attacks. This is because they have found the appropriate fit between the ethics and logic of legal spheres of discourse and the international desire to curb terrorism.[20] I find this line of action commendable and smart. However, there was not a similar fit between Lynch's use of moral discourse in the court of public opinion (BDS's primary sphere of action) and Shurat HaDin's attempts to transform perceptions of BDS from a galvanizer of public opinion into a legal entity that should be subject to judicial lawfare. It seems to me that Shurat HaDin did not realize how wrongheaded was their turn to the Australian legal system, and they did not heed the advice of Australian anti-BDS organizations to discontinue their Australian campaign.

When Shurat HaDin showed up in the Australian public sphere in July 2013, the coalition of anti-BDS advocates seemed to have been successful in marginalizing Lynch and his supporters. At this critical juncture, BDS activists were brought back to the public eye due to the publicity generated by Shurat HaDin. As reported in one newspaper, "But some leaders here [Australia] are understood to be privately fuming about the litigation by the Tel Aviv-based organization, fearing it is reigniting support for BDS in Australia soon after a broad counter campaign by Jewish leaders had won widespread support."[21]

Nitsana Darshan-Leitner, the founder of Shurat HaDin, immediately lashed back, accusing the Australian Jewish leadership of "not lifting a finger" in the battle against Lynch's actions.[22] This is a factual error.[23] She also accused Jewish leaders in Australia of having failed to "stand up for Jewish rights."[24] Jewish leadership had in fact conducted a successful campaign against the Australian BDS until the intervention by her organization, and in turning against them, Darshan-Leitner's accusations fit the mold of self-righteous moralism that I emphasized in my thinking about how good intentions become ill-conceived—at times, harmful—actions.

My lessons from being used by BDS protagonists are a mixture of the trivial and the consequential. Beginning with the trivial: I should not apply for fellowships at the last minute; I should run at least quick Google checks prior to contacting scholars with whom I seek to cooperate; and I should never assume that personal emails will remain personal. The consequential lessons are: the level of animosity directed at Israel is way above what I had imagined; the antiacademic BDS movement is by and large a feel-good movement characterized by self-righteous moralism; and this self-righteous moralism is channeled to an agenda that seeks to undermine the existence of Israel as a Jewish state. The events I witnessed indicate that when a political actor's actions are fueled by zealotry, he or she will find it easier and more self-inflaming to manipulate an image and address its imaginary characteristics than to meet a real, complex person.[25, 26]

DAN AVNON is an Associate Professor at the Hebrew University's Department of Political Science. In 2001, he founded the university's Gilo Center for Citizenship, Democracy & Civic Education, which he headed until 2007.

Notes

1. The notion of self-righteous moralism appears in Peter Euben, "Final Lecture: Political Freedom," *Political Science & Politics* 35, no. 4 (2002): 709–711.

2. See Philip Mendes and Nick Dyrenfurth, *Boycotting Israel Is Wrong: The Progressive Path to Peace between Palestinians and Israelis* (Sydney: New South Press, 2015), 92–98.

3. My own emails are lightly edited for minor mistakes that crop up in email. I did not change Professor Lynch's wordings.

4. Dan Avnon and Yotam Benziman, "Effective Plurality Despite Categorical Rigidity," in *Plurality and Citizenship in Israel*, eds. Dan Avnon and Yotam Benziman (London and New York: Routledge, 2010), 1–14.

5. See, for example, *The Australian* (December 8, 2012), and *The Jerusalem Post* (August 8, 2013), http://www.jpost.com/International/Sydney-U-against-BDS-but-not-taking-any-action-against-BDS-professor-322496 (accessed October 31, 2017).

6. For a comprehensive argument against the political rationale of BDS, see Mendes and Dyrenfurth, *Boycotting Israel Is Wrong*. For a diverse (at times, eclectic) range of essays critical of the BDS movement, see Cary Nelson and Gabriel Noah Brahm, eds., *The Case Against Academic Boycotts of Israel* (New York: MLA Members for Scholars' Rights, 2014).

7. BDSMovement.net, http://www.bdsmovement.net/bdsintro#sthash.iNhQOgyC.dpuf (accessed October 31, 2017).

8. For a philosophical presentation of this line of reasoning, see Martha Nussbaum, "Against Academic Boycotts," in *Case Against Academic Boycotts of Israel*, eds. Nelson and Brahm, 39–48.

9. UNRWA was established to take care of all "Palestine refugees" of the 1948 war. This implied both Arab and Jewish refugees. In 1952, Israel assumed responsibility for its Jewish refugees and UNRWA assumed responsibility solely for Arab refugees who became known as "Palestinian"—that is, Arab refugees from British-mandated Palestine. UNRWA is the sole UN agency dedicated to a single group of refugees, and its mandate has been repeatedly renewed for decades.

10. See, for example, the interview with Omar Barghouti, prominent BDS founder and activist: "Should People Boycott Israel," *The Real News* (August 29, 2010), http://therealnews.com/t2/index.php?option=com_content&task=view&id=31&Itemid=74&jumival=5547.

11. See the editorial "Abuse of Science: Hawking's Boycott of Israel Is Intellectually and Morally Disreputable," in *The Times* (May 10, 2013), http://www.thetimes.co.uk/tto/opinion/leaders/article3760693.ece.

12. Jake Lynch, "Why Academic Boycotts?" *The Daily Beast* (December 22, 2012, updated May 6, 2013), https://www.thedailybeast.com/why-academic-boycotts.

13. Mark Allan Powell, "The Religious Leaders in Luke: A Literary-Critical Study," *Journal of Biblical Literature*, 109 (1990): 93–110.

14. *NRG* (December 13, 2012), http://www.nrg.co.il/online/1/ART2/422/071.html. See critical response to Yemini's assertions in *NRG* (December 21, 2012), http://www.nrg.co.il/online/1/ART2/423/718.html.

15. See Yad Vashem, http://www.yadvashem.org/yv/en/exhibitions/vilna/during/ponary.asp (accessed October 31, 2017).

16. For examples, see Avnon and Benziman, "Effective Plurality Despite Categorical Rigidity," and Dan Avnon, ed., *Civic Education in Israel* (Tel-Aviv: Am Oved, 2012, in Hebrew).

17. Shurat HaDin is dedicated to "bankrupt terror, defend Israel from war crimes, and combat lawfare and the Boycott, Divest, and Sanctions movement." See Shurat HaDin, http://israellawcenter.org/about/overview/ (accessed October 31, 2017).

18. Statement of Claim—Form 17—Rule 8.06(1)(a). File Number: NSD2235/2013. File Title: *Shurat HaDin—The Israel Law Center & Ors v Jake Lynch.* New South Wales Registry—Federal Court of Australia, December 20, 2013.

19. The many interesting aspects of the Shurat HaDin intervention in this case merit a separate essay.

20. Shurat HaDin's lawfare tactics are a smart and timely initiative that adds pressure on terrorist organizations and limits their maneuvering space. See the ruling in their favor in *Sokolow et al. v. Palestine Liberation Organization et al.,* http://www.law360.com/cases/4d93a3f0010c44766e000001 (accessed October 31, 2017). It is regretful that Shurat HaDin squandered some of their hard-earned reputation in this ill-conceived Australian venture.

21. Dan Goldberg, "BDS Case Splits Australia's Pro-Israel Lobby," *Haaretz* (June 6, 2014), http://www.haaretz.com/jewish-world/jewish-world-news/.premium-1.597200.

22. Stuart Winer, "Australian Jewry Rebukes Sydney Professor over Israel Boycott," *The Times of Israel* (December 12, 2012), http://www.timesofisrael.com/australian-jewry-rebukes-sydney-professor-over-israel-boycott/.

23. See Peter Wertheim and Alex Ryvchin, *The Boycott, Divestment, and Sanctions Campaign against Israel* (Sydney: The Executive Council of Australian Jewry, undated).

24. Dan Goldberg, "BDS Case Splits Australia's Pro-Israel Lobby," op. cit.

25. Stanley Fish comments on the disingenuousness of academics who advocate academic boycotts in withering terms, similar in tenor to what I have in mind: "The idea that an academic becomes some kind of hero by the cost-free act of denying other academics the right to play in the communal sandbox (yes, this is third-grade stuff) is as pathetic as it is laughable. Heroism doesn't come that cheaply. Better, I think, to wear the 'ivory-tower intellectual' label proudly. At least, it's honest." Stanley Fish, "Academic Freedom against Itself: Boycotting Israeli Universities," *The New York Times* (October 28, 2013), http://opinionator.blogs.nytimes.com/2013/10/28/academic-freedom-against-itself-boycotting-israeli-universities/?partner=rssnyt&emc=rss.

26. I thank the trustees of the Sir Zelman Cowen Universities Fund Exchange Fellowship for enabling my visit to Australia; for promoting free exchange of ideas, faculty, and students across geographical, cultural, and, at times, political divides; and for their hospitality during my stay in Australia. My heartfelt thanks to friends and colleagues who commented on various versions of this essay: Daphna Avnon-Amit, Shahar Burla, Philip Mendes, Suzanne Rutland, Myer Samra, and Daphna Saring. This essay is a moderately revised version of my article "BDS and the Dynamics of Self-Righteous Moralism," *The Australian Journal of Jewish Studies* 28 (2014): 28–46. I thank the editors for their kind permission to use that material here.

2 Consensus, Canadian Trade Unions, and Intellectuals for Hamas

Julien Bauer

After a pro-Hamas, anti-Israel rally in Montreal, Julien Bauer dared to publicly criticize the "educated people" who participated, going so far as to characterize as antisemitic their Hamas-inspired calls for killing Jews and to express concern about intellectuals' propagation of highbrow antisemitism. Anti-Israel coalitions promptly rose to attack him. His office door was painted with antisemitic graffiti. Students called him a murderer and demanded his firing. Colleagues split into those who supported the witch hunt against him and those who opposed it, although most of the latter were intimidated against doing so publicly. The institutions that were supposed to protect him, the administration of his university and his labor union, not only failed to do so but the latter actively joined the campaign against Israel. Bauer's analysis places the incidents in the specific cultural context of Quebecois society, where the consensus culture is to silence those fighting antisemitic and anti-Israel bigotry.

On Sunday, November 17, 2012, a demonstration was organized in Montreal to condemn Israel's military operation in Gaza and support the Palestinian victims of blatant Israeli aggression. A few thousand people participated in the rally. Photos taken at the site show a predominance of Hamas flags, not Palestinian ones. At the end, some demonstrators screamed in Arabic, "*Ithbar Al Yahud*," slaughter the Jews.

The following day, I was interviewed on a private, populist radio station, CHOI Radio X Montreal. I stated that the people who demonstrated at this rally were not "for Palestinians and against Israel" but specifically for Hamas and its clearly antisemitic charter. I presented the view that the demonstrators were either ignorant or antisemites, or both. The journalist then asked, "How do you explain the number of educated persons who participate at this kind of demonstration?" My answer was not politically correct. I stated that intellectuals have a tendency to behave like prostitutes and support the worst kind of murderers if their ideology is perceived as progressive. In prewar France, many intellectuals were supporters of fascist regimes, in particular Hitler while others gave their obedience to Stalin. The intellectuals who were ready to publicly promote democratic regimes were a minority. After the war, in many democratic Western states, intellectuals were lauding the Khmer Rouge.[1] My conclusion was that I was saddened but not overly surprised by the participation of faculty and students of my university, Université du Québec à Montréal (UQAM).

The following day, my office door at UQAM was covered with antisemitic graffiti, including a "Heil Israel." It was the beginning of my fifteen minutes of fame.

Social media was full of personal attacks written mainly by intellectuals. The argument went as follows: on a live radio show, a Muslim woman had recently lamented that Hitler could not finish the job of getting rid of the Jews. Many people blasted the host for not answering or interrupting her. This tirade was antisemitic but was protected by freedom of opinion, the same way my views on Hamas were also repulsive but protected by freedom of opinion. According to this way of thinking, my calling terrorists what they are, terrorists, was equivalent to promoting genocide.

The political science graduate students of UQAM condemned me and asked for my resignation. This condemnation went viral on social media. A tiny point was missing: the motion, unanimous, was voted by 8 students present out of 240.

In case the message was not clear enough, I was publicly labeled a murderer by students I had never seen before when walking within the university.

CHOI Radio X was glad to be in the news, to have created such a commotion. It interviewed me a second time. Before answering the first question, I told the journalist, "I am an idiot, an incompetent, a promoter of hate propaganda." "What do you mean?" the journalist asked. "It is what is said and printed in social media, the student press, etc. Amongst my sins, one particularly repugnant one is to be interviewed on Radio X, a garbage radio." "What?" "It is what you are called." "I knew about it, but what do they believe they represent?" "People who are listening to this program are, by definition, morons, hearing the words of a scoundrel on a garbage program. Now I am ready to answer your questions."

This introduction did not win many fans in the politically correct crowd, but, surprisingly, quite a few people, including colleagues, students, and individuals from various backgrounds, expressed appreciation that at least a professor was refusing to be intimidated by the politically correct storm troopers.

The controversy, or rather the attack, went on. A student paper published an article accusing me of talking about antisemitism to hide my political vacuity. Even if I pretended to be a political scientist, it suggested, I was totally unable to analyze political facts in society, even less so when dealing with Israel. My bad faith, idiocy, incompetence, and, not to mention, my opposition to anything just, proper, and progressive all combined to make me a model "no-thinker." While the graffiti artists chose to remain anonymous, the character murderers, faculty and students, were proud to associate their names with a witch hunt against somebody repulsive enough to prefer Israel to Hamas.

A few days later, when it became clear that the condemnation by the political science graduate students was not representative of the student body, two of their leaders asked to see me. They let me know that they were not aware of all the ramifications of the story but that they maintained their objections to my ideas. I asked why they did not meet with me *before* their condemnation rather than after. Their answer was to suggest a public debate between supporters of Palestinians and myself under their aegis. I agreed to a debate but only if the students' association was not involved, as it was not neutral but a propagandist for one side. I reminded them—or rather taught them something they had never heard before—of the disputations between representatives of the Catholic Church and representatives of Judaism when they were brought together to debate their religions. It just so happened that Judaism was always found to be wrong. I stressed I was in no mood to participate in such a parody of a debate. A few people on social media took up this idea and lamented that I was not interested in a debate organized by "the students," as if 3 percent of the student body were the totality.

A repetition of the vandalism occurred in 2015. The differences were significant.

Instead of graffiti and a whole brouhaha, a few self-adhesive anti-Israel papers were plastered on my office door. It did not take days and a painter to repair the door, as in 2012, but just an hour to clean the door. The first time, the rector left a message in my voicemail expressing his strong condemnation of the antisemitic graffiti; this time, the new rector did not leave a message. The first time, security got in touch with me and seemed genuinely embarrassed by the situation. One consequence was to push for the introduction of cameras in the halls, stairs, and other such areas. Many people, including most of the faculty, were opposed to these cameras in the name of freedom. Those who were targets of vandalism were deemed guilty of promoting a police atmosphere in the university. This time, with cameras already installed, security could not determine who the vandals were. What was the use of cameras if they didn't show anything? Better, the head of security did not get in touch with me. His assistant and I left each other many voicemails. The most telling part was the following exchange: "Could you tell me what kind of action from you has triggered such vandalism?" I answered, "The mere fact I exist."

That was the extent of security involvement as far as I am aware.

As far as the media were concerned, most of them (except Radio Canada, see below) reported the first case but treated the second one in a low-key fashion, mentioning that a few professors of political science (myself included) had written an open letter condemning the intimidation tactics used by certain student groups but leaving out the specifically anti-Israel aspect. It was up to a daily, *Le Journal de Montréal*, a tabloid not averse to publishing critical news about Jews (from schools not respecting Quebec education laws to kashrut certification blamed for funneling the average consumer's money toward the Jewish community), to publish an article on intimidation at UQAM in general, with a reminder of the 2012 graffiti and noting that the "new ones are antisemitic."

The events presented above could take place anywhere on North American campuses—a professor accused of the worst sin, of not being an enemy of Israel. But in Quebec, it is better understood if we take into account a double French Canadian twist: the roles of consensus and trade unions.

Quebec society sees itself as a consensus society, where nuances do exist but not real divergences. In a departmental assembly, most resolutions are unanimous. The worst threat to this situation is to say, "I demand a vote." Quebec consensus, both on internal and external issues, is typically decided by a limited number of people: a few politicians, professors, and journalists constituting a network of friends who have attended the same schools and agree on most topics.

Radio and TV present a fascinating image of this consensus. Public radio and TV Radio Canada (RC), the French-speaking counterpart of the Canadian Broadcasting Corporation, should have aired news about antisemitic attacks in a university. We are talking about professors, students, links with international relations, and so on, the kind of news RC is supposed to cover. It was the only major source of information in Canada to not present the news! It happens that RC is highly critical of Israel. I am not. For the last ten years, in fact, I have been on their blacklist. I used to be interviewed from time to time but not anymore. Their experts are blatantly anti-Israel. RC is part of the official consensus.

Private stations, outside the consensus, have discussions and open interviews and are not above mocking university staff and other intellectuals who "know everything." They may not know that I am on the RC blacklist but are smart enough to notice that a professor who has published on the Israeli political system is never heard or seen on RC. Far from being a bad mark, this is a sign to them that I may have something to say on the topic.

The situation is quite paradoxical. RC, the official public network, has a head office clearly hostile to Israel. French-speaking programs all over Canada but outside of Montreal often resent the condescending tone of their big brother in Montreal, believe in news and not only in politically correct news, and do not hesitate to interview professors outside the consensus, myself included.

Private stations, specifically the populist ones, often exhibit a mixture of blatant ignorance of anything Jewish and admiration for Israel's tenacity.[2] Nonfaculty members of universities recognize ignorance and sometimes malice. A professional in charge of communication asked if I would agree to be interviewed by a private radio journalist about an illegal Jewish school. "But," said the professional, "I want to warn you that this journalist is a star, loves to ridicule university professors, and is known to use antisemitic arguments. I would not send a young professor or somebody not ready to fight. Are you interested?" I was, and I had the opportunity to debunk the pseudo-illegality. The journalist disagreed with me but was obviously happy to have a strong, if not brutal, exchange that showed he was not afraid of controversy. It worked because private networks are not part of the official consensus.

Another surprising case was about a botched Israeli secret service operation in an Arab emirate. Every day, the scandal grew, the number of spies spiraled, and the use of forged New Zealand passports was denounced. When I explained that the use of false papers is a common occurrence in intelligence services and that the number of persons involved seemed abnormally high, the journalist interrupted me to say, "You know, here, in our part of the world, we love Mossad; they are doing a good job. If they made a mistake this time, we wish them success in the future." Do I have to stress that such a journalist, listened to every day by hundreds of thousands of people, is not part of the official Quebec consensus on how to present events in the world?[3]

The second key particularity of Quebec is the role of trade unions.[4]

The American Federation of Labor and Congress of Industrial Organizations (AFL-CIO), the American trade union movement, was pro-Israel. In Canada, and even more so in Quebec, the position was more ambivalent. Quebec trade unions were divided into two streams, international and national. The former were union groups belonging to mostly US unions with a presence in Canada; they were politically center-left and supportive of free unionism in the world, particularly in Western Europe and Israel. The national trade unions were confined to Quebec, with a limited exposure to and interest in global affairs. Contrary to the international unions, which had a significant number of organizers and members who were Jewish, the nationals had hardly any Jewish members because they were founded by the Catholic Church and recruited mostly in civil service, education, and related fields where, at the time, there were very few Jewish workers, if any. The difference was blatant. At the annual meeting of the Quebec Federation of Labor, organizers would invite both the Israeli trade union, Histadrut, and what was left of the Jewish Eastern European socialist movement, Bund. At the same time, the two major national unions, the Confederation of National Trade Unions (CNTU) and the teachers' union Centrale de l'Enseignement du Québec (CEQ), were led by people hostile to Israel and critical of Jews.[5]

After the famous 1975 UN resolution declaring Zionism to be racism, Khadafi of Libya convened a conference in Tripoli in July 1976. There, a new group was founded, the International Organization for the Elimination of All Forms of Racial Discrimination. The announced goal was to fight racism; the reality was that more than half of its activities were attacks against Israel and Zionism. The

1976 meeting was the biggest antisemitic forum following the Second World War. Among the invited guests were Michel Chartrand, a leader of CNTU,[6] and Yvon Charbonneau, head of CEQ. This begs a question: why were these two union leaders invited?

The answer is perhaps that CEQ offered to accommodate, in its building, a branch of Khadafi's organization, the Quebec Movement against Racism, whose agenda was a continuous denunciation of Zionism. Further, CEQ attacked "the racist and expansionist Israeli regime" and proclaimed it the duty of teachers "to prepare new tools for education."[7] So, for over forty years, both the CNTU and the CEQ have been in the forefront of attacks against Israel. The conflict between Israel and the Palestinians was not presented as a national one or even a religious one but as a manifestation of imperialism where the capitalists, i.e the Jews, are using racism against the Arabs, i.e. the Palestinians. When the Quebec Movement against Racism asked, in 1961, "Should we talk about delicate questions such as racism against Jews and Arabs?", their answer devoted four more spaces to Israel racism than to the Holocaust. The message was clear.

As far as the Jews were concerned, "racism is a form of imperialism working for financially and economically powerful minorities" and "Jewish economic interests did not stop them from expelling many millions of Palestinians."[8] Jews, being, by definition, a wealthy minority, cannot be a target of racism.

The trade union involvement in anti-Zionism and antisemitism also coordinates with the consensus I spoke about earlier. Consider the career of Charbonneau. When head of CEQ, he was jailed with two other trade union leaders for defying a back-to-work legislation. His links with Khadafi and his group, its nonstop attacks on Israel, its treating Jews as a domineering people on the wrong side of history—all that did not prevent him from becoming a vice president for public relations of SNC-Lavalin, a jewel of the capitalist system he had regularly condemned (1990–1992); a liberal member of the Quebec National Assembly (1994–1999); a liberal member of the Parliament of Canada (1999–2006); and eventually Canada's ambassador to the United Nations Educational, Scientific and Cultural Organization (UNESCO) (2004–2006). When you are a member of the select group of consensus builders, the most outrageous comments are no impediment to a successful career.

The national trade union history continues to influence some unions today. In my case, when I phoned my union—Syndicat des Professeurs de l'Université du Québec (SPUQ), affiliated with the CNTU, a union whose membership is compulsory—and inquired what they were planning to do to defend the rights of a member, the answer was: "If you were attacked by the rector, it would be our duty to defend you. When colleagues and students condemn you, they exercise their freedom of speech."[9]

Are there lessons to learn from this case?

1. Consensus people do not like controversy. If nobody expressed deviant ideas, such as support for Israel, then everything would be fine. To express such ideas is a rupture of the consensus and encourages a backlash.
2. Recourse to intimidation is acceptable among at least two major unions and most consensus people.
3. Many people who combine blind support for anything Palestinian (including Hamas) and hostility to Israel are at ease with antisemitic tirades.
4. Colleagues and students who assured me of their support did so privately but were afraid to do it publicly. An amazing exception was a non-Jewish student, from another university, offering me free physical protection at any time!
5. Quite a number of members of the Jewish community offered their sympathy, and many warned me to be prudent.
6. The self-proclaimed official leader of the Jewish community, the Canadian Centre for Israel and Jewish Affairs, had nothing to say.

In conclusion, in the case of Quebec, it seems to me that professors who express opinions supportive of the Jewish people and pro-Israel do so at their own risk and peril and should not expect any help from the official Jewish leadership or the general human rights organizations. At the same time, the impact of such opinions is surprisingly high, because a large segment of the silent majority distrust the consensus position, RC, and some trade unions, and continue being supportive of Israel. An event within the walls of a university, therefore very limited in scope, has become, through information and analysis, a tool to keep a part of public opinion on the side of open mindedness.

JULIEN BAUER is a retired Professor of Political Science at the Université du Québec à Montréal. Specializing in public administration, public policy, religion, and politics, he is author of nine books, including works on Hassidic and Ashkenazi Jews. He is a fellow of the Canadian Institute of Jewish Research and a board member and former chairman of the Canadian Public Administration Institute (Montreal section).

Notes

1. For a presentation of this topic, see Julien Bauer, "Big Brother, Mythe et Technique," in *Orwell a-t-il vu juste?*, Henri Cohen, Joseph J. Levy, Sylvie Cantin, and Johanne Fortin (Quebec: Presses Universitaires du Quebec, 1986), 155–168.
2. The level of ignorance about Jews in the Canadian French media is astonishing. I remember an article in *Le Devoir*, the authoritative Quebec daily, on Yom Kippur. The

article was rather well written, except for a gem: "Jews, on Yom Kippur, wear a shroud in commemoration of Jesus' death"!

3. The difference of tone between public and private television channels is stunning. Even if both are regularly biased against Israel, only the public one and even more the French public one, Radio Canada, is obsessed with Israel and chooses its commentators on the Middle East exclusively among blatant anti-Israel propagandists.

4. When a majority of salaried people in an enterprise (professionals, blue collars, white collars, etc.) express their desire for a union, one and only one union is created. Everybody within the group has to pay an annual membership deducted from their salaries and directly sent to the union.

5. In 1921, the Catholic clergy in Quebec, faced by a growing trade union movement perceived as Protestant and Jewish, created the Confederation of Catholic Workers of Canada (CCWC). Each meeting of the union's section was conducted in the presence of a Catholic chaplain. In 1960, the CCWC secularized and took the name of Confederation of National Trade Unions. Meanwhile, CEQ has a history of hostility toward Israel, from giving the Quebec-Palestine Association offices in its own headquarters to refusing to attend an international convention of teachers unions because it took place in Israel. CEQ has also a peculiar view of antisemitism: in a pseudo-Marxist interpretation, Jews are bourgeois, capitalists, and privileged; therefore, to attack them is a normal response by oppressed workers.

6. Michel Chartrand (1916–2010) was himself a loud voice against Israel. His legacy is still noticeable in the CNTU. Among the three or four yearly positions taken on international issues, at least one is directed against Israel: condemnation of the "Israeli military attack on Gaza" (2014), joining the Boycott, Divestment, and Sanctions (BDS) campaign against Israel (2015), opposition to a motion at the Canadian parliament criticizing BDS (2016), and so on.

7. Yvon Charbonneau, "Representative of the International Organization for the Elimination of All Forms of Racial Discrimination, EAFORD, and Centrale de l'Enseignement du Québec," presentation at a Tripoli EAFORD seminar, presented to the 26th Congress of CEQ, 1978, under code 26ème Congrès CEQ-1978 (a78-co-9).

8. *Cahiers de pédagogie progressiste*, 1982 (jointly published by CEQ and Quebec Movement Against Racism).

9. All the professors of UQAM are members of SPUQ, and the mandatory fee is deducted from our salaries as a percentage. Lecturers have their own union following the same rule. The monthly CNTU magazine I receive as a member of SPUQ has, in nearly every issue, between a few lines and a full page of anti-Israel comments.

3   Bullies at the Pulpit

Doron S. Ben-Atar

Shortly after the American Studies Association's 2013 Boycott, Divestment, and Sanctions (BDS) resolution, Doron S. Ben-Atar announced at a faculty meeting that should Fordham's American Studies program fail to distance itself from that resolution, he would resign from the program and fight against it until it opposed bigotry. He promptly found himself the target of a Kafkaesque university investigation in which he wasn't informed of what the charges were or who was charging him and was told that his decision to seek legal counsel was an admission of guilt. He—who opposed BDS in the name of opposing bigotry—learned that he had been charged (bizarrely) with "religious discrimination" only when the final report came exonerating him. The process took months of his life and resulted in other retaliatory acts even after he was exonerated. Relations with fellow liberal leftists were destroyed, insofar as he did not toe the party line on the Israeli-Palestinian issue. Ben-Atar analyzes the kinds of BDS bullying that occur in the academy and shows how seamlessly anti-Israelism can blend into antisemitism.

THE EMAIL ARRIVED on the last Friday of the spring term shortly before 5:00 p.m. Anastasia Coleman, Fordham's director of Institutional Equity and Compliance / Title IX coordinator, wanted to meet with me. "It has been alleged," she wrote, "that you may have acted in an inappropriate way and possibly discriminated against another person at the university." I was stunned. My wife, kids, and friends have been warning me for years that my sense of humor and intellectual irreverence (my latest book is about bestiality[1]) could get me in trouble in these prudish times. I imagined myself brought before an academic disciplinary tribunal from Francine Prose's *Blue Angel*, where all my past transgressions would be marshaled to prove that I don't belong in the classroom. My mind raced, recalling the many slips of the tongue I had had in three decades of teaching. I perspired profusely and felt the onset of a stomach bug. What would I tell my mother?

"Did it have anything to do with a student?" I shot back anxiously, hoping to get a sense of my predicament before the director left for the weekend. I was lucky. Ms. Coleman responded immediately. "This does not involve students and is about your behavior regarding American Studies."

What a relief. But it was also very odd. The decision of the American Studies Association (ASA) to boycott Israeli universities in December 2013 had upset me. I wrote emails, circulated articles, and was pleased that my university's president quickly declared his opposition to the measure. I joined a national steering committee that set out to fight the boycott and participated in the drafting of a few statements. As an American historian who delivered in 1987 his first paper at the annual meeting of the ASA and served on the executive committee of Fordham's American Studies program, I wanted Fordham's program to sever official ties with the national organization until it rescinded the measure. Other programs have taken this courageous symbolic step, and I thought it proper for the Jesuit university of New York to take a moral stand against what most scholars of anti-semitism consider antisemitic bigotry.

I emailed Michelle McGee, director of Fordham's American Studies program, and asked for immediate action. She shot back some ill-informed cliché about the boycott's stand for Palestinian intellectual freedom, betraying both her ignorance of the complex reality in the region and her blind toeing of the party line. I asked for a faculty meeting to discuss our response. Fordham, as it turned out, was an institutional member of the ASA. The university administration decided that it was up to the American Studies program executive committee to decide on its position vis-à-vis the boycott. McGee, however, failed to form an executive committee, and thus, elections for a new executive committee had to take place. A slate of candidates was presented a few weeks later. The candidates, however, backed by McGee, refused to disclose their position about the boycott.

On February 24, 2014, the American Studies program held a faculty meeting chaired by the dean of the Faculty of Arts and Sciences to discuss the boycott. The meeting was sparsely attended. Fifteen percent of the affiliated faculty showed up. The attendees consisted of four of the five members of the program's new executive committee; a few opponents of the boycott; Glenn Hendler, chair of the English Department, who championed the boycott; and a couple of interested faculty. Nearly everyone spoke against the boycott, except, of course, for Hendler. Members of the executive committee did not say a word.

During the discussion about the appropriate response to the measure, I stated that should Fordham's program fail to distance itself from the boycott, I would resign from the program and fight against it until it took a firm stand against bigotry. The program's director, in turn, filed a complaint against me with the Title IX office, charging that I threatened to destroy the program. (As if I could. And what did this have to do with Title IX, which addresses sexual discrimination?) This spurious complaint (the meeting's minutes demonstrated that I did not make such a threat) ushered me into a bruising summer that taught me much about colleagues, liberal solidarity, and the price I must be willing to pay for taking on the rising tide of anti-Zionism on American campuses.

When Coleman appeared in my office to conduct her investigation, she demanded to know if I threatened to destroy the program. (Didn't she read the meeting's minutes?) I didn't think I did; it didn't sound like me, but the minutes of the meeting were not in front of me, and I wasn't sure. At the advice of my attorney, I said that I took the charges very seriously, that I could not respond to them at the moment, and that I would like to learn all I could about the charges before issuing my response. But Coleman refused to elaborate. Remaining vague, she hinted that others supported the complaint. "Who are the others?" I asked. Was the dean of the faculty who chaired the meeting involved? Was there anything more to the accusations beyond that supposed one sentence uttered in a meeting? She would not disclose. She warned me not to talk about the investigation with any colleagues and told me she would be in touch with my attorney, and we parted ways.

Meanwhile, the lack of candor by the executive committee of the American Studies program at Fordham came to light. None of its members expressed a position about the boycott prior to their election or during the February 24 meeting. At the end of the term, however, the executive committee issued a report that neither opposed nor supported the ASA position but concluded that the boycott was not an act of bigotry. It proposed to turn the program's blog into a forum for a discussion of BDS. Since no such forum had existed at Fordham before, the decision introduced BDS to the university and, in effect, endorsed the boycott. I resigned from Fordham's American Studies program because it refused to distance itself from bigotry. Five other Jewish members of the program did the same. I reached out to a few non-Jewish colleagues and asked them to join our protest so that the division within the program would not be between Jews and non-Jews. And while some nominal Jews of the affiliated faculty supported the ASA boycott, not a single non-Jewish member resigned in solidarity with our protest.

Over the next few weeks, Fordham's general counsel, Tom DeJulio, and my attorney engaged in a few friendly conversations in which we were led to believe that Fordham agreed I was perfectly within my First Amendment rights to oppose the boycott, resign from the program, and campaign for a change of policy. We informed DeJulio that I would be happy to meet with Coleman, even though we were still not informed what the specific charge was. Coleman never asked to meet me, and I assumed that the attempt to muzzle my opposition to the boycott had died down. In late July, however, I received Coleman's report, in which she cleared me of the charge of religious discrimination. It was the first time I had heard what I was actually accused of doing, although I'm still not sure how opposing the boycott could possibly amount to religious discrimination. But Coleman was not satisfied to leave things at that. She went on to write that I had refused to cooperate in the investigation (even though my attorney informed DeJulio weeks earlier of my willingness to meet her) and concluded that my decision to consult an attorney amounted to an admission of guilt. Coleman determined that in declaring I would quit the American Studies program and fight for a change of course should it not distance itself from antisemitism, I had violated the university's code of civility and recommended that the provost take disciplinary action against me.[2]

It was a sobering summer. I had to defend my reputation against baseless, ever-evolving charges from sexual to religious discrimination. I went through a Kafkaesque process in which I was never told exactly what I supposedly did wrong, nor was I ever shown anything in writing. Eventually, I learned that the charge was religious discrimination born out of my opposition to the ASA boycott. The implication is that antisemitism needs to be tolerated at Fordham and that those who dare to fight it run afoul of university rules. Administrators and colleagues failed to protect my First Amendment rights and fed the assault on my character. A person utterly unqualified to understand antisemitism sat in judgment of a scholar who publishes on and teaches the subject. A report was issued without letting me even defend myself. My choice to have legal representation was cited as proof of my guilt. Most painful was realizing that my commitment to fighting antisemitism, so central to who I am, had been held against me not only by the member of the faculty who filed the baseless charge but also by the office of the university counsel.

The provost did not discipline me. Over a cup of coffee, we exchanged our different perspectives on the episode. I told him that I planned to go public. He was not happy, pointing out the strong stand taken by the university's president, Joseph McShane, against antisemitism in all its forms and particularly against the ASA boycott. And he was right. Fordham has been a most welcoming university for me and for many Jews in the last few decades. It has featured many important interfaith dialogues and has undertaken many steps to make its Jewish students, faculty, and administrators feel part of the broader university community. I knew that if I went public, I'd be attacked and my lifetime-earned academic reputation would be tarnished. My family advised me to pocket the de facto exoneration and move on. But the entire episode centered on the effort by McGee and her allies to punish me for daring to challenge BDS. Staying quiet was not an option.

And so, in October, I published an article about my account of the episode in *Tablet*.[3] The response was surprisingly overwhelming. I received hundreds of supportive emails and letters from all over the world. Thousands shared the piece on Facebook, and numerous media outlets covered the story, usually aghast at the allegations and procedure. As expected, the bullying colleagues were not done. The chair of the English Department, Hendler, rose to defend the allegations and procedure. Hendler confessed to me in a personal email that he was probably the source of the false charge that I threatened to destroy the program. We've sparred before over politics. He was thrilled with the Occupy Wall Street movement, while I thought it smacked of adolescent New Left foolishness and worried about the appearance of traditional antisemitic tropes in some of its rhetoric. Now Hendler, unchastened by the way his malicious false allegation fed McGee's attack, launched an ad hominem attack on my integrity, accusing me of poisoning the atmosphere at the collegial meeting and declaring that as a Jew he gives the boycott movement (and a host of other anti-Zionist measures) a clean bill of health. And he brought up a new charge: that I campaigned against McGee personally, circulating charges that she was an antisemite.[4] I did nothing of the sort. McGee had no cause to file a complaint against me. I did not circulate emails about her. She was hardly on my radar. We teach on separate campuses and in separate departments. In my nearly two decades at Fordham, I might have had three conversations with her. We served together cordially on the faculty technology committee. And unaware of her complaints, I sought her assistance when I launched the inaugural Fordham Queer Seminar in the spring of 2014—after McGee filed the complaint but before I was confronted with the charge by Coleman—as both of us belonged to an ad hoc advocacy faculty group on gender and sexuality. As a lifelong liberal leftist, I thought we were allies. But it turned out that membership in the elite club of the principled and disobedient requires absolute obedience to the party line on the Israeli-Palestinian issue.[5] McGee decided to punish me by filing a complaint playing the Title IX card, and Hendler circulated the false information, fed McGee's flame, and invented a few more charges to boot in a nasty public personal attack.

McGee and Hendler at least put their names behind their attacks. Another English Department colleague found someone else to do her bidding. She and I once shared a panel on memoirs and thus read each other's works. We were on pleasant enough terms, and she was among the affiliated faculty I tried to enlist to join our protest. She rejected me angrily. She turned to an anti-Zionist activist, English professor Bruce Robbins of Columbia University, who was delighted to attack critics of the boycott on the infamous hate website *Mondoweiss*.[6] Robbins charged that in asking non-Jewish colleagues to join the protest against the ASA boycott, I implied that those who didn't were themselves antisemitic. Again, this is sheer nonsense. I wanted to build an antiboycott coalition that would transcend ethnicity. Since I believe BDS measures are antisemitic and that people of good conscience should take a stand against bigotry, shouldn't I have conveyed this sentiment to the colleagues I tried to persuade to join the protest?

Robbins, Hendler, McGee, and other academics of their ilk want to define the parameters of the argument in a way that allows them to cast antisemitic aspersions but denies others the right to call them on it. All three, for example, are on record as supportive of Steven Salaita, the scholar whose appointment to the University of Illinois was denied after a series of his antisemitic tweets came to light.[7] These so-called progressives found nothing obscene or evil in Salaita's bizarre statements. They were eager to protect his right to celebrate the transformation of antisemitism "from something horrible into something honorable."[8] (I don't doubt they would have felt differently had anyone dared to celebrate the turning of racism or homophobia into "something honorable.") Efforts to curtail the spread of antisemitism ran against their selectively applied cries for free speech—discriminatory free speech, of course; there is no censorship on the propagation of antisemitic bigotry, but if you dare to challenge bigotry, your freedom of expression becomes the ammunition for silencing dissent. Antisemitism is protected speech. Protesting antisemitism, however, is an actionable offense, to be punished by university administrators and their lawyers. That was the message conveyed to me and to all those daring to deviate from the new anti-Zionist orthodoxy: if you dare to speak up, we'll come after you; we'll spread false rumors and innuendos; we'll portray you as a sexist bully; we'll destroy your reputation; and we'll make you an outcast in your own department and university. The message was delivered loud and clear.

The Fordham tempest in a teapot is but one example of a growing trend in contemporary campus battles. Radical academics, opting for the moral narcissist discourse of virtue, have taken to threats and intimidation in their battle to establish anti-Zionism as the doctrinal orthodoxy. Dissenters are marginalized, harassed, threatened, and banned. Edward Said, the patron saint of postcolonial scholarship, showed the way in smearing Bernard Lewis with the tag of *Orientalist colonialist apologist* rather than address the substance of Lewis's criticism of Said's book, *Orientalism*.[9] The charges stuck. The trendy celebrity discredited the substantive scholar. Lewis had been rendered a scholarly anathema. Said's minions have adopted this cynical strategy with impunity. You no longer need to be an intellectual giant to incur the wrath of what the late Robert Wistrich called the Red-Green Coalition.[10] When the largest organization of professional humanities scholars, the Modern Language Association of America, began to debate the issue, its website, not surprisingly, quickly attracted multiple crude antisemitic expressions, as well as the verbal gymnastics of boycott supporters who package their prejudices in the language of virtue and justice.[11] (Antisemitism has always been packaged as a self-sacrificing stand for the sake of humanity.[12])

The bullying is even worse at the undergraduate level. A recent comprehensive study of American campuses found that "more than one-quarter of undergraduate respondents describe hostility toward Israel on campus by their peers as a 'fairly' or 'very big' problem and nearly 15 percent perceive this same level of hostility toward Jews."[13] In the University of California system, "almost every antisemitic act can be directly linked to BDS. And every BDS campaign has resulted in Jewish students reporting feeling threatened, harassed, bullied and unsafe."[14] At University of California, Los Angeles, a student's Jewishness was deemed a sufficient cause for denying her a post in the student government and students wishing to run for university offices had to sign an "ethics pledge" prohibiting trips to Israel with mainstream Jewish organizations.[15] Some concerned Jewish communities, in turn, hold workshops for high school juniors and seniors on how to deal with college antisemitism. It's probably an overreaction, but it reflects the profound anxiety over the abrasiveness of the anti-Zionist coalitions.

This brouhaha is different from the ordinary academic food fights because at its heart this is a struggle over an ideology that undergirds the upsurge in attacks against Jews all over the globe. The Anti-Defamation League's most recent comprehensive study shows antisemitism is growing at an alarming rate.[16] And at the core of the new hate is the dogma that focuses on the demonic evils of the new pariah—Israel. As Jewish blood is shed in Brussels, Bulgaria, Jerusalem, Kansas City, Paris, Tel Aviv, Toulouse, and Washington DC, American universities are experiencing a dramatic rise in antisemitic incidents, from mock expulsion notices delivered to Jewish students in their dorms at Northeastern, Rutgers, New York University, Harvard, Yale, the University of Michigan, Connecticut College, and more, to Nazi cartoons at Vassar.[17]

Many wonderful colleagues at Fordham privately expressed support for my stand and outrage at the proceedings. None, however, went public. The cost is simply too high. The situation is similar in many other liberal arts colleges. Loud cliques of self-righteous radicals are trying to control the intellectual public sphere and limit permissible discourse on the Israeli-Palestinian conflict to the perspective of the Red-Green alliance. Academics in the humanities, from graduate students to tenured professors, realize that future grants, promotions, and other aspects of career development depend on avoiding the fury of bullies who sit in judgment at the centers of power and unleash their wrath on those who dare to challenge their moral narcissism. They see what happens to those of us who speak up.

Administrators in institutions of higher learning are in a bind. Most recognize the bigoted nature of the campaigns, as evidenced by the loud and massive rejection of the ASA boycott by university presidents all over the country. When public outcry grows, they issue an occasional condemnation. Sometimes they overreach. Fordham's administration certainly did in December 2016 when it denied club standing to Students for Justice in Palestine (SJP), fearing that the SJP chapter would emulate others elsewhere that targeted and harassed Jewish students and faculty and bring the divisive scourge of BDS to campus. But Fordham's overreaction, which regrettably may have originated in the university's desire to avoid the public relations fiasco of the fall of 2014, is an exception. For the most part, university administrators sweep under the rug the fact that their institutions are becoming laboratories of the new hate. The same goes for the vast majority of non-Jewish members of university faculties. They protest bigotry against ethnic and sexual minorities but ignore the rising tide against Jews. The cynical purveyors of the new antisemitism, in turn, use this passivity to spread their hate and silence critics.[18]

Doron S. Ben-Atar is Professor of History at Fordham University and a playwright. In addition to publishing books and articles about early America, he authored, together with his mother, Roma Nutkiewicz Ben-Atar, *What Time and Sadness Spared: Mother and Son Confront the Holocaust.* He has, in recent years, turned his attention to the battles over Zionism in the American Jewish community with, among other writings, his satirical play *Peace Warriors.*

Notes

1. Doron S. Ben-Atar and Richard D. Brown, *Taming Lust: Crimes against Nature in the Early Republic* (Philadelphia: University of Pennsylvania Press, 2014).

2. A copy of Ms. Coleman's letter can be examined at William A. Jacobson, "Fordham Prof. faced 'religious discrimination' charge for calling anti-Israel academic boycott 'anti-Semitic'," *Legal Insurrection* (October 13, 2014), http://legalinsurrection.com/2014/10 /fordham-prof-faced-religious-discrimination-charge-for-calling-anti-israel-academic -boycott-anti-semitic/.

3. Ben-Atar, "Kafka Was the Rage," *Tablet* (October 13, 2014), http://www.tabletmag.com /jewish-news-and-politics/185511/kafka-was-the-rage.

4. Glenn Hendler, "University's English Department Chair Responds to *Tablet* Article: Israel Boycott Controversy Continues at Fordham," *Tablet* (November 14, 2014), http://www .tabletmag.com/scroll/186974/israel-boycott-controversy-continues-at-fordham.

5. Susan Sontag celebrated this elite club of resisters, connecting all "good" progressive causes in "The Power of Principle," *Guardian* (April 26, 2003).

6. Bruce Robbins, "Antisemitism at Fordham?" *Mondoweiss* (January 7, 2015), http://mondoweiss.net/2015/01/anti-semitism-fordham. *Mondoweiss* has been exposed as a hate website on numerous occasions as its editor, contributing writers, and commentators routinely employ stereotypical antisemitic tropes. For one recent expose, see David Bernstein, "'Mondoweiss' is a Hate-Site (UPDATED)," *Washington Post* (May 4, 2015), https://www.washingtonpost.com/news/volokh-conspiracy/wp/2015/05/04/mondoweiss -is-a-hate-site/.

7. Glenn Hendler and Michelle McGee signed the petition of the Palestinian Campaign for the Academic and Cultural Boycott of Israel to boycott the University of Illinois (August 19, 2014), http://www.pacbi.org/etemplate.php?id=2557 (accessed January 7, 2016). Robbins published a public letter titled, "Why This Jewish-American Can't Visit Urbana-Champaign," *Red Fury* (August 9, 2014), https://theredfury.wordpress.com/2014/08/09/uiuc-filmmaker/.

8. For Salaita's tweets of July 18 and 19, 2014, see Barry Deutsch, "Steven Salaida's [*sic*] Controversial Tweets about Antisemitism, with Context," *Alas! A Blog* (September 12, 2014), http://amptoons.com/blog/?p=19088.

9. Edward Said, "Orientalism: An Exchange," *New York Review of Books* (August 12, 1982).

10. Robert Wistrich, "Anti-Zionism and Anti-Semitism," *Jewish Political Studies Review* 16 (Fall 2004), http://www.jcpa.org/phas/phas-wistrich-f04.htm.

11. Jonathan Marks, "'Zionist Attack Dogs'? The MLA's Debate on Israel Might Go Viral," *Chronicle of Higher Education* (May 21, 2014), http://chronicle.com/blogs /conversation/2014/05/21/zionist-attack-dogs-the-mlas-debate-on-israel-might-go-viral/.

12. As philosopher Elhanan Yakira writes, "From its inception, antisemitism, as a specific historical phenomenon, has as its place of preference the ideology of spiritual leadership." See Yakira, "Virtuous Antisemitism," in ed. Alvin H. Rosenfeld, *Deciphering the New Antisemitism* (Bloomington, IN: Indiana University Press, 2015), 83.

13. See Leonard Saxe, Theodore Sasson, Graham Wright, and Shahar Hecht, *Antisemitism and the College Campus: Perceptions and Realities* (Waltham, MA: Brandeis University Maurice and Marilyn Cohen Center for Modern Jewish Studies, July 2015), 1.

14. Tammi Rossman-Benjamin, "Divestment Movement Inspires Threats to Jewish Students," *San Jose Mercury News* (January 14, 2016), http://www.mercurynews.com /opinion/ci_29376584/tammi-rossman-benjamin-divestment-movement-inspires-threats -jewish.

15. Larry Gordon, "UC Campuses Roiled Over Claims of Anti-Israel Bias," *Los Angeles Times* (March 7, 2015), http://www.latimes.com/local/lanow/la-me-ln-allegations-of-anti -israel-sentiments-rock-uc-campuses—20150307-story.html. Sharona Schwartz, "UCLA Responds to Shocking Anti-Israel Pledge for Student Gov't Candidates," *Blaze* (May 14, 2014), http://www.theblaze.com/stories/2014/05/14/ucla-responds-to-shocking-anti-israel -pledge-for-student-govt-candidates/.

16. "The ADL Global 100: An Index of Anti-Semitism" (May 13, 2014), http://global100.adl .org/public/ADL-Global-100-Executive-Summary2015.pdf (accessed January 7, 2016).

17. Harassment of Jewish students by posting eviction notices on their dorm's doors was a popular tactic of Students for Justice in Palestine in 2013 and 2014. The Anti-Defamation League compiled reports of such harassments. For example, see "Eviction Notices at Northeastern Kick Off Israeli Apartheid Week," ADL blog (February 27, 2014), http:// blog.adl.org/tags/mock-eviction-notices; William A. Jacobson, "Vassar Nazi Cartoon Reflects Campus Dehumanization of Israel," *Legal Insurrection* (May 19, 2014), http:// legalinsurrection.com/2014/05/vassar-nazi-cartoon-reflects-campus-dehumanization-of -israel/.

18. A portion of this piece was published as "Kafka Was the Rage," *Tablet* (October 13, 2014), http://www.tabletmag.com/jewish-news-and-politics/185511/kafka-was-the-rage. It appears here with permission.

4 A Traumatic Professorial Education: Anti-Zionism and Homophobia in a Serial Campus Hate Crime

Corinne E. Blackmer

As Israel defended itself from Hamas rocket fire, Corinne Blackmer, an openly lesbian, observantly Jewish Zionist, was targeted by hate crimes on her campus: her office door was defaced with antiqueer, antisemitic, and anti-Israel slogans; her voicemail was filled with threatening messages; and a swastika was carved into her car. Police, university authorities, and colleagues were quick to see the homophobic dimensions of the attacks but oblivious to the fact that she was also targeted for her Zionism. This episode demonstrates the selectivity of moral outrage: some of the very people who vigorously condemn bigotry against gays just as vigorously *commit* bigotry against Israelis and Jews. Blackmer subsequently chose to teach a course on the Israeli-Palestinian conflict and describes the pedagogical challenges of dealing with a rabidly anti-Israel student seeking to dominate the discussion. The student lodged a discrimination complaint against her after she required that he document an anti-Israel class paper with actual evidence. Blackmer ends with an analysis of the odd turn of the lesbian, gay, bisexual, transgender, questioning, queer (LGBTQ) movement against Israel and a scathing critique of the absurd "pinkwashing" charge levied by anti-Israel LGBTQ activists.

I. Anti-Zionist and Homophobic Hate Crimes

In March 2008, as Israel responded to Hamas and other terrorist groups firing Grad rockets onto Israeli citizens all over southern Israel, I became the target of a series of hate crimes on my campus. I found it next to impossible not to draw a link between these events, although in some ways they were far apart.

I am an out lesbian, an observant Jewish woman, and a Zionist. Proud of all these, my office door was covered with materials proclaiming my identities and convictions. I also teach courses in LGBTQ and Judaic studies. While my upper division courses are at times controversial, I always regarded this as to be expected in the course of things. The classes did not touch on disputes over Israel and Palestine but, rather, explored relations between Jewish and Christian identities in the context of the Hebrew Bible and contested meanings of sexuality difference. Further, my colleagues and my administration were enthusiastically supportive of my multicultural endeavors.

Therefore, I had nothing to prepare me when, one morning, a colleague approached and showed me that materials on my office door had been defaced—torn and scrawled over with profane, hateful language that was anti-LGBTQ, antisemitic, and anti-Zionist. Among the defaced things was the front page of the *New Haven Register* dated November 12, 2007, featuring a jubilant Jewish lesbian couple on the day that same-sex marriages became legal in Connecticut; a map of Israel; a photograph of myself holding flowers and wearing a *kippa* with my wife, Pilar; a picture of the Wailing Wall in Jerusalem; the Israeli and LGBTQ rainbow flags; a newspaper reprint of Iranian men being hung and Saudi Arabian men being flogged for being gay; and a photograph of a friend on the beach in Tel Aviv wearing a T-shirt proclaiming "Proud to be a Jewish Queer." The defacements were, in their fashion, meticulous, as each item had received its particular message, while the map of Israel was shredded into pieces without further comment. I also saw that I had received several telephone calls on the office line—among them three that contained implicit and explicit threats against both me and my wife. One consisted of a loud hammer banging down methodically, punctuated by a muffled voice intoning, "Pervert Zionist! Pervert Zionist!"

I saved the messages and called the campus police. I thought about how Israeli military operations, no matter how justified by Hamas's invidious acts of aggression, made me anxiously anticipate the inevitable stream of anti-Zionist protests; Boycott, Divestment, Sanctions (BDS) advocacy; biased pronouncements from the United Nations; anti-Israel social media campaigns; and wall-to-wall coverage out of proportion to that afforded analogous conflicts across the world. When the officer finally arrived, she took my statement and one scrawled-over photograph as evidence and asked me if I knew anyone who might have done this to me. I said I could readily imagine the *kind* of person who could do this to me and explained my identities and affiliations, but I could not name a specific person. I did not have any concrete enemies as far as I knew.

The officer's implicit, reflexive perspective on the crime also dismayed me. Throughout the interview, she seemed to assume that I had been the victim of *only* homophobic animus. All other threats and defacing were ignored, as if incidental, accidental, and, indeed, nonsignifying. I realized she could understand homophobia but, like my students, not anti-Zionism—which was *not* a recognized form of hate speech, as too many pro-Israel students, faculty, and staff at American college campuses have learned to their dismay. The personnel at my school were certainly not particularly to blame for this reaction, as I would encounter this mode of response throughout this experience among almost everyone. Only two parties, my family and the congregants at my synagogue, understood easily that someone could be targeted for being a Jewish lesbian Zionist simultaneously. Finally, and perhaps ironically, I realized I had myself contributed to a campus climate that could lead to such erasure by (a) failing to include Zionism as a protected form of diverse opinion and identity in our initiatives and (b) not bringing anti-Zionism up for discussion and critique, as I was fearful of the ways it could be used as a weapon against Jewish students, Zionists, and other allies of Israel.

I stumbled my way through the teaching day. I happened to run into a journalism professor I knew, and I told him about the episode. He promised he would do what he could to help. When I went back to my office later that afternoon, I had telephone calls from two Connecticut television networks wanting to interview me for the evening news, along with a reporter from the local newspaper. Again, I found myself perplexed by how they responded to the hate crime that had occurred. They, too, responded as if I had been victimized *only* as a lesbian. No one could or would hear me despite my protestations, and I realized that, placed in conjunction, the categories of "lesbian" and "Jew" (never mind Zionist—a concept that was simply off the map) did not make sense to them. There were many ways of understanding this, some more plausible than others. Perhaps they thought that a lesbian presenting herself as Jewish would offend Orthodox Jews watching the news. Perhaps they subtly employed homophobic perceptions of Judaism that could not apprehend a lesbian as *really* Jewish. Perhaps they understood anti-Zionism as a form of protected speech rather than hate speech. Perhaps "invariably" homophobic religion and sexual minority identity did not mix for them. Perhaps they preferred to evade the too-hot topic of Zionism. Or, perhaps the reporters, like the police officer, wished only to maintain a singular focus on the homophobia, to simplify their task.

I was left with only speculation. With these limiting assumptions, they were unlikely, I feared, to catch the perpetrator. It also occurred to me that my situation was not entirely unlike that of students who had once come to me for assistance, only to receive ambivalent messages about whether they were, as Jews and Zionists, actual victims of unjust religious and cultural prejudice or merely reluctant players in an international game of national politics. I felt uncomfortably like someone who had been cut into jigsaw pieces that did not fit back together.

Walking down the hall shortly after, I noticed the office door of a colleague. On it was the famous prohibition against men lying with other men in Leviticus 18:22 accompanied by passages about mixing fibers and stoning adulterers, meant to illustrate the sexist and homophobic primitivism of Jewish biblical law. My colleague only intended to show the humorous illogic of anti-LGBTQ animus, but in context, it struck me as unconsciously antisemitic and engaged in ideological Christian supersessionism. I felt angry and targeted, as Judaism was scarcely the sole or even major purveyor of homo-hatred in the Western world.

In the several days that followed, I sunk into contemplation of the *strange, unaccountable,* and, indeed, *unheimliche* nature of contemporary anti-Zionism.

While being a lesbian was more or less a continual but nominally tolerable prejudicial disadvantage, one could be, within the space of a single day, reminded of the sterling successes of the State of Israel and the respect accorded Jews, on the one hand, and the threats of extirpation and hatred both still faced, on the other. In contrast to the steady drone of homophobia, anti-Zionism was like an episodic series of traumatic shocks. I was worlds away from the historical catastrophes of pogroms and the Holocaust but, at the same time, could not but be aware of the unremitting efforts of anti-Zionists to perpetuate their hatred and warfare.

For instance, three days after the initial incident, I enjoyed a splendid Shabbat service at my synagogue, where the congregants offered their support and my rabbi, seeking to comfort me while speaking truth, reminded me that "the loathing for our people has never been personal." I spent part of the next day reading about remarkable Israeli technologies of de-desertification and innovative treatments for cancer. Then I arrived at school on Monday to see that the new materials I had placed on my door had also been defaced, and more hate-filled messages had been left on my office telephone.

I went through the same drill with the investigating officer, who now said she would set up a video camera to see if the perpetrator could be apprehended. That same afternoon, as I was walking toward my car to go home, I ran into faculty members who, along with some students, were protesting the recent military actions of the Israel Defense Forces (IDF) in Gaza. The reporters and police had erased my identities as a Jew and Zionist, while these folks now held signs accusing Israelis—by whom they meant Jews and Zionists—of being "Racist Western Colonialists," "Ethnic Cleansers," and "Nazi Zionists." One faculty member, who had heard about my being targeted, commiserated by telling me I had been the unfortunate victim of the "homo-hating patriarchy." While I reflected on the uncomfortable irony of this person targeting me in one way while expressing compassion for my being targeted in another way, I arrived at my car to see that it had been daubed with mud in the shape of a swastika.

Yet another visit to the police, feeling invisible and disconsolate.

The perpetrators of these hate crimes against me were never apprehended. I live with the realization that one or more people out there wish me harm, simply because I am lesbian, Jewish, and Zionist, and not necessarily in that order.

Further, because I doubt that the Jewish people would survive without the State of Israel, I have concluded that anti-Zionism ought to be perceived as a form of prejudice exactly on par with homophobia, sexism, and racism.

II. Subsequent Ordeal with an Anti-Zionist Student

Some months later, I began to consider whether there was something more proactive I might do to improve the campus climate for Jewish students, Zionists, their allies, and those interested in learning, in an objective and dispassionate fashion, about Israelis and Palestinians. I decided to teach a new course on the Israeli-Palestinian conflict.

When the semester arrived, I found the students in this class to be overall an uninformed, but pleasant, group. However, one student was an extreme anti-Zionist who explicitly supported terrorism as a legitimate response to "Israeli aggression" and whose writing expressed an assured zealotry and dead-serious conviction of rightness that gave me pause. The class progressed largely without incident, fortunately, except that this student objected nearly continually to even my blandest and most self-evident statements about the conflict. The other students eventually became irritated and impatient with his commandeering of the classroom. One could also see that they felt bullied and oppressed, particularly since he never engaged in give-or-take discussion or took into account other students' points of view.

When the student eventually discovered an opportunity to make trouble for me with the administration, I was not entirely surprised.

I had given the class an assignment to evaluate arguments based on facts and evidence that Israel had or had not engaged in genocide against the Palestinians. In his paper, my anti-Zionist student asserted vociferously that the Israelis had committed genocide against the Palestinians to eliminate their "enemies," who were the legitimate heirs to the lands the Israelis "illegally occupied." It was an enraged screed that provided no evidence whatever for its positions. Instead of giving him a failing grade for refusing to follow directions or deal with facts and evidence, I asked to see him in my office. There, I attempted to reason with him, but he soon marched out, accusing me of being an anti-Palestinian and anti-Islam racist who wanted to ruin his academic career because I was a Zionist.

Flummoxed, and somewhat worried, I was pulled aside soon after by my dean, who informed me that a student had come to her office and made "strident" comments against me. Although she recognized that these were out of character of what she knew of me, she had referred the student (as she was obliged to do) to the new director of the Office of Diversity and Equity.

The call came soon after. Here was someone whom I did not know and who took a very different attitude toward me than my dean had with respect to my anti-Zionist student. The director was reflexively, obviously, anti-Israel and inclined to give credence to accusations that I was anti-Islam and racist. The director asked me to complete a lengthy statement explaining my side of the story and then told me that I likely acted questionably in "threatening" to give a student a failing grade "simply" because he disagreed with my "subjective interpretations." I differed strongly with this view of the matter and gave my reasons. Accusations of genocide implicate human beings in the most profound ethical violations toward our sense of *humanity*, I argued, and the standard of evidence for them must be extremely high; casual and baseless accusations are both epistemically and morally unacceptable. The director subsequently arrived at the "remedy": to have this student graded by a different professor with whom he might, she concluded, "see more eye to eye."

I was at once relieved and deeply vexed by this solution, as it deprived me of legitimate pedagogical authority without cause and, at the same time, restored peace and good order to my class. I later had the limited satisfaction of seeing that this student did not receive a passing grade from the other professor, who also critiqued his work for lack of reasoned argument and evidence. Nevertheless, the strain of dealing with this student in the classroom, the need to take significant time to write a lengthy statement defending my pedagogical practices against false and egregious accusations of racism and bias, and his intransigent hatred of Israeli Jews and the mere existence of Israel exhausted and demoralized me.

III. Coming Out as a Proud, Queer, Jewish Pinkwasher

During that traumatic but transformative year, I also decided to heal and solve the puzzles of myself by, finally, integrating my multiple and often disjointed identities. I emerged from the largest and scariest closet I have ever lived inside: I came out as a proud queer Jewish pinkwasher.

Since 2008, I have become the Jewish lesbian who, rather than standing by chagrined and upset, cheers loudly for the Israeli LGBTQ delegation at gay pride parades. Other queer parade-goers, showing their instinctive antisemitic and anti-Israel animus, boo and heckle while moving away from me, my wife, and my friends, pariahs within our supposedly collectively oppressed community.

I am the Jewish lesbian who, as a professor, regularly shows Israeli LGBTQ films in my class in queer literature and film, including *Keep Not Silent* (2004, dir. Lil Alexander), about Orthodox lesbians, and *The Bubble* (2006, dir. Eylan Fox), about a love affair between an Israeli and a Palestinian gay man.

I am the Jewish lesbian professor who, when teaching sexuality and ethics, discusses the legal landscape for LGBTQ persons in the Middle East. In Egypt, same-sex sexual relations are punishable by seventeen years in prison with hard labor; in Libya, by amputation, imprisonment, or, for women, rape and forced marriage; in Iran, Sudan, Saudi Arabia, Bahrain, Oman, Yemen, and the United Arab Emirates, by flogging, the death penalty by hanging or decapitation, or both; and in Iraq and Jordan, while such relations have been decriminalized, honor killings, abuse, and silencing remain common.

In Israel, in bold contrast, the record of LGBTQ civil rights is not only sterling but also groundbreaking, preceding developments in the United States and much of Europe by years and, sometimes, decades. Israel banned workplace and housing discrimination against LGBTQ persons in 1992 and legalized open military service in 1993, same-sex relationships in 1998, inheritance rights in 2004, adoption rights in 2005, civil unions in 2008, and civil divorce in 2012. Further, in 2008, the Interior Ministry granted a gay Palestinian from Jenin a rare residency permit to live with his Israeli partner of eight years after he asserted that his sexuality jeopardized his life in the West Bank.

Given such an inspiring progressive record, which is an outstanding example of the success of the modern LGBTQ movement, why in the world would queers at gay pride parades in the United States (and Europe) volubly deride queer delegations from Israel? Why has Israel, with its struggles, achievements, and history of antisemitic persecution, become an outcast within the queer communities of America, Canada, Australia, and, to an even larger extent, Europe?

The answer lies not only in the sordid history of antisemitism and anti-Zionism but also in the portmanteau compound word *pinkwashing*. Although it's meant pejoratively, I have decided to wear this term with pride on my own terms.

Jasbir Puar, associate professor of women's studies at Rutgers University—most recently infamous for claiming, in a lecture at Vassar, that Israelis deliberately "stunted" the growth of and "harvested the organs" of Palestinians—first coined this term to find a way to castigate Israel for its strong LGBTQ civil rights record. Puar and others assert that Israel, concerned about its negative image abroad, actively attempts to cover up its misdeeds against Palestinian Arabs by touting its achievements regarding queer civil rights.

The absurdity and the underlying hate are palpable. You may as well argue that gay pride parades in the United States constitute a plot to conceal American foreign adventurism and the mistreatment of indigenous peoples. Puar spells out the details in her unfortunate screed, *Terrorist Assemblages: Homonationalism in Queer Times* (2007). There, she argues that queers in Western liberal countries, where they have been afforded significant civil liberties, have become co-opted into "homonationalism" and "homonormativity" and feel sufficiently privileged to voice complaints about *other* minorities, specifically Muslim immigrants, who are, in exaggerated fashion, accused of harboring homophobia. This strange effort to defend Islam from one very narrow form of critique, which Puar soon transforms into her attack on Israel, not only overestimates the extent to which queer persons have achieved acceptance in liberal Western states but also simply whitewashes the significant homophobia (as well as antisemitism and sexism) which many—but not all—Muslim immigrants share, given the normative precepts of Islam and social prejudice present in many or most Muslim countries. Puar then goes on to critique Israeli comparisons of the statuses afforded LGBTQ people in Israel and Palestinian territories—where gays have no legal protections and are subject to discrimination, abuse, shunning, honor killings, and murder—identifying them as instances of pinkwashing.

According to her, in effect, Israeli LGBTQ activists who labored long and hard to secure equal rights, often against entrenched ultra-Orthodox prejudice, did so only to cover up their nation's oppression of Palestinian Arabs. So, tainted, gay achievements in Israel can no longer be celebrated or praised, and it becomes taboo to suggest that Israel stands as a shining example for other countries in the Middle East or elsewhere to emulate. Instead, homosexual rights are transformed into an imperialist and anti-Palestinian Western phenomenon—despite the long histories of queer cultures in non-Western lands. Significantly, flying in the face of the traditional homoerotic subcultures that once flourished in Islamic nations, Puar advises that using the term *homosexual* within contemporary Muslim contexts would cause "unnecessary" divisions and "binary oppositions."

With activists like Puar and the many she has influenced, the animosity toward Israel and toward Jews within my own gay community becomes overt.

In 2008, I had to learn to confront head-on virulent loathing from two external sources: a perpetrator of serial hate crimes who detested Jews and LGBTQ people sufficiently to issue death threats and a student who despised the mere existence of Israel. However painful those experiences were, they paled beside the anti-Zionist and antisemitic pinkwashing accusers from within my LGBTQ communities. They constituted a different kind of enemy, now from the oppressed and marginalized group with whom I had always felt the most solidarity and for whose sake I had devoted much time and effort as an activist and advocate. They took all the liberal ideals of inclusion and respect for plurality in which I believe so deeply and used them against the Zionist and Jewish components of my identity. Already (obviously) excluded from the communities of my enemies, the religious bigots and the criminal haters, these haters threaten to exclude me from the community in which I had previously found refuge, mutual identification, and support.

This battle is far from over, but fortunately, I have discovered I am not alone in fighting it. Coming out of that capacious closet was the necessary first step for me. Since doing so, I have found a community of individuals who understand and support me and who, best of all, cherish me for who I am. More important, I have also discovered a community of allies among Israeli LGBTQ activists.

The battle is far from over, but we *will* recapture the liberal ideals that originally informed and motivated our community from those who hate Israel and who hate Jews and who, in attacking Israel, attack those very ideals.

CORINNE E. BLACKMER is Professor of English and Judaic Studies at Southern Connecticut State University, where she teaches Judaic studies, Hebrew Bible, and gender and sexuality studies. She has published widely on modernism and Judaic studies.

5 Slouching toward the City That Never Stops: How a Left-Orientalist Anti-Israel Faculty Tour Forced Me to Say Something (Big Mistake!)

Gabriel Noah Brahm

Gabriel Brahm went on a faculty research trip to Israel organized by his university. The trip turned out to be largely an anti-Israel hatefest aimed at indoctrinating the visiting professors about the evil Zionist entity. Brahm protested and asked for greater balance. Instead, he became the target of a disciplinary investigation that resulted from his refusal to go along with the anti-Israel propaganda. He was cleared of the charges in that case but, the following year, threatened with denial of tenure, even though his record of publication and teaching exceeded his university's requirements. Brahm appealed and won. Yet the case, as he writes, testifies to the "atmospheric antisemitism" that targets Jewish academics who are unwilling to denounce Israel. Since attachment to Israel is a foundational building block of identity for the vast majority of self-identified American Jews, the "normal repertoire of being Jewish," Brahm concludes, "makes you radioactive."

THE DELETERIOUS IMPACT of anti-Israelism on the academy is cumulative, multifaceted, and complex—the overdetermined product of loosely affiliated genres of ignorance, prejudice, resentment, venality, and intellectual laziness. Some of the hostility directed toward Israel on campus is openly ideological, while some is less explicitly doctrinaire and more atmospheric—the result of diffuse sentiment more than concentrated thought. In the former, manifestly political category, the works of Noam Chomsky, Ilan Pappé, and Edward Said stand out among many. But such often highly abstract anti-Israelism is generally not where the rubber actually meets the road in the workplace. Indeed, in the day-to-day academy, having much of an opinion about much of anything at all—other than politically correct approved opinions—can be dangerous. That is where the real censorship and abuse take place—from one colleague to another to another—in the halls of the Foucauldian academic archipelago of sites for the enforcement of regimented intellectual discipline. It is a corner of this treacherous space I now want to map in what follows.

Atmospheric Antisemitism, Radioactive Zionism

Anti-Israelism's most pernicious effects, as a practical matter, show up in what Michel Foucault called the "capillaries of power."[1] Off the kind of radar on which a relatively few big ideas/authors show up, many otherwise invisible microaggressions against Israel-identified Jews occur when Israel bashers and Judeophobes sense a target in range or smell blood in the water. Jews who loudly reject or quietly neglect (ignore) Israel are OK. But as soon as a Jewish person self-identifies as Zionist, he or she becomes vulnerable. In Mark Banschick's apt image, he or she becomes radioactive.[2] That's what happened to me.

It was early 2011, and I was the only Jew selected to participate in what turned out to be an anti-Israel academic study trip to the Middle East. (Although an Israeli-American colleague applied, she was rejected.) Of course, at the time, I didn't know it was an *anti*-Israel enterprise that I was getting involved with—I had thought, happily, Israel was just a part of the agenda. When finally it dawned on me that the bias I perceived was not merely a series of unfortunate accidents, and I thereafter objected to its pervasive ideological slant, I was then quickly branded a gadfly—a troublesome, typically annoying Jew, overly attached to Israel, too fond of debate[3]—and, as punishment, made to run a lengthy gauntlet of sado-bureaucratic reprisals brought on by those I had offended.

I call what I subsequently endured *atmospheric antisemitism* because it was a product of an environment in which being Jewish set you up for abuse—unless you quietly submitted to the hostility aimed at the central symbol of secular Jewish collective life today, the Jewish and democratic state of Israel. What happened to me could not have happened (it seems clear) to someone who didn't identify sufficiently with Israel to (a) know something about it and (b) feel a justifiable sense of indignation, at some point, when Israel was systematically smeared over a long period of time. *Structural antisemitism* and *institutionalized antisemitism* are closely related terms that also work to describe the same phenomenon. Whatever you call it, it's an example of what happens when holding on to certain ethnic traits that one cannot reasonably be expected to let go of—in this case, one's Jewish identity—puts one at risk. For many Jews, after all, maintaining a robust attachment to the Jewish State is simply an element in the normal repertoire of what it means to participate actively in Jewish life.[4]

The normal repertoire of being Jewish, in other words, makes you radioactive.

Antisemitic Anti-Israelism on Tour

We did not see Yad Vashem. We did not go to the Knesset. We walked around the gritty, grimy, thoroughly unlovely central bus station in Tel Aviv—the one that most people I know tend to avoid when traveling to and from the "city that never stops." (There is a nicer, open-air bus station in a better part of town, near the train at Arlozorov Street.) We were treated as well to a walk around the neighborhood—one of the poorest in Israel—and shown a smoke-filled room there, crammed with African refugees. The point? Not sure. We later saw a Palestinian sweatshop of some kind in Bethlehem and heard about the dismal working conditions there.

We traveled to a facility someplace in the West Bank that purportedly dealt with water issues, recycling, and peace. There, they fed us a traditional Arabic lunch of chicken and rice, demonstrating the locals' quaint tradition of hospitality—as the pervasive left-Orientalism we were soaking in tended to frame things. By *left-Orientalism*, I mean an exoticizing of the Orient that invariably works to condemn the West in the service of progressive, if not revolutionary, political purposes. And when I asked if we could next, maybe, for a change of pace, see what it was like for those living with Hamas rockets in Sderot, on the border with Gaza, my suggestion was taken and turned upside down. We went to Sderot and met with activists who claimed to be doing semi-clandestine solidarity work with Gazans.

In sum, it was one long litany of complaint against Israel. We saw nothing normal. For the sake of diversity, they took us to a settlement, where a stereotypically ideological settler from New Jersey gave us a not altogether ingratiating lecture. Of course, that too was a setup, calculated to be unappealing to liberal-minded faculty. To top things off, we met with a friend of our tour guide, the notorious Jeff Halper—mastermind behind the Israeli Committee against House Demolitions. Well-known to Israelis as a fringe character but new to my colleagues, Halper—presented as some sort of an expert—regaled us about Israel's many crimes. Speaking to our group of professors for more than an hour, he explained (among other things) how "the wall" (separation barrier, security fence) between Israel proper and the West Bank does not in fact save the lives of innocent Israelis by protecting them from terrorism but only serves to disrupt the lives of Palestinians. Intentionally so, of course! For it was all part of the Israelis' nefarious plan to steal land and nothing more. According to Halper, the Jewish and "democratic" state was utterly giving up on the latter adjective in preference to the former. The ostensibly defensive architectural impediment to terror, he said, had nothing to do with necessity due to the gruesome Second Intifada—a bloody series of events that most of my colleagues could not have told you anything about, either before or after Halper's polemics. He also predicted that Israel would utterly collapse (why and how wasn't so clear) within two years (this was in 2011). So, he was as accurate about the future as he was about the past.

We did not see any of the Israel Museum's magnificent exhibits, nor did we spend time at Tel Aviv's transplendent beaches. We didn't go to the Dead Sea (which at least would have been fun and iconic). We didn't see any architectural or archaeological sites, except for a sweaty jog around the Old City of Jerusalem. In keeping with the agenda, we saw nothing that reflected anything realistic, typical, much less positive, about the modern State of Israel. Other than ordinary poverty and misery, of the sort that you could find in pretty much any urban center anywhere—and which we were taken out of our way to find examples of in Israel—you would have thought the country was essentially devoid of any positive value post-70 AD.

This faculty research trip was rigged to smear the Jewish State, in short. Who perpetrated this cheap charade and why, I never fully understood. But it was partly the product of status-quo left-liberal hostility to Zionism and partly the product of political cronyism (along with no more than the standard measure of ordinary ineptitude as well, perhaps). The daughter of the then provost was working for a non-governmental organization (NGO) in the West Bank and had helped set things up, it was at some point whispered. Most such organizations, as Tuvia Tenenbom has demonstrated, obsess about finding Jews committing evil and are dedicated to blackening Israel's reputation.[5] But again, my colleagues could not have been expected to know that. Junior faculty at the time, I was invited because it was understood that I had some connection to Israel and Israel studies. This clearly shows there was some naiveté on somebody's part, at least—somebody who failed to distinguish between a person who actually knew something about Israel and the rest of the faculty. The rest of the faculty knew next to nothing and so were, by and large, ready and waiting (innocently or not) for anti-Israel indoctrination. That some were nonetheless too smart to fall for it was a testament to their intelligence and good character. But this could not be expected of everyone, alas. Nor should faculty have had to defend themselves against such an onslaught.

Eventually, after days of anti-Israel talking points, I had to say something. So, I objected to Halper's lecture in particular. I said it was wrong for him to speak as if he were a respectable authority on the matter. I pointed out some of his lies and distortions in real time. I urged the organizers to include other points of view. But they refused to allow anyone they defined as a "right-winger" into the conversation. I pleaded to have them take us to Yad Vashem at least, but we were driven instead to Jericho, where we were allowed to get out for—I kid you not—five minutes, before being driven back to Jerusalem, where we were then told it was "too late" to go to Israel's world-renowned Holocaust museum—the old "we just ran out of time" trick. The ruse certainly felt transparent, given our pointless excursion that same afternoon, which it seemed everyone was dumbfounded by. Insulting, even—considering what was sacrificed, as if it were nothing important. Moreover, it would have been terribly irresponsible, at a minimum—had the tour we were on actually been intended to educate about Israel.

By the time we got back to the United States, I was up on some kind of charges—unbelievable at the time. As absurd as our "visit" to Jericho. In true Kafkaesque style, I was told neither who accused me nor what exactly I was accused of. But I was investigated. For weeks, I and others who went on the trip were subjected to long interviews by the head of human resources. I was left in limbo for months, uncertain what would come of this inquiry. At the time, I was as yet untutored in the ways of intrafaculty squabbles, administrative ire (had I inadvertently stepped on the provost's toes, vis-à-vis her daughter?), and bureaucratic harassment. But I knew it was bogus. Unfair. Antisemitic "in effect if not in intent."[6]

In the end, I was cleared—naturally, since I hadn't done anything wrong! But that, as they say, is where my troubles began.

Shylock and the Conspiracy of Doofuses

Despite being exonerated of whatever I had been charged with, the black cloud continued to hang over me. When I went up for tenure the year *after* the trip and the investigation that had followed, I had to fight. Although no one with anything like my publication record (more than enough in terms of quantity and quality) and teaching evaluations (90 percent positive) ever had to push his or her case at my school the way I did, I was put through the wringer. In the good old-fashioned style one associates with corrupt, feudal-type governance.

The plan to teach this Shylock a lesson took its toll, alas, in the form of months of aggravation and emotional distress. It began when my department put my stellar tenure application forward with an utterly unprecedented *nonrecommendation*. Instead of saying *yea* or *nay*—as contractually mandated—the committee of my peers, overseen with a firm hand by my department head at the time, burped *meh*. Without a verdict either way, the dean (someone I then barely knew, but a good man, as it turns out, put in an impossible situation) was thus pressed to write a letter denying his support for my tenure, on the grounds that he couldn't confirm someone whose own peers didn't think well enough of to endorse.

So it was recommended that I be denied tenure—despite my record. Not a pleasant experience. But I persisted.

I appealed the outrageous judgment, compelled to make my case before a faculty committee charged with reviewing tenure and promotion cases. I readily demonstrated my credentials to this jury and was fortunate—having the facts on my side—to persuade them of my merit. Their decision was unanimous in my favor. Finally, after that, my tenure was grudgingly approved by the provost—by then, fortunately, a *different* provost from the one who had played a role in initiating the fateful trip and who had subsequently gone on to greener pastures at another school. Moreover, the new provost confirmed to me in a letter what should never have needed confirming—that there was "nothing in your record that should deny you tenure." It wasn't exactly the ringing endorsement I had dreamed of celebrating when I got into the profession, but it would have to do. I celebrated anyway. In sum, there was *nothing* to the trumped-up charge— engineered by those who had cherry-picked a handful of negative written comments by students over many years—that I was unpleasantly, and stereotypically, "bookish, wordy and contentious."[7] In other words, my persecutors claimed—against mountains of evidence accumulated in the course of a career—that students in my classes were suffering from an overly zealous gadfly's hectoring. They were not! Yes, I was (as I remain) a *bit* of a bookish, wordy, and contentious Jew. But no, that was not a reason to deny me, or anyone, tenure. In fact, my record of accomplishment was such that the diligent grievance officer of the American Association of University Professors at my campus said it was the strongest appeal he had ever seen and that my record was so good they "couldn't not" give me tenure, "even if they wanted to."

So why had they wanted to? Why was I put through this ordeal?

It was a direct result of my protest against the anti-Israel tour I was dragged into. The bottom line is that it all sprang from my having been the only Jewish faculty and the only faculty knowledgeable about Israel among a team of researchers (from librarians to mathematicians and economists) sent to study how to improve instruction about the Middle East, ostensibly. We were to learn this by going to the Middle East for two weeks—including our week of spring break, which we gave up for the cause. What we got for our trouble, however, was as described.

Did I fail to mention that Israel was not the only country we visited? Well, I should tell you about that, too, for it proves my point—dramatically. We also went to Turkey. Egypt had been scheduled initially but was scratched as the Arab Spring was sprung. Now get this: In Istanbul for several days, we saw national monuments, historical relics, and cultural treasures—the Blue Mosque, that sort of thing. We stayed in nice hotels. Unsurprisingly, we saw some very nice things about a fascinating place. In Israel, we had been put up by nuns in a bare-bones, bread-and-water type of operation. And saw the bus station.

Need I add that we saw nothing remotely critical of the Turkish republic, much less its Islamist, Muslim Brotherhood–affiliated government? As I write, several years later, that same government has recently imposed an extended state of emergency in response to a murky coup attempt and cracked down on journalists and universities, and most observers think it's the last gasp of democracy in Turkey for a while. No sir, Turkey was all sweetness and light—as opposed to devilish, if vibrantly democratic, Israel.

All in all, a remarkably consistent series of events, wouldn't you say?

Life Lessons, Double Standards, and the Half-Life of Bigotry

And what we do we learn from all this? That it's dangerous to be an "out of the closet" Zionist in academia these days. It's not so easy being Jewish either—that is, if you happen to be one of those Jews who admire the Jewish State and so don't pass the litmus test of being willing to denounce your heritage. In other words, Jews who want folks to boycott Israel are fine, but Jews who object to lies and defamation are troublemakers, worthy of careful scrutiny, witch hunts, and whisper campaigns.

One of the most troubling things about the whole episode is that it may well have started out largely as what Foucault called a "conspiracy without conspirators."[8] At least initially, pervasive implicit bias seems to have been the culprit more than anything. The expectation that Israel was naturally to be dealt with according to unstated double standards, simply as part of the normal way of doing business in politically correct academia these days, did a lot of the work by itself.

Only later did considerable human agency intervene to punish the one person who saw through the inherent antisemitism at work and said something about it. Years later, that tawdry aspect would be described to me, by a colleague in the know at the time when things were happening, as nothing less than a conspiracy, per se. But by then it was too late to matter. By the time I learned definitively that there had likely been a few who were literally out to get me, it was ancient history. The ringleader (tragically) had died of a heart attack, and as mentioned, the top administrator implicated had moved on to another institution. We had a wonderful new department head by then, so the department felt like a different place. A couple of disposable henchmen had retired, and even the human resources person—whose job description was rumored to include lying and bullying—had moved onward and upward as well. No one cared anymore, least of all me.

Indeed, without those four or five folks around, things had gotten better. I should stress that there are also some great, great people at my university— including a new generation of leadership in the new administration of my department, which superseded the former corrupt regime that had tried to punish me for speaking up. So, I was sick of the whole matter by the time a senior colleague, confiding in me, actually said those words: "It was a conspiracy." I'd moved on, content that living well was the best revenge (call it the Tel Avivian in me) and determined not to let the sordid affair grind me down any further.

That I won the battle in the end should serve as encouragement to all who bridle at the predominant intimidation into silence of pretenure Zionists. But minimal encouragement at best, I believe. For I remain somewhat radioactive still. And what's the half-life of bigotry, I wonder. To this day, there are colleagues who look askance at grant proposals from me that sound too Zionist to them, I fear. A proposal that was rated highly by the National Endowment for the Humanities, for example, was ranked dead last by some of my peers, who explained unabashedly to my face that I'm emotional about things like terrorism and boycotts. In fact, I am not. I do patient research on anti-Jewish activities, including boycotts, and identify these things for what they are.

That I had to *fight* for my promotion at all, for what was rightfully mine by dint of more than a decade's worth of accomplishments, can, I suppose, only add to the widely held impression out there nowadays that it's unsafe to challenge politically correct orthodoxy in the academy—especially when it comes to Israel.

For, again, *why* did my colleagues (a handful of them, anyway) seek to pull this? Why did they set me up for months of agony and time wasting in the mind-numbing ordeal of an appeal? Why was I forced to meet regularly for a semester with the grievance officer on campus (when I hadn't even known we had one of those or what a grievance officer was for before that)? Why was I forced to worry, for months on end, that I might be fired?

Make no mistake—this could *not* have happened had I *not* let them know I was an unashamed supporter of Israel.

This happened to me—

Because I'm Jewish.

That's the bottom line.

GABRIEL NOAH BRAHM is Associate Professor of English at Northern Michigan University, specializing in philosophical anthropology, literary theory,world literature and film. He currently serves as a senior research fellow at the Herzl Institute for the Study of Zionism and History (University of Haifa), a faculty fellow at Scholars for Peace in the Middle East (SPME), and a research fellow at the Schusterman Center for Israel Studies at Brandeis University. He has taught as a visiting professor at the Hebrew University of Jerusalem, and served as a visiting researcher at the Institute for National Security Studies (Tel Aviv University). He is editor (with Cary Nelson) of *The Case Against Academic Boycotts of Israel* and author (with Forrest G. Robinson) of *The Jester and the Sages: Mark Twain in Conversation with Nietzsche, Freud, and Marx.*

Notes

1. Michel Foucault, *Discipline and Punish* (New York: Penguin, 1977).

2. Mark Banschick, "BDS and Radioactivity: Alumni Confront Anti-Israel Rhetoric on Campus," *The Algemeiner* (November 10, 2016), https://www.algemeiner.com/2016/11/10/bds -and-radioactivity-alumni-confront-anti-israel-rhetoric-on-campus/.

3. According to Amos Oz and Fania Oz-Salzberger, in *Jews and Words* (New Haven, CT: Yale University Press, 2014), Jews are perceived as "bookish, wordy and contentious." I fear this may have been how I was seen by those who saw me as a menacing stereotype.

4. Kenneth L. Marcus, *The Definition of Antisemitism* (Oxford, UK: Oxford University Press, 2016).

5. Tuvia Tenenbom, *Catch the Jew* (New York: Gefen Publishing House, 2015).

6. An apt phrase coined by former Harvard president Lawrence Summers, characterizing the Boycott, Divestment, and Sanctions movement.

7. Oz and Oz-Salzberger, *Jews and Words*.

8. Michel Foucault, *Language, Counter-memory, Practice* (Ithaca: Cornell UP, 1977).

6 On Radio Silence and the Video That Saved the Day: The Attack against Professor Dubnov at the University of California San Diego, 2012

Shlomo Dubnov

Shlomo Dubnov's story highlights a common campus tactic of anti-Israelists: race-tinged libelous smearing of their opponents. Dubnov spoke against Boycott, Divestment, and Sanctions (BDS) at the student government's annual debate and promptly became the target of a campaign in which he was falsely charged with harassing an anti-Israel student "of color." Shockingly, university administrators and colleagues promoted the campaign against him even in the absence of any actual evidence of his wrongdoing. Only after the campaign had done its damage to him, personally and professionally, did video come to light that completely exonerated him—although even that didn't stop the attacks on him. Dubnov observes with dismay how Jewish academics are intimidated by anti-Israel activists and how difficult it is for Jewish students to be taught by so many professors who urge them to rethink their connections to Israel. Partly as a result of what happened to him, the following year anti-Israel forces prevailed in intimidating their campus opponents and finally passed a student government BDS resolution.

It was one of those almost routine events. February 2012. The annual BDS debate, loud and contentious, would go on all night at the University of California San Diego (UCSD) student government meeting. I expected it to be somewhat nerve-racking, and by knowing in advance that lies and false accusations against Israel were going to fly around and that I was going to hear over and over the same accusations of racism, genocide, and ethnic cleansing, I could mentally equip myself as I walked in there. I knew, or thought I knew, that the only decent response to the outrageous accusations would be to speak of tolerance, the need to negotiate, the principles of civil conduct, and so on.

I did not at all expect what ended up happening.

I came to UCSD more than a decade ago from Israel. Soon after my arrival, I organized a group of UCSD faculty as a local chapter of the academic organization Scholars for Peace in the Middle East (SPME). What I was going to say at that student government meeting was pretty much in line with how SPME framed its mission: "promoting academic integrity in the study of the Middle East, particularly with regard to the conflict between Israel and its Arab neighbors." It sounds good, decent, not too aggressive. I was also going to talk about the standards of academic free speech and was prepared to share a letter from forty Nobel laureates that read, in part:

> Believing that academic and cultural boycotts, divestments and sanctions in the academy are:
>
> - antithetical to principles of academic and scientific freedom,
> - antithetical to principles of freedom of expression and inquiry, and
> - may well constitute discrimination by virtue of national origin,
>
> We, the undersigned Nobel Laureates, appeal to students, faculty colleagues and university officials to defeat and denounce calls and campaigns for boycotting, divestment and sanctions against Israeli academics, academic institutions and university-based centers and institutes for training and research, affiliated with Israel.[1]

The letter goes on to encourage students, faculty, and university officials to promote and provide opportunities for civil academic discourse, and so on.

Yes, this letter was rather dry, academically written, and lacking the energy of students' typical battles in the marketplace of ideas—if one may refer in this way to the show trials of Israel that the student government was asked yearly to host by the pro-Palestinian student organizations. Nonetheless, sharing the letter and the ideas it expressed seemed the only decent thing one could do in that situation.

As for the evening itself, other colleagues of mine, including faculty and staff, also came out to speak for Israel and particularly to support the Jewish students who had more skin in the game, so to speak. At least that's what I thought: skin in the game but still a game. Some hardy pro-Israeli faculty even stayed there all night, but after a good half hour or so of accusations of racism directed at me as an Israeli professor who actually supports Israel—which I received with an ironic smile—I had had an adequate taste and left the hall. I met a colleague, a professor in the medical school, outside the room; we stopped to chat briefly with some of the Jewish students, and we left the building.

Walking to the bus, I thought more about this evil game that students had to play, to go through this volley of hate addressed at Israel and its supporters, where one side tries to achieve symbolic but vicious political gains, while the other side, feeling obligated through its heritage to defend Israel, themselves, and their people, had to stand there and take the beating. Many of the students spoke about how difficult it is to be a Jewish student on campus in such an atmosphere and how the student government's passing of the BDS resolution would isolate and alienate them. None of them really wanted to hit back at the other side, to go on the attack against them; it seemed to me that just standing there to confront the lies was heroic enough. After all, this is a university, a bastion of hypothetical imperatives, and the BDS resolution was only hypothetical, since everybody knew that the university administration would ignore any BDS demand by the student body. Even the chancellor assured me as much in person. So just being there and presenting an antithesis to the hate-filled calls for "Palestine from the river to the sea" should be enough, I thought, and proving the other side wrong in all its specific charges against Israel would be just a matter of facts and logic.

To my dismay and surprise, I was proven so wrong.

Perhaps I shouldn't have been so surprised, in light of the many campus activities in the years leading up to that night. I have regularly seen the Apartheid Wall filled with lies erected on campus. I have attended pro-Palestinian events, including one called "Palestine: Past, Present & Future" and a pro-Palestinian "Speak Out!" with lectures by people such as Alison Weir—who, according to her website,[2] is an expert in the "massive ethnic cleansing accomplished in Israel's War of Independence"—all organized by the UCSD Muslim Students Association and often even cosponsored by the UCSD Office of the Vice Chancellor of Student Affairs. Indeed, the difficult questions—of whether all this is hate speech, whether these attacks on Israel are also attacks on Jewish students and faculty, and whether these activities justify expanding the US Department of Education's Office for Civil Rights coverage to include Jews among those protected by the Civil Rights Act of 1964—had been debated feverishly among the Jews themselves and pretty much ruled out. Jews are not a protected category, some argued, because we do not need protection, and that was the prevailing spirit. The overall success of US Jewry, these people said, serves as proof. Still, they acknowledged in 2011 that standing up for Israel is not done lightheartedly. It can be and often is emotionally draining, as the events of that 2012 student government debate would make clear—the first hint of a new type of game on campus.

Nevertheless, wrote Kenneth Stern, the director on antisemitism and extremism for the American Jewish Committee, as he expressed the prevailing spirit among Jews at UCSD as of 2011, our moral ground was high enough that there was no need to "protect" Jewish students by imposing censorship.[3]

No, in retrospect, perhaps I should not have been surprised by what was to occur following that student government BDS debate in 2012. As one of the journalists in the *San Diego Jewish World* wrote afterward, attempting to explain what befell me: "These false charges [against Professor Dubnov] are a test tactic to counter the documented charges of harassment and violence by pro-Palestinian students at other campuses that have been deemed serious enough to be taken up by the federal government under Title VI of the Civil Rights Act. Recall that ten anti-Israel students were convicted [in September 2011] for their disruption of a [2010] speech by an Israeli ambassador at U.C. Irvine."[4]

And there were so many Jewish professors who came out to stand with those infamous anti-Israel students! One of our own UCSD faculty members, a member of Judaic studies and an expert on the Holocaust, had signed an open letter by thirty University of California (UC) Jewish studies faculty members defending the disruption by Muslim students of the 2010 UC Irvine lecture by Michael Oren, Israel's ambassador to the United States. As reported by the Gatestone Institute:

> Posted as "Stand With The Eleven" (the 11 being the offending members of the radical Muslim Student Union charged with a misdemeanor conspiracy to disturb a meeting), the letter states:

> "As faculty affiliated with Jewish Studies at the University of California, we are deeply distressed by the decision of the District Attorney in Orange County, California, to file criminal charges against Muslim students who disrupted Israeli Ambassador Michael Oren's speech on the UC Irvine campus last year. While we disagree with the students' decision to disrupt the speech, we do not believe such peaceful protest should give rise to criminal liability. The individual students and the Muslim Student Union were disciplined for this conduct by the University, including suspending the MSU from functioning as a student organization for a quarter. This is sufficient punishment. There is no need for further punitive measures, let alone criminal prosecution and criminal sanctions."[5]

This is the problematic spirit that was dominating the American Jewish community at that time, not just the Jewish faculty members in the UC system, including UCSD.

Of course, the vexed nature of the relationships between Israel, the Jewish people and "peoplehood," and the Diaspora goes well back. Ironically, my own grand-grand-grand uncle has been credited with putting the link between Israel as a state of the Jews and Jews as a people living in the Diaspora into question. In fact, David Myers, a prominent University of California, Los Angeles (UCLA) Jewish history professor who signed on to "Stand with the Eleven," published in 2011 an essay titled "Rethinking the Jewish Nation" in which the key questions of today were symbolized by the century-old debate between "the Zionist Ahad Ha'am (1856–1927) and the Diasporist Simon Dubnow (1860–1941)."[6] What Myers urges us to rethink is the "Statist Zionism" that "rests on the claim that nation and state are, or should be, equivalent." He writes that "in a globalized age of easy air travel, instantaneous cyber-communication, and far-flung cultural and economic networks," we need "to think of a new language and paradigm to revive the Jewish collective. The Statist Zionist model, which posits Israel as strong center and the Diaspora as weak periphery—itself a structural carry-over of the ideology of early Zionism—is a reflection neither of demographic realities nor of the kind of meaningful partnership of equals that this collective can or should be."

With *airplanes* and *cyber-communication*, this essay sounded to me like a futurist manifesto, only one hundred years too late and conveniently skipping some of the horrible events of history in between.

Ahad Ha'Am was also the name of a school near my childhood home in Petah-Tikva. And Dubnov was the name of a street in Tel Aviv near the opera, with a big parking lot bearing the same name. Whenever people would ask me if I was from Dubnov Street, I would say, "No, I'm from the parking lot." Both the school and the parking lot were physical realities. Dubnow's and Ha'Am's debates were metaphysical. Well, not totally metaphysical. Dubnow's picture was and is still hanging in my late father's study, and the ten volumes of his *World History of the Jewish People* were occupying a premium bookshelf location in his library. So, I knew Dubnow as an autonomist, territorialist, but also as a proud nationalist. His arguments with Ha'Am were discussed in our house but so was his admiration—apparently unappreciated by Myers—for the *Yishuv*, the Jewish settlement in the Land of Israel, as the greatest miracle in contemporary Jewish history.

Shamefully appropriating just one element of a scholar's thought in this way seems woefully common by Jewish studies faculty members (and others) in the United States these days. It amounts to presenting what are, in fact, their own political ideas by means of an eloquent technique of building partial historical narratives to their own advantage. This seems to work because many students fall for the eloquence rather than for the explicit construction of personal opinions and imperatives. With techniques like this, politicization of the classroom seems inevitable. Professors are, in effect, disseminating their own political convictions through their teaching.

It is in this confusing atmosphere that pro-Israel students have to operate on campus—an atmosphere where Jewish students go on Birthright trips to Israel and volunteer for the Israel Defense Forces (IDF) but, at the same time, are told by their professors how their Jewish Diasporic identity would be strengthened by rethinking the link to Israel. These students also regularly observe these same professors supporting aggressive actions in favor of the Palestinian cause. All that was the case already, even before the 2012 vote. Later on, I experienced that atmosphere directly for myself when another UCSD faculty member, Ivan Evans, a prominent sociologist, then head of the San Diego Faculty Association (SDFA) and today a provost of one of the colleges, posted accusations against me on the SDFA site. When these accusations were proven false, he refused to apologize; instead, he wrote me a private letter referring to my pro-Israel activity, telling me: "This is frightening patriotic rubbish—it has far more to do with the sort of police-state regimes that Nazis, Stalinists and Apartheid killers have inflicted on humanity than with democracy in complex societies such as Israel. In the 1960s, it was inconceivable to Afrikaners that Apartheid would one day consume dissenting members of *die volk*; by the 1990s, the unthinkable was routine."

That was the atmosphere in 2012. There was yet another BDS vote in 2013 for perhaps the fourth year in a row, and this time, the pro-Israel community, led by the Jewish student body, largely organized around Hillel, finally lost the BDS battle. Yes, in 2013, that same resolution was brought yet again, but this time, the Jewish students refused to allow faculty into the debate—perhaps responding to the troubling events of the previous year by distancing themselves from the non-students who had participated—insisting on handling the case on their own. Was I surprised that BDS passed? Not at all. As of today, the BDS resolution remains on the official record of the UCSD student government body.

Not that UCSD or the UC Board of Regents ever adopted the resolution's recommendations. But that didn't matter. The atmosphere was poisoned; the student government majority proclaimed Israel as guilty, and the Jewish student minority felt intimidated, silenced, no longer able to defend her. Conditions such as these—this silence, this inability to answer the charges—are very dangerous for the long-term prospects for American support of Israel. It is just such conditions that produce individuals like Simone Zimmerman, the short-lived Jewish outreach coordinator for presidential candidate Bernie Sanders, who, shortly after arriving at UC Berkeley, left her Zionist upbringing and American Israel Public Affairs Committee (AIPAC) youth activism to start siding with the Palestinian cause.[7]

Indeed, what is troubling is not merely that Zimmerman switched sides but how quickly it happened and how far she went. In roughly her first year at Berkeley, she went from pro-Israel enthusiast to slanderer of Israel, to rejecting even the alleged liberal Jewish motivation for BDS—to end the 1967 occupation and so save Israel from apartheid, but at least to save Israel—on to whole-hearted endorsement of the true goal of the BDS movement, which, according to the Palestinian Campaign for the Academic and Cultural Boycott of Israel, looks like this: "BDS is not about saving Israel as an apartheid state, giving up some occupied lands that are densely populated by Palestinians to make Israel a more pure apartheid, and to prolong the life of this apartheid for several more years. BDS is all about achieving Palestinian rights, paramount among which is the inalienable right to self determination, by ending Israel's three-tiered system of colonial and racial oppression: colonialism, occupation and apartheid."[8]

Or, in other words, ending Israel as a Jewish state the way we know it today.

So how exactly did this happen?

A *Jerusalem Post* opinion piece explains it this way: "At Berkeley, Zimmerman frequented Hillel, which presents itself as 'home away from home' [for Jews]. There, she encountered Kesher Enoshi, a Hillel group presenting programs demonizing

Israel and the IDF. Kesher Enoshi had been collaborating with Students for Justice in Palestine, a leading BDS campus group—on the Anti-Defamation League's top 10 list of anti-Israel groups in America. The Hillel director, Rabbi Naftalin-Kelman, supported and promoted Kesher Enoshi. Reviewing a sampling of the toxic IDF/Israel-bashing programs presented by Hillel and Kesher Enoshi illuminates the transformation Zimmerman, and numerous other students, underwent."[9]

It's not, of course, guaranteed that repeated exposure to Israel-bashing will convert a long-established Israel supporter—my own two older children were students at UC Berkeley at the time of that BDS campaign, present in the discussion hall, on the pro-Israel side, and they did not switch sides. But it's hard not to believe that it will have an effect on some or many—especially when it comes from within, from the "home within a home," from the Jewish community itself.

Zimmerman explains her switch by suggesting that her challenging questions about Israel were met by the Jewish community with "radio silence": "If my community is not going to give me the answers," she says, "then I need to find them elsewhere."[10] In the same interview, she acknowledges that her questions themselves were generated by listening to Palestinians complain for hours about Israel during the Berkeley BDS campaign, which tells you something about the effects of repeated exposure on a person. But more important, note, she did find the answers she sought—not only on the Palestinian side, but worse, from within, from the Jewish side, the progressive Jewish side.

What were those answers, and what is their logic?

If Israel is to be saved, it has to give up its Jewish nature, which in turn means that Jews in the Diaspora need to start building their own identity separately from that of the *Yishuv*, or whatever the Jewish population in the new Israel will be called. And if this is what is about to happen, it is better that it happens sooner rather than later. "If Not Now" is the name of Zimmerman's organization that aims to move the American Jewish day school curriculum away from support of Israel, to distance American Jewry from Israel. Cynical, yes, to take the Talmudic sage Hillel's dictum urging Jewish solidarity as the name for a movement to shatter that solidarity. Of course, our friend Myers seized the opportunity to proclaim, "Who is Simone Zimmerman? She is the future of American Jewry."[11] Two sides of the same coin: one just too young to conceal her slander, the other eloquent enough to rationalize it.

So, in Zimmerman's words, it was the "radio silence" of the Jewish community around the UC Berkeley BDS campaign that produced *her*. Ironically, that BDS campaign, yet another contentious anti-Israel hatefest, was eventually overturned through a veto of the president of the Berkeley student body. But again, the veto does not really matter. The atmosphere is poisoned; the community is further silenced. With each turn through the BDS grinder, it gets harder and harder for Jews to stand up and speak for Israel. Or maybe it makes it harder and harder for Jews to stand up and speak for themselves.

BDS has managed to cleave the Jews themselves, between Jewish national and spiritual aspirations. It offers a simple dualistic thinking where the complexity of the political situation is traded for Manichaean clarity with all the advantages and speedy spread that such theory offers. "Inspired by Jewish tradition to work together for peace, social justice, equality, human rights, respect for international law" appears as a slogan of Jewish Voice for Peace, which supports BDS.[12] "The humanitarian values of Judaism have been corrupted by the Israeli state's abuses of human rights" appears on the website of Jews for Justice for Palestinians, which also supports BDS.[13] It is painful to see how the websites of these organizations overflow with quotations from Torah and rabbinical sayings, marshaled against the sins of Israeli occupation. Good and bad. Dualistic thinking is simple. It is radical and righteous. It offers an opportunity for some Jewish and non-Jewish thinkers, if we can call them this, to run campaigns of extreme populism where advocating for the elimination of Palestinian suffering will also eliminate all antisemitism. This will make BDS disappear. They just do not realize that this is a Jewish dilemma, not a political solution or reality. Jewish group identity would be dissolved by the same process that would lead to the disappearance of BDS.

In this sense, perhaps Myers is right. Can more Simone Zimmermans be far behind?

And now to February 29, 2012.

A resolution was brought before the UCSD student government calling for university divestment from Israel. After seven hours of debate, it was defeated 20–13. During the meeting, I, like many others, expressed my opinions against the divestment. Two days after the resolution failed, Amal Dalmar, cochair of the Student Affirmative Action Committee (SAAC), sent an email signed by six other students to the UCSD administration, claiming that as "students of color," they were "verbally physically and emotionally attacked" during the debate. Josue Castellon, another cochair of SAAC, insisted that he personally witnessed divestment supporters being "verbally attacked and assaulted." His letter, titled "Subject: URGENT: Students of Color Attacked on Wednesday 2/29," was circulated by email widely across UCSD, with various allegations naming me as the attacking professor.

After saying they were "not going to allow such behavior to continue," the group demanded the university release $7,000 to them so they could bring a prodivestment speaker to campus. They then focused their wrath on me, accusing me of racist rhetoric and of verbally attacking a prodivestment student, whose name was not mentioned. Today, I know it was Noor el-Annan, president of the Arab Student Union. But it required an investigation of my own to find it out.

The accusatory email went like this: "University professor Shlomo Dubnov of the Music department followed a student outside of the 4th floor forum to verbally attack her and tell her that her narrative about surviving bombings in Lebanon was 'cheap and ridiculous.' [Dubnov and a university staff member] ended their diatribe by calling her a disgrace."

I and this staff member allegedly "used [our] positions as University employees to verbally attack the students and to even erase the existence of many individuals in the room." The staff member, whose name was spared from the letter, allegedly "went on to insult people of color." The letter continued, asking for the administration "to take a stance."

I was actually unaware of all that until an email arrived from the chair of the Academic Senate, telling me that severe accusations were being circulated against me and that I might be called to the senate to explain what happened. This started a barrage of libel. A field trial session was held with the Campus Climate Committee that accused pro-Israel professors, with reference to me in particular, as intimidating pro-Palestinian students. A web page against me was established on the SDFA website, including letters by pro-Palestinian professors to the chancellor demanding punitive action against me, and so on.

Since the accusations were done in a general manner and did not specify the name of the attacked student, it was practically impossible for me to battle these accusations. After trying to deny the accusations in private communications with the vice chancellor and the chancellor, who offered me no remedy to the libel, I went to the Office of Prevention of Harassment and Discrimination (OPHD) and filed a complaint against myself in order to start a formal investigation. Yes, I filed against myself since there was no name of a victim but there was a name of an attacker—Professor Dubnov. Since OPHD regulations encourage and even require third-party whistleblowing, I blew the whistle, accusing myself, in order to force the administration to actually launch an investigation. I hoped that by finding out the facts, not only would my name be cleared but also the false accuser would be reprehended.

The OPHD operated slowly, if at all. First, they could not identify the allegedly aggressed student, as no one would come forward. Luckily for me (it would turn out), the whole student government session was videotaped. That videotaping was even described in the original accusation letter, which didn't merely accuse me of the aggression but also accused the administration of allowing it to happen. Dalmar and Castellon wrote: "Furthermore, when we told you about all the individuals who videotaped and sent these videos out to other racists, classists, homophobic, sexists, bigots, we were right and you changed nothing. How can you all let that happen?"

So as *not* to allow that to happen, many pro-Palestinian faculty stepped in at this point. The director and associate director of critical gender studies, as well as the chair of ethnic studies, wrote to the chancellor and executive vice chancellor to immediately address their concerns about two members of the UCSD faculty and staff using their positions, in an abuse of power, to silence students of color, calling on the administration to publicly take a stance against this intimidation. The board of the SDFA wrote a letter—signed by Evans (the sociologist and now provost who would teach me how Israel advocacy compares to the police-state regimes of Nazis and Stalinists); Luis Martin-Cabrera, the vice president; and another six faculty members—demanding the chancellor "look into these offensive and shameful events ... and ... take action." My name and affiliation were posted on the faculty association website as the shameful person. Additional letters to the chancellor demanding that the administration take action came from other professors in sociology, visual arts, physics, literature, you name it.

My own letter to the faculty, a direct reply to the accusing students, and my appeals to the administration had no effect on dampening the public outcry. "The Board of SDFA stands behind its statement," wrote Evans. "We are particularly unwilling to engage with the hyperbolic and uncivil tone of Professor Dubnov's email and will not comment further on it." This is what he wrote in reply to my demand that they wait with their accusations at least until OPHD finished its inquiry.

So, with the help of some colleagues and friends—that is, those bigots and sexists who videotaped the events, according to the pro-Palestinian students—I launched an investigation of my own. Luckily, there were the videotapes. After going through the footage and doing some research, we were able to determine which student had made the allegations. I didn't know who she was, so I sent a screenshot of her from the video (talking about the Lebanon story that was mentioned in the accusation letters) to several Jewish students. Then I got a reply, not from the students but from the local Israeli *shaliach*, who wrote: "Hi Shlomo, one of the students forwarded me a picture you sent and asked who the student is. The student is Noor el-Annan, she was the President of the Arab Student Union."[14] I was surprised that the response came from him. "Tell me, are the students afraid of testifying against their peers? I'm sure they all knew who she is but I have not heard back from them," I wrote in reply. "Not sure if scared," he answered. "But I'm pretty sure they feel uncomfortable."

This was one of those little things that reveal more than you expect. "Feel uncomfortable." What?! I wrote to one of my friends who was and still is probably the most active and successful person in defending Jewish students in California:

> Just felt I need to share this with you.... I was trying to find out who was the student that alleged that I followed her and attacked her verbally after her talk. The university could not find out (apparently the Students for Justice in Palestine are not cooperating) so I asked our TFI [Tritons for Israel] students to help. I sent a note and a reminder to some of the students I spoke with during the meeting but got no response. So I had to remind them and eventually I got this.

I do not know how to react.... The fact that the Hillel and the Anti-Defamation League sat at the CCC [Campus Climate Committee] and did not prevent more slandering is already serious. But being afraid to reply to me is totally something I did not expect. I think we have a serious issue of trust and loyalty here and it is about time that we have a serious thinking of how we work with all Jewish campus players, especially with those who we are trying to protect.

So she was the president of the Arab Student Union, a graduate student. The footage also cleared my action: it showed me speaking, sitting in the hall, and then exiting with another faculty colleague. He later testified that we walked out of the building and did not speak to any student on the way. Only after this video was posted on the internet did the OPHD call me in to try to close the issue: "I wanted to let you know that the reference to a 'Music Department' faculty member has been removed from the San Diego Faculty Association website. This was done at the request of Noor el-Annan. In turn, it would be most helpful in putting this entire issue to rest if you could ask the parties who created the video highlighting 'Student N' to remove it from YouTube."

Soon after, an official letter closing the investigation was issued to me. It cleared my name but did not reprehend the false accusers, nor did it even mention their names or severity of such libel.

Even after this (unsatisfying) resolution to the false accusations levied against me, I have been receiving nasty communications from faculty members associated with the SDFA, not only refusing to apologize for their slanders against me, but also describing to me how their anti-Israel activities will now increase and how the issue of Israeli racism will now be included in the curricula of courses they teach at UCSD, even on unrelated subjects. As I said, one of the main faculty slanderers is now a provost, dispensing anti-Israel politics in the classroom. Meanwhile, the general fallout of this episode on the activities of pro-Israel faculty and students has been unfortunate. As I mentioned, the following year, the pro-Israel students avoided inviting faculty to talk before the student body on a repeated BDS vote, which then passed. In the dualistic battle between social justice, equality, and human rights and defending the Jewish home, the former won. Symbolically, ironically, but won.

Now you can perhaps appreciate why.

Epilogue

BDS is propaganda. It operates as such. Continuous repetition of simple messages is reinforced by threat of social alienation. It is surprising how well it propagates its message of diametrically opposite factors, the sources of good and the sources of evil. Is this antisemitism or anti-Israelism? The label is not important. What is alarming is that the problem of reconciling this dualism got into the heart of an identity problem facing the progressive Jewish community. It manifests itself through a parade of New Historians and pro-Israel, pro-peace writers that Judaic studies bring to UCSD. An American Jewish favorite, Ari Shavit, seems to have struck a gold mine in his recent book *My Promised Land* (2013)—admitting the guilt of Zionism while endorsing its history and the Palestinian tragedy as givens, embracing them as inevitable, necessary conditions of Israel's existence and reconciling them with current Jewish values.

But the obfuscating contradictions in Shavit's book do not drum up Jewish students to support Israel or break Zimmerman's silence. Even someone like Norman Finkelstein, a historian excommunicated from the academic community, finds that Shavit's book misses the target: "The question is whether Israel can yet again inspire American Jews after Shavit's inspired repackaging of no-longer-evadable facts. The answer is probably no. It both recycles too many shattered myths and confirms too many ugly truths to exhilarate anyone outside the depleting (and aging) ranks of Zion's worshippers."[15]

Finkelstein, an author of many poisonous anti-Israel writings, has been a frequent visitor to UCSD, invited on behalf of the Muslim students and by the Israeli Miko Peled's Israel-bashing Palestinian/Jewish-American dialogue group in San Diego.

Tammi Rossman-Benjamin introduced me to this group of activists committed to persuading Southern California Jews that Israel is a ruthless violent evil force. I met Dorris Bittar, an artist of Lebanese origin and a visual arts professor in one of the local universities, who makes a large part of her career showing mirrors from Lebanese homes shattered by Israeli bullets and who brought me to the dialogue group.[16] I met Marwan Arikat, who wrote to me: "As long as there is a slow demolition of Al-Aqsa mosque in the name of finding the Temple, As long as Israel keeps attacking its neighbors and possesses WMDs [weapons of mass destruction], As long as there are 'Jewish Only' Highways and most importantly, as long as there is no Palestinian state *on all the land of Palestine* then there will be NO PEACE!" And, of course, there is Peled himself, with whom I once was friendly. He was flabbergasted to hear that I served eight years in the IDF, something he considered a crime and I considered an honor. Later on, I learned that he wrote that the "IDF lusts for blood," has called the peace process "a process of apartheid & colonization," and has accused Israeli officials of "ethnic cleansing."[17] Since then, our ways have crossed at Finkelstein's campus events, on opposite sides.

But regardless of any political views, these events, and my personal encounters, which frankly carried some sense of personal sympathy for the other side's blunderers—at least until I realized how venomous their actions are on the minds of our kids—to me, all this paints most of all a gloomy picture of the Jewish situation and the future of the Diaspora.

Times change; tastes evolve. No one is going entirely under, and there are people out there working hard to ensure that. But we are losing our kids, not to the threat of annihilation, but to something much more subtle, something that operates on the sincere desire to be part of the progressive, moral, happy, socially accepted majority. Being Jewish is not categorical. It can be dispensed with when something more desirable comes along. Teaching skills of Israeli advocacy are also hypothetical, presupposing the student's actual desire to support Israel. So what is there? At least Israel itself is not hypothetical.

Maybe this is all that really matters.

And the battle goes on.

Evans wrote a letter to me, in which he credits my actions to leading him to change his course on South Africa and start promoting BDS, teaching about Israel as a racist state, and aiming overall to undermine the existing American view on the Israeli-Palestinian conflict:

> It is a pity that I have just decided to take a leave of absence for the Spring quarter and will not be teaching my regular course on South Africa. Frankly, it was in response to your correspondence that I had resolved to include a 2-week (4+ lecture) comparison of Apartheid and Israeli/Palestinian history and invite partisan academics from both sides of the debate. A comparison of the claim that attacking state policies is tantamount to sedition/racism was one of the topics I envisioned. The international boycott strategy was another. A third was the "foundational myths" of racial states. The 4th lecture would have been devoted to critical assessment and I was open to eliminating subsequent topics on the syllabus to accommodate more discussion. The premise of this module was to undermine the self-righteous and intimidating posture that distinguishes American dissections of Israeli/Palestinian politics. As best as I could determine from second-hand accounts, this includes your own contribution to the campus debate. I am happy to say that many Jewish colleagues on campus, including those (the majority) who object to an international boycott of Israel, have supported my characterization of your tone as over-the-top for an academic and counter-productive in general.

SHLOMO DUBNOV is a professor of music and computer science at UC San Diego and the director of a center for research on entertainment technologies at Qualcomm Institute.

Notes

1. Edward S. Beck, "In Light of the University of Johannesburg Boycott of Ben Gurion University, Please Endorse and Circulate This Statement by 41 Nobel Laureates Against Academic Boycotts: Faculty and Students Invited," *Scholars for Peace in the Middle East* (March 30, 2011), http://spme.org/spme-research/analysis/in-light-of-the-university-of -johannesburg-boycott-of-ben-gurion-university-please-endorse-and-circulate-this

-statement-by-41-nobel-laureates-against-academic-boycotts-faculty-and-students
-invited/9384/.

2. Allison Weir, http://alisonweir.org.uk/ (accessed November 2, 2017).

3. AAUP, "Cary Nelson and Kenneth Stern Pen Open Letter on Campus Antisemitism"
(April 20, 2011), https://www.aaup.org/news/cary-nelson-and-kenneth-stern-pen-open-letter
-campus-antisemitism#.WftAtxNSxE4 (accessed November 2, 2017).

4. Bruce Kesler, "A New Campus Tactic: Accusing Pro-Israel Professors of Intimidation,"
San Diego Jewish World (March 12, 2012), http://www.sdjewishworld.com/2012/03/12/a-new
-campus-tactic-accusing-pro-israel-professors-of-intimidation/.

5. "100 UCI Faculty Call on D.A. to Drop Charges Against Students Who Disrupted
Israeli Ambassador's Talk," UCI (February 9, 2011), https://news.uci.edu/2011/02/09/100-uci
-faculty-call-on-d-a-to-drop-charges-against-students-who-disrupted-israeli-ambassadors
-talk/ (accessed November 2, 2017).

6. David N. Myers, "Rethinking the Jewish Nation: An Exercise in Applied Jewish
Studies," *Havruta* (Winter 2011): 26–33, http://www.sscnet.ucla.edu/history/myers
/havruta%206%20page%2026-33.pdf (accessed November 2, 2017).

7. Isaac Luria, "Who is Anti-Occupation Activist Simone Zimmerman?" *Medium*
(July 25, 2016), https://medium.com/@isaacluria/who-is-anti-occupation-activist-simone
-zimmerman-a9a5a2077dcb.

8. Palestinian Campaign for the Academic & Cultural Boycott of Israel, "Debating
BDS: On Normalization and Partial Boycotts" (April 1, 2011), http://pacbi.org/etemplate
.php?id=1850 (accessed November 2, 2017).

9. Natan Nestel, "Simone Zimmerman: Pro-Israel Enthusiast Turned Anti-Isral Radical,"
The Jerusalem Post (April 27, 2016), http://www.jpost.com/Opinion/Simone-Zimmerman-Pro
-Israel-enthusiast-turned-anti-Israel-radical-452539.

10. Simone Zimmerman, "'My Israel Questions Were Met with Radio Silence'—
A Between the Lines Preview," YouTube Video (September 11, 2014), https://www.youtube
.com/watch?v=RMxdDCSDquU (accessed November 2, 2017).

11. David N. Myers, "Who is Simone Zimmerman?," *Jewish Journal* (April 19, 2016), http://
www.jewishjournal.com/david_n_myers/article/who_is_simone_zimmerman.

12. Jewish Voice for Peace, https://jewishvoiceforpeace.org/mission/ (accessed November
2, 2017).

13. Jews for Justice in Palestine, http://jfjfp.com/?page_id=2 (accessed November 2, 2017).

14. Israel sends emissaries to various communities to help forge connections between
Jewish communities. Such an emissary is called in Hebrew a *shaliach*.

15. Norman G. Finkelstein, "Finkelstein. Old Wine, Broken Bottle. Ari Shavit's Promised
land. OR Books. 2014" (October 24, 2014), http://temporaryehliss.blogspot.fr/2014/10
/finkelstein-old-wine-broken-bottle-ari.html.

16. Janet Saidi, "Art Shows Arabs, Jews Reaching Out," *Los Angeles Times* (February 2,
2003), http://www.dorisbittar.com/DB-Writings/04_LATimesSEMITESFeb2003.jpg; Hrag
Vartanian, "In Defense of the Boycott, Divestment, and Sanctions Movement," *Hyperallergic*
(February 8, 2016), https://hyperallergic.com/273340/in-defense-of-the-boycott-divestment
-and-sanctions-movement/.

17. Miko Peled, Wikipedia, https://en.wikipedia.org/wiki/Miko_Peled (accessed
November 2, 2017).

7 Fraser versus the University College Union: A Personal Reflection

Ronnie Fraser

Britain's teachers' trade unions have long been openly hostile to Israel and were among the first Western academic organizations to embrace BDS. The University College Union (UCU), in particular, opened the floodgates of bigotry when it officially (and nastily) rejected the European Union Monitoring Centre on Racism and Xenophobia (EUMC) "Working Definition of Antisemitism" (which recognized some forms of anti-Israelism to be antisemitic). Ronnie Fraser had had quite enough of the anti-Israel and antisemitic harassment pervading the union and bravely turned to the courts, accepting the pro bono representation of famed solicitor Anthony Julius (who had defended Deborah Lipstadt in the widely publicized David Irving libel trial). Fraser narrates the experiences that propelled him to take on his union and the deeply flawed judicial process that ultimately gave the stamp of legal approval to British antisemitism. Demonstrating the scope of antisemitic corrosion in Britain's academy and broader culture, he closes by relating the Far Left anti-Israel atmosphere in the unions to the antisemitism scandal that rocked Britain's Labour Party in early 2016.

THE INTERNATIONAL BOYCOTT, Divestment, and Sanctions (BDS) movement against Israel has probably found more support in Britain than in any other Western democratic society. Since 2002, British activists have been part of the international BDS campaign by initiating calls for academic, trade union, media, medical, architectural, and cultural boycotts of Israel. Britain's trade union movement works closely with the Palestine Solidarity Campaign (PSC) and is a key member of their British BDS campaign. Unions that are affiliated with and fund the PSC include Unite, Unison, the GMB, the National Union of Rail, Maritime and Transport Workers (RMT), the National Union of Teachers (NUT), and the lecturers' union, the UCU.

The UCU's support for the Palestinian cause can be traced back to the 1980s but only really took off during the Second Intifada, when British academics first called for an academic boycott of Israel.[1] I was a lecturer at Barnet College at the time and a member of the National Association of Teachers in Further and Higher Education (NATFHE), one of Britain's two trade unions for academics. The Board of Deputies of British Jews, of which I was a member, asked me to find out more about my union's support for the academic boycott of Israel. I soon discovered that the anti-Zionists within the union faced no organized opposition. I decided to stand up for Israel and formed the Academic Friends of Israel, the aim of which was to campaign against the academic boycott and antisemitism on campus. My efforts culminated a decade later in my taking legal action for unlawful harassment against the UCU.

In late May 2011, the UCU Congress met to debate the proposal to disassociate the union from the EUMC "Working Definition of Antisemitism."[2] I was in hostile territory. Throughout my two days at this congress, only one person, a UCU staff member, approached me to initiate a conversation. When I did speak to other delegates, the majority of our conversations were short and unfriendly. This led me to wonder if they had been instructed not to talk to me, the Zionist Jew. At previous congresses, people had spoken to me, although my speeches were always delivered to a silent audience. I never really understood why this was so but now believe this is a form of *blanking* by the audience, who were not interested in the views of the only pro-Israel Jew and wanted to return to the anti-Israel fest as quickly as possible. This silent treatment even continued in the hotel where we were staying. When my wife and I sat down for breakfast on both days, we noticed that fellow delegates moved away from us. When it was time for the debate on the antisemitism motion, I sat at the front of the hall directly facing the speakers, waiting for my turn to speak. I remember sitting there listening to what was being said, shaking my head in disbelief at what I was hearing, and feeling physically sick. Eventually, it was my turn to speak, and I made this passionate speech:

> I, a Jewish member of this union, am telling you that I feel an antisemitic mood in this union and even in this room. I would feel your refusal to engage with the EUMC definition of antisemitism, if you pass this motion, as a racist act.
>
> Many Jews have resigned from this union citing their experience of antisemitism. Only yesterday a delegate here said, "They are an expansionist people." It is difficult to think that the people in question are anything other than the Jews.
>
> You may disagree with me, you may disagree with all the other Jewish members who have said similar things. You may think we are mistaken, but you have a duty to listen seriously. Instead of being listened to, I am routinely told that anyone who raises the issue of antisemitism is doing so in bad faith.
>
> Congress, imagine how it feels when you say that you are experiencing racism, and your union responds: stop lying; stop trying to play the antisemitism card.

You, a group of mainly white, non-Jewish trade unionists, do not have the right to tell me, a Jew, what feels like antisemitism and what does not. Macpherson tells us that when somebody says they have been a victim of racism, then institutions should begin by believing them. This motion mandates the union to do the opposite.

Until this union takes complaints of antisemitism seriously, the UCU will continue to be labeled as an institutionally antisemitic organization. It's true that anti-Zionist Jews may perceive things differently. But the overwhelming majority of Jews feel that there is something wrong in this union.[3]

As I made my way back to my seat, I sensed that nobody looked me directly in the eye. It was an emotional and distressing experience. My speech was the only one to oppose the motion, and unsurprisingly, when the vote was announced, the UCU overwhelmingly rejected the EUMC "Working Definition of Antisemitism" with only four dissenting votes. The delegates gave themselves a round of applause. Immediately after the debate, I left the hall and sat with my friend, antisemitism scholar David Hirsh. Once we started talking, I realized I had been the victim of a racist act. I became so upset that I had to walk away in order to control my emotions. It took two additional days for me to regain my composure.

Once I was back in London, I spoke to several people, including solicitor Anthony Julius—well known for his 1996–2000 role defending Deborah Lipstadt from the libel charge brought by Holocaust denier David Irving—about the options available to me. He answered that, in his view, I could bring a claim against the UCU based on the Equality Act 2010 and that he would be delighted to represent me on a pro bono basis. He proposed applying for a declaration that the UCU's behavior was not acceptable to Jews and making the complaint at an employment tribunal. This would allay my concerns about cost because an employment tribunal rarely made an award for costs and then only in exceptional circumstances.

After nine years of standing up for Israel within the union, I felt that I had reached the point of no return. I was one of the few pro-Israel activists left at the UCU and the only one who attended the congress. Their disassociation from the EUMC definition of *antisemitism* was effectively the last straw for me because it eliminated the intellectual standard that guided my previous exchanges with the union. I sadly concluded that the UCU was no longer a place that was hospitable to Jews. The alternative to legal action was to resign from the union, a course taken by many others. I had considered resigning in the past, but my belief that you can only change things from the inside won out.

I accepted Julius's generous offer. My legal action against the UCU, which alleged "institutional antisemitism," went to court a year later in November 2012. My claim stated that I am an orthodox Jew with a strong attachment to Israel and that the union had *harassed* me by *engaging in unwanted conduct* relating to my Jewish identity (a protected characteristic), *the purpose and effect* of which had and continued to *violate my dignity* and had created *an intimidating, hostile, degrading humiliating and offensive environment* for me.[4]

My claim mapped out how the UCU's anti-Zionist and anti-Jewish activities amounted to institutional antisemitism. It also chronicled my opposition to their anti-Israel behavior since 2002, when I had founded the Academic Friends of Israel. To back up my claim, we found thirty-four witnesses who included current and ex-members of the union, Jews and non-Jews, academics, experts on antisemitism, union activists, Jewish communal leaders, and members of Parliament. In addition, we submitted some eight thousand supporting documents in evidence.

My complaints referred to: the annual congress boycott resolutions against only Israel, the conduct of these debates, the bullying and antisemitism that had taken place on the activists' email list, the UCU's failure to engage with people who raised concerns and their failure to address the resignations of Jewish members of the union, their refusal to meet with the Organization for Security Co-operation in Europe's (OSCE's) special representative on antisemitism,[5] the hosting of known antisemite Bongani Masuku,[6] and the repudiation of the EUMC "Working Definition of Antisemitism."

For some background, the UCU's support for the Palestinian cause began in the 1980s but really took off in 2002 during Israel's Operation Defensive Shield, when British academics first called for an academic boycott of Israel.[7] Although their initial attempt was thwarted, the boycotters, a group of left-wing academics, anti-Zionists, and members of the Socialist Workers Party (SWP), were determined to try again. They subsequently made several attempts to implement an academic boycott of Israel using their trade unions, the AUT, and NATFHE (which merged in 2006 to form the UCU), the first of which was at the 2003 AUT council meeting. Even though the debate was held late on a Friday afternoon just before the Jewish Sabbath, which denied orthodox Jewish members the opportunity to participate, the motion was defeated by a two-to-one majority.

The boycotters did not give up. The 2004 Palestinian Campaign for the Academic and Cultural Boycott of Israel (PACBI) provided them with a basis for their attempt to impose sanctions.[8] Sue Blackwell, who proposed the 2005 AUT boycott motions, admitted that "one of the reasons we didn't win last time was that there was no clear public call from Palestinians for the boycott."[9] After a short debate, the 228 AUT council delegates decided to boycott Haifa and Bar Ilan universities and distribute proboycott literature to its forty-eight thousand members.[10] Almost immediately, a campaign to reverse the AUT boycott decisions was started by union members Jon Pike and David Hirsh, who set up a group called Engage to that end and succeeded in a special AUT council meeting just a month later.[11]

The boycotters failed again in 2007 to persuade the UCU to implement an academic boycott, this time because the union received legal advice about Britain's discrimination legislation.[12] None of the AUT, NATFHE, or UCU academic boycott motions has ever been about building support for the Palestinians, nor have any targeted specific Israeli policies. The motions have been and still are an attempt by a small group of activists to delegitimize the State of Israel. Blackwell, who also initiated the 2010 UCU EUMC motion, regards the State of Israel as illegitimate[13] and has frequently said she is not antisemitic, but her actions in supporting motions that exclude from the threat of a boycott "conscientious Israeli academics and intellectuals opposed to their state's colonial and racist policies" cannot be seen as anything other than antisemitic.[14]

Two weeks later, I received an email that I reported to the police. It read: "*Let me tell you that Jews command no respect and deserve no sympathy, because they are evil by nature and rotten to the core.... I firmly believe that all Jews will burn in hell and in comparison Auschwitz will be like a holiday camp.*"[15] I am in no doubt that I received this email because of my known opposition to the boycott. The UCU had created an antisemitic atmosphere, and this was the result. Although I wasn't called to speak in the 2007 boycott debates at congress, two months later, I asked the UCU if it would be willing to distribute literature against the proposed academic boycott, as literature supporting the boycott had already been distributed. My request was turned down.

Between 2007 and 2011, the congress was gradually ethnically cleansed of any delegates willing to speak up on behalf of Israel and pro-Zionist Jews. By 2011, I was the sole remaining Zionist at congress.

One aspect of the UCU's failure to support their Jewish members was its lack of moderation of antisemitic comments posted on its online forum, the "Activists' List." Over a four-year period between 2007 and 2011, two thousand out of seven thousand threads related to Israel/Palestine, Jews, antisemitism, Anglo-Jewry, and the Holocaust; on these, there was constant abuse, insults, bullying, and intimidation, creating a hostile atmosphere for the handful of pro-Israel supporters on the list. Emails were posted with titles such as "cancelling Israel," "Would the Zionist care to defend this?" and "Another racist attack in Israel." Responses to my posting of the EUMC definition of antisemitism included "you are wrong" and "you cannot be serious about this 'definition.'"

In January 2010, anti-Zionist academic Keith Hammond posted a response to my posting about Holocaust Memorial Day that I thought was deeply antisemitic.[16] The post suggested that then UK prime minister Gordon Brown was "Israel's man in Number Ten" and implied that "Zionists" were responsible for university department closures. My complaint to the UCU about his post used the EUMC working definition to explain why it was antisemitic. I believe that my repeated effective use of the EUMC definition prompted boycott supporters to push for a union resolution against it.

The union treated me with contempt. It never interviewed me, failed to keep me informed about the progress of the investigation, and did not ask me to attend the panel hearing of my complaint.[17] Two of the three members of the panel were members of the UCU Left, and at least one was a proboycott campaigner. Eight months later, I discovered that the panel had cleared Hammond of all charges.

During the hearing of my action against the UCU, Julius asked Sally Hunt, the UCU general secretary, if "Mr. Fraser would be entitled to infer from this decision [clearing Hammond] that the union was not taking antisemitism seriously?" Hunt replied, "I think he would." But she argued that I could not be considered "an ordinary Jewish member of the union" because I had spent so much time working on the issues of anti-Zionism, antisemitism, and the UCU's proposed boycott of Israel.[18] By admitting that union policy marginalizes anyone who stands up for Israel and speaks out against antisemitism within the UCU, either she was upholding my claim of institutional antisemitism within the UCU or this was her own personal view, which would mean she held antisemitic views.

The tribunal hearing of my claim took place in November 2012 and lasted for twenty days. Anthony White, counsel for the UCU, took ten days to cross-examine twenty-nine of my thirty-four witnesses. I was cross-examined by White for a total of ten hours spread over three days, a bruising experience. The main point that he was trying to make in his questions to me was that my claim was not harassment but political discussion, allowed under academic freedom. Julius, my advocate, was given only three days to cross-examine five of the UCU's witnesses.

At one point during my cross-examination, I told the tribunal:

> This case is not about Israel-Palestine. It's not about me. It's about fellow Jews. We have been forced out. We have been humiliated. It has been horrendous and relentless against us.... I continued to put up with hurt and humiliation because my parents were refugees from the Holocaust and my grandparents died in Auschwitz as a result of the Nazi extermination of Jews and antisemitism. It is my way of saying, "Never again." I don't want my four children, my nine grandchildren, to have to suffer what they did.... That is my motivation for continuing to put up with everything, the way I've been treated by the union. I didn't want it to happen to them.[19]

The tribunal dismissed my ten complaints in March 2013. It ruled that one was "hopelessly out of time" and the other nine "wholly unfounded."

The tribunal said that it saw "almost the entire case as manifestly unmeritorious," describing some of the complaints as "obviously hopeless," "palpably groundless," and "devoid of any merit." The tribunal described the "gargantuan scale" of the twenty-day hearing and twenty-three volumes of evidence as a "sorry saga," which was "manifestly excessive and disproportionate," and added that the UCU should not have been put to the "trouble and expense of defending" the case. The tribunal accused me and my lawyer of "an impermissible attempt to achieve a political end by litigious means" and that "it would be very unfortunate if an exercise of this sort were ever repeated." We were charged with "a worrying disregard for pluralism, tolerance and freedom of expression, principles which the courts and Tribunals are, and must be, vigilant to protect."[20]

My first reaction was to question what we had done to deserve such a scathing judgment and how my lawyers could have gotten it so wrong. None of us— including me, Julius, and most of my witnesses—escaped censure, whereas the UCU's witnesses were described as "careful and accurate witnesses who related the facts rather than ventilating their opinions." From day one, Judge Snelson gave me the impression that he did not like Julius, whom he perceived as an eloquent, intellectual, arrogant Jewish lawyer, a point I noted at the time in my diary. In light of the harsh words in the judgment, the tribunal appeared to dislike also me and many of my witnesses.

The judgment warned others from trying a similar exercise and accused me of trying to curtail freedom of speech. The anti-Zionists have claimed many times during debates on the academic boycott and the EUMC definition that we were trying to curtail freedom of speech by raising the issue of antisemitism. This may not have been what the tribunal intended, but it seems to be an example of the Livingstone Formulation of antisemitism.[21]

Freedom of speech allows for calls to boycott Israel, as they are usually deemed not to be antisemitic or hate speech but political rhetoric. This means that as long as what is said is not against the law, people are free to fabricate and tell lies. Anti-Zionists can freely call for the delegitimization and destruction of the State of Israel or call Zionists "racists," as this is political rhetoric and not against the law. The line is only crossed when there are calls for violence against Jews, and then it becomes a hate crime. It is perfectly acceptable to substitute Zionist for Jew or conflate Israel and Jew, because that counts as political rhetoric and not hate speech.

Snelson argued that in taking offense at antisemitic critiques of Israel, I betrayed "a worrying disregard for pluralism, tolerance and freedom of expression, principles which the courts and Tribunals are, and must be, vigilant to protect." Clearly, he seems to be saying that it's OK to criticize Israel but it's not acceptable for Jews to say in response, "You have crossed the line into antisemitism." Where is *my* freedom of speech?

Shortly after the hearing had started, Snelson declared that he was not going to rule on antisemitism because it was not a public inquiry into antisemitism but a legal claim. This decision immediately undercut the heart of our case, which was all about what constitutes antisemitic provocation. How can one decide if there was unlawful harassment if you take out of the equation the antisemitism that we alleged had taken place? In my view, antisemitism, as defined by the EUMC, created the intimidating, hostile, and offensive environment that resulted in the unlawful harassment. By announcing he was not going to rule on antisemitism, he no longer had to decide if the relevant anti-Zionism was antisemitism. Without that, the judgment never got to the crux of the matter by discussing my claim that the atmosphere of antisemitism in the union led to unlawful harassment.

My claim was all about institutional antisemitism, with myself and my witnesses arguing that over the previous six years institutional antisemitism had taken place within the UCU. The 1999 Macpherson inquiry into the Stephen Lawrence murder introduced Britain to the concept of institutional racism.[22] The recommendations of that inquiry and its conclusions about institutional racism do not have any legal status, although the court of public opinion believes they do. One of the inquiry's recommendations was that if a person feels he or she has suffered racism or a racist act, he or she can make a complaint and the body or person that receives the complaint has to take the complaint seriously and investigate it. In my case, the tribunal did not take my complaint seriously. The double whammy of the "out of time" ruling and the decision not to rule on antisemitism meant that we were never going to win.

With the benefit of hindsight, the critical matter of "out of time" should have been dealt with at the start of the hearing. Julius argued that all my complaints were one cumulative complaint and therefore *not* out of time, because the most recent incident was within three months of filing the claim. The tribunal, however, chose to regard each complaint as a separate complaint, so all those incidents prior to the three months were out of time. To compound matters, the tribunal then accused us of wasting the court's time with a case of gargantuan proportions. So, unless any future legal actions involving institutional antisemitism take into account prior incidents of antisemitism over a period of time, it is unlikely that institutional antisemitism can ever be proved.

The judgment compared my actions as a campaigner and activist who accepted the risk of being offended or hurt on occasion by things said or done by my opponents to that of a rugby player who must accept his share of minor injuries. The judgment continued: "A political debate which by its nature is bound to excite strong emotions, it would, we think, require special circumstances to justify a finding that such involvement had resulted in harassment. We find no special circumstances here." The Jew, meaning me, is not willing to play by the British code of conduct. As Didi Herman put it in her study of Jews and English law, "The law is the perfect English gentleman, as compared to the feminized characteristics of 'the Jew' revealed in his impulsive, over-emotional, and disruptive 'Jewish voice.'"[23] Therefore, playing the game, playing rugby, keeping a stiff upper lip, is what it means to be an English gentleman. Is the implication here that as a Jew I am not really English and not playing the game as it should be played? My outbursts or campaigns are typically Jewish—impulsive, overemotional, disruptive—and by implication without substance and made in bad faith.

The tribunal refused to acknowledge the emotional bond between Jews and Israel. It ruled that "a belief in the Zionist project or an attachment to Israel cannot amount to a protected characteristic. It is not intrinsically a part of Jewishness." In one sentence, the tribunal rejected the most widely used definition of *antisemitism* in the world, the EUMC definition. Antisemitism, this definition states, is not only directed at the Jews but also at the Jewish State, the State of Israel, the homeland for the Jews. The tribunal ruled that it's OK to allege that Israel trades in Palestinian body parts, for example, but it's not acceptable, again, for a Jew to point out that this charge has crossed the line into antisemitic blood libel.

If, on the other hand, the tribunal had agreed that Israel and Zionism were an aspect of the "protected characteristic" of being a Jew, then it would have meant that much anti-Zionist expression could be actionable in law as "hostile environment harassment" for Jews. But that conclusion would not have served the tribunal's purposes.

This attitude is also at the root of the tribunal's failure to comprehend *Jewishness*. Jewishness is all about Jewish identity and what it means to be a Jew as distinct from Judaism. I am not qualified to talk about the definitions of *Jewishness* and *Jew* as used in English law,[24] but Israel is part of my Jewish identity. It is my understanding that the law upholds my right as a Jew to practice Judaism, but according to Snelson and his colleagues, that right does not include my attachment to Israel. Since no evidence was presented either for or against my attachment to Israel, it was obviously not enough for Julius to tell the court that I, along with "a significant proportion of the Jewish people have an attachment to Israel, which is an aspect of their self-understanding as Jews or Jewish identity."[25] English case law may not agree with my understanding as to what Jewishness means, but doesn't the tribunal's statement deny the right of the Jewish State to exist? Some people may feel that comment could be construed as antisemitic according to the EUMC definition.

The tribunal was determined to ignore the fact that Jews have been yearning for and attached to the Land of Israel for three thousand years, that this longing is spoken of in our daily prayers, and that the overwhelming majority of Diaspora Jews have a strong cultural and historical heritage that links us to the State of Israel.[26]

In writing this account four and a half years after the event, it is clear to me that I was never going to win. My legal team and I lodged a claim for unlawful harassment accusing the UCU of institutional antisemitism, which was heard by a tribunal led by a judge who said he was not going to rule on antisemitism and that all of my complaints were out of time. This meant that he and his colleagues never actually considered whether my complaints were justified or not.

Under UK law, it is not illegal to be an antisemite, and while antisemitic incidents are considered to be incitement of racial hatred, they are rarely prosecuted. Because there is no legal definition of antisemitism, the blood libels and Holocaust-denial are widely accepted as the standards. Therefore, not only was my definition of antisemitism different from that of others but also my view of where the line is crossed into antisemitism was different. I make this point because not only were we claiming that the harassment was antisemitic but also that it was "institutional antisemitism," which does not exist in the law. To make matters more complicated, the antisemitism we were complaining of was the "new antisemitism," where Israel is the substitute for the collective Jew—per the EUMC definition, which wasn't recognized by the UCU. The tribunal's decision, after all, was unsurprising, as no Jew has ever been successful in a discrimination claim brought against a non-Jew under the 1976 race-relations legislation.

The odds were therefore seriously stacked against our winning even before the claim was lodged.

The Aftermath

Hunt, UCU general secretary, said immediately after the judgment had been received that I would "be treated with respect within the union.... Now that a decision has been made I hope in turn that he, and others who share his views, will play an active part in the union and its debates rather than seek recourse to the law."[27] But we were not allowed to move on and resume our lives. With the ink hardly dry on that press statement, the UCU issued an application for their costs of $900,000 against me and Julius's law firm, Mishcon de Reya. We were to be bankrupted as an example to those in the future who might consider challenging the rising tide of antisemitism.

Six months later, in November 2014, my new counsel, David Craig, made an application to the court, accusing the tribunal of being biased and therefore ineligible to make an order for costs, because it had overstepped the mark in its judgment and had thus already prejudged the question of costs.[28] To everyone's surprise, Snelson said that the tribunal was recusing itself, because he agreed that there was a real possibility that the tribunal had overstepped the mark in what they had said in terms of "the tone of their indignation, their regret that the claim had been brought, and that the UCU should not have had to face the claim in the first place."[29] As a consequence, we were now in uncharted territory because it was difficult to see how a new tribunal could make a decision on the costs application if it hadn't heard the evidence and cross-examinations in the first place. It took another thirteen months of meetings with my legal team and several court hearings in front of a new tribunal before the UCU settled its costs application against Mishcon de Reya "on confidential terms to the satisfaction of both parties." As a result of the settlement, the UCU withdrew its costs application against me.[30]

UCU Leaflet "Challenging Antisemitism"

Seven months after the UCU Congress had voted to disassociate itself from the EUMC definition and my resulting legal action, the UCU hastily produced a leaflet titled "Challenging Antisemitism," which failed to recognize contemporary antisemitism or the links between antisemitism and anti-Israel hatred.[31] Three years later, in January 2015, this leaflet was revised to include four examples of antisemitism, two of which were questionable.[32] The first states: "Holding Jews collectively to blame, e.g., for the actions of the Israeli Government. Many Jews do not support the actions of the Government of Israel." This last sentence, making the link to anti-Israel bias, has no place in a leaflet raising awareness of the dangers of modern antisemitism. It was included for political purposes in order to placate the Far Left and the anti-Zionists within the union. The second, "Deliberate distortion, exaggeration, or misrepresentation of religious concepts and teaching," was a change from their original draft: "Distortion of religious concepts and teaching, e.g., an eye for an eye; the chosen people. Misuse of Jewish symbols such as the Star of David." One has to ask, "Why the changes?" Does the UCU seriously believe that flags and banners with swastikas embossed on the Star of David seen at the 2014 anti-Israel Gaza demonstrations were not antisemitic?

The first draft of their revised leaflet used a fifth example, which was removed from the final revision: "Judging Jews according to a different standard often manifests as explicit comparisons between what is perceived to be the collective action of Jews (usually the Israeli Government) and the action of Nazis." The removal of what is a perfectly good and relevant example of antisemitism begs the question once again: why? There can be no excuse for leaving out an example that equates the collective action of the Jews or Israel with the action of Nazis, especially as social media was awash in 2014 with such behavior. How can we take seriously a leaflet on the dangers of antisemitism that, for political reasons, purposely ignores and deletes examples of antisemitism in which Israel and the Jewish people are delegitimized, demonized, or subjected to double standards? But there again, the UCU couldn't possibly use examples from the EUMC definition, now could it?

Both the original and revised leaflet state: "Antisemitism at work is covered by the Equality Act 2010 … harassment (for example, offensive and hurtful comments directed towards any individual in the workplace, on account of their religion or ethnicity)." But as this was what legal action was all about, why didn't the

UCU admit they were wrong? Or more important, as this point was in Julius's skeleton argument, why did the tribunal prefer to rule the case out of time rather than uphold the law?[33]

UCU Congress Resolutions

The four years between 2012 and 2015, after my legal action started, saw a significant decrease in the frequency of anti-Israel resolutions adopted by the UCU. Why? It's not only the UCU, as most of Britain's trade unions have also been holding back. Perhaps the unions are now frightened with the prospect of having to foot massive legal bills and, as a result, are doubly cautious before adopting boycott policies. At the time of the latest Gaza war, in 2014, although all the main unions supported the anti-Israel demonstrations, the only anti-Israel resolutions came from the Trades Union Congress (TUC), the representative body for Britain's trade unions.

The 2015 UCU Congress once again debated and approved another BDS resolution.[34] To the delegates' surprise, the motion was declared "void and of null effect." The boycotters' intention was that all UCU members would be sent "a dedicated email, reminding them of [the UCU's] policy on Israel, and with a link to the PACBI [Palestinian BDS] guidelines and any misrepresentations of UCU's policy [would] be corrected publicly." If the UCU had gone ahead and sent out such an email, they would have been in breach of the legal advice they had received in 2007.[35] That the motion was declared "void and of null effect" invites the question: Does the UCU actually have a policy supporting BDS? I would suggest not, as they are effectively neutered since the UCU cannot directly or indirectly campaign for BDS. In addition, union officials cannot speak in favor of BDS when they represent the union at international bodies or rallies because to do so would leave the union in breach of their legal advice and infringe Britain's equality and discrimination legislation.

So, perhaps I won after all.

But only partly, as the UCU continues to support Hamas, whose founding charter cites the antisemitic *Protocols of the Elders of Zion*.[36] The UCU's strategy is perhaps more circumspect, but in essence, it still backs the delegitimization and destruction of the State of Israel. Although the UCU has said that it is opposed to antisemitism, the reality is that the union is only opposed to antisemitism as defined by its own political goals.

Final Thoughts

Ten years after the UCU was formed, the anti-Israel activists in the union are still trying to implement boycotts and BDS even though there are no Jews left to confront them at congress. This is what activists do. They do not move on as the rest of us do; they continue with the same anti-Zionist message and rhetoric. The culture within the union, which led to my case, is unchanged, especially on the "Activists' List," where the so-called apologists for Zionism, like myself, are still being blamed for our support of what they call Israeli crimes by controlling the media in order to limit its discussion of the issues as well as manufacturing and coordinating the crisis surrounding antisemitism in the Labour Party. Although they call us Zionists, it is clear they mean Jews.

With the benefit of hindsight, one can see that the election of Jeremy Corbyn as Labour Party leader in September 2015 provided his acolytes with the opportunity to demonize Israel and cross the line into antisemitism, by masking it as anti-Zionism. This is exactly what happened when the Far Left took control of the UCU in 2006. Back then, we saw it as a takeover by those on the periphery of labor politics, whose anti-Zionist policies made the union an intimidating, hostile, and offensive environment for Jews. It was, in reality, the prototype for what has since happened in the Labour Party: fringe racist anti-Israel policies have crossed over into mainstream politics with a resulting rise in antisemitism within the party.

Ever since I lost my legal action against the UCU four years ago, I have been campaigning for Anglo-Jewry to adopt a definition of *antisemitism*, because without a clear definition, anyone can deny that he is being antisemitic or guilty of racist or offensive remarks. Anglo-Jewry has been reluctant in the past to publicly adopt a definition, and as recently as February 2015, the *All-Party Parliamentary Inquiry into Antisemitism* report stated, "There was little if any pressure from the established representative bodies in the Jewish community to pursue the adoption of a definition of antisemitism."[37]

However, what happened in the spring of 2016 caught everyone by surprise. Amid public discussion of antisemitism within the Labour Party, which resulted in the suspension of fifty party members for alleged antisemitic and racist comments, the Chakrabarti inquiry was established to investigate. Much of the public discussion turned to whether anti-Zionism is antisemitism. The ignorance and lack of understanding of antisemitism, which the Chakrabarti inquiry discussed, are not solely the province of the Labour Party but a reflection on our wider society. While the inquiry report recognized right-wing antisemitism, it appears to have wasted an opportunity to investigate modern left-wing contemporary antisemitism surrounding the discussion about Israel.[38]

The Chakrabarti inquiry forced the anti-Israel movement to make submissions and put in writing what they understand to be antisemitism, as well as their belief that anti-Zionism is not antisemitism. The Palestine Solidarity Campaign (PSC) wrote that they believe that "antisemitism is hatred of or discrimination against Jewish people on the basis of their religion or identity" and that criticism of the Israeli government's policies and actions or Zionism is not antisemitic.[39] They also consider Zionism to be a political ideology rather than, as UK chief rabbi Ephraim Mirvis put it, "the right to Jewish self-determination in a land that has been at the center of the Jewish world for more than 3,000 years."[40] The PSC, along with other anti-Israel submissions, condemned the use of the EUMC definition, saying it denied their right to challenge the racism of the Israeli state.

Shortly after the Chakrabarti inquiry started its investigation, the parliamentary Home Affairs Committee decided to investigate the rise of antisemitism in Britain. It became clear that Anglo-Jewry had adopted a definition of *antisemitism* when Mirvis told the parliamentary committee, "we would like everybody to follow" the International Holocaust Remembrance Alliance (IHRA) definition of *antisemitism*.[41] His words were endorsed by the community's leading organizations, the Board of Deputies of British Jews (BOD), the Jewish Leadership Council (JLC), and the Community Security Trust (CST), in their oral and written submissions to both the parliamentary committee and Chakrabarti inquiry. The IHRA is an intergovernmental body comprised of thirty-one countries, including the United Kingdom. Although the CST recommends that we no longer use the EUMC definition, as that organization no longer exists, the IHRA's definition of *antisemitism* is a refined version of that definition.[42]

In December 2016 the UK government announced that it had adopted the IHRA definition of antisemitsim to counter the increase in antisemitic incidents in Britain. It has subsequently been adopted by the Jewish community, the Scottish government, the Welsh Assembly and several local authorities. The UCU is the only organization in Britain other than Far Left and pro-Palestine groups to condemn it. So, five years after I lost my legal action against the UCU, it is of some comfort to me personally that the community now has an agreed-on definition of *antisemitism* to refer to. If there had been a definition in place then, one wonders if the outcome would have been different.

RONNIE FRASER is Director of the Academic Friends of Israel, which campaigns against the academic boycott of Israel and antisemitism on campus. He is a mathematics lecturer and a member of the University and College Union (UCU).

Notes

1. The 2002 British call for an academic boycott of Israel was inspired by the 2001 Durban program. For more information, see the introduction to this volume and also Manfred Gerstenfeld's interview with Shimon T. Samuels, "Antisemitism and Jewish Defense at the United Nations World Summit on Sustainable Development, 2002, Johannesburg, South Africa," *Post-Holocaust and Anti-Semitism*, 6 (March 2, 2003).

2. UCU Congress 2011, "EUMC Working Definition of Antisemitism" (May 30, 2011), http://www.ucu.org.uk/index.cfm?articleid=5540#70. The EUMC "Working Definition

of Antisemitism" may be found at http://www.akdh.ch/AS-WorkingDefinition-draft.pdf (accessed December 21, 2015).

3. "UCU Condemned as Institutionally Antisemitic," *Academic Friends of Israel Digest*, 10, no. 4 (May 31, 2011), http://www.academics-for-israel.org/index.php?page=v10n4.

4. Fraser v. University & College Union [2013] ET 44. See, in particular, page 4, paragraphs 5-6.

5. Fifty-one countries are members of the Organization for Security Co-operation in Europe (OSCE). At its 2004 meeting, the OSCE acknowledged that antisemitism had assumed new forms and posed a threat to security and stability. This led to the publication of the EUMC "Working Definition of Antisemitism." Around May 2007, the OSCE became aware that UCU had called for a boycott of Israeli academics and institutions. The UCU refused to meet with its representative to discuss the problem.

6. Bongani Masuku is the international relations secretary for the Congress of South African Trade Unions and has been convicted in South Africa of hate speech against Jews.

7. Open letter published in *the Guardian* (April 6, 2002). In response to the Israeli offensive against Palestinian terrorist organizations in the West Bank, the *Guardian* letter, signed by Steven and Hilary Rose and over one hundred other academics, called for a European Union moratorium on funding for grants and research contracts for Israeli universities.

8. Palestinian Campaign for the Academic and Cultural Boycott of Israel (PACBI), "Call for Academic and Cultural Boycott of Israel," http://www.usacbi.org/pacbi-boycott/ (accessed September 21, 2017).

9. Polly Curtis, "Boycott Call Resurfaces," *Guardian* (April 5, 2005).

10. Polly Curtis, "Lecturers Vote for Israeli Boycott," *Guardian* (April 22, 2005). The AUT boycott resolutions may be found here: http://www.academics-for-israel.org/index .php?page=daut1 (accessed December 21, 2015).

11. *Report of the AUT Special Council 2005* (May 26, 2005), http://www.ucu.org.uk/index .cfm?articleid=1212.

12. "Israel Boycott Illegal and Cannot Be Implemented, UCU Tells Members" (September 28, 2007), http://www.ucu.org.uk/index.cfm?articleid=2829.

13. Phil Baty, "I've No Regrets. We've Touched a Raw Nerve," *Times Higher Educational Supplement* (May 20, 2005).

14. See Phil Baty, "I've No Regrets. We've Touched a Raw Nerve," *Times Higher Educational Supplement* (May 20, 2005), and PACBI, "Call."

15. The email was sent on June 19, 2007, by a Mr. Choudhury from Bradford, Yorkshire. Police arrested a man, but the case was dropped as they were unable to prove he had sent the email.

16. "Anti-Zionist and Antisemitic Emails Posted on UCU Activists List," *The Academic Friends of Israel Digest*, Vol. 9, No 1 (February 16, 2010), https://www.academics-for-israel .org/index.php?page=v9n1. See also Keith Hammond, "Keith Hammond on Holocaust Memorial Day," *Harry's Place* (January 29, 2010), http://hurryupharry.org/2010/01/29/keith -hammond-on-holocaust-memorial-day/.

17. When Harry Goldstein, one of my witnesses in my legal action against the UCU, made a complaint an antisemitic posting on the list in 2012, the UCU not only interviewed him about his complaint but also kept him fully informed of the procedure being followed.

18. Marcus Dysch, "Union 'Did Not Take Jew-Hatred Seriously,'" *Jewish Chronicle* (November 15, 2012).

19. Miriam Shaviv, "Tearful UK Jewish Academic Tells Court His Trade Union Has Crossed the Line into Antisemitism," *Times of Israel* (November 1, 2012), and Marcus Dysch, "Lecturer Sues Union over Antisemitism," *Jewish Chronicle* (November 1, 2012).

20. Fraser v. University & College Union [March 25, 2013] ET, https://www.judiciary.gov .uk/judgments/fraser-uni-college-union/.

21. The Livingstone Formulation, coined by David Hirsh, is the claim (by anti-Zionists typically) that charges of antisemitism are dishonestly raised only to suppress criticism of Israel.

22. "Report of the Stephen Lawrence Inquiry," https://www.gov.uk/government/uploads /system/uploads/attachment_data/file/277111/4262.pdf (accessed January 21, 2016).

23. Didi Herman, *An Unfortunate Coincidence: Jews, Jewishness, and English Law* (Oxford: Oxford University Press, 2010), 44.

24. On this, see Herman, *An Unfortunate Coincidence.*

25. Fraser v. University & College Union [2013] ET 44. See, in particular, paragraph 18.

26. The Jewish people's historical links to Palestine are confirmed in the Mandate for Palestine unanimously confirmed by the League of Nations in 1922 ("The Palestine Mandate," The Avalon Project, http://avalon.law.yale.edu/20th_century/palmanda.asp (accessed November 19, 2017), as well as in article 80 of the UN Charter (http://www.un.org /en/sections/un-charter/chapter-xii/index.html (accessed November 19, 2017)).

27. "UCU Cleared of Harassment in Landmark Tribunal," UCU (March 25, 2013), http://www.ucu.org.uk/6562 (accessed December 21, 2015).

28. "Academic Slammed over Harassment Claim Has Legal Costs Bid Delay," *Jewish News* 8 (November 2013).

29. Employment Tribunal letter setting out their reasons to recuse themselves, November 8, 2013.

30. Marcus Dysch, "Academic Settles Long-Running Legal Battle With Trade Union," *The Jewish Chronicle* (December 24, 2014), http://www.thejc.com/news/uk-news/127264/academic -settles-long-running-legal-battle-trade-union.

31. The original leaflet, which was produced without consulting the membership, let alone its Jewish members, uses a definition of *antisemitism* written by Dr. Brian Klug: "At the heart of antisemitism is the negative stereotype of the Jew: sinister, cunning, parasitic, money-grubbing, mysteriously powerful, and so on. Antisemitism consists in projecting this figure onto individual Jews, Jewish groups and Jewish institutions," http://www.ucu.org.uk /media/pdf/0/2/Anti_Semitism_Leaflet.pdf (accessed December 21, 2015).

32. The UCU consulted with its membership before publishing the revised leaflet, available at: http://www.ucu.org.uk/media/pdf/9/2/ucu_challengingantisemitism _leaflet_2015.pdf (accessed December 21, 2015).

33. Fraser v. University & College Union [2013] ET 44. See, in particular, page 32, paragraph 42.

34. UCU Congress 2015 Motion 43, "UCU and BDS Campaign—University of Brighton Grand Parade," http://www.ucu.org.uk/index.cfm?articleid=7521#43 (accessed November 19, 2017).

35. "Israel Boycott Illegal and Cannot Be Implemented, UCU Tells Members," UCU (September 28, 2007, updated December 14, 2015), http://www.ucu.org.uk/index .cfm?articleid=2829 (accessed November 19, 2017).

36. *The Protocols of the Elders of Zion* is an antisemitic forgery purporting to describe a Jewish plan for global domination. It was first published in Russia in 1903.

37. "Report of the All-Party Parliamentary Inquiry Into Antisemitism" (September, 2006), https://web.archive.org/web/20130822190807/ http://www.antisemitism.org.uk/wp -content/uploads/All-Party-Parliamentary-Inquiry-into-Antisemitism-REPORT.pdf (accessed November 19, 2017).

38. The majority of the report's recommendations suggested improvements to Labour Party procedures and rules relating to complaints of antisemitism. The report did not discuss anti-Zionism or definitions of antisemitism: The report is available at http://www.pearsinstitute.bbk.ac.uk/home/chakrabarti-inquiry-report-published/ (accessed November 19, 2017).

39. See "Submission from Palestine Solidarity Campaign for the Chakrabarti Inquiry," https://palestinecampaign.org/wp/wp-content/uploads/Evidence-from-PSC-to-Chakrabarti -inquiry-final-June-2016.pdf (accessed November 19, 2017).

40. Ephraim Mirvis, "Ken Livingstone and the Hard Left are Spreading the Insidious Virus of Antisemitism," *The Telegraph* (May 3, 2016), www.telegraph.co.uk/news /2016/05/03/ken-livingstone-and-the-hard-left-are-spreading-the-insidious-vi/.

41. House of Commons Home Affairs Committee, "Oral Evidence: Antisemitism, HC 136" (July 14, 2016), http://data.parliament.uk/writtenevidence/committeeevidence. svc/evidencedocument/home-affairs-committee/antisemitism/oral/35121.html, (accessed November 19, 2017).

42. International Holocaust Remembrance Alliance, "Working Definition of Antisemitism" (May 26, 2016), https://www.holocaustremembrance.com/sites/default/files /press_release_document_antisemitism.pdf (accessed November 19, 2017).

8 If You Are Not With Us: The National Women's Studies Association and Israel

Janet Freedman

Janet Freedman, a self-identified "progressive, feminist, pro-Israel, pro-Palestinian, pro-peace Jew," describes the transformation of the National Women's Studies Association (NWSA) from a vibrant inclusive organization into one that marginalizes Jewish women and embraces BDS bigotry against Israeli Jews. She documents how NWSA has mirrored other professional organizations in creating an environment in which dissent from the anti-Israel dogma is simply not tolerated. Along the way, many questionable tactics have been employed, including one-sided academic panels, the cutting off of pro-Israel voices, the organization's Jewish Caucus being ignored, key meetings being scheduled for the Sabbath, and so forth. Freedman notes that her "coming out" as a Zionist at the 2012 annual meeting was deemed a courageous act, as if the belief in the rights of Jews for self-determination was a badge of shame. She observes that the tactic of seeking out the exceptional anti-Israel Jewish woman to kosherize anti-Israelism "is one that has long been used to reinforce despicable racism and antisemitism."

IN LATE NOVEMBER 2015, the NWSA announced the results of the electronic poll of its membership on a resolution calling for the Boycott, Divestment, and Sanctions (BDS) of economic, military, and cultural entities and projects sponsored by the State of Israel. In all, 88.4 percent of the 35 percent who voted expressed support for the resolution.

I knew its passage was a foregone conclusion, but I was devastated nonetheless. I have a long history and deep connection to the organization. The annual conferences, publications, and email lists offered support and inspiration for me and many others initiating women's studies programs and campus women's centers. Meetings were frequently contentious, and there were many disagreements, but I perceived an intention among the members to be open to sometimes sharp criticism, particularly around issues of white, middle-class dominance of the women's movement and the association.

In recent years, the NWSA, like many other academic organizations, has urged its otherwise disputatious colleagues to come together on a single issue— BDS against the State of Israel. Preparing this essay has given me an opportunity to reflect on this phenomenon as one individual within one academic association. I'll begin with a short organizational and personal history.

That Was Then

Founded in 1977, the NWSA was created to support the women's studies programs that were developing on campuses throughout the United States. I regularly attended the annual conferences devoted to discussions of developing feminist theories and the ways in which these could be applied in curriculum development, teaching, research, and activism. Activist projects included work not only with campus-based women's centers but also with organizations and agencies beyond the campus that responded to the needs of girls and women, from K–12 schools to women's health centers, rape crisis programs, and domestic violence shelters.

As theoretical perspectives shifted, so too did the conference agendas. The initial focus on the words *woman* and *women* was critiqued as "essentialist," understood to mean that human behaviors could not be attributed to biology or even to differences in gender socialization. Creating more specific categories— for example, "Asian, disabled women"—could not resolve the problem of assuming that the experiences of members of that and other groups were uniform. Conference sessions began to emphasize cultural and historical variations that made universalizing impossible. Conference themes emphasized power and systems of privilege and the ways in which intersecting biases and oppressions function to perpetuate these.

The evolution is noted on the NWSA website:

> Women's Studies has its roots in the student, civil rights, and women's movements of the 1960s and 70s. In its early years the field's teachers and scholars principally asked, "Where are the women?" Today that question may seem an overly simple one, but at the time few scholars considered gender as a lens of analysis, and women's voices had little representation on campus or in the curriculum.
>
> Today the field's interrogation of identity, power, and privilege go far beyond the category "woman." Drawing on the feminist scholarship of U.S. and Third World women of color, Women's Studies has made the conceptual claims and theoretical practices of intersectionality, which examines how categories of identity (e.g., sexuality, race, class, gender, age, ability, etc.) and structures of inequality are mutually constituted and must continually be understood in relationship to one another, and transnationalism, which focuses on cultures, structures, and relationships that are formed as a result of the flows of people and resources across geopolitical borders, foundations of the discipline.[1]

Support for Palestinian rights has been a topic of concern for many years within the NWSA. But with the adoption of statements expressing the organization's commitment to transnational feminism and global concerns in recent years, the tempo has increased dramatically, and the NWSA conferences have become platforms for mobilizing around this issue.

Mirroring the behaviors of other organizations adopting statements in solidarity with Palestine and condemning Israel, the NWSA has *not* mounted campaigns against other countries. I can recall the 1989 conference when Chinese attendees called for solidarity with the prodemocracy movement that had spread across China and attracted a million people to Beijing's Tiananmen Square from mid-April to early June that year. The June 4 massacre of hundreds, perhaps even thousands, of participants and bystanders by government troops put a horrific end to that movement. I joined a small group in expressing outrage and sorrow, and I believe there was a statement of support from the association, but I do not recall any follow-up. Twenty-five years later, the brutal responses to the Arab Spring have received little attention in the form of plenary speakers, conference sessions, or resolutions.

Only Israel has been the focus of a sustained campaign and a resolution condemning its policies.

My own trajectory of activism often dovetailed with the NWSA agenda. I have been involved with the women's liberation movement since the late 1960s and, like many NWSA members, became active in feminist organizing after experiences in other progressive causes—antiracism, economic justice, peace and disarmament, and more. I integrated these concerns insofar as possible with my work as an academic librarian—for example, creating an alternative library of social change literature at a time when many colleges and universities were developing alternative libraries.

My family life, too, was affected by the climate of social change of that era. My then husband, two daughters, and I were part of a study group that included participants with a range of political positions. One of our members was active in B'reira, an organization critical of Israeli politics and often cited as a precursor to New Jewish Agenda (NJA), an organization seeking "a Jewish voice among progressives and a progressive voice among Jews" that was active from 1980 to 1992.[2] Both of these groups advocated for Palestinian rights.

There were a number of women who were active in the NJA's Feminist Task Force and attended the NWSA conferences and joined with non-Jewish feminists of color in challenging the historic domination of white perspectives within the feminist movement. They also brought to the fore within the NWSA the complex identities within the Jewish community—lesbian, gay, bisexual, transgender, questioning, queer (LGBTQ); black; poor; and Sephardic and other Jews—whose experiences were often subsumed by the dominance of the Ashkenazi. Many wrote for the journal *Bridges*, which, until it stopped publication in 2011, spread awareness of the diversity of Jewish feminism.

NJA feminists worked to advance the agenda of NJA's Middle East Peace Task Force. Members sponsored a well-attended discussion between an Israeli Jew and a Palestinian from Gaza at the Nairobi conference in 1985, the third in the UN Women's Forums. The session was seen as a positive rejoinder to the "Zionism equals Racism" resolution that had dominated discussion at the two previous UN international conferences.

I don't recall that the debates on whether attacks on Zionism equated with antisemitism, which were common in so many settings, took place within the NWSA. This was probably because there was an invisibility of Jews as an identity category within the organization, ironic in that they were so prominent in the women's liberation movement and disproportionately represented in the development and participation in women's studies programs. Efforts by Jewish feminists to include antisemitism in the NWSA's mission statement, which opposed racism and other forms of oppression, passed only after including both Arabs and Jews as targets of antisemitism, a distortion of the fact that the term was coined by German Wilhelm Marr in the 1870s to denote hatred of Jews as a particular racial group and has been used since that time with that meaning. This failure within the association to see Jews *as* Jews led some Jewish members of the NWSA to organize a Jewish Caucus in the 1980s.

The caucus became a place within the organization where Jews could discuss the issues that affected them within the NWSA and on their campuses and beyond. For several years, preconferences were held during which members met for a day to share aspects of their personal and professional lives and forge working connections and friendships. Conference sessions were planned and presented, including a plenary devoted to the diverse experiences of Jewish women. Shabbat services became a regular part of every conference. Since many within the association defined themselves as secular Jews, traditional ritual gave way to the celebration of a common culture.

Discussions of Israel were not a major focus of the gatherings in those early days of the caucus, but a significant number of participants were involved in activist work. I can remember a Shabbat at a conference in Akron, Ohio, in 1990 when a group of women from the local Jewish community brought challah, wine, and refreshments. A discussion on Israel began among a few attendees, during which tensions rose, and I felt that the community women left in haste and confusion.

The Death and Rebirth of the Jewish Caucus

I was probably naive in not recognizing the growing majority of those whose primary issue was Israel/Palestine within the NWSA and its Jewish Caucus.

As the years passed, membership in the Jewish Caucus waned. By the time I stopped attending the NWSA in the early 2000s, many Jewish women had left the association. I knew some who had moved to new careers, some who had retired, and some who shared their frustration with the turn toward postmodernism, even postfeminism, within women's studies programs—now renamed women, gender, and sexuality studies. I don't know whether the increased emphasis on Israel/Palestine was among the reasons. My own hiatus was primarily due to family concerns.

In 2009, I returned to the NWSA, where I renewed connections to several constituencies. My career included work as a library director, and I was glad to discover that the Librarian's Task Force was active. But I discovered that the Jewish Caucus had become inactive. I joined others in reapplying to the association for official recognition, and the caucus was reinstated, albeit with a much-reduced membership. Those who were still involved continued a commitment to meet, not for a full day, but for a gathering the evening before the conference, and we continued to sponsor a Shabbat service. Among the dozen or so who convened, probably more than half were engaged within and beyond the association in critiques of Israel and advocacy for Palestinians.

By 2012, in response to the growing attacks on Israel within the NWSA, I submitted a proposal to participate in a roundtable sponsored by the Jewish Caucus. My talk was titled "If I Am Not for Myself, Who Will Be for Me? If I Am Only for Myself, What Am I?" My short remarks acknowledged the separations, differences, and divisions that characterized discussions on Israel/Palestine and urged that reading, dialogue, and debate be the path to stronger advocacy for both Israeli and Palestinian rights.

I called for explaining the meanings of the words we use in our discourse about Israel and Palestine and advocated the reclamation of the word *Zionism*, the varied meanings of which must be explored to underpin discussions about the complex history of Israel, which often is unclear to both its supporters and detractors. I shared that my own efforts to listen and learn about the multiple connotations and historical shifts had led to new understandings and, sometimes, new contradictions that were illuminated by yet more reading, dialogue, and debate.

I recalled that my own notions of Zionism had been shaped by attending a Jewish summer camp where many of the dynamic counselors were secular labor Zionists who intended to make *aliyah*—to move to Israel—and help create a socialist utopia. Their vision not only influenced my view of Israel; it likely led to my attraction to democratic socialism as a path toward economic and social equality in this country as well.

I affirmed that much had changed since the establishment of the State of Israel, which much of the world celebrated. I stated that my support for Israel did not mean I was not critical of many of the policies of the state and those of many other countries, including my own. Yet my objections had not led me to the conclusion that Israel, or the United States, should be destroyed. Instead of denying Israel's right to exist, I exercised my right and responsibility to speak out, as many Israeli citizens can and do, to disagree with those whose approaches stood in the way of a two-state solution.

Antisemitism and Anti-Israel: Can They Be Separated?

In preparing my talk, I came face to face with the fact that internalized antisemitism had shaped my political activism. I realized that from the time I became involved in progressive and feminist movements, I often assumed the lead in embracing a radical position, sometimes repressing reservations I had about the prevailing opinion. For example, there were instances when I wanted to be the first to criticize certain actions taken by the State of Israel lest I appear to lack a proactive stance on rights for Palestinians.

I came to my decision to come out as a Zionist at the 2012 NWSA conference, in part by recognizing myself in the words of Jewish feminist activist Evelyn Torton Beck. Beck, one of the founding members of the NWSA's Jewish Caucus and the author of *Nice Jewish Girls,* recalled in that book her uncritical enthusiasm for Rita Mae Brown's novel *Rubyfruit Jungle*, one of the earliest mainstream fictional works about lesbianism. "As an emerging lesbian, I couldn't admit/protest that the leading fiction writer used age old antisemitic stereotypes. I simply couldn't afford to take it in. So I kept silent. In those early years of struggle it seemed unworthy to make a fuss. And worse, it seemed divisive. I could not yet claim my anger. I wanted too much to belong."[3]

I declared that I did not equate criticism of Israel with antisemitism, seeing such conjoining as another barrier to dialogue. But I observed that sometimes it is hard to separate the two when the word *Zionist* is hurled with derision and disgust, and that is why I was calling for the reclaiming of the word and for its explication, so that it is not thoughtlessly misused. And, while some would respond that *Jew* and *Zionist* are not the same, my personal knowledge that the existence of the State of Israel provided a home for Jews who would not have found another makes it hard not to link them.

I began my 2012 talk with a question I ask when I am determining how to work in solidarity with those who are seeking peace between Israelis and Palestinians.

"Do you think that the State of Israel should not exist?"

At my presentation in 2012, no one indicated they felt this way.

This Is Now

But in the several years since that talk, it became more difficult to feel welcome within the NWSA as a Jew who does not condemn Israel. Even though the

Jewish Caucus was revived, there was a paucity of conference sessions touching on Jewish themes *other* than Israel/Palestine. I attended most of these and was impressed by the quality of presentations, which included papers on Jewish poets and authors and readings of original works by Jewish members of the NWSA. Yet where Jewish women are eager to attend sessions sponsored by other caucuses and offered by diverse groups within the NWSA, few non-Jews attend the "Jewish" sessions. In earlier years, non-Jews often attended the annual Shabbat service, which always welcomes all conferees. I have observed that this lessened, too. An oversight by the organizational leadership to schedule a plenary session on Friday evening at the time the Shabbat service has traditionally taken place was also troubling. I've noted that I usually resist concluding that behaviors are antisemitic, but it is clear that Jews, unless they are involved in work for justice for Palestine, are, at the very least, irrelevant to the organization, many of whose members would be outraged if oversights affected other ethnic or religious groups.

The BDS Resolution

Following a proposal for a boycott of Israeli academic institutions by the American Studies Association and campaigns in other academic organizations, it was clear that the NWSA would follow suit. In 2014, the leadership of the NWSA, without consultation with the association's Jewish Caucus, sponsored official sessions in which speakers presented only one perspective on the BDS debate. These included a plenary on Israel/Palestine at which no Israeli was asked to speak and after which attendees who had heard a litany of remarks against Israel were asked to stand in support of "freedom and justice for/in Palestine."

Since the NWSA had not offered occasions to present a legitimate discussion on the pros and cons of the resolution, I felt it was important for me to accept an opportunity to speak for five minutes at the 2015 conference at a roundtable sponsored by the Jewish Caucus titled "Two Jews, Three Opinions: A Critical Query of the BDS Movement Against the Israeli Occupation." This offered a singular opportunity at the conference to present divergent viewpoints on the resolution. One other woman spoke against the resolution, and two spoke in favor.

I used my time to demonstrate how the frequently asked questions (FAQs) appended to the resolution and intended to allay concerns about its content instead provided the very reasons that it should be rejected.

The FAQ responding to apprehensions about whether the BDS resolution could be seen as antisemitic was addressed with this rejoinder: "[W]hat is really antisemitic is the attempt to identify all Jews with a philosophy that many find abhorrent to the traditions of social justice and universality that Judaism enshrines."[4] I observed that such presumptive, condescending language reprises the ancient appeal to the "good" Jew—in this case, one who sides with those who see Israel as a demonic entity. The tactic of seeking out the exceptional ones in a despised group is one that has long been used to reinforce despicable racism and antisemitism.

I also spoke against the egregious assault on academic freedom found in the explication in the FAQs of activities that would violate the boycott. Not only would a seminar talk in partnership with or sponsored by an Israeli institution not be allowed, but even telephone conversations were essentially subject to the boycott.

Since the time allotted was so limited, I did not have the opportunity to speak to the FAQ "Why is there no mention of Palestinian violence?" The response to this question was: "History shows us that oppressed people will resist their oppression (and are legitimized by international law to defend themselves against the brutalities of colonialism and occupation). Palestinians have responded to the Israeli Occupation with a wide range of strategies, including violent and non-violent means. Our support for BDS would pressure Israel to stop its violations of Palestinian rights and minimize the need of the Palestinian people to turn to violent resistance as a last resort against their colonization."[5]

If time had allowed, among many other points, I would have expressed that these rejoinders that valorize violence cannot possibly lead to a positive response from Israel.

As I had in my presentation in 2012, I asked if there were people in the audience who believed that the State of Israel should not exist. Where no one in 2012 indicated they felt this way, in 2015, one of my copanelists, a member of Jewish Voice for Peace, immediately interrupted to say the question was unfair. In the discussion following the panel, she acknowledged that she could not support the State of Israel in view of the nation's present policies.

As the conference proceeded, I became aware that the content of the resolution before the organization was irrelevant to most members. In fact, almost everyone with whom I spoke had not even read the resolution. In retrospect, I realize that support for both Israelis and Palestinians to live in peace and dignity and the encouragement of exchanges that respect all those involved were not the goals of this resolution.

If You Are Not With Us, You Are Against Us

My observations are that there is now a clear *us* and *them* within the NWSA. Supporting the BDS resolution was seen as a sign of solidarity with Palestinians; those who questioned that strategy, including some who might have been undecided on BDS, or were against the *particular* resolution placed before the membership are in the enemy camp, assumed to be opposed to justice and even made the objects of scorn and vitriol. Organizing efforts have become ends in themselves, unintentionally—and sometimes intentionally—based on the spreading of rumors and misinformation and challenging what I had once believed was a commitment to open dialogue within the association.

What I've Learned

The BDS movement as I experienced it within the NWSA directs our energy away from ways to find a peaceful solution that respects the humanity of both Israelis and Palestinians. It oversimplifies to the point of gross inaccuracies. The incredibly complex history and current conditions are obscured. The zeal with which many come to their position on BDS is often in contrast with a lack of awareness of history or of a respect for the accuracy of information brought to their advocacy. Supporters at the conference excoriated Israel, including, as I have noted, comments from some that Israel should not be allowed to exist. Palestinians were valorized and any criticism of egregious misdeeds on their part excused as a necessary response to Israeli aggression.

Now that the BDS resolution has passed, no affiliated Israeli scholars can present at the NWSA or even have a conversation with an NWSA member. But the shunning began before the resolution was passed. The organization, through its choice of conference themes, plenary speakers, and selection of sessions, repeatedly has advanced a position that castigates Israel and advocates for justice for Palestine.

Other than events sponsored by the Jewish Caucus, there has been no debate or discussion offered on Israel/Palestine.

While professing the challenge of interlacing systems of oppression that must be addressed together, antisemitism is usually excluded. The Jewish invisibility and antisemitism within the NWSA that led to the formation of a Jewish Caucus in the 1980s appear to have resumed after a period during which there was a somewhat more welcoming climate. In response to this, fewer Jewish women have sustained their commitment to the organization, and insofar as the NWSA contributes to the development of women and gender studies curricula, the varied histories, lives, issues, and activism of Jewish women are not being considered.

The voices of Jews and others whose positions are rooted in the right of Israel to exist as a state have been silenced. Following my remarks at the BDS roundtable, there was just one comment from the audience validating some of my points. But I received many private expressions of support and appreciation for my courage. Several people told me it would be damaging to their careers to openly express opposition to the resolution and support Israel. That was the saddest aspect of my experience at the conference.

I described myself to the 2015 NWSA roundtable audience as a "progressive, feminist, pro-Israel, pro-Palestinian, pro-peace Jew." Having a thorough, thoughtful exchange of what each of those words mean to me and others might have been the basis for a constructive dialogue on the Israeli-Palestinian conflict, but that has not occurred. Despite the passage of the BDS resolution, I still want that dialogue and intend to continue to seek solutions to this struggle based on deep reflection rather than simplistic, formulaic sound bites.

I know that I have more work to do to resist trying to ingratiate myself with the Left. I often observe in myself and others with many years of involvement in progressive politics, particularly Jewish colleagues, a struggle to be aligned with positions taken by other left-leaning individuals and groups. Even with the experience I have had within the NWSA, I initially thought—as have other, mostly Jewish, opponents to the excessive rhetoric of BDS resolutions in other organizations—that there could be an acceptable resolution that would acknowledge the multiple dimensions of the Palestine-Israel conflict. I need to disabuse myself and discourage others from seeking affirmation from those who, in reality, do not respect this approach and to relinquish the idea that it makes sense to invest time in trying to gain their approval by efforts to reshape resolutions intended to delegitimize Israel.

Although I am firm in my commitment to Israel, I feel it is important to bring continuing knowledge, understanding, and careful reflection to every action. Hillel's dictum that we do not do to our neighbor what is hateful to ourselves should be practiced within our own Jewish communities. As much as I am distressed by the knee-jerk reactions on the left, I am disturbed equally by the responses on the right. The abusive rhetoric that is exchanged on many websites is more than disheartening, especially the comments sections that often spew hatred against those who disagree with a stand. Nor is the vitriol limited to the specific remarks. When I wrote about my experiences at the NWSA, I was attacked because I was foolish enough to ally myself with "crazy feminists," and similar comments made me wonder where to build alliances around my pro-Israel, anti-BDS work.

In addition to finding ways to respectfully disagree, or at least be less hostile, we might pay heed to Hillel's urging that we "go and study" (Talmud Tractate Shabbat, 31a). Students and others often feel they must choose a side. Bringing together Jews—and Jews and non-Jews—with differing perspectives in study and discussion groups could allay the acrimony and perhaps yield paths toward more informed activism. I was recently told about the advice given to a college student who shared his concerns about signs that were posted on his campus attacking the Birthright Israel program. The administration advised him to write a letter to the college newspaper to express his opposition, a strategy that likely will result in counter letters rather than opportunities for meaningful face-to-face dialogue and the building of community. The response of that campus, like many others, often furthers polarized positions. Be it Israel/Palestine or other issues, there is an unfortunate tendency to try to get a balance by sponsoring speakers on one side or the other. This contradicts the mission of most academic institutions to explore the intricacies of human experience and its varied social, artistic, scientific, and political dimensions. Allowing discussions that assume that there are multiple perspectives could prove much more fruitful than sponsoring speakers on both sides of complex issues.

At the same time, as it is important to find approaches that avoid polarizing and even demonizing the "other," it is inescapable that the BDS resolutions and related efforts to discredit Israel are deliberate, hydra-headed campaigns that will spring ever new strategies. Recently, anti-Israel protesters in the LBGTQ communities have been accusing Israel of "pinkwashing." They charge that Israel is using gay-friendly policies to deflect from its egregious acts against Palestinians. In January 2016, two hundred people forced the cancellation of an event at the National LBGTQ Task Force Conference hosted by A Wider Bridge, a group seeking to build connections between North American and Israeli Jews. False accusations and double standards used as methods to fan the flames for a particular cause need to be documented and shared, and wherever hatred and discrimination exist against any individual or group, these need to be addressed forthrightly.

The current climate is distressing, but there are hopeful initiatives, too. In April 2016, I attended a conference at Smith College that brought together students from all the area colleges and universities for a day of community building around the theme "Calling In the Calling Out Culture." The idea for the conference came from Loretta Ross, who worked for many years for SisterSong, an organization for reproductive justice for women of color. The work of the day was to address how calling out—attacking ideas and people with which/whom we disagree—can take us to a place where we resemble what we are struggling against and to find alternatives to this now all-too-familiar dynamic. I discovered that the calling-in model is about finding ways to disagree with someone's politics without tormenting them. It encourages humility and the acknowledgment of imperfection and making mistakes from which we can learn. Calling in is about having conversations and building relationships and community. It is about asking ourselves, "How would I feel if someone said/did this to me?"

I'd like to end this essay by urging that if we have not already committed ourselves to such an approach, we begin immediately.

If not now, when?

JANET FREEDMAN, Resident Scholar, Brandeis University Women's Studies Research Center, and Professor Emerita, University of Massachusetts Dartmouth, is a longtime member of the National Women's Studies Association and a former chair of its Jewish Caucus. She is author of *Reclaiming the Feminist Vision: Consciousness Raising and Small Group Practice*.

Notes

1. National Women's Studies Association, "What Is Women's Studies?," http://www
.nwsa.org/womensstudies (accessed September 23, 2017).
2. "Proposed Mission Statement of New Jewish Agenda, 1987," in *American Jewish History: A Primary Source Reader* Gary Phillip Zola and Marc Dolinger editors (Lebanon, NH: Brandeis University Press, 2014), 355.
3. As cited in Lisa Maria Hogeland, *Feminism and Its Fictions: The Consciousness-Raising Novel and the Women's Liberation Movement* (Philadelphia: University of Pennsylvania Press, 1998), 53.
4. Janet L Freedman, "For the Women's Studies Association, the BDS Vote Was Over Before It Began," *The Forward* (November 30, 2015), http://forward.com/sisterhood
/325637/for-the-womens-studies-association-the-bds-vote-was-over-before-it-began/.
5. "National Women's Studies Association to Consider BDS Resolution at Upcoming Conference," US Campaign for the Academic and Cultural Boycott of Israel, http://www
.usacbi.org/2015/11/national-womens-studies-association-to-consider-bds-resolution-at
-upcoming-conference/ (accessed November 2, 2017).

9 Rhodes University, Not a Home for All: A Progressive Zionist's Two-Year Odyssey

Larissa Klazinga

From South Africa comes a narrative of persecution and harassment on an institutional scale. Larissa Klazinga, an alum of and staff member at Rhodes University, was approached by several Jewish students alarmed about an upcoming Israeli Apartheid Week. In solidarity with the students, Klazinga placed on her office door a poster of an Israeli flag with the words, "Wherever I stand, I stand with Israel," and dared to wear pro-Israel clothing to work. Anti-Israel activists promptly deluged her with abuse and insults, while the administration itself delivered an extended campaign to harass her, ultimately trumping up disciplinary charges to fire her over her support for Israel. Refusing to be bullied Klazinga fought back, with the support of the local Jewish community and lawyers, and won. She left Rhodes with her life destroyed but with a legal settlement and her head held high. Meanwhile, the campus remained riddled with antisemitic anti-Israelism, and not one of those who persecuted her was brought to justice.

THIS IS NOT an easy story to write; it's difficult to pinpoint the beginning, and the end is a fairly sad one. I suppose the long and short of it is this: Zionists can't really work at Rhodes University, and they probably aren't welcome to study there either.

For those of you unfamiliar with Rhodes, allow me to sketch the landscape. The demographic makeup of Rhodes is unlike other South African universities. Rhodes has very few Jewish students and even fewer Jewish staff members; factor in the number of those who openly identify as Zionists, and you are down to single digits.

Now to introduce myself. While I am no fan of labels, for the purposes of this story, permit me to use broad strokes: I'm a hearing-impaired Jewish lesbian vegetarian with a biracial Xhosa wife. No, I didn't just make that up. As you can imagine, I have come up against my fair share of snide comments and nasty glances, but I am forced to confess that until I came face to face with the Boycott, Divestment, and Sanctions (BDS) movement and its henchmen, I never really understood bigotry.

It was 2012 and time for a campus bombshell as I emerged from the proverbial leftist closet ... as a Zionist. OK, it was a poorly kept secret and not much of a shock to anyone close to me. I've been a Zionist for as long as I can remember. I was naive enough to believe it was an uncontroversial position; in fact, much like being proudly South African, it seemed like a no-brainer. I'd had discussions with progressive friends who disagreed with me, but the vitriol directed at me during my last two years at Rhodes, after I came out of that closet, came as a shock.

In addition to being a staff member, I was also an old Rhodian, and I used to be a proud one. After a brief stint elsewhere, I had returned to Rhodes, where I worked for more than a decade conceptualizing and organizing myriad transformation initiatives highlighting gender-based violence, xenophobia, racism, and other human rights abuses. I became the go-to person for anyone wanting to organize an awareness-raising event, and ironically, I also functioned as the university harassment officer, charged with assisting students facing discrimination and harassment and putting in place measures to counteract the problem.

Now that I've set the scene, let me describe the events that made me walk away from my alma mater and my career at the end of November 2013.

It all started in early 2012, when a new awareness-raising event reared its head at Rhodes: Israeli Apartheid Week (IAW). It was organized by a group of students and staff members ostensibly under the banner of the Faculty of Humanities, with evening film screenings, discussions, and lunchtime seminars hosted in the politics department. It was clear that these events were being directed by proponents of BDS.

From the outset, two things were evident: first, the event was actively underwritten by the university itself, and second, what was being promoted was not a debate but rather a diatribe, as the organizers would brook no dissent. Within days of the publicity materials blanketing campus, I had two separate incidents of Jewish students arriving at my office in tears after the students attempted to defend Israel and were subjected to ugly name-calling exchanges with some of the IAW organizers.

Both students were very upset by the grossly unbalanced nature of IAW. They asked for support as they tried to present a more balanced view of the Middle East conflict and proposed parallel events under the banner "Balance the Debate." One of those students, Ben K., contacted the national Jewish student association and asked for assistance. With its help, the students printed posters and T-shirts and organized a few events to highlight Jewish history, talk about antisemitism, and attempt to address some of the misinformation being disseminated by the BDS people for IAW.

I agreed to help them publicize their events, and because I realized how much pressure they were under, I agreed to attend the events with them when I was able. In an effort to constructively engage with their opponents, Ben and his small contingent of Zionist students committed to attending the IAW events, hoping that the IAW organizers would give them an opportunity to state their case and ask the kinds of questions that would open up genuine dialogue. The Zionist students also suggested to some of the IAW organizers that they host a joint event to encourage serious debate.

These attempts were rebuffed at every turn.

As the week of IAW dawned, I felt tremendous sympathy for these courageous Jewish students, a tiny minority at Rhodes, who confessed to feeling victimized because of their support for Israel but determined to speak out nonetheless. As one of only a handful of Jewish staff members and the only one who has ever expressed solidarity with Israel publicly, I felt honor-bound to support them. I believed that it was my duty, not only as a staff member tasked with supporting students against harassment, but also as a person of conscience and a Jew to stand up for what I believe in and to support others who do the same.

With that in mind, and after consulting with the Jewish students, I printed a large colored page featuring the Israeli flag and the words "Wherever I stand, I stand with Israel" and placed it on my office door. I did not anticipate that this would raise an eyebrow since I had put up a supportive poster during the Save Zimbabwe Now campaign three years earlier that had not elicited any comment. I understood that I couldn't actively arrange events in conflict with the official university calendar because I did not have the support of my line managers, so I reverted to indirect methods of support, such as the poster on my office door. I also decided to wear pro-Israel clothing to work, reasoning that I could go about my daily activities while still supporting the Jewish students who were taking more direct action.

I thought, based on previous political positions I had taken, that my actions were not controversial.

I returned the next day to find the page removed and shoved under my door with a note written on the back by Roger Adams, the deputy dean of students, asking me to discuss the matter with him immediately.

I arrived at his office wearing a pro-Israel shirt and was instructed to remove it as soon as possible and not to wear any "military or pro-Israel" clothing to work. I was told that using my office to further a political position was inappropriate, and I was instructed not to make any public statements in support of Israel.

I asked if that injunction applied to all staff and if it related to activities taking place after hours. I was informed that since I lived and worked on campus,

I was never in fact off duty and thus never entitled to voice my opinion on this issue. I asked why other staff members could pin their colors to the mast about Israel but I was silenced, and he answered that they were academic staff, entitled to academic freedom of expression, but as administrative staff, I was not.

I felt threatened and censored, and when I asked what made this issue different from any other, I was given no clear answer. I was, in fact, given the very clear message that to dissent on this issue would bring the office into disrepute and would be construed as insubordination. I argued with him as long as I could bear and then left the office shell-shocked.

Anyone who knows me will confirm that I am a stubborn person, so in order to honor my commitment to the small group of Zionist students, I took the next day off work, reasoning that this would ensure that I would not be seen to be acting in any official capacity. I attended a discussion hosted in the politics department seminar room led by John Rose (a BDS activist and visiting lecturer in politics) and Professor Robert van Niekerk. I sat at the back and wore nonpartisan clothing. I confess that for fear of being charged with insubordination, I did not speak at all during the meeting. Despite my silence, the following morning, I received a hostile email from a Rhodes staff member I had never met, aggressively questioning me due to my support of Israel.

And so it began.

The atmosphere on Rhodes campus during IAW 2012 was so vitriolic that it left no room to explore any common ground between the sides. I spent the week being insulted, harassed, and variously described as a racist, in favor of ethnic cleansing, an apartheid apologist, and (my favorite) the pied piper of misandry on campus, which, while inaccurate and defamatory (and frankly, I still fail to see how that relates to Israel), was certainly creative.

That initial anti-Israel email from the staff member began a nine-month battle to get Rhodes to take action against what emerged later to be a BDS-sanctioned witch hunt involving senior academics and extending all the way to Muhammed Desai, the national coordinator of BDS South Africa.

This national connection became apparent only a few weeks after IAW 2012, when I discovered a series of emails between IAW organizers, BDS South Africa activists, and Rhodes staff members, encouraging each other to gather "evidence in any medium: written, verbal, video … to collect data and people's personal experiences" against me because I was a danger to their agenda.

Believing this matter would be taken seriously, I met with the director of human resources, the staff harassment officer, and the dean of students, Vivian de Klerk, who was the head of my division. During these meetings, I was able to confirm that, on the one hand, Rhodes had a strong antiharassment policy and, on the other, no policy on staff political activity at all, leaving me confident that I had every right to speak out in support of Israel. After months of requests and finally with the help of my union representative, I secured a conviction against the author of the original anti-Israel email in October 2012.

No action was ever taken to address the BDS witch hunt against me.

Skip ahead to spring 2013, and IAW 2013 was more of the same, with the dean's office offering to sponsor IAW events at the invitation of Roger Adams. I was instructed to change the image at the top of the Rhodes student web portal to one promoting IAW. Meanwhile, a music department concert showcasing Israeli pianist Yossi Reshef was picketed.

Realizing that it was impossible for me to attempt any head-to-head confrontation, my partner, Charlene, aided by some Christian Zionists, put up a series of posters downloaded from the pro-Israel group StandWithUs around campus. These posters unleashed against us allegations of racism and resulted in angry phone calls from the members of the student government, official complaints to the dean of students office, and (I would say) an almost gleeful investigation into our supposed wrongdoing—which eventually ended in a hearing and a decision that the posters were protected by freedom of speech.

During this stressful period, I sought the help of the South African Jewish Board of Deputies (SAJBD) and the Zionist Federation. With their support and the support of certain key people (such as Leon Reich and Chuck Volpe), I raised enough awareness about the situation at Rhodes that a fact-finding visit to the campus was planned, incidentally coinciding with Yom HaShoah. On hearing about the impending SAJBD visit, my superior, de Klerk, warned me that my participation with it was ill-advised.

One can only conclude that the actions that soon followed were aimed at shutting me up or forcing me out. In fact, they began earlier, in Adams's official rebuke of me in March 2012, and were only reinforced when Deputy Vice Chancellor Sizwe Mabizela commented in the *Mail & Guardian* newspaper on the pro-Israel posters, stating that "the role and purpose of the Fairness Forum will be reviewed in due course and that action over a student who apparently put the posters up [in support of Israel], and the fact that a staff member [me] was also allegedly involved, shall follow due process."[1]

For months, I was silenced, harassed, and threatened with discipline. By June 2013, when none of that mistreatment was able to wring a resignation out of me, due process was followed, and I was served with a charge sheet consisting of eighteen separate counts, many related to my defense of Israel, some referencing my sexual orientation, and a number that were simply fabricated. These charges were drafted by the university's lawyer after a series of consultations with both Adams and de Klerk. They cited the authority of Vice Chancellor Saleem Badat for convening a relevant hearing, and they were signed by the director of human relations.

I was shocked by the scale of the onslaught and the mention of my partner and Zionism in the charges, but I was not unprepared. Thanks to the incredible support I received from the Jewish community, I did not walk into the hearing unrepresented, as de Klerk and company had hoped. Enter South Africa's top labor lawyer Michael Bagraim and High Court heavy hitter Izak Smuts. Without going into detail, let's just say that things swung in my favor with remarkable speed after they entered the fray.

The disciplinary hearing was aborted, and at the behest of the university, I entered into a confidential settlement agreement. I'm happy with the settlement and don't intend to breach it, so that is all I can say about that saga. Mazel tov! A happy ending!

Not so fast.

If you had asked me in 2011 if I thought Zionism would be the issue that defined my career at Rhodes, I would have scoffed. Even more surprising, as it turned out, my support for Israel was so unpalatable to my former colleagues that it voided any positive contribution I had ever made. I was subjected to bullying and harassment on a scale I had never experienced before. Throughout, I did my best to fight for my rights to freedom of speech, belief, association, and religion. I fought to maintain my health, and I struggled to come to terms with betrayals of loyalty and trust from people I used to admire.

I used to believe that discourse was possible in an academic setting and that once people started talking they'd see that Zionism and the belief in a Palestinian state could coexist and, in fact, support each other. I was wrong. There can be no dialogue, no understanding, no coexistence when there is fundamental intolerance based on double standards and blind hatred.

I say *double standards* and *blind hatred* because these progressive human rights activists are rabid in their anti-Israel rallying but completely silent about China's occupation of Tibet and about accepting Chinese state funding of a Rhodes language institute without so much as an angry note. They have not organized awareness events decrying Turkey's security wall, Saudi Arabia's oppression of women, or the Islamic State, or ever rallied in support of democracy and for an end to human rights abuses in Zimbabwe, our neighboring country. They only seem to object to Israel, leading me to conclude that their ethics are not universal, that their moral objections are limited to the only Jewish state in the world. That makes it old-fashioned, all-too-familiar antisemitism. Full stop.

This realization was particularly hard because I was a true believer in the ideal of academic freedom. I honestly thought that Rhodes was an institution that created spaces for intellectual exploration, for people to grow and change, and where ideas were valued above all. It is a difficult thing to admit to being naive, but I was. My alma mater became a totalitarian institution, where colleagues were encouraged to spy on each other, gather evidence, and work behind closed doors to get rid of people. It was a place where the deputy dean of students could look me in the eye and tell me that since I'm not an academic I'm not entitled to academic freedom ... without flinching or showing any signs that he might be uncomfortable saying it.

I was raised under Apartheid, but I never really understood what totalitarianism *felt* like until I was told that I was not allowed to speak, even in private, about a political belief. At Rhodes University. In 2012.

The *really* disappointing thing was that—despite a settlement that sent me packing and the vice chancellor's assurance that an investigation would be instituted to determine how an unconstitutional charge sheet was drafted on Rhodes letterhead—as far as I've been able to confirm, nothing ever happened; no one was brought to book; no heads rolled. De Klerk retired with full honors, Adams left with an unblemished reputation and was promptly employed by the University of Cape Town to carry on his good work, and worse still, two courses filled with one-sided anti-Israel propaganda continue to feature in the Rhodes curriculum.

The sad truth is that on Friday, November 29, 2013, I handed in my keys and I walked out of my office for the last time. I packed up my home, removed the mezuzah from the door, and walked away from a residence I helped found eleven years before. It felt like giving up. It felt like I let the bigots win—oh no, a really bad ending.

But wait, there's more!

This story would be incomplete if I failed to mention that Rhodes isn't monolithic. Yes, there are anti-Israel, homophobic bigots in abundance, but there are also some truly amazing people there.

I had the unwavering support of colleagues in Lilian Ngoyi Hall, of senior academics who reminded me never to cave in to bullies when I was at my lowest ebb, and of many other current and retired staff members who didn't know or didn't care much about Zionism but offered kind words and encouragement. I had the solidarity of several academics in the commerce faculty and of Christian Zionists like the Radloff family, who, as unashamed Zionists swimming against the academically popular tide, offered gentle reassurances and were brave enough to break rank and take a stand for Israel. I was inspired by the small band of Jewish students who put body and soul on the line to defend Israel, some at great cost. Rhodes really is where leaders learn, and as a country, we ignore that at our peril.

So, what did I learn?

I learned that freedom always comes at a cost, and it takes chutzpah to understand that and pay the price. It also takes good friends and the love of a good woman. I left Rhodes depressed and defeated, unemployed and homeless. I can report that things turned out well, and today I work with people I respect and for an organization that works every day to change the world for the better. I remain endlessly hopeful, reassured that there are things worth fighting for and people willing to stand with me and with Israel.[2]

LARISSA KLAZINGA is a Rhodes University alumna and former staff member. Currently, she is Regional Policy & Advocacy Manager at the Southern Africa AIDS Healthcare Foundation.

Notes

1. Ant Katz, "Rhodes Pays Dearly For Anti-Zionist Stand," *South African Jewish Report* (January 1, 2014), http://www.sajr.co.za/news-and-articles/2014/01/01/rhodes-pays-dearly-for -anti-zionist-stand.

2. An earlier version of this essay appeared in the *South African Jewish Report* and is reproduced with their kind permission: Larissa Klazinga, "Rhodes University: Not a Home For All," *South African Jewish Report* (January 1, 2014), http://www.sajr.co.za/news-and -articles/2013/12/31/rhodes-university-not-a-home-for-all.

10 Loud and Fast versus Slow and Quiet: Responses to Anti-Israel Activism on Campus

Jeffrey Kopstein

Jeffrey Kopstein brings a unique comparative perspective to the impact of anti-Israelism on campuses, having held leadership positions at the University of Toronto and, since 2015, the notorious University of California at Irvine. He describes his efforts to bring intellectual nuance to the Israeli-Palestinian conflict on campus while navigating the fraught politics, particularly as he attempted to bring three distinguished Israeli Supreme Court justices to campus. The first lecture he decided to cut short rather than allow the disruptive entry of protesters amassed outside. Regretting that decision, he instead brought the next visitor to campus secretly, to speak only to a private audience—but then felt ashamed at the indignity of treating a distinguished Israeli this way. Kopstein closes with an account of the widely reported May 2016 incident in which a large group of anti-Israel activists terrified a small group of pro-Israel students watching a film. At Irvine, it appears, Israel-related events must either be held secretly or only with significant police presence.

In my experience, campus organizations hostile to Israel are less interested in criticizing Israeli policy than in effacing and deleting its existence. The issue is not the occupation of 1967 but the occupation of 1948—that is, the very founding and existence of the state. The tactics of these organizations are first to obfuscate and twist the meanings of the words *Zionism* and *occupation* and then to use these redefinitions to prevent any normalization of Israel on campus. *Zionism* is redefined from Jewish self-determination to racist colonialism, and *occupation* is redefined as all land under Jewish sovereignty no matter where it is. From there, it is but a small step to tar every Israeli academic visitor, event, film, lecture, course, academic exchange, art exhibit, or cultural celebration as an expression of an unjust and illegal regime. It is a difficult argument to oppose. Most students and faculty members have scattered knowledge of the history and complexities of the region and therefore take the cognitive shortcut of identifying with the "out group."

Two responses to the generalized toxicity surrounding Israel on North American campuses offer themselves. The first is to counter speech with speech, to support Jewish students who encounter hostility by enabling them to talk about Israel, celebrate Israel, criticize Israel, and generally engage Israel. Jewish communities often support this approach and, through Hillel or other organizations, provide a steady stream of campus activities promoting the Israeli narrative. It is an approach with mixed success because high-profile events or even lower-profile ones that take place outside of the classroom and the normal curriculum do not diminish the ardor of anti-Israel activism. Just as often, it provides a focal point for anti-Israel activists. Countering speech with speech is important and theoretically sounds wonderful, but the reality is frequently less speech against speech than screaming against screaming and a generalized escalation of tensions (and toxicity) surrounding Israel on campus.

The second response is quieter and slower. With all the noise of campus politics, what can easily be forgotten is that the strong point of universities is teaching and research. It is surprising how few universities offer courses on the history of Israel, courses in the social sciences of modern Israeli politics and culture, or even courses on the intellectual history or philosophy of Zionism. Where an academic program in Israel studies exists and is well integrated across the curriculum, a large cohort of students has a deeper knowledge of the conflict. They are better able to situate what they hear on campus from activists within a broader understanding of Jewish and Middle Eastern history. They will not necessarily become Zionists, but their presence influences the broader campus in ways that the screaming matches of campus activism do not.

In summer 2015, I took up a new position as chair of the Department of Political Science at the University of California, Irvine (UCI), a campus with a reputation for beautiful weather, an innovative faculty, and anti-Israel activism. Of course, I had been warned, but I was confident that my five years as director of the Anne Tanenbaum Center for Jewish Studies at the University of Toronto had prepared me for anything I might encounter. Besides, I had been brought to UCI not to deal with campus Israel politics but to lead a political science department through issues that had nothing to do with matters Jewish and Israel. After so many years of navigating between right-wing donors and left-wing faculty members, in all honesty I was ready for a break.

Helping build the Center for Jewish Studies at the University of Toronto had exposed me to the politics of Israeli Apartheid Week (in fact, I believe it began in Toronto) and also the generalized weirdness associated with Israel on campus. What do I mean by *weirdness*? First was the reaction of my colleagues in the social sciences and humanities. All too often at Toronto, I detected on the faces of valued colleagues a look of pain whenever I mentioned Israel, when I proposed fairly innocuous meetings between my colleagues and visiting Israeli professors, or when I proposed deepening connections with Israeli institutions, which was, after all, one of the missions of my center. I knew what they were thinking: "Why would such a smart guy get involved in Jewish particularism; why would he derail his career in that way? He must be doing this out of nationalist or identity grounds rather than legitimate intellectual interest." Publishing any number of articles in mainstream journals of my own discipline did not seem to affect things. This was a strange detour, many friends insisted. No matter, my own interest in Zionism had evolved naturally out of my work on interwar East European politics, and I viewed my venture into Jewish studies as natural; if other sorts of ethnic studies were justified, how could my own not be?

The second bit of weirdness had to do with the view of the university administration on Jewish and Israel studies: it was frequently considered more a branch of fund-raising than scholarship. The tradition of Jewish philanthropy is strong, and universities tend to view Jewish and Israel studies as a loss leader to get donors involved in non-Jewish activities. Of course, the donors are perfectly well aware of this. Even so, it was telling that my main (and highly effective) contact in the university administration was an advancement officer rather than someone in the normal channels of academic administration. I tried to deflect the attentions of the advancement team, even while respecting what they had allowed us to do. The interest of advancement allowed the center to accomplish a great deal on campus and help out departments, but it also tended to reproduce stereotypes that I found painful. Department chairs would come to me and ask my center to intervene with the administration on personnel matters because, as one colleague put it, "You have access that others don't." Of course, I cringed when I heard this. As one equally startled colleague put it, "They think we have special Jew powers."

The donors, of course, are a special group. Toronto's Jewish community is large, more traditional, and more politically conservative than its American counterparts. Disproportionately of East European and Russian backgrounds with a sizable group of Holocaust survivors and their progeny, the city's Jewish community is well organized and highly effective and generous in Israel advocacy. Stewardship of such a community required a degree of diplomatic tact. Some of it was humorous, such as the time a community member called and offered us Hitler's sterilizer that her soldier father had looted from Berchtesgaden at the end of the war and was now sitting in a shoebox in her clothes closet. (Hitler was obsessed with germs and used this steamer-like device to sterilize flatware, pots, pans, etc.) She wanted us to put it on display at the center. The wisecracking associated with this offer became legendary (e.g., "We will use it to make lattes!").

But on the whole, there can be no doubt that the generosity of the donors allowed us to pursue our work across a variety of disciplines in a way that would otherwise not have been possible. For the most part, stewardship was easy and even pleasurable; donors did not interfere or try to interfere in any of our activities and were our biggest cheerleaders. Even so, I had to combat the impression among faculty and even some graduate students that they did interfere, especially when it came to Israel. One interesting feature of the donor relationship had to do with their reactions to our steady stream of visiting Israeli professors and graduate students, almost all of whom could be easily placed on the leftist part of Israel's political spectrum. Donors were occasionally shocked at the radical views of the Israeli academics but felt constrained in their criticisms not only by the intellectual quality but also by the clear impression that all criticism of Israel from these scholars came from a place of concern and love for their country. Academic radicals who served in Israel's elite Sayeret Matkal commando unit did not easily back down.

More problematic, of course, was the occasional outbreak of anti-Israel activism and the dreary annual ritual of Israeli Apartheid Week. Although this activism always remained a minority affair, the rhetoric was troubling and the toxic drumbeat persistent. It never actually disappeared. In my final year at Toronto, a small group of professors backed some graduate students in a meeting calling for an academic boycott of Israel. The meeting was disrupted by the Jewish Defense League, and the police came and put an end to the event. Although I did not comment at the time, my basic attitude was that the two groups sort of deserved each other.

Jewish advocacy groups would constantly call me and ask for my support when anti-Israel events occurred on campus (such as the showing of the play *My Name Is Rachel Corrie*), but my response was always that our job as a center was academic and not political ("If you don't like the play, you have the right to go and leaflet it" was my response during that incident). In fact, any advocacy or politicization on our part would diminish the effectiveness of our educational mission. Teaching the donor community the difference between Hillel (which serves Jewish students) and an academic center with a scholarly mission required constant work.

Israel events on campus, especially one-off events sponsored by the community, are part of campus life, but they also become the focal point of anti-Israel activism. Such events are loud and fast and frenetic and full of young people testing out their own views and trying to gain the approval of their peers. Many sympathizers of anti-Israel groups do not actually know very much about the Middle East. Few have traveled there. Almost none have been to Israel. My impression is that the friends of the boycotters are mostly looking for approval and view the boycott as part of the broader package of the Left. They may be loud, but their commitment is thin, and they are likely to move on to other issues as quickly as they come to anti-Israel activism. They frequently depend on faculty support to sustain their interest, but even when they find sponsors, they remain a small group.

Where I believe we succeeded is not in countering this small group of activists with our own equally loud voices. That would not, in any case, have been wise or effective; professors are not activists and politicizing the classroom is what we want to avoid at all costs. Instead, we did the slow, quiet, thoughtful, and unglamorous work of teaching thousands of students in a range of disciplines. Over time at the University of Toronto, this created a huge group of students on campus who actually knew something about Israel and understood the true complexity of the situation. Many had traveled there, even those whom I would classify as hostile to Israel, with the support of the Center for Jewish Studies. What we do well as professors—our business, if you will—is teach and research. Anti-Israel propaganda that edges over into antisemitism will probably never go away, but my experience at Toronto indicates that it can be relativized and put into context for the vast majority of students and faculty. It is done slowly and by cultivating connections with Israeli academic institutions and by teaching dozens and dozens of courses. This is how a climate is made and transformed. This may seem, I realize, like a triumphalist story, but my point is a simpler one: anti-Israel campus climates cannot be transformed by banning speech or by large, externally driven and funded events such as visiting soldiers or ambassadors. They are forged by making possible what we do best: teaching and writing.

And so it was with this in mind that I went to UC Irvine in July 2015, ready for a small break from Jewish and Israel studies. I say *small* because one of the items I negotiated before signing on the dotted line with UCI was permission to raise funds for a chair in Israel studies in the Department of Political Science. Although I had no contacts in Orange County, I did have experience articulating a compelling vision for Jewish and Israel studies and raising money, and I had confidence that creating such a chair could not help but improve what was well known as a neuralgic point of campus politics.

After several weeks in Southern California, I could finally find my office without a campus map. I had yet to see any sign of anti-Israel activism, but it was still summer. As happens each year, the UCI Department of Political Science did host a visiting professor from Israel sponsored by the Shusterman Foundation (and now by the Israel Institute), but the classes taught were small and, since the professorship lasted only a year, no momentum of student interest could ever be sustained. Students with a deeper interest in Israel could try to participate in the Olive Tree Initiative trips to Israel, which were less academic than experiential and catered to small groups of handpicked students.

The talented and highly energetic head of Hillel on campus came to me at the beginning of September 2015 to tell me of an exciting initiative involving three Israeli Supreme Court justices visiting UCI to deliver lectures at various points in the academic year. This seemed like a wonderful idea, an opportunity for the campus to put behind it what had become an infamous event in February 2010, when Israeli ambassador Michael Oren was invited to give a lecture on campus and, after being interrupted numerous times and shouted down by serial protesters who were removed from the room by campus police, a deeply embarrassed administration shut down the event. Eleven of the student protesters from the Muslim Student Union (MSU) were arrested and ten convicted of conspiracy and disrupting a public meeting, and UCI sealed its reputation as a hotbed of anti-Israel activism. The incident became a source of tension not only among students but also among the professoriate, some supporting the protesters and others signing a letter of concern for Jewish and pro-Israel advocates on campus.

In subsequent years, although the main student groups (MSU and Students for Justice in Palestine [SJP]) remained active, many on campus had come to believe a page had been turned, and the atmosphere was calm enough to invite three Israeli Supreme Court justices to speak: former chief justice Aharon Barak, Justice Dalia Dorner, and Justice Salim Joubran. Barak's reputation as justice and scholar with a razor-sharp mind gave me a bit of confidence that he would be allowed to speak. I had seen him in action before, in Toronto, so I knew that he could handle even the most hostile and aggressive questions. The fact that Dorner is a woman and Joubran an Arab also lent credibility and promise to the whole venture.

In mid-September, my dean called to say that neither he nor the dean of the law school could attend the lecture and asked me to chair the session. I thought little of it and suggested that questions be written on cards so as to avoid lengthy sermons from the audience. On the evening of the lecture, I introduced Barak to an audience of approximately eighty community members and twenty students, a modest crowd. The lecture was complicated and intellectually taxing but high octane—on the meaning of *Jewish* and *democratic* in Israeli jurisprudence—and there could be no doubt we had a large and active mind on our hands. About halfway through his remarks, the head of Hillel approached me and said a group of approximately twenty-five anti-Israel protesters were standing outside the lecture hall. They had made signs and wanted into the room; I was told they seemed less interested in listening to the speaker than in protesting the event. The police had been called and informed the head of Hillel that they had no reason to keep the protesters out of the room.

At that moment, a decision had to be made: allow the protesters into the room and hope that they were willing to engage in some sort of back-and-forth with Barak or stall for time, allow Barak to finish his remarks, and then finish the event then and there with no questions and no exchange with the audience. Perhaps I made the wrong decision—I do not know—but I decided to have Barak finish his remarks and then end the session. The audience was full of Jewish community members (some of whom considered Barak too left-wing for their taste), and the protesters looked young and vigorous. I did not know the players well, and I worried about public safety (multiple stabbings had occurred in these months in Israel). I still question my decision. Did I violate free speech? Were the protesters interested in speech? I erred on the side of safety, but in doing so, perhaps I made the situation appear more dangerous than it was. In the end, the (mostly) Jewish attendees filed out past the (mostly Muslim) protesters—the low point in my experience of anti-Israel toxicity on any campus. And I had only just started.

What about Justices Dorner and Joubran? How would they be brought to campus after what had transpired with Barak? With Dorner, I did something that I thought was clever. In the winter quarter of 2016, I taught an introductory class in political science with 190 students, and one lecture carried the title "Dilemmas of Liberal Democracy: The Problem of Terrorism." I told the class that a special guest lecturer would attend but kept the identity of the guest speaker a secret. With a large number of female students, and especially Muslim female students, the class would provide a wonderful venue to discuss the vexing issues of the ticking bomb, the use of torture, and individual rights (a problem that an Israeli justice faces all too often)—and all of this delivered by a remarkable woman from the Middle East. As it happens, the class itself was a huge success, and Dorner took challenging questions from the students. Several in headscarves came up to me afterward to thank me.

After the lecture, I did a sort of mental victory lap. What a wonderful experience for those students, something they will not soon forget: a female Israeli Supreme Court justice, a refugee, a humanist, a proponent of equal rights for all Israelis, a tough and committed Zionist. It was only later that the sense of shame started to set in. What had I done? Was it not humiliating to have to bring an Israeli Supreme Court justice to campus secretly? How undignified to fear my own course being disrupted and how cowardly of me not to request support from the campus administration. The lecture went well, but would I have kept it a secret if Dorner were from Egypt rather than Israel?

As it happened, I did not need to figure out what to do with Joubran. He refused to speak at UCI, and it was explained to me that he had to be extraordinarily careful, as a sitting Supreme Court justice, not to be seen as engaging in politics, something that the campus climate at UCI would not permit.

Such was my initial confrontation with the politics of Israel at UCI. I was relieved to let others take up the cudgel. UCI remained quiet for the remainder of the 2015–2016 academic year, until May 18 (while I was in Israel), when two events occurred on campus. A high-profile lecture by Stephen Smith of the USC Shoah Foundation was hosted by the chancellor and attended by several hundred community members and students. Across campus, however, a small group of Jewish students—approximately ten—held a screening of the film *Beneath the Helmet*, an Israeli film, as part of Israel Peace Week (which followed the Muslim Student Union's anti-Zionism week earlier in the month during which a sturdy Apartheid Wall was constructed and labeled pre-1967 Israel as "occupied territory"). Anti-Israel protesters from SJP had gotten wind of the screening, and approximately fifty stood outside the room screaming, "Long live the Intifada!" Some tried to push open the door, but the small group held the door closed. Some of the attendees felt trapped in the room. A female student who came late to the screening was intimidated and allegedly chased by the protesters. The protesters themselves demanded to be let into the room, claiming it was their right to enter. Pro-Israeli students claimed it was harassment, while the protesters claimed they had a right to disrupt pro-Israeli events on campus. Police ultimately escorted the (largely female) audience members away, while Chancellor Howard Gillman noted that the incident "crossed the line of civility," going on to affirm the university's support for free speech but clarifying that this "right is not absolute ... threats, harassment, incitement, and defamatory speech are not protected. We must shelter everyone's right to speak freely—without fear or intimidation—and allow events to proceed without disruption or potential danger."[1]

Gillman's statement was welcome, but the promised investigations—carried out by the office of student affairs and the police—must, of necessity, proceed slowly.[2] In the meantime, Jerusalem University, a pro-Israel advocacy organization, together with a number of other organizations decided to double down and rescreen the film on campus with a much larger community and official presence, including that of an Israeli Defense Force (IDF) officer who would answer questions following the film. The event went off without disruption, but the statement of one sympathetic eyewitness perhaps summed up the campus climate at its worst: "The UCI administration and police successfully secured the event with the presence of approximately 30 uniformed officers inside and outside of the Student Center Auditorium, bomb-sniffing dogs, physical barriers, and strict security protocols requiring pre-registration and identification in order to enter the venue."[3] Hardly the description of an atmosphere conducive to nonpoliticized learning.

These sorts of events will always be focal points for student activism, and my preference, on both moral and prudential grounds, is not to outlaw or curtail this activism. On academic and intellectual grounds, boycotts can be successfully opposed (we study places, even places we find distasteful; we don't boycott them). Free speech on campus, however, although not an absolute right, almost always entails the fast and loud mobilization of young voices. Our job as professors is to slow down the conversation and to engage in the long and incremental work of intellectual inquiry. In my experience, campus events surrounding Israel are frequently disrupted. Classes and courses, on the other hand, are rarely disrupted. That is where the real learning occurs and the discussion outside of the classroom acquires its tenor. Anti-Zionist voices that verge into the antisemitic will be with us for a long time to come, but the American campus is still a place where intellectual arguments carry weight. Our job is to provide students with the tools and knowledge to understand and make arguments. If enough students can do so, the dysfunctional climates surrounding Israel on campus can begin to change. But it is slow and hard work and must be undertaken from within rather than from outside the university.

JEFFREY KOPSTEIN is Professor and Chair of Political Science at the University of California, Irvine. In his research, Kopstein focuses on interethnic violence, voting patterns of minority groups, and antiliberal tendencies in civil society, paying special attention to cases within European and Russian Jewish history.

Notes

1. Howard Gillman, "Respecting the Lines of Civility," UCI Office of the Chancellor (May 19, 2016), https://chancellor.uci.edu/engagement/campus-communications /2016/160519-ssi-incident.php (accessed November 2, 2017).

2. In August 2016, the university released its investigation and concluded that SJP had violated student conduct policies for disrupting the event. They received a written warning and were required to hold an "educational program" as a penalty. (See Lea Speyer, "Students for Justice in Palestine at UC Irvine Issued Written Warning Over Recent Violent Anti-Israel Protest on Campus," *The Algemeiner* (August 19, 2016), https://www.algemeiner .com/2016/08/19/students-for-justice-in-palestine-at-uc-irvine-issued-written-warning-over -recent-violent-anti-israel-protest-on-campus/.)

3. "JFFS/Hillel – Successful Rescreening of 'Beneath the Helmet,'" Jewish Federation and Family Services, Orange County (June 6, 2016), https://jewishorangecounty.org/resources /news/jffshillel-successful-rescreening-of-beneath-the-helmet (accessed November 2, 2017).

11   A Controversy at Harvard

Martin Kramer

Martin Kramer describes his experience as the target of a smear campaign.
At a conference, he discussed another scholar's work on the relationship
between demographics and radicalism and, applying it to Gaza, speculated
that if Israel's sanctions on Hamas's Gaza should slow the runaway population
growth there, that would also diminish the demographic push toward jihadi
radicalization and terrorist activity. The anti-Israel website *the Electronic
Intifada* promptly framed Kramer's remarks as a genocidal call against
Palestinian births, and the smear campaign was under way. When Harvard's
Weatherhead Center, where Kramer was a fellow, issued a substantive rejection
of the charges, anti-Israel activists attacked the center itself as a racist defender
of genocide, showing that they also target institutions that do not capitulate
to their dogma. Kramer analyzes the administration's role in the affair,
arguing that while administrations generally should remain neutral in such
controversies, in this case, its substantive weighing in was warranted.

Guys, @Martin_Kramer is not calling for genocide against Palestinians.
I disagree with him on most everything, but he just isn't.

—Marc Lynch, Professor of Political Science, on Twitter[1]

LET US ASSUME that a faculty member has come under a tidal wave of criticism
for something he or she said in defense of Israel or against the Palestinians. Let
us assume that the responsible administrators, while not in agreement with the
faculty member, believe that the assault is over the top. Should the administrators come to the defense of the faculty member? Or should they adopt a stance of
strict neutrality?

In February 2010, I was at the heart of just such a controversy at Harvard
University, in the role of the faculty member. In comparison to some of the
controversies narrated in this book, it wasn't a high-stakes battle. At the time,
I was in the last stretch of a courtesy appointment at Harvard's Weatherhead
Center for International Affairs. An earlier three-year appointment as a senior
fellow had ended; I had shuttered my Harvard project (a strategy blog) and left
campus the previous November. When the controversy erupted, I was in Israel,

having resumed my full-time duties as president-designate of a new college. I experienced the controversy from a distance, through emails and the internet. It was the flap of the month at Harvard before another one came along, and it had no lasting consequences.

But this episode, minor though it may have been, reflected in miniature the dynamics of the much larger controversies over Israel and the Palestinians that have roiled American campuses. And if the conduct of administrators in this case deserves special attention, it is because, after all, we are speaking of Harvard—an institution expected by many to embody the best practices in American academe.

An Experimental Speech

What did I say that ignited the controversy? At the time, I was one of the few academics invited regularly to address the Herzliya Conference, a festival of speeches and networking, renowned as a venue where Israeli leaders make important policy statements. It was (and remains) a three-ring circus, with simultaneous panels on every aspect of national security. At the 2010 conference, I was assigned a slot on a panel titled "Rising to the Challenge of Radical Indoctrination." I wasn't the headliner; that spot was taken by Baroness Pauline Neville-Jones, who, a few months later, would be appointed Britain's minister of state for security and counter-terrorism. I'd obviously been invited to provide academic ballast—or, if you will, filler. My affiliation on the printed program was "Senior Fellow, Shalem Center; National Security Studies Program, Harvard University," a small unit under the auspices of the Weatherhead Center.

If you aren't a top-billed speaker at Herzliya, you have only five or six minutes to make your point, and a digital countdown clock is prominently displayed to you and the audience. If you want your talk to be remembered (so that you'll be invited back), it needs to be punchy and provocative. I decided (at the last minute, as I recall) to float a thesis I had encountered in an article about Gaza by a German scholar in the *Wall Street Journal, Europe Edition*. There, he argued that in "youth bulge" countries with high fertility rates, "young men tend to eliminate each other or get killed in aggressive wars." In Gaza, international aid had encouraged high fertility. He concluded:

> As long as we continue to subsidize Gaza's extreme demographic armament, young Palestinians will likely continue killing their brothers or neighbors.... One may argue that by fueling Gaza's untenable population explosion, the West unintentionally finances a war by proxy against the Jews of Israel.
>   If we seriously want to avoid another generation of war in Gaza, we must have the courage to tell the Gazans that they will have to start looking after their children themselves, without [United Nations Relief and Works Agency for Palestine Refugees] UNRWA's help. This would force Palestinians to focus on building an economy instead of freeing them up to wage war. Of course,

every baby lured into the world by our money up to now would still have our assistance.[2]

I thought this was an intriguing thesis and decided to peg my six-minute talk on its premise, with a nod to its author. There was nothing particularly controversial in the way I laid out the broader argument about the Middle East. As one critic later allowed, "There is no individual sentence in Kramer's remarks that is incorrect, and the internal logic is consistent: the high birth rate does lead to increased terrorist violence; aid groups are encouraging that high birth rate; and so on."[3] But it was my finishing flourish that would prove incendiary:

> Aging populations reject radical agendas, and the Middle East is no different. Now eventually, this will happen among the Palestinians too, but it will happen faster if the West stops providing pro-natal subsidies for Palestinians with refugee status. Those subsidies are one reason why, in the ten years from 1997 to 2007, Gaza's population grew by an astonishing 40 percent. At that rate, Gaza's population will double by 2030 to three million. Israel's present sanctions on Gaza have a political aim—undermine the Hamas regime—but if they also break Gaza's runaway population growth—and there is some evidence that they have—that might begin to crack the culture of martyrdom which demands a constant supply of superfluous young men. That is rising to the real challenge of radical indoctrination, and treating it at its root.[4]

I wasn't just calling for a UNRWA policy change—an unlikely prospect. I was making a provocative argument in support of Israel's sanctions against Gaza, at precisely the moment when they had become the subject of a growing movement of pro-Palestinian opposition. Even as I spoke, Turkish activists were purchasing a ship, the *Mavi Marmara*, that would attempt to run Israel's blockade of Gaza four months later.

So I was venturing into stormy waters. But to be candid, I hadn't anchored my argument in much scholarship, nor had I formulated it very carefully. The concluding punchline did sound sinister. I had succumbed to the temptation to be provocative, in a venue that encouraged just that. A critic later wrote that "Kramer may have brought the academic's correct love of experimental, extreme, half-held opinions into the unwelcome realm of politics."[5] That's a fair summation of my mood at the time. I also thought it would be interesting to push back against the title of the panel, with its assumption that terrorism came down to "indoctrination" (or, as often claimed in Israel, "incitement"). This was also why my talk fell flat in the "unwelcome realm" of *Israeli* politics. An acquaintance expressed his disappointment in me. "You're an expert on Islamist *ideas*," he said. "Why didn't you concentrate on *that*?"

In any event, my talk left no trace, until I uploaded a video of it to YouTube and posted it on my website. I succumbed to yet another temptation: even though my talk wasn't a finished product by any stretch of the imagination, a personal website must be fed with new content to keep the traffic up. So I posted it—and it seemed to disappear again. One journalist friend did repost it on his website, and it prompted a spirited discussion in the comments section. But his readers didn't focus on Gaza at all; they seemed interested only in debating the "youth bulge" theory of terrorism.[6] After that, even I forgot about my talk; my own research agenda lay elsewhere.

Genocide!

But two weeks later, *The Electronic Intifada* website discovered my post and ran a piece about my talk under this blaring headline: "Harvard Fellow Calls for Genocidal Measure to Curb Palestinian Births." The article claimed I had "called for 'the West' to take measures to curb the births of Palestinians, a proposal that appears to meet the international legal definition of a call for genocide.... The 1948 U.N. Convention on the Prevention and Punishment of the Crime of Genocide, created in the wake of the Nazi holocaust, defines genocide to include measures 'intended to prevent births within' a specific 'national, ethnic, racial or religious group.'"[7]

Genocide! Harvard! This would become the rubric for the controversy that followed—one that I watched unfold, from a distance, with growing incredulity.

Had a Harvard fellow (or was he a professor?) advocated genocide? The echo chamber around *The Electronic Intifada* answered with a resounding "Yes!" I won't list the various sources of this response or the many forms it took. (Suffice it to say, it produced quite a few demonstrations of Godwin's law.[8]) Israel's perennial adversaries were the most vociferous, parsing my words from every conceivable angle to show that they most certainly did constitute a call to genocide and insisting that Harvard dismiss me or dissociate itself from me.

It's not pleasant to be denounced as an armchair *génocidaire*. But my critics, in following this strategy, also succumbed to a temptation. They sought to be provocative as well, to draw maximum attention and compel a response. The *genocide* trope definitely achieved that aim. But once they had brought attention to my remarks, would reasonable people draw the same conclusion they drew?

Assuming they might, I girded myself for battle. I knew I had the tools—above all, my own website and social media—to put across my rebuttals. My strategy would be fairly straightforward: you might not like my views, but you have to concede that I've been smeared by extremists who have hurled false accusations driven by ignorance (of genocide) and malice (against Israel). I even laid down a first volley in a blog post titled "Smear Intifada." (Sample: "Being accused of advocating genocide by people who daily call for Israel to be wiped off the map of the Middle East is rich."[9]) I figured it would be a pitched battle and that I would be writing every day.

So I was taken by surprise when three directors of the Weatherhead Center—the then-current one, who was on leave, and the two acting directors in her stead—issued their own statement, changing the whole picture.[10]

They began by noting that they had heard the demands that the center dissociate itself from me. The center had hundreds of affiliates, the directors pointed out; it did not monitor or control their activities or take any position "on any issue of scholarship or public policy." This could have been cut-and-pasted from any administration statement in any controversy. But it was followed by this: "Accusations have been made that Martin Kramer's statements are genocidal. These accusations are baseless. Kramer's statements express dismay with the policy of agencies that provide aid to Palestinian refugees and that tie aid entitlements to the size of refugee families. Kramer argues that this policy encourages population growth among refugee communities. While these views may be controversial, there is no way they can be regarded as genocidal."

This constituted much more than a boilerplate defense of my right to express my views. It was a substantive refutation of the most defamatory distortion of them, as retailed by *The Electronic Intifada* and repeated by its camp followers across the internet. And there was more: "Those who have called on the Weatherhead Center to dissociate itself from Kramer's views, or to end Kramer's affiliation with the Center, appear not to understand the role of controversy in an academic setting."

That sentence crossed over into criticism of my critics. Yes, I had made *controversial* statements, but asking for my dismissal or even dissociation displayed an ignorance of the workings of the academy. The statement concluded: "It would be inappropriate for the Weatherhead Center to pass judgment on the personal political views of any of its affiliates, or to make affiliation contingent on some political criterion. Exception may be made for statements that go beyond the boundaries of protected speech, but there is no sense in which Kramer's remarks could be considered to fall into this category. The Weatherhead Center's activities are based on a firm belief that scholars must be free to state their views, and [the center] rejects any attempts to restrict this fundamental academic freedom."

So there *was* a boundary, the directors affirmed, but my "personal political views" fell squarely on the protected side of it.

"Baseless," "no way," "no sense"—this was strong stuff. I hadn't asked for this statement, or any statement, so I was surprised by it—especially since I suspected that the three signatories strongly disagreed with what I had said. But the accusation that they were harboring a *génocidaire* compelled them to consider the actual content of my remarks. The result was not only a defense of my academic freedom but also a rebuke to those who had launched a smear campaign based on the genocide charge.

At that point, it was game over as far as I was concerned. I could stand down—something I couldn't have done if the directors hadn't taken a substantive position on the definition of *genocide*. I posted the directors' statement verbatim on my blog without comment and went silent.

The next day, the student newspaper the *Harvard Crimson* ran an editorial echoing the Weatherhead statement. It was headlined "Weatherheading the Storm: Martin Kramer's Strategy for Curbing Extremism Is Repugnant, but Not a Call for Genocide." The student editorial board described my advice as "morally offensive," "strategically inept," and "ethically unacceptable." But they also believed that "the blogosphere clearly overreacted in perpetuating the genocide meme created by *The Electronic Intifada* and others.... Considering the content of Kramer's speech, labeling his policy as 'genocide' is unfair, and steers the debate away from his actual argument." They ended by noting that "a diverse view like Kramer's will certainly foster the sort of debate the [Weatherhead] center seeks to promote" and added that they would not question my continued presence at the center. They urged the blogosphere to follow suit.[11]

The Electronic Intifada, by putting the genocide charge front and center, thus guaranteed that reasonable people who disagreed with me, sometimes vehemently, would nevertheless reject the loudest accusation against me as "baseless" and "unfair." The excesses of my critics worked to my advantage. Admittedly, it might have turned out differently at a lesser university. Harvard faculty are devoted to the analysis of texts, enamored of their own powers of interpretation, and disdainful of the internet herd. This ensured that my words would receive a reasonably fair and informed hearing—and that the genocide claim wouldn't stick.

The directors' statement (and the *Crimson* editorial) also ensured that the controversy wouldn't make the leap to the *The Chronicle of Higher Education* or *Inside Higher Ed*, the usual course of out-of-control brushfires. And it obviated the need for higher administration to respond. In sum, the directors' statement was smart, and it had the additional merit of being the right thing.

Duty of Neutrality?

Or was it? The wrathful crowd now turned on the Weatherhead Center. A headline in *The Electronic Intifada* announced that the center "defends fellow's pro-genocide statements."[12] Bloggers denounced the "reprehensible statement defending Kramer."[13] Closer to home, representatives of sixteen student groups at Harvard wrote to the directors. They were "alarmed that rather than taking a dissociating or even strictly neutral stance against such extremist and hateful statements, the Weatherhead Center issued a defensive response." The directors' characterization of my "deeply racist" statements as merely "controversial" was "alarming." (Oddly, no mention was made of the alarming genocide charge, which had prompted the directors' statement in the first place.[14]) "Defend," "defending," "defensive"—the overall impression was that the directors had defended me, period.

One of the Weatherhead directors, a human rights scholar, was especially sensitive to this criticism, and she went to lengths to signal to my critics that she had upheld my academic freedom with reluctant resignation. I had no doubt she genuinely reviled my views, although it would have been more interesting had she made a reasoned critique of them. Instead, in two letters to editors, she attempted to parse the directors' statement in implausible ways.

"The center never exonerated Kramer from those who have disagreed with him"—a half-truth, since it certainly did exonerate me from the genocide charge.[15] "Do not make the mistake of concluding that the Weatherhead Center has defended Mr. Kramer's positions," she wrote in another letter. The Weatherhead statement "only makes the case that the speech in question is probably protected, for better or for worse."[16] But this wasn't the *only* case the directors made. If it were, I wouldn't have circulated their statement, and my critics wouldn't have denounced it.

I was tempted to respond, but this time, I resisted. If there was one thing I and my critics agreed on, it was our reading of the directors' statement. She also admitted she didn't speak on behalf of the other two directors; they remained silent. So, while she may have raised a clenched fist in solidarity with my critics, all that really mattered was that she, too, had put her signature on that statement. Indeed, without it, the statement could not have been issued at all. I decided that no more needed to be said.

The most important and interesting criticism of the statement came from a Harvard professor, Stephen Walt, a member of the Weatherhead Center's executive committee. Walt was no stranger to Harvard-class controversy: his 2006 Kennedy School working paper, "The Israel Lobby and U.S. Foreign Policy," coauthored with the University of Chicago's John Mearsheimer, had caused a firestorm. At the time, the Kennedy School issued a statement that "it stands firmly behind the academic freedom of its faculty, including Professor Stephen Walt." But somehow the Harvard logo disappeared from the paper, and a more explicit disclaimer replaced the usual boilerplate.[17] When accusations flew at Walt (a rebuttal in *the Washington Post* carried the headline "Yes, It's Antisemitic"), Harvard remained neutral. Given his own experience, how would he take this statement by his faculty colleagues?

In a post on his blog, Walt began by dismissing the genocide claim as a distraction: "I think the word 'genocide' has become a loaded term that gets tossed around too loosely, which makes it easy for Kramer and his defenders to portray legitimate criticism of his extreme views as over the top." In any case, he added, "what word you use to describe his comments is actually not that important"— they were "appalling," "horrific," "offensive," and "chilling" in their own right.

(On this point, my most vocal critics obviously disagreed. For them, the *g*-word had been the point of it all.) He allowed that "it would be wrong for Harvard officials to cut off Kramer because they disagreed with what he said or even found it offensive." That would be an infringement of academic freedom.

But he then made a very specific criticism of the directors' statement: "Notice that the Weatherhead Directors did not quite 'refrain from passing judgment' on what Kramer said. The appropriate stance to adopt whenever a faculty member or affiliated researcher takes a controversial or unpopular position is strict neutrality; the *institution*, or its official representatives, should take no position at all about the validity of the person's views. Therefore, they should have defended Kramer's right to say what he did but refrained from commenting on whether the accusations against him were 'baseless' or not."[18]

To my mind, Walt posed the only lasting question to arise from the entire episode, and I have given his opinion quite a bit of thought—partly because I have spent the years since this controversy as a college president, wondering what I would do were I confronted with a similar dilemma. It remains a theoretical question: my college is very small, and I haven't had a comparable controversy on my watch.

But as a matter of broad principle, as regards higher administration, I agree with Walt. In a research university, or even in a smaller college, higher administration cannot possibly be expected to determine what is baseless or not in the range of fields represented by the faculty. Only academic peers can begin to make that determination, and even they may differ. If such a determination is necessary, the appropriate approach of higher administration should be the appointment of a committee of peers to review the case.

But the Weatherhead directors were not higher administration. They constituted the mid-level academic leadership of a center for international affairs. And these three professors (of international relations and government) did not pass judgment on all the accusations against me, just a specific one: the claim that my statements were genocidal. Defining concepts such as *genocide* is one of the basic competencies of the Weatherhead Center's faculty. Who if not they? For Weatherhead's directors to have taken a position of strict neutrality on what constitutes a genocidal statement would have been unconscionable, especially as they agreed unanimously that my own statements didn't qualify.

So I would modify Walt's position. Yes, higher administration does have an obligation to practice strict neutrality. As a rule, it isn't equipped academically to do otherwise. But in the constituent units and departments of a university, academically qualified administrators have a right to take a position. To abstain is to forfeit their own ground to the blogosphere or Twitter, both teeming with activists animated by agendas. The administrators should exercise their right through the mechanism that governs all academic life, the committee of peers. In my case, the Weatherhead directors constituted just such an ad hoc committee.

They should also act expeditiously—if need be, within hours. "Rather than encouraging scholarly debate on this most grave of issues," complained one critic, "the Directors of the Weatherhead Center instead chose to invoke Dr. Kramer's academic freedom in order to suppress academic discussion of the matter." The complaints against me should have been "examined and discussed."[19] Obviously, examination and discussion are the essence of the academic enterprise (and nothing the Weatherhead directors did precluded it). But when controversies bleed into the internet and social media and become part of a news cycle, lack of swift action can do irreparable damage to the reputations of individuals and institutions. If academic administrators have an advantage during such controversies, it is because they are more likely to have thought through contentious issues already. If they can't act both judiciously and expeditiously in intellectual controversies, they have very little to commend them over professional bureaucrats.

Lessons of a Controversy

I write these lines six years after the affair. For me, it was a virtual controversy. It would have been very different had I been coming in each morning to the Weatherhead Center or crossing Harvard Yard or dining at the Faculty Club. I was half a world away, and my loose affiliation with Harvard was set to expire anyway. The episode (Walt called it a "ruckus") had no lasting consequences, either for my career or my reputation. Once, when I alluded to it in a conversation in Washington, my interlocutor said: "Yeah, I remember it. Some crazies came after you, but the university stood by you." If anyone beyond Cambridge recalls the episode, that is probably how it is (vaguely) remembered. The affair didn't follow me.

But I won't pretend that the ruckus didn't leave its mark on me. I had said goodbye to Harvard with a feeling of mission accomplished. That feeling dissipated. I also felt guilt (and gratitude) toward those who brought me to Harvard and who actively defended me behind the scenes after I left. For them, the controversy wasn't virtual at all, and they took their share of flak. I made one or two tactical compromises to make their lives easier; I wish I could have done more. Later, in May, the *Crimson* asked me if I would contribute an op-ed on the controversy to the commencement issue. I figured my friends had been through enough, and I took a pass.

I came away with three lessons, which I have tried to apply to myself but may be applicable more broadly. The first almost goes without saying. The Arab-Israeli conflict is not a place for thought experimentation. Don't take any positions or make any analyses that aren't thoroughly considered. There is nothing wrong with being provocative, and I have continued to provoke. One should never shy from controversy, and I haven't. But everything written and spoken should be the product of research and reflection. Academics shouldn't shoot from the hip, nor should they be tempted to reduce complex ideas to sound bites. I have become more deliberate (which may be why I'm no longer an invited speaker at the Herzliya Conference).

The second lesson: over-the-top accusations by your opponents are your best friends. For some reason, the Palestinian cause attracts more than its fair share of exaggerators, fantasists, and conspiracy theorists. In any given controversy, outlandish and nonsensical accusations will fly. Put the focus on them, highlight them, dispute them. There is a notion that even if they are untrue, something of them will stick. That is the entire premise of smear factories like *The Electronic Intifada*. But there will always be people in an academic setting who will feel that excessive claims, against Israel or against you, insult their intelligence. Deepen the sense of insult by shoving the most outrageous claims beneath their noses.

The third lesson: never apologize, retract, or delete. No one will rally to someone in retreat. If critics are spinning your words one way, spin them back the other way. Even if your original formulation was flawed, don't scrap it. Explain it, interpret it, elaborate on it, but don't walk it back. If administrators see you apologize, they will sigh in relief and sacrifice you to your opponents. If they see you are prepared to wage a long, drawn-out, take-no-prisoners battle, they just may make a statement to mollify you in order to bring the controversy to a swift end. If faculty and students see you are determined to fight, they are more likely to suspend judgment until you have had your say. If you can't persuade them that you are right, then try to plant a seed of doubt. Sometimes that's all it takes to win.

Risks and Rewards

I have focused here on the mechanics of a specific controversy, but what about the larger purpose of controversy? The Weatherhead Center directors, in their statement, said that those who demanded my dismissal "appear not to understand the role of controversy in an academic setting." What is that role?

It is to open a discussion that might otherwise never take place because the risks of opening it form a barrier. While a handful of academic gadflies weave in and out of controversies all the time, the vast majority of practicing academics do everything possible to avoid them. A controversy can make a career, but it can also break one, so why take the risk? And the more controversial a subject becomes in the political arena, the more risk attends to saying anything new about it in the academic one. This is true of Israel, the Palestinians, terrorism, Islam, and a host of topics related to the Middle East.

So why chance it? "Our own staff discussed your comments at length," I was told by the *Crimson* editor who solicited my contribution to the commencement issue, "and there were very different opinions on the matter. Many people submitted op-eds on the topic, and your statements elicited some of the best dialogue our page has seen all year."[20] That is controversy's reward, and perhaps that was my parting contribution to the intellectual life of Harvard. Students watched, listened, thought, debated. And while my intervention wasn't my scholarship at its best, it did bring out the best in the responses of some students.[21] If the affair incidentally caused some discomfort among administrators—well, this is exactly what they are paid to endure.

So in retrospect, I do not regret my Harvard controversy. It made some Harvard students think, and perhaps this retrospective can benefit faculty and administrators elsewhere. I don't recommend that those who believe they have something important to say about Israel actively seek controversy. For me, the costs of this episode ranged from very low to nil; for someone else, the costs might be appreciably higher. But there will always be openings—windows in time where there is greater receptivity to thoughtful ideas and less tolerance for crude polemics. These openings work to Israel's advantage and should never be wasted.

MARTIN KRAMER is President Emeritus of Shalem College in Jerusalem. During a twenty-five-year academic career at Tel Aviv University, he directed the Moshe Dayan Center for Middle Eastern and African Studies. He is author, most recently, of *The War on Error: Israel, Islam, and the Middle East.*

Notes

1. Marc Lynch on Twitter, February 24, 2010, https://twitter.com/abuaardvark /status/9598175486 (accessed November 13, 2017).

2. Gunnar Heinsohn, "Ending the West's Proxy War Against Israel," *Wall Street Journal Europe* (January 12, 2009).

3. Marc Tracy, "Harvard Affiliate Lambasted over Gaza Remarks," *Tablet* (March 9, 2010), http://web.archive.org/web/20100312102342/http://www.tabletmag.com/scroll /27775/harvard-affiliate-lambasted-over-gaza-remarks/?.

4. Martin Kramer, "Superfluous Young Men," *Sandbox* (February 7, 2010), http://web.archive.org/web/20100314085450/http://www.martinkramer.org/sandbox /2010/02/superfluous-young-men.

5. Tracy, "Harvard Affiliate."

6. Michael J. Totten, "'Radical Islam Is a Way for the Superfluous Sons to Enter History,'" *Michael J. Totten* (February 6, 2010), http://web.archive.org/web/20100210193340/http://www .michaeltotten.com/2010/02/%E2%80%9Cradical-islam-is-a-way-for-the-superfluous-sons -to-enter-history%E2%80%9D.php (accessed November 2, 2017).

7. "Harvard Fellow Calls for Genocidal Measure to Curb Palestinian Births," *The Electronic Intifada* (February 22, 2010), http://web.archive.org/web/20110709041625/

http://electronicintifada.net/content/harvard-fellow-calls-genocidal-measure-curb -palestinian-births/8692.

8. Godwin's Law is the adage that the longer an online discussion goes on, the probability of someone comparing someone to Hitler increases.

9. Martin Kramer, "Smear Intifada," *Sandbox* (February 22, 2010), http://web.archive .org/web/20100226084216/ http://www.martinkramer.org/sandbox/2010/02/smear-intifada.

10. Text of directors' statement archived at http://web.archive.org/web/20100303104811/ http://www.martinkramer.org/sandbox/2010/02/wcfia-at-harvard-accusations-are-baseless (accessed November 2, 2017). The signatories were Beth Simmons, Professor of International Affairs; Jeffry Frieden, Professor of Government; and James Robinson, Professor of Government.

11. "Weatherheading the Storm," *The Harvard Crimson* (February 25, 2010).

12. "Harvard Center Condemns, Then Defends, Fellow's Pro-Genocide Statements," *The Electronic Intifada* (February 23, 2010), http://web.archive.org/web/20110608120741/http:// electronicintifada.net/content/harvard-center-condemns-then-defends-fellows-pro -genocide-statements/8697.

13. Richard Silverstein, "Martin Kramer, Advocate of Genocide, Infanticide, or Just Plain Anti-Muslim Racism?" *Tikun Olam* (February 23, 2010), http://web.archive.org/web /20130827210749/http://www.richardsilverstein.com/2010/02/23/martin-kramer-advocate -of-genocide-infanticide-or-just-plain-anti-muslim-racism/.

14. John F. Bowman, Maryam Monalisa Gharavi, and Abdelnasser A. Rashid, "On Kramer's Statements," *The Harvard Crimson* (March 11, 2010).

15. Beth Simmons, "Harvard Center Thrives on Free Exchange of Ideas," *The Boston Globe* (March 10, 2010).

16. Beth Simmons, "Responding to Student Concerns About the Weatherhead Controversy," *The Harvard Crimson* (April 1, 2010).

17. Scott Jaschik, "War of Words over Paper on Israel," *Inside Higher Ed* (March 27, 2006), http://web.archive.org/web/20060505181301/http://insidehighered.com/news /2006/03/27/israel.

18. Stephen M. Walt, "Kramer vs. Kramer," *ForeignPolicy.com* (February 28, 2010), http://web.archive.org/web/20150222130627/http://foreignpolicy.com/2010/02/28/kramer -versus-kramer/.

19. Patrick Wolfe, "Dr. Martin Kramer's Allegedly Genocidal Remarks," *H-Genocide Discussion Logs* (February 27, 2010), http://www.webcitation.org/6gQcINhxe.

20. Private communication, May 18, 2010.

21. A good example is Jeremy Patashnik, "A (Somewhat) Modest Proposal, Literally," *HPRgument Blog* (February 24, 2010), http://web.archive.org/web/20150530053122/ http:// harvardpolitics.com/online/hprgument-blog/a-somewhat-modest-proposal-literally/.

12 Attempts to Exclude Pro-Israel Views from Progressive Discourse: Some Case Studies from Australia

Philip Mendes

Philip Mendes, for years at the forefront of the Jewish Left in Australia, which advocated for Palestinian rights and the two-state solution, notes that today most Australian Jews endorse the two-state solution while almost no pro-Palestinian activists do. The dominant position instead, that of eliminating Israel, he associates with the BDS movement's success in excluding pro-Israel voices from progressive debates, as several case studies illustrate. He describes his conversations with the Australasian Middle East Studies Association (AMESA) about fostering better relations with the Australian Jewish community, noting that when he called for discussion of the Israeli narrative he was purged from the organization. When he published an essay critical of suicide bombings, he was vilified by the pro-Palestinian Australian Left. A respected leftist journal also published a personal attack charging him with racism and following it with nasty libelous charges. The episodes demonstrate the now-mainstream leftist belief that even those Jewish or Israeli voices that are critical of Israeli occupation must be silenced, for only eliminationist discourse is acceptable.

I HAVE SUPPORTED a "two states for two peoples" solution to the Israeli-Palestinian conflict for over thirty-three years, since I was caught up as a naive seventeen-year-old first-year university student in the ill winds and polarization of the Lebanon War debate at Melbourne University. For me, two states has always meant simply the right of Israel to exist as a sovereign Jewish state within roughly the pre-1967 Green Line borders and equally the right of the Palestinians to an independent state within the West Bank and Gaza Strip. This means no coerced Jewish settlements within Palestinian territory and equally no coerced return of Palestinian refugees within Green Line Israel.[1]

My two-state position has long attracted criticism from extremists on both sides of the conflict. During the 1980s and early 1990s, prior to the signing of the Oslo peace accord, much opposition came from conservative Australian Jews who defended Likud's Greater Israel project and were intolerant of any political solution that involved legitimizing Palestinian nationalism. I have written elsewhere about the aggressive backlash that criticisms of Israel's West Bank settlements provoked in that period.[2]

Yet most Jews have shifted their position since the outbreak of the Second Palestinian Intifada and now endorse a two-state solution involving the creation of a Palestinian state alongside Israel.[3] It is relatively easy today to be pro-Israel and at the same time to espouse the two-state view traditionally associated with left-wing Israeli groups such as the Meretz alliance and the Peace Now movement.

In contrast, it has become very difficult, if not impossible, to be pro-Palestinian and support a two-state perspective. Many Australian leftists who strongly advocated peace and reconciliation in the Oslo era have instead regressed to the earlier pre-1988 Palestine Liberation Organization (PLO) position in favor of Israel's destruction. It is now called in this politically correct era the *one-state solution* instead of the earlier terminology of a *secular democratic state*. In practice, it means that Israel will cease to exist either by military violence or political coercion and will be replaced by a majority Arab state of Palestine, neither secular nor democratic, in which Jews will at best be allowed to remain as a tolerated religious, not national, minority. This extremist position has been accompanied by highly aggressive and shrill attempts associated with the Boycott, Divestment, and Sanctions (BDS) movement to exclude pro-Israel voices from progressive debates.

The three case studies that follow document attempts by pro-Palestinian advocates to misrepresent, demonize, and ultimately silence two-state advocates. The first attack occurred in 1998 at the height of the Oslo peace process within an academic association. The following two attacks, in 2003 and 2010, also involved academics acting either individually or via association with a journal or professional society. Noticeably, some anti-Zionist Jews were prominent in all three events.

I have noted elsewhere that a small number of Jews seem to play a prominent role in propagating extreme attacks on Zionism and Israel. One particularly contentious strategy used by Jewish anti-Zionists is to provide an alibi for antisemitic critics of Israel by arguing that Jews also share their views.[4] The opinions of these totally unrepresentative groups of anti-Zionist Jews are then opportunistically exploited by rabid anti-Zionists such as the sacked American academic Steven Salaita, who proudly called antisemitism "honorable."[5] The left-wing UK scholar David Hirsh rightly judges some of these Jewish interventions to be overtly racist: "Jews too can make antisemitic claims, use antisemitic images, support antisemitic exclusions, and play an important, if unwitting, part in preparing the ground for the future emergence of an antisemitic movement."[6]

Case Study One: Blocking a Zionist Takeover of the Australasian Middle East Studies Association

For nearly fifteen years, from 1987 to 2001, I was active in the left-wing Australian Jewish Democratic Society (AJDS). The AJDS position on the Middle East was very straightforward: a two-state solution as described above. AJDS utilized various strategies and networks to further that objective. One of the key strategies was to organize links with members of the local Palestinian and Arab communities.

Central to this strategy was showing the rest of the Jewish community that Jews willing to recognize Palestinian rights and aspirations would receive positive feedback from local Palestinians and Arabs. A further implicit motivation was that successful Jewish-Arab dialogue in Australia, based on mutual recognition and compromise, could perhaps be seen as a model for successful peace negotiations within Israel-Palestine.

I have noted elsewhere that this strategy was not particularly successful, at least in the pre-2000 period.[7] One exception, however, appeared to be the AMESA, an academic association consisting of both academics teaching in Middle East studies—some of whom were Arabs and others who were Anglo-Saxon—and members of the local Palestinian and Arab communities.

Throughout the period of the AMESA's existence (from about 1981 onwards), leading AJDS figure Norman Rothfield and other AJDS representatives had regularly been invited to speak at AMESA conferences and welcomed within AMESA circles. My own involvement in the AMESA had perhaps been less significant but had included presentations at two AMESA conferences, contributions to the Deakin University (and AMESA-linked) *Journal of Arabic, Islamic and Middle Eastern Studies*, and contributions to the *AMESA Newsletter*.[8]

In addition, I submitted in November 1997 (at the request of a key AMESA and Arab community figure) a witness statement to the Australian Human Rights and Equal Opportunity Commission supporting a case by the Australian Arabic Council against the News Limited–owned *Herald* and *Weekly Times* and the hawkish pro-Israel advocacy group Australia/Israel Publications (AIP). Briefly, the matter involved some allegedly racist anti-Arab statements made by a visiting AIP-sponsored speaker, David Pryce-Jones, which had been published by the daily Melbourne newspaper, the *Herald Sun*.[9] The matter was subsequently settled out of court, and the Australian Arabic Council thanked me in writing for "your very honest and powerful witness statement, and all your support throughout the two-year case."[10] I mention this in order to make the point that no one associated with the AMESA would have been left with any doubts regarding my goodwill and willingness (at least at that time) to critique not only Israeli extremism but also anti-Arab prejudice within the Jewish community.

Not only this, but two prominent AMESA and Arab community academics, Ray Jureidini and Christine Asmar, had approached me to draft a joint opinion piece on Jewish-Palestinian community relations in Australia. The article was intended to pinpoint the negative aspects of existing relations and the future potential for improving relations. For example, the emphasis was to be on the common interests of Jewish and Palestinian Australians around support for multiculturalism, opposition to racism, and opposition to media and public stereotypes regarding Middle East and non-Christian religions. Plans were even made for the publication of a joint monograph on Palestinian and Jewish experiences of otherness and racism in Australia.

It should be noted that the AMESA was always a highly contentious organization within the Australian Jewish community. There were two principal perspectives on the AMESA. One view—held by much of the mainstream Jewish community and particularly by AIP (which is now known as the Australia Israel Jewish Affairs Council [AIJAC])—was that the AMESA was a hardline pro-Palestinian propagandist body uninterested in any serious dialogue or debate with the Jewish community.[11] According to this view, any Jewish involvement in the AMESA was tokenistic and would merely be disingenuously used by the AMESA to deflect claims of bias. The organization was arguably beyond repair.

The second view—held by the AJDS and also other mostly left-leaning Jewish academics who participated in AMESA activities—was that the AMESA was a broad organization that was open to significant Jewish involvement and input. For the AJDS particularly, the AMESA was a testing ground for the theory that Jews committed to Israeli-Palestinian peace and justice would provoke a positive response from local Palestinian and Arab intellectuals and activists. And conversely, that greater Jewish participation would help to marginalize the propagandists and extremists and ensure that the AMESA acted as a genuinely impartial academic body.

My own experience within the AMESA would suggest that the AIJAC was almost certainly right and the AJDS and others were wrong.

In late 1998, I was invited by the president of the AMESA, Asmar, to contribute an article to the *AMESA Newsletter* exploring how the AMESA might improve its relations with the Jewish community. The submitted piece made the following points: that there was at best token representation of Jews in the AMESA, that there appeared to be a built-in structural bias against Jewish representation within the AMESA, and that, nevertheless, there were different views within the Jewish community about the AMESA, including some interest in identifying common ground.

In order to facilitate constructive engagement, I suggested the following:

- The AMESA adopt for its 1999 conference the theme of "Jewish/Arab dialogue and friendship, historically and today"

- The AMESA invite the Executive Council of Australian Jewry to nominate two representatives to participate in the Conference Planning Committee
- The AMESA invite the Israeli ambassador and the Palestinian National Authority ambassador to co-open proceedings
- The AMESA invite a mainstream Israeli writer or academic as a keynote speaker
- The AMESA invite the editor of the *Australian Jewish News* and a commensurate Arab community newspaper to speak at a joint session on Australian media presentations of Jews and Arabs and on possibilities for joint action against racist coverage
- The AMESA publicly debate the merits of electing a Jewish supporter of Israel as president within the next five years

I suggested that these proposals would "probably constitute the minimum needed to convince the Jewish community that the AMESA is genuinely becoming what it has always claimed publicly to be: an impartial academic body committed to encouraging Jewish/Arab dialogue and discourse, rather than to promoting the Palestinian cause, or any other narrow ideological or political agenda."[12]

To my surprise, the AMESA chose to publish six responses to my article in the same issue of their newsletter without either my prior knowledge or permission. Three of the responses, from Orit Shapiro, Clive Kessler, and the AMESA Committee, were broadly positive. For example, the AMESA Committee recommended organizing a panel for their next conference jointly with the Australian Association of Jewish Studies on Arab-Jewish relations.[13]

However, the other three responses—from academics Ray Jureidini, John Docker, and Ned Curthoys—were vociferously critical.[14] Their common concern seemed to be that my proposals would transform the AMESA from a pro-Palestinian organization into potentially a pro-Israel organization.

Jureidini later informed me that he had not been told that my piece was commissioned by the AMESA and would probably have responded very differently if he had been aware.

But Docker, a long-standing Jewish anti-Zionist, was the main concern.[15] He argued absurdly that my intention was to "intimidate, threaten and marginalize Jewish intellectuals" who did not conform to the Jewish community consensus. He claimed that my proposals would lead to the policing of ideas and to surveillance and control of the AMESA by powerful Zionists who had also allegedly suppressed free debate and discussion in the Australian media. Similarly, Docker's son Ned Curthoys, another anti-Zionist fundamentalist, argued bizarrely that my proposal was "grotesque" and reflected a totalitarian vision for society.[16]

Both Docker and Curthoys were fully aware that their ad hominem criticisms totally misrepresented my viewpoint. I had argued since the early 1980s, both within and outside the Jewish community, for the legitimacy of Palestinian national aspirations, for the creation of an independent Palestinian state alongside Israel, and for a free and tolerant Jewish debate around these issues. I was the last person who could reasonably be accused of wanting to censor anyone.

But worse was to come. I wrote a short, careful, and arguably measured response to the six responses, pointing out the negatives and positives and trying to focus again on the desired objective of achieving better relations between the AMESA and the Jewish community. My reply was critical of Docker et al., but not exceptionally so. Initially, Asmar indicated that she would have to cut my letter to one page, to which I reluctantly agreed. She also indicated at the same time that our proposed joint paper on Palestinian-Jewish relations would not go ahead. Too busy, she claimed, but I later wondered whether she had been warned off by someone in her own community.

One month later, I was informed by the new *AMESA Newsletter* editor, Aileen Keating, that she had cut and rewritten (without consultation) my letter to 150 words. I subsequently wrote a protest letter to the AMESA president but to no avail. The organization had closed ranks, and I was purged. My experience of Jewish-Arab dialogue was over.

I subsequently discussed my experience with a number of Jewish friends and acquaintances of varying viewpoints. The general consensus seemed to be that Jewish-Arab dialogue was a waste of time given that local Palestinian and Arab groups seemed to have little interest in promoting moderate and peaceful outcomes. On a personal level, the AMESA experience convinced me that local Arabs and Palestinians (with some exceptions) were only interested in one-sided dialogue—that is, talking to Jews who offered unilateral criticism of Israel, rather than criticism of both sides.

Case Study Two: Using Personal Attacks to Silence Pro-Israel Views

Many Jewish Left groups and individuals were profoundly affected by the outbreak of the Second Palestinian Intifada in September 2000 and the associated breakdown of the Oslo peace process. There was no uniform Jewish Left response to the Second Intifada. Some groups and individuals embraced the pro-Palestinian Left and became enthusiastic advocates of the so-called Right of Return and later the BDS movement. But others, including myself, responded to the violence and terror perpetrated by Palestinians during the 2000–2004 period by constructing a more critical analysis of Palestinian views and actions, politically and historically.[17]

In early 2003, I wrote and circulated a structural critique of Palestinian suicide bombings that was later published in the left-wing American journal *Jewish Currents*.[18] The article argued that there was no progressive justification for suicide bombings, which constituted a reactionary response to oppression that failed to target the real causes of Palestinian disadvantage. The article appeared to have upset some pro-Palestinian apologists on the Left who believed that suicide bombings should be understood or even endorsed as a reasonable response to the structural oppression of the Palestinians rather than condemned outright.

Consequently, a left-wing Jewish academic critical of Israel, whom I will call by the pseudonym of Bob Cohen, wrote a letter to the social work department at Monash University dated April 17, 2003, attacking my academic integrity and demanding that I desist from further commentary on Middle East politics. Cohen added in a brief follow-up letter that he was a committee member of a group called Jews for a Just Peace (J4JP) and implied he was writing on their behalf. The J4JP was a short-lived group formed in May 2002 to oppose Israel's West Bank occupation and promote the establishment of a Palestinian state alongside Israel. The J4JP was a slightly more radical organization than the AJDS and arguably acted as a ginger group within the AJDS with a view to encouraging the society to move further to the left in its criticisms of Israel.

The letter writer implied that I knew nothing about Jewish affairs (even though I held an adjunct position in the Monash University Center for Jewish Civilization) and little about politics in the Middle East or elsewhere (even though my doctorate involved a political and historical analysis of a social policy advocacy group and I had published numerous articles on Israeli-Palestinian politics in scholarly journals). The letter ended with an implied threat of legal action if I did not accede to this demand.

Following receipt of the letter, I contacted the official spokespersons for the J4JP group, Sandra Goldbloom Zurbo and Barry Carr. They were clearly embarrassed by Cohen's actions and clarified that they had not known about the letter beforehand and did not endorse either its contents or method of delivery. They added that they endorsed a civil public debate between Jews with different points of view but did not state any intention to reprimand Cohen for his actions aimed precisely at silencing scholarly debate.

Eventually, Cohen wrote me an apology, regretting the "tone and substance" of his earlier letters and acknowledging his "error of judgement." He did not indicate any understanding as to why it might be ethically inappropriate to write to an academic's employer questioning his integrity and threatening legal action to stifle his voice in a public debate. Nor did he comment on the importance of protecting freedom of speech for all opinions on the Israeli-Palestinian conflict.

While this episode on its own is rather minor and generated no serious harm, Cohen's behavior did suggest that the pro-Palestinian lobby was increasingly determined to censor any views other than their own.

Case Study Three: Turning Scholarship into an Anti-Israel Platform

Overland is a Melbourne-based academic journal formed by ex-communist Stephen Murray-Smith in 1954 to promote progressive and democratic debate. Although Murray-Smith published a powerful critique of Soviet antisemitism in 1965, *Overland* has rarely covered Jewish-related issues. To the best of my knowledge, it rarely, if ever, published material on Israel until 2007.

However, under the editorship from 2007 to 2014 of Jeff Sparrow, founder and longtime activist in the Far Left Trotskyist group Socialist Alternative, which aggressively opposes the existence of Israel, the pro-Palestinian lobby captured *Overland*'s agenda. For example, extreme anti-Zionist articles appeared in issues 184 and 187 by Ned Curthoys, 193 by Antony Loewenstein, and 198 by Michael Brull. These formed a mad hatter's picnic of fanatical attacks on Israel and supporters of Israel.

The most concerning and strident polemic was arguably that of Brull, a blogger for the tiny anti-Zionist group known as Independent Australian Jewish Voices, which oddly claims to support a two-state solution while regularly demonizing Israel and supporters of Israel. Brull's particular contribution was rambling, repetitive, contradictory, and of a standard that one might expect to find on a blog devoid of editorial oversight, not as an article in a refereed intellectual journal. Particularly bizarre were his final four paragraphs, which consisted of ad hominem hysterical abuse of myself and others. In particular, he accused me of "poisoning public discourse with vicious and unwarranted charges of antisemitism."[19] This misrepresentation of my views and opinions on the nature of the relationship between anti-Zionism and antisemitism (which I have always portrayed as reflecting complex historical and political influences) is not surprising since Brull has regularly levied similar ridiculous accusations on his blog.[20] What is surprising is that a serious journal chose to publish this unsubstantiated nonsense.

In response to this one-sided discourse, a group of six Australian academics (consisting of Douglas Kirsner, Andrew Markus, Bill Anderson, Bernard Rechter, Nick Dyrenfurth, and myself) sent a polite but firm private letter to the *Overland* editor, editorial board, and patron, Barry Jones. The letter questioned why *Overland* chose to highlight the most extreme voices who "contribute only fanatical polemics and represent nobody in either the Jewish community or the Left, and chose to ignore or actively censor the large group of Jewish (and broader Left) voices who support two states, strongly oppose Israeli settlements and expansionism, but also totally reject the simplistic 'Israel oppressor, Palestinians victim' argument presented by Curthoys et al., and seek to promote Israeli-Palestinian peace and reconciliation rather than continued violence and enmity. Their views represent the majority of the Left, but seem to have been deliberately excluded from the pages of *Overland* magazine."

The *Overland* editor, Sparrow, immediately published this letter on the *Overland* blog without our permission. He then launched into an inflammatory polemic, claiming erroneously that we had argued that *Overland* excluded contributors on the basis of ethnic or religious affiliations.[21] Our letter, in fact, made no reference to antisemitism, and Sparrow's argument conformed to a long-standing Far Left political strategy whereby any criticisms of anti-Zionist fundamentalism are deliberately misrepresented as allegations of antisemitism. The intention behind this strategy is to delegitimize any critique of hardline pro-Palestinian arguments as involving "crying wolf" tactics and hence not deserving of a serious response. This also neatly allows the target to avoid an objective analysis of the existence of some serious linkages between anti-Zionism and antisemitism.

Sadly, the final shameful contribution came from the once-moderate AJDS, which historically supported two states but is increasingly using the language and arguments of the anti-Zionist fundamentalists. The AJDS's new media officer, Les Rosenblatt, who was formerly a committee member of the now-defunct J4JP group, issued a statement of unequivocal support for *Overland*'s pro-Palestinian orthodoxy. He bizarrely claimed that *Overland* was actually seeking to broaden rather than limit the range of views in the debate and, even more strangely, cited with approval Brull's article in favor of the AJDS's concern to promote "civility and respect in debate on political differences over the issue and strongly oppose the vilification and abuse that often follows expression of radical or minority opinions."[22] The AJDS clearly did not even bother to read the content of Brull's article, for otherwise they would have realized that they were endorsing personal abuse instead of a diversity of opinions.

Conclusion

The majority of the international Left supports a two-state solution, which encapsulates recognition of both Israeli and Palestinian national rights. Those anti-Zionist fundamentalists who advocate the elimination of the State of Israel and its replacement by an Arab state of Greater Palestine represent a small, if vocal, minority. These zealots frequently accuse pro-Israel activists of utilizing tactics of intimidation and hate, but this seems to be a case of the pot calling the kettle black.[23] The case studies cited above suggest that this minority group is actively attempting to censor and exclude any Left voices in favor of the continued existence of Israel. And any means are justified to achieve this outcome, including the ad hominem abuse of individual academics and a horrific lowering of intellectual and scholarly standards. The pro-Palestinian lobbyists are willing to throw out the most basic academic conventions regarding accurate presentation of evidence and correct citations and referencing if they don't serve the interests of the Palestinian cause.

PHILIP MENDES teaches social policy and community development and is Director of the Social Inclusion and Social Policy Research Unit (SISPRU) in the Department of Social Work at Monash University in Victoria, Australia. His most recent publications include *Jews and the Left: The Rise and Fall of a Political Alliance* with Nick Dyrenfurth, *Boycotting Israel Is Wrong* with Pamela Snow, and *Australia's Welfare Wars*, third edition.

Notes

1. Philip Mendes, "Transitioning from a Pro-Palestinian to Pro-Israel Perspective," *Drum Opinion* (July 21, 2011).
2. Philip Mendes, "Censorship or Pluralism: Some Personal Reflections Concerning the Australian Jewish Debate on Israel," *Generation: Australian Jewish Life & Thought* 6 (1997): 64–69; Philip Mendes, "Dissent and Intolerance in the Melbourne Jewish Community," *Arena* 96 (1991): 18–21.
3. Philip Mendes, "The Two-State Switch: Why Jews Changed Their Minds and Why It Matters," *Australian Broadcasting Commission Religion and Ethics* (February 28, 2014).
4. Philip Mendes, *Jews and the Left: The Rise and Fall of a Political Alliance* (Houndmills, UK: Palgrave Macmillan, 2014), 282–283; Philip Mendes and Nick Dyrenfurth, *Boycotting Israel Is Wrong* (Sydney: New South Press, 2015), 74–79.
5. Steven Salaita, *Uncivil Rites: Palestine and the Limits of Academic Freedom* (Chicago: Haymarket Books, 2015), 118–119.
6. David Hirsh, *Anti-Zionism and Antisemitism: Cosmopolitan Reflections* (New Haven, CT: Yale Initiative for the Interdisciplinary Study of Antisemitism Working Paper Series, 2007), 13.
7. Philip Mendes, "Australian Jewish Dissent on Israel: A History of the Australian Jewish Democratic Society," *Australian Jewish Historical Society Journal* 15 (November 2000): 468–470.
8. Philip Mendes, "Jewish Journals in Australia," *AMESA Newsletter* 4 (December 1996): 6–7; Philip Mendes, "An Historical Controversy: The Causes of the Palestinian Refugee Problem," *Journal of Arab, Islamic and Middle East Studies* 3 (1996): 83–102.
9. David Pryce-Jones, "Back to Rule by the Gun," *Herald Sun* (November 7, 1995).
10. "Apology by Australia Israel Publications," *Herald Sun* (December 23, 1997).
11. See the comments of Michael Danby, *Australia/Israel Review* (November 22, 1984): 2–3; Nicole Gershov, "The Pantomine Continues," *Australia/Israel Review* (September 1, 1988); David Bierman, "A Pro-Israeli Fronts Up at AMESA," *Australian Jewish News* (October 15, 1993); Michael Kapel, "Kessler Totally Misses the Point," *Australian Jewish*

News (November 4, 1994); Tzvi Fleischer, "Will the Peace Process Finally Transform AMESA?" *Australia/Israel Review* (November 2–21, 1994); David Bierman, "A Matter of ...," *Australia/Israel Review* (October 5–26, 1995); Daniel Mandel, "AMESA Trouble," *Australia/Israel Review* (September 29 to October 20, 1998).

12. Philip Mendes, "AMESA and the Jewish Community: Towards New Directions," *AMESA Newsletter* 10 (November 1998): 5.

13. "The AMESA Committee Replies," *AMESA Newsletter* 10 (November 1998): 6. See also Clive Kessler's response on pp. 6–7, and Orit Shapiro's reply on p. 12.

14. Ibid., 8–9, 12.

15. On Docker's long-standing extreme hostility to Israel, see Philip Mendes, "Denying the Jewish Experience of Oppression: The Jewish Anti-Zionism of John Docker," *Australian Journal of Jewish Studies* 17 (2003): 112–130. Docker later co-coordinated an Australian petition for an academic boycott of Israel. See Mendes and Dyrenfurth, *Boycotting Israel Is Wrong*, 86–89.

16. Mendes and Dyrenfurth, *Boycotting Israel Is Wrong*, 63; Philip Mendes, "AMESA and the Jewish Community," 9, 12.

17. For one example of this perspective, see Philip Mendes, "End of the Line," *Diplomat* 1 (December 2002 to January 2003): 32–33.

18. Philip Mendes, "Suicide Bombings: Oppression Is No Justification," *Jewish Currents* 5, (September–October 2003): 6–7.

19. Michael Brull, "But What About Zionism?" *Overland* 197 (2009): 98.

20. For my views on anti-Zionism and antisemitism see, for example, Philip Mendes, "Reflections from Australia: Are Anti-Zionism and Antisemitism One and the Same?" *Covenant* 2 (2008): 7–16, and Philip Mendes, *Jews and the Left*, 88–95.

21. Jeff Sparrow, Jacinda Woodhead, Rjurik Davidson, Kalinda Ashton, Alex Skutenko, and John Marnell, "Overland Bias: A Response to Some Critics," *Overland* (May 3, 2010), https://overland.org.au/2010/05/overland-and-bias-a-response-to-some-critics/.

22. Les Rosenblatt, "AJDS Statement of Support for Overland Editorial Response to Some Critics," May 6, 2010; "Overland and Bias: A Response to Some Critics," *Overland* (May 3, 2010), https://overland.org.au/2010/05/overland-and-bias-a-response-to-some-critics/.

23. Steven Salaita, "How to Practice BDS in Academe." In Ashley Dawson and Bill V. Mullen, eds. *Against Apartheid: The Case for Boycotting Israeli Universities* (Chicago: Haymarket Books, 2015), 135–139.

13 Anti-Israel Antisemitism in England

Richard Millett

Richard Millett was not surprised by the 2016 antisemitism scandal in Britain's Labour Party, as he has spent the last eight years documenting Far Left anti-Israel events, many of which were sponsored or featured appearances by Labour Party officials. His experiences demonstrate that anti-Israel antisemitic bigotry has metastasized from the British academy into the highest echelon of the cultural and political elites and is now to be found at schools, churches, charities, theaters, trade unions, academic bodies, and even at allegedly impartial non-governmental organizations (NGOs) such as Amnesty International. His exposing the disreputable fabrications and murderous wishes of antisemitic anti-Israelists has often gotten him into trouble, where the antagonists attempt to discredit him through lies and smears. He is particularly disturbed by the situation on British campuses, where, he observes, a whole generation of students is now being brought up on a hateful anti-Israel diet.

AS I WRITE this, the opposition Labour Party in the United Kingdom has finally become convulsed in a crisis of antisemitism.

Many Far Left Labour Party members have been suspended for various statements, the most high-profile of whom is the ex-mayor of London, Ken Livingstone, for suggesting on national radio that Hitler was a Zionist because Hitler had, according to Livingstone, supported a Jewish national homeland in British-mandated Palestine (despite Hitler's ultimate plan to murder every last Jew anywhere).

Another high-profile suspension was Member of Parliament (MP) Naz Shah for suggesting on Twitter that the best solution for the Israeli-Palestinian conflict was to relocate Israel to America.[1] Vicki Kirby, MP, was suspended for tweeting that Hitler was a "Zionist God," "We invented Israel when saving them from Hitler, who now seems to be their teacher," "I will never forget and I will make sure my kids teach their children how evil Israel is," and that Jews have "big noses."[2]

There are about another thirty suspensions being considered as I write, and a Labour Party inquiry into antisemitism will commence soon. This has all come to light since the Far Left politician Jeremy Corbyn, MP, was elected leader of the Labour Party after Labour lost the 2015 general election to David Cameron's Conservatives.

I am not surprised by these statements and suspensions. For eight years, I have been attending Far Left anti-Israel events and demonstrations in order to record them for my blog. I have written about these horrendous events and posted photos, footage, and audio recordings. Many of these events have been arranged by Labour MPs, including Corbyn himself, and many have had Corbyn as the main speaker.[3]

In August 2012, I witnessed Corbyn speak at the annual Al Quds Day demonstration in central London.[4] Al Quds Day was inspired by Iran's Ayatollah Khomeini to claim Jerusalem for the Islamic world. At the annual demonstration, activists come adorned in Hezbollah flags while sporting some of the most obscene statements about Israel. Hezbollah is an antisemitic organization whose main objective is to destroy Israel and murder Jews.

I have photographed placards stating: "We are Hezbullah," "Israel listen, leave!!!" and "Israel is a disease, we are the cure."[5]

At the previous year's Al Quds Day protest, I photographed placards stating, "For world peace Israel must be destroyed," "Israel your days are numbered," "Death to Israel," and "The world stopped Nazism, the world stopped apartheid, the world must stop Zionism."[6]

I witnessed Labour MP Martin Linton say during a Friends of Al Aqsa event at the houses of Parliament in 2010: "There are long tentacles of Israel in this country who are funding election campaigns and putting money into the British political system for their own ends."[7] The symbol of tentacles is a hangover from the Nazis, who propagated the notion of a huge Jewish octopus controlling the world.

At the same meeting, I witnessed Labour's Gerald Kaufman, MP, say, "Just as Lord Ashcroft owns one part of the Labour Party, right-wing Jewish millionaires own the other part."

There are no arenas where anti-Israel polemics do not appear. Universities, schools, churches, NGOs, charities, theaters, trade unions, and academic bodies are all fair game for a minority of activists who now delight in putting out anti-Israel messages on behalf of their professional bodies.

Theater and Education

My most haunting memory was when I visited the Royal Court Theatre in London in February 2009 for Caryl Churchill's infamous *Seven Jewish Children*. There were thirteen performances of this ten-minute play. Entrance was free, and the performances took place after Marius von Mayenburg's play *The Stone*. Churchill had cleverly secured a ready-made audience for her play.

As I watched *Seven Jewish Children* for the first time, I saw unfold Churchill's portrayal of the Jewish people traveling out of the ashes of the Holocaust to become oppressors and murderers of Palestinians. The whole Jewish race had lost all morals because of the Holocaust and had now become just as bad as their Nazi oppressors.

At the end, the audience applauded enthusiastically. I couldn't comprehend how intelligent, cultured people could applaud a play in which Jews were portrayed as murdering Palestinian children and laughing at the sight of dead Palestinians. I had a sudden glimpse of how easy it was for those who hated Jews in the past to stir up the hatred of the general public, which then led to the pogroms.

Seven Jewish Children continues to be performed all over the country in schools, churches, and such, free of charge. Naive and immature minds are getting early exposure to this anti-Israel/anti-Jewish propaganda.

This approach is already producing negative results. No doubt fifteen-year-old schoolchild Leanne Mohamad has seen Churchill's play. Mohamad won a regional final of the "Speak Out" Challenge 2015–2016. These are a few of the lines from her winning speech: "Since 1948 to this very day more than 30,000 innocent Palestinian children have been killed." "Since the start of the Palestinian-Israeli conflict Israel has been fighting Palestine with the most advanced weapons while Palestine has no army, no government, no money, nothing." "Palestinians should not be discriminated for who they are. Every day their homes, schools, hospitals are destroyed. They're left with nothing. Not even their basic human rights."[8]

Compare Churchill's *Seven Jewish Children* of 2009 and Leanne Mohamad's speech of 2016, and the parallels are unmistakable.

When Israeli actors and dancers have come to the United Kingdom to perform, I have witnessed the constant disruption of their live shows. In September 2011, I watched as the Israeli Philharmonic Orchestra's performance at the London Proms, conducted by the great Zubin Mehta, was regularly interrupted. Anti-Israel protesters in the audience shouted abuse before being taken out by security.[9] In May 2012, I watched as Habima's (Israel's national theater) production of *The Merchant of Venice* at the Globe Theatre was similarly interrupted.[10] And in November 2012, I sat through a stunning performance by the youth wing of the Batsheva ensemble dance group while they were repeatedly interrupted with chants of "Free, free Palestine."[11]

Churches and Israel

One of the most distressing exchanges I have had was in October 2011 after the Palestine Solidarity Campaign event at the Rivercourt Methodist Church in West London.

I went to hear what anti-Zionist Christian preacher Stephen Sizer had to say. I filmed Sizer claiming that church leaders refuse to speak out about Israel's "crimes" because of "guilt for the Holocaust" and that churches that side with the occupation and Zionism have "repudiated Jesus, have repudiated the Bible, and are an abomination."[12]

As I left the church, I got involved in a conversation with a woman, which I recorded.[13] She claimed that there were no gas chambers during the Holocaust and that Jews merely died after having had their "foreskins chopped off." She told me that "a few hundred thousand" died in the Holocaust. "You're using it [the Holocaust] to fucking kill the Palestinians," and "I see the Jews in Israel as total Nazis."

Although the Palestine Solidarity Campaign condemned her remarks, they went on to say that she had been "harangued" by me.[14] The lie that I harass, or harangue, people, so forcing them into making such vile comments, will be a common theme in this essay.

For Christmas 2013, St. James's Church in Piccadilly, at a cost of £30,000, built an imposing life-size replica of Israel's security wall in its courtyard. The church invited members of the public to write messages on it. Despite the actual wall built by Israel having saved untold thousands of Israeli and Palestinian lives, St. James's Church beamed slogans on to their own replica wall that made statements such as: "In 2002 the [Israeli] government began construction of the barrier. Its stated aim was the security of Israeli citizens. In 2004 the International Court of Justice in The Hague stated the wall was illegal and it should be dismantled."[15]

The Law and Academia

I trained as a lawyer some twenty-five years ago. I had my final award ceremony at the Law Society on Chancery Lane in central London. That was where I was awarded my certificate of qualification as a solicitor. It was a very special day for me.

However, in November 2010, I was back in the same room of the Law Society to witness the Russell Tribunal on Palestine (RTOP) take place. RTOP is a weak attempt to give anti-Israel activism legal backing. RTOP hears evidence about some aspect relating to Israel before passing judgment—usually one of guilt.

One weekend in November 2010, this kangaroo court convened at the Law Society to hold an anti-Israel trial. The room was set up like a court with a so-called jury listening to evidence. Those on trial were companies that were accused of complicity in Israeli war crimes. RTOP already took for granted that Israel had committed war crimes.

Companies on trial were G4S (British company that helped run checkpoints), Elbit Systems (Israeli company that makes drones and conducts business with British companies), Caterpillar (American company that makes bulldozers), Cement Roadstone Holdings (Irish company that manufactures cement used by Israel for the security wall), Dexia (Franco-Belgian company that helped finance Jewish settlements), Veolia Transport (French company involved in building the Jerusalem Light Rail), and Carmel Agrexco (Israeli company that exports agricultural produce from the West Bank).

The trial lasted two days. Witnesses were called, and evidence against these companies was heard. None of the companies chose to appear. This kangaroo court then reconvened the following day for the verdict at the headquarters of Amnesty International in central London.

I was in the audience as, surreally, everyone stood up in silence while the RTOP jury filed onto the stage. The jury consisted of: Stéphane Hessel, French diplomat; France Mairead Corrigan Maguire, Nobel Peace laureate, 1976; John Dugard, former UN special rapporteur on human rights in the Palestinian territories; Anthony Gifford QC, UK barrister; Ronald Kasrils, South African political activist; José Antonio Martin Pallin, Spanish judge; Cynthia McKinney, American political activist; and Michael Mansfield QC, UK barrister.

Mansfield read out the verdict, in which he said the jury had found

> compelling evidence of corporate complicity in Israeli violations of international law, relating to: the supply of arms; the construction and maintenance of the illegal separation Wall; and in establishing, maintaining, and providing services, especially financial, to illegal settlements, all of which have occurred in the context of an illegal occupation of Palestinian territory. It is clear from the evidence of witnesses that this conduct is not only morally reprehensible, but also exposes those corporations to legal liability for very serious violations of international human rights and humanitarian law. What distinguishes the present situation from others in which international action has been called for, is that in this case both Israel and the corporations that are complicit in Israel's unlawful actions are in clear violation of international human rights and humanitarian law.[16]

Mansfield then described to the audience at Amnesty International what could happen next in light of this judgment. He suggested that activists actively demonstrate within the United Kingdom against these and other companies, and if they were prosecuted for any criminal offense, then the activists could employ the defense of "necessity."[17] In other words, they could argue that they only committed the crime out of necessity to stop another crime (in this case, complicity in Israel war crimes) from taking place.

Mansfield then directed the audience to such a protest that was taking place as he was speaking, at the Israel-owned AHAVA natural minerals shop in London's Covent Garden district. AHAVA sells products from the Dead Sea and, at the time, had a factory employing Palestinians and Israelis in the

West Bank (Judea/Samaria). Its shop in Covent Garden sold these Dead Sea products. It had been subjected to violent attacks, protests, and invasions over the previous two years by anti-Israel activists. This included harassing AHAVA's staff, daubing the frontage with red paint, gluing up the lock on the front door, protesting noisily every other Saturday outside the shop, and invading the shop and locking themselves to a heavy object they had brought with them, which caused the shop to close while these activists were removed by police.

This last action, which could lead to a criminal conviction for aggravated trespass, was again taking place that Monday at the AHAVA shop. This time, it was seemingly being approved by Mansfield himself, one of the United Kingdom's most famous barristers.

I immediately left Amnesty International, and when I arrived at the shop, I witnessed two anti-Israel activists, Jessica Nero and Christopher Osmond, sitting on the floor of the AHAVA shop. They had handcuffed themselves to a concrete block, making it impossible for them to be removed.

The shop had to close for three hours while the situation was dealt with. A special police unit had to be brought in to cut Nero and Osmond loose, and they were eventually led out to a police van under arrest.[18]

Nero and Osmond faced trial along with two other suspects who had similarly invaded the AHAVA shop on a previous occasion. All four were convicted of aggravated trespass (although Nero and Osmond were later acquitted on appeal on a technicality).[19]

The AHAVA shop eventually closed down when its landlord refused to extend its lease at the behest of neighboring shopkeepers who had found their Saturday takings reduced due to the noisy Saturday anti-Israel protests outside AHAVA.

I complained to the Bar Standards Board (BSB, the official body of barristers) about Mansfield's advice to the audience at Amnesty International. My main complaint to them was that Mansfield had incited the crime of aggravated trespass with his words.

But the BSB replied: "The BSB does not have the power to consider allegations of criminal conduct. If you consider that Mr. Mansfield QC is guilty of a criminal offense, you should refer the matter to the police in the first instance. I would also point out that Mr. Mansfield's comments were made in his personal capacity and not in connection with the provision of a legal service."[20]

Right.

Medicine and Academia

I have also witnessed and recorded various attempts in the medical field to delegitimize Israel.

In December 2013, I witnessed the *Lancet*, the world-renowned UK medical journal, present a 2013 publication of the work of the Lancet-Palestinian Health

Alliance (LPHA). The event was held at the Royal College of Pediatrics and Child Health in central London.

Richard Horton, the *Lancet*'s editor, accused Israel of denying safe passage to pregnant Palestinian women. Another presenter, Iain Chalmers, who had initiated the LPHA in 2009, presented a cartoon of Ehud Olmert in a swimming pool of blood and bones. The pool was in the shape of Gaza.

Chalmers finished with this incredibly dark statement: "I was asked to write a commentary for the *Lancet* after the Cast Lead attack. I ended it by saying a self-defined Jewish state now controls the lives of almost as many non-Jews as it does Jews. What will that Jewish state do with six million, *it is an interesting figure*, the six million non-Jews whose lives it controls? You answer that question."[21]

Was he suggesting that Israel might kill those "six million non-Jews whose lives it controls"?

In April 2014, I attended the launch of the UK-Palestine Mental Health Network at the Guild of Psychotherapists in central London. It was a meeting of trained health specialists discussing how best to whip up support for a boycott of Israeli psychotherapists.

Andrew Samuels, a lecturer at Essex University, complained that "the psychotherapy world is two-thirds pro-Israel ... we have to have the fight." And he suggested that "histrionics, the worst case scenario, emotional blackmail, and all that kind of thing" should be used.[22]

Samuels and his colleagues, it seems, wished to spare nothing and no one in their efforts to isolate Israeli psychologists. So much psychological help is needed for both Israeli and Palestinian civilians, but it is hard to understand the cynicism of those who would wish to deprive those who can help two war-stricken peoples, the Israelis and the Palestinians, access to the wider world to further their learning.

Amnesty International

As noted above, the RTOP used the offices of Amnesty International in London to deliver their kangaroo court verdict. Amnesty International continuously offers its headquarters for such anti-Israel events. I have witnessed many there, including one with film director Ken Loach in November 2010. Loach criticized Tony Blair and Gordon Brown for being patrons of the Jewish National Fund, which Loach claimed collected money to buy land on the basis of "racial purity." Loach then claimed that the effluent of Jewish settlers flowed downhill onto the land of the Palestinians, making it unusable for farming. He finished off by claiming that David Ben-Gurion preferred to save half of the Jewish children from Germany if it meant transporting them to Israel rather than all of them if it meant transporting them to Britain.[23]

But the one event at Amnesty International that really stands out for me was in April 2011.

Various speakers showed the usual photos and slides claiming that Israel had committed murder and human rights breaches. One slide accused Israel with this: "Destruction of toilets, cisterns, and other wash-related infrastructure makes water and sanitation physically inaccessible for the communities affected."[24]

One presenter, Asad Khan, claimed that Palestinians are arrested in their hospital beds and taken away by Israeli soldiers while accompanied by Israeli doctors. Then another presenter, Ala Abu Dheer, showed a photo of a young Palestinian boy with a Star of David seemingly carved into the flesh of his forearm.[25] The photo was dated April 30, 2003, and headed: "The soldier, checking the student's ability to bear pain, took a piece of glass and broke it and taking Qasem's arm, cut into it a Star of David."

At the end, I asked Dheer about the photo, seeing that it was such a serious accusation. My intention was to report the soldier to the Israeli authorities if this was all true. The photo was taken eight years ago, so why hadn't action been taken by now, I wondered. I knew at the back of my mind the photo was a hoax but wanted to make sure.

Dheer assured me that the photo wasn't faked. I asked whether Qasem could be traced to give evidence against the soldier. I handed Dheer my email address, and he assured me he would contact me with all the relevant details about the incident.

Kristyan Benedict, the Amnesty International employee who regularly organizes these anti-Israel events, confronted me, calling me a "war crimes denier." He then threatened me, the personal details of which I won't go into. After an investigation, Benedict was eventually forced to apologize to me by Amnesty International.

Needless to say, I never received that email from Dheer about the alleged cutting incident with the Israeli soldier. It was presumably staged, but if so, to have such a staged photo displayed openly at a human rights NGO like Amnesty International is shocking and undermines the credibility of other evidence produced by Amnesty International concerning real human rights abuses.

That photo looked wrong anyway. The Star of David is perfectly formed. This would have been impossible on a screaming boy writhing in agony. Also, the plaster to cover the supposed wound is in an improbable position.

Benedict continued his tirade against Israel. In 2012, during Operation Pillar of Defense, he tweeted the following about three British MPs who are Jewish: "Louise Ellman, Robert Halfon and Luciana Berger walk into a bar … each orders a round of B52s … #Gaza."[26]

And in 2014, Benedict compared Israel to the Islamic State while the Islamic State was still being referred to as ISIL (Islamic State in the Levant). He tweeted:

"Israeli regimes [sic] response to our Gaza report: Amnesty 'a propaganda tool for Hamas and other terror groups' (#JSIL?)." By "JSIL" Benedict presumably meant Jewish State in the Levant.[27]

In July 2017 I received an email from Amnesty International informing me that "based on past behavior" I was permanently banned from attending any more events at Amnesty's London office. I had been covering their anti-Israel events there for seven years. I requested examples of my alleged "disruptive" behavior. They could not provide any specific examples to me.

Three London University Campuses: Kings College London, London School of Economics, and the School of Oriental and African Studies

The real anti-Israel problems are on campus, where young students away from home looking for a cause to attach themselves to are easy prey for those wanting to swell the ranks of anti-Israel activists. This is where it has also been quite violent in terms of language used and physical threats.

On Tuesday, January 19, 2016, I was queuing outside King's College London (KCL) alongside 150 students waiting to hear Ami Ayalon, an ex-director of Israel's Shin Bet, an ex-Labour member of the Israeli Knesset, and a potential peace-maker. Ayalon cofounded with Palestinian Sari Nusseibeh a peace initiative called The People's Voice. Ayalon wanted to talk to KCL students about the steps he believed Israel could take to secure peace.

Unfortunately, I didn't make it into the room where the talk was due to take place, as it only accommodated some fifty-six people. As soon as the room was full, the doors to the building had to be shut, and I was outside the building on the street along with one hundred others. Among us were twenty angry anti-Israel activists from the Palestine societies of KCL, London School of Economics (LSE), and the School of Oriental and African Studies (SOAS).

While we were queuing for the talk, these activists handed us leaflets. The leaflets viciously attacked Ayalon by falsely incriminating him in war crimes. The leaflets also attacked him for his support of a two-state solution to the Israeli-Palestinian conflict. Not even the creation of a Palestinian state would satiate these activists, whose sole objective was the end of the Jewish State.

The words on their leaflets were unambiguous: "To argue Israeli Jews must always be a majority and to deny the Palestinian right to return implies the two-state solution is preached due to a fear of losing the ethnic and colonial supremacy Israel has enjoyed since 1948. Thus his position makes him no different from the more overtly racist Zionists in the Israeli government."

For these activists, Ayalon's support for Israel's existence as a Jewish state makes him "overtly racist."

It wasn't long before a window was smashed as these twenty agitated activists outside Ayalon's talk continuously pounded their hands and fists hard on the door and windows of the building.[28] They also scaled the windows and held a large Palestinian flag for Ayalon to view. A fire alarm in the building was activated, which led to an adjoining building being evacuated.

Inside the building, a female organizer was physically assaulted and chairs were thrown. The police eventually arrived to protect the building and those inside, but the continuous noise and disruption made it almost impossible for Ayalon to be heard during his talk, so he ended his talk prematurely.

Events like these are almost par for the course on campus. While British universities offer safe spaces where discussion should be allowed to take place without fear of violence, interruption, or insult, such safe spaces are absent where Israeli diplomats, politicians, and academics are concerned.

On Holocaust Memorial Day, January 27, 2015, it was the language of some students that was violent as opposed to their behavior. This time, I was at a joint event of the Palestine society and the feminist society at LSE, where the killing of Israelis was sickeningly glorified.

Rana B. Baker, a student from SOAS, praised Sana'a Mehaidli, whom Baker said "deserves a standing ovation." Baker told a packed student audience how in south Lebanon in 1985 Mehaidli "drove a car full of explosives and blew it up near an Israeli convoy killing two Israeli soldiers and injuring between 10 and 12 more." Baker described Mehaidli as "the first female to carry out a suicide bombing in south Lebanon" and said Mehaidli was "more admirable for not being well known and for not being Palestinian." Baker concluded her presentation by telling how Mehaidli's will called "men and women to armed struggle against a colonial regime based on violence."[29]

And if that wasn't enough hatred for a student audience to imbibe, Zena Agha, another student, also portrayed Israelis as rapists of Palestinian women. She declared that "in Israel the view of Palestinian women is very derogatory and that rape had become a very prevalent idea. Rape for Israelis is almost a weapon of war against Palestinian women."[30]

So this was why the feminist society was part of the proceedings; not only was there an apparently heroic woman who devoted her life to murdering Israelis, but LSE students were also being fed the notion that all Israeli men were ideological rapists!

Trade Unions

Another chilling moment for me came when I sat next to a trade unionist at an event held at SOAS.

One night in November 2011, the Rail, Maritime, and Transport (RMT) union held an event at SOAS. After a few speakers, we heard from Steve Hedley, then RMT's London regional organizer. There had been a few pro-Israel comments from an audience member, and Hedley didn't like what he heard. He stood up to address the person who made the comments.

Staring intently, he pointed at the person and shouted angrily: "The attack on those innocent women and children who you starved and turned into the biggest concentration camp on earth ... you're an absolute disgrace to the Jewish people.... You're a modern day Nazi!"

After he took his seat next to me, I asked him if he felt better after shouting.

I recorded Hedley's response: "Better than you, obviously. But, then again, you're one of the Chosen People so you might feel better than me, huh?"[31]

This "Chosen People" remark was a horrendous antisemitic comment. It is one of many I have heard or had aimed at me. Hedley also compared Israelis to Nazis, another common feature of the anti-Israel dynamic among the Far Left in Britain. Palestinians and the Bedouin in Israel are regularly compared to the Jews of Nazi Germany. These are clearly antisemitic comparisons.

As for the phrase *Chosen People*, Chris Elliot, the *Guardian*'s former readers' editor, has explained: "It has never meant that the Jews are better than anyone else. Historically it has been antisemites, not Jews, who have read 'chosen' as code for Jewish supremacism."[32]

In response to my calling out Hedley for his antisemitic comment on my blog, he responded with a libelous attack on me, which is still up on RMT's website.[33] In his own blog, Hedley admits his use of the phrase *Chosen People* was unwise, and he apologized "to anyone who may have been offended by this remark."[34]

But, echoing the Palestine Solidarity Campaign's empty apology about the Rivercourt Methodist Church incident described above, Hedley claimed that he was "provoked." He also claimed that I had called him a Nazi and that this had upset him. Of course, I didn't call him a Nazi.

He then finished his blog post with another lie: that I had to register my blog "outside the UK because [I] have been sued for slander and libel by other victims of [my] maniacal denunciation of everyone who dares to speak out against the Israeli state's role in the Middle East."

My blog, being run by WordPress, is automatically registered in America. I have no choice as to where WordPress is based.

Summary

My eight years of blogging about anti-Israel events in the United Kingdom have led me through some quite frightening and humiliating experiences.

I have now been banned from taking photographs or filming at SOAS in London, where, incidentally, I studied for my master's in politics and society in the Middle East.

In May 2012, I went to a Palestine society event at SOAS where the anti-Israel journalist Abdel Bari Atwan was due to speak. Atwan had once declared, "If Iranian missiles hit Israel, I will dance in Trafalgar Square,"[35] so I felt I had to be there to record what else he had to say about Israel's destruction to an audience of students.

As soon as I started to film, I was pounced on by a group of students ordering me to stop filming. They tried to snatch my camera out of my hand, and one said to me, "You're a typical Israeli, you know that." I'm English.

They wanted me to leave the auditorium, but I refused. It was my right to be there and to witness what was being said. It was a public event. They then removed my coat and bag from the seat next to me so I had no option but to leave and try to retrieve them.[36]

You won't be surprised to read that the statement released by the SOAS Student Union to defend the Palestine society had a paragraph about me, which read: "By now, we are well aware of his intentions. He first provokes, intimidates, and insults (including racially) speakers, organizers, or members of the audience and violates generally accepted conventions of public meetings."[37]

I then received an email from SOAS banning me from using my camera under threat of being banned from SOAS itself and possible legal action. I was informed that in the future I should ask in advance for permission to take photographs or film at any SOAS events, but I have been refused every time I have since asked.

Similarly, a month before, I was also at SOAS to hear Amal Jamal, an Arab Israeli lecturer at Tel Aviv University, tell his student audience how downtrodden Arabs are within Israel.

When it came to the Q&A after his talk, I asked Jamal how it was that he succeeded in Israel if Arabs were, in his view, so downtrodden.

Professor Gilbert Achcar, who runs the Center for Palestine Studies at SOAS, immediately branded me a professional disrupter in front of everyone; announced that had he known I was attending the event, he would have barred my entry; and then told everyone that I had left insulting messages on his answering machine.[38]

Over eight years of blogging, I have had so many negative experiences like this, publicly surrounded and humiliated and asked to leave, all for wanting to record for posterity what was being said about Israel, Israelis, and Jews, or for merely asking a challenging question.

On campus, I have heard demands for the Jewish State to disappear,[39] Israelis compared to the German citizens who failed to confront their Nazi government at the time,[40] and constant Holocaust minimization in the form of comparing the Palestinians and Bedouin of today to the Jews in Nazi Germany.[41]

I have also been asked at anti-Israel events how much I am paid for what I do, as if someone defending Israel can only do it if he is paid handsomely.

A whole generation of students are being brought up on this diet. These are the students who will be our future political leaders and opinion formers. We are not providing these students with Israel's narrative, sadly, and I don't know why this is not being made a priority.

For all we know, Corbyn, who was not expected to be elected Labour Party leader in 2015, could be elected prime minister in 2020. To have a prime minister who has described Hamas and Hezbollah as friends would be a huge blow to British Jewry.

I would have to say that the most scared I have ever felt was not on campus. In July 2014, I was at a huge anti-Israel demonstration in central London taking a photo of a protester wearing a shirt emblazoned with the words: "Auschwitz Iraq Dachau Palestine."[42]

As I was walking away, someone grabbed me and shouted, "He's a Zionist." I managed to summon up all my strength to break free.

But on university campuses throughout the United Kingdom, anti-Israel propaganda continues unabated and virtually unopposed. In May 2016, I heard the most surreal statement made by author Tariq Ali to a student audience at the University of London Student Union. Ali told them, "The end of Israel will benefit all Israelis."[43]

Right.

RICHARD MILLETT is a nonpracticing qualified solicitor. For the last eight years, he has been writing about and documenting anti-Israel events in and around London and the United Kingdom and held at various universities, NGOs, professional bodies, theaters, and churches.

Notes

1. Anonymous, "Labour MP Naz Shah Backed Plan To 'Relocate Israelis To America'," *The Jewish Chronicle* (April 26, 2016), https://www.thejc.com/news/uk-news/labour-mp-naz-shah-backed-plan-to-relocate-israelis-to-america-1.64398.

2. Anonymous, "Labour Suspends Vicki Kirby Pending Investigation," *The Jewish Chronicle* (March 15, 2016), https://www.thejc.com/news/uk-news/labour-suspends-vicki-kirby-pending-investigation-1.61589.

3. Richard Millett, "'Neo-Nazi' Talks at Max Blumenthal's Anti-Israel Event In Parliament: Clip Update," *Richard Millett's Blog* (October 10, 2014), https://richardmillett.wordpress.com/2014/10/10/neo-nazi-talks-at-max-blumenthals-anti-israel-event-in-parliament-clip-update/.

4. Richard Millett, "Hezbollah Marches through London Again on Al Quds Day," *Richard Millett's Blog* (August, 17 2012), https://richardmillett.wordpress.com/2012/08/17/hezbollah-marches-through-london-again-on-al-quds-day/.

5. Ibid.

6. Richard Millett, Lauren Booth, "Lebanon, Jordan and Egypt Must Liberate Jerusalem," *Richard Millett's Blog* (August 22, 2011), https://richardmillett.wordpress.com/2011/08/22/lauren-booth-lebanon-jordan-and-egypt-must-liberate-jerusalem/.

7. Richard Millett, "Free Palestine, Vote Labour," *Richard Millett's Blog* (March 24, 2010), https://richardmillett.wordpress.com/2010/03/24/free-palestine-vote-Labor/.

8. See the speech on YouTube (posted January 21, 2017), https://www.youtube.com/watch?v=GhU1W5q2dFg (accessed November 16, 2017).

9. Richard Millett, "Why Did The BBC Pull Last Night's Live Transmission of the Israeli Philharmonic Orchestra At The Proms?" *Richard Millett's Blog* (September 2, 2011), https://richardmillett.wordpress.com/2011/09/02/why-did-the-bbc-pull-last-nights-live-transmission-of-the-israeli-philharmonic-orchestra-at-the-proms/.

10. Richard Millett, "Habima's Merchant Of Venice Rocks London's Globe Theatre," *Richard Millett's Blog* (May 29, 2012), https://richardmillett.wordpress.com/2012/05/29/habima-rocks-globe/.

11. Richard Millett, "Protests Fail to Disrupt Batsheva Ensemble's Deca Dance Show at Sadler's Wells," *Richard Millett's Blog* (November 20, 2012), https://richardmillett.wordpress.com/2012/11/20/protests-fail-disrupt-batsheva-sadlers-wells/.

12. Richard Millett, "Sizer, the Rivercourt Methodist Church and Holocaust Denial," *Richard Millett's Blog* (October 9, 2011), https://richardmillett.wordpress.com/2011/10/09/sizer-the-rivercourt-methodist-church-and-holocaust-denial/.

13. Richard Millett, "Palestine Solidarity Campaign Defends Holocaust Denier," *Richard Millett's Blog* (October 14, 2011), https://richardmillett.wordpress.com/2011/10/14/palestine-solidarity-campaign-defends-holocaust-denier/.

14. Ibid.

15. Richard Millett, "St. James's Church, Piccadilly, Installs Life Size Replica Of Israel's Security Wall During 12 Days Of Christmas," *Richard Millett's Blog* (December 24, 2013), https://richardmillett.wordpress.com/2013/12/24/st-jamess-church-piccadilly-installs-life-size-replica-of-israels-security-wall-during-12-days-of-christmas/.

16. "Finding of the Final Session of the Russell Tribunal on Palestine" (March 16-17, 2013), http://www.russelltribunalonpalestine.com/en/full-findings-of-the-final-session-en (accessed November 16, 2017).

17. Richard Millett, "Bar Standards Board Clears Michael Mansfield QC of Professional Misconduct Over Anti-Israel Speech," *Richard Millett's Blog* (January 12, 2012), https://richardmillett.wordpress.com/2012/01/12/bar-clears-michael-mansfield-over-anti-israel-speech/.

18. Richard Millett, "Ahava Shut Down Again; Two Arrested," *Richard Millett's Blog* (November 22, 2010), https://richardmillett.wordpress.com/2010/11/22/ahava-shut-down-again-two-arrested/.

19. Richard Millett, "Anti-Ahava Activists on Trial: A View from the Public Gallery," *Richard Millett's Blog* (March 26, 2011), https://richardmillett.wordpress.com/2011/03/26/anti-ahava-activists-on-trial-a-view-from-the-public-gallery/.

20. Richard Millet, "Bar Standards Board Clears Michael Mansfield QC of Professional Misconduct Over Anti-Israel Speech," *Richard Millett's Blog* (January 12, 2012), https://richardmillett.wordpress.com/2012/01/12/bar-clears-michael-mansfield-over-anti-israel-speech/.

21. Richard Millett, "The Lancet, MAP and Sir Iain Chalmers' 'Interesting Figure' of Six Million," *Richard Millett's Blog* (December 6, 2013), https://richardmillett.wordpress.com/2013/12/06/the-lancet-map-and-sir-iain-chalmers-interesting-figure-of-six-million/.

22. Richard Millett, "British Psychotherapists Gear Up for Racist Boycott of Israeli Psychotherapists," *Richard Millett's Blog* (April 3, 2014), https://richardmillett.wordpress

.com/2014/04/03/british-psychotherapists-gear-up-for-racist-boycott-of-israeli
-psychotherapists/.

23. Richard Millett, "Russell Tribunal on Palestine Presents Ken Loach at Amnesty,"
Richard Millett's Blog (November 9, 2010), https://richardmillett.wordpress.com
/2010/11/09/russell-tribunal-on-palestine-presents-ken-loach-at-amnesty/.

24. "Joint Parallel Report Submitted to the Emergency Water, Sanitation and Hygiene
Group (EWASH) and Al-Haq" (September 2011), https://unispal.un.org/DPA/DPR/unispal.ns
f/0/25404F8138A8FEA5852578FC0050F939 (accessed November 16, 2017).

25. Richard Millett, "Amnesty Event: 'Israeli Soldier Used Broken Glass to Cut Magen
David into Palestinian Boy's Forearm,'" *Richard Millett's Blog* (April 13, 2011), https://
richardmillett.wordpress.com/2011/04/13/amnesty-event-israel-soldier-used-broken-glass
-to-cut-magen-david-into-palestinian-boys-forearm/.

26. Ben White, "Zionists Smear Amnesty over 'Cocktail' Joke,'" *The Electronic Intifada*
(January 11, 2013), https://electronicintifada.net/blogs/ben-white/zionists-smear-amnesty
-over-cocktail-joke.

27. Richard Millett, "Now Amnesty International's Kristyan Benedict Compares Israel
to Islamic State," *Richard Millett's Blog* (November 5, 2014), https://richardmillett.wordpress
.com/2014/11/05/now-amnesty-internationals-kristyan-benedict-compares-israel-to-islamic
-state/.

28. Richard Millett, "Police Prevent Activists Smashing into Ami Ayalon Talk At King's,"
Richard Millett's Blog (January 19, 2016), https://richardmillett.wordpress.com
/2016/01/19/police-prevent-activists-smashing-into-ami-ayalon-talk-at-kings/.

29. Richard Millett, "Israeli Deaths Glorified At LSE on Holocaust Memorial Day,"
Richard Millett's Blog (January 28, 2015), https://richardmillett.wordpress.com
/2015/01/28/israeli-deaths-glorified-at-lse-on-holocaust-memorial-day/.

30. Richard Millett, "Israeli Deaths Glorified At LSE on Holocaust Memorial Day,"
Richard Millett's Blog (January 28, 2015), https://richardmillett.wordpress.com
/2015/01/28/israeli-deaths-glorified-at-lse-on-holocaust-memorial-day/.

31. Richard Millett, "Threatened and Told I'm 'One of the Chosen People' at Anti-Israel
Trade Union Event," *Richard Millett's Blog* (October 25, 2011), https://richardmillett.wordpress
.com/2011/10/25/threatened-and-told-im-one-of-the-chosen-people-at-trade-union-event/.

32. Chris Elliott, "The Readers' Editor on… Averting Accusations of Antisemitism," *The
Guardian* (November 6, 2011), https://www.theguardian.com/commentisfree
/2011/nov/06/averting-accusations-of-antisemitism-guardian.

33. Richard Millett, "RMT's Steve Hedley Defames Me Trying to Save His Own Skin,"
Richard Millett's Blog (November 9, 2011), https://richardmillett.wordpress.com
/2011/11/09/rmts-steve-hedley-defames-me-trying-to-save-his-own-skin/.

34. "Statement from Steve Hedley," *RMT londoncalling* (November 8, 2011),
http://rmtlondoncalling.org.uk/node/2579.

35. Jonny Paul, "London Editor Prays for Nuclear Attack on Israel," *The Jerusalem Post*
(August 28, 2007), http://www.jpost.com/International/London-editor-prays-for-nuclear
-attack-on-Israel.

36. Richard Millett, "Camera Grabbed, Rucksack Snatched and Racially Abused at
SOAS," *Richard Millett's Blog* (May 15, 2012), https://richardmillett.wordpress.com
/2012/05/15/camera-grabbed-rucksack-snatched-and-racially-abused-at-soas/.

37. Richard Millett, "SOAS Update," *Richard Millett's Blog* (May 22, 2012), https://richardmillett.wordpress.com/2012/05/22/soas-update/.

38. Richard Millett, "Smearing of Pro-Israel Questioners Gathers Pace at SOAS' Centre For Palestine Studies," *Richard Millett's Blog* (April 17, 2012), https://richardmillett .wordpress.com/2012/04/17/smearing-pro-israel-questioners-gathers-pace-soas-centre -palestine-studies/.

39. Richard Millett, "Ghada Karmi Calls For 'The End of a Jewish State in our Region,'" *Richard Millett's Blog* (January 16, 2011), https://richardmillett.wordpress.com /2011/01/16/ghada-karmi-calls-for-the-end-of-a-jewish-state-in-our-region/.

40. Richard Millett, "Mavi Marmara's Ken O'Keefe Compares Jews to Nazis: the Footage," *Richard Millett's Blog* (February 27, 2012), https://richardmillett.wordpress.com /2012/02/27/mavi-marmaras-ken-okeefe-compares-jews-to-nazis-the-footage/.

41. Richard Millett, "American Professor Tells British Audience 'Israel Is Heading Into an Abyss'," *Richard Millett's Blog* (November 13, 2013), https://richardmillett.wordpress .com/2013/11/13/american-professor-tells-british-audience-israel-is-heading-into-an-abyss/.

42. Richard Millett, "Protesters Compare 'Palestine' to Auschwitz and Dachau Outside Israeli Embassy," *Richard Millett's Blog* (July 12, 2014), https://richardmillett.wordpress .com/2014/07/12/protesters-compare-palestine-to-auschwitz-and-dachau-outside-israeli -embassy/.

43. Richard Millett, "Tariq Ali: 'The End of Israel Will Benefit All Israelis'," *Richard Millett's Blog* (May 10, 2016), https://richardmillett.wordpress.com/2016/05/10/tariq-ali -the-end-of-israel-will-benefit-all-israelis/.

14 Conspiracy Pedagogy on Campus: BDS Advocacy, Antisemitism, and Academic Freedom

Cary Nelson

Cary Nelson analyzes the impact of ideological anti-Israelism and BDS tactics on the professional academy and the classroom. Graduate students and young faculty are afraid to even *attend* sessions devoted to boycott discussion for fear they will expose their views and so subject themselves to harassment and intimidation and potentially jeopardize their careers. Antisemitism has found a home in the humanities and social sciences, taking over entire departments and disciplines. The classroom is turning into a space not for exploring the complexities of the Middle East but for indoctrinating students to view Israel and Zionism as the embodiment of modern evil. Nelson illustrates this with an analysis of anti-Israel syllabi from Columbia University and an examination of recent widely publicized anti-Israel incidents at Vassar and Oberlin. While BDS activities are unlikely, in the short run, to affect the investment portfolios of universities, anti-Israel curricular and campus activities are shaping the hearts and minds of "tomorrow's teachers, businesspeople, professionals, religious leaders, and politicians."

Introduction

There is now a substantial body of scholarly literature and political commentary explaining why Boycott, Divestment, and Sanctions (BDS) is dangerous. It demonizes, antagonizes, and delegitimizes Israel and uncritically idealizes the Palestinians. That will inhibit negotiations, not promote them. Despite some naive followers of the movement who believe otherwise, BDS misrepresents its goal, which is not to change Israeli government policy but rather to eliminate the Jewish State.[1] It thus offers no specific steps toward a resolution of the conflict and no detailed peace plan. Moreover, it does not seek to negotiate a Palestinian "Right of Return" to the West Bank but rather to impose a right for all Palestinians to return to Israel within its pre-1967 borders. BDS falsely claims to imagine a nonviolent route to ending the conflict. But there is no nonviolent way to achieve its goal of eliminating the Jewish State. Indeed, BDS demands an end to all efforts to build mutual empathy and understanding between Israelis and Palestinians. This antinormalization campaign rejects the communication, dialogue, negotiation, and unconditional interchange necessary to achieve a peaceful resolution of the conflict. The year 2016 became the year in which BDS-allied groups decided it was a matter of pride to block dialogue by interrupting and silencing pro-Israeli campus speakers. In addition to consistently undermining academic freedom with its boycott agenda and its effort to silence speakers, BDS actually offers nothing to the Palestinian people, whom it claims to champion. Perhaps that is the single most cruel and deceptive feature of the BDS movement. Its message of hate is a route to war, not peace. With these general conditions as a context, this essay will review the most widely publicized BDS agendas on campus and in professional associations, then move on to its special concern, the increasing anti-Israel politicization of humanities and soft social sciences classrooms and the degree to which this suggests antisemitism has found a pedagogical home.

The battles over boycott proposals in academic and professional associations have grown increasingly more difficult since about 2012, not only because the number of BDS faculty and graduate students attending annual meetings to promote boycotts has grown, but also because in some cases the detailed reports supporting the resolutions have grown in both length and the number of accusations leveled. But while it only takes a sentence to register an accusation, it may take weeks of research and many pages to refute it definitively. The 130-page pro-BDS report issued by the American Anthropological Association (AAA) in October 2015 is a prime example.[2] Nonetheless, the strategies necessary in response, beginning with good information and continuing with tactics, rhetoric, timing, outreach, arguments, and organizing, are familiar and well tested. There is a tremendous amount of work involved, but at least the nature of the work is well understood, even if its success cannot be guaranteed.

On college campuses, BDS initiates divestment resolutions that have no impact on college investment policy even if they succeed. But the resultant battles do turn some students against Israel and promote some antisemitic perspectives. Those students become tomorrow's teachers, businesspeople, professionals, religious leaders, and politicians. In addition to promoting anti-Israel sentiment that migrates to Jews in general, this presents a long-term challenge to US policy and thus a long-term security risk to Israel. BDS often takes over the public spaces on American campuses and drives pro-Israel students to retreat to the safe spaces of their Chabad or Hillel chapters or to their work in less politicized areas like engineering or the sciences. But the institutional impact of BDS has been still deeper and more troubling. It has helped turn some entire academic departments and disciplines against Israel and some faculty members in the humanities and soft social sciences into anti-Israel fanatics. Fanatics do not just oppose policies;

they indulge in corrupting passions and biases. Anecdotal evidence, public hate speech, and examples of representative syllabi now demonstrate that this trend has spread to the classroom itself.[3] There, the task of responding is infinitely more difficult—infinitely, not only because the classroom is not a public space in the same way a professional association or a campus quad is, but also because it is more thoroughly protected by academic freedom.

But the main topic here—the political corruption of the classroom—must be prefaced with a simultaneous warning about the fragility of academic freedom in the contemporary university. In the early 1970s, about two-thirds of higher education faculty were eligible for tenure and thus a high degree of job security. In the new millennium, that percentage has declined to one-third. Most college teachers are now at-will employees subject to nonrenewal. They lack strong, if any, academic freedom protections. In departments with a pro-Israel or anti-Israel bias, contingent or adjunct faculty can be at risk of nonrenewal if they refuse to embrace their colleagues' politics in a syllabus. Many adjunct faculty consequently realize they are safer if they avoid controversial course topics. That is a depressing conclusion, but it nonetheless reflects reality. The links between academic freedom and job security are now widely broken. That some in the BDS movement are willing to sacrifice the university's principles and its future in the service of their political agenda does not mean that those who oppose them should do the same. Political struggles are usually fought by deploying whatever weapons are available. That has never been the best strategy in higher education. Perhaps Israel's defenders, including university administrators and Israel's non-academic allies, should show some reticence about using what power and influence they may have in campus conflicts.

War by Other Means: The State of the American Campus

One can recognize the problems at stake in some classroom assignments and in the level of unqualified hostility toward Israel that some faculty members express in their public statements on campus and elsewhere. When faculty members say publicly that Israel is a settler-colonialist, genocidal, racist, and apartheid state, there is reason to conclude that they believe these are factual statements, not hypotheses to be debated. Some likely present these political opinions as fact in classroom lectures as well. There is little doubt that students would be better off, that the mission of higher education would be better served, and that the reality of Israeli-Palestinian and worldwide politics would be better represented if these accusations were to be treated as debatable, with students provided access to opposing views. But that is commonly not the case. These accusations are being debated in the public sphere, and thus, they should be treated as contestable claims in the classroom as well, no matter what political opinions teachers may hold. That is not because it is a universal principle that one must cover the character of debates, especially given that some positions are discredited and become irrelevant over time, but rather because attitudes toward the Israeli-Palestinian conflict are currently inseparable from the competing arguments that shape them. It should be helpful to put these issues into context, offer some examples, and reflect on what this means.

When University of California (UC), Santa Barbara sociology professor William Robinson sent an email to the students in his 2009 Sociology of Globalization course that had photos of the 2008–2009 Israeli assault on Gaza set up as parallel to photos of the German occupation of the Warsaw Ghetto during the Second World War, some people urged he be fired.[4] His Nazi/Israel comparisons were irresponsible history and deplorable pedagogy, but academic freedom protected his right to say such things. Were he a job candidate, one might also have defended his right to say what he pleased, but a search committee could certainly have decided not to hire him. But you cannot fire a tenured faculty member for saying things that are commonplace in given academic disciplines. Comparisons between Israel and Nazi Germany may be despicable, but they were not categorically rogue opinion in 2009, and they are not so now. They have a history not just in the United States and Europe but also in Israel. Similarly, like it or not, we are long past the point where claims that Israel is a settler-colonialist apartheid state are outliers. That means we can and should contest them, but punitive options for advocating such views—as opposed to careful professional evaluation—are largely unavailable. The BDS movement did not initiate these claims, but it has widely promoted them and has helped install them as self-evident truths. And that means some faculty members feel free—indeed, responsible—to treat them as truths. Unfortunately, that can intimidate some students and inhibit them from presenting opposing opinions. When entire disciplines are consumed by such views, students who differ can easily be silenced, and they can certainly experience those disciplines as antisemitic.

The Robinson case concerns an explicit communication with the students in his class, but debates about the Israeli-Palestinian conflict in academic associations also point to the state of the academy more broadly and suggest how the issues will be handled in class. At the December 2014 annual meeting of the AAA, those in attendance were confronted by hundreds of ferociously anti-Israel young graduate students excitedly voting down a resolution opposing academic boycotts. They were spurred on by faculty members presenting anti-Israel papers at formal academic sessions scheduled by the organization. One tenured faculty member read a paper making an antisemitic claim that Jews and non-Jews, not citizens and noncitizens, are separated on arrival at Israel's Ben Gurion airport. That slander was met with audience applause, a chilling display of mass ignorance. A year later, those same faculty and graduate students voted for an academic boycott by a margin of 1,040 to 136.[5] All these young students did not acquire their convictions exclusively in extracurricular settings. They had to be carefully taught.

During a 2014 AAA annual meeting session devoted to small-group discussion, a table with nine anthropology faculty and graduate students engaged in analyzing the pros and cons of academic boycotts. There was unanimous sentiment that anthropologists had to do something, that inaction was unacceptable, and on that basis alone, some felt an academic boycott was justified. Someone sensibly asked what the impact of adopting a boycott resolution would be on anthropology as a discipline. I suggested that people consider what had happened to the American Studies Association (ASA) after it voted to boycott Israeli universities in December 2013. Not one other person at the table even knew about the ASA resolution, let alone what the national response was.[6] Yet they considered themselves well informed enough to proceed with their own disciplinary debate. There was nonetheless a clannish conviction that only anthropologists should be heard from, that people outside the discipline had nothing relevant to say about how boycotts violate universal principles of academic freedom.

When a boycott resolution came up for debate on a California State University campus in 2015, students reported that faculty members used classroom time to advocate for the resolution. Some faculty members refused to let students voice opposing views, a clear violation of academic freedom. Most of the courses in which faculty urged support for the resolution had nothing to do with history or political science, let alone the Israeli-Palestinian conflict.

This essay will take up the topic again later, but it is worth recalling here that the policy of the American Association of University Professors (AAUP) has for more than half a century warned against bringing politically extraneous material into the classroom. In 1970, the AAUP sensibly modified its stand by introducing a standard of persistence. In that light, a home economics or veterinary medicine professor could urge students to vote for or against Israel so long as he or she did not do so repeatedly. But any such faculty advocacy must also welcome alternative student views. Although most students and faculty do not realize this, failure to do so could justify disciplinary action. For a tenured faculty member, the consequences could range from denying an annual raise to delaying a promotion decision, although not termination. Needless to say, no sanctions of any kind were applied in the California case. We need to better educate the campus about faculty responsibilities and the way they limit academic freedom, a concept that does not free you to intimidate students.

At the January 2016 meeting of the Modern Language Association (MLA), a number of those in attendance routinely met pro-Israel graduate students and young faculty who were afraid even to *attend* sessions devoted to boycott discussion or debate for fear they would be asked their opinion, thereby exposing their views and potentially jeopardizing their careers. At that same meeting, when an anti-BDS speaker accused the BDS movement of antisemitism, the seventy or so BDS supporters in the room broke out in spontaneous laughter. For years, accusations of antisemitism have met with outrage, denial, and anger. Perhaps we have turned a corner and laughter now replaces anger.

Early in 2016, David Makovsky, an adviser to John Kerry's 2013–2014 Mideast peace initiative, visited the University of Illinois at Urbana-Champaign as part of a national tour. The sponsors could not find one member of the current faculty willing to attend an invitation-only seminar with him. At his public lecture that evening, not one current member of the faculty of two thousand was in attendance. Several emeritus faculty members came, but otherwise, the faculty stood in solidarity with the campus atmosphere of anti-Israel intimidation.

We need to gather the stories of pro-Israel graduate students and young faculty who decided not to go into Israel studies for fear they would never get a job in departments or academic fields now dominated by BDS and suggestions of antisemitism. All this is supplemental to the widely reported—but also hotly debated—anti-Jewish atmosphere in public spaces reported on some campuses by undergraduates, an atmosphere that helps convince students that passionate departmental attacks on Israel may be antisemitic, even if they are not. Although the intimidation of graduate students and young faculty members is less widely known than the antisemitic incidents on campus, the increasing examples of career intimidation are deeply troubling. An undergraduate can often keep her or his head down or retreat to Hillel to avoid hostile social confrontations over Jewish identity, a retreat that encourages the ghettoizing of pro-Israel sentiment on campus. And an undergraduate can move on with his or her life after graduation. A prejudicial classroom, however, is another matter. It can shape the perception of intellectual life long term. So, obviously, do decisions about what kind of work will be the focus of one's career. For over forty years, many faculty members have urged students to follow their hearts, to choose the specializations and research interests to which they are most deeply drawn. In some disciplines, like Middle East studies, that advice is no longer wise. A June 2016 essay in *Legal Insurrection* analyzing the close AAA vote against a boycott of Israeli universities ends with this statement: "The author is a graduate student who must write under a pseudonym for fear of retribution from pro-BDS faculty."[7] Another graduate student writes that his

> concern is to get BDS-supporters who have power over me to just stop bothering me, and let me pursue my career in peace.... Because of the success of BDS in North American Anthropology Departments, doing archaeology in Israel is becoming increasingly difficult for young archaeologists. Most North Americans who do archaeology in Israel via secular universities are Jewish. In effect, BDS is holding my career hostage to the actions of the Israeli government. I am not the only young Jew in academia who is in this situation. In my

case, it has gotten to the point where I am considering making *aliyah* so that I can pursue my academic career more easily.[8]

Discipline-wide intimidation represents a threat to the character of the academy and to the meaningful exercise of academic freedom.

And ad hominem attacks also play a substantial role in intimidating others. BDS has not been able to shut down Russell Berman, Alan Dershowitz, Todd Gitlin, Rachel Harris, Jeffrey Herf, David Hirsh, Sharon Musher, Andrew Pessin, Martin Shichtman, myself, or its various other committed opponents, but over-the-top BDS rhetorical assaults on visible faculty are very effective in silencing many who have so far remained quiet. As we have seen in Donald Trump's Republican primary campaign, delivering insults instead of confronting arguments is an effective tactic. In BDS's case, it purports to replace fear with contempt. Since I don't want to disseminate slander about others, I'll cite a couple of remarks about me. Consider comments like these from UC Riverside history professor Mark LeVine, posted on Facebook but quoted widely:

> People like Cary Nelson and other *"machers"* [Yiddish for a self-important person] in the American Jewish community get up in arms about BDS. Well, Cary Nelson and the rest of you: F--- you. Call me uncivil, but still, f--- you. F--- all of you who want to make arguments about civility and how Israel wants peace when this is what Israel does, it's "mowing the lawn" and "defending" freedom. This is, in no uncertain terms, genocide. If you want to argue about it, come to Gaza with me. Come look at Palestinians in the eye and talk about how uncivil Steven Salaita is and how you are in fact a "critic" of Israel. There is only one criticism of Israel that is relevant: It is state grown, funded, and feeding off the destruction of another people. It is not legitimate. It must be dismantled, the same way that the other racist, psychopathic states across the region must be dismantled. And everyone who enables it is morally complicit in its crimes, including you.

And University of Michigan history professor Juan Cole: "Cary Nelson, a powerful faculty member at the University of Illinois Urbana-Champaign and pro-Israel fanatic who supported Salaita's firing later said that he thought it would be fair to give Salaita a settlement of a million dollars to go away. That is, it was worth $1M of state money to Nelson to avoid having on campus a colleague with whom he disagrees. Nelson had, scarily enough, been high in the AAUP's Academic Freedom Committee for years. I very much doubt that he would have defended my freedom of speech."[9]

These kinds of remarks began months and years before the Salaita affair—Joan Scott of Princeton's Institute for Advanced Study began severely criticizing me for Israel-related actions in 2006—but then escalated, with hyperbole spreading to more presentable scholars like Cole, in his case leading to implicit denial of the many times I defended pro-Palestinian scholars and indifference to the many statements of principle I wrote or coauthored for the AAUP.[10] One might not expect better of some, but one would expect better of Cole, which demonstrates how the politics of the anti-Israel constituency drives people to abandon factuality. A number of faculty members who privately stated their support for my views about Israel made it clear they had seen these or other comments and were not about to speak out themselves. Faculty willingness to support Israel publicly is severely curtailed by years of BDS hostility. Imagine the effect on vulnerable graduate students, contingent faculty, and untenured colleagues. Meanwhile, *Inside Higher Ed* informed me that it had refused to post the numerous violent responses to my publications there. On some campuses, it is difficult to find a faculty member even willing to reserve a room for a pro-Israel lecture.

These ad hominem remarks reflect a broader phenomenon both in the academy and in the public sphere. Not in living memory have we seen a political issue that has divided people so decisively as the debate over the Israeli-Palestinian conflict. With surprising frequency, people are willing to sever personal relationships over their differences about Israel. A number of people I have known for decades will no longer respond to emails from me, although I've never expressed any hostility toward them. Even during the Vietnam War, one did not see such widespread personal bitterness in the academy. For some academic disciplines, disputes about Israel are not only politically but also personally decisive.

We may have reached a tipping point in the politicization of humanities and soft social science disciplines, not only here but also in Britain and perhaps in some European countries. It is helpful in this context to step back a moment and remember that it is more than thirty years since we had largely completed the disciplinarization of the academy. Instead of thinking of themselves as members of the professoriate as a whole, faculty members today think of themselves as members of the engineering, computer science, anthropology, or English professions. Many disciplines present an inadequate, uninformed, or misleading knowledge base on which to judge the complex historical, political, religious, and cultural conflicts between Israelis and Palestinians. And yet the ethics of disciplinarity essentially says that you are only bound to teach both sides of an issue when disciplinary consensus does not exist. A biologist does not have to give equal time to those who oppose the theory of evolution. A historian has no reason even to mention Holocaust denial. A sociologist might be expected to cover debates about global warming, but a climate scientist could well choose either to give bare mention of disbelievers or to make it clear that truth resides on only one side of the debate.

What this suggests is that some disciplines—without having the requisite expertise—have reached a virtual consensus about the truth of Israel and the Israeli-Palestinian conflict. Moreover, it appears that the number of disciplines and subdisciplines where the balance has been tipped and consensual anti-Israel truth reigns is increasing. A political scientist might recognize the need to acknowledge both the Israeli and Palestinian narratives and treat them each as possessing validity. In cultural anthropology; throughout literary studies and ethnic studies; in much of African American studies, Native American studies, and women's studies; and of course, throughout Middle East studies, that is no longer the case.[11] In many areas of the academy, there is substantial social and professional support for faculty devoted to demonizing the Jewish State. They feel justice and the truth of history reside entirely on one side of the conflict, and they consequently feel quite righteous in teaching that perspective. They may have no awareness whatsoever that they have turned their classrooms into propaganda machines. That students experience all this as antisemitic is unsurprising.

The lopsided votes in favor of academic boycotts in some disciplines are a good indication of the state of not only of political but also pedagogical consensus. In some disciplines, to be sure, the balance of power is local. A given department may have jettisoned differences of opinion and a climate for debate that prevail in the discipline at large. Jewish studies is a particularly telling example of that phenomenon, for some Jewish studies programs have become centers of anti-Israel politics and conviction.

There is good reason to argue that requiring certain individual colleagues to make an effort to portray both sides of the Israeli-Palestinian conflict fairly, to embody "balance" in the classroom, is pointless. The effort by some organizations to urge universities to compel political balance in individual courses is misguided. Would there be any point in asking Judith Butler, Nadia Abu El Haj, Angela Davis, Barbara Foley, Grover Furr, Neve Gordon, Barbara Harlow, Gil Hochberg, Joy Karega, David Lloyd, Sunaina Maira, Joseph Massad, Bill Mullen, David Palumbo-Liu, Ilan Pappé, Jasbir Puar, Bruce Robbins, Malini Schueller, Steven Salaita, Gayatri Spivak, Gianni Vattimo, or Cornel West to do so? Moreover, the list above amounts to a subset of BDS's intellectual elite; even less presentable acolytes are surely out there. There might be more clarity for students if such tenured faculty simply embodied their unqualified malice in their teaching. But then the rest of us have great need to make certain that teaching based on mutual empathy is powerfully in evidence in the curriculum as a whole. We cannot win the day by countering pro-Palestinian fanaticism with pro-Israeli fanaticism. The best that does is strengthen or install ideological war on campus. And in many disciplines, we would lose that war; indeed, in some quarters, it is already lost. There are moral, professional, and tactical reasons to choose another way.

The bottom line is this: a university has a responsibility to ensure that the curriculum as a whole, not individual courses, displays an appropriate degree of balance. Campuses need to have a conversation about the character of the balance they seek.

A Representative Anti-Zionist Course

It will be helpful to look in detail at a recent course in Middle East studies by a well-known scholar at a major university. The required books for Joseph Massad's fourteen-week spring 2016 Columbia University undergraduate course Palestinian and Israeli Politics and Societies, a copy of the syllabus for which was supplied by a Columbia student, make the course's perspective perfectly clear: Edward Said, *The Question of Palestine*; Rashid Khalidi, *Palestinian Identity*; Joseph Massad, *The Persistence of the Palestinian Question*; Theodor Herzl, *The Jewish State*; Theodor Herzl, *Altneuland*; Shlomo Sand, *The Invention of the Jewish People*; Ghassan Kanafani, *Men in the Sun*; Kanafani, *Returning to Haifa*; Sara Roy, *The Gaza Strip: The Political Economy of De-Development*; Neve Gordon, *Israel's Occupation*; Jeroen Gunning, *Hamas in Politics*; Israel Shahak and Norton Mezvinsky, *Jewish Fundamentalism in Israel* (2004 edition); and Ali Abunimah, *The Battle for Justice in Palestine.*

Herzl is there less to represent the varieties of historical Zionism than as a foil for the course goal of demonstrating how Zionism has gone wrong. Other than that, the Jewish writers here either endorse BDS (Neve Gordon) or are fiercely hostile to Israel (Shlomo Sand, Israel Shahak). The result is a coherent course embodying overall only one point of view, a negative one that excludes any positive commentary on Israel or any recognition of Israel's achievements. Massad's course is designed to show that everything originating in historical and contemporary Zionism is fundamentally deplorable and destructive. Thus, the course in no way fulfills Massad's description, which claims comprehensiveness:

> This course covers the history of Zionism in the wake of the Haskala in mid-nineteenth century Europe and its development at the turn of the century through the current "peace process" and its ramifications between the state of Israel and the Palestinian national movement. The course examines the impact of Zionism on European Jews and on Asian and African Jews on the one hand, and on Palestinian Arabs on the other—in Israel, in the Occupied Territories, and in the Diaspora.... The purpose of the course is to provide a thorough yet critical historical overview of the Zionist-Palestinian encounter to familiarize undergraduates with the background to the current situation.

Massad's course is about convincing students that his political opinions are correct and in urgent need of adoption. Since some of the readings entertain conspiracy theories about Israel or about Jewish history and culture, some students would find them to be antisemitic; whether that can be claimed of the course as a whole is impossible to say. The essays and book chapters that Massad adds to various weeks' readings do a good deal to flesh out Palestinian self-representation and the racial and ethnic tensions in Israeli society, but they can hardly be accounted a fair representation of the varieties of Israeli culture or Jewish Israeli self-understanding. He assigns Ella Shohat's "Sephardim in Israel: Zionism from the Standpoint of Its Jewish Victims," but this represents the view of a tiny minority. Massad's "Zionism's Internal Others: Israel and the Oriental Jews" and a chapter from Sami Chetrit's *Intra-Jewish Conflict in Israel: White Jews, Black Jews* only reinforce the course's mission to prove that Zionism's whole legacy is corrupted by colonialism and racism.[12] One would not guess from Massad's choices that there are Mizrahim and Druze, to cite a couple examples, who actually support the state or that there is a large and distinctive Russian population.

The fourteen weekly topics are:

1. <u>The Haskala and Early Zionism</u>. The week is split between Regina Sharif's *Non-Jewish Zionism* and Michael Selzer's polemical anti-Zionist *The Aryanization of the Jewish State*.
2. <u>Zionist Foundations</u>, for which the week's reading includes both Herzl and Sand.
3. <u>Zionism and European Jews</u>, with Herzl's novel *Altneuland* and Sand figuring again. A nineteenth-century utopian novel can easily seem misguided to today's students.
4. <u>Zionism and Nazism—Zionism and Asian and African Jews</u>, which opens with Walter Laqueur and Hanna Arendt, but moves on to Lenni Brenner's *Zionism in the Age of the Dictators*, which purports to detail Jewish collaboration with Hitler. Brenner notably is a source for discredited former London mayor Ken Livingston's antisemitic remarks, remarks that led to him being suspended from the Labour Party.[13]
5. <u>Zionism and Asian and African Jews, and the Palestinians</u>. Readings by Khalidi, Massad, and Edward Said offer a range of anti-Zionist and anti-Israel views.
6. <u>Zionism and the Palestinians I</u>. Readings are limited to Khalidi and Massad.
7. <u>Zionism and the Palestinians II (in Israel and the Diaspora)</u>. Readings include Schechla's "The Invisible People Come to Light: Israel's 'Internally Displaced' and 'Unrecognized Villages'" and Massad's "Producing the Palestinian as Other: Jordan and the Palestinians."
8. <u>Palestinians in the Diaspora</u>. Selections from Said's *The Question of Palestine* are supplemented by a Yasser Arafat speech and a Massad essay.
9. <u>Palestine and the Palestinians</u>. The week is devoted to Ghassan Kanafani and Neve Gordon. Kanafani's novel *Men in the Sun* has been described as "an allegory of Palestinian calamity in the wake of the Nakba in its description of the defeatist despair, passivity, and political corruption investing the lives of Palestinians in refugee camps."
10. <u>Palestinians in Gaza</u>. Readings are limited to Sara Roy.

11. <u>Religion in Israel</u>. Gunning's *Hamas in Politics* (2007) was completed before the civil war in Gaza between Hamas and Fatah commenced. Although he occasionally recognizes Hamas's violence, Gunning tends overall to credit it as a resistance, rather than a terrorist, organization.

12. <u>Women in Israel and Palestine</u>. The twelve essays assigned for this week include five essays about Palestinian women activists.

13. <u>The Peace Process</u>. There are numerous books about the peace process, but none of them are assigned here. Instead, there are readings by Massad, Gordon, Roy, and Gunning.

14. <u>The End of the "Peace Process"</u> concludes the course with BDS advocate and the *Electronic Intifada* founder Ali Abunimah, who believes the Jewish state must be brought to an end.

This is not to suggest that all of these reading assignments are inappropriate. Many faculty members, including myself, would want students in a course on the Israeli-Palestinian conflict to read Khalidi and Said. I quote Khalidi in my *Dreams Deferred*, and I quote Palestinians in an effort to honor their Nakba narratives, although I would not assign Brenner, Sand, Selzer, or Shahak, among others—unless of course I wanted to provide some examples of misguided or fraudulent work. They are widely regarded as irresponsible and unreliable; they are here because they share Massad's relentless anti-Zionism. The fundamental problem is that Massad uses a course claiming comprehensiveness as part of a biased anti-Israel political campaign. The coercive social, political, and intellectual force of the assigned readings and lectures, moreover, would make it extremely difficult for a student to voice an alternative perspective and equally difficult to gain a hearing for one; there are, after all, no assigned readings on which to ground a different historical narrative. Massad is perfectly within his rights to teach the course this way, as a pro-Palestinian and anti-Israel polemic, but a university needs other points of view if it is to mount a responsible curriculum.[14] A department dominated by courses like Massad's has effectively chosen to be a political, rather than an academic, enterprise. Massad's academic freedom to teach the course the way he wants does not, however, protect him from other faculty faulting his course. Just as publications are open to criticism and debate, so too are courses and their syllabi.[15]

Syllabi are already on occasion part of departmental conversations. They are evaluated during job searches and contract renewal and promotion and tenure decisions. Faculty members routinely make suggestions to one another about potential reading assignments. Writing about her own course on the Arab-Israeli conflict, Donna Divine observes that her "task as instructor is to help students develop their analytical and critical abilities as well as make available to them the body of knowledge necessary for making their own informed judgments"[16] about the subject. One may reasonably ask whether Massad's course fulfills such aims. If not, does it meet other useful pedagogical goals? Challenges about such matters are appropriate components of professional life.

Conspiracy Pedagogy

University instructors are at least to some degree accustomed to helping people improve their teaching. We can also channel people into the kinds of teaching they do best. But we have no model of how to address political fanaticism in the classroom, let alone ideological fanaticism endorsed by a community of faculty believers. The goal has always been good teaching across the institution. Now we are left with borrowing the compensatory and corrective model from scholarship: to counter bad teaching with good teaching.

That can only take place in an environment in which we combine forthright condemnation of the demonization of Israel with firm criticism of Israeli government policy when it is merited. Again, faculty can voice their political opinions in class, but they must welcome open debate from their students. If they repress, ridicule, or disparage opposing student opinion, they should risk exposure and sanction. Persistently using a class on an entirely unrelated topic as a vehicle for promoting either pro-Israel or anti-Israel views, however, is unacceptable.

We must remember that many faculty members with strong views on the subject teach in fields with no connection to the conflict, and it is fair to assume that most of those faculty members never deal with it in class. Many faculty members keep their politics separate from their teaching and are quite capable of signing a pro-BDS or pro-Israel petition without bringing their views to class or trying to persuade students to adopt them. Signing a BDS petition may be a warning sign, but it is not proof of classroom bias. A faculty bias against sharing their political views also still carries a good deal of weight in the academy, but anti-Israel passion is seriously eroding that tradition in some fields. If you believe Israel is the root of all evil in the world, as some on the hard Left do, then that conviction can trump all the restraints on propagandizing that have sustained the profession for so long. And it can lead to vitriol that cannot readily be distinguished from actual antisemitism.

Unfortunately, as the debates unfold, the evidence suggests the tide has begun to turn on the system of values and restraints that have long shaped the ethics of teaching. The prevalence of vicious anti-Israel classroom proselytizing is increasing. At the anthropology meeting in 2014, attendees encountered graduate students who seemed to be basically brainwashed, and it is rather worrying that they are the next generation of teachers. But some of these teachers are already on the job.

In February 2016, Jasbir Puar, a tenured Rutgers University faculty member in women's studies, presented a talk at Vassar College devoted to an antisemitic claim that Israel has a formal policy of maiming and stunting the Palestinians in the West Bank and Gaza.[17] She added to it a claim that Israel regularly harvests the organs of dead Palestinians. She made similar assertions at Dartmouth in May. The Vassar lecture was recorded by audience members, transcribed, and widely distributed.[18]

There are conspiracy theories that obsessively find clues everywhere; the project is to interpret myriad facts through a paranoid lens that turns them into proof. And there are projects, like Puar's, that find evidence, let alone proof as ordinarily understood, irrelevant. Neither proof nor evidence was at stake in the blood libel, still alive in Arab countries, that Jews added Christian blood to matzah dough. The existence of the matzah itself was all that was needed for anti-semites to imagine any ingredient and add it rhetorically to matzo's preparation. And so with women's studies professor Puar. Some Palestinians are maimed in confrontations with the Israel Defense Forces (IDF), so by extension, Israel wants to stunt and maim all of them, keeping them alive as conveniently disabled enemies. According to Puar, Israelis can then bewail their own victimhood without being in any actual danger from the Palestinians. From this antisemitic perspective, there is no need to find documents supporting such a policy. All you have to do is play out the logic behind the slander. The sequential reasoning constitutes scholarship. One can respond in part by marshaling counterevidence; her claims about excessive birth defects and stunting in Gaza can be readily countered.[19] The statistical evidence refutes her global assertions. But her accusations will spread and be welcomed by those already conditioned to find them appealing.

For now, Puar still represents the lunatic fringe of the BDS movement, but many in the audience at Vassar applauded her, and others around the country have disputed accusations about the antisemitic character of her work, as though criticism of Puar's claims amounts to an attack on academic freedom. In fact, faculty have a responsibility to condemn slander packaged as academic reasoning. We have a responsibility to counter the impact her work has on the impressionable students who applaud her talks. Otherwise, her views and those of others will become more widely adopted and normalized within some academic communities. Unfortunately, the lunatic fringe is welcome throughout the BDS movement. It is increasingly at the heart of the matter. Some will endorse her theories out of political solidarity.

One may try a thought experiment. Do we suppose that in teaching about Gaza and the West Bank, Puar would feel inclined, let alone professionally compelled, to reframe what she presented in lectures as factually true and treat it as hypothetical or open to debate? Would she pause before the antisemitic aura of her accusations against Israelis? There is certainly no hint in her lecture or in her publications that she feels the charges of stunting and maiming are open to debate. Quite the contrary.

If these claims represent the lunatic fringe of BDS thinking, what should we make of the extremist elements of BDS cited earlier that are shared by many of its loyal soldiers, including the conviction that Israel's aims are genocidal? Add to those the claim that Zionism equals racism. It's not that long ago when that motto was considered an outlier in the humanities as a whole, despite its adoption by parts of the Left. Evidence that students have been affected by campus assertions like that is now common.

But lunatic opinion is still more lunatic. Oberlin College professor Joy Karega's online syllabus for her fall 2015 rhetoric course Writing for Social Justice includes a section on the Israeli-Palestinian conflict.[20] The rationale for the course is interesting; it has its own trigger warning: "You may not always feel comfortable in this classroom. Social justice work is not generally geared towards making people feel comfortable. Social justice work attempts to enact social change, and that can be quite threatening and uncomfortable on many fronts. Also, polemical and agitation rhetorics are strategies that some social justice writers employ. As such, I will not discourage their usage in your own writing. We will also examine in this course several iterations of these kinds of rhetorics at work in the writings of social justice activists."

The readings include Rania Khalek's "How Today's Liberal Zionists Echo Apartheid South Africa's Defenders" and Bruce Dixon's "Cowardly, Hypocritical, Subservient Congressional Black Caucus Endorses Israeli Apartheid and Current War Crimes in Gaza," along with a long, combined reading on intersectionality. There are no readings listed that are sympathetic to Israel, but then this is a training course in writing for social justice, and social justice, as the BDS movement tells us, is embodied in only one side of the conflict. Most of the course is focused on US-based activism on racial issues, but antagonism toward Israel is integral to the course's concept of social activism and apparently to classroom discussions. It is not a course that simply studies the topic. It trains you to participate from a particular point of view. There is no evidence that the course includes the lunatic antisemitic topics she pursues on social media, even if the two are related by her core convictions.[21] But she certainly employs the "polemical and social agitation rhetorics" she trains her students to use in her public persona. She does assign four chapters from Christian Fuchs' book *Social Media*, but whether Karega points to her own use of social media one cannot say with any certainty, although it's easy to imagine that Karega's own uses of social media would come up for discussion. Would students struggle with her advocacy? Not if they are self-selected in sympathy with her anti-Israel hostility. In any case, the syllabus is perfectly rational, arguably more troubling because of that, because it's a course that could easily be emulated. Just how rational her classroom discussion of Israel would be is another matter.

The contrast between the delusional and nakedly antisemitic character of Karega's Facebook posts and the rational but politically charged character of her syllabus gives us a pretty good guide to how faculty who are basically unhinged opponents of Israel can make themselves academically respectable.[22]

But the antisemitic Facebook posts are still part of her public persona; they are part of Oberlin's public profile and part of the gateway to her courses. The academic profession has yet to deal with the reality that faculty members can establish a public presence through social media that completely outstrips anything they could typically achieve through teaching and research. The AAUP has—in my view, unwisely—taken the position that faculty statements on social media are not part of their professional profile, even if the arguments and subject matter clearly overlap with their teaching and research.[23] Those legislators who have reacted with hysteria to faculty members who make a couple of intemperate remarks on Facebook or Twitter are clearly out of line, but we need to think seriously about those faculty who make persistent use of social media in the same areas in which they teach or do research.[24] In such cases, faculty members should be academically responsible for what they say.

The relationship between Karega's teaching and her social media activism, however, is still deeper, because she is effectively training students to emulate her. Not all of us would consider a for-credit tutorial on how to participate in extremist activism an appropriate college course, but some departments now would. There is yet another issue that student support for Karega suggests may be embedded in her course—a call to bind identity with a perceived social justice issue. That, however, is how the academy has evolved in recent history. Its roots go back decades, having now produced consequences we hardly imagined.

This is a personally painful subject for me not only because I do not welcome hearing Israel demonized but also because I have long argued that articulate, rational, well-supported advocacy has a place in the classroom.[25] It can help model intelligent argumentation for students. It can show students what academia brings to controversy that Washington politics often does not. But I did not have in mind Palumbo-Liu's opportunistic anti-Israel sarcasm and his repeated indulgence in antisemitic tropes or Lloyd's anti-Israel harangues, let alone Puar's elaborate hate-based conspiracy theories or Karega's antisemitic demagoguery. And it does not help matters that black students at Oberlin included a demand that Karega be automatically guaranteed tenure among the December 2015 list of demands they gave Oberlin's president.[26] At least in some quarters on the American campus, there are no limits to the venom that will be embraced.

BDS thus did not invent this problem. It reflects the degradation of some disciplines over decades. But BDS influence is advancing the problem. And unfortunately, BDS's lunatic fringe is increasingly evident in some disciplines. What still counts as unquestioned lunacy—like Karega's Facebook posts—meanwhile helps make somewhat less rabid opposition to Israel seem reasonable. One hopes Karega could not get applause from a general audience for her claim that the

Mossad was behind the Charlie Hebdo massacre or for continuing to promote the antisemitic charge that Israel was behind the assault on the World Trade Center, but Puar's madness was well received by some and strongly defended by others.

All one can do about Puar, who is tenured, is to employ the fundamental practice of intellectual critique. But the call to counter defective speech with better speech does not cover all our responsibilities. We do not argue that it is fine to hire or tenure an idiot so long as we compensate by hiring or tenuring someone smart. Based on her dissertation, there were clearly reasons to question the wisdom of hiring Karega. Her reliance on interviews with her father as her primary source is a viable strategy for a personal book but not necessarily for a doctoral research project. Karega, of course, is untenured, which means that there are two occasions when the adequacy of her teaching and research will be reviewed—first in her third year and then in her sixth. Calls for her summary dismissal reflect a failure to understand and honor the standards for due process necessary to preserve academic freedom. Putting her on paid leave prior to the completion of a faculty review is also highly problematic, unless the faculty have already reached preliminary conclusions.[27]

If Rutgers faculty decide that Puar promotes delusional standards of evidence in the classroom, there is not much they can do save to assign her courses where her convictions will not be in play or compensate with better courses taught by others. Karega, notably, teaches the basic rhetoric course. That means faculty across campus have a vested interest in whether she supports or undermines generally accepted academic standards in her teaching. Faculty members could file a complaint separately from her formal reviews, and that could produce action at any time. Whether the result would be reassignment or something more serious is impossible to say. In any case, full due process would apply. Given that her responses to public events appear not to be rational, it is also possible that problems with her public persona could recur.

Because of the risks to academic freedom and the potential for unwarranted criticism, we need to tread very carefully in examining the pedagogical practices of individual faculty. We certainly have no comprehensive evidence of antisemitic teaching to present, not even broad access to appropriate syllabi, but we have enough evidence to know that the problem exists. Some of what is cited here is anecdotal. But developments at public meetings in academic associations, the character of numerous events on campus, and the evidence of key course syllabi are sufficient to demonstrate we have a problem we need to consider how to confront. On campus, the public sphere and the classroom are only partly discontinuous spaces. At the very least, they interact and overlap. Competing accounts of the campus climate for Jews, however, remind us that students can proceed on separate tracks, with some who become involved in campus governance or devote themselves to more politicized disciplines encountering considerable stress and antagonism and others who concentrate on their engineering major or socialize at Chabad, finding the campus mostly hospitable.

There is too much evidence of the political corruption of academic disciplines, however, to treat pedagogy as sacrosanct. To ignore the issue, moreover, will be to watch the problem rapidly get worse. How often we confront anything so simple and unidirectional as indoctrination—especially given the complex pluralism of much of campus life—is very much open to question, although Massad's syllabus is clearly an effort to persuade and perhaps to indoctrinate. But there is no question that the campus devotion to civil discussion and debate is frequently under assault and that in many local settings the campus has become inhospitable to presentable intellectual activity. The increase in BDS efforts to silence pro-Israel speakers is especially clear evidence of that trend. Some disciplines no longer promote self-critical intellectual reflection. The time to confront these trends is now.

Perhaps our responsibility begins with broader forms of disciplinary critique. We need to take responsibility for the state of our own academic disciplines and subject them to serious scholarly critique. That means producing well-supported and thoughtful analyses. And it means mixing the critique of individual faculty with disciplinary contextualization. Tempting though it is, just going after Puar or her equivalents without interrogating the cultural and professional developments that have made her possible is inadequate. But it is equally unacceptable to cower before the BDS intimidation campaign claim that criticizing someone's work constitutes a violation of academic freedom and a suppression of free speech rights. That message disavows the core purpose of academic research and debate, eviscerating the educational mission.

For now, we can say with some certainty that in many quarters things are going to get worse and that there is no evidence they will get better. It will, unfortunately, take real courage for people within the more degraded disciplines to do the kind of informed analysis we need. And it is unrealistic to anticipate that some pervasively biased disciplines will reform themselves any time soon. Instead, some departments will choose new colleagues as part of an effort to impose a single anti-Israel political perspective on what is actually a complex, unresolved issue. It then becomes necessary for colleges and universities to approve hires in such a way that students are likely to be exposed to multiple perspectives. Some departmental propaganda machines may need to be mothballed, denied hiring rights until they can be reformed or their members retire. But that should not be a unilateral administrative decision; the faculty senate needs to be involved in a thorough program review and a resulting decision, not only to preserve academic shared governance, but also because the campus as a whole will not learn anything from an administration decision that can be discounted on procedural, rather than substantive, grounds. We will need a multidisciplinary critique that draws on the resources of the academy as a whole if our educational institutions are to be insulated from the political conformity that BDS allied faculty too often seek to impose on their students.[28]

CARY NELSON is Jubilee Professor of Liberal Arts and Sciences and Professor of English at the University of Illinois at Urbana-Champaign and an affiliated professor at the University of Haifa. His most recent books are *The Case Against Academic Boycotts of Israel* and *Dreams Deferred: A Concise Guide to the Israeli-Palestinian Conflict and the Movement to Boycott Israel.*

Notes

1. Although the main BDS website does not make this explicit, every major BDS spokesperson has been clear in lectures and in print that this is their aim. As I write in the introduction to my *Dreams Deferred: A Concise Guide to the Israeli-Palestinian Conflict and the Movement to Boycott Israel* (Bloomington, IN: MLA Members for Scholars' Rights / Indiana University Press, 2016),

> BDS founder Omar Barghouti has argued, "accepting Israel as a 'Jewish state' on our land is impossible." California State University political scientist As'ad AbuKhalil, among many other BDS leaders, echoes those sentiments: "Justice and freedom for the Palestinians are incompatible with the existence of the state of Israel." In *The Battle for Justice in Palestine* Ali Abunimah the Chicago-based cofounder of the *Electronic Intifada*, confidently concludes that "Israel's 'right to exist as a Jewish state' is one with no proper legal or moral remedy and one whose enforcement necessitates perpetuating terrible wrongs. Therefore it is no right at all" (44).... As I detail in an extended essay on her work, Berkeley literary theorist Judith Butler aims to have Israelis abandon their commitment to a Jewish state and a homeland of their own.... Although the rhetoric employed in each of these examples varies, the end result, as Barghouti has put it, is the same: "euthanasia" for the Jewish state.

2. See American Anthropological Association, "Report to the Executive Board: The Task Force on AAA Engagement on Israel-Palestine" (2015), http://s3.amazonaws.com/rdcms -aaa/files/production/public/FileDownloads/151001-AAA-Task-Force-Israel-Palestine.pdf (accessed November 13, 2017).

3. In 2012, a controversy erupted after University of Pennsylvania English professor Amy Kaplan suggested that faculty might well look for opportunities to insert anti-Israel material into courses that offer a potential thematic link with the Israeli-Palestinian conflict. She used the examples of a general course on prison culture and politics that could be enhanced with a section on Israeli treatment of Palestinian prisoners or a general literature survey that could include a section on Palestinian literature. See "University of PA Responds About Amy Kaplan's Politicizing of Her Courses," *Elder of Ziyon* (February 10, 2012), http://elderofziyon .blogspot.com/2012/02/university-of-pa-responds-about-amy.html.

4. See Scott Jaschik, "Crossing a Line," *Inside Higher Ed* (April 23, 2009), https://www .insidehighered.com/news/2009/04/23/ucsb.

5. See Elizabeth Redden, "Big Night for Boycott Movement," *Inside Higher Ed* (November 23, 2015), https://www.insidehighered.com/news/2015/11/23/anthropologists -overwhelmingly-vote-boycott-israeli-universities.

6. See Sharon Ann Musher, "The Closing of the American Studies Association's Mind," in Cary Nelson and Gabriel Noah Brahm, eds. *The Case against Academic Boycotts of Israel* (Chicago & New York: MLA Members for Scholars' Rights / Distributed by Wayne State University Press, 2015), 105–118.

7. See "Anti-Israel Boycott Resolution Fails at American Anthropology Association," *Legal Insurrection* (June 7, 2016), http://legalinsurrection.com/2016/06/anti-israel-boycott -resolution-fails-at-american-anthropology-association/?utm_source=feedburner&utm _medium=feed&utm_campaign=Feed%3A+LegalInsurrection+%28Le·gal+In·sur·rec·tion%29.

8. See "What Israel's Nightmare Trajectory May Mean on Campus," *Third Narrative* (March 20, 2016), http://thirdnarrative.org/bds-does-not-equal-peace-articles/what-israels -nightmare-trajectory-may-mean-on-campus/.

9. Juan Cole, "How the Israel Lobbies Hurt U of Illinois-U. C. & 1st Amendment (Salaita Case)," *Informed Comment* (August 15, 2015), http://www.juancole.com/2015/08/illinois -damaged-amendment.html.

10. For an account of some of my efforts to defend pro-Palestinian faculty, see my *No University Is an Island: Saving Academic Freedom* (New York: New York University Press, 2010).

11. [An October 2017 study documented that some 90% of campus anti-Israel events are sponsored by departments of ethnic studies, gender studies, and Middle East studies: "New Study Reveals How Faculty Who Boycott Israel Increase Likelihood of Antisemitism," AMCHA Initiative (October 14, 2017), https://amchainitiative.org/new-study-faculty-boycott -israel-increase-antisemitism-pr-102417.—eds.]

12. For a recent example of Massad's views, see his "Palestinians and the Dilemmas of Solidarity," *The Electronic Intifada* (May 14, 2015), https://electronicintifada.net/content /palestinians-and-dilemmas-solidarity/14518.

13. See Paul Bogdanor, "An Antisemitic Hoax: Lenni Brenner on Zionist 'Collaboration' With the Nazis," *Fathom* (June 10, 2016), http://fathomjournal.org/an-antisemitic-hoax -lenni-brenner-on-zionist-collaboration-with-the-nazis/.

14. The Faculty Action Network has a new website (www.israelandtheacademy.org) that includes, among its four hundred syllabi in Israel studies and Jewish studies, a significant number that aim to teach the Israeli-Palestinian conflict in a way that represents both sides fairly.

15. My own university requires that each department keep copies of all current course syllabi publicly available.

16. Donna Robinson Divine, "How to Teach all Sides of the Arab-Israeli Conflict Without Taking Sides," *History News Network* (January 17, 2010), http://historynewsnetwork .org/article/122054. This essay is also available on the Faculty Action Network site (www.israelandtheacademy.org).

17. For detailed comments on (and extensive quotations from) the Puar lecture, see William A. Jacobson, "Vassar Faculty-Sponsored Anti-Israel Event Erupts in Controversy," *Legal Insurrection* (February 8, 2016), http://legalinsurrection.com/2016/02/vassar-faculty -sponsored-anti-israel-event-erupts-in-controversy/. See also Mark G. Yudof and Ken Waltzer, "Majoring in Antisemitism at Vassar," *The Wall Street Journal* (February 17, 2016),

and Ken Waltzer, "BDS Scholars Defend the Indefensible," *The Times of Israel* (March 13, 2016), http://blogs.timesofisrael.com/bds-scholars-defend-the-indefensible/.

18. [In November 2017 Duke University Press published Puar's book asserting these claims: Shiri Moshe, "In Upcoming Book, Controversial Rutgers Professor Accuses Israel of Sparing Palestinian Lives in Order to Control Them," *The Algemeiner* (October 22, 2017), https://www.algemeiner.com/2017/10/22/in-upcoming-book-controversial-rutgers-professor -accuses-israel-of-sparing-palestinian-lives-in-order-to-control-them/—eds.]

19. See David Stone, "Has Israel Damaged Palestinian Health? An Evidence-Based Analysis of the Nature and Impact of Israeli Public Health Practices in the West Bank and Gaza," *Fathom* (Autumn 2014), http://fathomjournal.org/wp-content/uploads/2014/12/Has -Israel-damaged-Palestinian-health.pdf (accessed November 14, 2017). Also see Elihu Richter, "Selective, Biased and Discriminatory: The American Anthropological Association Task Force Report on Israel-Palestine," The Louis D. Brandeis Center for Human Rights Under Law (April 6, 2016), http://brandeiscenter.com/blog/selective-biased-and-discriminatory-the -american-anthropological-association-task-force-report-on-israel-palestine/.

20. Syllabus for Writing for Social Justice: Rhetoric 204 at Oberlin, taught by Joy Karega, https://new.oberlin.edu/dotAsset/04cd95b3-51a0-4807-b1b9-5e8c24f86209.pdf (accessed November 14, 2017).

21. Karega's blatantly antisemitic Facebook posts were widely publicized in March 2016: Andrew Pessin, "Oberlin Alumni Outraged Over 'Growing Tolerance for Antisemitism' at Alma Mater," *The Algemeiner* (March 1, 2016), https://www.algemeiner.com/2016/03/01/oberlin -alumni-outraged-over-administrations-tepid-response-to-antisemitism-at-alma-mater/.

22. Screenshots of Karega's Facebook posts are reproduced in David Gerstman, "Oberlin Professor Claims Israel Was Behind 9/11, ISIS, Charlie Hebdo Attack," *The Tower* (February 25, 2016), http://www.thetower.org/3012-oberlin-professor-claims-israel-was -behind-911-isis-charlie-hebdo-attack/.

23. Had the AAUP's Committee A on Academic Freedom and Tenure been responding to social media interventions about a subject other than Israel, it might have been willing to take a more serious look at the issues involved in the changed world in which all of us are living. By the time the issue arose, however, two opponents of Israel, both supporters of academic boycotts, had been appointed to the group. It did not help matters that one proceeds by intense ad hominem attacks and the other by way of personal sarcasm. That did not encourage a free and open discussion. During the course of drafting and revising the AAUP's investigative report on the Salaita case, there was considerable staff and appointed committee member support for claiming that Jewish donors had shaped the university's decision to withdraw Salaita's offer. In conversation with me, one senior staff member cited the Sami Al-Arion case in Florida as an example of Jewish donor intervention proving that that was always what such people do, even though there had been no significant evidence of donor influence at the University of Illinois. In the end, there was enough disagreement that the accusations against donors were removed from the report. But the AAUP refused to seriously consider the idea that a faculty member's social media interventions in areas of his or her teaching or research might be part of his or her professional profile.

24. On the relevance of social media to a faculty member's professional profile, see Don Enron, "Professor Salaita's Intramural Speech" and Cary Nelson, "Steven Salaita's Scholarly Record and the Problem of his Appointment," both in *AAUP Journal of Academic Freedom* 6

(2015), https://www.aaup.org/reports-publications/journal-academic-freedom/volume-6 (accessed November 14, 2017).

25. See my "Advocacy Versus Indoctrination," *Journal of College and University Law* 39 (2013): 749–768.

26. See Blake Neff, "Oberlin Students Release Gargantuan 14-Page List of Demands," *Daily Caller* (December 17, 2015), http://dailycaller.com/2015/12/17/oberlin-students-release -gargantuan-14-page-list-of-demands/.

27. [After this essay was submitted, Oberlin put Karega on paid leave and subsequently fired her: "Oberlin Professor Dismissed over Antisemitic Facebook Posts," *The Algemeiner* (November 16, 2016), https://www.algemeiner.com/2016/11/16/oberlin-professor-dismissed -over-antisemitic-facebook-posts/—eds.].

28. My thanks to Sharon Musher, Kenneth Stern, and Kenneth Waltzer for comments on a draft.

15 When Did We Abandon Academic Integrity for Academic Freedom?

Denise Nussbaum

Denise Nussbaum's narrative shows what happens when anti-Israelism gets out of control. She describes the activities of her campus chapter of Amnesty International, which for years relentlessly sponsored anti-Israel events. When the group won campus funding to bring Boycott, Divestment, and Sanctions (BDS) activist Miko Peled to speak, Nussbaum decided to act. She documented Peled's lack of academic credentials and his fabrications and falsehoods. She stated that he was not a peace activist but sought the destruction of Israel, and she proposed preparing a more balanced presentation or organizing a bona fide academic panel. For this, she was rewarded with a smear campaign using lies and misrepresentations to represent her as a racist, an Islamophobe, and a bully opposing free speech. The university ignored her formal complaints of workplace harassment. Refusing to be silenced, Nussbaum protested at a faculty meeting. One of her colleagues got so worked up that he crossed the line from verbal to physical abuse, and nobody intervened. Now a pariah for resisting anti-Israelism on her campus, Nussbaum has filed suit against both her attacker and the school.

I AM A professor of sociology at Mt. San Jacinto College (MSJC) in Southern California, where I have worked for seventeen years. I have worked for equality and justice my whole career and am published in the fields of diversity, discrimination, and pedagogy. I am the founder and director of BEAR (Bias Education, Advocacy & Resources). I am the recipient of the Stanback-Stroud Diversity Award from the Academic Senate for California Community Colleges. I am the matriarch of a large Jewish family that has dealt directly with antisemitism. I am also an alleged Islamophobe.

In February 2015, I was asked by a fellow faculty member to look into a guest speaker who had been invited to our campus by the campus adviser for Amnesty International and who, through the adviser, was being sponsored by our Diversity Committee. That speaker was Miko Peled, a leading voice of the BDS movement. After twenty-two years of fighting for the minority rights of others, the fight for my minority group—for Jews, for Israel—came to my campus.

Initially, I was not concerned. I thought that once I informed my colleagues on the Diversity Committee who this man was—a BDS advocate who calls for the destruction of Israel—surely they would rethink their support. Certainly, they would see the danger in bringing such hateful speech to our campus, *especially* without any balanced or scholarly discussion. This was not about free speech or academic freedom but about academic integrity. I argued that the Diversity Committee should not sponsor a speaker who openly calls for, and regularly justifies, violence against innocent Israelis. I endeavored to educate my community through letters, literature, and speeches. As I pursued ethical and legal measures, my anti-Israel colleagues began a campaign of hate and lies so vicious that within two months our campus was a seriously hostile environment, not only for Jewish students and faculty, but for *anyone* who spoke out in favor of Israel. In the end, I was publicly attacked at a faculty meeting—verbally and physically—as my colleagues and administrators watched ... and did nothing.

This is my story.

Amnesty International Brings BDS to MSJC

Over the past few years, I had begun to hear, from students and colleagues, about the anti-Israel bias of our campus chapter of Amnesty International. A quick look at the organization's events over the previous eight years revealed an average of four anti-Israel films, speakers, or events per year. The number of pro-Israel events: zero. Films or events vilifying any state or country besides Israel for human rights abuses: zero.

While walking across campus early in the spring semester in 2015, my colleague informed me that our very own Diversity Committee, which she and I had cofounded fifteen years earlier, had voted to sponsor an event with Peled. The Amnesty International adviser had told the Diversity Committee that Peled was a world-renowned peace activist and likened him to Gandhi and Martin Luther King, Jr. The committee voted to give Peled the bulk of their yearly budget: $2,500.

The few professors and students who were familiar with BDS were upset that we were paying to bring what we considered to be hate speech to our campus. I decided I would do everything within my power to educate our campus on the true nature of BDS and Peled.

I began by going to San Diego City College to see Peled's presentation there. I wanted to prove that my opposition to Peled was not simply a knee-jerk defense of Israel. My intention was to document the historical inaccuracies he would surely present there in order to show how inappropriate he was as a campus speaker and to garner support for a cosponsored, genuinely *academic* panel on the Palestinian-Israeli conflict.

Peled did not disappoint. In the course of his one-hour presentation, he made 166 remarks that were anti-Israel, often crossing the blurred line into antisemitism.[1] Peled constantly used terms like *apartheid, occupation, colonialism, ethnic cleansing, racist, oppressors, Nazi, terrorist, baby-killer,* and so forth to describe Israel and Israelis. Additionally, I counted no fewer than twenty-six gross historical inaccuracies and at least six specific calls to action against Israel. In the name of academic integrity, it seemed obvious to me that MSJC should not sponsor the presentation of destructive political propaganda disguised as history. My counter-suggestion of an academic panel was met with silence, however, even when I offered my opponents the choice of a moderator. They apparently had no interest in any joint event.

I wrote a letter to the Amnesty International faculty adviser, Shahla Razavi. I honestly believed that if she were aware of BDS and Peled's dishonest advocacy, she would rescind her offer and invite an academically more qualified speaker. When that failed, I endeavored to make Peled's presentation part of a larger academic discussion on campus. I informed Razavi that I opposed Peled's coming to campus because he was *not* a peace activist and because his one-sided presentation would do more harm than good to our campus community. What we needed, I wrote, was "an open-minded, honest, factual and academic discussion. If we are to bring this hot topic to campus, it must be in a balanced and scholarly manner." This, again, was one of several times I suggested we do some joint, balanced event.

Razavi was not interested. Rather than respond to me, she sent a letter to the Diversity Committee (thirty-plus members), scores of our colleagues, and countless others, accusing me of intimidation and bullying and of being an Islamophobe. She wrote:

> Miko Peled is an Israeli military veteran, now a peace activist ... who advocates for the rights of the indigenous peoples of the Holy Land. Apparently, one of our faculty members has approached a few of our faculty and opposed the funding of this event.... Is Miko Peled a controversial figure? He probably is. There are countless examples in our history of controversial figures who were ahead of their time and called on their governments to take actions to bring peace and justice to oppressed peoples [like] Nelson Mandela.... Unfortunately, *our faculty member opposing this event is using her power to intimidate not only myself, but the whole committee in what seems to me like academic bullying* [emphasis added].[2]

Though Razavi also wrote, "Academic freedom in teaching means that both faculty members and students can make comparisons and contrasts between subjects taught in a course and any field of human knowledge or period of history," she herself *refused* to include "comparisons and contrasts" as I had proposed, via an academic panel, instead choosing to present solely the Palestinian perspective. She further claimed that academic freedom "gives both students and faculty the right to study and do research on the topics they choose and to draw what conclusions they find consistent with their research." Peled's lectures, however, were not actually based on facts or research but instead were political diatribes to advance the BDS narrative under the guise of humanitarianism. Razavi quoted the Diversity Committee Mission Statement that I myself had written fifteen years earlier, claiming that the Peled event was consistent with our goals: "In our commitment to the furthering of knowledge and fulfilling our educational mission, the MSJC Diversity Committee seeks a campus and community climate that embraces, celebrates, and promotes respect for the entire variety of human experience. In our commitment to diversity, we welcome people from all backgrounds and we seek to include knowledge and values from many cultures, in the curriculum.... *We will also develop and communicate policies and promote values that discourage intolerance and discrimination* [emphasis added]."[3]

Razavi here inverted the situation, labeling *me* as intolerant and discriminatory. In what way does Peled's call for the destruction of Israel embrace, celebrate, or promote respect? How does hateful speech against Israel and the Jewish people "promote values that discourage intolerance and discrimination," particularly when recent research reveals a clear connection between the presence of anti-Israelism on campuses and antisemitism?[4]

Razavi continued: "I would like to state that Miko Peled, like thousands of other Jews, is a peace activist advocating for equal rights for Israelis and Palestinians." But, in fact, BDS does *not* argue for equal rights for Israelis. Its proponents call for the end of Israel and the removal of the Jewish people from their homeland.

Then this:

> After decades of conflict, the world has come to the understanding that an end to the conflict between Israelis and Palestinians can only be brought about by open dialogue and engagement, and that is why many Jews along with many Palestinians and non-Jews are working so hard to bring peace to this land. Miko Peled stands as one of them. I end with affirming my right to academic freedom and that *this faculty member is infringing on it and is threatening me with "rallying thousands of Jews" against this event.* Well, in response, I am going to also rally thousands of "academicians" who respect academic freedom [emphasis added].

The misrepresentations throughout her letter are stunning. Razavi speaks of "open dialogue and engagement," yet refused to even reply to my request for just that. She deflects the actual issue, academic integrity, to one of academic freedom. She falsely accuses me of abuses of power and academic intimidation and bullying. To the contrary, these were in fact the techniques that she and her BDS and Students for Justice in Palestine (SJP) constituents would use against *me.* At the time, I did not know this email was going around *outside* the Diversity Committee as well as off campus to countless anti-Israel activists. However,

I knew something had happened. Literally overnight, colleagues, students, staff, and administration began making snide comments and accusatory remarks to me. "Here she comes, the troublemaker"; "Why do you hate Palestinians?"; "Why are you attacking Shahla?"; "I hate to see professors against each other"; "I would have figured you for a proponent of free speech." Every day. All day. For months.

As I later learned—through materials acquired as part of the discovery process in my lawsuit—Razavi had repeatedly stated to colleagues, staff, students, and even our college president that I had threatened her and was "out to get her." She alleged that I was trying to silence her, that I was bullying her and junior faculty, and that I was trying to restrict her academic freedom. Razavi's supporters claimed that I, along with the congressmen who had written letters opposing Peled, were puppets of the American Israel Public Affairs Committee (AIPAC) and, therefore, stooges of Israel.[5] Razavi vilified me using hyperbole and outright lies to convince all who would listen that I was an Islamophobe and an oppressor.[6]

Razavi's narrative was so outrageous I felt compelled to defend myself. However, my response went only to the Diversity Committee, since (as I mentioned) I didn't know she had distributed her letter widely. In my letter, I explained to the Diversity Committee that Razavi's email both misquoted and misrepresented me. I told them that I believed the Palestinian-Israeli conflict deserved an open-minded, honest, factual, and *academic* discussion. I argued that Peled's approach was not consistent with the mission of the Diversity Committee and that they should rescind their support.

Particularly deceitful was Razavi's accusation that I was "threatening [her] with rallying thousands of Jews" against this event. What I had actually written to her was that I was "strongly opposed" to Peled being sponsored by the Diversity Committee as a "peace activist" and that his talk would be opposed by "1000s of educated Jews, Christians, and Muslims." Razavi's deletion of "educated" and "Christians, and Muslims" was clearly deliberate and inflammatory. Her deceitful misquote turned the debate into a Jewish issue rather than a scholarly issue for *all* people. It was this lie that turned the tide against me, I believe. Her overt manipulation made me look like I was just another Jew with an agenda, throwing my weight around and bullying my colleagues, rather than someone arguing for academic integrity.

After I sent this letter, I buried myself to prepare for the next Diversity Committee meeting, three weeks later. I spent the weeks summarizing studies; gathering news clips, YouTube videos, and historic photos; and painstakingly preparing an FAQ sheet (about Israel, the Palestinians, BDS, Peled, etc.) with careful answers, documenting each and every line to be sure my scholarly colleagues could trust that I was presenting valid knowledge. For a shared governance committee, all documents had to be submitted to the chair forty-eight hours prior to the meeting for proper, balanced dissemination. Following the rules, I did so.

What I did not know was that while I was naively aiming to present my case through academic and ethical conduct, my detractors were using unethical and perhaps even illegal measures to spread their narrative.

For example, Razavi sent documents directly to members of the Diversity Committee lobbying for Peled, despite strict rules stating that documents were to be submitted only to the chair. Razavi and her supporters called and emailed countless colleagues and coworkers, as well as people off campus, accusing me of academic bullying, of threatening Razavi, and of trying to silence pro-Palestinian voices. One untenured supporter of mine received messages from senior faculty that made her fear for her own promotion and, therefore, her livelihood: "Be careful, you're not tenured," "I wouldn't get involved if you're not tenured," and such.

The Campaign to Silence and Delegitimize Dissent Blossoms

Despite the ongoing vilification and ostracization, I persisted in my preparations for the Diversity Committee meeting. In the days preceding the meeting, the climate on campus became charged and uncomfortable for Jewish and/or Zionist students and faculty. It really hit me the day one of my students came to me fearful that our Holocaust Remembrance Day film addressing Nazi ideology and antisemitism would cause an uproar and make it appear that she had an agenda. She told me that, given everything that was going on, she didn't want to offend anyone and that she had changed her presentation from one that addressed anti-semitism to one that celebrated the role of American GIs in freeing the Jews. This is the climate at MSJC today: students afraid to discuss antisemitism and the Holocaust for fear of being labeled a Zionist.

In March, as I entered a faculty meeting, a female colleague, a woman I had served with for years on the academic senate, saw me and said, "There she is, the troublemaker!" I was shocked but didn't react right away. By the end of the meeting, I was shaking. After the meeting, I asked her why she had called me that. She laughed and said she didn't mean anything by it. She claimed she had the utmost respect for me as a scholar and a faculty leader. When I pressed her, she admitted she had "heard something" about a speaker I was trying to keep off campus. I told her that that was not an accurate statement, and I explained to her the issues involved. I said, "You know me. You know I have led the fight for minority rights at this college for sixteen years. You know I support free speech and academic freedom." She agreed with me. Then she said, "But I have a Palestinian student and ... I just don't know."

The day of the March Diversity Committee meeting arrived. The tensions on campus had been so high that the college president had me and my family escorted by armed police officers to and from our car. The meeting was linked by satellite between the two main campuses of MSJC. My opponents and their supporters were on the other campus. However, Razavi's husband came to *my campus*, and in a large, almost empty room, sat down directly behind me and my family. He sat there, arms folded, glaring at me. Later, two separate female faculty leaders commented on his "menacing stare" and "intimidating presence."

Razavi pulled some other last-minute shenanigans. She attempted to have her pro-Palestinian supporters Skype in with their comments, despite having been told repeatedly that it was against the bylaws. All throughout the meeting, Razavi was "out of order": talking over people, speaking out of turn, going off on rants. She even accused the academic senate president of impropriety and discriminating against her. She loudly alleged that I had choreographed the entire meeting and that it was a personal attack on her. She repeatedly claimed that I had threatened her and coerced the committee members.

Razavi's supporters spoke of the "Israel lobby" and of "abuses of power." Two women in hijabs spoke of Palestinian victims and the "truth" of the Israeli "occupation." Public comments on my behalf included a former Israel Defense Forces (IDF) soldier who spoke of the evils of the BDS movement and my sixteen-year-old daughter, Aliya, who spoke with passionate opposition to antisemitism and hate speech. This was no dry, scholarly debate. This had become very personal. My family stood beside me.

The Diversity Committee voted to rescind its financial support of Peled's lecture.

At the next scheduled meeting, a month later, the Diversity Committee voted further to remove their name entirely from the event because it was not consistent with their stated mission.

Our side was thrilled with the decision. What we did not know was that the nightmare had just begun.

Razavi was furious. She continued to allege widely that I had bullied, coerced, quashed free speech, and rejected academic freedom. In April, I made two formal complaints of workplace harassment. The first was a result of the persistent comments made to me by faculty and students as a result of Razavi's campaign. On April 3, 2015, I submitted a formal complaint to my college president and other senior administrators, writing, "The harassment by Razavi, her husband, and their supporters has caused a hostile work environment.... As administration, you are in a position to put an end to the harassment, or to facilitate the harassment."[7] The next day, the president emailed in reply, "We will be treating your most recent communication as a formal complaint of harassment and a hostile work environment, and as such, we will have the Human Resources (HR)

Department take the lead on this matter.... An investigator will be in contact with you shortly." I had three private phone conversations with the president, who said that he had my back and that my opponent was "batshit crazy" and "out to get" me. (He later denied all of this in a deposition.) He and the vice president of HR promised that an independent investigator had been assigned. Weeks went by, and nothing was done.

Meanwhile, Razavi and her supporters made several attempts to gain financial support for Peled's visit from other campus sources. They appealed to the Student Government Association (SGA). The SGA did their homework and declined. Then the History Club was asked to sponsor Peled. Again, our students declined. Having exhausted all other sources, my opponents decided to sponsor Peled through the organizations they themselves controlled: Amnesty International and our college newspaper, *Talon Talks*, which ran a hit piece on me three months after Peled's visit.[8]

The ongoing campus tensions finally came to a head at our April faculty meeting.

As Razavi's harassment had continued and MSJC was showing no signs of acting on my formal complaints, I felt increasingly silenced. I made a sandwich board to have my voice—and Israel's voice—heard. It was actually my students' idea. We had been studying the civil rights movements in class, and they had suggested I do it as a mode of peaceful protest. Together, as a class, we decided what the sandwich board would say. On the front, it said, "When did we abandon academic integrity for academic freedom?" We chose other quotes as well. From Martin Luther King, Jr. we chose, "The whole world must see that Israel must exist and has the right to exist, and is one of the great outposts of democracy in the world." From Gandhi, we chose, "What is really needed to make democracy function is not knowledge of facts, but right education."

I wore my sandwich board to a mandatory meeting with more than one hundred faculty members and administrators present. My first encounter as I entered the building was with a political science professor who self-identifies as "Black" (from the Black Power movement) and corrects anyone who calls him "African American." It was he who had warned the anti-Israel leader on campus of my opposition to Peled in the beginning by forwarding a personal email from me about the topic. In the past, he and I had cotaught two classes: History of Race & Ethnicity in the US and Black History. I had called him friend for over sixteen years before I spoke up for Israel. I was now the enemy.

When he saw me, he laughed and proclaimed, "Here comes trouble!" I responded, "You are calling *me* trouble? I am simply defending our pro-Israel students and speaking up for the rights of the Jewish people. I would think you of all people would understand." "All right, all right," he said. "I didn't mean anything by it."

As I entered the meeting, I walked the entire length of the large room to a reception of stares and whispers. As I set my stack of carefully researched literature on a table, a fine arts professor came over to me with his camera. As he approached, he appeared to be reading my quotes about peace and education then said to me, "I hate to see professors against each other." I was unclear how this could be his interpretation of my sandwich board, which included only positive statements. Clearly, he had heard Razavi's allegations against me. I replied, "The only thing I'm against is hate." As he left, I pushed a packet of literature into his hand and implored, "Read this if you want the truth." He took it reluctantly. As the meeting was about to begin, I removed my sandwich board and leaned it on the wall behind me, about twenty feet away.

During the next hour, I could feel the stares and sense the hostility. Each time I looked up, I saw several of my peers, some of them former friends, glaring at me. The most chilling part was how blatant it was, the unconcealed antagonism. I was so unsettled that I moved to leave at our first break. I turned to get my sandwich board and saw that it was gone.

I immediately went to our vice president of instruction who, after a few minutes, found it among my opponents, being held by Razavi's partner in Amnesty International. I marched over to the group, which immediately surrounded me. I grabbed my board and asserted, "This is private property!" The group erupted in a mass of voices. One man aggressively asked me if I had proof of Peled's words. I told him I had it all on video and would be happy to share it with him. He seemed perturbed that I had done my research. He asked Razavi, "So this is the one?" A history professor told me I wasn't making any sense about the BDS narrative and that I didn't know what I was talking about. Another history professor then entered the verbal assault. I knew this man because I had received complaints about misogynistic comments he'd made in the classroom in the past. One complaint had come to me just that week. I turned to him and told him to stay out of it, that he had embarrassed himself and the college with his misogynistic rantings at the honors seminar the previous week. He started screaming at me, "Who told you that?! ... What is her name? Bring her to me! I bet she won't say it to my face!" I yelled back, "There's no way I'm telling you who she is. You're a bully, and she's afraid of you!" When I turned to leave the group, this man grabbed my left arm tightly between my wrist and elbow. I yanked my arm to get away from him, but he was holding on tightly. I looked directly into his eyes and loudly, slowly, and deliberately said, "LET. GO. OF. MY. ARM!" As the others stood by and watched, he screamed, "NO! I WANT TO TALK ABOUT THE HONORS SEMINAR!" I tugged my arm again to get free, but he held on tighter, screaming at me to "bring me the girl!" I roared, "TAKE YOUR HANDS OFF ME!" and yanked my arm a third time, finally wrenching free. I grabbed my sandwich board and stormed out of the large, packed room.

I sat in my car, shaking and crying in the parking lot ... and waiting—waiting for a security guard, an administrator, a colleague. No one came. I left the property about five minutes later. I was a faculty leader, a scholar, and an expert in diversity and discrimination. I was an academic senator. I was a full professor! How could it possibly be OK to treat me this way, to verbally attack and physically grab me in front of faculty and administration?

Only one answer made sense to me.

I am a self-proclaimed Zionist.

Later, many of my colleagues admitted to hearing "something" or "a ruckus" or "Denise yelling," but no one came forward. I learned that two female colleagues approached my abuser during the next break and asked, "Did you put your hands on Denise?" According to their reports, he "smiled like a Cheshire Cat" and replied proudly, "Yes!" The next day, I had a large bruise on my arm where my colleague had grabbed me, about four inches long and two inches wide. What followed were a failure to investigate, obstruction of a police investigation, coercion, collusion, a good old-fashioned cover-up, and finally, retaliation. I recently learned that immediately after the event, my faculty association president, who is friends with both Razavi and my attacker, contacted our president, telling him that something had happened, but it was no big deal and I was going to blow it out of proportion. These facts came out in the president's deposition the following summer.

Three days later, I had not been contacted by anyone from MSJC regarding the incident. Finally, I filed a written complaint with human resources, the college president, and our union president. My union president forwarded my confidential complaint to my opponents, *including my abuser*, within minutes of receiving it. They all spoke to the president, gave him their side of the story, and the investigation stopped right there. My president later said in his deposition that he just happened to have "incidental meetings" where these people "felt compelled to tell" him their stories, which led him to believe my complaints were "no big deal" and he would "let the process play itself out." The college president spoke to all of my opponents about the issue, but he never spoke to me. Ever. They had closed ranks. Once an insider, I was now on the outside looking in. A pariah.

A Zionist.

I asked the district to reprimand my abuser. They did nothing. I asked that they send him to anger management. Nothing. I asked that they send him to sexual harassment training. They claimed he had been, as everyone had been, per district rules. I knew that was not true, because I was on the committee that organized the sexual harassment training. When the district could not prove he had attended the mandatory training, they sent a certificate of completion, dated the previous day, of his completion of an online course. Knowing I was getting no support from my district, I hired my own attorneys and sued my abuser for battery.

From there, things went from bad to worse. The day my abuser was served with the lawsuit, he began making phone calls to defend himself. I remained silent, following the rules, trusting justice would prevail. I was told by one untenured female that he called her and threatened to sue her for slander if she spoke ill of him. I am aware of a tenured professor to whom he made the same threat. Weeks later, I learned that the college, where I had led the fight against discrimination and harassment for sixteen years, made the decision to defend my abuser and hired lawyers *for him*. The district's lawyers proceeded to schedule interviews with *my supporters*, telling them falsely that they were representing the college, when in reality they were representing my abuser. My supporters later reported, and complained to the district, that they had no idea these lawyers were defending my abuser. These respondents gave interviews under false pretenses, all the time believing it was an independent, impartial investigation.

Later, the district's independent investigator claimed he never received the picture of the bruise on my arm, despite the fact it was sent with other documents he did receive and then re-sent three additional times. When shown the time- and date-stamped photo of my bruised arm in deposition and asked what he saw, the investigator responded, "Blue and green discoloration." My attorney asked, "So you do see the bruise on Dr. Nussbaum's arm, then?" The investigator said, "No, I didn't say that. I don't know why it's discolored. It could be anything." The campus police department would not return my phone calls or emails for several months, until finally, when contacted by my attorneys, they falsely reported that I had dropped the case.

The discovery phase of my lawsuit revealed my opponents had colluded via email. In defense of my abuser, Razavi—a self-proclaimed feminist—wrote that she witnessed him grab me but that it wasn't hard enough to have left a bruise and that I was exaggerating. *She admitted he had grabbed me.* Later in her interview with the investigator, she reported he did not grab me. She claimed he "lightly touched" my arm "as if to say, 'let's chat.'" The others who had formerly been discussing the "grab" via email all reported my abuser had "lightly touched" me in their official reports. They all used similar phrasing.

As I write this, it is sixteen months after I first learned that BDS was thriving on my campus. A little over a year ago, I spoke up for Israel and I spoke out against BDS. Today, I have been relegated to online teaching only and have been excused from any of my duties as professor or department chair that require my physical presence on campus. I had to resign my positions as academic senator, chair of the Salary Advancement Committee, and chair of the Bias Education, Advocacy & Resources Committee. I may never return to my career of twenty-two years. To make things worse, we have attorney bills approaching six figures.

We have now included the district in our lawsuit, including charges of harassment and retaliation. I will not give up this fight. Mine is just one battle in the war against BDS on college campuses all over North America and Europe. I will not be silenced.

DENISE NUSSBAUM is Professor of Sociology at Mt. San Jacinto College in Southern California. She has published in the areas of diversity, discrimination, and pedagogy and speaks publicly on bias in mass media. In addition to teaching and writing, Dr. Nussbaum serves on the board of the American Truth Project, a nonprofit organization dedicated to educating the public on issues affecting US foreign and domestic policy.

Notes

1. For the relationship between anti-Israelism and antisemitism, see the US State Department definition of *antisemitism* (http://www.state.gov/j/drl/rls/fs/2010/122352.htm) and Tammi Rossman-Benjamin, "First Hard Evidence Released That Anti-Zionism Fueling Escalation in Campus Antisemitism: BDS, SJP, & Faculty Boycotters Strongest Predictors of Antisemitism at Schools Nationwide," AMCHA Initiative (March 2016), http://www .amchainitiative.org/bulletin-first-hard-evidence-antizionism-fuels-antisemitism (accessed November 15, 2017).

2. Shahla Razavi, "Re: Miko Peled," email to Diversity Committee (February 16, 2015).

3. Ibid.

4. Rossman-Benjamin, "First Hard Evidence."

5. Public comments made at Diversity Committee Meeting (March 5, 2015), Mt. San Jacinto College.

6. Razavi, "Re: Miko Peled."

7. Denise Nussbaum, "Formal Complaint of Workplace Harassment," email to Roger Schultz and Bill Vincent (April 3, 2015).

8. "Professor Fights Free Speech," *Talon Talks* (August 5, 2015).

16 BDS and Zionophobic Racism

Judea Pearl

Judea Pearl was thrust into the public eye by the brutal 2002 murder of his son, reporter Daniel Pearl, by jihadi radicals in Pakistan whose hate was focused on Daniel's Jewishness. Pearl and his family went on to establish the Daniel Pearl Foundation to continue his son's "life-work of dialogue and understanding and to address the root causes of his tragedy." Pearl's global reputation for moral rectitude, intellectual clarity, and great dignity inspired us to invite his contribution to our volume. In this essay, he analyzes the moral bankruptcy of the BDS movement and exposes its venomous goals, unabashedly identifying it as a racist movement. On the relationship between BDS and freedom of speech, Pearl is particularly decisive, writing, "A racist movement that shows no respect for truth or other people's identity can hardly be expected to respect the sanctity of academic freedom."

Preface

My contribution to this volume builds heavily on an article I wrote for the *Los Angeles Review of Books* (LARB) titled "BDS, Racism and the New McCarthyism."[1] It was written three years ago, when the Boycott, Divestment, and Sanctions (BDS) movement was still an enigmatic phenomenon and only a handful of writers recognized its hypocritical and downright racist character. Things have changed in the past three years. On the global sphere, BDS has managed to reveal its agenda and to galvanize the Jewish community in an unprecedented wave of unity and determination. If the Jewish people ever needed a name for its sworn enemies, a name that negates the core of Israel's existence, free of secondary issues of territories, antisemitism, or political grievances, BDS has given it to us. In fact, it was BDS and the gullible intellectuals who joined its bandwagon that revealed to the world the persistent and uncompromising nature of Arab rejectionism. Even some of my J Street colleagues, who never miss an opportunity to spoil Jewish consensus, managed to find a reason to oppose BDS.

In the microcosm of my own campus, while BDS cronies continued to harass fellow students and silence pro-coexistence voices, the word *BDS* became synonymous with "toxic nuisance" and essentially disappeared from the public square. Even BDS-controlled groups such as Students for Justice in Palestine (SJP) and the Muslim Student Association (MSA) now try hard to hide any association with their mother ideology, BDS, pretending to be working independently. More revealing yet, Hillel's students at University of California, Los Angeles (UCLA) began urging me not to write anti-BDS op-eds anymore, lest they receive undue attention and wake up from their blissful slumber. The recent defeat of a pro-BDS resolution at the Modern Language Association (MLA), the traditional stronghold of anti-Israel academics, testifies to a movement gone stale, kept alive by its adversaries more than its supporters.

It was not BDS's fictional call for an economic boycott of Israel but its threat to the Zionist idea itself that galvanized this broad resistance and has helped people discover what values unite them all, liberal and conservatives, orthodox and secular, and how central the existence of Israel is to Jews and to people of conscience everywhere. With this context in mind, I here submit a revised version of my earlier article.

Imagine a forum on the spread of Islamophobia. The first thing that comes to mind is: "Yes, we should measure the magnitude of this phenomenon, understand the origins of its ideology, examine what drives its advocates, unearth who funds them, assess the dangers they pose to society, and so on."

Similar expectations came to mind when I was invited to participate in the LARB forum on BDS.

Now, imagine my surprise on discovering that this forum did not intend to investigate the inner workings of the BDS movement but to be a "balanced debate" on the merits of its objective: an academic boycott of Israel. Moreover, some of the contributors to the forum were active leaders in the BDS phenomenon and longtime delegitimizers of Israel.

My thought was: should I bestow academic credibility onto an ideology that accuses me of crimes as ridiculous as ethnic cleansing, apartheid, and colonialism when I do research at my alma mater, the Technion, in Israel?

I further thought: why have the editors chosen to give a stage to advocates of a morally deformed movement that even anti-Israel advocate Noam Chomsky describes as a "hypocrisy rising to heaven,"[2] and arch Israel-hater Norman Finkelstein characterizes as a "hypocritical, dishonest cult" led by "dishonest gurus"[3]? It would be like hosting a balanced debate between supporters and detractors of the Flat Earth Society (FES), or, God forbid, the Americans for the Restoration of Slavery (ARS). Evidently, the editors of LARB had deemed some of the BDS arguments to be semirational or even debatable.

Despite these misgivings, I accepted their invitation, hoping to prove them wrong on both counts.

The BDS Arguments and Tactics

The core of the BDS appeal seems compelling in its simplicity[4].

- The Israeli-Palestinian conflict has been going on for too long; it has caused much suffering and must come to an end.
- Israel is guilty of prolonging the conflict, be it via action, inaction, or by merely continuing to exist.
- Boycotting is a nonviolent way of pressuring Israel to act the way we (BDS) think she should.

As many of us have witnessed, BDS tactics are brilliant. Boycott has never been its aim; what university would go along with such a childish, antiacademic idea? Its aim has always been to bombard campuses with an endless stream of anti-Israel resolutions. The charges may vary from season to season, the authors may rotate, and it matters not whether a resolution passes or fails, nor whether it is condemned or hailed. The victory lies in having a stage, a microphone, and a finger pointing at Israel saying, "On trial!" It is only a matter of time before innocent students, mostly the gullible and uninformed, will start chanting, "On trial!" It worked in Munich, and it has worked on some campuses. The effect will be felt among the next generation of policy makers.

The Facts Behind the Rhetoric

Everyone agrees that the Middle East conflict has inflicted unimaginable suffering on both Palestinians and Israelis, that the status quo is not sustainable, and that it must end through some sort of healing and compromise. However, note a fundamental difference in optics between the BDS spokespersons and their opponents. The former see one and only one type of suffering; the latter see suffering on both sides.[5]

Some human beings are endowed with an amazing capacity to filter reality and see only that which fits their agenda. BDS advocates see the checkpoints, the separation wall, the night raids, and the home demolitions in the West Bank. They do not see the innocent victims of terror. They do not see the innocent babies who owe their lives to the wall. They certainly do not see the anxiety of 7.9 million human beings living under the shadow of hundreds of thousands of deadly rockets, aimed at their civilian populations.

BDS followers possess infinite capacity to remember every horror of the 1948 war that led to the Palestinian refugee problem but zero capacity to remember another refugee problem. Between 1936 and 1940, the British government succumbed to mass Palestinian riots and blockaded Jewish refugees from entering Palestine—thus sealing their fate in Auschwitz. My grandparents were among them. Perhaps it is hard for BDS supporters to acknowledge these refugees because they are not with us to testify. What they should be able to acknowledge, though, and rarely do, is the 1948 Arab attack on the newly created nation of Israel, which, by all historical accounts, was genocidal in intent and left deep scars on the Israeli psyche. I mention these scars because they are deliberately ignored by those who urge one side to undo injustices of the past. Scars on both sides beg for healing; seeing some and not others is seeing none.

The one-way prism worn by BDS advocates is most glaring when it comes to the issue of self-determination. Some of their intellectuals preach for hours and hours on the moral right of Palestinians to self-determination. At the same time, they intentionally forget, wish away, or deny the moral right of their neighbors to that same self-determination. In the old days, we used to label such intellectuals *racists* and shun them from the company of those of goodwill. Nowadays, the label *racist* is reserved primarily for Islamophobes and white settlers, real and imaginary, while the distinct racist character of the BDS ideology is rarely condemned for what it is. It is time to change that.

Israel's Exclusive Guilt of Action and Inaction

It is true that the occupation is an ugly predicament. However, anyone who sees Israel as the sole culprit for this unfortunate entanglement is guilty of blindness or dishonesty. Israel has been pilloried elsewhere in this forum, I am sure, so I am going to focus on the Arab contribution that prolongs this conflict. Often overlooked by Israel's detractors is that the Arab side has taken what should have been a diplomatic negotiation on borders and resources and turned it into an almost unresolvable security issue. How? By nurturing a culture in which coexistence means defeat and ending the conflict is a cardinal sin.

Of course, settlements present a roadblock to a two-state solution. But how can an honest person fixate on a roadblock and not notice the white elephant ahead—the deeply entrenched, triple-tier, hundred-foot wall of Arab rejectionism that blocks all roads to this or to any other solution?

Assigning guilt to one side only and rushing to issue an indictment, a verdict, and a sentence—as BDS has done—is dishonest, reckless, and probably racist. Most people of conscience understand that Israel derives no pleasure from controlling another people's lives. The current situation is imposed on Israel by neighbors who continue to announce that they wish her dead and lifting the occupation would only embolden their wishes. BDS's complaints about travel restrictions on students in the West Bank appear grotesque compared to the daily existential threats that Israelis are enduring.

The BDS Agenda: From Slander to Elimination

Some people are of the opinion that supporters of the boycott are "decent people whose main motivation is to create the conditions for genuine intellectual exchange."[6] This is indeed what one may be tempted to conclude from reading the texts of their resolutions and proclamations on campuses and in public—a glorious hymn to human rights, peace, brotherhood, and social justice. However, this is not the purpose for which these proclamations are being used.

The leaders of the BDS movement do not hide their real purpose: In every conversation with them, they admit that their ultimate goal is not to end the occupation, and surely not to promote peace or coexistence, but to choreograph an arena in which the criminality of Israel is debated and her character defamed. In other words, their goal is not to win a debate but to stage one, in which the words *boycott Israel* are repeated time and again to slowly penetrate listeners' minds, thereby tarnishing Israel's image with a stain of criminality. Net effect: bullying pro-coexistence voices into silence.[7]

Omar Barghouti, cofounder and top ideologist of BDS, repeatedly has stated that ending the occupation is not the end of BDS. BDS will continue its struggle until Israel's legitimacy is eroded and its sovereignty dissolved. In a video dated September 29, 2013, for example, he states: "Colonizers [read: Zionists] are not entitled to self-determination by any definition of self-determination."[8] In his lecture at UCLA on January 15, 2014, he stated again that Jews in Israel are not entitled to any form of self-determination, on any piece of land, however slim. "They are not a people," he proclaimed (with a straight face), "and the UN principle of the right to self-determination does not apply to them."[9]

Consider the implications of committing 6.4 million human beings to eternal statelessness, stripped of their protective sovereignty, in a neighborhood that is boiling with genocidal designs. In so doing, Barghouti has, in effect, defined BDS as a racist, if not genocidal, movement. His statements were not disavowed by any BDS activist that I know of and certainly not by my esteemed colleague Professor Robin Kelley, who introduced Barghouti at UCLA with reverence befitting a reincarnated Mandela. Kelley is a distinguished professor of history, specializing in social movements, poverty, colonialism/imperialism, and race, and has other noble credentials. To charge such professors with racism or bigotry would normally be considered heresy of the first degree. But should it be? Shouldn't they be reminded that words and actions have consequences, that there are human beings affected by those consequences, and that the cruelty of those consequences can exceed that which is inspired by acknowledged racists and bigots?

Who Is Indigenous, and Who Is a Colonizer?

When a student stood up at Barghouti's UCLA lecture and said that he was a tenth-generation Israeli and therefore indigenous, Barghouti scoffed, "You aren't indigenous just because you say you are." So, what does Barghouti accept as a qualification for indigeneity? You guessed correctly: race! According to Barghouti, that young student could be indigenized at the end of a few generations if his family intermarried with the Arab claimants of the land.[10]

This genetically defined conception of ownership is not uncommon in BDS circles; it is endemic to societies lacking historical narratives and traditions on which to base claims.[11] While modern norms no longer accept racial criteria as a basis for claims, BDS intellectuals are still playing the race card when it comes to Israel. The idea that indigeneity, peoplehood, and nationhood are based on collective memories and continuity of historical narratives, not on genetic lineage, must be as foreign to BDS intellectuals as history itself.

It is not surprising, therefore, that misrepresenting Israel as a "white settlers colonialist society" has become a cornerstone of BDS ideology and propaganda. UCLA's James Gelvin, for example, another history professor turned BDS propagandist, continues to teach this white settlers ideology to unsuspecting students year after year, with full knowledge of his department. Readers are invited to count the number of times these labels are used in essays written by BDS supporters.

And, while counting, readers should ask themselves if they can recall:

- One case of white settlers moving into a country they perceived to be the birthplace of their history
- One case of white settlers speaking a language spoken in the land before the language spoken by its contemporary residents
- One case of settlers whose holidays commemorated historical events in the land to which they moved—not in the lands from which they came
- One case of settlers who did not name towns like New York, New Amsterdam, and New Wales (Israeli towns are not named "New Warsaw," "New Berlin," and "New Baghdad"), but after names by which those towns were known in ancient times.
- One case of settlers who narrated their homecoming journey for eighty generations in poetry, prose, lore, and daily prayers

Modern philosophers of political liberalism (like John Stewart Mill in "On Liberty"), after rejecting race as a basis for settling territorial claims, have identified collective memory and historical continuity as far more reasonable bases for defining boundaries between groups and nationalities. Today, these collective states of mind are the strongest forces that tie functional societies together—among them the pluralistic, secular, multiethnic, and multiracial society of Israel. They cannot be replaced by the old glues of common blood, common color, or common place of residence.

Why Pick on Israel?

Some of my colleagues find contradiction in BDS's relentless attacks on tolerant Israel, while obvious violators of human rights, such as Iran, Saudi Arabia, or Palestine, enjoy BDS silence, if not favors. I for one am not surprised. For BDS, human rights is merely a slogan to rally the uninformed around the banner of Israel bashing. What is puzzling to me, however, are the intellectuals who have read a chapter or two in the history of the Middle East yet buy into this deception. I can only conclude that there must be some deeply ingrained animosity that turns such intellectuals against Israel. What is it?

I believe the answer lies in what Israel represents to BDS followers and to the world.

To most of the civilized world, Israel represents the ideas of nation-building, historical continuity, and man's victory over repression and death. Marxist-leaning intellectuals (most BDS followers), on the other hand, see Israel's success as a failure of their ideology. It is a pillar of their belief that nationalism is an evil and anachronistic myth. The success of the Zionist experiment refutes this belief. It has unveiled the infinite energy that can be unleashed through that anachronistic and mythical idea called *peoplehood*, as it emerges from the unifying and creative force called *shared history*. It has demonstrated to the world how scattered tribes of beggars and peddlers can lift themselves from the margins of history and transform themselves into a world center of art, science, and entrepreneurship. Marxist intellectuals will never forgive Israel for proving their textbooks wrong.

The entire neural architecture of BDS intellectuals is wired around the hated image of white settlers who have long disappeared from the earth (not counting the Falkland Islands). Israel is hated because the white settler must be reinvented to fit the villain script. These intellectuals cannot stomach Israel's narrative of "a nation rebuilding its historical homeland," which has inspired so many communities to seize control over their destinies and strive for freedom and excellence. They cannot forgive Israel for giving new meaning to man's existence, a meaning that transcends class struggle and racial strife and, instead, unites people and propels them to move forward and dare the impossible. It is no coincidence that despite the daily threats to her existence, Israel is one of the most optimistic nations on earth.

The Anti-Academic Issue

Some of my colleagues are surprised that BDS has chosen to cross the red line of academic freedom and call for a boycott of Israeli universities. They claim that any university that does not officially denounce the occupation is guilty of a crime and should therefore be punished by boycott. (It is as if any American university that does not officially denounce the Tea Party or abortion clinics deserves punishment.)

I am not a bit surprised, because, as we have seen before, it is not the veracity of the charges that matters but their music—in the grand opera of BDS's slander machine, it is not the libretto that matters but the stage and the megaphone. A racist movement that shows no respect for truth or other people's identity can hardly be expected to respect the sanctity of academic freedom.

One academic organization that was lured by the siren song of BDS was the hapless American Studies Association (ASA), which in 2014 passed a resolution calling for an academic boycott of Israel. This turned the whole notion of academic freedom on its head, and naturally, it generated an immediate backlash: over two hundred college and university presidents condemned the ASA for their resolution.

The backlash was, in fact, so profound that, at UCLA, SJP, the campus proxy of BDS, had to change tactics and distance themselves from the BDS movement when they tried to convince the student council to vote for a divestment resolution. They failed—because the tactic was transparently dishonest—and the resolution was defeated seven to five. The important lesson is that, from the students' perspective, affiliation with BDS has finally turned into a liability. One can only hope that this perspective will become the norm on all US campuses. Nevertheless, BDS proxies continue to harass pro-coexistence students and others who do not share the BDS agenda, as we have witnessed in the case of Milan Chatterjee, former president of the Graduate Students Association, who ultimately felt forced to leave UCLA after months of harassment.[12]

What Can University Administrators Do?

My own position on academic boycotts is summarized in an open letter I wrote to John Sexton, president of New York University (NYU):

January 20, 2014

Dear President Sexton,

I am writing to you as an alumnus of an NYU-affiliated school who is deeply concerned with the recent boycott resolution by the American Studies Association (ASA) and its adverse impact on the reputation of NYU.

I received my Ph.D. in 1965 from the Polytechnic Institute of Brooklyn, which last month became part of NYU. In November 2013, I was awarded the Distinguished Alumnus Award from NYU-Poly, an honor that made my association with NYU stronger and full of pride. I was disappointed therefore to learn that the leadership of the ASA, which pushed through a resolution that threatens the very fabric of academic life, is so intimately connected with NYU, both academically and administratively.

Four ASA National Council members (25%) are affiliated with NYU and vocally campaigned for the resolution. In particular, the ASA President-elect, Lisa Duggan, is NYU Professor of Social and Cultural Analysis. This means that in the next couple of years, NYU will become the semi-official host to most activities of this organization, and will be perceived as the academic lighthouse from which this group will be broadcasting its irresponsible, anti-coexistence and anti-academic ideology.

I represent a group of professors who are particularly affected by the ASA boycott resolution. As part of my recent appointment to Visiting Professor at the Technion, Israel Institute of Technology, I am engaged in joint scientific projects with the Technion and its research staff. I also collaborate with Israeli universities on journalistic projects, named after my late son, Daniel Pearl, which aim at bringing Israeli and Palestinian journalists together.

I think you can appreciate how demoralizing the ASA action has been for me, as well as for other professors in my position. It is not that we view the ASA action as a danger to the continuation of our research projects—scientific collaboration has endured many hecklers in the past, much louder than the ASA drummers, and the latter are clearly more interested in defamation than in an actual boycott. What we do consider dangerous is the very attempt to contaminate our scientific explorations with a charge of criminality, and to bring that "criminality" for a so-called "debate" in the public square, on our own campuses. We view this attempt as a new form of McCarthyism that is aimed at intimidating and silencing opposing voices, and thus threatens academic freedom and the fundamental principles of academic institutions.

When a group of self-appointed vigilantes empowers itself with a moral authority to incriminate the academic activities of their colleagues, we are seeing the end of academia and the end of the sacred academic principles that have been painstakingly developed over centuries.

It is for this reason that I was personally disappointed with your letter which, while expressing opposition to boycotts in general and the ASA resolution in particular, failed to identify the ASA action as an imminent threat to NYU's reputation. Your letter did not state whether the ASA will be able to continue using NYU facilities and services as its de facto national headquarters, and what action you plan to take to restrain its leaders from re-staining the name of NYU with similar actions in the future.

In the name of many NYU alumni who wish to remain proud of their alma mater, I strongly urge you to remove NYU's name from the ASA "institutional member" list (as other universities have done), and to voice a strong and unequivocal condemnation of the pro-boycott activities of the ASA leadership.

Sincerely,

Judea Pearl
UCLA

This letter to President Sexton was intended to close a gap between what university administrators say about the boycott and what they have done about it thus far. If the boycott stands contrary to basic academic principles, then, surely, boycott advocates are undermining those principles and should be exposed.

Of course, no one expects university administrators to discipline professors who violate academic principles; academic freedom survives by leaving its principles vulnerable to abuse. What one nevertheless expects campus leaders to do is to *define* the norms of a desirable campus environment and to identify activities that do not contribute to such an environment. I hope that activities that undermine academic principles are classified in this category.

I have recently come to understand how campus norms are shaped by willing administrators without infringing on anyone's free speech and without curtailing anyone's academic freedom. It came to my attention in a letter that the chancellor of UC Davis sent to the campus community. The occasion was an event planned for January 13, 2017, featuring Milo Yiannopoulos, an editor at Breitbart News, known for his provocative anti-leftist commentary. In a masterfully worded letter, Davis's interim chancellor, Ralph J. Hexter, said this: "A university is at its best … when it listens to opposing views, especially ones that many of us find upsetting or even offensive." Thus, Yiannopoulos is a welcome guest. But then came the punchline: "This does not mean, however, that we take an approving or even neutral position with respect to speech intended to express hate or to denigrate or offend others.… Such speech we unequivocally condemn." In other words, we are not censoring nor excluding, not even condemning, this ugly speaker, not least because doing so will invite complaints, if not legal action, from organizations such as Council on Islamic-American Relations (CAIR) and the American Civil Liberties Union (ACLU). No. We are noble, inclusive, and absolutely viewpoint-neutral. What we can do, however, is tell the campus community which speakers we believe are radioactive and which are safe, and we do so only if it is true that their "speech [is] intended to express hate or to denigrate or offend others."

I call this approach selective neutrality. The neutrality is just right, I think, and both wise and effective. But why selective? Because such a message was not sent by Davis's chancellor in the week preceding the anti-Zionist speech of Azka Fayyaz, who spoke at UC Davis in January 2015 at the invitation of the SJP. Nor was such a letter sent by the UCLA chancellor in the day preceding the offensive appearance of Roger Waters on November 30, 2016, who spoke at UCLA at the invitation of the SJP.

A first step for university administrators who are serious about restoring campus civility, then, must be to internalize the equation: Zionophobia = Islamophobia. The antipathy to Jewish self-determination is no less heinous than the antipathy to Islam and to Muslims. Religion, in other words, has no monopoly on human sensitivity. All identity-defining symbols should be equally respected, and equal protection should be applied against all forms of discrimination, including anti-Zionism, Islamophobia, white supremacy, and more.

Selective neutrality should be the instrument with which the university administration distinguishes those who contribute to a respectful campus climate and productive discourse and debate from those who disrupt such a climate and discriminate against various identities. It must be selective, not in the sense of being inconsistent but in the sense of defining and shaping appropriate campus norms. So understood, it is perhaps the only legitimate means by which academic norms can be reestablished on campus.

Peace and the Future of Israel/Palestine

For those who are curious about my own thoughts on the prospects of peace in the Middle East, they can be summed up in one sentence:

"Two states for two peoples, equally legitimate and equally indigenous."

When Palestinian leadership gathers the courage to utter the magical words *equally indigenous*, peace will become unstoppable—not even BDS will be able to stop it.[13]

JUDEA PEARL is Chancellor Professor of Computer Science and Director of the UCLA Cognitive Systems Laboratory. Known internationally for his contributions to artificial intelligence, human reasoning, and philosophy of science, he is a member of the National Academy of Sciences and a founding fellow of the Association for Artificial Intelligence. Pearl is also the father of slain *Wall Street Journal* reporter Daniel Pearl and president of the Daniel Pearl Foundation. With his wife, Ruth, he edited the book *I Am Jewish: Personal Reflections Inspired by the Last Words of Daniel Pearl*, winner of the 2004 National Jewish Book Award.

Notes

1. Judea Pearl, "BDS, Racism, and the New McCarthyism," *Los Angeles Review of Books* (March 16, 2014), https://lareviewofbooks.org/essay/bds-new-mccarthyism/. Material appears here by permission.

2. Dave Markland, "Chomsky on BDS: A Transcript," *Z Blogs* (July 4, 2017), https://zcomm.org/zblogs/chomsky-on-bds-a-transcript/.

3. Marcus Dysch, "Finkelstein Disowns 'Silly' Israel Boycott," *The Jewish Chronicle* (February 16, 2012), https://www.thejc.com/news/uk-news/finkelstein-disowns-silly-israel -boycott-1.31716.

4. See the official website of the BDS movement: https://bdsmovement.net/what-is-bds (accessed November 14, 2017).

5. I invite readers to examine the essays in the original *Los Angeles Review of Books* collection and note this glaring asymmetry.

6. David N. Myers, "U.S. Academics Should Not Boycott Israeli Universities," *Jewish Journal* (December 18, 2013), http://jewishjournal.com/opinion/125482/.

7. Indeed, this LARB "forum" was itself a great achievement for BDS: it provided a public arena where the words *boycott Israel* were repeated many times and, unless taken humorously, helped achieve their subliminal goal on unsuspecting readers.

8. Benjamin Doherty, "Watch: Omar Barghouti on 'Ethical Decolonization' and Moving Beyond Zionist Racism," *The Electronic Intefada* (September 29, 2013), https://electronicintifada.net/blogs/benjamin-doherty/watch-omar-barghouti-ethical-decolonization-and-moving-beyond-zionist-racism.

9. Roberta Seid, "Omar Barghouti at UCLA: A Speaker Who Brings Hate," *Jewish Journal* (January 16, 2014), http://jewishjournal.com/opinion/126186/

10. Eyewitness report by Roberta Seid in Ryan Torok, "Eritrean Solidarity Rally Underscores Community Divisiveness Over Israel," *Jewish Journal* (January 22, 2014), http://jewishjournal.com/news/los_angeles/126278/.

11. A Columbia professor, George Saliba, became famous for allegedly scolding a green-eyed Jewish student for tracing her ancestry to Semitic roots and biblical times. Saliba claimed that the green-eyed student, as well as most Jews of European origin, are descendants of the medieval Khazars and, therefore, have no claim to Middle Eastern lands. See Aymen Jawad, "Middle Eastern Christians and Antisemitism," *The Jerusalem Post* (August 1, 2011), http://www.jpost.com/Opinion/Op-Ed-Contributors/Middle-Eastern-Christians-and-anti-Semitism.

12. See chapter 26 in the current volume.

13. Acknowledgment: This article benefited substantially from discussions with David Brandes.

17 Friday, November 13, 2015, at the University of Texas, Austin: Anti-Zionists on the Attack

Ami Pedahzur and Andrew Pessin

In November 2015, a group of anti-Israel students loudly disrupted a lecture at the Institute for Israel Studies at the University of Texas. Ami Pedahzur, the institute's director, allowed them a few minutes to express their hate for Israel and then pleaded with them to sit and listen to the speaker. They refused and continued their intervention, chanting for intifada, the destruction of Israel, and the dismantling of the entire institute on their campus. At one point, Pedahzur stood face to face with their leader as the latter shouted at him. Immediately after the event, the disrupters launched a social media campaign smearing Pedahzur, using heavily edited video footage to generate a false narrative of an aggressive Zionist racist professor assaulting peacefully protesting victims. The campaign went viral through anti-Israel networks, bringing worldwide calls for Pedahzur to be punished or fired, as well as threatening messages. Pedahzur endured a months-long ordeal as the university undertook an investigation. Though he was exonerated in the end, the personal and professional damage was done. No word was given on whether the disrupters were ever disciplined.

Part I: The Event[1]

Andrew Pessin

BACKGROUND

On Friday, November 13, 2015, the Institute for Israel Studies (IIS) at the University of Texas (UT) at Austin hosted Gil-li Vardi from Stanford University, who presented her critical study "The Birth of the Israeli Defense Force's Military Culture."

Although the IIS has been active since 2012, none of their many previous events had ever been interrupted. Moreover, neither the university authorities nor the police had warned them that this event might be compromised. Thus, when Ami Pedahzur, the director of the IIS, saw a group of young men and women wearing *keffiyehs* entering the seminar room and taking seats, he was delighted, anticipating a vigorous learning experience for all. He recognized one member of the group, Patrick Higgins, who had been a student in his graduate seminar in the fall of 2014. Higgins had always been polite and had never made political statements in class. It didn't occur to Pedahzur to think these individuals were members of any particular group (in this case, the Palestine Solidarity Committee [PSC]) or that they had come for any other reason than to listen to the speaker and engage in an intellectual conversation.

The event had required RSVPs so they could order a sufficient number of box lunches. Although these attendees did not RSVP, Pedahzur invited them to eat and make themselves comfortable.

Friday, November 13

Noon

As soon as Pedahzur introduced the speaker, the whole group stood up as one and formed a human wall at the rear of the room. Many of them pulled out their cell phones and started recording and taking pictures. Others, including Higgins, held up a Palestinian flag. Later, the leaders of the group were identified as law student Mohammed Nabulsi, graduate student Higgins, and graduate student Katie Jensen (who also teaches her own classes at UT).[2]

Nabulsi, apparently the main leader, announced, "We want to introduce [the speaker] as well. We are making an intervention." He then began to read from his cell phone a statement regarding the "ethnic cleansing of the indigenous population of Palestine" and continued on to include inflammatory and derogatory remarks about the invited speaker, the IIS, and the State of Israel. (All this, and much of the disruption, can be seen in the heavily edited video that the group would release forty-eight hours later.[3])

As soon as the students began their disruption, a member of the audience—a military veteran who was a PhD candidate at the Lyndon B. Johnson School of Public Affairs—attempted to intervene in their intervention. He stood directly in front of Nabulsi repeating, "I am a scholar, and I want to hear what this speaker has to say!" At one point, he attempted to swipe Nabulsi's phone from him, and at another, he ripped away the Palestinian flag held by one of the disrupters. This man, who was neither Israeli nor Jewish, would not be targeted later by the disrupters, who instead would go on to falsely claim that it was Pedahzur who took these actions. The campaign they would soon launch directly targeted only the Israeli Jew, Pedahzur, and the IIS itself.

While the preceding was occurring, Pedahzur approached Higgins and told him that he had some nerve coming to an event of his former professor's and behaving that way. Pedahzur told Higgins that he was being disrespectful, and he asked Higgins to leave the room. Higgins refused.

Nabulsi stepped in. Responding to Pedahzur's repeated urging that they sit and listen, he said that they were not interested. "We don't want to listen to your whitewashing. We know who you are." Pedahzur asked him, "How do you know? What do you know?"

Surrounded by his supporters, Nabulsi returned to reading his statement from his cell phone. He directed his angry words at the invited speaker. Pedahzur asked him to stop and either sit down and learn or leave.

Ignoring Pedahzur and diverging from his written statement, Nabulsi began to talk about his "great-grandfather who was murdered by Zionist militias, leaving eight children behind." When Pedahzur realized that they were intent on ruining the event, he told Nabulsi, "Say what you have to say and then leave." Nabulsi raised his voice and said, "We want to talk about the fact that the [Institute] for Israel Studies exists on this campus to whitewash the State of Israel's crimes against the Palestinian people."

Again, Pedahzur pleaded with him to listen to their speaker, and his response was that Pedahzur, the speaker, and others were all former Israel Defense Forces (IDF) soldiers. (All Israelis are required to serve in the military.) "You are a former IDF soldier. We don't listen to you; you have nothing to say to us about the Palestinian experience."

When Pedahzur asked Nabulsi how many years he had spent in Palestine, Nabulsi answered, "How many years has my family lived in Palestine?" "No, *you*," Pedahzur repeated, asking where was he born, to which Nabulsi said, "Dallas, Texas."[4] Pedahzur asked him, "So what do you know about Palestine?" He responded, "I know everything." One of Nabulsi's followers said, "He knows everything. He is a Palestinian." To Pedahzur's question, "So this makes him an expert on Palestinian issues?" Nabulsi answered, "Yes. It makes me an expert." So apparently having a Palestinian great-grandfather makes a Dallas-born American student an expert on the Israeli-Palestinian conflict. Think of the university tuition one could save with those credentials!

Then the female student leader, Jensen, took the lead. Throughout this next phase, Pedahzur did not stop pleading with the group to sit down and learn.

Jensen, who was very confrontational, started shouting, "Free, free Palestine!" and the whole group joined her.

Then a female next to her took the lead. She shouted, "Long live the Intifada!" As is well known, *intifada* literally means "uprising" and refers specifically to the violent uprisings in which Palestinians have murdered many hundreds of Israeli Jewish civilians. In that particular context, at that particular time, it was impossible not to understand it minimally as a call in support of the months-long wave of violent stabbings of Jews by Arabs in Israel, which many were calling the

"Knife Intifada." More disturbingly, since intifada violence is directed at Israeli Jews and Israeli Jews were present in the room, it also appeared to be an implicit threat of violence against those present.

This female was agitated to a degree of physical trembling. The leader, Nabulsi, became increasingly agitated himself. Pedahzur decided spontaneously to stand in front of Nabulsi and make him shout directly into Pedahzur's face.

Nabulsi was surrounded by his followers. One of them, a young female, pushed Pedahzur away. This section of the students' video was edited carefully to remove this woman's pushing him, although you can see that some disruption has occurred and you hear Pedahzur saying, in response, not to touch him. Pedahzur attempted to return to his position in front of Nabulsi but was held back.

Next, the students began shouting, "We want forty-eight; we don't want two states." This was a call not merely against the peace process between Israel and the Palestinian National Authority (which is predicated on the two-state solution) but also for the annihilation of the State of Israel. It was impossible in context not to understand that as a direct call for violence against Israeli Jews.

Then the students suddenly left.

A second video shot from outside the room was posted later on the blog *Legal Insurrection*, catching the same moments and the shouting as it was heard from the corridor.[5] Laura Evans, the administrator for the IIS, is heard in this video saying to an unidentified person that she has called the authorities.

Nabulsi is seen exiting the room, coming out into the hallway, followed by his group. A member of the group can be heard talking about collaboration between the Zionists and the Nazis. Pedahzur came out after them and said that it would have been great to have them participate in the event. Their response was the cynical "We did participate." Higgins shouted loudly in response to Pedahzur's plea, "Free Palestine!" They resumed their angry chants of "Long live the Intifada!" as they disappeared down the stairs.

Pedahzur tried to talk to one of them, a younger male, in a last attempt to convince him to join the lecture. The young man responded that the group prevented him from staying.

Then the police arrived.

Pedahzur was asked by a police officer to identify himself and describe the events. The officer also asked if Pedahzur wanted to press charges. Pedahzur declined. Rather, he asked the officer to invite the protesters back as he remained interested in opening a channel of academic communication with them.

Pedahzur stayed outside the classroom door to guard it while the speaker finally gave her talk, and he left after about thirty minutes, when it became apparent the students would not return. On leaving the building, he saw the students sitting at the entrance to the building with several police officers standing next to them. Higgins was separated from the rest.

3:37 PM

Pedahzur posted a message on Facebook and on the IIS website: "To the protestors who interrupted our event today. We are sorry that you stormed out and chose not to listen to our brilliant speaker. We invite you to contact us. We are interested in listening to you and engaging in a respectful and enriching academic exchange."

4:41 PM

Jensen posted her first message on Facebook. The message named Pedahzur and claimed that Pedahzur (along with a PhD student) assaulted two members of the group in retaliation for the PSC's "peaceful disruption of an event glorifying the Israel Defense Forces (IDF) and normalizing ethnic cleansing." Jensen implicated herself as a participant in the event. She also appeared in the group's video. Unlike the rest of the group, however, she did not identify herself to the police and evaded their questioning, according to the publicly available police report filed later.

6:02 PM

While Pedahzur was hosting the guest speaker for dinner at his house, he began to receive messages indicating that the group had launched a social media campaign against him. Ignoring the horrific news that was just arriving about the massacre in Paris, and using an out-of-context photo capturing the moment in which Nabulsi and Pedahzur were face to face with each other, Nabulsi posted a Facebook message describing himself as the victim and Pedahzur as the aggressor. In this message, Nabulsi failed to mention he was surrounded by his followers, who were pushing Pedahzur, as well as the aggressive manner in which his group had taken over the room and were shouting for violence. Nabulsi concluded by promising to release a video that would prove that Pedahzur escalated the situation. Apparently, he considered responding to his disruption to be a form of escalation, suggesting that he believed that the people scheduling the lecture had no right to resist his disruption.

Nabulsi posted his Facebook message publicly under the name Georges Abdallah, a known terrorist.[6]

The social media campaign against Pedahzur ignited over the next several days. Hundreds of Twitter and Facebook messages began circling the globe, carrying variations on the theme that the Zionist Israeli professor Pedahzur had intimidated and violently assaulted peaceful nonviolent student protesters, suppressing their free speech. In none of these messages was it mentioned that the students themselves initiated the conflict by crashing the event without RSVPs, hijacked the public event, prevented a speaker from speaking, angrily made slanderous claims about Israel, and chanted slogans calling for violence against

Israeli Jews (which included those present in the room) and for the destruction of the only Jewish state in the world. There were immediate calls for Pedahzur to be disciplined and fired. In short, the students: (1) complained that their free speech was being infringed on, when they were in the process of infringing on others' free speech; (2) demanded the right to intervene in and disrupt another group's event without resistance; and (3) cried foul when the group being attacked actually intervened in their intervention and disrupted their disruption.

Saturday, November 14

4:00 PM
On Saturday, after learning that not only Nabulsi but also Higgins publicly bore the online identities of known terrorists, Pedahzur filed a report with the University of Texas Police Department (UTPD).

On that same day, someone who described himself as a "Muslim friend" used an untraceable number and left a message on Pedahzur's voicemail. He said that he prayed that God would lead Pedahzur to take the right path, to support freedom for *all* people. That the person had Pedahzur's personal phone number was very creepy, and it was hard not to interpret the message as a veiled threat.

Sunday, November 15

5:12 PM
The students released their edited and defamatory video, in which they explicitly accused Pedahzur of "assaulting students." The video went viral immediately and fueled the many hateful and threatening messages that Pedahzur would receive over the coming weeks. (As of May 2016, the video had surpassed 180,000 views.)

5:32 PM
Shortly after the group posted its video, Pedahzur posted his first and only response online, on his personal Facebook page and the IIS website. The most relevant portions are reproduced below:

> Dear Friends and colleagues,
>
> I never imagined that my academic research on terrorism and my administrative role as the Director of the Institute for Israel Studies would coincide in such a chilling way.
>
> Less than forty-eight hours after the horrific attacks in Paris, I feel that it is my responsibility to ask you to join me in an attempt to confront the radicalization process on campuses and to protect students, staff, and faculty members from intimidation and violence.
>
> On Friday, November the 13th, 2015, our institute hosted Dr. Gil-li Vardi from Stanford University....

[Pedahzur presents some background on the IIS, its scholarly work, its support of and collaboration with Arabic studies and Palestinian scholars, and the Arab and Muslim students who have taken their classes enthusiastically. He then begins describing the students' disruption of their event.]

Then their leader, who I later learned is a UT Law student named Mohammed Nabulsi, attempted to hijack the event.

It is important to pause here for a second and underscore the fact that Mr. Nabulsi's online name is Georges Abdallah, of the Lebanese Armed Revolutionary Factions who murdered American Lieutenant Colonel Charles R. Ray, and Israeli diplomat Yaakov Bar-Simantov in Paris, France in the summer of 1982.

After some more research we learned that Nabulsi was not the only member of the group who assumed the identity of a murderer online. For example Mr. Patrick Higgins, a former student in my graduate seminar, who recently completed his MA in Middle East Studies, refers to himself as Edward Despard, a British officer of Irish descent, who radicalized, joined the Irish rebellion, and plotted to assassinate King George III.

Back to Friday's events … Nabulsi … claimed that he knew everything about our speaker and referred to her as a war criminal due to her service in the IDF…. [The group] refuses to talk to Israelis who are all war criminals…. Meanwhile, I kept on telling them that based on their comments, they seem to know nothing about the history and politics of Israel and Palestine and I pleaded with them to stay and listen. I stood in front of Mr. Nabulsi in an attempt to make him shout directly at my face. I didn't touch Nabulsi. Quite the contrary, his followers who surrounded him started pushing me around. A minute or two later they suddenly left.

Later that evening, as the news from Paris was arriving, I received several emails indicating that the group had executed a carefully planned media campaign … [launching] a social media blitz that was a complete lie. Mr. Nabulsi, for example, wrote an inciting and self-serving message. Using a heavily edited picture in which we are facing each other, he described himself as the victim and me as the aggressor…. He also failed to mention that we were surrounded by his followers who were pushing me back.

Initially, I thought that the members of the group had a genuine interest in human rights and justice. Gradually, I realized that they are part of a group who have a long history of launching manipulative campaigns that aim at intimidating and terrorizing those who they perceive as their enemies.

What I saw was a tight group of young men and women who follow a charismatic leader who admires a notorious murderer. After spending two decades of learning how people turn to terrorism, I fear that what I witnessed on Friday should raise many red flags.

I believe in the First Amendment and in full academic freedom. However, neither the law nor its moral foundation protects coercion or direct attempts to impede freedom of speech and academic discourse.

We cannot let such individuals terrorize us.

I appeal to my friends and colleagues as well as to students and individuals who believe in freedom to stand up and counter this campaign of terror and intimidation.

Ami Pedahzur

Pedahzur, it should be mentioned, is a scholar who specializes in the study of terrorism and radicalization, including Jewish extremism. You should observe how careful Pedahzur's letter here is. The Paris massacre had just occurred. He, an academic expert on radicalization, had simultaneously had his institute's lecture invaded and disrupted by hostile students calling for violence against Israeli Jews, whose leaders publicly took the online names of terrorists. You don't need much of an imagination to appreciate how intimidating and terrifying such an invasion and disruption is, nor to be concerned that such intimidating and terrifying behavior, in the service of a radical agenda calling for violence against Israeli Jews (including those present in the room) and in clear violation of campus norms and possibly the law, might raise some "red flags."

6:42 PM
Nabulsi immediately responded on his own Facebook page: "I have never in my life felt so dehumanized, does this video in any way reflect what he says?" Shortly thereafter, Nabulsi, Higgins, and Jensen deactivated their Facebook accounts or deleted their posts. One wonders whether they were already receiving legal advice.

We might observe again here that while the PSC strongly believed in their own freedom of speech to slander Israel and Israeli Jews, accusing such Jews of being war criminals and committing horrific crimes, they were outraged when one of the people who stood up to their attack used his own free speech to express *his* opinions about *their* behavior.

Monday, November 16

9:00 AM
Pedahzur went to the police station for the second time. In light of the students' escalating smear campaign and the threats and the hateful comments that were appearing online, he asked the police to protect the IIS offices as well as the class that he was scheduled to teach the next day. UTPD promised to have their patrol go through the IIS offices twice each shift and to protect Pedahzur's classes until the end of the semester. They also offered to conduct a safety survey in the IIS offices, so that the IIS would know what kind of safety measures they should install. On behalf of the IIS, Pedahzur happily accepted. As far as could be determined, the IIS was the only campus organization that required heightened security measures.

10:22 AM

After coming back from the police station, Pedahzur received an email from Richard Flores, the senior associate dean of the College of Liberal Arts, asking him to come in for an immediate meeting. The dean instructed Pedahzur to refer any inquiries from the media to UT's director of public affairs. From this moment forward, Pedahzur was essentially silenced by UT, leaving him incapable of defending himself from the smear campaign and vulnerable to the ongoing defamation and distortion of the facts.

11:27 AM

The following email was sent to Pedahzur's supervising chair and dean.

> From: BDS Reddit
> Date: Mon, Nov 16, 2015 at 11:27 AM
> Subject: RE: Professor Ami Pedahzur
> To: Randy Diehl, Robert G. Moser
> Cc: Pedahzur, Ami<pedahzur@austin.utexas.edu>, Palestine Solidarity Committee
>
> Dear Dean Diehl and Professor Moser,
>
> By now I am sure that you were aware of the incident that took place on your campus on November 13, 2015. Professor Pedahzur assaulted and intimidated students at a public event. A video of the incident is here [link]. This behavior is not professional, and has no place anywhere on a public university campus. More troubling, the Professor has made a post on his personal website implying that the students at your University are terrorists and compared them to the people behind the horrendous attacks in Paris [link]. I strongly advise you to fire Professor Pedahzur and remove him from campus immediately. I am currently in contact with students at Yale and the University of Missouri who have had to deal with the same kind of abusive behavior from racist elements. Similar protests will be taking place at the UT-Austin soon if the University deals with this in a tone-deaf manner.

Note that they make their goal quite clear: to fire Pedahzur. In their view, Pedahzur "assaulted and intimidated," when in fact all he did was (literally) stand up against *their* intimidating assault on a lecture and on all Israeli Jews. Nor did Pedahzur's post imply the students *were* terrorists but merely pointed out that their behavior displayed the same kind of radicalization that could ultimately lead to terrorism. Again, these students who explicitly called for violence against Jews and took the online names of terrorists were outraged that someone was concerned about their becoming radicalized.

4:52 PM

Pedahzur received a message from Flores, asking him to remove the students' names from his post. According to the dean, names were restricted directory information and protected by The Family Educational Rights and Privacy Act (FERPA). Pedahzur immediately complied. Later, Pedahzur received an opinion from Fordham University law school professor Joel Reidenberg, rejecting Flores's claim.

Given the carefully planned nature of the students' attack, Pedahzur assumed that it was the students themselves who notified the legal department at UT about their FERPA claim.

Meanwhile, while Pedahzur had no way to defend his reputation and following the university's statement that it was looking into the matter, the student group moved to the next phase of its campaign.

Tuesday, November 17

10:00 AM
Pedahzur was approached by numerous journalists—local, national, and international. As instructed, he referred them to UT's director of public affairs.

Noon
Although the students had complained that Pedahzur's use of their names in his Facebook post violated their privacy, they went on to hold a very public press conference.[7] (Somehow their concern for their privacy didn't stop them from producing the video of their disruption and promoting its wide distribution over the internet either.) Falsely and misleadingly depicting the events and repeatedly smearing Pedahzur's name, they announced that they were filing a civil rights complaint against him to the university. Their attorney asserted that their treatment at the lecture was a "complete violation of their First Amendment rights," somehow oblivious to the fact that it was the students who, in disrupting a public lecture, were themselves violating First Amendment rights.

We end the chronology here. According to *Legal Insurrection*, the students' civil rights complaint was never made public, nor was it obtainable under a "Texas open records" request, since the university claimed student privacy.[8] Nor did the students' attorney choose to share the complaint when asked.

During the several months of investigation that followed, Pedahzur had to sit by quietly, silenced, powerless to respond to the students' ongoing smear campaign. He had to deal with the stress of continuing to teach his classes and had to continue interacting professionally with Arab and Muslim students even while he stood accused of assaulting pro-Palestinian students, while dealing with ongoing concern for the safety of himself and his family, as well as for the IIS, which was compelled to increase its security profile. He was given very little information about what was going on at the university's administrative level.

More than three months later, the University of Texas finally announced the results of their investigation in a March 9, 2016, press release.[9] UT officially declared that Pedahzur had neither violated the university's nondiscrimination policy nor engaged in "harassment" of the student organization. This was followed by a strong statement of support for Pedahzur from UT president Gregory Fenves, who included praise for UT's commitment to free speech.

According to *Legal Insurrection*, no indication has been given of whether the students who so grossly violated the freedom of speech of others were disciplined or reprimanded.[10]

After UT announced its results, the students' lawyer, Brian McGiverin, said, "I don't think they really did an honest investigation. They certainly talked to a lot of people, but he [Pedahzur] took actions that were rooted in part on the student's national origin.... If he [Nabulsi] had been an Irish kid or a Japanese kid or someone from Sweden, I don't think the professor would have accused him of displaying red flags of terrorism."[11]

McGiverin admits the university "talked to a lot of people," but for some unspecified reason, he denies the investigation was honest. He then oddly accuses Pedahzur of singling Nabulsi out because of his Palestinian heritage, somehow not noticing that Pedahzur's Facebook post had specifically named both Nabulsi *and* Higgins and referred to their own explicit admiration for terrorists.

Nabulsi also complained about the result on his Facebook page, accusing the university of "blaming the victim"—because it found Pedahzur's actions to be motivated not by ethnicity but by the students' actions—and accusing Pedahzur anew of "vilifying me and my Arab and Muslim comrades as 'terrorists.'" Nabulsi also seems not to notice that Pedahzur specifically named both him and Higgins and that his two coleaders in the group were Higgins and Jensen, neither of whom is Arab or Muslim.

Part II: Foundations for a Research Proposal

Ami Pedahzur

I am a scholar, and I cannot but respond to the events described above *as* a scholar. What happened at the University of Texas was one aspect of the larger Boycott, Divestment, and Sanctions (BDS) movement and must be understood as such.

BDS formally emerged in 2005. Within ten years, it has become a global phenomenon. So far, it has had little concrete success in attaining its stated goals. Nonetheless, it has become perhaps the most vocal adversary of the State of Israel in Western democracies. Scholarly attempts to understand the ideology, structure, and modus operandi of the movement have, to date, yielded inconsistent conclusions. Part of the reason for this limited success is rooted in the approaches and methods that scholars have applied in their analyses. BDS is very much a product of the social media era. This is both a strength and a weakness. The social media proficiency of BDS activists has allowed them to spread their messages rapidly, to aggregate anti-Israel and antisemitic activists under a single loose organizational umbrella, and to initiate coordinated operations. However, the public nature of both BDS and its network structure also provide an opportunity for researchers who are interested in looking closely into its mechanisms.

In the immediate weeks after the events described above, I was consumed by an attempt to find out more information about the PSC, which functions as the BDS chapter at my campus. Since I had not even been aware that the group existed, the attack they launched against me took me by surprise and was overwhelming. Within the first forty-eight hours, they managed to smear my name and reputation all over the internet. Through Facebook and Twitter, their story arrived in many countries, and I was bombarded by hostile emails and social media attacks. On the third day, they added the edited video to their arsenal. This was a game-changer. People tend to believe visual materials more than written ones and are more easily influenced by them. Even some of my closest friends referred to the heavily edited video as if it were an accurate depiction of the events. In a matter of hours, the video went viral, and as mentioned above, by May 2016, it had surpassed 180,000 views.

It took me more than a week to understand that the whole incident was in fact a premeditated media production. I immediately began to read the literature on viral social media campaigns to get a sense of the basic foundations of the group's strategy. Unlike their activist predecessors of the 1960s, who sought to gain media attention through mass mobilization and demonstrations, contemporary activists follow a cheaper, highly controlled, and often extremely effective procedure. They are the scriptwriters, actors, filming crew, editors, and disseminators of their materials. I believe that the students timed their assault against the Institute for Israel Studies at UT Austin so that it coincided with riots and demonstrations occurring on other campuses. They were hoping to advance their cause by jumping on the bandwagon of the upheavals at Missouri, Yale, and Brandeis. (Some evidence for this can be seen in the November 16 email reproduced above.)

Their audiences were not ultimately the individuals who were actually subjected to the assault but rather the masses who follow their feeds on social media and, as importantly, share these feeds. It is important to note that the entire active campaign lasted less than a week. They followed the known rule of campaigners who advise their clients to focus their campaigns on an individual, in this case me, rather than an organization or institute. Once their aggression had flushed out an individual to serve as their target, they went to work. In order to hamper or even eliminate my ability to respond to them, the group filed a long list of false complaints against me with the university. In response, the administration asked me to be silent, thus allowing the students to operate their media blitz with no public response or pushback from me.

But I did begin my private response, the way I know how, as a scholar.

Much of my work is on extremism and terrorism. Relying on years of experience in studying radical social networks such as those, I began by mapping out the group and its followers using publicly accessible materials from their own platforms—namely, Facebook, Twitter, and YouTube. Additionally, I gathered thousands of emails that I received in the aftermath of the event. I relied on computer-assisted mixed-methods data analysis software to answer the following questions.

(1) Who are the members of the group?

The data that they share on Facebook allowed me to map out the 508 members of the PSC at UT Austin and identify the leadership clique, its supporting network, and the ties that they have to other groups on and off campus. I supplemented the network analysis with individual-level data. To my surprise, the data showed me that the overwhelming majority of the group's members were undergraduate students who were born and raised in the United States and had no Arab or Muslim roots. Most of them were not even students of the Middle East. Although this is not the context in which to analyze this result, I do think it extremely important for understanding the movement.

(2) What do they want?

Text analyses of Facebook, Twitter, and blog feeds demonstrated that the PSC at UT Austin follows an elusive set of ideas. The leaders of the group reject the two-state solution and instead openly endorse the annihilation of the State of Israel. Moreover, they denounce the Palestinian National Authority and call on their activists to support groups such as the Popular Front for the Liberation of Palestine, Hamas, and the Palestinian Islamic Jihad. The more I read about the group, however, the clearer it became that it lacks a focused ideological backbone. It, in fact, provides a virtual home for postmodern anticolonialist views, communism, and even Jihadism. Mostly, it provides a reference group for young students who look for social ties and a sense of self-significance. Not surprisingly, though, the strongest ideological denominators among many of the activists were anti-Israelism and antisemitism.

(3) How can a small group from Austin, Texas, reach hundreds of thousands of people all over the world?

Again, I was surprised by what I found. First, I searched for the most common words and expressions that they used in their media campaign. Later, I applied sentiment analysis. The results demonstrated that the group uses terminology that fits into the jargon that is used by other minority protest groups in the United States. Most significantly, immediately after the event and regardless of the fact that they had initiated it and acted in an aggressive and proviolence manner, they depicted themselves as victims of racism and Islamophobia.

By turning the victimizer into a victim, they managed to draw the attention of like-minded bloggers and reporters, who subsequently allowed them to perpetuate their campaign and exert political pressure on the university.

Part III: Personal Observations and Recommendations

Ami Pedahzur

I fear that the prevalence of such events is likely to increase in the near future, and unfortunately, they will not be limited to the Israeli-Palestinian context.

These provocations are a new phenomenon that feeds off the new media revolution. In the past, political activists focused on mobilization in their immediate environment. Today, such mobilization is no longer significant. National and international networks of political activists provide platforms to disseminate narratives and messages swiftly. They instruct their local representatives to generate social-media-oriented events.

In my case, the activists of PSC followed a carefully devised script that has been applied in previous cases:

- To maintain the element of surprise, they deliberately refrained from announcing their plans in advance or registering with the dean of students.
- Their leaders used the disorientation and fear that they inflicted on the participants in the seminar to dominate the event for fifteen to twenty minutes.
- As soon as they had acquired the footage that they needed for the subsequent campaign, they left.
- The campaign was carefully timed. They launched it over the weekend on Facebook and Twitter. They waited for Sunday night before they uploaded their heavily edited video to YouTube.

I should mention that I believe that the University of Texas operated throughout in good faith and worked hard to do the right thing when confronted with a complicated and fast-moving chain of events.

If I were to provide universities with advice, however, with the clarity of hindsight, I would recommend replacing the narrow but lengthy legal process that occurred here with a swifter and more comprehensive one.

I understand universities' well-justified wish to protect themselves from potential lawsuits and negative publicity. However, I doubt that the legal arena is actually the main battlefield. Moreover, I believe that the assumption that the public interest in the issue would subside during the investigation is misguided. Today, activists no longer depend on traditional media outlets. They have their own outlets. They can keep things going as long as they desire.

Practically, I would make the following recommendations.

(1) As soon as the campus safety office or another office at the university learns about such an event, the threat assessment team should be alerted. Representatives of the provost and dean of students should be on call and immediately deploy to the location. This would provide the university with a proper understanding of the nature of the event and would allow it to devise an appropriate response. From my perspective, this would have been ideal. For instance, the university would have known instantly who instigated the event and who the target was and so would properly understand just who was the aggressor and who was the victim. This simple information would help put everything else in the right context.

(2) The same representatives should follow up with both the faculty and the students. I would have benefited tremendously from knowing that I had someone working with me whose role is to liaise between me and the university. The sense of uncertainty about just what was going on at the university level was one of the biggest burdens that I had to carry.

(3) The first few days are especially crucial. I had questions about ensuring the safety of my students and my family. My superiors had no answers. Therefore, I approached the police myself and asked for advice.

Other issues that came up over the first seventy-two hours pertained to the smear campaign. The event took place on Friday. While the students engaged in character assassination, I was told not to respond to media inquiries but to refer interested media to the university's public relations director. Journalists told me later that they either couldn't reach him or that he declined their requests for comments. For ten days, the activists had a nearly complete monopoly over the media. I emphasize this point due to the rapid nature in which social media operates. Within forty-eight hours, their YouTube video was viewed more than 100,000 times. The amount of damage that student activists could do in that time to their target's reputation, and to the university's, is enormous, not to mention the amount of danger to which they could subject their target and his or her family.

(4) The university should form a task force for new media that would utilize the same tools that the activists use, in order to counter such campaigns and to offer an accurate depiction of the facts.

(5) The dean of students' office should warn activists of the potential consequences of defamation.

(6) Other important roles that a faculty liaison officer could fulfill would be to provide assistance with information about lawyers. I did not know if I should retain a lawyer and was clueless as to what kind of lawyer I needed. In retrospect, I believe that it's better to be safe than sorry, and a targeted faculty member should obtain a lawyer as soon as possible.

(7) It is also imperative to offer faculty medical and mental support. Loneliness and fear are overwhelming. I was threatened, harassed, investigated, and left in the dark. While these events are unfolding, you don't know who is with you and who is against you. A stronger network of support and continuous communication with the university would have been invaluable.

(8) Finally, it is imperative for the university to devise concrete guidelines for faculty and students about academic freedom and acceptable behavior. I have spoken to many colleagues. None of them knew what to do if something like that happened to them. Other universities, such as the University of Chicago and University of Wisconsin, have recently adopted and issued such guidelines. It seems to be self-evident that freedom of speech includes the freedom of speakers and their audiences to speak without disruption. Let dissenters attend and voice objections during discussion, or let them protest outside the room. But the freedom to disrupt is just a violation of freedom of speech.

AMI PEDAHZUR is Professor of Government and the Arnold S. Chaplik Professor in Israel and Diaspora Studies at the University of Texas at Austin. He is also Founding Director of the Institute for Israel Studies at UT Austin. His books include *The Triumph of Israel's Radical Right, The Israeli Secret Services and the Struggle against Terrorism, Jewish Terrorism in Israel* (with Arie Perliger), and *Suicide Terrorism*.

ANDREW PESSIN is Professor of Philosophy at Connecticut College and Campus Bureau Editor of the *Algemeiner*. Author of many academic articles and books, a philosophy textbook, several philosophical books for the general reader, and two novels, his current research is focused on philosophical matters relevant both to Judaism and Israel.

Notes

1. Most of the information reported here was obtained from the blog *Legal Insurrection*, which covered the affair closely. For example, see William A. Jacobson, "UT-Austin Rejects Discrimination Claim by Anti-Israel Students Who Disrupted Event," *Legal Insurrection* (March 9, 2016), https://legalinsurrection.com/?s=pedahzur&image.x=0&image.y=0.

2. William A. Jacobson, "Why Hasn't UNEDITED Video of UT-Austin Israel Studies Disruption Been Released?" *Legal Insurrection* (November 29, 2015), https://legalinsurrection.com/2015/11/why-hasnt-unedited-video-of-ut-austin-israel-studies-disruption-been-released/.

3. https://www.youtube.com/watch?v=46W4S3lr9HU&feature=youtube (accessed December 27, 2017). This video was posted on Sunday November 15, 2015, at 6:00 PM. It was assembled by cutting and pasting footage from six different cell phones.

4. This answer was silenced in the video, in order perhaps to lay the ground for Nabulsi's later complaint against Pedahzur based on the Family and Educational Privacy Act (FERPA).

5. William A. Jacobson, "New Video Supports UT-Austin Israeli Studies Prof. After Confrontation By Protesters," *Legal Insurrection* (November 17, 2015), https://legalinsurrection.com/2015/11/new-video-supports-ut-austin-israeli-studies-prof -after-confrontion-by-protesters/.

6. https://en.wikipedia.org/wiki/Georges_Ibrahim_Abdallah (accessed October 30, 2017).

7. *Spectrum News* (November 18, 2015), http://www.twcnews.com/tx/austin /news/2015/11/18/pro-palestine-ut-students-claim-civil-rights-were-violated.html.

8. William A. Jacobson, "UT-Austin Rejects Discrimination Claim by Anti-Israel Students Who Disrupted Event," *Legal Insurrection* (March 9, 2016), https://legalinsurrection .com/2016/03/ut-austin-rejects-discrimination-claim-by-anti-israel-students-who-disrupted -event/.

9. "Statement on University Review of Nov. 13 Incident," *UT News* (March 9, 2016), https://news.utexas.edu/2016/03/09/statement-on-university-review-of-nov-13-incident.

10. William A. Jacobson, "UT-Austin Rejects Discrimination Claim by Anti-Israel Students Who Disrupted Event," *Legal Insurrection* (March 9, 2016), https://legalinsurrection .com/2016/03/ut-austin-rejects-discrimination-claim-by-anti-israel-students-who-disrupted -event/.

11. Mary Ann Roser, "University of Texas Finds No Wrongdoing in Professor's Treatment of Palestinian Students," *The Jerusalem Post* (March 13, 2016), https://www.pressreader.com /israel/jerusalem-post/20160313/281595239636914.

18 Colonel Richard Kemp at the University of Sydney, Australia, March 11, 2015

Jan Poddebsky, Peter Keeda, and Clive Kessler

Jan Poddebsky et al. tell of another hostile disruption where the victims also got portrayed as the aggressors and vice versa, this time in Australia. British colonel Richard Kemp, a well-known military expert and advocate of Israel, was speaking at the University of Sydney when protesters stormed the room, shouting nasty accusations through megaphones and taking over the floor. In the melee that followed, Poddebsky and Peter Keeda, mature-age audience members, confronted the invaders, standing up to them or, in Poddebsky's case, mocking them. In response, the university brought in a legal firm to investigate and initiate disciplinary measures, not for the invaders but *Poddebsky and Keeda*. Their narration, supplemented with Clive Kessler's analysis, exposes the hypocritical way that politically correct university culture fails to protect the basic rights of Jewish and pro-Israel students, faculty, and staff.

Part I

Jan Poddebsky

I am a mature-age doctoral candidate at the University of Sydney.

I attended a lecture by Colonel Richard Kemp at the university on March 11, 2015. Kemp was described on the poster as "perhaps the United Kingdom's most highly respected analyst and commentator on the rules of war and the Middle East conflict." The title of his talk was "Ethical Dilemmas of Military Tactics in Relation to Recent Conflicts in the Middle East: Dealing with Non-State Armed Groups."

Five weeks later, the vice chancellor of the university would respond to the widespread criticism of the orchestrated disruption of Kemp's lecture by publicly emphasizing "the importance of our commitment to academic freedom, the freedom of speech, and the right to protest."[1]

Preamble

The Kemp lecture was a public lecture held at lunchtime, and anyone could attend. Given the Charlie Hebdo massacre just two months earlier and the Paris massacre just eight months later, Kemp's topic was as relevant then as it is now. I catch myself reflecting on how everyone pays attention to those killings but not so much to the killings in the Parisian delicatessen, the murders of a rabbi and his family in a Jewish center in Mumbai, and the ongoing killings of Israelis by car-rammings and knife attacks.

A large banner greeted those arriving to the lecture. Held up by three individuals, it read, "Cut Ties With Israeli Apartheid" across the top, centered over adjacent blocks of print reading, "Sydney Uni Staff For BDS" and "Boycott, Divest, Sanction." As I arrived, I realized that one of the people holding the banner was Professor Jake Lynch, director of the Center for Peace and Conflict Studies (CPACS). According to the university provost, Professor Stephen Garton, CPACS is the *home* of the Boycott, Divestment, and Sanctions (BDS) movement against Israel on our campus. According to Lynch, he and CPACS are supporters of this policy. I became familiar with the building that houses CPACS when I attended lectures there several years ago. One of the staff had a map on his wall of "Greater Palestine," a Palestinian state without Israel.

For just a bit more background, CPACS conducts a course in peace journalism where students learn to pirouette the news. Lynch himself has a background in journalism. One of the lecturers at a conference on peace journalism at CPACS in 2012 was Professor Wendy Bacon, who is a contributing editor to the left-wing journal *New Matilda*. In March 2015, *New Matilda* published a lengthy apologia for the disruption by Dr. Nick Riemer, a senior lecturer in English at Sydney, responding to the Kemp affair.[2] Riemer argues that disruption is not only desirable but a moral imperative to be used selectively. I do not know if he likes having his life disrupted.

We were also greeted by pamphlets as we arrived, courtesy of the Sydney Staff for BDS. One of these expressed demands for legal equality and human rights for Arabs in Israel. I looked for equivalent demands for legal equality, freedom of speech, and human rights for women, homosexual persons, non-Muslims, and persons with varied political and religious affiliations within Gaza (governed by the genocidal Islamist organization Hamas) or within the territories administered by the Palestinian Authority, but there were none. Apparently, struggling for the rights of these folks does not rate according to the proponents of BDS. They have different priorities.

Another pamphlet at the entrance described the aims of the Sydney Staff for BDS as "exerting pressure on the university to withdraw all institutional and financial support from Israeli academic and research institutions," "showing solidarity with the Palestinian university communities," promoting "the academic and cultural boycott of Israel," and "supporting the global BDS movement" more generally. The pamphlets announced that the group's weekly meetings were held at CPACS, in the bosom of the university. The center provides moral, physical, and economic support for BDS on campus and is part of the University of Sydney. I wondered who pays for their publicity.

Although the university's vice chancellor emphasized "the importance of ... academic freedom [and] freedom of speech," Sydney Staff for BDS apparently do not, at least not for Israelis. I wondered if they also boycott Palestinians who attend and work at Israeli institutions.

After perusing one of the BDS pamphlets, I asked its distributor, "So why don't you boycott this event?"

He answered, "We are here for a free and fair debate."

I commented to Lynch that his people were present for a free and fair debate. He is a public figure whose pronouncements on BDS are well known. He has been quoted in newspapers exhorting students to take part in anti-Israel street demonstrations. I think we can describe him as a leader of sorts. He paused and said to me, whom he had never met and about whom he knew nothing except that I was attending this lecture, "And your people?"

Five weeks later, again the vice chancellor would state that he was "most keen to preserve [the university as a] forum for the free debate of difficult and often confronting ideas."[3]

But alas, freedom, fairness, and debate were not to be; orchestrated confrontation, disruption, and mayhem took their place.

THE MAIN EVENT

Kemp was introduced and started his lecture. Shortly into it, the room was invaded. The invaders arrayed themselves in front of Kemp, faced the audience, and started screeching anti-Israel slogans full blast into a megaphone. Kemp discontinued his lecture and waited. At first, we were stunned and disbelieving. The megaphone was not an invitation to discuss or dialogue. The noise was loud and distorted and overwhelming. I felt assaulted, repeatedly assaulted, by each and every one of them. They invaded. We heard what they were screaming at us. They screamed, "Colonel Kemp, you can't hide; you support genocide."

They were looking me in the eye, and I felt that I was being accused of genocide.

Despite his later denials, I saw one academic not only participating in the disruptive chanting but running around conducting it. One invader justified the disruption of the lecture on the grounds that the university had earlier refused permission for the radical Islamist group Hizb ut-Tahrir to speak on campus.

Another screamed that the Jews were doing to the Palestinians what the Nazis did to the Jews. Another accused a fellow student of murder.

I could not stop the invasion and the disruption. I could not out-scream the invaders, but I could witness and photograph them, and they would know they were being witnessed and photographed. I got up out of my seat and approached the screaming invaders, stood in front of each one, and photographed them. I continued moving around and photographing as the line broke up and reformed. In the course of the confusion, one invader attempted to hinder my movement and tried to prevent my taking photographs, even though many others in the room were filming, including Lynch. One fixed camera was operated by a staff member of the School for Biblical Hebrew and Jewish Studies. These records were later used during the investigation. I was harassed, leaned over, and pursued. Another invader in a religious uniform pushed my hand away. I realized that I had encountered this person on the occasion of the Sydney University–Israel Research Partnership Forum of October 31, 2011, when she distributed pamphlets containing the blood libel that Israel used the body parts of Palestinians for organ transplants. That time, she fled in front of the camera. She had grown confident in the intervening years.

I thought it was possible that my camera might be wrested from me or damaged in the course of these encounters, and I resisted. I pushed back—with a finger. I performed a dance to stand my ground. The melee became physically violent as security officers attempted to remove invaders from the room and they resisted. I had not previously witnessed this kind of physical tussle in person.

It was shocking to a seventy-year-old woman with various frailties.

The vice chancellor was keen to preserve the university as a forum for free debate. Was this invasion screaming the BDS agenda a version of free debate? Later, it was supported in the student paper, *Honi Soit*, and at a subsequent meeting called at the university where students and academics perpetuated the myth that this was a political demonstration and that it was about freedom of speech. Selective freedom of speech.

There were no bullets and no bloodshed, perhaps.

And there was no debate.

The trauma of the fracas itself, where I witnessed virulent hatred masked as academic and political freedom, was intense. It was followed by a period of persistent rerunning of the events in my mind. The continuing aftereffects efficiently derailed my studies the remainder of the semester.

THE AFTERMATH

I was so distressed by the confrontation that I wrote to the vice chancellor and offered to give evidence at the investigation he had announced after receiving many complaints, including from Kemp and former minister for education

Peter Baldwin, who was present at the lecture. Because I believed that the invasion and organized disruption were so obviously wrong, I did not invite legal representation to accompany me. I did not expect to require legal protection. I was told that the investigation's terms of reference were to find out what had happened and how it affected me. However, during that interview, I developed an intuition that it was about my participation. This was confirmed when I myself subsequently had to face allegations of breaching the university's code of conduct.

I confess that until then I had received a bachelor's degree, master's degree, and diploma in education at this university without reading the code. My own code of conduct had not brought me into contact with the university's code.

On April 15, five weeks after the lecture, the university announced that its code of conduct provided clear statements of its expectations concerning the behavior of its staff, students, and affiliates. The code requires all individuals to be tolerant, honest, respectful, and ethical at all times.

As can be easily understood, interpretations of the code are fluid. How much tolerance is expected when harassed, attacked, and pursued? Are there no limits to what must be respected? How should one react to blatant dishonesty? What behavior is construed as lacking in respect or unethical?

For example, I was accused during the investigation of doing a dance. Dancing was a risky business in Australia in 2015. An indigenous footballer and Australian of the year in 2014, Adam Goodes, was vilified for doing an indigenous dance on the sports field.

My dance, the dance of a seventy-year-old woman standing her ground in the face of harassment, pursuit, and unwelcome body contact, was deemed a breach of the code. And why? Because it was deemed to be mocking. My pursuer had made a mockery of the lecture, the lecturer, the audience, the situation, and the values of the university. But I was supposed to respect him.

I was supposed to respect the behavior of Lynch, who waved a five-dollar note in the face of an elderly Jewish visitor. He denied that it was an antisemitic gesture on his part. We saw what he did. We cannot prove it was an antisemitic gesture. However, even if that was not his intention, one might expect a man of Lynch's sophistication to realize how offensive it was, especially in that context. Antisemitic or not, whatever his intention, it was offensive and read so by those witnessing it. It is hard to view that gesture as tolerant and respectful. Nevertheless, students, academics, visitors, and Green politicians all rushed to support him.

On April 15, the university announced that the investigation found that one staff member, five students, and two affiliates may have engaged in conduct that breached the code. The conduct of five members of the public also fell short of standards required by the university of visitors to its campus.

I was reprimanded under the code. I felt that I was reprimanded for dancing, for objecting to a campaign of purposeful disruption emanating from within the university, and for asserting my right to listen to what I chose to hear. I have no idea what happened to Lynch and the invaders, although he did announce that he was exonerated from the accusation of antisemitism.

I later spoke to a younger Jewish student who told me that someone had approached him at a university party and called him a Nazi. It seems that most of his friends have experienced incidents of this kind on campus. Young Jewish students on campus are growing up with this kind of abuse as their norm. My informant was much more tolerant than the invaders of the Kemp lecture. About his abuser he said, "Free speech."

Targeted abuse of Jewish students is called free speech.

The university conducted its investigation, but I do not feel safer. I recall an anecdote in Fanny Stang's *Fräulein Doktor*. She recounts an incident when she was confronted by a student friend on campus at the University of Vienna. He had been attacked by university Nazis and was bleeding, but if he was caught by police outside the university gates, they would arrest him for being involved in a brawl.[4]

Part II

Peter Keeda

> "Do not rejoice in his defeat, you men. For though the world has stood up and stopped the bastard, the bitch that bore him is in heat again."
>
> Bertolt Brecht (*The Resistible Rise of Arturo Ui*)

As a mature-age research student at the University of Sydney, I rarely attend lectures. However, the Kemp lecture on "Ethical Dilemmas of Military Tactics" looked particularly interesting, and as I needed a break from hours at the computer, I decided to attend. Unfortunately, we did not hear much of the promised ethical dilemmas, but since the incidents of that day, I have been faced with many.

As I approached the lecture hall, I saw a group of students with a large sign protesting Israel's occupation of Palestine. I did not stop to talk with them, as I came to hear a lecture by an expert in his field and found little point in trying to engage with a group of young students who already seemed to have all the answers. They pushed some papers in front of me, but in consideration of the environment, both the physical and metaphorical, I did not take any.

I entered the lecture hall and noticed about fifty members of the audience already seated. I greeted several I knew and made my way to sit next to someone I had not met before.

After being introduced, Kemp commenced his lecture. The lecture hall's doors had been closed to shut out the noise from the outside. About ten minutes into the lecture, a group of ten to twelve students burst into the lecture hall and stood at the front of the hall in front of Kemp with a megaphone at full volume, screaming and chanting, "Richard Kemp, you can't hide; you support genocide." Kemp stepped aside and waited quietly for the commotion to subside. This continued for about ten minutes, at which time the university's security guards tried to evict the demonstrators, who physically resisted.

At the early stages of the screaming and shouting, I noticed that a youngish person sitting behind me was joining in screaming slogans. I turned to him and suggested that this was not appropriate behavior for a young academic, to which he replied, "Don't patronize by calling me 'young.' I am not so young." To which I retorted, "I am not patronizing you by calling you 'young.' I am patronizing you by calling you an 'academic.'"

I was stunned and horrified by the intrusion, by its intimidating and terrifying nature. At some point, another group of hostile students burst into the lecture hall. It seemed to me that the security personnel had lost control and were not keeping us safe. At this point, I thought it was a good idea to close the lecture hall doors and thus separate the two groups of protesters. When I tried to close the door, my foot became jammed between the door and the wall—it was quite painful—so I turned to the young man who seemed to have pushed the door against my foot, who promptly protested, "Don't touch me, or I will call the cops!" In the meantime, a young female student stood in my face and shouted, "Fuckin' murderer, fuckin' murderer!"

When order was eventually restored, Kemp continued to talk for about ten minutes before opening the floor for questions. In response to a question from Lynch—the director of the Center for Peace and Conflict Studies—Kemp asked Lynch what he thought Israel could have done differently in the circumstances, to which the venerable professor retorted something to the effect of, "I don't know. You are the expert." Kemp tried to respond but was interrupted by Lynch, who, after all, did seem to know better. "But you just said that you did not know," was Kemp's response, "so just keep quiet and listen."

I left the lecture hall distraught and disturbed. The following day, I sent this letter to the university's vice chancellor:

March 12, 2015

Dear Dr. Spence,

I wish to express my deep concern at the events that occurred yesterday on campus while Col. Richard Kemp tried to deliver his presentation on ethical dilemmas. The mob frenzy of the so-called protesters has left me traumatized and distraught.

I am a mature-age post-graduate student at the University of Sydney, having recently completed an MA degree (with merit) and have now commenced further studies towards an MPhil. My specialty is Holocaust studies and the screams and abuse that we suffered yesterday by the mob was so reminiscent of the early days of the Nazis' rise to power in Germany.

My mother and her parents came to Australia as refugees from Germany where most of their family perished in the Holocaust. The trauma of yesterday's "protest" has left me sleepless and wondering how I can raise my grandchildren when such events can manifest themselves in so-liberal Australia.

The slogans shouted (over a bull-horn) by the mob were offensive and their pushing and shoving left me in despair.

I am told that this disgrace was orchestrated by a member of the Academic Staff of the University and I am wondering whether the University will take steps to curtail his influence over susceptible students.

Yours truly,

Peter Keeda

A few days after the incident, I was invited to give evidence about the event. However, I was still very distraught, so I answered that I would not be able to attend. Two weeks later, I went overseas for a holiday, which my wife and I had been planning for six months.

A few days into our holiday, I received an email from LF (a legal firm hired by the university to conduct the investigation) advising me that I had been accused of "misconduct" and that I should attend an interview the following week. LF advised that they had been engaged by the university to conduct an investigation into alleged misconduct by alleged wrongdoers at the March 11 incident, among whom I was one. I advised LF that I was overseas and would be returning in six weeks' time.

Our long-planned holiday was severely marred by learning that I was being investigated for misbehavior. For the next six weeks, I spent many sleepless nights trying to understand how it was possible that I innocently went to a university lecture, was abused and vilified by a mob of slogan-shouting hooligans, and because I responded to their outrageous comments and behavior, was accused of misconduct!

On returning to Sydney, I was given a date for my *interview*. I use this term reluctantly as I had no idea of what the specific charges were (although they had given me some vague information), what my rights were, and under what framework the investigation was being carried out. To this day, I do not know who my accusers were, nor do I know what cases have been brought against the twenty or so protesters who forcibly entered an academic lecture and screamed abuse at all. Some of the academics who joined the protesters—or possibly instigated the protest—were questioned but, from all accounts that I have read, were exonerated.

I made contact with the Executive Council of Australian Jewry, one of the organizers of the Kemp lecture, and asked for legal assistance. They helped me draft a response to the accusations and suggested that I contact a barrister who could help me pro bono and possibly accompany me to the interview. The barrister was quite helpful over the phone but unavailable to accompany me, so I was most fortunate to have Professor Clive Kessler, an old family friend, take up the task. Unfortunately, we had little idea of what the rules of procedure were, nor what my specific rights were. The LF lawyer disregarded a lot of my testimony and, in fact, initially was not even willing to allow me to record the interview. On this point, Kessler and I insisted, and fortunately, the lawyer eventually relented. This was indeed fortunate, as LF's record of the event had many omissions and errors.

There was even an official video of the incident, although I had not been warned prior to the interview. The lawyer could not, or would not, answer my question as to who ordered this "official video" (his terminology), who filmed it, and who edited it. I was only shown brief, carefully selected excerpts. At the end of the interview, the lawyer offered to show me the entire video, which, he said, was about twenty minutes long. Since the entire event itself was about an hour, this twenty-minute clip must just have been some edited version, so I declined. It eventuated that this video formed the basis for the allegations against me; however, I still do not know who made the video and why.

In the ensuing weeks, I tried to make sense of what happened and how it was possible that the systems that should have worked to protect me, in particular those within the university, failed so miserably.

In reading about the event in the press, I learned that a very courageous seventy-five-year-old woman had stood up to some of the academics who seemed to be egging on the students, and in response to her, Lynch had waved a five-dollar bill in her face. Was he implying that, as a Jew, she could be bought? Of course, he denied that his act was antisemitic, claiming (according to the press) that he was merely threatening to sue the woman after she kicked him "in the meat and two veg."[5] In the ensuing investigation, the university accepted his claim. Some might consider his claim that she had kicked him in that sensitive area unlikely, as she was a frail seventy-five-year-old woman and he was a rather large man at least twenty years her junior. Nevertheless, the press reported that the university in its infinite wisdom sanctioned this brave woman and refused to say what action they took with regard to the provocative and inciting behavior of their academic staff.

Five weeks after my interview, I received a notification from the university of their findings, with an added admonition that their findings were confidential. I am left wondering:

- What should I have done under the provocative circumstances with which I was faced?
- What should other Jewish students do when faced with this rabid hate and vilification? There seems little point in expecting any sort of protection from the university.
- Who was the source of the official video, and why was it only twenty minutes long when the whole incident lasted over an hour?
- What penalties has the university imposed on those who deliberately and with premeditation disrupted an invited lecturer on campus and terrified those students and academics who came to learn and discuss?
- What has the university put in place to ensure the free speech of students (and academics) even when they have the temerity to defend Israel?
- And a final question—where was the organized Jewish community in all this? The Jewish Board of Deputies, the Executive Council of Australian Jewry, the Zionist Council of NSW, the academic staff of the University of Sydney ... ?

Postscript

Clive Kessler

What was wrong, morally and politically, about the way that the University of Sydney handled the aftermath of the violent disruption of the Kemp lecture?

Basically this.

In treating alike those who resorted to calculated violence and intimidation and those who responded as best they could—perhaps indecorously and impulsively—to that traumatizing assault, the University of Sydney displayed a splendid capacity for even-handedness: a magnificent impartiality that recalls Anatole France's sublime remark that "in its majestic equality, the law forbids rich and poor alike to sleep under bridges, beg in the streets, and steal loaves of bread."[6]

In its official response, the University of Sydney seemed intent solely to uphold a similar "majestic equality."

More, and worse, by placing itself in the aftermath of those events, via its contracted specialist industrial relations consultants, as the arbiter and judge over offenders from the two sides—the violent intruders and those who reacted in shock and dismay to their actions—the University of Sydney artfully exonerated itself. It dodged and fudged essential consideration of a principal cause of those ominous events, as they unfolded—namely, its own failure to provide and ensure a safe and secure campus, free from abusive intimidation, for its students, staff, and all members of the university community.

Why proceeding in this way made good and proper administrative sense to the University of Sydney is an interesting question.

The intruders acted violently, with intimidatory intent. Those who reacted to their sudden intrusion acted, at worst, indecorously and perhaps imprudently. Yet the two failures to conform to the university's code of ethics were equated and treated identically. Why?

When people are unprotected and threatened and are made to feel publicly and institutionally abandoned, they may react impulsively, perhaps imprudently, and in ways that fail the highest standards of etiquette. Of course, by the time people began to react to the violent intruders in this case, those on the other side had already decisively jettisoned and repudiated the standards of etiquette. They had rejected the canons of decent behavior from the outset; that was the very nature and defining character of their action on that day.

This fact alone ought surely to have reduced, even negated, the force of any charge that the university might have been inclined to make of indecorous behavior against those who were subjected, and reacted, to that sudden, traumatic intimidation.

The University of Sydney, then and now, ought to recognize and accept that those who are made to feel undefended will react and may seek to defend themselves as they see fit and are best able—and that, when they do, they cannot be faulted over-fastidiously by those, the very people, who failed to protect them and ensure their security from such intimidation and intimated violence in the first place. Whose obligation is it to maintain a safe campus, after all: the students' or the university's?

This point applies to everybody, to all who might be made to feel publicly abandoned and left institutionally unprotected. It applies with a special force to people of a certain background. Like me—and this is my point of identification and solidarity with them—at least two of the three *discourteous* reactors who were subjected to the university's disciplinary procedures were not young students but mature-aged people of my background and generation, people whose parents barely escaped the mid-twentieth-century destruction of the Jews of Europe, who were raised by such parents, and who grew up and whose identities were formed under the shadow of those terrible events.

We are people, in other words, who from childhood were intimately shaped by the oppressive, immediate, and pervasive but largely unspoken presence of the industrial extermination of the Jews of Europe. Since then, we have spent our entire lives—while going about our mundane business—also brooding over and coming painfully to terms with those terrible events, with what they mean for the world generally, or ought to, and also how they powerfully informed, overshadowed and threatened to maim, our own intimate personality formation. Now, six decades and more later, we are still wrestling with, are even haunted by, those demons. They are not things that we even now live with easily. Yet when we find ourselves under assault, a genteel university and its genteel managers expect us to respond decorously, with fine manners and nothing more stringent than soft, polite demurrals. As the new Cossacks descend on us, we are urged to recall the idealized Christian practice of turning the other cheek.

This, on top of all else, is in itself a moral scandal and outrage.

There once was a time when a broadly sympathetic understanding of the deep wounds left by recent history, not indifference or an implacably unfeeling or hostile attitude, was characteristic of university authorities and the so-called educated public and could be expected of them.

No longer.

Why not?

These days—as the modernist, Enlightenment paradigm has collapsed, and Jews are no longer seen as both the exemplars of modernity and then as the tragic scapegoats for the rancid discontents that it generated, and we are now subjected to the obligatory thrall of postmodernist doctrine and its postcolonialist canons of contemporary political correctness—we now find a very strange situation on campuses worldwide, including those here in Australia.

You may not give any form of deemed offense to indigenous or third world people (not that any of us wish to cause such offense), nor may one say anything at all that questions the proprietary monopoly that certain kinds of Muslims and their allies have established over the public discussion of Islamic society, history, and civilization.

Those are absolute no-nos.

But it is quite in order, in fact, even *de rigueur*, not just to offend Jews but to abuse them and threaten them with violent intimidation—to attempt to make our universities no-go areas for all Jews, or at least all Jews who will not submit to this grotesque new moral order.

And, regrettably, university administrations, in the procedures that they now routinely follow in these cases, such as after the Kemp lecture, do not stand aside from but embrace—and in that way further validate recourse to—this disgraceful moral failure.

Why do they do so?

There are many possible explanations.

One is that they simply lack the guts, the moral and political courage, to say, "No!" to the current zeitgeist and its putrid political tastes.

Many explanations are possible. That is the kindest of them.

Jan Poddebsky is a doctoral candidate at the University of Sydney.

Peter Keeda is a research student at the University of Sydney, enrolled in a master of philosophy degree.

Clive Kessler is Emeritus Professor of Sociology and Anthropology at the University of New South Wales in Sydney. In 2000, he was elected Fellow of the Academy of the Social Sciences in Australia.

Notes

1. University of Sydney statement (April 15, 2015), http://sydney.edu.au/news /84.html?newsstoryid=14820.

2. "Disruptive Protest and Freedom of Speech: A User's Guide," *New Matilda* (March 19, 2015), https://newmatilda.com/2015/03/19/disruptive-protest-and-freedom -speech-users-guide/.

3. University of Sydney statement (April 15, 2015), http://sydney.edu.au/news /84.html?newsstoryid=14820.

4. Fanny Stang, *Fräulein Doktor* (Sussex: The Book Guild, 1988).

5. "Sydney University Investigating After Associate Professor Waves Money in the Face of a Jewish Woman at a Recent Protest on Campus," *The Daily Telegraph* (March 13, 2015), http://www.dailytelegraph.com.au/news/nsw/sydney-university-investigating-after -associate-professor-waves-money-in-the-face-of-a-jewish-woman-at-a-recent-protest-on -campus/news-story/8f6456966a185515b4163a98871d7e89.

6. Anatole France, *The Red Lily* (1894), Chapter 7.

19 "Oh! Now I've Got You!": In the Sights of Anti-Israelists at the Claremont Colleges

Yaron Raviv

Yaron Raviv was in his office when a distraught Jewish student informed him of being harassed at a mock Israeli checkpoint blocking access to a dining hall. Raviv, attempting to make sure that the demonstration did not infringe on others' rights to enter the building, was accosted by one of the anti-Israel students to whom he angrily responded with a profanity. He was thereafter subjected to a smear campaign by anti-Israel students and faculty that falsely painted him, both on and off campus, as a racist Israeli bullying peaceful Palestinian students—a libelous campaign that did great personal and professional harm and brought threatening messages to Raviv and his family. Shockingly, college administrators participated in and promoted the defamation, breaking various campus rules along the way. The defamatory smearing continued even after an investigation definitively cleared him of any wrongdoing. This incident demonstrates again the unethical ways that Boycott, Divestment, and Sanctions (BDS) activists seek to demonize and silence their opponents, as well as their cynical use of academic disciplinary processes to create an intimidating campus atmosphere.

"Hitler had the right idea, he was just an underachiever. I thought you might enjoy that since you seem to be such a huge supporter of genocide. Cheers."

"I am one of your students. What right do you have to call one of my colleagues a 'cockroach,' you filthy Israeli cunt? Please, could I ask you to leave the U.S. and return to the land of Zion-Nazis where you can slaughter innocent cockroaches at whim? See you in class you wasted inbred."

The Initial Event

On March 4, 2013, I was sitting in my office at Claremont McKenna College (CMC) grading a midterm exam.[1] It was around 5:20 PM, and a student from Pitzer College (PC)—another college in the consortium known as the Claremont Colleges—suddenly popped in. He told me with some concern that there was a demonstration going on at the dining hall. I accompanied him downstairs, but once we got on the main sidewalk near the dining hall, he took a turn because he was afraid to be seen with me.

When I got to the dining hall, I saw a couple of students handing out fliers, and I saw a line of students blocking the entrance. I also saw a couple of students standing on the side of the dining hall and crying.

I approached the dining hall. The students were standing shoulder to shoulder, and I could not pass. They told me, "Show us your ID." I said, "What?" "Yeah, yeah, this is an Israeli checkpoint. Show us your ID if you want to come inside." I said, "I'm not going to show you my ID. Have you ever seen an Israeli checkpoint?" One of the students said, "Yeah, yeah, I saw an Israeli checkpoint." I said, "Who is your leader? Who brought you here?" Then they told me, "We don't have a leader. We've come by ourselves, and this is an approved demonstration." I said, "OK, OK, let me in." So at this point, they let me in without physical contact.

I went inside the dining hall to look for the dining hall manager. I told her, "The students have the right to demonstrate—they probably have approved that—but they cannot block the entrance. Please move them ten feet aside. They can do their political activity there. Just move them ten feet aside so they will not block the entrance and hassle students. That's illegal."

She went outside, and she talked with the students, and at first, they complied. They took off the ropes along the side of the dining hall, and they moved away. However, the moment the manager went back inside, they immediately blocked the entrance again. I went back inside the dining hall. This time, I could not find the manager, so I went to the cashier and asked to use her phone. I called Campus Safety, and I told the dispatcher, "The students have the right to demonstrate, but you need to send someone to move them ten feet aside. They cannot block the entrance."

The Campus Safety officer arrived, and he parked his cart thirty to forty feet south of the dining hall entrance. I started to walk toward him, to explain what was going on, when a student from the demonstration approached me and said in my face, "Who are you? Show me your ID! Are you faculty or a visitor? If you are a visitor, you cannot be on campus after 5:00 PM. Show me your campus pass!"

I told him, "I will not show you my ID. It's not your business who I am. I can be a faculty or a visitor; it's not your business." I kept walking toward the Campus Safety officer, and this guy pushed in my face aggressively. I started to talk with the officer and said, "The student event has been approved for this demonstration, but they cannot block the entrance. You need to move them ten feet aside." To give some weight to what I was saying, I pulled out my faculty ID to show the officer. The student who was in my face said, "Oh, you are faculty! I will hunt you down!" And I said, "What? You will hunt me down? You're a fucking little cockroach."

The student heard that and said, "Oh! Now I've got you!"

The moment he said that, I was really concerned—not because of the "cockroach" but because of my use of the f-word. I immediately disengaged. I went back to the PC student who had originally asked for my help. I told him, "Campus Safety is here. They will take it from here."

And I left.

"Immediately after the above incident, students and faculty mainly from Pitzer College began disseminating false and defamatory information about me: wrongly accusing me of racism, harassment, and the violation of students' rights to organize and protest. This smear campaign against me continued even after a CMC investigation decisively cleared me of these accusations. Making matters worse, the smear campaign was clearly motivated by hostility towards me based on my ethnicity as a Jewish Israeli" (ZOA). As a direct result of these activities, my family was subjected to tremendous pressure, anxiety, and fear.

I found out later that the reason a couple of students were crying near the dining hall was because when they had tried to enter the hall, some of the demonstrators had told them, "Fuck off, Jews!" I would give this information to Jim Marchant, then vice president for student affairs at PC, who, to the best of my knowledge, would never do anything with or about it.

The Immediate Aftermath and the Reframing

"Two individuals in particular engaged in the vendetta against me: Najib Hamideh, the former PC student who had the verbal exchange with me, and Daniel Segal, professor of anthropology and history at PC who was advising Hamideh" (ZOA). Additional malfeasance on the institutional level was committed (as we shall see) by Marchant, just mentioned, and Laura Trombley, then president of PC.

"The entire incident occurred" (LLM) in the area around a Claremont McKenna dining hall. "Accordingly, CMC has complete jurisdiction" (LLM) over the event and its consequences. Correspondingly, CMC's former dean of students Mary Spellman conducted a thorough investigation "during which 11 witnesses were interviewed including several students from Students for Justice in Palestine (SJP)" (LLM)—the student group responsible for the demonstration—the dining hall manager, the Campus Safety officer, myself, and Hamideh.

On April 19, Pamela Gann, then CMC president, released the results of the investigation, finding that:

(1) The professor's conduct was inappropriate and below the standards of CMC behavior, but given the context, his behavior did not constitute "harassment."

(2) The SJP demonstration violated both the CMC and the 5C (Claremont Colleges) Demonstrations Policies. Both bar "actions in which there is a deliberate disruption or an impedance of access to regular activities of the College or of the College Community, including those which restrict free movement on the campus."

(3) The faculty member had not inappropriately interfered with the demonstration and had not tried to shut down the demonstration.

"Although these were the findings by the college that had jurisdiction and undertook the thorough investigation, the public narrative both within the campus and without was a very different one. This was due to a publicity campaign instigated almost immediately not only by the SJP students but by Prof. Daniel Segal" (LLM). Segal was central to this process throughout. Serving not merely as faculty advocate for Hamideh, he actively reframed the incident to suit his and Hamideh's agenda and then spread that false narrative to the Pitzer faculty, through emails and via media outlets. Along the way, he ignored the confidentiality rules by which, as a faculty advocate, he was bound.

"According to Segal, and therefore according to most initial media accounts, what happened on March 4 was this: (1) a 'staunch Zionist' Jewish Israeli professor intentionally interfered with, and tried to block the free speech rights of, Arab pro-Palestinian students at a pre-approved demonstration at CMC; (2) my exclamation to Najib Hamideh was a vicious racist slur by a Jewish Israeli 'Zionist' against a Palestinian student; and (3) CMC was revealed to be biased against Arabs" (LLM).

In spreading his narrative, "Segal stated as facts things about which he had no independent knowledge" (LLM), as he had not been present at the demonstration and relied only on what the students told him. He also discussed the incident with outside media "before and during the investigation process" (LLM), without waiting for its conclusion, and publicly released confidential documents that "were part of the investigation process. Further, he sought and spread information about PC's own internal investigation from Jim Marchant, information that probably should have remained confidential" (LLM).

What were Segal's ultimate motives? I believe his zeal to advocate for Hamideh was fueled by his personal perception that "evil Zionists are out to demonize Arab students and deprive them of their constitutional rights, and that CMC is a 'biased institution'" (LLM), which, in focusing on the students' violation of the demonstration rules rather than on the "Zionist's racist attack," produced a "materially misleading" report.[2]

"Eventually, CMC informed Segal that he could not continue to serve as Hamideh's faculty advocate because he had violated confidentiality requirements outlined in the CMC handbook. That decision was contested by Segal and outside legal counsel providing him assistance, the Center for Constitutional Rights. Shortly after CMC issued its review and findings, Hamideh filed a formal grievance against me with CMC. On May 7, CMC rejected the grievance, allegedly because Hamideh was unwilling to abide by the confidentiality requirements of the grievance process" (LLM).

Pitzer's Investigation and Rejection of My Grievance

Despite CMC's jurisdiction over the incident, Pitzer College also undertook an investigation.

"In an April 26 letter to the PC community, President Trombley revealed that Pitzer's findings were very different from CMC's. Trombley stressed the only undisputed fact—that I used inappropriate language (which I had readily admitted)—but rejected any allegation of inappropriate conduct either by Hamideh" (LLM) or his fellow SJP demonstrators.

While CMC found that the SJP students had repeatedly violated the demonstration policy because they kept returning to block the dining hall entrance, "Pitzer concluded that they did *not* violate the policy because the three times they were asked to move, they did.... Trombley also informed the community that Jim Marchant, Vice President for Student Affairs, had rejected a grievance I filed against Hamideh" (for multiple violations, see below) "because he 'determined that there was no merit to the complaint based on his investigation of the incident'" (LLM).

What investigation was this?

Whatever investigation he did of the episode or with respect to my grievance did not include any discussion with me.

Even Segal, when informed about this anomaly, told the *Jewish Press*, "That can't be right" (LLM). He then said he would ask his "good friend" Marchant about it. So Segal was "good friends" with the person investigating an incident in which Segal had taken a direct personal stake. Segal then followed up with the *Jewish Press* to explain that Marchant said he "did not need to speak with Raviv" about my grievance because he "had already heard what Raviv had to say during the CMC investigation" (LLM). One can only ask, with Lori Lowenthal Marcus: "Is that an impartial investigation by a College administrator?" (LLM)

There are many parts of the Segal/SJP narrative that are just impossible to believe, which makes me question deeply not merely the entire Pitzer process but the ready acceptance of their narrative by so much of the community at large.

First, Hamideh claimed he went after me as I approached the Campus Safety officer because it was after 5:00 PM and he did not recognize me as someone permitted to be on campus. "But the incident took place at CMC and Hamideh is not a CMC student" (LLM), so why should he have recognized me? And why "would he consider it *his* responsibility to determine whether I should be on campus, given that I was at that very moment approaching a Campus Safety officer?" (LLM).

But far more disturbing was the ready acceptance of the Segal/SJP claim that I had made a racist remark.

"In an effort to show that 'cockroach' is a racist slur against Arab Palestinians, the advocates of this narrative had to go back to 1982 to find a time when an Israeli used the term to refer to Arabs. More importantly, while my own background is obvious as soon as I open my mouth—my Israeli accent is very strong— Hamideh neither looks Middle Eastern nor has any accent. I had no idea he was anything but American. Further to this point, in his original description of what I said, Hamideh claimed I also referred to all Pitzer students as cockroaches. If that were the case, then since only a tiny percentage of PC students are of Arab descent, I certainly was not using the term as a negative term for Arab Palestinians" (LLM).

Unless I knew Hamideh was a Palestinian, and only if the term *cockroach* was "regularly used to refer to Palestinians" (LLM), my choice of words could not constitute racial harassment either under current law or in the Claremont Colleges handbook. "For Segal and the SJP students and others to repeatedly suggest otherwise was at best disingenuous," at worst straightforward dishonesty and lying, and "possibly slander under California law" (LLM).

Indeed, Segal/SJP's effort to cast the incident as my effort to deny free speech rights to Arab Palestinians is nothing less than absurd. "Even the PC report— which found fault only with me and none with Hamideh or SJP—did not find that I attempted to shut down the SJP's demonstration" (LLM). And of course, the CMC report found that I had not improperly interfered with the demonstration, because I hadn't.

"Finally, both Pitzer and the SJP students stressed the fact that the students had obtained permission to stage the 'mock Israeli checkpoint' demonstration. But that was beside the point. Obtaining permission for the demonstration in advance does not immunize any bad behavior that violates school policy at the demonstration" (LLM).

Their entire narrative was simply absurd and should have been dismissed immediately. The facts that: (1) it was taken seriously at all by the administration and community at large, (2) my grievance against Hamideh was so coarsely dismissed, and (3) Segal was permitted to run such a malicious and defamatory campaign against me are all profoundly disturbing.

Najib Hamideh's Conduct

Consider the fact that Hamideh violated at least five different elements of the Pitzer Code of Student Conduct, each of which deserves a grievance process of its own:

(1) Hamideh, and SJP, violated the rules on demonstrations. This is the explicit conclusion of the CMC investigation, which had jurisdiction.

(2)   Hamideh personally threatened me when he said, "I will hunt you down." The CMC investigation notes that there was at least one other person who heard him say that.

(3)   Hamideh lied during the official investigation, claiming that I could identify him as a Palestinian because he was wearing a keffiyeh. However, photos from the incident show him dressed in typical student attire: jeans and a T-shirt.[3]

(4)   Hamideh violated the confidentiality requirement of the grievance and investigation processes. In a letter to the Claremont College community dated May 7, 2013, President Gann confirmed that there were documented "breaches of confidentiality" by Hamideh.

(5)   Hamideh defamed me and helped spearhead the smear campaign against me. He repeatedly and falsely painted me as a racist, falsely claimed that I interfered with students' constitutional rights, and even falsely accused me of criminal conduct.[4] "These false accusations against me were surely motivated by his ethnic bias against me. He repeatedly referred to my Israeli origin when disparaging me" (ZOA), claiming that my alleged misbehavior toward him reflected Israeli behavior. According to Pitzer's student handbook, invoking someone's national origin as evidence of their racism and aggressiveness should constitute ethnic bias.

And yet Marchant and Pitzer were willing to overlook all this. Why is that?

Pitzer Vice President Jim Marchant's Conduct

In his handling of this episode, Marchant demonstrated a lack of professionalism, failure to fulfill his duty, failure to keep the investigation fair and neutral, and violation of confidentiality. To the best of my knowledge, his decision to dismiss a faculty grievance against a student without any serious investigation is unprecedented at the Claremont Colleges.

The PC administration appeared biased against me from the start. To minimize the damage of the defamatory emails that Segal was sending to the PC community, I requested early on to meet with the PC administration to give them my account. Their reply, as we have seen, was that they didn't need to meet with me because they knew what happened.

I filed a grievance against Hamideh, requesting that he be held accountable for his numerous violations of the PC Code of Student Conduct. PC gave this no serious consideration. Only one week after receiving it, Marchant wrote me that "there is not sufficient information supporting your allegations to proceed with charging Najib Hamideh with any violation[s]." He reached this conclusion without interviewing me or conducting an independent inquiry.

Marchant said he didn't need to meet with me because CMC had already done an investigation. But then he also contended that my claim that Hamideh said, "I will hunt you down" had not been substantiated—when it had been substantiated by the very CMC investigation Marchant cited!

"Marchant claimed that there was insufficient evidence to support my charge that Hamideh had falsely accused me of hate speech" (ZOA). But when I brought him the publicly available photo proving that Hamideh had lied about being identifiable as a Palestinian, "Marchant admitted that he had not seen it or any other photos of the event—demonstrating the lack of seriousness of his 'investigation' into my grievance" (ZOA).

Even after seeing the photo, Marchant then claimed that it was not substantive to the complaint I submitted. But of course it was: it proved that I had been falsely accused of hate speech, since I could not have known Hamideh was a Palestinian.

The photo also demonstrated that the students were blocking the entrance to the dining hall, but Marchant chose to overlook that.

Marchant also apparently chose not to act on the information (above) that the demonstrating students had said, "Fuck off, Jews!"

I cannot know what Marchant's motives were, but it is natural to wonder whether they have something to do with his relationship to his "good friend" Segal, mentioned above—who at various moments relayed confidential information to reporters that he only could have obtained from Marchant. Indeed, at one point "Hamideh somehow obtained a copy of the Campus Safety report about the incident, which he then passed on to Segal who circulated it to PC faculty. If Marchant gave the report to Hamideh, then that is serious impropriety" (ZOA).

Daniel Segal's Conduct

In my opinion, Segal's smear campaign against me was motivated by ethnic bias against my Jewish Israeli origin.

Examples of his unprofessional conduct and harassment are provided below. These are all the more egregious as he repeatedly accused me of serious misconduct at the demonstration—despite his not having been present. He simply accepted the students' false version of events and propagated it uncritically.

"On March 13, 2013, he emailed PC faculty accusing me of verbally attacking Hamideh, even though he knew that the accusation had not yet been investigated or substantiated. Later, he obtained the Campus Safety report from Hamideh, in violation of confidentiality requirements. Segal then disseminated the report with his email to PC faculty members, claiming that Hamideh authorized him to circulate it. Segal must have (or should have) known that Hamideh had no such authority, and thus that he himself had no such authority" (ZOA).

In his email, Segal provided a link to what he called "a useful news account of the incident" that allowed "other faculty and Pitzer administrators [to] confirm … that the person who attacked the students as 'cockroaches' is Professor Raviv" (ZOA). Again, nothing about an "attack" could be "confirmed" at that point since an investigation was barely underway. Moreover, that "useful news account" was in fact a one-sided story on the *Electronic Intifada*, a virulently anti-Israel site that shared Hamideh's narrative but noted that "I and officials at CMC and Pitzer had declined to comment, due to the pending investigation" (ZOA).

Further, "when some PC faculty members advised Segal to stop his malicious campaign against me in light of the ongoing investigation, Segal continued anyway. One faculty member cautioned him about 'rabble rousers' who 'want to stir troubles before facts are known.' But Segal brushed this aside, stating proudly that it was 'a badge of honor' that he might be considered a 'rabble rouser'—at my expense" (ZOA).

Segal's ongoing attempts to malign me reveal, in my opinion, "that he was motivated by his own ethnic bias against me as a Jewish Israeli. In an email he sent to Pitzer faculty on March 14th, he referred to me as a 'Zionist faculty member' who was 'trying to interfere with a legitimate exercise of speech rights by Palestinian identified students.' 'Zionist' is often used pejoratively to refer to all Israelis and even to many Jews, which is the way that Segal plainly used it since he did not know me or anything about my personal political beliefs" (ZOA). As to his claim that I tried to interfere with "speech rights," again, one wonders if Segal typically accepts as facts one-sided allegations before bothering with an investigation, or whether he reserved this behavior for this incident.

And of course, the CMC investigation soon proved that his accusation was false.

Segal's ethnic bias was also present in his media statements. As support for his charge that I am a racist, for example, Segal repeatedly claimed that I am a "staunch Zionist" and "a staunch, uncritical defender of the state of Israel." When asked why he called me a "staunch Zionist," he responded, "because [Raviv] served in the Israeli military."[5]

Segal disseminated the documentable falsehood that Hamideh had been wearing a keffiyeh at the demonstration to support the lie that my remark was directed at Hamideh's ethnicity.

"On March 14th, Segal also circulated a draft motion to the Pitzer faculty accusing me of having violated professional ethics standards and committed harassment, in violation of CMC policies" (ZOA). These accusations were based on as-yet uninvestigated and unsubstantiated claims and defamed me in a manner that undermined the fairness and neutrality of the investigatory process and helped poison my colleagues against me, creating a very hostile work environment.

On March 19, only days after President Gann had issued a clear directive for a fair and neutral investigation, Segal maligned me to the media. He told the *Electronic Intifada* that my "behavior was 'clearly harmful' to the educational environment," accused me of "corrod[ing] and degrad[ing] the educational context of the colleges; it's an attack on the students, it's also an attack on our community," and claimed that I was "clearly in violation of [the college's] handbook" due to my allegedly bias-related targeting of Hamideh and the other students.[6]

As the CMC investigations shortly made clear, every one of these accusations was false.

One cannot help but wonder: What kind of person pursues inflammatory campaigns like this without waiting for the facts to be ascertained? What kind of *scholar* makes claims like these without allowing even the minimal degree of due process?

Indeed, Segal continued to smear me, as well as interfere with and attack CMC's investigation itself, while the investigation was ongoing.[7] "Even *after* the investigation established that his accusations were false, he continued to make them. In an 'open letter' to CMC faculty, Segal continued to promote the falsehood that I 'improperly interfered' with the SJP demonstration, and that I subjected the SJP students to 'a verbal, dehumanizing attack'" (ZOA).[8] Although the CMC investigation was as thorough and impartial as anyone could hope, Segal simply adopted uncritically the students' narrative and complained that the CMC's report "blamed the victims in this incident: the SJP students" (ZOA).

It is hard for me not to conclude that Segal's conduct was racist, bigoted, and unconscionable. "His actions show a lack of professionalism and serious misconduct" (ZOA). He adopted a false narrative that suited his agenda, then disregarded every proof of its falseness. And he engaged in verbal harassment against me, attempting to poison my faculty colleagues at CMC as well as our sister institutions, and the public at large, against me.[9]

"According to the PC Faculty Handbook, all of this wrongdoing merits Special Review" (ZOA). However, when I asked for a Special Review of Segal's behavior, my request was dismissed without addressing any of the concerns I raised above.

Pitzer President Trombley's Conduct

One week after President Gann emailed the Claremont Colleges Community the summary of CMC's investigation, PC president Trombley "issued a statement to the Pitzer College community, taking issue with CMC's conclusions. According to Trombley, as we saw above, SJP did not violate the demonstrations policy because the students moved" (ZOA) every time they were asked to.

Any neutral observer surely should wonder about this.

First, PC had no jurisdiction here. So why were they weighing in at all?

Second, Trombley could not know what really happened because Pitzer hadn't done a proper investigation. Indeed, when she sent that message, she hadn't seen any photos from the event, so she could not evaluate whether SJP was blocking the entrance.

Third, most bizarrely, she *acknowledged* that SJP repeatedly blocked the entrance even *after* being asked to move, yet somehow found a way to excuse them from violating the policy against blocking the entrance.

Why, we must ask, were my grievances against the many misbehaviors of PC student Hamideh and PC faculty member Segal, described above and readily documented, simply dismissed without investigation?

In October 2013, the Zionist Organization of America (ZOA) sent a letter to Pitzer College inquiring about their handling of the incident, sharing all of the details above.

Pitzer ignored it completely.

Then the ZOA sent another letter in which they wrote: "Your silence strengthens the perception that Pitzer College tolerates a hostile antisemitic campus environment, tarnishing the reputation of the entire community of The Claremont Colleges. We ask to hear from you by no later than Monday, November 25, 2013."

Trombley's response was dismissive, completely disregarding all the facts so painstakingly laid before her. In her letter, she states merely, "Regarding the incident that occurred on CMC campus last March, a full investigation was made by the College and the matter has been concluded."

Subsequently, I asked Trombley for a copy of the Pitzer investigation report, curious about it since I had not been interviewed for it.

Her reply: "The College has already responded to your inquiry and has no further comment at this time."

I was never given a copy of the report.

My Conclusions

Four days after the incident, while the investigation was taking place, Hamideh disseminated his narrative through the student newspapers. He falsely accused me of hate speech and tried to damage my reputation and relations with other students and faculty. His claim that I insulted him because of his racial background was pure slander and reflective, I believe, of *his* racist hostility toward Israeli Jews. He spread his slander widely, not merely damaging my reputation and relations, but also putting my family in danger.

I received nasty emails and phone messages. For example: "Hitler had the right idea, he was just an underachiever. I thought you might enjoy that since you seem to be such a huge supporter of genocide. Cheers." And: "I am one of your students. What right do you have to call one of my colleagues a 'cockroach,' you filthy Israeli cunt? Please, could I ask you to leave the U.S. and return to the land of Zion-Nazis where you can slaughter innocent cockroaches at whim? See you in class you wasted inbred."

Radical terrorists are always looking for Israelis outside of Israel, and for them, I may be a good, and easy, target. Not only am I an Israeli Jew, but I am allegedly one who is racist against Palestinians. After publishing my name, it was easy to find my home address. We lived in terror for months. My wife was scared to start the car while our kids were inside it. The school one child attends was made aware of the incident and increased their security. The Claremont Colleges Campus Safety and the Claremont police were alerted as well.

I will not detail the severe physical and psychological distress I suffered during this period. Nor can I even adequately describe how difficult it was for me to continue teaching during this period, particularly since I had several Arab students in my classes, including one of Palestinian descent. What were they thinking, I wondered, helpless to say or do anything because I was committed to the confidentiality of the investigation process. Imagine trying to have normal interactions with students or colleagues when you are being publicly accused of racism and you are unable to defend yourself properly.

Did Hamideh and Segal desire this outcome, that a member of their community should become so alienated from that community and have to live in fear for his safety and that of his family? I cannot answer that question, but this outcome is the clearly foreseeable outcome of the dishonest widespread public campaign to defame me as a racist Israeli Jew.

Even if this was not their intention, the damage they inflicted on me personally and professionally was enormous and only exacerbated by the dishonest manner in which they conducted their campaign.

The "Oh! Now I've got you!" continues to haunt me.

And it wasn't only damage to me but to the community as a whole, in particular the Jewish community on our campuses who experienced an overall culture of fear. A Jewish faculty member at PC sent an email to PC faculty early on, describing verbal attacks on Jewish students both directly and on social media, as well as antisemitic graffiti, noting that one religious student had stopped wearing her Star of David out of fear.

Here are several things I have learned from the ordeal.

Since public opinion is determined quickly, it is important to have your side of the story disseminated as soon and as widely as possible. To the contrary, I maintained public silence, believing naively in the investigative process, as well as abiding by the confidentiality rules. Moreover, the school administration explicitly asked me not to discuss the issue publicly. My attackers did not abide by these rules, choosing to damage me publicly without bothering to wait for, and then even after, the results of the investigation.

Further, I believe there should be a designated agency that gathers information regarding similar attacks on Jewish or pro-Israel students and faculty at other campuses. This agency should also be able to provide real and prompt assistance. I was overwhelmed when these events happened. I felt lost and didn't get any real support initially from any agency, despite initial efforts to contact several. Indeed, one reason I have chosen to contribute to this book is to help create public awareness that these sorts of attacks are occurring and hopefully help create support mechanisms for those being targeted.

Outside of my family and my faculty support person, there were eventually two people who helped me tremendously. First, Lori Lowenthal Marcus from the *Jewish Press*, who not only interviewed me at length but also then referred me to Susan Tuchman from the Zionist Organization of America. Susan was both supportive and extremely helpful, referring me to a lawyer and writing letters to the administration on my behalf (much of which I have borrowed in composing this essay).

Get a lawyer and be ready to sue. I believe I made a mistake by not hiring a lawyer immediately and filing lawsuits. Initially, I was abiding by the rules of the grievance filed against me, which precluded outside counsel. Later, after consulting with an attorney, I considered two types of lawsuits: one against Hamideh and Segal for defamation and reputational damage, and a second against PC for the cursory dismissal of my grievance against Hamideh. These actions may well constitute a violation of my civil rights due to my country of origin.

In the end, there were two reasons I decided not to pursue legal action. First, the lawyer told us that the case would become even more public than it already was and would probably be covered by mainstream media. After the tremendous ordeal we had suffered, we felt what we needed most was quiet, not more publicity. Second, legal action would be extremely expensive. Unfortunately, not many have the resources, psychological or financial, to take legal action in cases like these.

A last lesson is for students and their parents.

When considering where to go to college, or whether you want to work at a college, you ought seriously to consider its political atmosphere. For example, prospective Jewish students may consider whether they would be comfortable at Pitzer College in light of its behavior in this incident, in which the college seemed simply to accept racist defamatory claims against an Israeli Jewish professor while ignoring all the evidence that the racism was actually in the opposite direction.

YARON RAVIV is Associate Professor of Economics at Claremont McKenna College.

Notes

1. During the episode, I shared most of the details that appear in this chapter with Lori Lowenthal Marcus from the *Jewish Press* and Susan Tuchman from the Zionist Organization of America (ZOA). Based partly on that information, Marcus published the articles cited in the chapter and Tuchman wrote a private letter to the presidents of the Claremont Colleges, dated October 18, 2013. Quotations from one of Marcus's articles ("'Cockroach' as Anti-Arab Slur and Other Narrative Creations," *The Jewish Press* (May 28, 2013), http://www.jewishpress .com/news/cockroach-as-anti-arab-slur-and-other-narrative-creations/2013/05/28/0/), slightly modified for stylistic purposes, I signify in the text by "LLM"; quotations from the ZOA letter, similarly modified, I signify by "ZOA."

2. [David Rosen, in chapter 20 of this volume, describes Segal as a "BDS leader" and describes Segal's organization of a boycott of a Claremont Colleges talk by visiting Israeli anthropologist Moshe Shokeid.—eds.]

3. Lori Lowenthal Marcus, "Cockroach Curses and Jew-Hunting in California Colleges," *The Jewish Press* (May 10, 2013), http://www.jewishpress.com/news/cockroach-curses-and -jew-hunting-in-california-colleges/2013/05/10/.

4. Gabriel Schivone and Nora Barrows-Friedman, "Israeli Professor Working in US Calls Palestinian Student 'Cockroach,'" *The Electronic Intifada* (March 19, 2013), http://electronicintifada.net/content/israeli-professor-working-us-calls-palestinian-student -cockroach/12296.

5. Lori Lowenthal Marcus, "'Cockroach' as Anti-Arab Slur and Other Narrative Creations," *The Jewish Press* (May 28, 2013), http://www.jewishpress.com/news/cockroach -as-anti-arab-slur-and-other-narrative-creations/2013/05/28/0/.

6. Gabriel Schivone and Nora Barrows-Friedman, "Israeli Professor Working in US Calls Palestinian Student 'Cockroach,'" *The Electronic Intifada* (March 19, 2013), https://electronicintifada.net/content/israeli-professor-working-us-calls-palestinian -student-cockroach/12296.

7. Carlos Ballesteros, "SJP Vigil Calls For CMC Response," *The Student Life* (April 12, 2013), http://tsl.pomona.edu/articles/2013/4/12/news/3899-sjp-vigil-calls-for-cmc-response.

8. The letter was initially posted at http://www.claremontportside.com/prof-segal -on-sjp-incident-an-open-letter-to-cmc-faculty/, but as of April 2016 the link was dead.

9. See Brad Richardson, "Scripps, CMS Faculty Exchange Blows on Raviv Incident," *Claremont Independent* (June 26, 2013), http://claremontindependent.com/scripps-cmc -faculty-exchange-blows-on-raviv-incident/.

20   The Magic of Myth: Fashioning the BDS Narrative in the New Anthropology

David M. Rosen

David Rosen provides a behind-the-scenes look at the Boycott, Divestment, and Sanctions (BDS) movement within the American Anthropological Association (AAA). Despite a multiyear effort by anti-Israel activists, including the leadership of the AAA, in 2016 the membership voted BDS down by a razor-thin margin of thirty-nine votes. Rosen documents the many questionable tactics of the anti-Israelists, showing how a small cadre of committed radicals can nearly take over an entire organization. He explores the abuse of the notion of complicity by which activists seek to justify their bigoted boycott and shows how their interest is not in engaging in debate with anyone but in demonizing and silencing their opponents instead. "To impose pariah status on the Jewish State, they are more than willing to tear apart the freedoms and protections American academics have created over centuries." Anyone who does not advocate the end of Jewish self-determination is rendered complicit in the alleged crimes of the Jewish State. Although BDS lost this time, the challenge isn't over: BDS activists have announced that their efforts will continue.

On June 7, 2016, the AAA announced that its members rejected a proposed BDS boycott of Israeli universities and academic institutions by a vote of 2,423 to 2,384—a slim margin of just 39 votes. Fifty-one percent of the association's approximately 9,353 members voted, the largest voter turnout in its history. It was a hard-earned victory for boycott opponents. Only six months earlier, at the 2015 annual meeting of the association and one of the biggest moments for BDS in academe, members of the association had voted 1,040 to 136 to place the boycott resolution on the spring ballot. The carnival atmosphere at that meeting, with all the symbolic trappings and paraphernalia of a BDS political pep rally, made victory over BDS seem almost impossible.

Had the boycott vote succeeded, the AAA, the largest association of anthropologists in the world, would have become a party in the Israeli-Palestinian conflict. It would have marked the final transformation of the AAA from a professional scientific organization into a radical nongovernmental organization (NGO). With the defeat of the boycott, this has not occurred—yet. However, even with the failure of the boycott resolution, significant damage to the profession has been done. Major departments of anthropology are still in the grip of the boycott ideology and continue to impose conformity or silence from dissenters, faculty, and students. Boycott supporters vow that they will continue the boycott on an individual basis, thereby ensuring that a silent boycott against Israeli institutions and scholars will continue to operate. In the most Orwellian sense, boycott supporters have, as Richard Shweder has pointed out, turned BDS's discriminatory animus into a public and private virtue. Equally important, the elected leadership of the AAA continues to claim that there is a consensus within anthropology for condemning Israel and continues to promote views on the conflict between Israelis and Palestinians that begin and end with Israeli culpability for every issue. Despite the vote, the battle within anthropology is hardly over.

So, it is crucial to understand how BDS functions within anthropology and the wider academy.

There is no doubt that over the last several decades anthropology has become a highly politicized discipline. From its earliest days, many individual anthropologists have held strong political positions. What is new is the degree to which forces within anthropology have demanded that the entire discipline take a unified position and that the association transform itself into a political entity. Equally important, the current leadership of the AAA has embraced this idea and systematically privileged the boycott movement's central place in the association's affairs.

The formal public process of valorizing BDS within the association began with the 2014 annual meetings in Washington, DC. Shortly after the deadline for submissions for those meetings, the leadership announced that something had to be done in anthropology regarding Israel-Palestine. What it did was package and promote a series of panels and events put together by BDS activists under the cover of promoting a conversation within the association. When the leadership of an association takes it on itself to address any controversial issue, basic fairness suggests that all interested parties be given notice of the association's intentions and that all parties be given an opportunity to be heard. These fundamental tenets of fairness and equity were set aside as the association showcased a series of panels that functioned as mini political rallies of BDS stars and supporters. Dissenters from within the association were left shouting from the sidelines, completely ambushed by these events, which were announced only after the deadline for the submission of panels had closed. No contact was made with the Israel Anthropological Association or even Israeli members of the American

Anthropological Association. The 2014 meetings and their panels were simply a stalking horse for a boycott, creating a de facto exclusion of both dissenters and potential victims of a boycott from the entire so-called conversation. The symbolic importance of these actions by the association's leaders cannot be over-stated. Their actions advertised to the entire association the political synergy between the elected AAA leaders and those of BDS.

Following the 2014 meetings, the association created a task force to investigate and report back to the association on the situation in Israel and Palestine. The task force on Israel/Palestine was charged with developing "principles to be used to assess whether the AAA has an interest in taking a stand on these issues. This may include providing a comprehensive and neutral overview of arguments for and against a range of specific possible stands (including no action)."[1] Inherent in this charge is the idea that the task force should adhere to reasonable standards of neutrality. Nonetheless, from the beginning, it was evident that the report of the task force would be shaped by the assumptions of Israeli culpability and Palestinian innocence. Indeed, when the first chair of the task force resigned, he was briefly replaced by a publicly declared BDS supporter until a colleague and I protested this appointment. But the end result was the same: a report that is rife with cherry-picked data and citation bias.[2] The citation bias shows up very early in the report, where the task force cites a petition in support of a boycott by BDS supporters in anthropology but blatantly omits any mention of a petition signed by other anthropologists in opposition to the boycott.[3] The pattern continues throughout the report, with the result that the overwhelming preponderance of anthropologists cited in the report are self-declared supporters of BDS. As expected, the report makes little effort to disguise its hostility to Israel.[4]

Had the association joined the BDS boycott, it would have established, for the first time in its more than one-hundred-year history, an ideological litmus test for participation in the academy. Endorsing a political test for speech is a step on a dangerous path for American anthropologists. As University of Chicago president Robert Zimmer put it, boycotts are an "assault on the fundamental principles of open discourse, exchange of ideas, and free argumentation, principles that lie at the very foundation of the academy and its missions of discovery, search for understanding, and education."[5] Little wonder that academic boycotts have been rejected by the American Association of University Professors and more than one hundred major higher education institutions across the country, including the American Council on Education, the Association of American Universities, and the Association of Public and Land-Grant Universities. All these institutions recognize that an academic boycott opens the door to the general political suppression of speech in the academy. They recognize that if academics no longer uphold the principle of free speech in the university, neither will anyone else.

For BDS activists, these concerns remain a mere trifle. The niceties of academic freedom are a minor concern at best and, at worst, an obstacle to be surmounted. They seek to demonize Israel so thoroughly and to place it so far outside the boundaries of normal academic discourse that it can be discussed only in the language of immorality and criminality. To impose pariah status on the Jewish State, they are more than willing to tear apart the freedoms and protections that American academics have created over centuries, principles that have served as the first line of defense for personal freedom and autonomy. Their eyes are on one goal: eliminating Jewish sovereignty and the Jewish State. As British historian Simon Schama has put it, "Criticism of Israeli government policies has mutated into a rejection of Israel's right to exist; the Fatah position replaced by Hamas and Hizbollah eliminationism."[6] Had the AAA subscribed to BDS tenets, it would have completely divorced itself from the long history of struggle by people, institutions, and groups to uphold academic freedom in the United States.

Boycott: An Intellectual Crisis

The boycott movement represents an intellectual crisis for anthropology as a discipline, which has its roots in the erosion of the AAA's commitment to science.

When the association voted in 2010 to strip the word *science* from its long-range plans, much of anthropology had already become thoroughly politicized. There is no doubt that a huge amount of serious anthropology is still taking place in the profession. But by the same token, the politicization of the discipline has led to an erosion of rigorous intellectual standards that had, historically, combined skepticism of established truths with constant openness to alternatives. The result of this erosion is that where anthropology is needed most, in helping solve difficult problems such as the conflict between Israel and Palestine, it has become the least useful. Anthropology is increasingly dominated by a perspective shaped by intellectuals who provide scripted and clichéd postmodern and postcolonial analyses of problems. The emergence of scripted narratives has led many evidence-based scholars, such as archeologists and physical anthropologists, to all but abandon the association, and even many cultural anthropologists have walked away in disgust at the replacement of empiricism and rigorous analysis with narrative form and political aesthetics. In many areas of anthropology, all that is left are the trace marks of a past discipline and a perspective that has little patience for science or for rational debate. The new anthropology is about political advocacy. It frames the world largely in terms of victims and victors, oppressors and oppressed. Data are now cherry-picked to fit the narrative. There is significantly less room for the careful analysis, thick description, and nuanced understanding that have long been the hallmarks of good anthropology. But in the new postempirical anthropology, it is the narrative—not the data—that actually counts. Like all forms of propaganda, the truth is a function of its emotional persuasiveness. If it fits the narrative—it is true.

The BDS Attack on Anthropology

The targeting of Israeli anthropology by BDS was an attempt to mobilize the power of the AAA and focus it on a tiny group of Israeli academics. There are no independent departments of anthropology in Israel; Israeli anthropologists typically constitute a junior discipline in joint departments of sociology and anthropology. At last count, there were only about 120 anthropologists in the entire country, and only a fraction of these hold full-time academic appointments. Even fewer are members of the AAA. Nevertheless, for most Israeli anthropologists, American academic organizations have been significant gateway institutions that facilitate the participation of this small community of scholars in world anthropology.

Ironically, Israeli anthropologists are probably the most likely to agree with many of the concerns that motivate many grassroots supporters of BDS. Like them, Israeli anthropologists overwhelmingly favor a fair and just solution of the problem of occupation, oppose the settlement movement, and support the creation of an independent Palestinian state. But this is not the ultimate goal of BDS's leaders, who see the realization of Palestinian rights as contingent on the end of the Jewish State. Accordingly, like all persons calling for Israeli and Palestinian cooperation and dialogue in achieving peace, Israeli anthropologists have become anathema to the leadership of BDS and its antinormalization campaign, which opposes the right of Jewish self-determination and the very existence of the Israeli state. BDS founder Omar Barghouti's recent call that Israel be "euthanized" makes plain that BDS's increasingly hysterical and irredentist vision for the Jews of Israel is not a two-state solution or even a one-state solution—but rather a no-state solution.[7] Moreover, Barghouti and company cannot be unaware that this language itself resonates with images of the Final Solution.

Suppressing moderate voices is central to BDS's antinormalization campaign, which is designed to shut down debate and drive out the voices of dialogue and moderation. But no one should be surprised. All radical movements demand simple binary oppositions: a world made up of oppressors and oppressed, good guys and bad guys. All radical movements have "if you're not with us, you're against us" positions. BDS is no different. Its own ideology—the destruction of Jewish sovereignty in Israel—cannot abide even the existence of liberal, tolerant, pluralistic, and progressive Israeli institutions and actors. The BDS antinormalization project is specifically designed to eliminate all cooperation with centers of progress and reform in Israel. All of these become subsumed under the mantras of the regressive Left, such as "settler-colonialist state," "complicity," and, of course, the evil specter of "Zionism." Once upon a time, this kind of thinking by slogans was anathema to anthropology. Now it has become commonplace.

In this light, BDS launched a two-pronged attack on academic freedom within anthropology more generally: first redefining academic freedom as a privilege conditioned on the acceptance of the BDS agenda and worldview, then marginalizing and demonizing those whose opposing views render them unprivileged to speak. It is a process of blacklisting and stigmatization. In BDS's morality play, there are only virtuous Palestinians and wicked Israelis. The only Israelis who can be tolerated are those who are willing to erase their national identity and surrender the right of Jewish self-determination. In this, BDS seeks to reverse history and re-create the political climate at the end of the Six-Day War as embodied in the Khartoum resolution of 1967: No Peace, No Recognition, and No Negotiation.[8]

The BDS Guidelines and the Politics of Complicity

Understanding BDS's ideology of complicity is central to understanding how BDS works in anthropology. BDS continuously uses the term *complicity* to describe the ways individuals and institutions are said to be implicated in the Israeli occupation of Palestine. The term *complicity* appears eight times in the academic boycott guidelines created by the Palestinian BDS National Committee, which serve as the foundational charter and catechism for the BDS movement.[9] It is crucial to examine the BDS doctrine of complicity and how it functions as a component of BDS rhetorical stratagems.

For BDS, complicity operates at three distinct levels. These are: (1) individual complicity, (2) Israeli institutional complicity, and (3) non-Israeli institutional complicity. Israeli institutions are regarded as presumptively complicit, as we'll see below. Other individuals and institutions are deemed complicit by virtue of their activities and actions. According to the guidelines, such persons or institutions can be deemed complicit through one of five separate modes of action and thought. These are: (1) silence, (2) justification, (3) whitewashing, (4) diversion, and (5) direct collaboration with complicit academic institutions. These fifteen BDS-defined forms of complicity comprise BDS's template of culpable thought and action.

Individual Complicity

BDS's guidelines claim that it supports the universal right of academic freedom and that the mere affiliation of Israeli scholars with an Israeli academic institution is not grounds for applying an individual boycott. But as Todd Gitlin has noted, the S in BDS is best understood as meaning *slippery*.[10] BDS paeans to academic freedom serve as a Potemkin village of the mind, functioning only to imitate and mislead. The actual details and operations of the BDS guidelines render these assertions meaningless. Central to this deception is the BDS assertion that all academics, Israel, American, or anyone else, are subject to so-called commonsense boycotts that "conscientious citizens around the world may call for in response to what they widely perceive as egregious individual complicity in, responsibility for, or advocacy of violations of international law (such as direct or indirect involvement in the commission of war crimes or other grave human rights violations; incitement to violence; racial slurs; etc.)."[11] While couched in the grandiose language of violations of international law, it is actually impossible to know to what actions and statements the guidelines really refer. Indeed, at face value, the guideline justifies the boycott and blacklisting of virtually any member of the public or the academy. Clearly, there should be no tolerance for racial slurs, but when did such slurs, offensive as they are, become the subject of international law? BDS's slippery slope of sanctionable offenses is completely open-ended and culminates in the final offensive category: "etc." BDS's slipperiness is further amplified in the now-rejected resolution brought forward by BDS to the AAA annual meeting, which states that "individual anthropologists are free to determine whether and how they will apply the boycott in their own professional practice."[12] If we examine how this actually works, we can see that it opens up a whole world of self-authorized vigilante boycotts of scholars for any reason.

Take, for example, the case of Moshe Shokeid, an Israeli anthropologist with strong Left political leanings. He is most well known in recent years for authoring highly regarded ethnographies of gay life in New York. During the First Intifada (1988–1993), along with other colleagues at Tel Aviv University, he initiated and chaired the organization Ad Kan (No More), a university-based peace movement that organized conferences, protests, and public demonstrations and advertised lists of many academics who advocated negotiations with the Palestine Liberation Organization (such advocacy was a punishable offense at that time). Members of the movement also visited Yasser Arafat in Gaza and Ramallah. Shokeid himself met Arafat twice. In 2008, Shokeid was a signatory to a petition criticizing actions by the Israeli government that were said to be infringing on the academic freedom of academics in the occupied territories, a petition that was lauded by the Palestinian Campaign for the Academic and Cultural Boycott of Israel (PACBI).[13] By any reasonable standard, Shokeid has a long history of progressive engagement with the issues of the Israel-Palestine conflict.

In 2012, Shokeid was invited to give a lecture at Pomona College in California. Daniel Segal, a local anthropologist and BDS leader, initiated an effort to boycott Shokeid's talk by circulating a public letter stating that he was refusing to attend Shokeid's talk because, in some of his early work, Shokeid had "participated in Zionist representations of Palestinians as antithetical to, and outside of, a modernizing, rational Israel."[14] That claim could be made about many anthropological descriptions of indigenous groups throughout the world, a fact that appears to have been no barrier to Segal's eager-beaver boycott efforts. Had it been about any other place in the world, Shokeid's early work would ordinarily have been regarded as common scholarly argument about indigenous peoples and modernization of that era. Instead, the BDS approach was to demonize Shokeid's work and make it a pretext for assigning individual complicity and for attempting to blacklist and exclude him from the academic community. What is crucial here is that BDS dogma provides any individual with an off-the-shelf pretext for leveraging normal scholarly disputes into moral grandstanding. The so-called guidelines provide the trappings of legitimacy and coherence to what is fundamentally an out-of-control discriminatory animus, grounded in guilt by association, which shuts down the free exchange of ideas for no other reason than the national origin of an individual scholar.

The vigilante character of these self-authorized boycotts is also illustrated by Hebrew University political scientist Dan Avnon's experience in seeking a sabbatical appointment at the University of Sydney's Center for Peace and Conflict Studies.[15] That center, led by BDS advocate Jack Lynch, apparently concocted its own foreign policy of blacklisting Israeli academics. The University of Sydney has no policy authorizing boycotts, yet faculty members in a department ostensibly felt free to create their own boycott while administrators remained mute. In this instance, there was no attempt to make even a sham case for individual complicity. Like Shokeid, Avnon was blacklisted merely for being an Israeli. Avnon later learned that shortly after Lynch sent him an email rejecting him, Lynch emailed the news to numerous colleagues, trumpeting his achievement at blacklisting an Israeli.

Lynch's conduct came under scrutiny again in March 2015, when he was involved in a BDS protest that disrupted a guest lecture at the university by British colonel Richard Kemp, who has defended the military conduct of the Israeli Defense Forces (IDF) in Gaza.[16] Among his other disruptive actions, Lynch was accused of making an antisemitic gesture—waving money in the face of an elderly Jewish woman at the lecture. In the end, the university determined that it was not clear that Lynch's conduct "constituted antisemitic behavior or unlawful harassment on the grounds of an individual's religious belief (or perceived religious belief),"[17] but he was still warned that he could face disciplinary action for possible breaches of the university's code of conduct, under which staff must treat visitors "with respect, impartiality, courtesy, and sensitivity."[18] Lynch still remains the director of the center. These episodes raise many questions about the leeway given to faculty members to engage in a wide variety of forms of speech suppression under the banner of BDS.

Israeli Institutional Complicity

Beyond these individual blacklists, BDS guidelines provide what is termed an *overriding rule* that all Israeli academic institutions, unless proven otherwise, are subject to boycott because of their alleged "decades-old, deep and conscious complicity"[19] in maintaining the Israeli occupation and denial of basic Palestinian rights. As mentioned above, BDS asserts that institutional complicity involves five different modes of action. Although the guidelines treat these in connection with academic institutions, an examination of BDS rhetoric shows they are routinely applied to individuals and nonacademic groups as well. An example is whitewashing, which covers almost any issue or topic in which Israel might, directly or indirectly, be cast in a favorable light. In BDS rhetoric, *whitewashing* is the term used to stigmatize progressive and liberal practices in Israel that the BDS narrative defines as existing merely as a cover for Israeli crimes and a diversion from the occupation. As an example, it was used recently to describe the activities of the West-Eastern Divan Orchestra founded by Daniel Barenboim and the late Edward Said, an iconic figure in Palestinian resistance to Israeli occupation.[20] It's a cliché that revolutions eat their own children, and with the BDS demonization of Said's orchestra, BDS has taken its first bite.

A simple Google search shows that BDS supporters employ numerous variations on whitewashing: *pinkwashing* (Israel's gay rights movement); *greenwashing* (Israel's environmental movement); *genderwashing* (Israel's feminist movement); *brownwashing*, *blackwashing*, and *redwashing* (advocacy by members of minority groups on behalf of Israel); *healthwashing* (Israeli medical outreach in crisis zones); *animalwashing* (Israel's animal rights movement); and *veggiewashing* (Israeli vegetarian advocacy). In parallel with BDS attacks on individuals, these BDS rhetorical strategies are designed to mark out and dismiss virtually all activities in Israel, which elsewhere are regarded as normal and/or progressive, but which BDS rhetoric demonizes as a form of complicity. Such categorizations are attempts to close down all ordinary forms of discourse.

Non-Israeli Institutional Complicity

The doctrine of complicity is also used by BDS to describe relations between Israeli institutions and non-Israeli institutions. For example, the guidelines tell us that a variety of forms of scientific cooperation constitute complicity: the United States–Israel Binational Science Foundation; the EUREKA Initiative, a European intergovernmental initiative set up in 1985 that includes Israel; and the Britain–Israel Research and Academic Exchange Partnership (BIRAX). The most important target for BDS is Horizon 2020, the largest European Union research program ever undertaken, which will make available more than eighty billion euros in research funding over a period of seven years. BDS is seeking to exclude Israel, arguing that such scientific cooperation amounts to a whitewashing of the complicity of Israeli universities.

It is not clear how much anthropological research is actually supported by the Horizon 2020 research program. The vast majority of Horizon 2020 projects are located in the hard sciences, including neurobiology, genetics, oncology, and a smattering of archeology. Nevertheless, BDS demands that all projects of these kinds be brought to an end under the doctrine of complicity. BDS supporters in anthropology, however, are eager to close down any anthropological research involving Israel under Horizon 2020. Indeed, Niko Besnier, a member of the AAA task force, presumably taking his clues from the PACBI guidelines, has cited Horizon 2020 in his written request that the European Association of Social Anthropologists take a stand against Israel on the grounds that "neutrality is no longer possible."[21]

Vicarious Complicity

Beyond this, anthropologists themselves have manufactured a new form of complicity—vicarious complicity—in which complicity exists largely in the imagination. An especially intriguing example is the way a particularly dubious critique of Israeli archeology has been leveraged into an even more dubious attack on Israeli anthropology. The location of archeology in the social sciences and the humanities varies greatly in different parts of the world. Briefly, in the United States, certain kinds of archeology are treated as subfields of anthropology, while elsewhere in the world, archeology is more likely to be an independent discipline or a subfield of other disciplines. This means that in the United States, archeologists often train in the same departments as anthropologists and, in the past, were often members of the AAA. Today, many archeologists in the United States, even those trained in anthropology departments, seek their professional homes outside the AAA.

In Israel, as in much of Europe, there is a scant connection between anthropology and archeology programs. Archeology is a distinct discipline, unconnected to anthropology. But the fact that anthropology and archeology are connected in the United States has served as the pretext for BDS's conflating anthropology and archeology in Israel. Moreover, as practicing archeologists have tended to drift away from anthropology, some anthropologists have reinvented themselves, not as archeologists, but as creators of a critical discourse about archeology. This critical discourse is shaped less by the actual methods of archeology itself or even of anthropology but more by the canons of literary criticism. The practice of archeology, in this way, becomes a kind of text on which unrestrained postmodern, postcolonialist interpretations are imposed.

Attention to Israeli archeology began with the 2001 publication of Nadia Abu El-Haj's *Facts on the Ground*.[22] The phrase *facts on the ground* originally referred to a cardinal principle of the post-1967 Israeli settler movement, which held that by building and occupying settlements in the newly controlled West Bank, it would be able to create an undeniable dominion over Palestinian lands that would be impossible to dislodge. El-Haj's book uses the phrase to refer to the entire archeological enterprise in this region of the world, which she charges, beginning in the nineteenth century, invented a mythological story of Israelite and Jewish historical presence in the Land of Israel, and she imbues that story with the false aura of factuality that has also proven impossible to dislodge. In her view, archeology is a "colonial science" whose main goal has been to intellectually erase the history of Palestinians from the land.

Facts on the Ground began as a critical analysis of the role of nationalism in archeology. Indeed, long before its publication, there was criticism within Israel of attempts to use archeology for nationalist purposes, even if much the same can be said about archeology in Europe, China, the former Soviet Union, and nearly everywhere else that archeology is practiced.[23] At the time of its publication, the book engendered controversy. But nowadays, it seems to have been an opening in the ideological salvo in BDS's attack on Israeli anthropology. Some responses have been quite predictable. It would be hard to imagine that passions would not be raised by such a broad attack on two centuries of archeology in this region. But the book has also been the subject of serious and sober scholarly reviews, both in Israel and abroad—some harshly critical, others more laudatory. One of its harshest critics, the Israeli archeologist Aren Maeir, regards the book as having virtually no scientific merit and describes it as simply a "political manifesto."[24] But even more sympathetic archeological reviewers, such as Tim Murray of La Trobe University in Australia, describe the analysis of archeological theory and sociopolitics of the discipline itself as limited and idiosyncratic.[25] These reviews suggest that the book demonstrates a poor grasp of archeological theory and practice. In stark contrast, numerous nonarcheologist anthropologists have described it as sophisticated, meticulous, and important. The cleavage between the archeologists and nonarcheologists is profound. How can a work that apparently demonstrates clearly defective understanding of the archeological sciences be regarded as excellent anthropology?

Part of the explanation can be found in the current hostile political climate in anthropology toward Israel, where the wildest accusations about Israel are treated as fact. But politicization also derives from the impact of literary criticism and cultural studies on anthropological methods. *Facts on the Ground* is profoundly shaped by Said's book *Orientalism*, which clearly rejects the idea of the objectivity of knowledge.[26] Said's view is that science itself was developed in the context of colonialism. By locating the scientific enterprise within the colonial, it becomes possible for writers like El-Haj to create labels such as "colonial science" that treat archeology in much the way old-line Marxists created the doctrine of "bourgeois science" to try to expunge Mendelian genetics from Soviet scientific thought. Like genetics, archeology is treated as suspect, because it allegedly serves the interests of ruling groups.

But the problems with this approach actually run much deeper. In *Orientalism*, Said argued that the traditional scholarly study of the Middle East constituted a racist and imperialist discourse. As borrowed from Foucault, the concept of discourse refers to a set of interconnected ideas. One of the most distinctive conceptual elements of discourse is that it is not rule-bound; its connective threads are neither empirical nor logical but political and often comprise a disparate collection of ideas strung together in a come-what-may manner. Small wonder that Jacques Derrida, one of the framers of the concept of discourse, was immediately attracted to Claude Lévi-Strauss's concept of *bricolage*. The term *bricolage* refers to the notion that thought processes are often highly improvisational. It is related to the French word *bricoler*, which means "to tinker." In his classical study of mythology, Lévi-Strauss argued that all myths are essentially a bricolage—their stories, characters, and conceptual elements constructed willy-nilly out of what was at hand. Derrida married the study of myth to the study of discourse by arguing that not only myth but all modes of thought could be understood as bricolage. But almost in imitation of its subject, indeed almost in self-parody, postmodern, postcolonialist studies, cultural studies, and their anthropological progeny have now adopted bricolage as their primary methodology. Borrowing thoughts and ideas indiscriminately from the worlds of literary criticism, literature, law, politics, and in this instance, from archeology, they construct their analyses with little concern for empirical or logical connectedness. Like Lévi-Strauss's mythmaker, they are masters of the found object and pull in anything to create a story. It's a method in which the intellectual Rube Goldberg machine trumps Occam's razor at every turn. This methodology has no connection to science. Its power lies in its politics and its aesthetics, not in such boring ideas as validity and reliability.

It is within this framework that *Facts on the Ground* is situated. Postcolonialist discourse has intellectually colonized much of the anthropology of the Middle East. As a form of bricolage unburdened by rules of evidence or proof, it pulls together snippets of anything and everything to weave its dismal tale of unfettered nationalism and colonialism. The task is made easier by the book's definition of *archeology*, which intentionally conflates professional and scientific practices with popular and political uses of archeological material. As El-Haj states, "Rather than maintaining a sharp distinction between professional and scientific practices, on the one hand, and popular or political ones on the other, in this book I understand the work of archeology to be situated among a variety of actors and institutions that, together with archeological practice and practitioners, instituted archeology and rearranged contemporary historical reality in Palestine and Israel."[27]

In other words, Israeli archeology constitutes both scientific archeology and anything else bearing on the contemporary history of Israel and Palestine.

Imagine the results if this definition were applied to cultural anthropology in the United States. Every use of anthropology, from the crackpot to the sublime, could be attributed back to the profession. And so it goes: a potsherd here and a potsherd there, a bizarre comment by a tour guide, a film in a museum exhibition, all become grist for the mill.

The book is rife with instances of this mode of analysis. For example, *Facts on the Ground* takes issue with the archeological exhibition at Burnt House, a museum located in the Jewish Quarter of Jerusalem's Old City. The official interpretation is that Burnt House is the home of a wealthy Jewish family, possibly of the priestly class, that was destroyed during the Roman siege and conquest of Jerusalem in 70 CE. El-Haj participated in a tour of this museum and other related sites along with an "American writer" and a "British archeologist," both of whom are unnamed. El-Haj recounts that during the tour, the unnamed and uncited American writer whom she describes as "having authored several books and articles on the politics of archeology in Israel" objected to the established narrative of Burnt House. He argued that the destruction of the house might have resulted from class conflict among Jews in Jerusalem, the result of the simmering anger against Jerusalem's nobility by working class laborers whom Herod the Great had imported to build the temple. He postulated that Burnt House might have been burnt down by an angry Jewish mob long prior to 70 CE. The curator countered that a coin found at the site and dated to approximately 66 CE suggests that the house was burnt close to the 70 CE time period. El-Haj counters that this evidence does not preclude the possibility that the site, including the house, may have been burnt down more than once. The unnamed British archeologist apparently adds another view by asserting that "most cities burn every twenty to twenty-five years."

The point here is that El-Haj suggests there are possible interpretations other than the established narrative. If the museum were to present either the class struggle narrative or the natural cycle of fire narrative as alternative possibilities, it would, in her view, be a strong corrective to the narrative of national loss and ascendance that she believes wrongfully pervades Israeli archeology. But the text offers no evidence that either of these alternate narratives is probable or even plausible. What weight would any scientific study accord to this exchange other than it demonstrates a passion for contested narratives? It certainly offers nothing probative of the existence of any facts different from those now presented at Burnt House. Certainly, it would be interesting and important if El-Haj were actually able to demonstrate that the ethos of Israeli nationalism screened out important and contradictory data. But she offers nothing stronger than anecdote to make the case. Given its methodology—bricolage—*Facts on the Ground* accords carefully constructed archeological evidence and off-the-cuff anecdote exactly the same weight.

Since anthropology and mythology now occupy the same epistemological space, there are few barriers to spinning tales out of whole cloth to create the illusion that somehow the real archeology of Israel and Palestine had to be rescued from the Zionists. The next step was to pin the blame on the anthropologists. This particular twist was given prominence by one of the many peculiar and troubling voices within the BDS movement in anthropology, that of the fictional character Isaiah Silver, whose writings feature prominently in the popular anthropology blog *Savage Minds*. The name Isaiah Silver, with its obviously Jewish shadings, is claimed to be the collective pseudonym of two members of the AAA who have lived and worked in Israel and Palestine and who describe themselves as "proud Jews." And so it is as a proud Jew that Isaiah Silver points his accusing finger at Israeli anthropologists, charging them with all manner of crimes against Palestinians.

As a former insider, Isaiah Silver, the renegade proud Jew, lends the aura of authenticity to BDS's accusations. In reality, the emergence of the character of Isaiah Silver is reminiscent of what the late Richard Hofstader dubbed the paranoid style of American politics, in which the renegade figure—formerly the ex-Communist and now the anti-Israel Jew—plays a central accusatory role. But why choose a pseudonym? After all, anyone remotely familiar with American anthropology knows that you don't exactly need to be Braveheart to condemn Israel in front of a crowd of American anthropologists. But the pseudonym adds to the aura of staged victimhood, as these BDS propagandists demand that their identities be protected as they seek to destroy the careers of their Israeli colleagues.

Silver, however, outlines the anthropologists' archeological rescue mission. "The AAA," he asserts, "has a history of defending the discipline from those who would misuse it for their own ends." He goes on to declare that "maintaining the organization's tradition of defending ethical uses of anthropology is just one of the ways that an academic boycott would uphold the best traditions of the AAA."[28] Unlike Isaiah Silver, the AAA task force on Israel and Palestine actually acknowledges that anthropology and archeology in Israel are completely separate disciplines.[29] But this has not stopped the task force from giving archeology prominent place in its report, without questioning whether it was even possible for people of one academic discipline to directly influence the course of affairs of another. Finally, one could reasonably ask why anthropology has never attempted to rescue archeology from other nationalisms throughout the world. But there will never be an answer to this question for anthropologists who are hell-bent on demonizing the Jewish State.

Shortly before the 2014 meetings of the AAA and the clear signals of BDS dominance over the association's leadership, a small group of anthropologists, myself included, worked to muster opposition to BDS. We organized a group of American and Israeli anthropologists called Anthropologists for Dialogue on Israel and Palestine.[30] The central tenets were to recognize the severe anguish and human tragedy in Israel and Palestine and to promote the use of anthropology's critical theories and methods in working toward peace and social justice in Israel and Palestine within the context of a two-state solution. To this end, our goal was to enlist anthropology into active support of dialogue and engagement among Israelis, Palestinians, and others in the region. We recognized that our approach would be anathema to the BDS leadership, with its implacable hostility to even the idea of an Israel, but we hoped to appeal to the large number of anthropologists who valued peace and conciliation in an area of the world where cooperation and compromise are rare commodities.

Using our website, Facebook site, antiboycott counterpetitions, blogs, and articles in the public media and social media, we tried to build a counternarrative that promoted the role of anthropology in helping solve rather than exacerbate the conflict. We created alliances with other organizations whose social media presence would help amplify our message. We were well aware of BDS's intention to sponsor a resolution calling for a boycott of Israeli academic institutions at the 2015 annual meeting of the association in Denver. Nevertheless, at that meeting, we sponsored two antiboycott panels and also offered an alternative resolution that would put the power of the AAA behind peace and reconciliation. But our efforts were soundly rebuffed at a meeting where the organized presence of BDS activists, and the hostile carnival atmosphere they created, ensured that boycott and estrangement would be favored over dialogue and engagement. Our antiboycott speakers were hissed at and given short shrift and curt treatment by the then-president of the association, who quickly cut off debate and allowed BDS supporters a resounding victory.

Despite our defeat at the annual meeting, a second antiboycott group, called Against the Boycott, formed.[31] This group took no official position on the Israeli-Palestinian conflict but focused almost entirely on the damage that an academic boycott would cause to academic freedom and the discipline of anthropology. Part of the impetus in forming this group was precisely the dismissive treatment of antiboycott speakers by the AAA leadership. By January 2016, both these groups were engaging in separate but parallel efforts to persuade members of the AAA of the dangers of BDS.

The central theory of the anti-BDS strategy remained consistent. Both groups believed that the more people who could be convinced to vote, the more likely it would be that BDS would be defeated. Anthropologists for Dialogue on Israel and Palestine initiated a video campaign with which we hoped to reach a large number of AAA members; the campaign consisted of short videos of Israeli and American anthropologists that both challenged BDS demonology and established a human face for Israeli anthropologists. We hoped that

American anthropologists would see the people as colleagues wrestling with complex political and moral challenges both in and outside the academy. We also showcased prominent American anthropologists who were opposed to the boycott. Against the Boycott initiated a communications campaign, continually reminding anthropologists of BDS's threat to academic freedom and professional integrity. We were not at all convinced that we could win, but we hoped to work around the AAA leadership and BDS activists to reach as many anthropologists as we could and hope for the best.

We won by thirty-nine votes.

For the moment, the anthropological boycott of Israeli academic institutions has been staved off, but the association remains divided. We have a great deal of work ahead of us to show that dialogue, engagement, and academic freedom can triumph over radicalization and suppression.

DAVID ROSEN is Professor of Anthropology at Fairleigh Dickinson University. His main research interests largely relate to issues surrounding child soldiers and how they are represented legally, historically, and in popular culture. His publications include *Child Soldiers in the Western Imagination: From Patriots to Victims, Child Soldiers: A Reference Handbook, Armies of the Young,* and *Child Soldiers in War and Terrorism.*

Notes

1. See American Anthropological Association, "Report to the Executive Board: The Task Force on AAA Engagement on Israel-Palestine" (2015), http://s3.amazonaws.com/rdcms -aaa/files/production/public/FileDownloads/151001-AAA-Task-Force-Israel-Palestine.pdf (accessed November 13, 2017).

2. American Anthropological Association, "Report to the Executive Board" (2015).

3. Anthropologists against the Boycott of Israeli Academic Institutions, "The Statement," https://anthroantiboycott.wordpress.com/ (accessed October 31, 2017).

4. Harvey E. Goldberg, "An Evaluation of the Report to the Executive Board by the Task Force on AAA Engagement on Israel-Palestine" (April 13, 2016), http://media.wix.com/ugd /c9faad_96671ab4b33e44c4a7eb7c0dcb0c774e.pdf.

5. Robert Zimmer, "Letter to UK's University and College Union" (July 31, 2007), https://president.uchicago.edu/page/letter-uks-university-and-college-union-ucu.

6. Simon Schama, "The Left's Problem with Jews Has a Long and Miserable History," *Financial Times* (February 16, 2016), http://www.ft.com/intl/cms/s/0/d6a75c3c-d6f3-11e5-829b -8564e7528e54.html#axzz4osjfz0fh.

7. Monica Osborne, "'Academic Boycott' Is an Oxymoron," *The Chronicle of Higher Education* (February 19, 2016), http://chronicle.com/article/Academic-Boycott-Is-an /235350?cid=rc_right. See also John Glancy, "A Polite Hatred, Part IV," *Tablet* (March 25, 2015), http://www.tabletmag.com/jewish-news-and-politics/189623/a-polite-hatred-4-british-left.

8. League of Arab States, "Khartoum Resolution" (September 1, 1967). See the Israel Ministry of Foreign Affairs, http://www.mfa.gov.il/mfa/foreignpolicy/peace/guide/pages /the%20khartoum%20resolutions.aspx (accessed November 13, 2017).

9. Palestinian Campaign for the Academic and Cultural Boycott of Israel (PACBI), "Guidelines for the International Academic Boycott of Israel" (Revised July 2014), http://pacbi.org/pacbi140812/?p=1108.

10. Todd Gitlin, "There Is No Victory without Anguish: On the Logic and Illogic of Boycott, Divestment and Sanctions," *Tablet* (January 20, 2016), http://www.tabletmag.com /jewish-news-and-politics/196749/no-victory-without-anguish.

11. PACBI, "Guidelines for the International Academic Boycott of Israel (Revised July 2014)," http://pacbi.org/pacbi140812/?p=1108.

12. American Anthropological Association, "Resolution to Boycott Israeli Academic Institutions" (2016), http://s3.amazonaws.com/rdcms-aaa/files/production/public/AAA %20Resolution%20to%20Boycott%20Israeli%20Academic%20Institutions%20w -submitters%20for%20posting.pdf (accessed November 13, 2017).

13. PACBI, "Academic Freedom for Whom?," http://pacbi.org/etemplate.php?id=792 (accessed October 31, 2017).

14. Netta van Vilet, "On the Academic Calls to Boycott Israel, Part II," Public seminar at the New School for Social Research (September 10, 2015), http://www.publicseminar .org/2015/09/on-the-academic-calls-to-boycott-israel-part-ii/#.Vp-Ttvl96M8 (accessed November 13, 2017).

15. What follows is drawn from Avnon's account of his experience, published previously and revised and reprinted in chapter 1 of the current volume. See Dan Avnon, "BDS and the Dynamics of Self-Righteous Moralism," *Australian Journal of Jewish Studies* 28 (2014): 28–46.

16. This episode is also discussed in the current volume, in chapter 18.

17. Peter Munro, "Academic Jake Lynch Cleared of Antisemitism in Ugly Stoush at Sydney University," *The Sydney Morning Herald* (April 27, 2015), http://www.smh.com.au /nsw/academic-jake-lynch-cleared-of-antisemitism-in-ugly-stoush-at-sydney-university -20150426-1mtdk1.html.

18. Peter Munro, "Academic Jake Lynch Cleared of Antisemitism in Ugly Stoush at Sydney University," *The Sydney Morning Herald* (April 27, 2015), http://www.smh.com.au /nsw/academic-jake-lynch-cleared-of-antisemitism-in-ugly-stoush-at-sydney-university -20150426-1mtdk1.html.

19. PACBI, "Guidelines for the International Academic Boycott of Israel (Revised July 2014)," http://pacbi.org/pacbi140812/?p=1108.

20. "PACBI: West-Eastern Divan Orchestra Violates Boycott," *The Electronic Intifada* (March 24, 2010), https://electronicintifada.net/content/pacbi-west-eastern-divan-orchestra -violates-boycott/1040.

21. Niko Besnier, "European Anthropology in Israel/Palestine," *Social Anthropology* 23 (2015): 501–503.

22. Nadia Abu El-Haj, *Facts on the Ground: Archaeological Practice and Territorial Self-Fashioning in Israeli Society* (Chicago: University of Chicago Press, 2001).

23. Philip L. Kohl, "Nationalism and Archeology: On the Constructions of Nations and the Reconstructions of the Remote Past," *Annual Review of Anthropology* 27 (1998): 223–246; Phillip L. Kohl and Claire Fawcett, *Nationalism, Politics and the Practice of Archeology* (Cambridge: Cambridge University Press, 1996).

24. Aren Maeir, "Review of Nadia Abu el-Haj, *Facts on the Ground: Archeological Practice and Territorial Self-Fashioning in Israel Society*," *Isis* 95 (2004): 523–524.

25. Tim Murray, *Australian Journal of Anthropology* 14 (August 2003): 265–266.

26. Edward Said, *Orientalism* (New York: Vintage Press, 1979).

27. El-Haj, *Facts on the Ground*, 21.

28. Isaiah Silver, "Digging the Occupation: The Politics of Boycotts and Archeology in Israel (BDS pt. 3)," *Savage Minds* (July 6, 2014), http://savageminds.org/2014/07/06/digging -the-occupation-the-politics-of-boycotts-and-archeology-in-israel-bds-pt-3/.

29. American Anthropological Association, "Report to the Executive Board" (2015).

30. http://www.anthrodialogue.org/ (accessed October 31, 2017).

31. http://www.againstanthroboycott.org/ (accessed October 31, 2017).

21 Retaliation: The High Price of Speaking Out about Campus Antisemitism and What It Means for Jewish Students

Tammi Rossman-Benjamin

Tammi Rossman-Benjamin became alarmed as departments and student organizations at the University of California, Santa Cruz (UCSC) sponsored anti-Israel events and lectures exclusively. The rhetoric in these events and in the classroom called for violence against Israeli Jews and against their American supporters. Approached by Jewish students who felt threatened, Rossman-Benjamin asked administrators not to endorse such hatefests. To her surprise, rather than protect the university's Jewish students, the faculty senate opened an investigation against *her*, charging that her work on behalf of Jewish students violated the freedom of speech of the anti-Israel activists. Rossman-Benjamin soon became the target of a massive student-led national campaign to paint her as a racist Islamophobe and to destroy her career.

Introduction

I have been a lecturer in Hebrew at the University of California, Santa Cruz since 1996 and a vocal advocate on behalf of Jewish students on my campus for most of that time. I am also cofounder and director of AMCHA Initiative, an organization dedicated to investigating and combating campus antisemitism throughout the country. As a result of my advocacy work on behalf of Jewish students, I have, on several occasions, come under personal attack from students, faculty, administrators, and anti-Israel groups outside of the university. This essay will focus on the sustained campaign of harassment, intimidation, and defamation that was carried out by an anti-Israel student group on my campus, the Committee for Justice in Palestine (CJP), and members of affiliated Students for Justice in Palestine (SJP) groups on other University of California (UC) campuses.

The campaign in question ostensibly focused on remarks I had made during a talk I gave in June 2012 at a synagogue in Stoughton, Massachusetts. Like most of the numerous presentations I make before groups in the Jewish community, my Stoughton talk included a survey of campus antisemitism and a discussion of one of its primary sources: Muslim and pro-Palestinian student organizations—in particular, the Muslim Students Association (MSA) and SJP. I described how some members of these groups engage in behavior unlike members of other student groups on campus, behavior that has created a hostile environment for Jewish students. I mentioned that a number of MSA and SJP members have been responsible for physically harassing and assaulting Jewish students, vandalizing Jewish communal property, disrupting pro-Israel speakers, and aggressively confronting Jewish students at pro-Israel events; that some MSA and SJP chapters consistently sponsor speakers, films, and exhibits that engage in discourse or use language considered antisemitic by the US State Department; and that some MSA and SJP chapters have associated with individuals and organizations that are linked to terrorist activity and call for violence against Jews. Finally, I emphasized how difficult campus life can be for Jewish students who are not ready for such confrontations and who are, in general, not nearly as motivated to defend Israel as MSA and SJP students are to attack it.

In February 2013, Rebecca Pierce, the head of the UCSC CJP group and a former student of mine, used a two-minute clip that she had created from an online recording of my Stoughton talk as a pretext for launching an extensive campaign accusing me of having made openly racist and Islamophobic comments about SJP and MSA students. With the help of her CJP group and SJP members throughout the UC system, Pierce coordinated a series of actions that included: posting and promoting a defamatory online petition accusing me of racism and censorship and calling on the UC president to condemn me;[1] posting hundreds of defamatory flyers about me on the UCSC campus;[2] posting a dozen videos about me on YouTube that wrongfully accused me of being hateful, dangerous, and Islamophobic;[3] calling for SJP students UC-wide to fill out hate/bias reports against me on their respective campuses;[4] and calling for the passage of libelous resolutions condemning me for my "inflammatory, hateful, and racist assumptions" in the UC Berkeley,[5] UC Santa Barbara,[6] UC Davis,[7] and UC Irvine[8] student senates. Anti-Israel online publications (e.g., *Electronic Intifada*[9] and *Mondoweiss*[10]) picked up the story and widely circulated these defamatory allegations.

This campaign of harassment and defamation, which continued for several months, affected me both professionally and personally. On a campus like UCSC, there are few more damaging allegations than racism. I was deeply concerned that these slanderous charges against me would have a negative impact on my relationships with students, colleagues, and supervisors and would impede my ability to do my job. I was also anxious about my physical safety, in light of the history of violent behavior shown by radical activists on our campus and others. A few years earlier, UCSC biology professors who had been singled out in a similar but far more limited campaign of public vilification had their homes firebombed by animal rights activists. One of the targeted professors was my neighbor.

Despite my repeated calls for support throughout the student-led campaign against me, top UCSC administrators—my employers—failed to enforce university policies proscribing such student behavior and did not defend my right to freedom of expression. Indeed, some university officials even supported the CJP students' defamatory accusations against me. In order to understand the far-reaching implications of such a campaign for the safety and well-being of both faculty and students across the country, it is important to provide some background.

A History of My Advocacy on Behalf of Jewish Students and Backlash to It

Early Unsuccessful Efforts at UCSC

From early 2001, roughly coinciding with the start of the Second Intifada, I became aware of the virulently anti-Israel sentiments of many of the humanities and social sciences faculty on my campus. I also grew concerned at seeing multiple academic departments, administrative offices, and residential colleges cosponsoring numerous public lectures, symposia, and academic conferences about the Israeli-Palestinian conflict that were egregiously biased against Israel and often included highly tendentious and unscholarly rhetoric that demonized Israel and encouraged members of the audience to engage in actions to harm it. For instance, one conference titled "Alternative Histories Within and Beyond Zionism," sponsored by eight academic departments and research groups and two residential colleges, featured talks by four professors and one graduate student who promoted the following unsubstantiated and defamatory claims:

- Zionism is racism.
- Israel is an apartheid state.
- Israel commits heinous crimes against humanity, including genocide and ethnic cleansing.
- Israel's behavior is comparable to that of Nazi Germany.
- Jews exaggerate the Holocaust as a tool of Zionist propaganda.
- Israel should be dismantled as a Jewish state.
- Morally responsible people should actively engage in mounting an opposition to the Jewish State, by, for instance, joining in the divestment campaign.

During the same time period, there were no department-sponsored events that promoted a countervailing narrative about the conflict.

Often, pro-Israel Jewish students who attended these events told me that they were extremely upset by the official university sponsorship, especially when the students' own departments or residential colleges were among the sponsors. A history major told me she was shocked that her own department sponsored the Alternative Histories event, and another expressed outrage that her university tuition was supporting what she felt was a demonization of the Jewish State. In addition, many of my Jewish students reported to me that in some of their classes they felt emotionally and intellectually harassed and intimidated because of their perceived support for Israel. Some students said that they stayed away from, or dropped out of, courses they would otherwise have been interested in taking, because they knew from fellow students that the professor was biased against Israel and intolerant of alternative legitimate points of view. One student described feeling personally assaulted by her professor when she tried to defend Israel in class. Another student left a class in tears; after she had shared her research paper on the topic of Zionism, her fellow classmates chastised her and accused her of being a Nazi—and her professor stayed silent.

For several years, I advocated on behalf of my students, who were reticent to confront their professors, department chairs, or university administrators regarding these issues for fear of retaliation. I often worked together with my husband, Ilan Benjamin, a professor of chemistry at UCSC. We wrote many letters to department chairs, divisional deans, college provosts, and four successive chancellors regarding specific events or classroom incidents. Those letters that were answered—and at least one-third were not—received similar responses, namely, that academic freedom protected individual faculty, departments, and even administrative offices from the kinds of criticisms we were raising about the inappropriateness of inserting such clear anti-Israel political advocacy into the university's academic programing and its harmful and discriminatory impact on Jewish students.

Adopting a more systemic approach, in May 2007, my husband and I submitted to the UCSC Academic Senate Executive Committee (SEC) a fifteen-page report documenting a clear pattern of political bias and advocacy—predominantly, although not exclusively, anti-Zionist—in classrooms and at department-sponsored events since 2001. We argued that such bias and advocacy were antithetical to the academic mission of the university and had a negative impact on students, and we urged the academic senate to investigate this problem.[11] The SEC agreed to look into our inquiry and sent it to the Committee on Academic Freedom (CAF) for consideration. In May 2008, we received the CAF report,[12] along with a letter indicating that the SEC fully endorsed it. Unfortunately, the report ignored our primary concern and instead twisted the committee's charge into an investigation of my husband and me for alleged violations of academic freedom. This was made clear in a letter sent by the chair of the CAF to eight UCSC professors soliciting reports on their negative interactions with my husband or me, which was included as part of an appendix to the CAF report: "Our committee does not plan to investigate incidents of this alleged bias, but seeks rather to determine if, connected to the complaint in any way, including the activities of those making the complaint, there is anything that threatens academic freedom on our campus."

The appendix also included testimonies from four professors accusing my husband and me of infringing on their academic freedom. Although the CAF report ultimately upheld our right to freedom of speech, we believe that their including an investigation of us in the report amounted both to discrediting us and to threatening retaliatory investigations against us or other faculty members who might push for further inquiry into the matter.

Then, in January 2009, Cowell College, one of ten residential colleges at UCSC, hosted and sponsored A Pulse on Palestine, which included a screening of the anti-Israel propaganda film *Occupation 101* and a panel discussion by two anti-Zionist community activists moderated by a UCSC professor well known for his anti-Israel sentiments. The film and panel discussion featured rhetoric that used classic antisemitic tropes to demonize and delegitimize Israel and its supporters, condoned terrorism, and promoted anti-Israel activism such as supporting a boycott of Israel.

In the weeks leading up to the event, I sent numerous emails to and met with Cowell College administrators to inform them of the egregiously anti-Israel, potentially antisemitic nature of the Pulse on Palestine program and the harmful impact it would have on Jewish students. I urged them to remove the college's sponsorship. The administrators, however, were not persuaded by our concerns and reaffirmed their right to sponsor the event.

Jewish students themselves engaged in efforts to communicate with administrators their serious concerns about how the college-sponsored event would contribute to a hostile environment. A petition signed by ninety Jewish UCSC students requesting that the college "not sponsor the event A Pulse on Palestine because it is politically biased and discriminates against the Jewish student population" was presented to Cowell College administrators. But the administrators were not swayed, and the event proceeded as planned. Adding insult to injury, when a distraught Jewish student asked two top college administrators who had attended the event whether they still felt that it was appropriate for Cowell College to have sponsored it, they both said they had no regrets. Cowell College administrators' unwillingness to even acknowledge the offensive nature of the program and their blatant insensitivity to Jewish student concerns—an insensitivity they would have shown to no other racial, ethnic, or gender minority on campus, I believe—caused me to think about bringing significant outside pressure on the university to address the long-standing and pervasive problem of anti-Jewish discrimination at UCSC.

Turning to Title VI of the 1964 Civil Rights Act

Federal antidiscrimination law enforced by the Department of Education's Office of Civil Rights (OCR), Title VI of the 1964 Civil Rights Act, requires that schools receiving any federal funding ensure they are free from discrimination based on "race, color, or national origin" or risk losing their federal funding. For many years, the law's applicability to protecting Jewish students was unclear since religion was not a protected category under Title VI, and antisemitism did not easily fit under the rubric of racism or national origin discrimination. In 2004, the OCR announced a new policy of covering Jewish and other religious minority students under Title VI. The first test of this new policy came soon after: a lawyer for the Zionist Organization of America (ZOA) filed a complaint on behalf of Jewish students at UC Irvine, alleging they had been subjected to a long-standing pattern of antisemitic harassment by members of pro-Palestinian student groups. After a three-year investigation, the OCR dismissed the ZOA's complaint, not because it didn't find antisemitic harassment—in fact, it did—but because the OCR leadership had apparently changed its mind and decided that Jewish students were no longer protected under Title VI. The ZOA appealed the OCR's ruling in 2008, a response to which was still pending when I was contemplating how best to address anti-Jewish bigotry on my own campus.

Inspired by the ZOA's example, in June 2009, I filed a twenty-nine-page Title VI complaint on behalf of Jewish students at UCSC, alleging that anti-Israel discourse and behavior in classrooms and at university-sponsored events was a form of institutional discrimination against Jewish students that had created an atmosphere of intellectual and emotional harassment and intimidation.[13] Besides providing extensive documentation of the problem, I also chronicled the failure of numerous efforts that others and I had made to encourage faculty and administrators to address it. For more than a year, my complaint languished at the OCR, apparently a victim of the same indecisiveness that plagued the ZOA complaint at UC Irvine. It seemed that the OCR could not decide whether Jewish students were or were not covered under Title VI.

Meanwhile, the Jewish organizational world had become engaged in the effort to ensure federal antidiscrimination protection for Jewish students. In March 2010, thirteen national and international groups—including International Hillel, the Religious Action Center of Reform Judaism, and the Orthodox Union—wrote to US Secretary of Education Arne Duncan, urging him to enforce the 2004 policy of affording Jewish students protection under Title VI, and a few months later, thirty-eight members of Congress sent him a similar letter. In October 2010, the

OCR issued a "Dear Colleague" letter that finally made clear that Jewish students would be protected under Title VI. In March of 2011, I received word that the OCR would investigate my complaint.

Soon after the investigation became public, pro-Palestinian activists turned to discrediting my complaint. Rebecca Pierce, a leader of the UCSC SJP-affiliated Committee for Justice in Palestine—who in 2013 would play a central role in the campaign portraying me as a racist and Islamophobe—publicly condemned my Title VI complaint on at least three occasions prior to the 2013 campaign. Less than a week after my complaint was opened for investigation in March 2011, Pierce called my complaint "wrong and offensive" in an article in the anti-Zionist blog *Mondoweiss*.[14] In another article published in August 2012, she bemoaned the fact that "the current Title VI complaint and federal investigation into 'anti-semitism' at our University is chilling criticism of Israeli policy."[15] And then in a video she made in September 2012, with help from members of SJP and MSA on multiple UC campuses—which attempted to convince the UC president to table a report he had commissioned detailing the hostile climate for Jewish students on several UC campuses—Pierce spoke of "the current Department of Education Title VI investigation at UC Santa Cruz that alleges antisemitism [that] is actually being used to stifle Palestinian-related speech on campus."[16]

By the fall of 2012, numerous West Coast chapters of SJP, MSA, and associated legal and advocacy nongovernmental organizations (NGOs) had launched a campaign against my Title VI complaint and two others filed on behalf of Jewish students on UC campuses—one at UC Irvine and the other at UC Berkeley—which were also under investigation by the OCR at that time. They claimed that all three of the Title VI complaints were politically motivated attempts to shut down the freedom of speech of Arab and Muslim students and Palestinian human rights activists. In the case of my complaint, that charge was patently false, as my allegations were wholly centered on UCSC faculty and administrators and never challenged the speech of students. Nevertheless, from the beginning of their campaign, my complaint was falsely charged with having violated the First Amendment rights of Muslim, Arab, and pro-Palestinian students and having created a "hostile environment" for them.

Here are some highlights of that campaign:

- On October 11, 2012, SJP West, a coalition of West Coast SJP chapters, published on their website a poster[17] titled "The University of California Record of Censorship," which included my picture and name and insinuated that my having petitioned the US Department of Education to "investigate 'anti-Israel' discourse at UC Santa Cruz" was an attempt to "censor students and faculty who stand up for human rights on UC campuses." Linked to that webpage was a "fact sheet"[18] titled "The Systematic Attempt to Shut Down Student Speech at the University of California," which specifically named my Title VI complaint as one of five federal complaints attacking the free speech of SJP and MSA students.

- On November 7, 2012, twenty-three MSA and SJP groups from California universities sent a letter[19] to the US Commission on Civil Rights decrying the "abuse of Title VI to silence political groups and marginalize Arab and Muslim students," specifically mentioning my complaint at UC Santa Cruz as one of three "baseless, Islamophobic Title VI complaints" on UC campuses.
- On December 10, 2012, the American Civil Liberties Union (ACLU) of Northern California sent a letter to the San Francisco OCR office investigating the UC Title VI complaints that focused on the UC Berkeley complaint, arguing that it was "in violation of fundamental First Amendment principles." At the end of their seven-page letter, the ACLU disingenuously targeted my Title VI complaint for similar First Amendment violations: "OCR has been investigating allegations of an antisemitic educational environment at UC Santa Cruz since March 2011. That investigation is based on a 29-page complaint that almost exclusively references expressive activities and campus debate about the Israeli-Palestinian conflict. That such protected free speech activities have been part of an investigation for 20 months is disturbing in view of the chilling effect that it can have on students who want to join, or continue to participate in, similar political activities in the future."
- On December 12, 2012, five pro-Palestinian legal and civil rights organizations—Asian Law Caucus, American Muslims for Palestine, Council on American Islamic Relations–San Francisco Bay Area, Center for Constitutional Rights, and National Lawyers Guild International Committee—submitted an issue statement titled "The Misuse of United States Law to Silence Pro-Palestinian Students' Speech"[20] to the United Nations Human Rights Committee. These organizations claimed that pro-Israel organizations were filing frivolous Title VI complaints, including my own, as part of a coordinated campaign to trample the free speech of Palestinian human rights activists on college campuses and that this campaign was creating a hostile environment for Arab and Muslim students. Furthermore, the legal groups claimed that the US Department of Education was complicit in this abuse of Title VI to silence pro-Palestinian voices, and they called on the UN Human Rights Committee to intervene.

Considered against the backdrop of these concerted efforts by many of the same individuals and groups involved in the campaign of harassment and character assassination that would be directed against me a short time later, I believe that anti-Israel activists targeted me personally in retaliation for having filed a federal complaint on behalf of Jewish students. It seemed they were trying to make a lesson of me to others who might consider standing up against campus antisemitism in this way. Indeed, the online petition calling on the UC president to condemn me for my "openly racist" and "Islamophobic" remarks, which turned out to be the opening salvo in the defamatory campaign against me, contained statements specifically deprecating my role in combating antisemitism at the UCSC campus and beyond, including my having filed the federal complaint.[21]

The efforts to have my Title VI complaint and the other two UC complaints dismissed by the OCR continued well into May 2013 and perhaps beyond.[22] On August 19, 2013, the OCR dismissed all three of our complaints despite the very different nature of each of them.[23] In all three dismissal letters, the OCR invoked the First Amendment to justify closing our cases, using language strikingly similar to that of the West Coast SJP and MSA groups and the legal and advocacy groups supporting them. Much to my chagrin, the OCR rejected my argument that Jewish students at UCSC deserve to be protected from antisemitic hate speech.

The Campaign against Me

Seeking Help within the University

A few days after becoming aware of the online petition against me, I informed[24] UCSC chancellor George Blumenthal of the retaliatory campaign being perpetrated against me by members of a UCSC-registered student group. I also pointed out that Debra Ellis, a UCSC administrator who had played a large role in the Pulse on Palestine event, was among the signatories of the petition. The language of the petition portrayed me, an untenured language instructor, as a menace to the UCSC community:

> Numerous students, faculty and staff, at University of California, Santa Cruz have been the target of hate speech and intimidation by Tammi Rossman-Benjamin and her supporters. The language she uses in the video and on campus is Islamophobic, racist, inaccurate and hateful... There will always be a "Tammi Rossman-Benjamin." Responsibility lies with The University of California and the Office of the President to confront and condemn this type of language and misrepresentation of the University by one of its employees. The world is watching. Will The University of California protect targeted students or remain silent and risk being seen as an Islamophobic, racist, and

hateful institution of higher learning? Please support diversity and inclusion and condemn hateful attacks on our Muslim/Arab students.[25]

In addition, I let the chancellor know that this wasn't only about me; there were students who were also stigmatized and silenced for speaking out about anti-Jewish bigotry, and I provided several recent examples. I asked the chancellor to describe what steps he intended to take to ensure the physical, emotional, and intellectual safety and freedom of expression of us all.

After ten days without a response to my email, and as the campaign of harassment and defamation rapidly escalated, I sent a second email[26] reminding the chancellor that as a Title VI complainant, I was entitled to whistleblower protection from precisely the kinds of actions that were presently being directed against me. I wrote that unless he took concrete steps to protect me and others who spoke out about anti-Jewish bigotry at UCSC, I would be initiating another complaint with the OCR, this time accusing the university of retaliation against me for having filed my original complaint. Within a day, I received a reply, albeit a disappointing one, from the associate chancellor, affirming the free speech rights of both the CJP students and the UCSC administrator and indicating that the UCSC administration would do nothing to help me.[27]

Although UCSC eventually hired a lawyer to investigate claims I had made in a subsequent email[28]—namely, that CJP students may have violated specific university policies prohibiting "harassment" and "expression with intent to intimidate"—the lawyer found no fault with either the students' behavior or the university's response to it. Furthermore, in her report, the attorney gratuitously noted that it was "not surprising" that my statements at the Stoughton synagogue had elicited the students' "vigorous outrage" and "spirited" condemnation, arguably implying that the students' campaign of harassment and defamation against me was actually justified.

Frustrated by the nonresponsiveness of UCSC administrators and its implications for Jewish students on my campus, I sought help from a different quarter of the University of California—the Office of the President. In an eight-page letter to then UC president Mark Yudof in May 2013,[29] I described the CJP/SJP assault against me and documented the overall pattern of behavior of SJP and MSA. I pointed out that these university-registered student organizations engaged in the following behaviors:

- Targeting Jewish (and other) students who identify or sympathize with the Jewish State for harassment, intimidation, and, on occasion, physical aggression
- Expressing religious and political animus and intolerance toward another national identity and ethnic group on campus

- Attempting to shut down free speech
- Retaliating for speaking out against antisemitism
- Hosting events that include speakers, exhibits, and behaviors that are antisemitic
- Associating with individuals and organizations that are linked to terrorist activity or call for violence against Jews

I called on President Yudof to investigate these groups system-wide for violations of university policy and the law, as well as to publicly affirm the right of all members of the campus community—students and faculty—to speak out against anti-Jewish bigotry without fear of harassment, demonization, or defamation. But the central administration of the UC system proved equally unresponsive. The UC vice president for student affairs turned down my request, reasoning that UCSC was already addressing my concerns and smearing me again with the charge that I wanted to limit freedom of speech, writing that the university "cannot and does not engage in the censorship of protected speech."[30] In other words, the Office of the President would not be investigating the antisemitic and hostile behavior of SJP and MSA groups system-wide, nor would President Yudof be using his free speech to speak out on my behalf or on behalf of Jewish students whose freedom to express their concerns about antisemitism was being suppressed through harassment, intimidation, and defamation.

Actions speak louder than words. In June 2013, the UC regents announced that they had nominated UC Berkeley senior Sadia Saifuddin to be a student regent in 2014–2015.[31] A leader of her campus MSA group and a member of student government, Saifuddin was a central figure in campus anti-Zionist activities and a cosponsor and spokesperson for the anti-Israel divestment resolution adopted by the UC Berkeley student senate in April 2013.[32] Prior to that, she had been active in efforts to delegitimize Jewish student reports of anti-Jewish hostility on UC campuses. For example, in July 2012, Saifuddin was one of the few individual signatories of a letter sent by the Council on American-Islamic Relations, the National Lawyers Guild, and seventeen UC SJP and MSA groups to UC president Yudof, which denounced the UC Jewish Student Campus Climate Report commissioned by Yudof.[33] The letter dismissed out of hand one of the report's chief findings—that Jewish students were confronting "significant and difficult climate issues as a result of anti-Zionist campus activities"[34]—claiming that the report was simply a ploy "to suppress speech critical of Israel" by Jewish student groups and faculty and even by Yudof himself. That same month, Saifuddin told the *Daily Californian* that she would work to undermine civil rights complaints filed on behalf of Jewish students, saying, "Cal SJP, Cal MSA, and our civil rights partners will work to ensure that these complaints are dismissed and the legacy of UC Berkeley as the birthplace of free speech is protected."[35] Most relevant to me personally, however, was that in March 2013, Saifuddin had been the sole author of the unanimously approved UC Berkeley student senate resolution that targeted me by name and accused me of "inflammatory, hateful, and racist assumptions" and "Islamophobic hate speech."[36]

The announcement of Saifuddin's nomination for UC student regent was met with a firestorm of criticism from the Jewish community. Pro-Israel advocacy group StandWithUs issued an open letter to the regents saying that Saifuddin had shown "marked callousness" to the concerns of Jewish students and was "ill suited to be student regent."[37] The Simon Wiesenthal Center urged its supporters to sign a petition protesting Saifuddin's appointment.[38] Both organizations not only highlighted the divisive role that Saifuddin had played as a Boycott, Divestment, and Sanctions (BDS) leader on her campus, they also described her efforts to "discredit and silence" me.

I naively believed that if the regents understood what appeared to me to be the retaliatory nature of Saifuddin's behavior and were reminded of my status as a federally protected whistleblower, they would not approve her appointment. By that time, I had secured the legal assistance of Kenneth Marcus, president and general counsel of the Brandeis Center for Human Rights Under Law, and on July 15, Marcus sent a letter to the regents on my behalf.[39] In the letter, Marcus argued that Saifuddin's appointment to the UC Board of Regents "would exacerbate the unlawful retaliatory campaign that Ms. Saifuddin and others" were waging against me and that UC had a duty "to protect civil rights complainants from retaliation under Title VI of the Civil Rights Act of 1964." The regents never responded to the Brandeis Center letter and, at their July 17 meeting, confirmed Saifuddin as the 2014–2015 student regent with a near-unanimous vote.

Turning to the OCR

Having exhausted my options within the university, I decided it was time to invoke the whistleblower protection afforded me as a Title VI complainant. According to federal law, no recipient of federal education funds, such as UCSC, "shall intimidate, threaten, coerce, or discriminate against any individual ... because he has made a complaint ... or participated in any manner in an investigation, proceeding or hearing."[40] I had clearly been the victim of a campaign of harassment and defamation as a result of my Title VI complaint against my university, and I felt certain that the law applied to my circumstances. So, on my behalf, the Brandeis Center submitted to OCR a Title VI Retaliation Complaint against UCSC.

A letter sent to the OCR in August 2013 detailed the students' campaign of retaliation against me that had begun soon after my Title VI complaint became public knowledge. It described the ways in which certain UCSC administrators actively participated or openly condoned the students' retaliatory campaign, and it demonstrated how UCSC administrators and even the UC regents purposefully disregarded the students' campaign and failed to address it. In addition, although not the focus of the current essay, it is important to mention that the letter included descriptions of three separate instances of what I believed were retaliatory actions taken against me by the cochairs of the Jewish studies program with which I was affiliated.[41] Finally, the complaint noted the consequences of not adequately addressing such acts of retaliation: "When an OCR complainant is subject to retaliation for availing herself of OCR's process, the unlawful retaliation not only restricts the core rights which Americans are legally and constitutionally guaranteed, but also discourages witnesses and future complainants from participating in OCR's enforcement programs."

These consequences became quite real for me when, a few weeks later, I received the OCR's response to my complaint: although one of my allegations regarding retaliation against me by a Jewish studies cochair was to be opened for investigation by the OCR, my allegation that the university had failed to protect me from the retaliatory actions of students and administrators was summarily dismissed. The OCR refused to acknowledge that I was a victim of retaliation and denied me relief under federal law, instead claiming that the university had acted "appropriately" and "adequately." Sadly, not only had my civil right to avail myself of OCR's process been violated with impunity, OCR's unwillingness to protect me from such vicious retaliation would surely discourage others from using Title VI on behalf of Jewish students.

The Retaliation Campaign in Perspective

My story may be extreme, but it is not unique. Across the country, students and faculty who speak out about antisemitism are being attacked by members of anti-Zionist student organizations and their support network, both on and off campus, and university administrators and the OCR are doing nothing about it. It is important to put the behavior of each of these actors into perspective.

The slanderous personal campaign against me sought to undermine the credibility of my Title VI complaint and was part of an even more extensive campaign to undermine Title VI protection for Jewish students. But the efforts of anti-Zionist activists did not stop there. They extended to organized attempts to torpedo any official initiative seeking to address the serious and growing problem of campus antisemitism, particularly on California campuses. For example, contemporaneous with their campaign against Title VI, UC SJP members organized efforts to discredit two landmark documents acknowledging and condemning the existence of antisemitism and a hostile environment for Jewish students on some California campuses.

The first document was the UC Jewish Student Campus Climate Report, published in July 2012.[42] It described the results of a fact-finding mission authorized by UC president Mark Yudof, which included meetings and interviews with Jewish students on seven UC campuses. According to the report, "Jewish students are confronting significant and difficult climate issues as a result of activities on campus which focus specifically on Israel, its right to exist, and its treatment of Palestinians. The anti-Zionism and Boycott, Divestment, and Sanctions (BDS) movements and other manifestations of anti-Israel sentiment and activity create significant issues through themes and language which portray Israel and, many times, Jews in ways which project hostility, engender a feeling of isolation, and undermine Jewish students' sense of belonging and engagement with outside communities."

Soon after its release, the SJP at UC Berkeley launched a well-coordinated campaign demanding that President Yudof reject the report.[43] The campaign included a petition,[44] articles in virulently anti-Israel publications,[45] a letter from attorneys at two anti-Israel organizations—the Council on American-Islamic Relations and the National Lawyers Guild—on behalf of SJP/CJP and MSA/MSU groups on eight UC campuses,[46] and a similar letter from the California Scholars for Academic Freedom, a group of 134 California academics who support the academic boycott of Israel.[47]

To this day, UC administrators have not adopted the report or its recommendations.

In August 2012, the California State Assembly unanimously approved California House Resolution 35 (HR-35),[48] a landmark resolution acknowledging and condemning antisemitism on California campuses. The resolution specifically identified as antisemitic activities such as campaigns to boycott and otherwise harm Israel. It recognized that student groups that encourage support for terrorist organizations such as Hamas and Hezbollah and openly advocate terror against the Jewish State are engaged in antisemitic activity and noted their suppression and disruption of speech in support of Israel.

Almost immediately after HR-35 was approved, SJP groups on UC campuses launched a campaign similar to their previous assault on the Jewish Campus Climate Report. This time, they demanded that California State Assembly members revoke HR-35. The SJP's efforts included successfully lobbying for resolutions condemning HR-35 to be passed in the UC-wide student assembly[49] and the UC Berkeley graduate student government[50] and coordinating letters to state assembly members from the California Scholars for Academic Freedom[51] and numerous anti-Israel groups and SJP groups from four UC campuses.[52] Although HR-35 called on the University of California and California State University (CSU) to take "actions to confront antisemitism on [their] campuses," no UC or CSU administrator has ever acknowledged support for the resolution or willingness to implement its recommendations.

Considered together, these efforts suggest that combating any and all criticism of their behavior, particularly charges of antisemitism, is a central strategic goal of anti-Zionist student activists. It is interesting to note that in each of the campaigns described above, the students and their supporters adopted a similar multipronged strategy for deflecting criticism of the antisemitic nature of their behavior:

- They portrayed their speech as legitimate criticism of Israeli policy and their conduct as morally justified human rights activism.
- They portrayed themselves as victims of a malicious campaign to silence their activism and to denigrate their character.
- They portrayed charges of antisemitism as malevolent attempts to shut down legitimate criticism of Israel and to intimidate and harass Muslim and Arab students and their supporters.
- They portrayed those who raised concerns about their antisemitic behavior—including the authors of the UC Jewish Student Campus Climate Report, the state assembly members who approved HR-35, and Title VI plaintiffs such as myself—as members of the "Israel Lobby," McCarthyites, racists, and Islamophobes.

Conclusions

Unprecedented in their scope and aggressiveness, anti-Zionist student campaigns are successfully deflecting legitimate accusations of antisemitism. As a result, Jewish students are becoming the single most vulnerable ethnic group on campus; often the direct target of the antisemitic behavior of anti-Zionist activists, they have no redress, as complaints about antisemitism are routinely dismissed by university administrators and OCR officials. Jewish students may well be subject to additional harassment and denigration for even daring to speak out about the bigotry they are experiencing, and such retaliatory behavior is unlikely to be addressed by either school administrators or civil rights officers.

Recently, some progress has been made at the University of California. In March 2016, the UC regents unanimously approved a groundbreaking statement of principles against intolerance, which identified antisemitism and antisemitic anti-Zionism as "forms of discrimination that have no place at the University of California" and highlighted the urgent need for UC administrators to address the problem.[53] Anti-Zionism has now been linked to antisemitism and other bigotries and condemned by the most prestigious public university system in the world. This is a significant step forward, which will benefit Jewish students across the country.

Nevertheless, much more needs to be done to guarantee that Jewish students, and those who speak out on their behalf, can exercise their constitutional right to protest antisemitism knowing that they will be protected from bullying, harassment, intimidation, and defamation. University leaders must vigorously defend the rights of those who speak out against anti-Jewish bigotry and swiftly and forcefully condemn all acts of retaliation. At the federal level, Title VI whistleblower protection for complaints regarding campus antisemitism must be significantly strengthened and the Jewish community assured that complainants are fully protected. Without such safeguards, there is little hope of defeating the growing scourge of campus antisemitism.

TAMMI ROSSMAN-BENJAMIN is a lecturer in Hebrew and Jewish studies at the University of California, Santa Cruz and the cofounder and director of AMCHA Initiative, a nonprofit organization devoted to monitoring and combating campus antisemitism in America. She has written and lectured widely about academic anti-Zionism and antisemitism on college campuses.

Notes

1. "Demand that UC President Mark Yudof Speak Out against Hate Speech!" (poster, University of California, Santa Cruz, 2013), https://www.change.org/p/University-of -california-president-mark-yudof-condemn-ucsc-lecturer-s-hateful-attacks-on-muslim -arab-student-groups (accessed July 15, 2016).
2. For example, see images at http://amchainitiative.org/wp-content/uploads /2013/04/photo-2_1.png (accessed November 1, 2017).
3. See UCSC CJP channel, https://www.youtube.com/channel/UCuL7ZzGgx_K _K2yszoxVpuA?feature=watch (accessed November 1, 2017).
4. For example, see http://amchainitiative.org/wp-content/uploads/2013/04/Tom -Pessahs-email-re-filing-hate-bias-complaints.pdf (accessed November 1, 2017).
5. "A Resolution Condemning Islamophobic Hate Speech at the University of California," http://amchainitiative.org/wp-content/uploads/2013/04/A-Resolution -Condemning-Islamophobic-Hate-Speech.pdf (accessed November 1, 2017).
6. https://www.as.ucsb.edu/senate/resolutions/a-resolution-condemning-islamophobic -hate-speech-at-the-University-of-california/ (accessed July 15, 2016).
7. "ASUCD Senate Resolution #21" (presented April 11, 2013), http://www.amchainitiative .org/wp-content/uploads/2013/05/SR.21.Spring.13.pdf.
8. "ASUCI Resolution R48-61" (presented April 25, 2013), http://www.asuci.uci.edu /legislative/legislations/print.php?cnum=R48-61&gov_branch=ASUCI.
9. Nora Barrows-Friedman, "US University Lecturer's Shocking Hate Speech Against Arab, Muslim Students Condemned," *The Electronic Intifada* (February 12, 2013), https://electronicintifada.net/blogs/nora-barrows-friedman/us-University-lecturers -shocking-hate-speech-against-arab-muslim.
10. Alex Kane, "Caught on Tape: California University Lecturer Smears Student Activists as Antisemites With Ties to Terrorists," *Mondoweiss* (February 21, 2013), http://mondoweiss .net/2013/02/california-University-terrorists/.

11. "Letter to Senate Executive Committee" (May 20, 2007), http://www.amchainitiative .org/wp-content/uploads/2016/06/Report-to-SEC.pdf (accessed November 1, 2017).

12. UC Santa Cruz, Committee on Academic Freedom Annual Report, 2007-08, http://senate.ucsc.edu/committees/caf-committee-on-academic-freedom/caf-annual -reports-folder/CAFar0708scp1575.pdf.

13. Letter to OCR (June 25, 2009), http://www.amchainitiative.org/wp-content /uploads/2016/06/Title-VI-Complaint-6-25-09-no-address.pdf (accessed November 1, 2017).

14. Rebecca Pierce, "A Jewish Student Responds to the Charge of Antisemitism at UC Santa Cruz," *Mondoweiss* (March 21, 2011), http://mondoweiss.net/2011/03/a-jewish-student -responds-to-the-charge-of-anti-semitism-at-uc-santa-cruz/.

15. "UC Report on Jewish Campus Climate: Results Marginalize, Misrepresent Students Critical of Israel," *The Jewish News of Northern California* (August 24, 2012), http://www .jweekly.com/article/full/66225/u.c.-report-on-jewish-campus-climate-results-marginalize -misrepresent-stude/.

16. "Students and Critics Respond to Controversial UC Campus Climate Report" (September 4, 2012), https://www.youtube.com/watch?v=cerl2jWqPqg&t=5m52s.

17. "Timeline – The University of California Record of Censorship," SJP West (October 11, 2012), http://sjpwest.org/2012/10/11/timeline-the-University-of-california-record/.

18. "Fact Sheet: Shutting Down Student Speech at UC," SJP West, http://sjpwest.org /wp-content/uploads/2012/10/FACT-SHEET-Shutting-Down-Student-Speech-at-U.C._fn _DISTRIBUTE.pdf (accessed November 1, 2017).

19. Letter to US Commission on Civil Rights (November 7, 2012), http://sjpwest.org/wp -content/uploads/2012/11/UC-MSA-SJP-Letter-to-USCCR-11.8.2012-Final-Version_corrected .pdf (accessed November 1, 2017).

20. ICCPR Issue Statement Submission: "The Misuse of United States Law to Silence Pro-Palestinian Students' Speech" (December 17, 2012), http://www2.ohchr.org/English /bodies/hrc/docs/NGOs/26-USHRNetwork_AsianLawCaucusCoalition.pdf (accessed November 1, 2017).

21. "Demand University of California President Mark Yudof Condemn UCSC Lecturer's Hateful Attacks on Muslim, Arab Student Groups," online petition, https://www.change .org/p/University-of-california-president-mark-yudof-condemn-ucsc-lecturer-s-hateful -attacks-on-muslim-arab-student-groups (accessed July 15, 2016).

22. See: Letter to OCR, San Francisco (May 14, 2013), http://ccrjustice.org/sites/default /files/assets/files/2013%2005%2014_LTR%20to%20SF%20OCR%20w%20ATTACHMENTS .pdf (accessed November 1, 2017); Letter to Department of Education (May 14, 2013), http://www.adc.org/fileadmin/ADC/2013_05_14_LTR_to_DOE_HQ_w_ATTACHMENTS .pdf (accessed November 1, 2017).

23. See: OCR Letter of Findings (August 19, 2013), http://www.amchainitiative.org/wp -content/uploads/2013/10/OCR_letter-of-findings-no-address.pdf (accessed November 1, 2017).

24. Letter to Blumenthal (February 14, 2013), http://www.amchainitiative.org /wp-content/uploads/2016/06/Letter-to-Chancellor-Blumenthal-2.14.13.pdf (accessed November 1, 2017).

25. "Demand University of California President Mark Yudof Condemn UCSC Lecturer's Hateful Attacks on Muslim, Arab Student Groups," online petition, https://www.change .org/p/University-of-california-president-mark-yudof-condemn-ucsc-lecturer-s-hateful -attacks-on-muslim-arab-student-groups/c/12417257 (accessed July 15, 2016).

26. Letter to Blumenthal (February 25, 2013), http://www.amchainitiative.org/wp-content/uploads/2016/06/Second-letter-to-Blumenthal-2.25.13.pdf (accessed November 1, 2017).

27. Letter From Vice Chancellor (February 28, 2013), http://www.amchainitiative.org/wp-content/uploads/2016/06/letter-from-Vice-Chancellor-2.28.13.pdf (accessed November 1, 2017).

28. Letter to Blumenthal (March 25, 2013), http://www.amchainitiative.org/wp-content/uploads/2016/06/Letter-to-Chancellor-3.25.13.pdf (accessed November 1, 2017).

29. Letter to Yudof (May 8, 2017), http://www.amchainitiative.org/wp-content/uploads/2013/05/Letter-to-Yudof-with-appendix8final_updated2.pdf (accessed November 1, 2017).

30. Letter From UC Vice President for Student Affairs (June 6, 2013), http://www.amchainitiative.org/wp-content/uploads/2016/06/JKSakaki-Rossman-Benjamin-Ltr-6-6-13.pdf (accessed November 1, 2017).

31. Larry Gordon, "Next UC Student Regent Hopes to Freeze Tuition on the 10 Campuses," *Los Angeles Times* (June 6, 2013), http://www.latimes.com/local/lanow/la-me-ln-student-uc-regent-20130606-story.html.

32. SB 160, "A Bill in Support of Human Rights in the West Bank and Gaza Strip," http://senator.kleinlieu.com/wp-content/uploads/2013/04/SB160FinalDraft.pdf (accessed November 1, 2017).

33. Letter to Yudof (July 10, 2012), http://www.nlginternational.org/report/LtrYudofFreeSpeech.pdf (accessed November 1, 2017).

34. President's Advisory Council on Campus Climate, Culture, & Inclusion, University of California Jewish Student Campus Climate Fact-Finding Team Report & Recommendations (July 9, 2012), https://cascholars4academicfreedom.files.wordpress.com/2012/07/jewish-climate-fact-finding-report-july-2012-final.pdf (accessed November 1, 2017).

35. Karishma Mehrotra, "Lawsuit Alleging Antisemitism Against Campus, UC Dropped by Plaintiffs," *The Daily Californian* (July 12, 2012), http://www.dailycal.org/2012/07/12/lawsuit-against-uc-settled/.

36. Sadia Saifuddin, "A Resolution Condemning Islamophobic Hate Speech at the University of California," http://amchainitiative.org/wp-content/uploads/2013/04/A-Resolution-Condemning-Islamophobic-Hate-Speech.pdf (accessed November 1, 2017).

37. Open Letter to the UC Board of Regents Regarding the Nomination of Sadia Saifuddin, StandWithUs, http://www.standwithus.com/news/article.asp?id=2798#.UeSdRG1Gxno (accessed November 1, 2017).

38. "ACT NOW: Protest Proposed Appointment of a Leading Anti-Israel, Anti Free-Speech Student to UC Regents" (July 15, 2013), http://www.wiesenthal.com/site/apps/nlnet/content2.aspx?c=lsKWLbPJLnF&b=4441467&ct=13221517#.V3SjJVeQcVQ (accessed November 1, 2017).

39. Letter to Regents (July 15, 2013), http://www.amchainitiative.org/wp-content/uploads/2016/06/Final-Letter-to-California-Regents-7-15-13.doc (accessed November 1, 2017).

40. Code of Federal Regulations, Title 34, Subtitle B, Chapter I, Part 100, Section 100.7, https://www.law.cornell.edu/cfr/text/34/100.7 (accessed November 1, 2017).

41. The three instances of alleged retaliation at the hands of the cochairs of my university's Jewish studies program, which were documented in the August 2013 letter to the OCR, were as follows: In February 2012, I was publicly humiliated in front of hundreds of students at an event held on campus to discuss campus antisemitism, at which I was to speak about the history of my Title VI complaint. One of the Jewish studies cochairs, who was also a panelist at the event, loudly berated me from the podium just before the event was to begin, harshly criticizing me

for my unwillingness to allow another Jewish studies faculty member to participate in the event because of his intention to speak out against my complaint. A month later, I was castigated at a faculty meeting in front of my Jewish studies colleagues by both of the program's cochairs, who accused me of causing a loss in donations to the program and for giving UCSC and the Jewish studies program bad reputations as a result of publicity connected to the civil rights allegations I had made. Finally, in October 2012, I was denied the right to teach a course in biblical Hebrew that I had developed and taught exclusively for the previous ten years. Despite my strenuous protests, the course was given to another faculty member to teach.

42. University of California Jewish Student Campus Climate Fact-Finding Team Report & Recommendations (July 9, 2012), http://www.amchainitiative.org/wp-content /uploads/2013/05/campus_climate_jewish.pdf (accessed November 1, 2017).

43. "Tell Yudof to Reject the Campus Climate Report," http://calsjp.org/tell-yudof-to -reject-the-campus-climate-report/ (accessed July 15, 2016).

44. "Demand the President of the University of California Table the Student Campus Climate Report and Recommendations," online petition, https://www.change.org/p /president-of-the-University-of-california-table-the-jewish-student-campus-climate-report -and-recommendations (accessed July 15, 2016).

45. Nora Barrows-Friedman, "Bogus Allegations of 'Antisemitism' Create Real Climate of Fear Arab, Muslim Students in US," *The Electronic Intifada* (August 8, 2012), https://electronicintifada.net/content/bogus-allegations-anti-semitism-create-real-climate -fear-arab-muslim-students-us/11563.

46. Letter to Yudof (July 10, 2012), http://www.nlginternational.org/report /LtrYudofFreeSpeech.pdf (accessed November 1, 2017).

47. California Scholars for Academic Freedom, Letter to UC President Yudof regarding Campus Climate Report on situation of Jewish, Muslim and Arab Students, https://cascholars4academicfreedom.wordpress.com/category/academic-freedom/ (accessed November 1, 2017).

48. California Legislature HR-35 (2011-12) (August 29, 2012), http://leginfo.legislature .ca.gov/faces/billTextClient.xhtml?bill_id=201120120HR35 (accessed November 1, 2017).

49. Jacob E. Brown, "UCSA Calls Contentious Anti-Semitism Resolution a Limit to Free Speech," *The Daily Californian* (September 17, 2012), http://www.dailycal.org/2012/09/17/ucsa -calls-contentious-anti-semitism-resolution-a-limit-to-free-speech/.

50. The Graduate Assembly, Resolution #1210b, https://www.documentcloud.org /documents/501924-graduate-assembly-resolution-1210b.html (accessed November 1, 2017).

51. California Scholars for Academic Freedom, "An Open Letter From California Scholars for Academic Freedom to California Assemblymembers Linda Halderman, Bonnie Lowenthal, and 66 Co-authors of California House Resolution 35," https://cascholars4academicfreedom.wordpress.com/2012/09/24/an-open-letter-from -california-scholars-for-academic-freedom-to-california-assemblymembers-linda -halderman-bonnie-lowenthal-and-66-co-authors-of-california-house-resolution-35/ (accessed November 1, 2017).

52. Letter to Assemblymembers (August 28, 2012), http://files.ctctcdn.com /730585a6001/8a0316ef-932a-41e2-8e47-3e95fa6dc558.pdf (accessed November 1, 2017).

53. Committee on Educational Policy, "Adoption of the Report of the Regents Working Group on Principles Against Intolerance" (March 24, 2016), http://regents .Universityofcalifornia.edu/aar/mare.pdf.

22 A Field Geologist in Politicized Terrain

Jill S. Schneiderman

Vassar College has seen some ugly anti-Israel incidents in recent years, including hosting, to great applause, Professor Jasbir Puar's infamous 2016 lecture accusing Israel of deliberately maiming and stunting Palestinians and harvesting their organs. In 2014, geologist Jill Schneiderman's class trip to Israel/Palestine to study water issues was itself subject to a smear campaign, simply because it dared to include Israel in its itinerary. Schneiderman, a leftist critic of Israel and advocate for Palestinian rights, had aimed to "promote respectful dialogue among students before, during, and after the trip so that our students might be able to participate in ongoing work toward a just peace." Instead, anti-Israel activists campaigned to have the class canceled, picketed the class meetings, harassed class members, sponsored a hostile public forum that put the class on trial, and regularly depicted the situation in terms of a conflict between privileged white Jews and marginalized people of color. Such a toxic atmosphere feeds anti-Jewish hostility, strongly discourages the open exchange of ideas on campus, and produces a climate of fear inconsistent with academic values.

IN MARCH 2014, I led a study trip to Israel/Palestine. The trip elicited strong reactions from my campus community, reactions that could be characterized as anti-Zionist bullying. The kind of behavior that resulted from the controversy threatens academic freedom. This chapter recounts and comments on these events.

Introduction

In March 2014, two colleagues and I led a two-week study trip to Israel/Palestine, "The Jordan River Watershed." The trip was the centerpiece of a course designed to engage the hydropolitics of the Levant from a geoscientist's perspective. In response to the annual call for proposals to lead Vassar's International Studies (IS) Program study trips for the 2013–2014 academic year, I worked with the director of the IS Program as well as other faculty members throughout the

2012–2013 academic year to develop the course. My study trip would follow the format of previous IS study trips to locations such as Germany, Russia, Vietnam, and Cuba in which six weeks of classroom instruction were followed by travel to the region of focus.

As conceived, after six weeks of book learning, my students and I would travel mostly within the Jordan River watershed to try to appreciate the hydro-geological reality of life in a region of hydrologic and topographic extremes.[1] As a newly minted professor of geology at Pomona College in 1987, I had learned the imperative of a pedagogical approach of this nature from taking students to observe water distribution and engineering projects in Las Vegas and the Mojave Desert. Likewise, I surmised that in the Middle East it would be difficult for students from water-rich places to appreciate the situation of West Bank villagers sharing meager water supplies from springs, while Israelis enjoyed recreational opportunities like swimming pools in the desert, or to imagine solutions to these problems without seeing the situation on the ground. I was motivated to propose and teach the course because, from my perspective as an earth scientist, I understand how daily and future access to clean water in ample supply is one of the key issues about which people in the region fight. It is also a problem on which Arabs, Jews, Jordanians, Palestinians, and Israelis have worked together with integrity and compassion.

Vassar's curriculum committee approved the proposal as endorsed by the faculty members of the IS faculty steering committee. I was delighted. The trip epitomized the methodology of the field sciences, as well as the "go to the source" approach that has long been a defining feature of a Vassar education.[2]

Although I am a geologist by training, I am also an interdisciplinarian with scholarly publications in science studies. As a student of the late geologist and historian of science Stephen Jay Gould (who claimed to shun the politics of science), I am well versed in the truths revealed by studies at the intersection of science and society. I was inspired partially to teach the IS study trip by the work of Munqeth Mehyar, Nader Khateeb, and Gidon Bromberg, respectively, the Jordanian, Palestinian, and Israeli codirectors of EcoPeace Middle East (formerly Friends of the Earth Middle East), a nongovernmental association of Israelis, Palestinians, and Jordanians that works to solve environmental challenges in the Middle East, especially water supply and sanitation problems. The use of diplomacy on water issues by EcoPeace Middle East taps into the physical interconnectedness of water, soil, and air—a basic principle of earth science. Through interactions within the EcoPeace network, I hoped that my students and I would learn enough to speak knowledgeably about the resource realities of this conflict-ridden place so as to be potential agents for positive change. We hoped to promote respectful dialogue among students before, during, and after the trip so that our students might be able to participate in ongoing work toward a just peace.

Study Area

The Jordan is Israel's longest river. It flows south from its headwaters near Mount Hermon into the freshwater Lake Tiberias,[3] which is a main source of freshwater for the country. The river forms the boundary between Jordan and Israel and the West Bank territory and terminates in the Dead Sea.

Israel's mountain aquifer and coastal aquifer are the two main sources of groundwater for the country. Water is conveyed to different parts of the country via the National Water Carrier run by Israel's national water company (Mekorot) that extracts surface water from Lake Tiberias and groundwater from aquifers at various depths.

Methods

Near the beginning of the fall semester 2013, approximately one hundred students attended a meeting for students interested in the spring 2014 course. The meeting revealed the intellectual focus and logistical details of the course. We outlined our goal—by the semester's end, students would understand the basic hydrogeology of Israel and how issues of water sourcing and delivery and management of other natural resources are critical to peaceful coexistence. Also, we explained that the course would have a broader scope than exclusive study of the geology of the Jordan River watershed.

At the meeting, we clarified that the watershed would be a lens through which to look at questions of place in the State of Israel and the Palestinian territories. We wanted students to appreciate the fact that ways of thinking about place involved consideration of politically constructed boundaries and ancient historical and physical geographic features of land itself. While ours would be an educational trip, not an explicitly political one, we expected that we would engage political realities along with geological principles and historical and cultural issues. In sum, we anticipated that the course would illustrate that boundaries, natural ones, such as watersheds, and political ones, such as the Green Line and the separation barrier, profoundly affect the region as they demarcate processes and practices that define, unite, and divide people and places.

After the meeting, roughly eighty students submitted applications for thirty seats. We selected students based on an application letter, declared academic interest, and class year. We aimed to enroll students representing a variety of academic interests and years in college. Most of the students who were offered a seat accepted that spot. Initially, one or two students were admitted from the waitlist.

When the spring semester opened, we began six weeks of study to prepare for our trip. Students read journalist Ari Shavit's *My Promised Land* and articles on the region's geology and geography, boundary-making in the modern world, Greek influence and Roman occupation, and the founding of the State of Israel, its demography, and its cultural output. Students viewed films including *The Band's Visit, Encounter Point,* and *The Bubble.*

Before travel, students needed to attend all pre-trip classes, write a paper about Shavit's book, and construct responses to readings and films. We spelled out our hope that participants would contemplate contentious views about Zionism and cautioned that the trip would be about study, not service; in other words, participants would not undertake activities aimed at helping in the border region.

On our return, we would discuss our experiences in additional classes. We expected students to create poster presentations to share with the campus community in the College Center—a central gathering place—near the semester's end. The quality of the poster presentations would count toward final grades for the course.

Results

The Trip

Twenty-eight students and three faculty members embarked on the study trip on the first day of spring break. The composition of the group differed from the original one because of last-minute withdrawals from the course. However, we benefited from a more international group, including a student from a Lebanese family. On our first day, we visited the holy sites of Islam, Christianity, and Judaism in Jerusalem and laid the groundwork for appreciating the passionate global discourse about the disposition of this contested terrain.[4] Next, led by Palestinians, Jordanians, and Israelis affiliated with EcoPeace Mideast, we visited the Arab village of Battir and a nearly century-old Palestinian hilltop farm, Tent of Nations, as well as the Dheisha refugee camp in Bethlehem; these localities provided bird's-eye views of resource issues in the Palestinian territory of the West Bank.

After our introduction to the complicated mixture of communities in this tiny area, we traveled north toward the Lebanese border to the contested volcanic heights of Israel/Syria and familiarized ourselves with the water sources that feed the upper reaches of the Jordan and the Sea of Galilee, the largest freshwater body in the region. Students were surprised by the high rate of water discharge into the headwaters of the Jordan with its attendant waterfalls and lush vegetation; their observations ran contrary to their vision of the region as thoroughly arid. They also appreciated that water surface and groundwater flow do not recognize political and geographic boundaries—that is, water is a transboundary issue. While in Galilee, we visited Nazareth and the ancient Roman city of Sepphoris, remarkable for the archaeological record it provides of Romans, Jews, and Christians coexisting peacefully for hundreds of years.

Over the next days, we traveled along the Jordan to its terminus in the Dead Sea. With the assistance again of EcoPeace Middle East guides, we encountered the stark reality of dammed tributaries, water in sensitive agricultural practices, inadequate sewage treatment facilities, wetland reclamation efforts, land subsidence, mineral extraction industries, and, especially notable, unequal access to surface water conduits and groundwater aquifers. Our trip concluded in the Negev, where we met people trying to live in harsh desert terrain by employing solar power, dry composting, permaculture farming, and mud-plaster building.

Throughout the trip, we encountered Israelis, Palestinians, Jordanians, Christians, Muslims, and Jews working toward justice using nonviolent means. These individuals, nongovernmental organizations (NGOs) (such as the Emergency Water and Sanitation-Hygiene group), and educational institutions (such as Auja Eco Center and Arava Institute for Environmental Studies) validated our desire to inhabit the gray area between radical extremes. We met brave people on both sides who, despite charges leveled against them, consistently asserted the imperative to sustain conflicting narratives simultaneously. As Sulaiman Khatib—a representative from the binational NGO Combatants for Peace who served ten years in an Israeli prison for armed resistance—put it, "Every stone has at least two stories." Khatib's line became our mantra as we strove to occupy the murky but potentially productive middle space between binary extremes.

Campus Reaction

The maelstrom of reactions to the course began just after the informational meeting in late September 2013 and continued until the end of the academic year.

The first hint of trouble came when a concerned student informed me in October 2013 that Students for Justice in Palestine (SJP) were displaying posters in the College Center claiming that the study trip was an act of greenwashing. According to Urban Dictionary, *greenwashing* is the use of propaganda to distract from corporate malfeasance in environmental policy, to give the impression that the degraders care about the environment.[5] Although not an apt analogy for the study trip, the placard-bearing students were suggesting that we were attempting to use environmental collaboration between Israelis, Palestinians, and Jordanians on water and other natural resource issues to distract from Israel's oppressive policy toward Palestinians and Israeli Arabs.

Reactions intensified in December 2013 with news of an impending vote by the American Studies Association on whether to support a Boycott, Divestment, and Sanctions (BDS) boycott of Israeli academic institutions.[6] Some students enrolled in our course for the spring semester withdrew from it. Sadly, a loss to all of us, one student who withdrew had spent a junior year abroad in Jordan studying irrigation in arid regions. That individual explained that he or she felt conflicted about taking the course because of the numbers of his or her respected friends that were SJP members.

Events took a turn for the worse once the spring semester began. In early February 2014, SJP picketed our course, thrusting flyers at our students on their way to class that urged them to drop the course. On entering the space of the classroom, some of our students spoke of feeling harassed and intimidated. One pro-Israel blogger interviewed some participants and described the situation this way: "Protestors were lined up side-by-side across the lobby such that [one of the professors] and the students in the class had to push through the line to get to the classroom. While not physically blocked, [they] described that this required [them] to physically cross the protest line, as the protesters created a space to walk through.... The protestors made loud ululating sounds."[7]

We wrote to the relevant college administrators about the situation, stating that we objected to the picket because of its negative effect on our students, who already felt beleaguered by ill-informed criticisms across campus. Also, the students asked us to relay to the acting dean of the college and the director of the International Studies Program their request for a facilitated discussion with SJP members. Despite our repeated requests for such an intervention, none transpired.

Dear Students of International Studies 110,

You are *not* just taking a class, you are making a **political choice**! The simple act of entering and moving within the state of Israel is a freedom denied to over five million Palestinian refugees who were ethnically cleansed from their homes by the Israeli state. Your participation in this class financially and symbolically supports apartheid and the degradation of Palestinians. You may be critical, but your physical presence in the occupied country of Palestine is an endorsement of the systematic violation of human rights.

The indigenous people of Palestine do NOT want you to come!*

Do your research, engage with the realities of settler colonialism, and support BDS by opting out of this class!

We encourage you to join your peers at SJP General Body Meetings on Sundays at 6pm in the Women's Center!

*CALL FOR ACADEMIC AND CULTURAL BOYCOTT OF ISRAEL, 2004

"We, Palestinian academics and intellectuals, call upon our colleagues in the international community to comprehensively and consistently boycott all Israeli academic and cultural institutions **as a contribution to the struggle to end Israel's occupation, colonization and system of apartheid.**"

Flyer distributed directly outside the classroom to students taking the study trip to Israel.

Electronic dialogue among involved colleagues ensued. Some members of the college community characterized our objection to the picket as our use of white privilege to target students of color. Furthermore, one side argued that whether or not the SJP students conducted themselves in an appropriate or respectful way, they were exercising their rights to freedom of assembly and speech and did nothing illegal. Others contended that even if SJP had not acted illegally, as an educational community there needed to be some protection of the classroom as a sacred space. In their, and my, opinion, harassing students for attending a course that the college curriculum committee had approved violated what should be a protected right on campus. We relocated our upcoming classes to another building and continued our educational endeavor.

Tensions peaked in an event sponsored shortly afterward, in early March, by the faculty Committee on Inclusion and Excellence (CIE). Initially billed as an "open discussion" on "The International Studies Trip and Student Protest at Vassar," it surprised us since neither my coteachers nor I had been informed that CIE planned such a public conversation about "the ethics" of our course. We contacted our CIE colleagues and requested that the forum be deferred until our return, as we were preparing for our imminent departure. We also contested the title and description, for they read, to our minds, as a public referendum on the course, which felt inappropriate to us. We were told that the forum would be held despite our request, but the title was changed to "The Ethics of Student Activism and Protest at Vassar College." Because the forum would go on with or without us, we agreed to participate. I planned to describe briefly the origin of this particular study trip and our itinerary.

The Committee on Inclusion and Excellence presents:
The International Studies Trip and Student Protest at Vassar
Join us for an open discussion about the International Study Travel trip to Israel and the response from students. Representatives from the Dean of Students office, the International Studies Program and Travel class, and Students for Justice in Palestine will kick off a conversation on the ethics of the travel trip, the rights of students to protest on campus and other related issues.
Monday, March 3rd
5:30 to 6:30 pm
Multi-purpose Room, College Center

Original announcement for the public forum.

The Committee on Inclusion and Excellence presents:
The Ethics of Student Activism and Protest at Vassar
Join CIE for an open conversation on the ethics and possibilities of student activism and the rights of students to protest on campus. This open dialogue, while not limited to, will include a conversation about the International Study Travel trip(s) and responses from students. Representatives from the Residential Life office, the International Studies Program, Travel class, Students for Justice in Palestine, and J Street will kick off the conversation.
Monday, March 3rd
5:30 to 7pm
Multi-purpose Room, College Center

Revised announcement for the public forum.

Just prior to the forum, our dean wrote to those faculty intimately involved in it reminding us per the college governance that academic freedom accords faculty complete liberty of instruction, safeguards the right of all to free speech including the right to protest, and dedicates us to freedom of inquiry in the pursuit of truth.[8] He expressed the hope that the forum would be about academic freedom, activism, and the difficulties surrounding travel to many places. He also commented that although he hoped the forum would be respectful and result in fruitful conversation, he could not control what went on in the room.

Students in our class, SJP members, and numerous faculty members, including those who approved the course as members of the IS Program, among others, attended the forum. One of the chairmen of the CIE began the forum with a statement that "cardboard notions of civility" would not guide the session. In a packed room, the statement set the tone for a session filled with belligerence, vilification, intimidation, and rage against Israel.

A number of issues were raised about the trip. One of the chairs of CIE questioned the ability of all students of different nationalities to avail themselves of the trip: would some students be refused entry to Israel or subsequently encounter trouble returning to their home countries had they been known to have traveled to Israel? Faculty referred to generalized struggles against racism and the military-industrial-prison complex as a motivation for boycotting Israel and protesting the trip. Students criticized us for planning to use roads to travel through Israel on which Palestinians could not traverse. The idea that the issue of travel for study to other countries where oppression exists was not explored. That the Arava Institute receives funding from the Jewish National Fund and is affiliated with Ben-Gurion University also drew ire. No senior administrators attended except for the acting dean of the college, who did not speak during the forum. Most faculty members, including the head of the IS Program, also remained silent. Despite the fact that he had no teaching responsibilities at our college, one mid-level administrator in the student life division spoke as a "man of color" about what he would have done if his office had been picketed.

What happened at the forum was widely reported in the media.[9]

One prominent pro-Israel blogger summarized it as a "campus forum in which the professors and Jewish students were belittled, heckled, and mocked in such crude ways that it left even critics of Israel shaken."[10] The reference to "critics of Israel" is to the anti-Israel blogger Philip Weiss, who attended the forum. In an essay titled, "Ululating at Vassar," Weiss first noted an earlier blog post of mine about the forum in which I'd said I was "knocked off-center by a belligerent academic community dedicated to vilifying anyone who dares set foot in Israel," and then he acknowledged:

> [The forum] was truly unsettling. Over 200 students and faculty jammed a large room of the College Center, and torrents of anger ripped through the gathering. Most of them were directed at Israel or its supporters.... The spirit of that young progressive space was that Israel is a blot on civilization.... If a student had gotten up and said, I love Israel, he or she would have been mocked and scorned into silence.... I left the room as soon as the meeting ended. The clash felt too raw, and there was a racial element to the division (privileged Jews versus students of color).[11]

After the event, members of the campus community communicated with us or about us. A particularly disturbing aftereffect was a Facebook post by one of the CIE chairs that mocked the powerful emotions of some people present and castigated the individual who reported the post to the dean.

> "Them shits burn water and move mountains. All praise is due to white tears."
> This is what a white student turned me in to the dean for.
> Thank yall for caring. I didnt let you down. I wont be getting called in again for what I write on facebook And neither will any other black and brown professors burdened with cleaning other folks mess.
> —
> Them shits burn water, move mountains and get niggas sent to the deans office. All praise is due to white tears.

Facebook post by a chair of the CIE, one of two with over two hundred likes after the public forum. Post was later taken down.

Wow. Students sending my facebook posts to the Dean of Faculty now? Fam, I haven't friended one person on facebook. If you came on my page, you friended me. And if you friend me, and don't like what I say, that's cool, but you in my yard. I don't know who folks think they're dealing with. I'm too black, brilliant, beautiful and loving to kiss white ass. Ever. Ever. So I'm going to talk to the Dean later and if you wanna send something else his way before I get there, send this, too. Fuck you, and be happy you get to share the same space with us. It's not going down like you think it is. It's just not.

"If white American entitlement meant anything, it meant that no matter how patronizing, unashamed, deliberate, unintentional, poor, rich, rural, urban, ignorant, and destructive white Americans were, black Americans were still encouraged to work for them, write to them, listen to them, talk with them, run from them, emulate them, teach them, dodge them, and ultimately thank them for not being as fucked up as they could be."

Facebook post by a chair of the CIE, one of two with over two hundred likes after the forum. Post was later taken down.

Dismay was expressed and apologies delivered for not stepping up to take responsibility for the decision by the IS Program and the curriculum committee to approve the course. Some colleagues characterized the conversation as a show trial at which they were appalled by the "grueling and exhausting spectacle." Others reported that students, even some from SJP, were embarrassed by the rude and ungenerous behavior of some people present. One sympathetic colleague wrote, saying that comments made about the significance that Israel and the boycott had assumed in their lives were reminiscent of antisemitism past and present. That individual continued that he or she was unimpressed with confusing and vain arguments that were made seemingly to burnish the revolutionary credentials of the speakers. We were told that amidst the "upsetting process" in which "scores of people were silent, watching and listening" to "deeply unfair criticisms" even though they could see what was happening, we handled the situation extraordinarily well—addressing questions and comments with "clarity, honesty, generosity, poise." Expressions of concern came to us from administrators who were not present but received reports about the event. One of them wrote to us, posing the question, "Why can't we have conversations about difficult issues that don't become personal and intimidating?"[12]

Despite the turmoil, we left on our trip as planned. Our departure coincided with an all-campus email from the president:

Students, faculty, and staff,

As we start our Spring Break, I wanted to acknowledge the work of many on campus who in recent weeks have been part of challenging discussions on a range of issues related to Israel and Palestine. These can be difficult, emotionally-charged conversations that require care as we express our own views and as we listen to others. Some in our community have felt distressed with a lack of respectful discourse, and some have felt that their views are marginalized. Different members of our community have different ideas not only on the substantive issues but also on what constitutes productive discussion. We may never reach consensus on these issues, but we will benefit from continuing to explore useful ways to talk about them. Otherwise, many will choose not to engage in these important conversations, which would be a loss for our entire community.

I look forward to working with many of you on opportunities for continuing our discussions when everyone returns later this month.

Nonetheless, we returned after spring break to find that the rabbi who was the adviser to Jewish students on campus had announced her retirement, and we heard reports of a still-simmering BDS-SJP situation and an inflamed community of alumnae and alumni. As a result, we decided to amend our final assignment for the course. Rather than have public poster presentations by our students on their topics of study, we shared our presentations only among classmates.

In December 2014, not quite one year after the debacle I have described, the president appointed "as advisors to the President and the senior administration on issues of race and inclusion" one of the CIE faculty chairs who initiated and presided over the forum on our course.[13]

Discussion

The events leading up to the study trip to Israel marked an unprecedented low for me in nearly thirty years as a college professor. One especially vexing aspect of the criticism leveled at my coteachers and me was that it was racialized. Our objection to the SJP protest steps from our classroom door was unfairly characterized as the response of white women to feeling threatened by brown and black bodies. Our students—many of whom belong to racial and ethnic minority groups—were as surprised as we were that the group of SJP protesters was characterized as being of color. If given the opportunity to be listened to, we would have made clear that we supported the right of SJP students to protest in any number of ways but not inside an academic building at our classroom door. If anyone had thought to speak with us before stereotypically labeling us, multiple competing narratives would have emerged. For example, while we have indeed benefited from the privilege of being seen as within the white majority in our society, we were at the same time in sympathy with the concerns of SJP. Because members of the community were quick to attribute our behavior to racist views, an educational opportunity was lost. Because course participants were condemned for choosing to study in Israel, the larger campus community missed the opportunity to learn from our experiences.

With regard to the forum itself, perhaps we should have chosen to not participate at that moment in time. However, given the rebuff of our expressed desire to engage in such public discussion on our return, we felt we had no choice but to speak at the planned forum on behalf of our educational endeavor. Although we were prepared to engage in challenging dialogue, we were concerned that the description of the event seemed designed to put our course on trial. Furthermore, the gathering was to be held a mere five days before we would set off on our trip. We worried that a contentious open forum less than one week before our departure might destabilize our diverse group of students. Such a turn of events could make it more difficult to have a safe and productive travel trip. When the forum was opened with the invitation to speak freely because "the notion of civility is a tool of the oppressor," in retrospect, perhaps we should have gotten up and left the room. It seems fair to say that the situation in the room went from bad to worse. It's not just that students and faculty were behaving badly but that faculty seemed to encourage and support the students' behavior. Facilitators of the forum became advocates for a certain set of students. Furthermore, the rage unleashed disrespectfully at my coteachers and me at the forum had a gendered and racial dimension. At the end of the evening, it seemed that we had lost all sense of what it means to be part of an educational community.

Throughout this ordeal, members of our college community from both the Left and the Right personally attacked my co-instructors and me. In one account, we were "white settler-colonialists" oppressing the Palestinians; in the other, we were "self-hating Jews" pursuing an "anti-Israel agenda." In fact, people who made little, if any, effort to examine the details of our course subject and itinerary reduced us to stereotypical caricatures. If their narrative was that we were bent on destroying Israel, it was because our support for many of the goals of SJP and the Open Hillel movement seemed irreconcilable with our involvement in our Jewish communities and support (albeit critical) of Israel. If their narrative was that we supported a white colonialist regime in Israel, then perhaps they refused to look at the ways in which we were committed to fighting injustice against Palestinians. Although unsurprised by these reactions, they saddened us, particularly as educators.

Students and faculty have expressed their concern that in recent years a climate of fear has descended on campus.[14] What might be the source of some of that fear? In the case of our course, some people caricatured our students as having been greenwashed by the trip itinerary. Students in our course were victimized by spurious depictions that underestimated their intelligence. Perhaps one way to begin countering the climate of fear on many college campuses around the country where similar events have transpired is to work harder campus-wide to engage one another with intellectual openness. In our case, a starting point for such an endeavor might have been to talk with any one of the twenty-eight breathtakingly thoughtful students who devoted their spring break to the study trip. In fact, one colleague addressed what transpired at the forum in his or her class the next day because one of the students in that class was a "bright-eyed freshman" in the study trip course, while another student in the class was a member of SJP and had been "wearing her or his convictions on her or his shirt." Purportedly, a number of the students on the proboycott side came to understand more about the virtues of the trip and harbored fewer reservations about it. Such a result is the upside of complicated and possibly painful discussions.

Still, an episode such as the one I have described in this chapter invites the questions: Why can't members of academic communities have conversations about difficult issues that don't become personal and intimidating? Why do people think it is acceptable to behave in this manner? How do we change an academic culture that condones belligerence? How do we get faculty to speak up and hold each other accountable? Academic freedom does allow for protest. Students should protest and argue about positions with which they disagree. But academic freedom does not imply that differences of opinion may be voiced via taunts, nor does it suggest that intimidation is a legitimate and productive means to affect change. Academic freedom does not mean that students should be pressured to avoid unique and difficult educational opportunities because others impugn them. To tackle specific controversial ideas, we must agree on ideas about what it means to be civil, to dissent respectfully, and to work collaboratively on difficult issues.

Conclusion

Vassar is one of many US colleges and universities where, instead of working to engage debate and refute contentious ideas, students and faculty are shutting down avenues of inquiry and blocking the attempts of others to examine difficult issues.[15] Such bullying stymies learning and is anti-intellectual. Although it came at great cost, I decided to stick to my educational principles, and I'm glad I did. By learning on the ground from Palestinians, Israelis, and Jordanians about hydropolitics in Israel, my students and I came to appreciate why water issues are central to the conflict in the region. We also learned lessons about principled stances, forms of protest, and academic freedom that I never would have thought to put on my syllabus.

The events I've described have caused me to ask, "How do I continue my professional life as a Jewish faculty member committed to the idea of academic freedom and the right to pursue ideas that some might consider risky?" The episode has had ramifications in my professional life at the college. Relationships with colleagues in my home department are strained. Faculty and students new to the college may not know of me first as an individual with a record that reflects a lifelong commitment to social justice nor as a dedicated teacher of earth science. Of course, this is impossible to prove, but I wonder sometimes about my electability for college committee work or my draw as a teacher. Nonetheless, I hope to take inspiration for wisdom regarding social change from the idea articulated by Frances Kissling, former president of Catholics for Choice, that one must "approach differences with this notion that there is good in the other"; one must "absolutely refuse to see the other as evil."[16] In seemingly intractable dilemmas regarding Israel, I hope that both sides might use Kissling's approach to nurture the ability to contemplate simultaneously conflicting ideals.

JILL S. SCHNEIDERMAN is Professor of Earth Science at Vassar College, has authored many papers on wide-ranging subjects including studies of sediment transport mechanisms, feminist approaches to environmental justice, and critical Anthropocene studies. She has also edited *The Earth Around Us: Maintaining a Livable Planet, For the Rock Record: Geologists on Intelligent Design, Exploring Environmental Science with GIS: An Introduction to Environmental Mapping and Analysis,* and *Liberation Science: Putting Science to Work for Social and Environmental Justice.*

Notes

1. The course did not involve explicit study of the use of desalination, the process of converting seawater into potable water. Use of the process ramped up in Israel beginning in 2014; as of March 2016, five desalination plants operated in the country. According to a 2016 report, as a result of these measures, Israel has been able to supply itself with the approximately 528 billion gallons of water it requires each year (Alina Dain Sharon, "How Israel Survived the Mediterranean's Worst Drought in 900 Years," *The Algemeiner* (March 22, 2016), https://www.algemeiner.com/2016/03/22/how-israel-survived-the-mediterraneans -worst-drought-in-900-years/). Approximately 15 billion gallons of that water Israel provides to Palestinians living in the West Bank—almost double the amount that was agreed on in the Oslo Accords—and just under 15 billion gallons also is provided annually to Jordan. Israel also directs water to Gaza at a price equal to the cost of desalinating water and transporting it. Israel constructed a supply pipeline extending to Israel's border with Gaza in order to deliver that water. In March 2015, Israel announced plans to double the amount of water it delivers to Gaza in order to help mitigate the major water crisis there. Whether or not these measures to supply water to Palestinians are sufficient remains a matter of debate.

2. "Vassar Traditions," *Vassar Encyclopedia,* https://vcencyclopedia.vassar.edu /traditions/ (accessed November 1, 2017).

3. Also known as the Kinneret and the Sea of Galilee.

4. Our itinerary included these stops: Old City Jerusalem, Mahane Yehuda; Tsur Hadassah/Wadi Fuqeen, Bethlehem; Hermon Stream (Banias) Nature Reserve, Agamon Hula Nature Reserve; Tzippori National Park and Nazareth; Alumot Dam and Peace Island, Al 'Auja; Masada National Park, Ein Gedi and the Dead Sea; Tel Aviv; Ein Avdat and Wadi Aricha; Makhtesh Ramon Nature Reserve and Coral Beach Nature Reserve; Kibbutz Ketura; Kibbutz Lotan.

5. "Greenwashing," Urban Dictionary, http://www.urbandictionary.com/define .php?term=greenwashing (accessed November 1, 2017).

6. "What Does the Boycott of Israeli Academic Institutions Mean for the ASA?" American Studies Association, http://www.theasa.net/what_does_the_academic_boycott _mean_for_the_asa/ (accessed November 1, 2017).

7. William A. Jacobson, "Anti-Israel Academic Boycott Turns Ugly at Vassar," *Legal Insurrection* (March 27, 2014), http://legalinsurrection.com/2014/03/anti-israel-academic -boycott-turns-ugly-at-vassar/.

8. "A Documentary Chronicle of Vassar College," http://chronology.vassar.edu /records/1923/1923-06-11-new-governance.html (accessed November 1, 2017).

9. William A. Jacobson, "Anti-Israel Academic Boycott Turns Ugly at Vassar," *Legal Insurrection* (March 27, 2014), http://legalinsurrection.com/2014/03/anti-israel -academic-boycott-turns-ugly-at-vassar/. Philip Weiss, "Ululating at Vassar: the Israel/ Palestine Conflict Comes to America," *Mondoweiss* (March 20, 2014), http://mondoweiss. net/2014/03/ululating-israelpalestine-conflict/; Jonathan Marks, "'Shut Up,' BDS Explained: An 'Open Forum' at Vassar," *Commentary* (March 26, 2014),https://www .commentarymagazine.com/culture-civilization/popular-culture/shut-up-bds-explained -an-open-forum-at-vassar/; Joshua Levitt, "Vassar Profs Who Brought Students to Israel Describe Campus 'Climate of Fear'," *The Algemeiner* (April 14, 2014), https://www .algemeiner.com/2014/04/14/vassar-profs-who-brought-students-to-israel-describe -campus-climate-of-fear/.

10. William A. Jacobson, "Anti-Israel Academic Boycott Turns Ugly at Vassar," *Legal Insurrection* (March 27, 2014), http://legalinsurrection.com/2014/03/anti-israel-academic -boycott-turns-ugly-at-vassar/.

11. Philip Weiss, "Ululating at Vassar: the Israel/Palestine conflict comes to America," *Mondoweiss* (March 20, 2014), http://mondoweiss.net/2014/03/ululating-israelpalestine -conflict/; Jill S. Schneiderman, "Vassar College Study Trip to the Jordan River Watershed and Surroundings," earthdharma.org (March 4, 2014), https://earthdharma.org /2014/03/04/vassar-college-study-trip-to-the-jordan-river-watershed-and-surroundings/.

12. All the quoted material in this section of the chapter comes from documented personal communication with me.

13. Letter from President, https://president.vassar.edu/letters/141215-letter.html (accessed June 16, 2016).

14. One Vassar colleague has recently expressed her concern about a growing "anti-Jewish" atmosphere on our campus: see Andrew Pessin, "Non-Jewish Pro-Israel Vassar Professor Says 'Anti-Jewish Atmosphere' on Campus 'Starting to Have Long-Term Effects'," *The Algemeiner* (March 23, 2016), https://www.algemeiner.com/2016/03/23/non-jewish-pro -israel-vassar-professor-says-anti-jewish-atmosphere-on-campus-starting-to-have-long -term-effects/.

15. Jonathan Cole, "The Chilling Effect of Fear at America's Colleges," *The Atlantic* (June 9, 2016), http://www.theatlantic.com/education/archive/2016/06/the-chilling -effect-of-fear/486338/; Wort News Department and Darien Lamen, "Alice Dreger And Academic Freedom Under Siege," WORT (March 1, 2016), http://www.wortfm.org/alice -dreger-and-academic-freedom-under-siege/; Abby Ellin, "Studies in the First Amendment, Playing Out on Campus," *The New York Times* (June 22, 2016), http://www.nytimes .com/2016/06/23/education/studies-in-the-first-amendment-playing-out-on-campus .html?smprod=nytcore-iphone&smid=nytcore-iphone-share&_r=0.

16. Quoted by Krista Tippett in *Becoming Wise* (New York: Penguin Press, 2016).

23 Fanatical Anti-Zionism and the Degradation of the University: What I Have Learned in Buffalo

Ernest Sternberg

Ernest Sternberg examines the decidedly nonacademic antisemitic tropes that dominate academic discourse at his university and beyond. Falsehoods, misrepresentations, and slanders against Jews and Israel are uttered and accepted with minimal interest in facts, evidence, or argument. The theme of the Jews as demonic Nazis is repeatedly uttered, along with modern incarnations of the blood libel as a kernel of truth about an Israeli pathologist morphs into enormous charges of institutionalized organ harvesting by the Jewish State. Academics not only don't resist this morphing process but openly contribute to it. Sternberg challenges some of these claims, showing how even minimal effort can easily debunk these lies—an effort that too many academics don't bother to exert. These slanderous claims about Israel and Israeli Jews, he concludes, are not "ordinary claims, to be answered with argument, evidence, and reason.... They are solidarity-building rituals of execration." That they are thriving in the academy reveals "the university's intellectual debasement, its corruption as an institution of higher learning."

On the fanatical, bizarre, and irrational hatred toward Israel that some professors and students espouse, my wake-up call came on April 28, 2004. It was during a lecture on my campus, the University at Buffalo (UB), by the anti-Israel activist and then DePaul professor of political science Norman Finkelstein, who in those years spoke by invitation at dozens of colleges. He was just one of what is now an entire industry of Israel antagonists invited to American campuses to foment extreme anti-Zionism—in essence, to describe the Israeli Jew as the execrable enemy, the global fiend, the new Nazi.

In the pages below, I use this and other UB occurrences to show how anti-Israel events on academic campuses turn into decidedly un-academic nightmares of demonization. I should say now that in my analysis of these events I have gained particular insight from Bernard Lewis, who explained that antisemitism is rather more than ordinary racism. It attributes to Jews, and by extension, to the Jewish movement known as Zionism, cosmic evil, and it judges them by standards applied to no other.[1] In the decade and more that has elapsed since that ugly evening, I have struggled to understand the form of malice that his talk exemplified and to decide what my ethical obligation was in response.

An Evening of Hate

Addressing around 150 people crowded into an auditorium that night in 2004, Finkelstein initially contended that Jewish authors such as Elie Wiesel and institutions such as the Simon Wiesenthal Center were peddling the Holocaust story. Their reason: of course, what we would expect of Jews, to make money. Thousands of books about the Holocaust appeared after 1967, the year of Israel's victory in the Six-Day War, Finkelstein said, because Jewish leadership needed a new way to defend what he alleged was Israel's oppression of Palestinians. He did not explain what kind of entity—what shadowy emanation of the Elders of Zion—could give marching orders to so many scholars to write books on this terrible subject.

As it happened, I had searched Finkelstein's name on the internet before his speech and found in the online Israel-bashing site *CounterPunch* an interview in which he commented on the then-recent Post-Soviet migration, which led Israel to give entry to Russian migrants, some of whom turned out not to be Jews. The "reason why," Finkelstein declared, "is because the Israeli establishment likes the blue-eyed, blond-haired Aryan types as a racial group."[2]

In the Q&A just after his talk, I asked what evidence he had to indicate that Israelis wanted to racially transform themselves into Aryans. He hesitated. Some works of pro-Israel literature had blond and blue-eyed characters, he finally said. By way of example, he continued, was Leon Uris's *Exodus* (1958) with its blond and blue-eyed protagonist Ari. And that name, Finkelstein said in front of an audience of academics, is short for Aryan.

Like many of us who make our lives in academia, I had up till then entertained the pleasing thought of the university as a place where intelligent people devote themselves to the search for knowledge, seeking the truer or better through dedication to evidence, good reasoning, and open debate. Yet this speaker, Finkelstein, was warmly introduced by a professor of English who, after hearing what I have related, would send Finkelstein an effusive letter of thanks. Another English professor, this one holding the distinguished rank, had financially cosponsored the event and never subsequently distanced himself from it. An ostensible peace group, the Western New York Peace Center, had also cosponsored the event and would not later apologize or distance itself, even after requests do so. Nor, certainly, did the other cosponsors: a suburban church, an Arab or Muslim student association, and the Marxist-Leninist Study Group. At the evening's end, excepting the few who had come for the reason I did and sat in silence, the audience responded with rousing applause.

Most of the Arab students and students from other Muslim countries would have had little previous exposure to Jews or Israel. With some luck, they could have still returned from this hate-filled auditorium to their dorms and just forgotten it, as they would have forgotten any bad lecture. But I could not help but notice, as I looked around, faces that were emotionally engaged, giddy with excitement, as if flushed with a new and intensely meaningful knowledge. There could not be doubt that for some this was a moment of indoctrination—the moment at which the realization dawns about the world's great evildoer.

I'm almost embarrassed to feel obliged to answer that night's crazy accusations, on the off chance that a reader might stumble on the present essay and wonder. Israelis seek to be like Nazis—that's what Finkelstein wanted to slip into tender minds, so that they would then naturally slide into believing that Israelis *are* like Nazis. Let's point out that during the period that real Nazis held sway in Europe, the Jewish population—how should we put it?—declined. During the time that the Israelis have had a country, Palestinians in Israel and the world have enjoyed some of the world's highest population growth rates. Israeli Arab children are born alongside Jewish ones in Israeli hospitals; the Jewish and Arab mothers lie in beds and delivery rooms side by side (compare this to the Israeli Apartheid accusation). Despite challenges arising from cousin marriage, childbearing by very young mothers, and other factors lowering the Arab population's health, the shocking disparities in Arab and Jewish childhood survival that Israel inherited with statehood have steadily declined under the Israeli medical system. The survival rate among Israeli Arab Christian children now exceeds that of Israeli Jews and is close to the top in the world. The survival rate of Palestinian children under Israeli medical care exceeds most of those in the Arab world.[3]

As for the name? Ari is the diminutive for the ancient Hebrew name Aryeh, which means "lion." The word *Aryan* comes from the Sanskrit (and is, as a point of information, the source of the word *Iran*). "Aryan race" as a category of beings is a Nazi myth; it is not at all clear how even people who wanted to would actually go about turning themselves into one. It would take only modest attempts at communication with Israeli or Diaspora Jews—just the tiniest modicum of investigation—to discover that they abhor Nazi race theory. The assertion that Jews would name a child Aryan or would want to become Aryans is imbecilic. Yet there it is. A professor invites a professor to say such things on an American campus, a distinguished professor uses State University of New York money to cosponsor the event, and students applaud.

The Jew As the Nazi

It is worth adding parenthetically that this would not be the only time in which Finkelstein publicly put forth the idea that Israelis were Nazis or were like Nazis or wanted to be Nazis. After children studying in a yeshiva were massacred by terrorists in Jerusalem in 2008, news photos showed the children's blood splattered on Talmudic texts. Along with a group of other faculty members, I signed a letter of condolence and shock. Finkelstein wrote, "Nazi professors mourn death of *übermenschen*," suggesting that we regretted the lost opportunity to breed Hasidic children into a master race.[4] Finkelstein's claim, in short, was that the American academic signatories to the petition had hoped to turn yeshiva children into Aryan supermen.

Such talk did not prevent Finkelstein's UB hosts from honoring him with a return invitation to lecture at the university in April 2011.

There are many variations on the Jew-is-Nazi motif, and I now mention another one with a Buffalo connection, just one small sample in the vast genre of professorial hate literature. Published online in the *Electronic Intifada* in late 2009, an article by UB professor James Holstun and a then-recent student concerned an Israeli brigadier general who had visited Buffalo.[5] The article claims boldly, "Colonel Efraim (Fein) Eitam was only following orders when he told his troops to beat Ayyad Aqel in 1988. They beat him to death." Merciless Israelis, relishing blood.

It took me only minimal investigation to discover what a clutter of disconnected quotes and jumbled time lines the article was. To keep it brief: Aqel was a Palestinian detainee abused by four Israeli soldiers in Gaza. For this, the soldiers were court-martialed and sentenced under Israeli military regulations to terms of imprisonment. The court did not find their commanding officer, Eitam, to have been culpable, although the soldiers' defense attorney had attempted that argument. Separately, at some unspecified time and in an unspecified context, in reaction to an attack of some kind, Prime Minister Rabin allegedly said, "Break their bones!" Presto: the Jew general is a Nazi, obeying kill orders à la Eichmann.

Even a barely cognizant reader could see in this rubbish that the soldiers, who violated standing orders on the treatment of prisoners, were court-martialed for *disobeying* orders.[6] Contradiction notwithstanding, it was perhaps not surprising that the article was reposted again and again on Islamist, militant, Western radical, and blatantly antisemitic sites.

What was surprising was that it was written by people with university affiliations.

In the long history of antisemitic libels, the Jew-is-Nazi slur is a comparatively new one. It is used with abandon in anti-Zionist speech generally; the Buffalo incidents are merely a few local examples. But irrationalism and outright absurdity are no obstacles to anti-Zionists because of the power of that image, its compelling nature. In our time, the Nazi is the ultimate in secular evil. How delicious it is to apply the epithet to the Jew. The Jew-is-Nazi slur must be used, and will inevitably be used, because it so naturally expresses the accuser's need to depict the Zionist, the Israeli, and the Jew as the cosmic evildoer.

Jews Dressed Up as Christians to Kill Muslims

The blood libel is a venerable tactic, a slur that stands out among slurs, achieving its power through the dramatic contrast of the monstrous, scheming evildoer and the innocent, defenseless child. It appears in several modern forms, of which I will mention only two, one being a somewhat unusual and obscure instance. It took place at UB on October 22, 2010. With the university's English department as cosponsor, the evening event was ostensibly meant to commemorate those killed at the Sabra and Shatila refugee camps near Beirut in 1982.[7] We do know that at least ten times as many were killed in the same year in the city of Hama in neighboring Syria by the Syrian regime, portending the catastrophe that would come thirty years later. That the Hama atrocity would not be memorialized on our or any other campus, and the Sabra and Shatila would be, reveals what the motive was: not to express concern for the victims of massacres or learn something about how to prevent atrocities but to depict Israeli Jews as monsters.

In September 1982, the military wing of the Lebanese Front, made up mainly of members of a Maronite Christian party called the Phalange, entered the camps and killed close to one thousand people, mostly civilians. By almost all accounts, they were taking revenge for the assassination a couple of days earlier of their leader, Bachir Gemayel, and for the Palestinian Liberation Organization's (PLO's) massacre of five hundred people in a Christian village in 1976. While the Sabra and Shatila atrocity was occurring, Israeli troops controlled the outskirts of the camps. An official Israeli investigation castigated the Israeli military for not having anticipated the massacre or acting rapidly to stop it upon receiving information that it was occurring.

The evening in Buffalo twenty-eight years later first featured harrowing descriptions of the killings by a man introduced as a survivor. Then, guest speaker Don Wagner, a Presbyterian minister (described in posters as an eyewitness to the event) claimed that "most likely many Israelis were in the Phalangists' military uniforms and they denied responsibility." The claim was novel; not even PLO-affiliated historians had made it.[8] Given the global prevalence of anti-Zionist ferocity, with the United Nations itself providing a privileged stage for it, it was rather a surprise that a new blood libel would make its debut here in Buffalo.

To the students and activists in the audience, the evening's lesson was clear: the dead bodies, the babies under rubble, and the stench of death were the crimes of Israeli Jews. To contrast with the blood-soaked, demonic Israelis, the Presbyterian minister had no trouble identifying with the innocents. "There is an enormous nonviolent movement in Palestine, and many are paying a heavy price, so resist in all kinds of ways! Don't concede!" he advised the crowd, which was heavily made up of Arab and/or Muslim students. The audience was soon at the boiling point. Speakers and audience members quickly called for sanctions, boycotts, and divestments. Boycott anything you think is Israeli Zionist, one voice said; boycott Starbucks, said another, for some reason (it has no branches in Israel but has a Jewish CEO). Still others agitated for academic boycotts. So it is that fabricated accusations of collective murder—blood libels—are used on campuses to directly incite students into a paroxysm of hatred.

One can actually find as internet flotsam rare references to a Phalangist fighter or two who says, in effect, "It was not I who murdered; it was a Jew dressed like me." For the accused in Lebanon, that would be the best available expedient to save oneself from opprobrium and worse. In the face of the Arab world's sectarian divisions, in which hatred of the Zionist Jew has been the only reliable commonality, this—the blaming of the Jew—was long the expedient of choice, until the 2010s, when it could no longer hold back the reckoning. It is hardly a surprise that an accused mass murderer would try to save his skin by resorting to it. But what is a surprise, again—perhaps it should stop being a surprise by now—is that professional academics would accept these claims so easily. Indeed, those who believe these claims must practice a highly selective credulity. Despite normally being careful investigators, they have the willingness, the eagerness, to believe anything that depicts Israel as a monstrous evil. No matter how transparently self-serving the Jews-dressed-as-Christians-to-kill-Muslims accusation, no matter how unsubstantiated the accusation is by reputable historiography, there are academics fanatical enough to use it to incite students.[9]

The Jewish Murderer for Organ Transplants

The murder-for-organ-theft libel gained notoriety in 2009, when the Swedish newspaper *Aftonbladet* claimed that, as part of an international syndicate involving rabbis and Jewish doctors, the Israeli military hunted down and murdered young Palestinians and slit open their bodies so as to harvest their organs either for sale or for insertion into needy Jewish bodies. The defamation spread quickly and gained legs. Soon, Israelis were accused of kidnapping Ukranian children (twenty-five thousand no less!) to steal their organs, not to mention Algerian children, and not least, Haitian children, whose bodies these single-minded Israelis plundered while pretending to help the Haitians recover from a devastating earthquake.

The author of the Swedish article was altogether evasive about when and where these macabre crimes took place; he relied in part on memories of an event occurring seventeen years before. The sourcing is a hodgepodge of fragments. Take, for instance, an ugly claim about Israeli medical behavior: it comes from a second article regarding a third article, which has a partial truncated translation from a Hebrew fourth article, the original, which discusses a responsible and ethical conversation between doctors about organ transplantation and has no relation to the slanderous impression the Swedish article wishes to give.

Central to the narrative is an allegedly innocent Palestinian "stone thrower" who was hunted for weeks by Israeli troops, who finally cornered him and shot him several times in the legs. Where to begin with the ridiculousness? According to a later investigation by the American organization, Committee for Accuracy in Middle East Reporting in America (CAMERA)—which subsequently published a *Wall Street Journal* op-ed exposing the fraud[10]—the poor victim was hard to identify from the article but appears to have been a leader of Palestinian vigilantes who murdered Palestinians for collaborating with Israel. Contrary to typical behavior by those shot in each leg, the man kept running—the Swedish article casually reports—until soldiers shot him in the back. As described, the marauding Israeli soldiers then dragged the body (let's imagine it, bump, bump, bump) up the steps, loaded it into a helicopter to whisk it to a morgue to have his organs plucked out, and stuck inside a Jew, one whose luck—as we shall see—would be no better than that of the deceased vigilante.

For one thing, bullets to the man's upper body would likely have damaged items of interest for eventual transplantation; caused hemorrhaging and denied blood to living organs, which would soon cease functioning; and burst the intestines, releasing contents that would poison any organs that the bullets had spared. The bumps up the stairs would have scrambled them some more. And this mess would have been taken to the morgue, an unsanitary place in the best of times, where—to continue this bizarre story—a waiting Jew (wouldn't you have to check for matching antigens? a scientist might ask) would have been given a dead or infected organ that would very likely have killed him. A Harvard surgeon and international transplant expert quoted in the CAMERA piece declared the alleged scenario, a shooting preceding the supposed organ harvesting, to be "not feasible from a surgical vantage." A Johns Hopkins University medical faculty member of Swedish background described the allegation as "medically impossible."[11]

It is marginally consoling that this accusation did not actually make its way into a public lecture at UB (although a variation did appear at an academic lecture at Vassar).[12] Instead, a faculty member in my university spread it through a campus listserv to some two hundred faculty and staff members, who normally discussed union matters. The message also referenced a then-eight-year-old case, in which an American academic had recorded Israeli pathologist Dr. Yehuda Hiss saying he performed "organ harvesting." Not a native English speaker, Hiss credulously uses the term introduced by his interrogator, a rather persistently anti-Zionist academic from Berkeley.

To make sense of all this, one must note the contrast with the kidney, liver, heart, etc. that are desperately needed by patients with failing organs. After a qualified donor has died, the organ of interest, say the kidney, must be extracted under sterile conditions and properly refrigerated and handled. Tests must be performed on the organ for infection such as HIV and for blood type and other antigens to establish a match with the prospective recipient. If rapidly refrigerated, the organ remains viable for about two days but deteriorates as the hours pass.

It takes only a little bit of attention to realize that what Hiss was referring to was the removal not of organs but of skin samples, heart valves, and corneas from the corpses of about 125 cadavers for transfer to medical facilities. His words caused a shock in Israel's orthodox community, since the removal of body parts is generally religiously prohibited. And clearly he did not seek informed consent. Obviously of a secular or anticlerical bent, Hiss seemed proud that he was disregarding mere religious strictures to help patients recover eyesight or recover from burns or to help provide anatomical samples by which to train medical students. In his only nod to concern about consent, Hiss claimed that for each cadaver he had permission for an autopsy.

In autopsies around the world, a medical examiner typically snips apart organs and vessels, weighs and examines them, and then either puts them back in the body cavity in some order or just incinerates them. Since the body tissue has already been scrambled and respect for the body's integrity already undermined, a morgue worker may not think it too much of an ethical jump to then send off some of the tissue for medical use.

Some reports indicate that Hiss's rogue operation charged for these items. Contrary to scandal-mongering in both the Israeli religious press and in the anti-Zionist outpourings that gleefully exploited it, the prices quoted in the report resemble interhospital transfer fees, far below black market prices found in the world organ trade. Moreover, such removal of corneas and other tissue was then legal in many places. According to reporting in 2006, twenty-eight US states had "presumed consent" laws by which certain tissue, such as corneas and heart valves, can be taken from cadavers without explicit consent, often by funeral homes.[13] By those states' standards, Hiss's actions would not even have been illegal.

The interviewer tries hard to get Hiss to say he is involved in the removal of more interesting organs. Thinking her to be his admirer for his progressive rescuing of items for medical use, Hiss tries to be helpful. Maybe she can find something of the sort in Russia, he suggests. He assumes that the interviewer must know what to anyone with medical training is obvious: it would be deadly to take an organ from a corpse in a morgue and transplant it into a living human body. The morgue is far too unsanitary, the corpses have lain too long, the organ would likely have deteriorated and died, and the medical systems would be missing.

The Israel-hating blog *CounterPunch*, which published the transcript, now takes the necessary next step: it inserts next to Hiss's statement about removing corneas from Oriental patients the square-bracketed term *Arabs*. One needs only passing familiarity with Israelis of Hiss's generation to know that they have not read Edward Said and instead use the word to mean "Oriental Jews," as the adjoining discussion of funerary ritual makes clear—the context discussed Sephardic customs of putting sand into the eyes of the deceased. Nonetheless, the damage was done: Israel-hating propagandists would now widely claim that Hiss had confirmed the *Aftonbladet* report on the murder of Palestinians for the theft of their organs.

UB professor James Holstun's message of February 3, 2011, takes the same tack: "There was an explosion of charges of 'blood libel' after a Swedish newspaper ran an article claiming that Israeli medical personal [*sic*] were stealing organs for transplant from the bodies of Palestinians. But the claim was true, as Dr. Yehuda Hiss, the Israeli organ thief, confirmed [there follows an internet link]." Since the Swedish article claimed purposeful killing for the sake of organ theft, Holstun seems to depict Hiss's statements about his waylaying of anatomical tissue as admission that murder for organ theft actually took place.

Imaginatively combining both the organ-theft blood libel and the Jew-is-Nazi slur, New York City *Indymedia*, a mouthpiece for the radical Left, titled its report on the Hiss affair as "Dr. Mengele Work Continues in Israel." It showed a doctored photograph of a tile-walled clinic, in which a man in a doctor's coat stands in front of an operating table. We are told by the caption that he represents Mengele. He is putting on rubber gloves, evidently getting ready to abuse a shriveled patient cowering under him on the table. A Star of David is prominently displayed on the clinic wall. Boston *Indymedia* ran a variation on the Haitian organ-theft libel. Both articles were reposted at numerous politically sympathetic sites.

By 2010, the internet literary magazine *Camera Obscura* brought the blood libel full circle: it claimed child murder. The magazine awarded a prize to Elaine Chiew's story about little Ahmed, narrated as if from Ahmed's brother's point of view. Shot for throwing fireworks on the street, Ahmed is "flown out, across the wire, to a hospital in Haifa." We now switch scenes to a little boy named Aviv, evidently Jewish, whose heart condition won't let him live past ten. Sure enough, he receives a new heart, from the source we immediately guess at, and his tongue soon erupts in foreign words, like *Muassalam* in Arabic. "This is what comes from accepting a contaminated goyim heart, the father yells." Yes, Ahmed's heart is now in Aviv, his liver in a fifty-seven-year-old Israeli woman, and his kidney in someone else. The brother-narrator ends that he would, if he could, write a message with Arab street boys' spilled blood, would write it for Ahmed over and over, "Don't forget me. I am everywhere."[14]

There you have it: in one story, the innocent Palestinian child's body plundered; in another, cackling Mephisophelean Doctor Hiss; in each, a Nazi-Jew doctor who plucks out still-beating hearts to give monstrous new life to a Zionist Jew. A ghastly tale, a modern blood libel, somehow gracing an allegedly academic mailing list.

Tissue Trade and Double Standards

I began by referring to Bernard Lewis's definition of *antisemitism*, as the attribution to Jews of cosmic evil, and one more matter, which I would now like to take a few paragraphs to illustrate: the holding of Jews to standards that apply to no other, even by the educated and the academic elites, who surely ought to know better. How has the world responded to cases outside Israel in which body parts were, to variously unethical or illegal extents, diverted from cadavers in autopsies to labs or medical facilities?

Take the discovery in the early 2000s at Liverpool's Alder Hey Children's Hospital. According to investigators, hospital personnel had removed, stored, and transferred body parts from 850 infants, without authorization or family permission. The Alder Hey scandal led to the discovery of more abuses nationwide. Examining such cases, the *Medical Law Review* reported in 2005 that there had been tens of thousands such cases in Britain, where tissue was used for "transplantation, research, drug testing, clinical audit, cell-line development and trade."[15]

In the authors' words in *Medical Law Review*, the "54,000 organs, body parts, stillborns, and fetuses that were retained between 1970 and 2001 are just a small proportion of the total quantity of stored tissue specimens in the U. K."[16] The numbers far exceeded anything ever reported for Israel—by orders of magnitude. It may even be speculated that some of the displaced body parts in Britain belonged to Irish persons, since the period of abuse coincided with the Northern Ireland troubles. Other organs may have come from minority Britons or third world immigrants.

Al Jazeera, which made many of the allegations about Israel, failed to find the topic important enough to report on. The *Guardian* did report in 2005 but was matter of fact about it. It did not use the provocative term *organ harvesting*, with which it described Israeli practices.

In Britain, this turned out to be an episodic scandal, because on December 19, 2009, it flared up again. Despite the tightened regulations, British authorities were discovering more postautopsy bodies with missing organs. In some, the brains had been misplaced or removed at mortuaries and pathology labs, for reasons not made clear. Although the *Guardian* would report just one week later on Israel's ten-year-old Yehuda Hiss case, it found this story unnewsworthy. The antisemitic MP George Galloway took up space in a Scottish newspaper to compare what was by then fantastically mythologized Israeli actions to Auschwitz but for the far larger events much closer to home—by what I have been able to find—had no comment.[17]

In the United States, the National Organ Transplant Act of 2006 prohibits commercial transactions for human organs and tissue in interstate commerce. But the author of one of the most detailed law reviews of the subject writes that the prohibition is largely illusory. He asserts with multiple citations that "hospitals, organ procurement organizations, medical schools, coroners, and crematoriums are all sources of human tissue trade." And consent may be illusory: "Hospitals, for example, may condition treatment on a patient waiving her right to recover or destroy her tissue, including placentas."[18]

Even in the countries with the finest medical systems, namely Britain, the United States, and Israel, there is a netherworld of anatomical parts daily generated in medical facilities, anatomical parts demanded but unavailable in other branches of the same facilities or elsewhere, and various illicit, intermittent, and shadowy operations to match one to the other. This trade comes to light occasionally in these countries thanks to their free press, which extracts from them their full potential for scandal, after which they melt away again. What goes on in countries with less systematized medical establishments and media less open to broadcasting public scandal, we can just suspect.

What we do know is that those alleged scholars who find themselves aghast at a long-ago incident in an Israeli morgue seem to have no curiosity about much more extensive incidents around the world. And when such events are exposed, as at a facility in Britain, no one concludes that Britons and Britishness are thereby cosmically accused. Yet when it's Israelis? The global literati transmogrifies them into organ-plundering demons, and the professors follow suit.

Anti-Zionism at the Repulsive Extreme

There is a specter haunting the university. It appears more frequently at California universities but finds its way to campuses all over, even to my town, Buffalo. There it is at the boycott rally, the atrocity lecture, the global justice discussion group, the academic mailing list. It's the Zionist/Jew-as-Nazi, the Jew-dressed-as-Christian-to-kill-Muslims, and the Jew-as-murderer/organ-thief—the cosmic evildoer come back to haunt us, on campuses of all places, which is where, you would hope, the power of rationality and critical thinking would make it decidedly unwelcome.

Yes, it is just an ugly superstition. For anyone with a modicum of research capability, and even for someone like me educated in urban planning, it doesn't take much investigation or clarity of mind to debunk it. As with a sighting of an alien, however, to show it to be bunk is a more painstaking, detailed, and boring exercise than to originally claim it. It is far more memorable to accuse Israelis of being organ thieves than to trace ridiculously misleading newspaper citations, present data on the excellence and ethics of Israeli medicine, find details of a decades-old court-martial, or explain the medical inadvisability of organ transplant after bacterial growth in body cavities. It takes some added effort that the modicum of wrongdoing in Israel's minor scandal is outweighed by far larger incidents of similar kinds around the world, yet those elicit little or no comparable fury.

Israel's moral stand must be rather good, if her enemies would assault her with accusations so fatuous that any researcher of modest abilities can reveal them to be nonsense. That would be consolation, however, only if we could be sure that the university would remain the institution through which reasoned researchers disrupt the spread of nonsense. The evidence now is that we cannot be sure. That these irrational extremes are celebrated on campus is a sign, not just of fanatical hatred spreading among students and faculty, but of the university's inability to resist it—of the university's intellectual debasement, its corruption as an institution of higher learning.

In search of conclusions, let me return to the Finkelstein 2004 event that for me both started it and epitomizes it all, because it is what first woke me from the comfortable slumber under which I had until then lived my academic life. I was shocked awake, literally. It became one of the few nights in my life when I was so agitated I could not sleep at all. While my children slept, I paced the living room.

No doubt my reaction occurred in part because of what I knew of my parents' experiences in western Romania and the experiences of grandparents, uncles, aunts, and cousins whom I would never get to meet. Even in the years preceding the Holocaust, as I had heard from those most dear to me, odious claims about Jews were common parlance, and a simple train ride could, for a Jew, turn into mortal danger from those who had internalized the vile beliefs and bloodcurdling tales about Jewish perfidy. That the Jews of Nagyvárad were forced to wear the yellow star, made to live in a fenced-in ghetto, and then one day in 1944, ordered to the train station at gunpoint and shipped for three days with no food to arrive at Auschwitz had its origins in virulent, bigoted speech not at all dissimilar to what I was hearing on my own campus.

There was a further reason for my agitation. I could already, by that night listening to Finkelstein, sense that slurs, when accepted on campus as if they were an intellectually defensible position—indeed as claims that would somehow contribute to global justice—undermine an entire framework of belief. I had believed in knowledge cultivated through a lifetime of academic training, in academic colleagues' good faith in the search for knowledge, and in the campus as a bastion of intelligent dialogue. Like many in academia, I was a perspectivist of sorts; I made a practice of treating others' positions respectfully, or at least tactfully, on the expectations of some reciprocity and the hope that perspectives in dialogue would lead to a better and fuller view.

But the specters of Israelis turning into Aryans, the Israeli general compared to Eichmann, the Jews masquerading as Christians to kill Muslims, the murderers for organ theft—these are a crock. A slur, lie, or fabrication is not a perspective; it is the obscurer of perspective, the crusher of dialogue, the defeater of knowledge.

Like many of us who had gone through the gauntlets of PhD defense, scholarly publishing, and the tenure process, I was also used to intellectual modesty and to public self-effacement. It was my habit of mind. With academic colleagues, I just wanted to get along and receive some little regard for accomplishment in the intellectual fields in which I had specialized. The world was complex, my knowledge puny. I was wary of stating opinions about topics, such as Israeli politics or transplant medicine, in which I was not educated. But in the face of fanatical hate speech, my inclination to be self-effacing seemed like an escape from the moral obligation to speak.

By morning, I managed at least to pull together a letter of protest to the campus paper; indeed, it is with reference to that letter that I draw my recollections of that night.[19] I was also on my way to a small measure of understanding. I started realizing that the explanation for the slurs was already there, in the ugly meeting in which I witnessed them.

Take the Jew-is-Nazi claim. In our time, the secular representation of evil is the Nazi. The claim adds marvelously to the repertoire of accusations against Jews, since it defiles Jews with the greatest crime committed against them and makes the memory of that crime a form of oppression against all those who suffer the world's evils. Not least, it allows intellectuals to wallow in ancient hatred while dressing themselves as the most progressive of humanitarians. To the very many in the world, and especially to many students, who seek answers for the world's miseries, how satisfying it must be to find it in the ugly fellow, the Zionist Jew.

It took me some time to understand the Jew-is-Nazi trope's appeal to the group that assembled that night in 2004. It is the same that appeals to all Boycott, Divestment, and Sanctions (BDS) campaigns, Apartheid Weeks, and similar Israel hatefests on all the campuses. For motley Marxists and self-proclaimed pacifists, crusading humanitarians, disoriented Arab and Muslim youth, intellectuals besotted by opaque theory, and confused students seeking answers to diverse disgruntlements, the appeal is in the thrill of solidarity achieved through the identification of the cosmic enemy. It is this world-unifying feature of the Jew-is-Nazi slur that gives it its power to overcome reason, overturn history, and inspire malice.

Hence my lesson from that evening. Zionists as Nazis, Zionists as harvesters of Palestinian organs for transplant into Jews, Zionists as the imminent destroyers of the world, Zionists as controllers of government and media, Zionists as destroyers of the World Trade Center, Zionists as secret puppeteers of ISIS, Zionists as inhumane mass killers—these should not be treated as if they were ordinary claims, to be answered with argument, evidence, and reason. They are something else entirely.

They are solidarity-building rituals of execration, and they must be understood, and exposed, as such.[20]

Those of us who care not only about justice for Israel in the face of global hatred but also about the safeguarding of reasoned debate in the university cannot allow ourselves to retreat to our old habits of restraint. The academic world is under assault, from the inside. In answer to malicious slurs against a people depicted as a collective evil, our moral task is to step outside our zones of comfort, beyond the topics in which we have been educated and beyond limited roles to which we have confined ourselves as specialized academics, to publicly expose and denounce the fanatical movements that are subverting the university.

It is time we speak.

ERNEST STERNBERG is Professor of Urban and Regional Planning at the University at Buffalo. His usual topics of research are planning theory, history of planning thought, regional economic development, disaster planning, and infrastructure planning. The last of these is the topic of his recent book, with George C. Lee, *Bridges: Their Engineering and Planning.*

Notes

1. Bernard Lewis, *Semites and Antisemites: An Inquiry into Conflict and Prejudice* (New York: W.W. Norton, 1999), 129 and 194.

2. Don Atapattu, "How to Lose Friends and Alienate People," *CounterPunch* (December 13, 2001), http://www.counterpunch.org/2001/12/13/how-to-lose-friends-and-alienate-people/.

3. David Stone, "Has Israel Damaged Palestinian Health?" *Fathom* (Autumn 2014), http://fathomjounral.org.

4. Reported by several sources, Finkelstein's pronouncement "NAZI PHDs FOR PEACE Mourn Death of *Übermenschen*" was on Finkelstein's website but is no longer posted. Sources that refer to it include Heribert Schiedel, "Norman Finkelstein in Vienna? – Open

Letter to the Rector of the University of Vienna," Scholars for Peace in the Middle East (May 14, 2009), http://spme.org/news-from-the-middle-east/norman-finkelstein-in-vienna -open-letter-to-the-rector-of-the-university-of-vienna/6853/, and Gary Fouse, "Norman Finklestein Posting on a Terror Attack in Israel," *Fousesquawk* (March 26, 2009), http:// garyfouse.blogspot.com/2009/03/norman-finklestein-posting-on-terror.html.

5. Jim Holstun and Irene Morrison, "'We Will Have to Kill Them All': Effie Eitam, Thug Messiah," *The Electronic Intifada* (November 25, 2009), https://electronicintifada.net/content /we-will-have-kill-them-all-effie-eitam-thug-messiah/8555.

6. I wrote a little exposé: "Trafficking in Slurs: Buffalo Professor and Peace Activist Incite Antisemitism," *SPME Faculty Voices* (March 2, 2010).

7. I should say that after the evening I depict, I wrote a letter of complaint to the chair of the English department. She expressed anger that one or more faculty members had used the department's name without her or her faculty's permission to organize the event. However, she declined to publicly condemn or apologize for the event. The department remains on the record as a cosponsor.

8. None of the many encyclopedia entries I consulted, not even the ones whose antagonism to Israel was transparent, said that Israelis masqueraded as Phalangists. Nor did Rashid Khalidi, author of *Under Siege: PLO Decisionmaking During the 1982 War* (New York: Columbia University Press, 1986), although he was no friend of Israel and had extensive access to people on the ground and to PLO documents and leaders.

9. Ernest Sternberg, "Israelis Dressed up as Christian Militiamen to Kill Palestinians! A New Blood Libel Debuts at the State University of New York at Buffalo," *SPME Faculty Voices* (February 2, 2011).

10. Andrea Levin, "Anatomy of a Swedish Blood Libel," *The Wall Street Journal* (October 14, 2009), http://www.wsj.com/articles/SB10001424052748704107204574470712953449876.

11. Andrea Meyerhoff, "Israel Organ Harvesting Scandal 'Medically Impossible,'" *Local: Sweden's News in English* (August 31, 2009), http://www.thelocal.se/20090831/21798.

12. See William A. Jacobson, "Vassar Faculty-Sponsored Anti-Israel Event Erupts in Controversy," *Legal Insurrection* (February 8, 2016), http://legalinsurrection.com /2016/02/vassar-faculty-sponsored-anti-israel-event-erupts-in-controversy/.

13. Michele Goodwin, *Black Markets: The Supply and Demand for Body Parts* (UK: Cambridge University Press, 2006), 16.

14. Elaine Chiew, "Brother Heart," *Camera Obscura Journal* (January 2010), http://www .obscurajournal.com/bridge-Elaine-Chiew.php.

15. Kathleen Liddell and Alison Hall, "Beyond Bristol and Alder Hey: The Future Regulation of Human Tissue," *Medical Law Review* 13 (Summer 2005), p. 175.

16. Kathleen Liddell and Alison Hall, "Beyond Bristol and Alder Hey: The Future Regulation of Human Tissue," *Medical Law Review* 13 (Summer 2005), p. 175.

17. George Galloway, *Daily Record* (December 28, 2009).

18. Michele Goodwin, "Empires of the Flesh: Tissue and Organ Taboos," *Alabama Law Review* 60, no. 5 (2009): 1219–1248, 1234–1235.

19. Ernest Sternberg, "Finkelstein Speech Criticized," *Reporter* 35, no. 33 (May 6, 2004): 5.

20. I have expanded on this logic elsewhere. See Ernest Sternberg, "The Origin of Globalized Anti-Zionism: A Conjuncture of Hatreds Since the Cold War," *Israel Affairs* 21, no. 1 (2015): 1–17; and "Purifying the World: What the New Radical Ideology Stands For," *Orbis* 54 (Winter 2010): 61–86.

24 What Is It Like to Be an (Assertive) Israeli Academic Abroad?

Elhanan Yakira

Elhanan Yakira, an Israeli philosopher, documents the growing refusal of
the academy to engage even with the moderate Zionist Left. Demonstrators
prevented him from speaking in Paris, American scholars refused to read
an essay of his even though they had assembled for that purpose, and the
nongovernmental organization (NGO) Oxfam concluded it was not "ready,
or ripe, to meet and talk to an Israeli mainstream—namely, not anti- or
post-Zionist—intellectual." Yakira describes meeting with Israeli graduate
students studying in Europe who were too intimidated to speak up for Israel
on their campuses. Yakira's book *Post-Zionism, Post-Shoah: Three Essays on
Denial, Repression, and Delegitimation of Israel* led to a vigorous conversation
in Israel about the relationship between anti-Zionism and Holocaust denial
but has been all but ignored abroad. The silencing of Israel's voice, of any
unapologetic Israeli voice including those on the Left, according to Yakira,
is an "outrage" meriting "the most explicit denouncement" by those of
conscience—but for now appears to be a victory for the anti-Israelists.

A FEW YEARS ago, I published a book in which I tried to undermine the intellectual
and/or moral pretensions of the then so-called post-Zionists and to show, as it
were, that the emperor had no clothes.[1] At the time, post-Zionism was a name
given to a set of ideas or maybe of discursive practices common to a group of
Israeli intellectuals who pretended to question the hegemonic Zionist narrative.
In fact, some of the post-Zionists simply denied the moral, political, ideological, and historical pertinence of Zionism. In other words, they cast a generalized
suspicion on the idea of a Jewish state, as well, of course, on the state itself. In the
years that passed since the publication of this book, many things have changed.
The particular post-Zionist group I was talking about has more or less dissolved,
and its messages have been marginalized. Many of its leaders have left the country, and even those who remained are more active outside Israel than inside it.
They talk, it seems, more to audiences in California, New York, Paris, Berlin, or
London and are also more listened to there. Some of its members participate in

Boycott, Divestment, and Sanctions (BDS) or other anti-Israeli campaigns and contribute to its legitimation in ways reminiscent of the useful idiots of twentieth-century Communists. While the more straightforward anti-Zionist discourse seems to have migrated to Europe and the United States, the critical discourse inside Israel has camouflaged into a pseudo-theoretical discourse about the one-state solution. Based on a mixture of ideological and allegedly pragmatic claims, the extreme Right and Left meet here in a common rejection of the two-state solution. For some, it is the divine promise of the entire Land of Israel or the refusal of the Palestinians to reach a reasonable compromise; for others, it is the expiry of the nation-states era or the irreversibility of the settlements project. In both cases, it amounts to a denial of the right for self-determination—either of the Palestinians or the Jews.[2] By and large, however, post-Zionist discourse has transformed itself into being less ideological and more political. It is now more anti-occupation than anti-Zionist, directed against Israeli conduct and policies rather than against the basic premises of the original Zionist claim for the establishment of a Jewish state in Eretz Yisrael. What distinguishes it from other forms of criticism is the double tendency to demonize Israel and to hold it as the sole party responsible for the lamentable—described often as catastrophic—condition of the Palestinians.

When *Post-Zionism, Post-Shoah* first appeared in Israel, it provoked a small, but heated, controversy. It coincided with the gradual fading and marginalization of the older post-Zionist subculture. There were some very harsh attacks but also a considerable amount of support. In fact, this book is still alive in Israel. In sharp contrast to Israel, its reception in both the Anglophone and the Francophone worlds has been a kind of nonreception. It was indeed met with a rather general silence. Besides a couple of reviews (mostly positive) in internet journals and a very negative one in an academic printed journal (there may, of course, be more), to the best of my knowledge, no one took heed of it. To give a fuller picture, I should add that the book seems to have made a certain progress and to have acquired a certain presence below the surface, but its audience apparently consisted mainly of readers inclined to pro-Israeli and anti-BDS attitudes. Outside this rather small circle of sympathizers, I met a refusal to hear my voice, which is probably more a paradigmatic than personal matter. I shall come back to it at the end of this essay.

The refusal to hear an Israeli voice can assume different forms—from violent attempts to blow up public discussions and debates to the very polite, the very (politically) correct and academic dismissal. Since I have become, after the publication of my book, an active player in the public debate about Israel, I can tell about my own experience. Here are a couple of examples. A few years ago, I was invited to participate in a roundtable in the most prestigious French institute of higher education, the École Normale Supérieure in Paris. The topic was

"What Is Zionism?" Upon my arrival, it was immediately clear that something unpleasant was about to happen—on the sidewalks leading to the building we could see some blatant anti-Israel graffiti, and in the hall, there were very few people waiting, among them two very visible, huge security agents. The moment the person chairing the panel (a professor of political philosophy from the Sorbonne) began to talk, a group of youngsters rose up and began to shout slogans such as "Israel murderer," "Child murderer," "Away with Israel!" and more. The youngsters—they all looked to me younger than twenty years old—were visibly organized. Three or four older ones, scattered in the hall, silently orchestrated the show, which lasted some three-quarters of an hour. The group then left, leaving almost no time and certainly no will for conducting a civilized and fruitful discussion.

Evidently I, as the only Israeli participant, was the target and my presence there the cause of this rather ridiculous and pathetic show. There was no violence in the air, no real passion, and despite the extreme language used and the fact that the small shouting band succeeded in preventing the discussion, at no point did any of us, on the podium or in the hall, feel menaced. The kids—belonging to some leftist group and probably taking themselves to be revolutionaries—looked quite docile and even sweet. It was much less frightening than other such events lately reported from campuses in the United States, United Kingdom, or elsewhere. And yet, the event was not only unpleasant and distasteful but also significant, and beneath its apparent harmlessness, there was much that deserves attention. Thus, during the forty-five minutes I was sitting idle looking at what was going on before me, I could not help thinking that there was something familiar in it, a kind of *déjà vu*. There were a number of young men (also women) in the audience, but none of them moved. The security agents also did not move, only regarded, visibly quite amused, the event unfolding in front of them. The bottom line: mission was accomplished, and an Israeli professor was denied the possibility to speak at the most respected of French educational institutes. The revolutionaries had their way, and no one stood up to protest, let alone throw them out.[3] Not less, perhaps more, significant is the fact that the event received almost no attention outside the room. Besides a very polite, but also subdued, personal letter of apology I received from the director of the establishment, the school did not find the event worthy of more public reaction.

Silencing an unwelcome voice can be done in more subtle ways as well. Shortly after the publication of *Post-Zionism, Post-Holocaust*'s English version, a colleague, a professor at an important American university, concerned and dismayed by the vicious anti-Israeli atmosphere on his campus, invited me to a couple of encounters with faculty, students, and others at his university. The first meeting was organized by Jewish studies and was, as expected, rather pleasant. The next day, however, I was invited to appear before a small discussion group consisting of faculty from different departments, destined to discuss issues linked to the Arab-Israeli conflict. The few members of this group were supposed to read an article distributed in advance, discuss it briefly, and then discuss with me a chapter from my own book. The meeting was polite and calm, but after a short while, it became clear that the members of the group had no intention of listening to me. The article they read was written by the notorious anti-Zionists Daniel and Jonathan Boyarin and contained an apology of Neturei Karta and, especially, of their anti-Zionism.[4] It was also evident that, not surprisingly, none of the participants, including, notably, the woman charged with presenting the article and leading the discussion, had the slightest idea of what they were talking about—of either the group itself or of the stakes of its ideology—let alone giving it anything resembling a critical reading. They were, for example, quite surprised when I explained to them that the ultra-orthodox community in Israel, of which the Neturei Karta are the most extreme sect, is, on the whole, the most hateful of Arabs, among the Jews of Israel. This, however, was more or less the only thing I was allowed to say, and the planned discussion of my criticism of post- and anti-Zionism never materialized.

When we were about to leave the room, everyone still very polite and correct, one of the participants approached me and very silently, practically whispering, told me that she was completely on my side but that she felt she was not in a position to intervene. If I understood her correctly, she was afraid. I believe no further comment is needed.

My exposure to anti-Zionist closed-mindedness actually came before my book appeared. Some fifteen or more years ago, I chaired the philosophy department of Hebrew University. A graduate student in our department, who was (and still is) a central figure in human rights, anti-occupation, and other so-called leftist NGOs, approached me with an odd request from Oxfam, the antihunger organization. Oxfam has its headquarter in an Arab village near Jerusalem. It also has a website titled "Oxfam in the Occupied Territories and in Israel," although the organization in this part of the world directs its aid exclusively to Palestinians, even though there is no hunger in the West Bank. (Palestinian standard of living and life expectancy, at least in the West Bank, have been rising consistently since 1967.) Oxfam, like most other NGOs, devotes considerable resources to the Palestinian cause. The student told me that the people of Oxfam decided they wanted to meet some mainstream Israeli and try to understand such a person's views on the Arab-Israeli conflict in general. He suggested to them meeting the chair of the philosophy department of Hebrew University, on the face of it, not a fanatic, racist, Arab hater. He thus asked me if I would meet them. Of course, said I. They will call you, said he, and will fix a date and place. Sure thing. Days go on, and no one calls. After a while, I asked the intermediary, "What happened?" Visibly embarrassed, he explained to me that the heads of the Oxfam bureau in

Israel (or Palestine) decided they were not yet (sic!) ready, or ripe, to meet and talk to an Israeli mainstream—namely, not anti- or post-Zionist—intellectual. Again, no commentary seems to me to be needed.

But the Oxfam people do meet non-Arab Israelis and talk to them. The man who acted as an intermediary between them and me is one example. As happens to many activists in such NGOs, this young man has become very quickly an international figure, contributing in different ways to the Israel-bashing campaigns. Indeed, Israelis participating in BDS or demonization-delegitimization campaigns are not rare. Our intermediary does not consider himself anti-Zionist but a true Israeli patriot. But his acceptance as a valid interlocutor by the Oxfam people is probably conditioned upon his relentless activity in various anti-occupation and human rights groups, which often play an important role, willingly or not, in the anti-Israel campaigns. Among the less-than-small number of their activists, many of them have become rather well-paid professionals, not only valid interlocutors for organizations like Oxfam, but also welcome guests in all kinds of institutions abroad, academic or otherwise. Not all Israelis, however, are so comfortable outside their country, especially students in Western universities. The adviser of a graduate student at another important American university, working on a PhD in political philosophy, suggested to her to avoid talking too much about Israel, especially if she felt she wanted to defend it. This message, explicit and more often implicit, is what many Israeli students are receiving during their years of study abroad.

A couple of years ago, I was asked by a group of such students, studying different disciplines at different institutions in London and in its vicinity, to talk to them about the delegitimization issue. I told them, in essence, not much more than that they should not be ashamed of being Israelis and that they could be critical of certain, even many, aspects of their government's policies or their country's conduct without being frightened into some generalized guilt about the essence, as it were, of their being Israeli. There was nothing either very original or profound in this talk. The reaction of the audience, however, was quite amazing. Most of the young people who attended this meeting were deeply moved, thanking me, sometimes practically with tears in their eyes, for conveying this (rather banal, I think) message: do not be ashamed to be Israelis. Your Israeliness is not a human or moral stain.

Many of the young Israelis who study in Europe and North America enjoy their years abroad. Some would settle there. But they all share the same experience: better not be too explicit about your support of Israel or, rather, better not be too loud about your opposition to the delegitimization and/or demonization of your country. The reactions to this message vary considerably; some would keep quiet, some would resist, others would join the party, but all live, insofar they are Israelis, in a hostile environment.

To conclude, I wish to return to my opening remarks about the reception—or nonreception—of my book outside Israel. As someone told me some time ago, we—Israelis, Jews, defenders of Israel and of Zionism—apparently speak mainly to ourselves. Most people have other matters to deal with, know very little or next to nothing about the history of the Middle East, and understand even less its present. Besides this "we," those who are interested in Israel (or rather Palestine) are quite often the very committed anti-Israel crowd. The interest some of them show looks sometimes like an obsession. More often than not, they would be immune to the kinds of argument their adversaries bring forward.

Along the silencing, rejection, and refusal exemplified in the anecdotes told above, there is one more thing I should mention here. I think that my experience as an author may be of some significance. As I mentioned above, there was nothing on my book in the printed press. I received, mostly on a personal basis, quite a few positive reactions to my book. Some of them were even surprisingly so, but the public scene was mute. So far, nothing worth mentioning. What is, however, less trivial is the fact that a couple of journals that share the general outlook, or can be considered allies, of what is called in Israel the Zionist Left and that, on the face of it, should have found an interest in the messages contained in the book actually refused to publish reviews of it.

I define my own political position as roughly that of this Zionist Left. Neither the Oxfam people, nor the learned professors of the important American university, nor the Parisian pathetic little revolutionaries know anything about this, and if they do, they do not care. Two fundamental elements of the Zionist Left's political outlook have to be emphasized here: *Zionist* refers to the belief that the establishment and the continued existence of Israel as a Jewish state is fully justifiable—from moral, humane, historical, political, and geostrategic points of view. *Left* refers to the firm conviction that the so-called two-state solution—namely, the creation of a Palestinian state alongside the Jewish state—is the only acceptable solution, again, morally, historically, politically, and strategically.

What may have caused the refusal to publish anything concerning my book? I have been asking myself this question ever since I found out about it. My personal feelings aside, given the big difference between this shyness on the one hand and the animated discussions that still take place in Israel around it on the other, one may wonder if there may not be here something more general, even paradigmatic, but also more significant and, indeed, disquieting. One reason for the reticence to deal publicly with my book may have been its very polemic and straightforward not politically correct style. My guess, however, is that not less important is its utterly nonapologetic nature. Such a nonapologetic voice may be hard to accept, even for many friends of Israel. Can this fact—if this is indeed the case—be considered as at least a partial victory of the attempt to silence us? I am not convinced. The culture of silencing Israel's voice, as exemplified in the cases I wrote about here, is an outrage. Those doing the silencing deserve nothing but the most explicit denouncement. Facing the demonization of Israel with any kind of apologetics or with semi-complicity with its alleged critique is not only countereffective, it is also immoral.

ELHANAN YAKIRA is Professor Emeritus in the Department of Philosophy of Hebrew University of Jerusalem. His main fields of interest and work have been early modern philosophy and, in more recent years, twentieth-century phenomenology and French thought and political philosophy. He is the author of numerous scholarly articles and a number of scholarly books, including *Post-Zionism, Post-Shoah: Three Essays on Denial, Repression, and Delegitimation of Israel.*

Notes

1. *Post-Zionism, Post-Shoah: Three Essays on Denial, Repression, and Delegitimation of Israel* (in Hebrew) (Tel Aviv: Am Oved, 2006). The book was later translated, with considerable revisions, into English and French, under the same title by Cambridge University Press in 2009 and Presses Universitaires de France in 2010.

2. As Doron S. Ben-Atar commented to me personally on this point, "A very important transformation has taken place [. . . and] Human Rights discourse has replaced self-determination as the utopian ideal." Talking of the latter may thus look like belonging to an already obsolete discourse, not relevant anymore in our allegedly postnational era. Without getting into any discussion of this matter, I would only remark here that respecting the right of the two peoples sharing the territory between the Mediterranean and the Jordan River for self-determination is the only way of ensuring human rights to all concerned in this territory as well.

3. Actually one man, a well-known Jewish journalist, tried to silence the shouting kids and then left the hall in anger and disgust.

4. The Neturei Karta (literally, the Guardians of the City) is an extremely orthodox group, in fact fundamentalist. It is known for its venomous anti-Zionism and hatred of Israel, which they conceive as a work of Satan. One of their members served for a while as a minister for Jewish affairs in the Palestinian Authority; a few participated in the Holocaust deniers' convention in Teheran in 2005. It is hard to think of an ideology more opposed to anything that falls under the title of "human rights." Undoubtedly, the only thing that can make the Neturei Karta of any interest to the brothers Boyarin is their hope for the demise of the State of Israel.

II. Students' Essays

25   A Wake-Up Call at the University of Michigan

Jesse Arm

In the middle of campus, pro-Palestinian activists erected a large mock separation wall decorated with slogans and images glorifying Palestinian violence and calling for the destruction of Israel. Jesse Arm, a student government representative, debated the protesters and suggested they organize together a joint event expressing solidarity against the violence on both sides. Instead, the pro-Palestinian students launched a public campaign to remove him from office, replete with assaults on his character. A student government investigation eventually cleared him of the bogus charges brought against him, but the incident sent a clear message to others: challenging the anti-Israel position will bring personal attack and university procedures to silence dissent.

The Incident

On Thursday, November 19, 2015, two terror attacks occurred in Israel,[1] in the early days of what would become a months-long terror spree called by some the Knife Intifada. The perpetrator of the second attack that day was a Palestinian man armed with an Uzi submachine gun. Among the three people he murdered was an American Jewish student studying abroad named Ezra Schwartz. Schwartz was a contemporary of mine, a member of my broader community with whom I shared many friends. He was abroad on a gap-year program that I seriously considered attending before deciding to enroll at the University of Michigan. His story was my story.

What happened to him could easily have happened to me.

On that same date, in the University of Michigan Diag (a large central area on campus), members of a group called Students Allied for Freedom and Equality (SAFE) were holding a demonstration. Although their name implies very general and ideal aims, in fact they are a Palestinian solidarity group whose Facebook page is filled primarily with anti-Israel information and events.[2] On that day, they stood costumed as Israeli soldiers next to a massive wall constructed with images of a dove being targeted by a sniper, Arabic writing across the entire map of Israel, a Palestinian flag, a depiction of a series of maps about Jewish land appropriation that some call The Map That Lies,[3] and the phrase "To Exist Is to RESIST" in enormous red letters.

I approached the protesters and objected to the use of that phrase in particular because I believe it to be a plainly regressive way of looking at the conflict no matter which side you are on. Resistance is a code word for violence. That much is plain to everyone. To exist should not be to resist but to coexist. To exist should be to dialogue. To compromise. To strive toward peace. To reject these values is to threaten lives on both sides of the struggle.

And these values, at the very least, are the ones that govern (or should govern) a university community, where individuals with very different interests, needs, and perspectives live and study together and try to get along.

I also felt that these protesters had co-opted a central campus location that should serve as a safe space for all Michigan students. I don't mean *safe space* in the sense that has been greatly targeted of late, such as "safe from different opinions." I mean *safe space* in the sense of civility and respect, a space where no one feels marginalized, much less directly threatened. And so I questioned the taste, timing, and appropriateness of a display that seemed to call for violence, to make violence an essential feature of one's being, in light of all the terrorism that had been inflicted on innocent civilians around the world over the prior few weeks and most of all in Israel.

Indeed, they were supporting and glorifying violence against Israel on the very day that Schwartz had been murdered by someone who believed in that same violence.

It was hard not to feel that they were supporting and glorifying Schwartz's murder.

That they would support and glorify my murder, for Schwartz's story could have been my story.

I specifically proposed an alternative to them. Instead of putting on their incendiary display portraying Israeli soldiers as terrorizers and instead of promoting the violence of resistance, they could use their time to hold a moment of silence along with pro-Israel student groups, expressing a solidarity against the violence that had taken too many lives on both sides. I then offered my phone number to their leader, to continue the conversation.

He told me he was uninterested in continuing a dialogue.

Instead, SAFE went to the Central Student Government (CSG), on which I serve, to call for my forced removal from the assembly on the basis of failing to be representative of their views as students.

The Investigation

Many of the members of CSG were absent that evening, as it was the last Tuesday evening meeting before Thanksgiving. The presence of pro-Israel representatives was particularly low. The first half of the meeting was dominated by members of SAFE making accusations regarding my "racist views," "blinding privilege," and physically threatening stature and sharing other anecdotes about the alleged mistreatment of Palestinians on campus and across the world. A couple of CSG members were persuaded to request an Ethics Committee investigation into my alleged misbehavior as a CSG representative.

This was to be the first Ethics Committee investigation in CSG history, despite the fact that CSG representatives had been arrested for protests and other questionable activities in the past.

Apparently my behavior—questioning, through dialogue, the decision of a student group to promote or glorify violence—merited an unprecedented ethical review.

The accusations that I had engaged in hate speech or any form of physical or verbal abuse were, of course, simply untrue. In fact, I believe that my actions constituted precisely the type of exchange to be desired from and expected of a representative of the student body. I disagreed with the decisions made by the student activists, and I voiced my concerns. I acted as a representative of students who felt marginalized or threatened by SAFE's public demonstration, which seemed to endorse and promote violence.

My actions came from my own place of hurt, as a Jewish student and supporter of Israel, and from the hurt felt by a sizable portion of my constituents. I was not merely angry but also saddened that my role as a student government representative was called into question by virtue of my opposition to a purposefully inflammatory protest. I hoped, as a member of student government and also as a person committed to reason and mutual civility, to pursue respectful dialogue with those who disagreed with me, and I hoped to serve as a model for students on both sides of this issue. I never wished to silence any members of SAFE, as much as I disagreed with their perspective. I only asked that they make their arguments in a fashion that was respectful and considerate to Jewish, Israeli, and other Zionist students.

It is also noteworthy that one of the participants in the SAFE demonstration was also a representative on CSG. That this person was not called up for an ethics investigation was remarkable, for clearly if it was potentially unethical for me, as a CSG representative, to challenge a student demonstration when my opinion might not represent the views of all students, then it was equally potentially unethical for another representative to participate in a demonstration that might not represent the views of all students.

The Ethics Committee interviewed multiple members of SAFE. Because I was denied a right to counsel during *my* interview—due to CSG regulations—I chose not to deviate from previously written remarks and not to answer any questions. I was pressed to name the CSG representative who took part in the

SAFE demonstration and to offer names of pro-Israel witnesses to the exchange in the Diag but did not feel as though doing either would be appropriate.

Fortunately, for me, there was a video available of the incident, which demonstrated that the charges against me were false.

The final report of the Ethics Committee concluded: "Representative Arm did not engage in unethical behavior or engage in conduct unbecoming of a representative."[4]

Further, to their credit, they acknowledged that had they had that video in the first place, they would never have brought the charges: "Speaker Betman and Ethics Chair Hislop chose to accept the ethical question before video of the confrontation was made available. A Representative of the Assembly posed the question, and after deliberating, Speaker Betman and Chair Hislop decided that the matter was worthy of an investigation. At the time, this action seemed appropriate. Video evidence of the incident called into question the need for a thorough investigation."

Reflections

No, the ethics charges should never have been brought.

Indeed, the implication that a student government representative must either shed all ideas or stop expressing them or that a basic requirement for CSG leadership would be either to have no ideas or simply to remain silent is inimical to the very idea of a free democracy. Isn't the very purpose of a campus demonstration to provoke thought and expression and dialogue about the issue in question? Or at least *shouldn't* that be the purpose of campus demonstrations? Wasn't I doing exactly what the demonstrators presumably were inviting me to do—looking at the display and having it evoke feelings and thoughts and subsequently dialogue?

Unless, perhaps, none of that was the purpose of the SAFE demonstration.

I am a fervent believer in political pluralism and freedom of speech. It is impossible that all members of CSG will please all students all the time. Some students will inevitably disagree with us and feel disdain for the decisions we make and the votes we take. The same is true of all democratically elected officials everywhere. To suggest that I am not suited to be a member of Michigan's CSG because of my opposition to SAFE's demonstration on the Diag, in the public center of campus, would be to undermine the core principles of democracy and pluralism on which the University of Michigan is grounded, not to mention our entire nation.

Nevertheless, at the meeting in which the Ethics Committee issued their decision in my favor, SAFE, along with CSG members who shared their ideology, immediately denounced the decision and began to inquire about the procedural route toward calling for my censure on some other basis.

For SAFE, taking up this battle was a win-win scenario. SAFE has been leading efforts, year after year, to have the University of Michigan divest from the State of Israel, dating back long prior to my own matriculation. My removal from the CSG would have brought SAFE one vote closer to achieving that divestment goal—not by the legitimate democratic process of persuading people on the basis of reason and evidence, but by simply removing the people who disagree with them.[5]

It seems to me that American college campuses are becoming extremely hostile places toward Israel and free speech generally. The American Jewish community, which has a strong propensity toward political liberalism, must ensure that it is not complacent on this issue. Jewish students simply do not fight for their cause with the same dedication and passionate intensity that pro-Palestinian students do. This is a reality that I have witnessed firsthand and have had confirmed by fellow pro-Israel advocates on other college campuses throughout the country.

I hope that my story will serve as a wake-up call for the American Jewish community about what is currently festering on college campuses. Influential alumni and students alike should not allow this assault on free speech to become the new campus norm. This battle must be taken up soon, now. If we cannot preserve the free exchange of ideas in our academic institutions, then we will lose the ability to foster the young minds of our future leaders in the most fundamental American values.

JESSE ARM, University of Michigan 2018, is majoring in political science and international studies with a focus in political economy and development and minoring in entrepreneurship.

Notes

1. Raoul Wootliff, "3 Killed, Several Wounded in Etzion Bloc Shooting Attack," *The Times of Israel* (November 19, 2015), http://www.timesofisrael.com/3-dead-several-wounded-in-etzion-bloc-shooting-attack/.

2. Students Allied for Freedom and Equality (SAFE), https://www.facebook.com/SAFEUmich/ (accessed November 3, 2017).

3. "The Map That Lies—and One That Doesn't," *Elder of Ziyon* (March 9, 2011), http://elderofziyon.blogspot.com/2011/03/map-that-lies-and-one-that-doesnt.html.

4. "Report of the Ethics Committee," https://csg.umich.edu/files/2015/CSG%20Ethics%20Committee%20Report%20on%20Representative%20Arm.pdf (accessed January 4, 2016).

5. In the fall of 2016, BDS was defeated at the University of Michigan for the tenth time, in response to which members of SAFE rejected overtures of dialogue from the pro-Israel

side: Lea Speyer, "Following BDS Defeat, Activists at U of Michigan Reject Outreach Efforts by Pro-Israel Peers, 'Normalization' With Jewish State," *The Algemeiner* (November 17, 2016), https://www.algemeiner.com/2016/11/17/following-bds-fail-activists-at-u-of-michigan -continue-to-reject-normalization-with-jewish-state-pro-israel-peers/. As this book went to press student activists were launching their eleventh effort at BDS, which finally succeeded: Shiri Moshe, "After 10 Defeats, Divestment Resolution Targeting Israel Passes at the University of Michigan," *The Algemeiner* (November 15, 2017), https://www.algemeiner .com/2017/11/15/after-10-defeats-divestment-resolution-targeting-israel-passes-at-university -of-michigan/.

26 On Leaving the University of California, Los Angeles, Due to Hostile and Unsafe Campus Climate

Milan Chatterjee

As the graduate student body president at the University of California, Los Angeles (UCLA), law student Milan Chatterjee saw the divisiveness of BDS campaigns elsewhere and wanted to spare the graduate student government from wasting hours over matters not directly relevant to campus life. His efforts to keep his administration neutral on BDS, neither endorsing nor rejecting it, were rewarded with a public smear campaign by anti-Israel activists and their own efforts to remove him from his elected position. UCLA administrators not only failed to defend him from that dishonest campaign but ultimately enabled and supported it. Chatterjee was forced to obtain legal representation and, after months of harassment, chose to leave the school. The Chatterjee case testifies that even those who try to stay above the fray are bullied by anti-Israel activists and sharply exposes the failures of administrators to ensure a safe campus climate for all.

August 24, 2016

VIA E-MAIL AND FEDEX
gblock@conet.ucla.edu
chancellor@ucla.edu
Chancellor Gene Block
University of California, Los Angeles
Chancellor's Office
Box 951405, 2147 Murphy Hall
Los Angeles, CA 90095-1405

RE: Leaving UCLA Due to Hostile and Unsafe Campus Climate

Dear Chancellor Block,

I write to inform you that I have decided to complete the final year of my UCLA School of Law program at a different institution. The hostile and unsafe campus environment I am facing at UCLA has left me with no choice but to move away from this university at great additional expense to me and my family.

Since November 2015, I have been relentlessly attacked, bullied, and harassed by BDS-affiliated organizations and students. The smear and harassment campaign started with the false accusation that I (an Indian-American Hindu) was not "viewpoint neutral" when allocating funds, in my capacity as Graduate Student Body President, to a diversity event. What really occurred is that my administration and I abstained from supporting either a pro- or anti-BDS agenda. This condition was explicitly approved by a UCLA administrator. The event took place on November 5, 2015 and a variety of campus viewpoints were actively represented, including both sides of the issues raised by the BDS movement. Dean Erwin Chemerinsky—one of America's leading constitutional law scholars—and four legal organizations concluded that my administration and I acted in a viewpoint-neutral manner.

Subsequently, BDS activists wrote defamatory articles about me and led a grassroots campaign against me on the UCLA campus. They even tried, on multiple occasions, to remove me as Graduate Student Body President. I reached out to senior members of your administration—many times—for guidance and support to defuse this situation. Furthermore, I believed that these administrators would be especially sensitive given the public outcry caused by similar BDS-led efforts against UCLA students Rachel Beyda, Avi Oved, Lauren Rogers, and Sunny Singh. I could not have been more mistaken. Your administrators were non-responsive and unhelpful.

In fact, when Palestine Legal and the ACLU circulated a legal letter defaming me on the internet, had their attorneys write a libelous article about me in the Daily Bruin, and sent lawyers to Graduate Student Association meetings to attack me personally, I contacted the Interim Vice Chancellor of Legal Affairs many times for help. Not only did she decline to provide me with the necessary legal support, but she told me that I needed to get my own attorney. Finally, I was connected to the American Jewish Committee, who found the situation serious enough to refer me to pro-bono counsel.

In late February 2016, my new attorney, Peter M. Weil, of Glaser Weil LLP, sent you and several senior members of your administration a lengthy letter detailing the constant bullying, harassment, and attacks to which I was being subjected. Your administration chose to not take any action or even investigate this matter.

To make matters worse, at the behest of pro-BDS organizations, the Vice Chancellor of Equity, Diversity and Inclusion (EDI) launched a three-month-long investigation of me. His office wrote a defamatory, 27-page report which has been heavily condemned by seven major organizations.

In reality, this report was an attempt by your administration to publicly scapegoat me for their systematic failure to adopt and implement University of California policies, and provide the necessary guidance to me and other student organizations when we approached them for help. Your administrators fell asleep on the job and decided to blame me—a student—for it.

But the desire to vilify me did not stop there. Although the report was designated as "Confidential," no reasonable safeguards were adopted to preserve the report's confidentiality. It was readily foreseeable that pro-BDS organizations—whom your administration freely made this "Confidential Report" available to—could and would leak it. No efforts were made to prevent this and, of course, this is precisely what occurred.

In violation of confidentiality and retaliation policies, Students for Justice in Palestine openly and unlawfully leaked the EDI report onto the internet. When I filed a complaint about this violation, your administration declined to investigate it. Worse yet, the Vice Chancellor of EDI, on his blog, urged the public to read this leaked confidential report, and gave them access to it. As recent as August 22, 2016, there was a scurrilous op-ed piece in the Daily Bruin attacking me and relying extensively on the socalled Confidential Report.

UCLA is one of the finest universities in the world. It is unfortunate, indeed, that your administration has not only allowed BDS organizations and student activists to freely engage in intimidation of students who do not support the BDS agenda, but has decided to affirmatively engage in discriminatory practices of its own against those same students. Whether you choose to acknowledge it or not, the fact is that the UCLA campus has become a hostile and unsafe environment for students, Jewish and non-Jewish, who choose not to support the BDS movement, let alone support the State of Israel.

I implore you to acknowledge the reality of this regrettable situation and take corrective action that not only remedies my grievances but addresses the current hostile and unsafe campus climate generally so that other students are not forced to leave UCLA. It is too late for me, but I sincerely hope that it will not be too late for those students who follow me.

I will be returning to Los Angeles as often as necessary in order to pursue the discrimination grievance that I filed pursuant to UCLA Procedure 230.l.

Sincerely,

Milan Chatterjee

MILAN CHATTERJEE was a law student at UCLA and President of its Graduate Student Government before transferring to complete his degree at New York University.

27 Boycott, Divestment, and Sanctions and Antisemitism at Stanford University

Molly Horwitz

Molly Horwitz, as a Jewish Latina, particularly sought the endorsement of the Students of Color Coalition (SOCC) in her campaign for the Stanford senate but was confronted with a litmus test over her position, as a Jew, on Boycott, Divestment, and Sanctions (BDS). The widely publicized scandal triggered an international discussion of antisemitism on American campuses. Horwitz then found herself in the middle of another international incident the following year, when she brought up a bill about antisemitism for senate action. A fellow senator objected, stating that comments about "Jews controlling the media, the economy, the world, etc." weren't antisemitic but material for a "very valid discussion." That such straightforward antisemitism could be seen as "valid"—and that this senator subsequently received five hundred student votes toward reelection—shows the slippery slope between anti-Israelism and antisemitism in campus discourse. Support for Israel is simply part of the Jewish plot to control the world.

IN ORDER TO explain how I've become who I am today, a fresh Stanford graduate and fierce Jewish Zionist, I must first describe where I came from.

I was born in Asuncion, Paraguay, in 1993. While my birth mother was unable to support me, she was able to give me the greatest gift of all: a new beginning. I was put up for adoption, and shortly afterward, an amazing woman from over five thousand miles away in Milwaukee, Wisconsin, overcoming both a divorce and cancer treatment, arrived to take me home.

I was engulfed in love from my family and my mother's friends from the moment the plane touched down. My mother made sure that I was welcomed into the Jewish community by helping me complete the orthodox conversion process. We began keeping kosher and observing all the Jewish holidays. Warmth enveloped my childhood from all corners of my family. Both of my grandparents were proud Zionists who had traveled to Israel with their children shortly after the Six-Day War, to visit a son studying at the Weizmann Institute. Two of our family friends had survived Auschwitz-Birkenau to live exemplary lives, sharing joy with their daughters and many grandchildren. My grandfather had also served in the US military and helped liberate concentration camps. My grandmother taught herself Hebrew and fell in love with the State of Israel. With such inspiring role models, I embraced my Jewish heritage and thrived in my Jewish day school, becoming passionately interested in learning more about Israel.

It wasn't until high school that I began wrestling with the complexities of being Jewish while also wanting to be more involved in the Latino community. There was a schism between the small Jewish student group and the other ethnic groups, which made me feel like I had to decide which single part of my identity to embrace. Not that embracing either was simple. My peers told me I was not a real Latina while also claiming it was my Latina ethnicity that got me into Stanford. I felt both not Hispanic enough and too Hispanic. Similarly, some people would say I didn't look Jewish, while others would confront me with antisemitic comments, such as alluding to the stereotype of Jews being obsessed with money. Such experiences made me cling to and take pride in my Jewish identity yet sometimes also made me afraid to say I was Jewish.

At Stanford, I found a community in which I felt understood. The diversity of this community allowed me to explore and embrace all aspects of my identity. But I also learned how many Stanford students grapple with the many manifestations of racism. I felt my experience as a member of two different oppressed minority groups—Jews and Hispanics—gave me unique insight into the challenges students of color face. I decided during my junior year to run to serve on the following year's Stanford senate, primarily to address problems I saw in Stanford's mental health-care system. One of these is a lack of diversity among counselors at Counseling and Psychological Services (CAPS). In preparation for my campaign, I decided it was advisable to scrub my Facebook page of my pro-Israel postings, not because I'm not proud of my Zionism (I am), but because I felt I couldn't do maximal good unless I won, and I wasn't sure I could win if my pro-Israel inclinations were widely known. In any case, my position on Israel seemed irrelevant to my candidacy for student government, so it was an unnecessary distraction.

Or so I thought.

In my campaign, I was eager to obtain the endorsement of the Students of Color Coalition, since I felt that my candidacy and SOCC had many goals in common. SOCC decided to grant me an interview. The interview was held on Friday, March 13, 2015, in the basement of the Native American Community Center. I entered the room apprehensive but hopeful. I would leave it shocked and devastated.

Across from me in the room sat eight SOCC members, who took notes throughout the interview. Partway through, the lead interviewer asked me, "Given your strong Jewish identity, how would you vote on divestment?" I couldn't quite process that I had actually been asked this question. Did my being Jewish somehow call into question my qualifications to serve on the senate? Did SOCC have an official litmus test on Israel that all candidates had to pass? Would they have asked a non-Jew his or her position on Israel, or was it only Jews they were worried about? Did SOCC doubt my commitment to serving students of color on the basis that I am Jewish? Were they prepared to put a candidate's views on Israel ahead of her or his qualifications to serve the interests of students of color?

Somewhat stunned, I asked for clarification. The SOCC interviewer responded that she had noticed I talked about my Jewish identity in the application and was wondering how this would affect my decision on divestment. I wanted to cry. I had spent so much time trying to move past the feeling that I was not Latina enough, that I was not Jewish enough, that I was too Jewish, that I was too Latina, that I couldn't be both Jewish and Latina, that my identities were in conflict. And now here they were, apparently forcing me to choose between being a Latina who stands up for the rights of Hispanics and being a Jew who stands up for the rights of Jews.

I responded honestly. I told SOCC I was upset that the senate had voted for divestment, but that regardless I was proud of the democratic nature of the vote. I explained that I believed that Stanford students sincerely wanted peace in the Middle East, even if we disagreed on how to get there.

The rest of the interview was a blur. I barely kept it together. As soon as I left the interview room, I began shaking. I replayed the incident over and over in my mind. It was bad enough that SOCC had asked me about divestment but even worse that they appeared to think that my Jewish identity might make me a poor senator. "As a Jew," they seemed to ask, "can you really be trusted to vote the right way on important issues like criticizing the Jewish State?" Of course, there are Jews who support divestment, there are Jews against it, and there are Jews who do not take a position. My involvement in Hillel, my praying in synagogue, my love of the Hebrew language, my study of Talmud, my celebration of Rosh Hashana and Hannukah and Purim and Passover have nothing to do with divestment.

My Jewish identity should never have come up in that interview.

For a while, I debated whether I should come forward about it. I consulted with many members of the Jewish community at Stanford as well as back home in Wisconsin. The most jarring moment for me occurred when the Hillel director at Stanford urged me to keep quiet. She felt, as a director, that her goal was to attract more Jewish students, and associating Stanford with antisemitism would only do the opposite. I was flabbergasted. After hanging up the phone, I was in dreadful doubt of the amount of support I would be able to garner from the Jewish community at Stanford.

Ultimately, I decided it was necessary for me to address inequality and discrimination wherever it occurs. I embraced the values I grew up reading about in Jewish studies classes and followed the example my mother set for me as a specialist in discrimination law. I was reminded of a quote by Rabbi A. Y. Kook, "I don't speak because I have the power to speak; I speak because I don't have the power to remain silent."[1] I was and am very concerned about the treatment of Jewish students on Stanford's campus. As a potential student senator, I felt that I had an obligation to speak up for the communities that I represented on campus and to better the quality of student life. So, I spoke up. I reported the episode to the elections commissioner, to the associate dean of students and director of student activities and leadership, to the Anti-Defamation League (ADL), and to the *Stanford Review*, a conservative student newspaper. Reliving the experience repeatedly was incredibly difficult for me. But it was necessary.

I was immediately faced with the consequences of achieving a higher level of fame. I received multiple insulting and threatening messages via Facebook and email and became a central topic of conversation among the supporters of Boycott, Divestment, and Sanctions (BDS) at Stanford and nationally. I soon had to relinquish my social media accounts to my friend to protect myself from the wave of hateful criticism that I received.

But there was a brighter side. I also received many emails and messages of support from the greater Jewish community across the world and especially from those who, like me, identified as having multiple ethnicities. After a month, I had gotten better at answering even immensely personal questions with poise and was invited to speak at an ADL event. My improvement at public speaking also translated into being elected to the senate with the fourth highest number of votes. The student voice had risen up to speak out against discrimination and to connect communities. Knowing that the majority of students supported me, I felt inspired to speak out against similar instances of discrimination at Stanford. While I was in Israel volunteering over the summer, I eagerly accepted an invitation to speak at the Jewish Federations of North America General Assembly in November. I had newfound confidence to return the following school year and begin my year as senator.

My largest goal for my senior year was to pass a senate resolution that would reaffirm the fight against antisemitism at Stanford and allocate funds for educational purposes. I decided to wait until a later point in the academic year to submit the resolution. During spring break, I made the finishing touches and began working to get sponsors. I was able to get Chabad at Stanford, the Jewish Students' Association, J Street U, Alpha Epsilon Pi, and Cardinals for Israel (my own advocacy group) to sponsor. It wasn't an easy process to get everyone to agree to the language in the resolution. But eventually everyone did, and I put the resolution up for debate. In Stanford's senate, a resolution must be debated for at least one week before being put to a vote.

During the first week of debate, we spoke mainly about the resolution's affirmation of the US State Department's definition of *antisemitism*, which deems as antisemitism the demonization and delegitimization of, and application of double standards to, Israel. J Street U eventually became unhappy with this part of the resolution, and the senate voted to require a new definition of *antisemitism*. The new definition merely listed examples of antisemitism, such as making demonizing comments about the power of Jews as a collective or accusing the Jews of exaggerating the Holocaust or calling for the killing of Jews. These examples are important manifestations of antisemitism, but they do not address the line that is often crossed between anti-Israel sentiments and antisemitism on campuses. Toward the end of the discussion, then-senator Gabe Knight took issue with the resolution's examples of antisemitic language and commented, "[The resolution] says, 'Jews controlling the media, economy, government, and other societal institutions,' and it cites this as a fixture of antisemitism that we theoretically shouldn't challenge. I think that that's kind of irresponsibly foraying into another politically contentious conversation. Questioning these potential power dynamics, I think, is not antisemitism. I think it's a very valid discussion."[2]

In his view, in other words, asserting that Jews control the media, etc. is not antisemitic but, to the contrary, a very valid discussion to have.

Aghast, I sat back in my seat and waited a moment or two to gauge others' reactions to what he had said. Only four of my friends and I reacted negatively. The rest of the room snapped their fingers in approval. A group of enlightened Stanford students all enthusiastically believed it was valid to discuss whether Jews control the economy, the government. The meeting concluded shortly after, and I rushed out of the room to meet up with my friends. We sat there silently in a separate room for about five minutes before beginning to process what had occurred.

What Knight said didn't surprise me, ultimately, because before he deleted his Facebook account in response to the media storm, it had contained many posts complaining about Israel's oppression of the Palestinians and their systematic ethnic cleansing. But I was most irate about those bystanders who emphatically approved Knight's shockingly inappropriate remarks. If those people didn't understand what was wrong, then there desperately needed to be greater education about antisemitism on campus.

To kick that off, a freshman who was also running for senate, Matthew Wiggler, single-handedly arranged a rally against antisemitism the following day. Other senate candidates spoke, as did Jewish students, about their own experiences with antisemitism at Stanford. There was immense communal support at the event, which I really appreciated. It is now my goal to set up an educational series on antisemitism for next year at Stanford. I've already planned a training program for the incoming senate. It remains clear to me that this is necessary because—despite (or perhaps because of) his widely reported comments—Knight received roughly five hundred votes from the student body toward his own reelection. Knight did eventually suspend his senate campaign and was officially censured by the senate. But before that, only two organizations that had endorsed him withdrew their support. The SOCC was one of the organizations that continued to support Knight until the elections ended.

Now, what can people do to help? It can be extremely difficult to be Jewish, let alone a Zionist, on a college campus today. I know the surrounding Jewish community is extremely welcoming, so it would be wonderful to invite student leaders into the local community. Providing that sense of community and overall support will help the students do what they do best. Despite trying their hardest, many students don't have the same resources that you in the community may have. Offering these resources to pro-Israel student leaders can decrease the amount of work that they have to devote toward reaching out to various organizations for support. I have spent countless sleepless nights slaving over projects for Cardinals for Israel.

Most of all, though, you can stand firm in your belief that there is a bright future for student leaders and pro-Israel advocates on campus. As Mahmoud Darwish, a beautiful Palestinian poet, said, "Without hope we are lost."[3]

It is not the best of times for campus Zionists, but we are far from lost.

MOLLY HORWITZ, Stanford 2016, majored in religious studies and minored in Jewish studies.

Notes

1. Quoted at *Ve'ahavta*, https://veahavta.org/veh-home/quote-rabbi-a-y-kook/ (accessed November 3, 2017).

2. Yair Rosenberg, "Stanford Student Senator: Saying 'Jews Control the Media, Economy, Government' Is 'Not Antisemitism,'" *Tablet* (April 7, 2016), http://www.tabletmag .com/scroll/199362/stanford-student-senator-saying-jews-control-the-media-economy -government-is-not-anti-semitism.

3. Quoted at 95Quotes, http://95quotes.com/mahmoud-darwish-quotes.html (accessed November 3, 2017).

28 On Being Pro-Israel, and Jewish, at Oberlin College

Eliana Kohn

Eliana Kohn describes the uncomfortable atmosphere for non-Israel-haters at Oberlin College. Antinormalization and intersectionality have created a hostile orthodoxy where Zionist students must meet only in secret, are excluded from participating in social justice causes, are condemned as white and privileged and for being racist toward persons of color (including Palestinians), are not allowed to have ethnic-themed Shabbat dinners lest they be guilty of cultural appropriation, and so on. Meanwhile, open antisemitism isn't merely tolerated but actively defended—most notoriously during the spring 2016 discovery of offensive Facebook posts by Oberlin professor Joy Karega. In an inversion of reality, many on campus saw Karega not as a despicable racist but as a victim targeted *by* racists (i.e., Jews). The endless demonization of Israel on campus, Kohn feels, expresses and fuels the antisemitism, allowing not only a Karega to say such vile things about Jews—"but for an enlightened liberal arts community to accept them."

I HAD EXPERIENCED anti-Israel sentiment during high school, but I never felt uncontrolled animosity until attending Oberlin College. Throughout my first year at Oberlin, I felt a range of awful emotions that I would have never thought to associate with being a pro-Israel Jewish student. I felt ashamed of myself and my beliefs, scared for how I would be treated by my peers, and incredibly angry and hurt.

The shame began at the very start of school, when someone asked me what my Israel Defense Forces (IDF) T-shirt was referring to and then gave me weird and discouraging looks when I explained. In that moment, I learned not to mention the IDF, or even Israel itself. When I returned to my dorm, I shamefully stuffed the T-shirt into the bottom corner of a drawer, never to be worn at Oberlin again. It was really horrible to realize that I felt uncomfortable wearing this very meaningful shirt in the place I was to call home for the next four years. I decided to wear my bullet necklace from the Ayalon Institute Museum in Israel every day, because it was a less noticeable way to show my support for Israel, and keep it close to my heart.

Later that same week, I heard about a Free Palestine event. I felt compelled to go because the poster said open mic. I wanted to voice my support of Israel, but my friends (both Jewish and non-Jewish) convinced me not to go because they worried that it would make people hate me or start a fight. So I stayed in my dorm, feeling ostracized, alienated, confused.

I thought that Oberlin's Hillel might offer a safe space to talk about Israel without those worries. Yet it did not give me an outlet. When someone tried to bring up Israel at a Hillel meeting, the subject was shot down. We were told that the place for discussing Israel was at a J Street meeting, a group I believed to be more pro-Palestinian than pro-Israel. For me, that moment when even Jewish students pushed Israel away was one of my worst. After that meeting, my feelings of detachment from my Jewish peers really grew. I started to question and second-guess myself. Maybe I had been wrong my entire life. Maybe the feelings of comfort and of belonging I experienced during my first trip to Israel were just a mirage in the Negev. When you are an outcast, you feel like you should be ashamed of what you think and where you stand. With hostility toward Israel coming from non-Jews and Jews alike, I felt silenced, afraid of all the hate that would come at me the second I opened my mouth.

The rest of that first semester was mostly calm, until mid-December of 2015, when a black student organization issued a list of its demands.[1] When it first came out, I really wanted to sign it because of how much I supported their cause. Yet I couldn't sign it because it also contained this: a demand for "the immediate divestment from all prisons and Israel." This statement casually connected the idea of America's problematic prison system to the idea of Israel, which without a doubt intentionally demonized Israel. Israel had nothing to do with the situation of black students at Oberlin, let alone America; it was so out of place in their list of demands that including it could only serve to support and promote hate toward Israel. Yet I felt that if I voiced my opinion against the anti-Israel statement, I would be faced with students calling me a racist. That seemed all the more upsetting to me, because I care about and believe in the Black Lives Matter movement. Unfortunately, this intersectionality idea—that all forms of oppression are somehow connected—presents a great challenge at Oberlin, since it prevents students from supporting social justice causes unless they also take an anti-Israel stance.

This intersectionality strategy is intentionally pursued by Oberlin's Students for a Free Palestine (SFP) group. They deliberately get people to associate the words *Zionism* with racism and *Israel* with apartheid and/or human rights violators. They thus connect Palestinian issues with black student issues, such that it is now impossible to be pro-Israel and support black students, as just noted. Joining those issues together causes Oberlin students to look at Israel through a lens of hate, without any effort at understanding; they only focus on negative aspects of Israel, instead of the whole picture and the wonderful meaning of Israel's existence.

SFP not only deliberately perpetuates *mis*understanding about Israel, they then refuse, in the name of "antinormalization" or "nonengagement," to have any open and effective student dialogue. So they set up demonstrations and posters that vilify Israel and lie about Israel and then refuse to engage with anyone who wants to argue against something written or said or even talk with someone who just has a challenging question. Add to this the fact that most Jewish students are afraid to speak up for Israel, and there's little meaningful debate indeed. Add in further that many Oberlin students claim there is a clear distinction between being anti-Israel and being antisemitic, while somehow not appreciating just how antisemitic their unbridled anti-Israel language often sounds.

Intersectionality has reared its head in other problematic ways here as well. Students are focused on the problem of white privilege and immediately lump Jews into the privileged category, simply because most of the Jews here are white. But this completely disregards non-white Jewish students. In past years, Jewish students of color, including Latinx, Asian, and black students, have requested and/or participated in Hillel Shabbats that have had food themes relating to those ethnicities. All of these events have been met with complaints that Hillel was appropriating other cultures. Not only was that wrong, but it was also completely ignorant. The Oberlin idea of Jewish people is that we are all just rich white people. Never mind that half of Israel's Jews are Sephardic or Eastern Jews of color, there are even Jews of color right here on this campus. And this ignorance is not only harmful to them but also to all Jewish students as a whole, because we are seen as people who cannot possibly be affected by discrimination and oppression. When the campus allows just a single narrative, the open-minded students do not seem so open-minded anymore. They have already made their decisions on who is oppressed and who is not. It's no surprise that when you've decided that Jewish students are privileged white kids, you've decided that antisemitism is impossible—even as you demonstrate it yourself.

During the winter term of 2015-2016, a group of concerned alumni wrote an open letter, available for anyone to read and sign. The letter called attention to the anti-Israel and antisemitic activity on campus, starting a chain reaction that gained much attention when I returned to Oberlin for spring semester. I, of course, had signed the letter, and Hillel staff noticed and reached out to me. I met with a couple of staff members, and we decided that an Oberlin Zionist group needed to restart. The number of signatures on the letter showed that pro-Israel students did exist on this campus, and there was all the more reason to start the group given the number of students that did not sign because they were too afraid. Honestly, I was almost too scared to sign the letter myself, but I had grown tired of not speaking up for Israel.

So a small group of us showed up to an unadvertised, rather secret, meeting in the Hillel room to talk about Oberlin Zionists. There were maybe ten of us, tops, but we all wanted this safe space to discuss Israel. Having a space where we would not face scrutiny or be marked as horrible people was comforting. Our main goal was to make Israel-supportive people feel less alone at Oberlin and to teach other students to look at Israel through a fairer and more accurate lens. Yet right away, we ran into the debate on whether we would be aggressive activists or merely aim to maintain this safe space. Most students who came were too nervous to be visible and to advertise the group, much less bring in a speaker. For most of that semester, we did not create any public events.

While some students in Oberlin Zionists kept in contact with some of the alumni, other Jewish groups felt that the alumni had overstepped their boundaries. Some alumni had run-ins with J Street on campus, for example, and the J Street students blamed us, although we had nothing to do with it. I did not even know about that conflict until I received an email, inviting me to meet with other Jewish student leaders over lunch. When I sat down at the table, there were two Hillel staff members (one of which I knew had no idea what was about to happen, and the other, I am not so sure) and three J Street student leaders.

The email had suggested a friendly meeting, but that quickly turned into a three-against-one scenario. All three of the J Street students became very aggressive and lectured me that Oberlin Zionists was a terrible group that was tearing the Jewish community apart. They argued that J Street was supposed to be where everyone feels welcome, that it was the main Jewish organization on campus, that I was discrediting something they had worked so hard to build, etc. They also conveyed how awful it was that we were affiliated with the alumni who they felt had attacked them. They caught me completely off guard as I found myself defending Oberlin Zionists to *Jewish* students. I felt astounded that they thought a pro-Israel group was destroying the community. I had to explain that Oberlin Zionists was not affiliated with the alumni and that if every Jewish student really did feel comfortable and safe at J Street, then I would not have been sitting with them at the moment. Although one of the students sent me an apology email later that day, it was an appalling experience, and I felt absolutely betrayed.

I also felt deep dismay and distress that the anti-Israel hatred surrounding us, by pressuring Jewish students to conform, was dividing us.

Although second semester started off rocky, Hillel had scheduled several events regarding Israel, and this offered some potential comfort. Unfortunately, they did not always go as well as planned. One was a meeting to discuss just how to talk about Israel that was disappointingly unproductive. A woman I was paired with simply had nothing to say, basically refusing to talk about Israel even though she had come to a meeting to do just that. It continued to alarm me how

Jewish students found pro-Israel sentiment to be so taboo, even when they were in a safe environment to express it.

It was about a month later that the Professor Karega scandal erupted.

After the *Tower* broke the story, her antisemitic Facebook posts were discussed in articles all over the internet, and most students at Oberlin found out what happened extremely quickly.[2] She had posted outrageously absurd statements, claiming that ISIS was really Mossad, that Zionists were behind 9/11, and that people calling her antisemitic were just bullying her. Yet perhaps most disturbing of all was the way that students reacted to the story. On their own Facebook pages, students were arguing that Karega should *not* be fired. Their reasons included: she is one of the few black professors, she is a mentor to many black students, she is a good professor, and her posts were not antisemitic. I was angry. I do not care how great a teacher or mentor a professor is. If someone spouts hateful nonsense, he or she should not be allowed to teach and influence students, particularly impressionable liberal arts students. If this were a white professor posting anti-black racist statements on Facebook instead, the student body would be up in arms trying to get her fired, which obviously should happen. But here was a black woman making antisemitic libels, and they were defending her. Oberlin's president Krislov's lack of a substantial response was equally distressing, not least because he is Jewish too. He offered absolutely no support to those sorely wounded by Karega's comments and sent out an incredibly weak email merely citing academic freedom. That email alone indicated that Oberlin as an institution would not even take blatant antisemitism seriously.

This situation represents the epitome of the dangers of intersectionality, and it infuriates me. This campus is so driven to look at Israel with hate that it cannot seem to see the good anymore. What Israel originally stood for, the return of an indigenous people to their ancestral homeland and a safe haven for Jews after the terrors of the Holocaust, have been replaced by false accusations and demonizations. All this demonization expresses, and fuels, the antisemitism. There exists such a high level of double standards, demonization, and delegitimization of Israel that it makes it possible not only for a Karega to say such vile things about Jews—but for an enlightened liberal arts community to accept them.

After an extremely uncomfortable spring semester, I was glad to leave campus for the summer and to learn, via a campus email over the summer, that the administration had decided to put Karega on paid leave until her contract expired and then make a final decision about her. Sending the email while students were off campus was a smart move by Oberlin, because it minimized the student response.

In contrast, when the final decision was made to officially fire Karega just a few months later, in November 2016, school was fully in session and everyone was back. With the announcement coming shortly after the controversial presidential elections, most students were already fired up and angry about Trump's win, and some nonwhite students were even lashing out at their white classmates, Jewish and non-Jewish. The news about Karega poured more fuel on this fire, really angering the already infuriated black / people of color community. Posts began lighting up Facebook, claiming that Oberlin had betrayed them and did not care about black lives. Some posts blamed the alumni; other posts claimed that Oberlin took antisemitism more seriously than other issues, without naming specifics. It was as if the students were ignoring the fact that the evidence against Karega was not only extensive but also widely publicized internationally. A few hours later, Jewish students began writing posts claiming that they understood why the people of color community would feel hurt, but they absolutely had to acknowledge the fact that Karega was antisemitic. Then many people started commenting on each other's posts, either fervently agreeing or ardently disagreeing, creating an awful "Us versus Them" dynamic that seemed more destructive than productive.

Two days after the Karega announcement, a Jewish professor's home was vandalized with antisemitic and threatening language.[3] My immediate reaction was to connect the events, but no other information was given, so nothing can really be confirmed or denied. Additionally, some Jewish friends informed me that there were small swastikas drawn in bathroom stalls in one of the buildings on campus. Yet perhaps the most troubling aspect of these hate crimes was that no one on campus besides the administration, Jewish organizations, and Jewish students had a reaction. The social media silence was deafening. After a few days of this silence, an outspoken Jewish student posted on Facebook stating that he or she no longer felt safe on campus, that Jews are in fact an oppressed group, and that students should not pride themselves on fighting against and protesting oppression unless they fight for all oppressed groups. Many Jewish students have now followed suit by simply sharing that status or writing their own, but radio silence remains from the non-Jewish students who typically post enraged statements about the oppression of minorities and other hate crimes. Once more, the degree to which Oberlin students disregard antisemitism and anti-Israel hatred is made clear.

Israel is not perfect, no democracy is. No government is above criticism. Yet it should not be held to double standards and delegitimized, especially by my peers, who know so little about the complicated history of the Middle East. There were many times throughout the school year that I questioned whether I made the right choice in choosing Oberlin. If I had known how antisemitic the campus was, maybe I would not have come. There were some days when I seriously considered transferring somewhere else, but then I thought, "If people like me do not stay and try to help and make a difference, who will?" So, I returned to Oberlin this year, as a cochair of Oberlin Zionists and an Israel on Campus

Coalition Grinspoon fellow, and I will be more prepared for this year and my upcoming years.

When we permit the anti-Israel hostility, we permit the antisemitism.

We can no longer permit it.

ELIANA KOHN, Oberlin 2019, plans to major in psychology and minor in creative writing.

Notes

1. Letter to Board of Trustees, http://new.oberlin.edu/petition-jan2016.pdf (accessed November 6, 2017).

2. David Gerstman, "Oberlin Professor Claims Israel Was Behind 9/11, ISIS, Charlie Hebdo Attack," *The Tower* (February 25, 2016), http://www.thetower.org/3012-oberlin -professor-claims-israel-was-behind-911-isis-charlie-hebdo-attack/.

3. Lea Speyer, "'Gas Jews Die' Note Found on Mezuzah of Oberlin Professor's Home," *The Algemeiner* (November 21, 2016), https://www.algemeiner.com/2016/11/21/gas-jews-die -note-found-on-mezuzah-of-oberlin-professors-home/.

29 Battling Anti-Zionism at City University of New York John Jay College

Tomer Kornfeld

Tomer Kornfeld provides a chilling account of the tactics of Students for Justice in Palestine (SJP) on his campus. These anti-Israel activists have adopted the antinormalization policy, refusing to engage in any way with Jewish students' groups. Instead, they repeatedly intimidate non-Israel-hating students, sponsoring die-ins, co-opting others' causes for their own ends (such as converting antiracism rallies into anti-Israel diatribes), producing maps that remove Israel, and so on. Their coalitions with radical students of color and others regularly paint Israel as the epicenter of racist oppression. Kornfeld himself was targeted for social media abuse by one activist, leading him to conclude that "the Jewish student on campus who feels connected to his ancestral homeland is automatically [seen as] evil for that fault alone."

BIGOTRY AGAINST ISRAEL and against Jews is growing dramatically on college campuses, where Israel is regularly demonized, delegitimized, and held to double standards. It is happening here at John Jay College of Criminal Justice in Manhattan, and this essay is meant to give you a glimpse of what it looks like through the eyes of a student.

As a rising freshman in September of 2013, I was determined and focused on ensuring I had the best four-year college experience possible. Unlike perhaps most high school students, I was already aware of what was happening on campuses. Still, I felt prepared for it, ready to be on the front lines of the war against Israel being waged on college campuses, as I had done some training for it through high school with the help of several organizations, most notably the StandWithUs High School Internship. Nevertheless, even I was stunned to discover just how real, pervasive, and strong the hostility is to Israel and to Jews on campus.

Before I even arrived on my campus, I experienced my first battle—with the Middle Eastern Club. Researching the club online revealed that Israel was wiped off the map on its Facebook page and replaced with Palestine. I experienced this almost personally as a slap in the face, as an attempt to deny or delegitimize my identity as a Jewish student with strong Israel ties. I immediately reached out to StandWithUs, who helped me compose a letter to the president of the club. He responded promptly and removed the map. With that issue resolved and feeling confident from this small victory, I came to campus to begin my college years.

Little did I know this was the first battle of many.

I promptly became involved with Hillel at John Jay. In December of 2013, we attempted to set up a mock peace talk with Students for Justice in Palestine, to be moderated by the United Nations club. Perhaps we were naive, but we were peace-loving students, sick and tired of hearing about war and conflict, and we wanted to try to bridge the divide at least on our campus. Perhaps, we thought, if we could get along with those on the other side here, that would be one small step toward helping the antagonists get along better over there, in the Middle East. At the bare minimum, each side could get to understand the other side a little more clearly.

SJP simply rejected our olive branch.

They refused even to dialogue with us. Instead of participating in a peace talk, they sponsored an important workshop, with a "prominent civil rights attorney and Palestinian activist," Lamis Deek, on the topic of "normalization with Zionist groups."[1] Their promotional announcement for the workshop indeed helped us understand their side a little more clearly. They wrote: "Many of you have suggested that we work with Zionist groups on campus (like Hillel) and have a debate or something of the sort. If you do not understand why we refuse to cooperate with such groups, this would be the perfect learning experience for you."

I was very appreciative of their concern for our learning experience. One thing I did learn was that they were not very interested in getting to understand *our* side.

In October of 2014, SJP, as well as other campus groups, combined to hold a die-in/vigil for Ferguson and Gaza. Although the connection between Ferguson and Gaza is not very clear to me, I suppose they can do whatever they want. A die-in, of course, is when students lie on the ground covered in sheets soaked in "blood." This particular die-in included the spewing of many lies, such as "Israel trains police officers on how to use their weapons to kill innocent people." You can imagine how pleasant it is to walk past or through something like this, on your college campus, and observe it spreading malicious and hateful lies about your people.

SJP members and other participating students also hurled insults directly at us, the pro-Israel students. These ranged from someone reaching for my Israeli flag and asking if they could "wipe their a**" with it to screaming that the flag I carried was "stained with blood." It is one thing to spread lies about Israel in general but another to directly target students on your campus in this way. In their minds, I and my peers were seemingly directly responsible for a conflict that is nearly six thousand miles away. There is no other side of the story to them. For us to support Israel is for us to be complicit in all the offenses they accuse Israel of.

With these insults, they were attempting to intimidate us, me, into silence and delegitimize my identity, or at least attack me on the basis of my identity. It takes a lot of courage to continue advocating for Israel on campus at this cost. I say this not to boast about myself or my peers but, really, to partly explain why so few Jewish students are willing to stand up for Israel.

Somehow we overcame this dreadful bigoted event and responded a week later with our own event. We played music, handed out food and fact sheets about Israel and the conflict, and brought a good vibe to campus, one free of intimidation. Once again, we attempted to stress coexistence and peace on our campus, instead of intimidation and hatred.

In December of 2014, SJP once again used another group's event to further their own agenda. This time, they partnered with the African Students Association and rallied in solidarity, not merely with Ferguson and Gaza, but also with Mexico. Once again, they took time supposedly devoted to the treatment of people of color in the United States and Mexico to spew lies and incite hatred toward Israel.

What is going on here is pretty clear, at least to me. There is no genuine connection between Ferguson, Mexico, and Gaza. But they don't care about that. What they care about is trying to spread the lie that Israelis (Jews) are white and Palestinians are of color. The truth is that Israelis and Jews are of many different colors, that half of Israeli Jews are Sephardic and quite indistinguishable from many Arabs, and that many Palestinians are also quite fair-skinned. But most college students won't know this and will accept those lies, especially when they are shouted with such anger and conviction.

This is all part of SJP's larger agenda. They form these alliances, based on false premises, not only to get many campus groups to hate Israel, but also to make it seem as if Israel is a racist, apartheid state. It doesn't matter that the facts prove them false, that Israeli-Arabs serve in the Knesset, in the Supreme Court, and in almost every single professional field in Israel. They aren't interested in the facts, and most of the students they are influencing don't know the facts.

One wonders how organizations that don't care about truth and facts are permitted to operate on college campuses, where you would think that truth and facts are important values.

In March of 2015, swastikas and other hate graffiti were discovered on our campus. This was not the first time swastikas had been found here. Hillel responded to the bigotry by holding our first ever, and now annual, Diversity Seder for Passover. The seder was an attempt to bring our community together, especially after homophobic, anti-African-American, and anti-Arab hate speech and symbols were also found on campus. Perhaps we remain naive, but we remain committed to taking positive steps toward peace and coexistence.

At least officially, John Jay agrees with our approach. We won an award for an "outstanding multicultural event" from the school for this event.

In November of 2015, we were faced with another SJP rally. This time, they held a protest in solidarity with the University of Missouri students who were protesting racism on their campus. As usual, SJP used the rally for their own purposes. Many pro-Israel students felt particularly intimidated by this rally, feeling like nearly the entire student body was somehow united against us. The fact is, we actually wanted to support this rally, because we do genuinely stand in solidarity with the University of Missouri students, and we are vigorously opposed to racism in all its forms. But we were effectively excluded from participating in this rally because it had also been converted into a rally against *us*.

Still not completely deterred, or perhaps still naive, we at Hillel responded by organizing for later that month a Coexistence & Diversity event with two officers from the New York City Police Department—one Muslim and one Jewish—with the aim of spreading their ability to peacefully coexist to our student body. We were thrilled when the John Jay Muslim Students Association (MSA) agreed to cosponsor the event, feeling that our message would be heard.

It was not to be.

As the dean of students, Kenneth Holmes, put it in a student newspaper article about the affair, "The MSA pulled out last minute because of the negative backlash they were receiving from their neighborhoods and family."[2]

And not just their "neighborhoods and family"—the campus SJP was vigorous in its opposition to MSA participation as well. In a Facebook post at the time, an SJP leader wrote, "I am GREATLY disappointed at the MSA for moving forward with this event, especially when the MSA president has openly said they will support Palestine no matter what and has collaborated with our SJP chapter before and understood the implications and harms of normalizing."

Happily, the event went on as scheduled, without MSA's sponsorship, and the two police officers did a wonderful job spreading their message of getting along despite their differences. (And to his credit, the MSA president came to the event, participated, and even said a word of thanks to the officers afterward for taking time to speak to our campus.)

In February of 2016, I was personally targeted by the Israel-haters.

Another student decided to post a screenshot of only part of a conversation we had had, with my profile picture and name included. In the textbox he wrote, to characterize the conversation, "When you just want to talk to people and understand their perspective but you're big, black, and sharp so it's easy for them to be afraid of you." This was preposterous, suggesting that I wouldn't talk to him because he was "big" and "black" and I felt threatened by him. I stopped talking to him because, as I wrote explicitly, he had already made his judgment of me, so there was no *point* in talking to him.

In any case, it wasn't this absurdly racist charge that was so troubling. It was the subsequent thread of students commenting on our conversation, including individuals from SJP, and personally attacking me. One wrote, for example, "yo he's an avid zionist which inevitably means he's a racist, white supremacist, religious supremacist colonizer."

My complaint with the fellow who posted the conversation was that he had already made his judgment about me. There was no point in talking to such a person whose mind was fixed, or worse, pre-fixed. What SJP shows repeatedly is that they are the same way, except with their pre-fixed minds they have no interest in talking to anyone on the other side.

To be a Zionist, to support Israel, is automatically to be a "racist, white supremacist, religious supremacist, colonizer."

The Jewish student on campus who feels connected to his ancestral homeland is automatically evil for that fault alone.

TOMER KORNFELD, CUNY John Jay College of Criminal Justice 2017, majored in law and society.

Notes

1. These and the following quotations are from an email sent by SJP dated December 4, 2013.
2. Timothy Wilson, "Clash of the Cultures: Cultural Conflicts Almost Stop Event," *The John Jay Sentinel* (November, 2015, precise date unavailable).

30 Students for Justice in Palestine at Brown University

Jared Samilow

Jared Samilow sketches the anti-Israel climate at Brown University, another recent hotspot. Particularly troubling was a 2016 incident involving the campus visit of a well-known transgender activist. Students for Justice in Palestine (SJP) campaigned for her to renounce the cosponsorship of a Hillel group, complaining that that made her complicit in Israeli "pinkwashing." Although the event had nothing to do with Israel and the Hillel group was devoted to social justice, SJP still found the group too tainted to be permitted to sponsor *anything*. The activist's capitulation only helped foster an atmosphere in which anything connected to Israel is seen as toxic. This puts great pressure on Jewish students to disaffiliate from Israel. The problem, Samilow argues, is that academic rigor has been replaced on campus by identity politics. He then locates anti-Israelism in the context of broader leftist movements, concluding that for anti-Israel activists, facts don't matter—all that matters is resisting oppression and marginalization.

At the end of January 2016, Natan Sharansky and Michael Douglas came to Brown University to speak about their Jewish heritage at a Hillel event called Jewish Journeys. Sharansky's stint as a political prisoner in the Soviet Union is legendary, as is Douglas's movie career, so the event was quite high-profile. The president of Hillel International was there, as were many figures in the New England Jewish community. A few days before the event, it was brought to our attention—we being pro-Israel Jewish students at Brown—that Students for Justice in Palestine was planning a protest. SJP had launched a Facebook campaign urging Brown students to "protest [the] egregious display of Settler Colonial apologism," apparently understanding a conversation about Jewish heritage as being indistinguishable from endorsement of the Zionist project. Although only about twenty-five students had indicated that they'd join the protest, we knew that the possibility for disruption was something to keep in mind.

At around 7:00 PM on Thursday, January 28, attendees began to file into the packed Salomon Center at Brown. As expected, we were greeted by SJP's welcoming party. Protesters carried signs hurling all the classic, almost ritualistic slurs. Apartheid. Ethnic cleansing. Occupation. Murder. Charitably, one assumes it was only the Israeli government they were charging with these crimes, not all Jews or Israelis, even though (again) the event was about Jewishness.

The event began at 7:30 PM, and despite the protest, it seemed like we were in for an uneventful evening. SJP was free to protest outside, but the event staff and campus police prohibited them from entering the auditorium where Sharansky and Douglas were speaking. But about one-third of the way through the lecture, chants of "Free Palestine" broke into the room. Rather than returning home once the event began, SJP's recruits had snaked around the building and were shouting from outside an emergency exit door.

The hysterical yells persisted for about a minute, then died down. Sharansky and Douglas finished their bits without further disruption. SJP had had its fun, but at least in this instance, it did not wield a heckler's veto. They made their mark—but for perspective, they'd mustered a whopping turnout of twenty-five anti-Israel fanatics out of a campus population of more than six thousand.

Still, it was enough to have an influence. Sharansky altered his talk to address Boycott, Divestment, and Sanctions (BDS) and anti-Israel activity, ultimately concluding that while they don't hurt the Israeli economy, they do exact a significant social and personal cost among Diaspora Jews. He said that he worries that the ugly political storm that follows Israel around discourages younger Jews from learning about and feeling proud of the world's only Jewish country. They may have had only a minor influence that night, but who can say what kind of subtle influence they are having on the Jewish students who hear them?

In fact, I'd suggested something similar in Israel's newspaper *Haaretz* back in November 2015: "So what do anti-Israel protestors on campus hope to accomplish? To exact a cost for expressing or associating with pro-Israel views. It's classic realpolitik and the million-dollar prize is control. The presence of bitter controversy around even the most innocent of presentations cloaks the Jewish state in a tenor of untouchability. This makes pro-Israel students shrink from public expression and makes the college environment uncomfortable for Israel's supporters."[1]

But Brown's SJP was not done for the year.

Several weeks later, in March 2016, a social justice group within the campus Hillel, along with several other student groups, invited Janet Mock to come speak. Mock is a transgender woman of color, a major activist, and something of a pop icon among left-wing college students. But even her progressive bona fides could not shield her from backlash for having the audacity to associate with a campus Hillel. SJP launched a petition to get her to renounce the sponsorship of the Hillel group, complaining that accepting the sponsorship of a group affiliated with a pro-Israel organization made her complicit in Israeli pinkwashing—referring to the theory among Israel-haters that Israel only engages in or promotes its progressive attitudes in order to deflect attention from its many crimes.

Even though the event had nothing to do with Israel, and even though the Hillel-affiliated group was devoted to the pursuit of social justice, and even though many members of our Hillel are extremely critical of Israel, SJP still found the group too tainted to be permitted to sponsor *anything* progressive on campus.

Instead of ignoring SJP, Mock capitulated and canceled the event altogether. SJP didn't win in one sense: Mock did not simply renounce the Hillel group's sponsorship, as they had demanded. In fact, SJP very much wanted Mock to speak, just not under the auspices of Hillel. But her capitulation did allow them to win in another sense, for episodes like these help foster an environment in which Israel is seen as an abnormal country, a plague outside the bounds of polite discussion and not worthy of the respect of which all other human societies are worthy.

And ironically, so much of the campus hostility comes from the left, where Jews have historically been pioneers and where so many contemporary Jewish students would like to locate themselves. Now Jews are increasingly unwelcome in the most progressive quarters. And if the Overton window—the window of permissible public discourse—shifts, as it seems to be doing and support for Israel becomes taboo within the center-left, quite a few Jews, forced to choose, will pick leftism over Israel. It's worth remembering that American Jews are so wedded to being progressive that a higher percentage of Jews than Hispanics voted against Donald Trump in the 2016 election.

I put it this way in December 2015, in *Haaretz*:

> Left-leaning young Jews are a weak link in the American Jewish community's relationship with Israel. As any exit poll can tell you, American Jews do not, on the whole, vote based on Israel. American Jews vote for candidates who share their liberal social values. Thus, liberalism trumps pro-Israelism for most secular Jews. What will be when liberal Jewish students are forced to choose between their allegiance to Israel and their commitment to social justice? What will happen when not supporting BDS is seen as a fatal tribal weakness? The answer should frighten anybody concerned with the future of the Diaspora's relationship with Israel.[2]

The incidents above didn't come out of nowhere, as the drip-drip of anti-Israelism has been occurring on our campus for some time, sometimes operating in bizarre and unexpected ways. In November 2015, for example, Brown experienced a wave of student activism for Syrian refugees. Ben & Jerry's ice cream store was rejected as a venue for a student meeting after someone posted a Facebook article accusing the company of operating in Israeli settlements. The taint of Israel is so dangerous that you can't even enjoy some ice cream while doing some good. This was (again) particularly painful for Hillel students who were actively involved in advocating for Syrian refugees.

That same month, SJP launched a petition to remove Sabra products from campus dining locations at Brown. They circulated it on their Facebook page and set up an information table in the Blue Room, a popular campus café. Nothing much came of it, fortunately, which I credit partly to our group—Brown Students for Israel—choosing not to respond and breathe life into it. But then again, even where an individual effort fails, it may well fertilize the soil for the next operation. Drip-drip irrigation long enough, and perhaps the anti-Israelism will take root next time.

Why does all of this happen? What makes a campus so hospitable to a bizarre obsession with a small besieged country thousands of miles away?

One reason is that academe's tradition of scientific inquiry has been replaced by an identity politics hierarchy. At a university, the logic or substance of a particular argument does not determine how successful it will be. What matters is only the identity of the arguer. The vast majority of American Jews are, in collegiate language, *privileged.* This contrasts with *marginalized.* At a university, the more marginalized you are, the more your opinions count. The more privileged, the less.

When young Jews move into college dorms, they quickly discover that despite what they have learned about Jewish history, Jews are now oppressors, not victims. Jews are part of the white privilege superstructure that needs to be dismantled. Palestinians, to the contrary, are lionized as victims of European colonialism and imperialist US foreign policy. Nothing more needs to be said.

Is the anti-Israelism on campus antisemitic? I think it is, but it's not the classical antisemitism our grandparents were accustomed to. It's a more sophisticated variety that draws inspiration from critical race theory and postcolonialism and rejects the Jewish State itself as a form of anti-Arab racism. The anti-Israelists have successfully convinced people—many Jews too—that opposing Israel is not about being against Jewish national aspirations but about working for Arab civil rights. So deluded, many Jews can thus feature prominently in the anti-Israel movement and still feel proud of their Jewish heritage. Indeed, most anti-Israel fanatics, Jewish or non-Jewish, probably do not see themselves as motivated by antisemitism.

In my view, anti-Israel campus activism needs to be viewed as part of a broader global left that sees itself as struggling against Western imperialism. Its leaders are often radical left-wing firebrands, not people who hold mainstream political views. They hate the Western nations for their imperialism and colonialism, and they hate Israel because they see it as an ethnic state made possible by that imperialism and colonialism. It's no wonder that they are not impressed by Israel's otherwise excellent progressive credentials and that they invent such obnoxious terms as *pinkwashing*. Radical leftists don't give Western nations credit for any of their progressive triumphs; why would they extend any credit to these nations' imperialist offspring?

It doesn't matter whether their conception of Israel is accurate or fair. Logic doesn't matter when the goal is resisting oppression and marginalization. Part of the reason it's so hard to defend Israel is that facts and truth have lost their importance and been replaced by feeling and emotion. In February 2014, for example, the *Harvard Crimson* published an article arguing that professors should not have jobs if they or their work opposes the goals of identity politics leftism (what she called justice). This was no idle philosophy but a demand to institutionalize what is already a social norm. Dissenting opinions are accused of erasing the identities of the oppressed. Free speech is valued only to the extent it can promote the marginalized and weaken the privileged. Speaking up for Israel does the opposite. And that inflicts psychological harm and perpetuates oppression. You can't defeat such claims with reasoned polemics because it's all a matter of personal feeling. You can't instruct someone on what he or she ought to feel.

We're fighting an asymmetric war because the Zionist Jew in fact is *not* privileged. We can be attacked, and we are attacked, but we can't effectively respond without being accused of supporting injustice and inflicting psychological distress on other students. It recalls how Israel must struggle to defeat what are in fact much weaker enemies (like Hamas and Hezbollah) because the rules of war are not the same for both sides.

I am fortunate to have fared well so far, personally, on this otherwise inhospitable campus. But anti-Israel prejudice still presents a formidable challenge, and not everyone is so lucky. One of my friends is a political science major who takes Middle East studies classes pass-fail because he is guilty of the thoughtcrime of supporting Israel and worried about the potential impact on his grades. Another wants to major in Middle East studies but keeps his support of Israel hidden, thinking not just about Brown but about going to graduate school later on. Given some of the faculty panels that have taken place, my friends' fears are more than reasonable. Brown's Middle East studies department has few Israeli professors, and I know of at least two who openly and enthusiastically support the BDS movement against Israel. In the fall of 2014, for example, the Middle East studies department held a panel on Gaza featuring three pro-BDS speakers and one liberal Zionist.

When the ISIS attacks in Paris occurred in November 2015, some students designed a banner-cum-monument as a memorial to victims of terrorism in, among other places, Syria, Nigeria, Paris, and Beirut. Readers may recall that at that time Israel was itself in the midst of the stabbing intifada. A student from Hillel saw fit to add by permanent marker the Jewish State to the banner, which hung on a concrete wall across from the student center. We found Israel's name scratched off a few days later.

JARED SAMILOW, Brown University 2019, is majoring in applied mathematics. He is also a columnist for *Haaretz*.

Notes

1. Jared Samilow, "On Campus, Pro-Palestinian Activists Want to Cow Israel-Supporters into Silence," *Haaretz* (November 30, 2015), http://www.haaretz.com/jewish/the-jewish -thinker/.premium-1.689197.
2. Jared Samilow, "This Is What Happens When BDS Infiltrates Social Causes That Have Nothing to Do with Israel," *Haaretz* (December 29, 2015), http://www.haaretz.com/jewish /the-jewish-thinker/.premium-1.694396.

31 Battling Anti-Zionism at the University of Missouri

Daniel Swindell

Daniel Swindell documents his ongoing battles with the pervasive anti-Israel forces on his campus, including entire departments. There's a biology professor who devotes his time to Israel-bashing and who attempts to teach a course called "Perspectives on Zionism" that offers only negative perspectives. Department after department makes up reasons not to sponsor Zionist speakers whom Swindell wants to bring in, instead bringing in speakers with minimal credentials to promulgate fabrications and deceptions and call for the destruction of Israel. The Peace Studies Department hosts such events every semester, somehow not understanding that destroying Israel would not be a peaceful endeavor. In doing this, they repeatedly use false maps alleging Jewish theft of Palestinian lands, propaganda presented as academic material, and lies presented as facts, a clear sign that the university, as a place of learning and scholarship, has gone astray. How can students emerge from this environment with anything other than anti-Israelism, when this is what masquerades as education?

To MAKE A long story short, I did not grow up thinking of myself as Jewish, although my mother is Jewish. However, in 2012, I met some orthodox Jews, one of whom said, "I don't care if you are a Muslim eating a cheeseburger, if your mother is Jewish, then you are Jewish." They invited me to study in Israel. A two-week visit turned into a year. During my stay, I wanted to see the Gaza Strip. The closest option was an Israeli border town I had never heard of, Sderot. I learned about a man named Noam Bedein, the founder of the Sderot Media Center, which offers scheduled tours. Although I arrived off-hours, Bedein was kind enough to offer me a private tour.

While I was in Sderot, the town was pleasant and quiet. I saw the skyline of Gaza from a distance of a few miles, but I learned that a few miles is in the range of rocket fire. Sderot has been hit by thousands of rockets from Gaza. I saw a school with huge black marks above the main doors, from a rocket explosion. Bedein explained that if the school had not been designed as a bomb shelter, then the rocket would have gone through the wall and killed the children. In Sderot, bomb shelters are as common as mailboxes.

At the end of the tour, Bedein asked only one thing of me: "Be our voice when you get home." His voice was not desperate, but his statement stayed with me. In 2013, I returned to Columbia, Missouri, where the University of Missouri (MU) is located. I had graduated from MU in 2010, and while there, I did not think much about Israel-related issues. However, after my year abroad, I wanted to learn how Israel was being presented on campuses.

A few months later, a biology professor named George Smith hosted the anti-Israel film *5 Broken Cameras*. I did not know it at the time, but Smith and I were going to become rivals for the next three years. At the film, Smith explained that the attacks from Gaza were trivial, and therefore, the Israeli blockade on Gaza was not justified. I raised my hand and asked him how he could refer to twelve thousand rockets as trivial. Smith responded, "The rockets are only symbolic." I could not believe a professor, or really anyone, could say such a thing.

I remembered Bedein asking me to be his voice.

I felt convinced that I needed to bring him to MU. I tried to find a group to sponsor him—I even asked the Israeli embassy—but no one was willing. Finally, the local rabbi introduced me to the president of the MU Christians United for Israel (CUFI) club, Destiny. I hadn't heard of the group before, and they were only three members. Destiny's faith moved her to stand up for Israel, and she had already taken a few punches. During Operation Cast Lead in 2008, someone took her picture and wrote, "This Christian supports the slaughter of Palestinian children," and shared it on Twitter. Bravely, Destiny agreed to sponsor the event.

To host the event, we needed a $1,000 honorarium. Surprisingly, the university agreed to give us the money. The geography department even cosponsored. Sadly, Smith showed up and distributed a flier that said that the rocket attacks were justified because the average Palestinian has to "go through a checkpoint every time he has to take a sh*t." Despite his crude protest, there was a form of poetic justice because Bedein spoke in the same room where Smith had hosted the anti-Israel film. Unfortunately, this event would prove to be the sole exception; afterward, the support dried up.

The next two years were not so favorable. In the fall of 2014, MU CUFI hosted a British Muslim named Kasim Hafeez. Hafeez was to speak about his transformation from being raised in an antisemitic home to becoming a supporter of the Jewish State. I requested cosponsorship from several departments. None was willing. CUFI is sometimes accused of being composed of religious zealots who believe that the Palestinian people are standing in the way of the return of the Messiah. However, Hafeez, a Muslim, spoke about his support for the creation of a Palestinian state beside the Jewish one. In contrast, the same semester that no one would cosponsor Hafeez, six departments cosponsored a lecture called, "The Everyday Occupation of Palestine," by Dr. Saree Makdisi. Makdisi is a professor of comparative literature at University of California, Los Angeles (UCLA) and the nephew of Edward Said. At the event, Makdisi advocated for Israel to be removed from the map and replaced by a new binational state.

Immediately after Makdisi's talk, a Palestinian graduate student gave his own minispeech. The MU Glo Co, a diversity-oriented student group, reported on the event: "Hanish Shraideh, an MU student who arrived … three months ago from Palestine, said that the talk resonated with him. A former water engineer for the Palestinian Authority, he spoke about the demolition of 40 wells in his home of Gaza simply because it was decided the region had access to too much water. 'It's not about calories, not about rockets, not about Hamas, it's about occupation,' Shraideh said."[1] But, that is not all he said. To the whole audience, he explained that Israel was a fanatical religious state exactly like ISIS and that Israel was trying to cleanse its territory of other ethnic groups.

I wanted to scream, "But Hamas calls for the murder of all Jews!" But I found myself unable to talk. I could not even bring myself to ask Makdisi a question. I think it was probably because the room had about one hundred people, and perhaps only my friend and I were supporting Israel. I felt crushed. Over the next few days, I couldn't stop thinking about it. So, I wrote a letter to the local paper. It was perhaps the first time I referred to myself as a Jewish person in a public statement: "As a Jewish alumnus of MU, words fail to express the moral disappointment of knowing six departments sponsored a man who came to inspire students to work for a world without Israel."[2]

Next semester, in the spring of 2015, MU CUFI hosted an African-American pastor named Dumisani Washington to give a lecture called, "Dr. Martin Luther King's Pro-Israel Legacy." Washington is the author of the book *Zionism and the Black Church*. I wrote to Dr. Richard Callahan, the chair of the Religious Studies Department (RSD), requesting that they cosponsor the event. Callahan responded, "We … as a Department do not support events tied to particular religious purposes, or that are not academically focused." I responded, "I am disappointed. You see … last semester, Religious Studies co-sponsored Saree Makdisi. Makdisi is an advocate with Students for Justice in Palestine, with no academic degrees in Religious Studies." Callahan responded, "Makdisi is a professor who was here … to discuss his academically-oriented work that also grounds his political views." In other words, RSD sponsored a political activist with no degrees in religious or political studies but claimed to have a rule against sponsoring speakers who are not "academically focused" when CUFI requested sponsorship.

I also asked the Black Studies Department (BSD) to cosponsor Washington's lecture. I was aware that some black student organizations revise the history of Dr. King's support for Israel. I included a flier from the Black Students Organization at Columbia University, complaining that Zionists co-opt the black liberation struggle.

I wrote, "There is a distinct difference between this flier and Pastor Washington's presentation. The flier does not quote Dr. King … while Washington uses only direct quotes." I produced the quotes, and I also sent a description of a document supporting Zionism signed by two hundred civil rights leaders, including Dr. King's wife.

BSD did not cosponsor the event.

The next semester, the fall of 2015, BSD cosponsored instead a lecture called "Racism in Israel," by Israeli-Canadian journalist David Sheen. Sheen is well known for radical statements such as comparing the housing conditions of African immigrants in Israel to Auschwitz. I organized a group letter and sent it to BSD requesting that they cancel their sponsorship, explaining, "Sheen commits an egregious iniquity when he equates the temporary housing conditions of undocumented Africans to 'Auschwitz.' … This comparison is actually a well documented form of antisemitism known as 'Holocaust Inversion.'" I sent another letter explaining that "the treatment of African refugees does *not* include forced cattle car transport, starvation, slave labor, crematoria, and the systematic gassing and murder of millions." I received nothing in response.

I vowed not to be silent as I had been at the Makdisi lecture. Sure enough, here is how the MU *Maneater* reported the event: Sheen "compared the late Israeli leader Meir Kahane to Adolf Hitler. The emotional remarks struck MU graduate Daniel Swindell particularly."[3] Apparently, I was fairly loud when I confronted Sheen at the end of the lecture. (A few days later, a friend told me, "I saw you yelling at the event.") The *Missourian* reported, "An audience member asked Sheen about his thoughts on a possible two-state solution for Israel and Palestine…. Sheen responded that he did not support such a compromise, and said if Palestinians acknowledged Israel as a 'legitimate Jewish state,' then it would be 'a license (for Israel) to be even more discriminatory.'"[4]

I was not the only person affected by this lecture. I saw a Jewish girl sitting a few seats behind me, and at one point, she was crying softly. I also spoke with another Jewish student named Evan. He told me he was so distraught the day after the lecture that he had called his brother and spoke with him about transferring to another university.

One reason there is such a disproportionate sponsorship of anti-Israel events, I believe, is that the conflict is wrongly conceived of not as an academic subject but as a social justice issue, linked to other issues such as racism, oppression, apartheid, and even genocide. It's grossly oversimplified, so that Israelis are the oppressors and the Palestinians the oppressed, period; Israel is simply wrong the way we all recognize that sexual assault is wrong. In fact, Israel is so obviously wrong that a speaker discussing the conflict need not have scholarly expertise on the subject—he or she need only be a good person concerned about human rights.

This truth was brought home to me when the MU Socialists and the MU Muslim Student Organization cosponsored the anti-Israel film *The Wanted 18*.

The film is an animated documentary about Palestinians' efforts to start a dairy industry during the First Intifada.

The film was followed by a conversation moderated by Dr. Valier Kaussen, a professor of French and film studies. Kaussen explained that the Israelis create all the problems, then find ways to blame the Palestinians. Israelis "don't allow people to work, and then they call them lazy." She explained that the West Bank, also known as Judea, was "occupied" and "colonized." This claim was false in my opinion, as the legal status of the West Bank is not "occupied" but "disputed." In any case, here we have a French professor cosponsored by two student groups to lead a discussion on the Palestinian-Israeli conflict. No one really cared about credentials. It did not matter if the professor's facts were fuzzy. The students' goal in sponsoring the event was to raise awareness about injustice, and fuzzy facts about Jewish colonizers would do just fine.

Another aspect of seeing the conflict only as a social justice issue is the advent of the activist professor who makes the Palestinians his personal cause. Reenter biology professor George Smith. In the fall of 2015, Smith attempted to teach a course called "Perspectives on Zionism." I wrote a blog post in the *Times of Israel* attacking MU for allowing him to teach the course.[5] The issue gained public attention, and the *Columbia Tribune* interviewed Smith and me. Smith defended himself, "I know huge amounts about contemporary and modern Jewish history."[6] The *Tribune* reported, "MU alumnus Daniel Swindell ... helped organize a letter-writing campaign that sought to cancel the class ... [and] included signatures from 16 different organizations."

Here is how my blog post started:

> Smith's ... perspective is that the entire history of Zionism has been "shameful" and that the Jewish State needs to be destroyed.... Smith has protested, written, and hosted events against Israel for years. It is impossible for the administration to claim ignorance of his beliefs.... Is it ethically responsible to allow a professor of biology who calls for the destruction of Zionism to teach a course on Zionism? How about a man who protested a talk given by an Israeli eyewitness of terrorist attacks with a crude joke? [At a 2013 event featuring Sderot resident Noam Bedein] Smith distributed a flier which joked that ... rocket attacks [on Israelis] were justified because the average Palestinian has to "go through a checkpoint every time he has to take a sh*t."

While I (along with sixteen organizations) was attempting to cancel Smith's class, many people accused me of having a personal beef with Smith. A Jewish student who wore a kippa accused me of being dishonest in my depiction of Smith.

I thought long and hard about this. Allow me to examine an obscure letter in the *Columbia Tribune*, written by Smith, as proof that it was not a personal problem. The letter appears to have gone entirely unnoticed. It was about the murder of five members of an Israeli family, the Fogels, and titled, "Piece about Slain

Israelis Omits Facts."[7] On March 11, 2011, in the Israeli settlement of Itamar, five members of a Jewish family were murdered in their beds: the father was stabbed in the neck, the mother was stabbed and shot, an eleven-year-old had his throat slit, a four-year-old was strangled, and a three-month-old infant was decapitated. The bodies were discovered by the twelve-year-old daughter of the family who arrived home around midnight after a youth outing.

In early April of that year, before the suspects were confirmed, the Israeli consul general made some statements mourning the victims. Smith's letter was a response to those comments. Smith claimed also to mourn the victims and stated that nothing justified the massacre, then immediately justified the massacre. Smith explained that the consul general "omits a key fact: Itamar is a Jewish-only settlement in the West Bank ... established by a 44-year campaign of land confiscation and violent repression of the resident Palestinian people." Smith explained that this fact "does not excuse the grisly crime at Itamar but surely helps explain it." He concluded, "When you oppress people, they naturally resist—sometimes, though rarely in the case of Palestine, with hideous violence."

Personally, I do not understand why the newspaper published this letter. Even if the settlements were an obstacle to peace, for the sake of argument, isn't this perhaps the single occasion not to blame Israel? But the hard facts are these: after Smith heard about five family members being chopped up and an infant decapitated, he felt the need to explain that Israelis should "naturally" expect consequences when they "oppress" the Palestinians.

That is why I opposed Smith's course.

The dispute began to get more coverage. "Nancy West, director of MU's Honors College, told *JNS.org* ... 'Smith has a 30-year record of being an outstanding teacher who is very well respected. We trusted that record and trusted him.... I stand behind George's course.'"[8] In the end, the class was canceled, officially due to lack of enrollment, but JNS also reported, "Nonetheless, it is unlikely that the course will ever be offered again ... an affidavit is being prepared by Jewish community activists, in conjunction with the University legal department, that would help ensure Smith will be turned down next time he tries to teach about Zionism."

To this day, I have mixed feelings about how the situation concluded. I know that many people celebrated this as a victory. However, the letter from the sixteen organizations amounted to a national declaration by representatives of the Jewish people that the university's approval of Smith's class in the first place was a disgrace. The university itself ignored that declaration, canceling the class only due to lack of enrollment.

It's even worse when the activist professor is propped up by an activist department. The MU Peace Studies Department (PSD) worked with Smith many times on their mission to attack Israel. During the 2014 Gaza War, a group called

Mid-Missouri Fellowship of Reconciliation hosted a protest against Israel. The press release was shared on the PSD Facebook page. Hamas was innocent, it declared, for "the crisis was initiated by Israel"; somehow, experts in peace studies were unable to conceive of twelve thousand rocket attacks and the kidnapping and murder of teenagers as nonpeaceful actions. Hamas was in "a struggle for equality and human rights, not for sovereignty over land." Finally, "Israeli Jews have a right to live securely in their homeland. But they don't have a right to a Jewish ethnocracy." PSD would promote this call for Israel's destruction relentlessly. From 2014 to 2016, PSD hosted four events, one every semester, advocating for the replacement of Israel as a Jewish state with a binational state, which everyone knows means Arab-majority state.

PSD's ongoing attack on Israel is perhaps best captured in their repeated use of a series of maps allegedly showing Palestine's shrinking at the hands of the Jewish people.[9] In the spring of 2015, PSD cosponsored a lecture by Smith called "Palestine in Context." The flier for the event showed the four false maps. When I saw the fliers, I organized a letter to the chancellor signed by several people, one of whom was the author of a book titled *U.S. Policy on Jerusalem*. The letter explained precisely how the maps were fabrications and intentionally misleading. "The maps show a nonexistent country [Palestine]," the letter concluded, "and then shows the Jewish State destroying this 'country.'... The fliers should be taken down, and it should be made clear that the map cannot be shown at the event." To think that an academic department would advertise an event with such dishonest material.

The chancellor responded that the department would look into the issue. I eventually received a message from Dr. Lo, the chair of PSD, who explained that, "The maps you mention and the name labels represent the political beliefs and future aspirations of some Palestinian groups rather than picturing the existing geopolitical lines and names at different historical periods. A notice to this effect appears on the Peace Studies official website." The response was both false and incoherent. The images were maps labeled as named territories existing from 1947 to the present day. I responded to Lo, "I cannot follow the explanation, the maps give no indication of future years." I also emailed the chancellor, whom I believed should know that an academic department was distributing straightforward propaganda, "Where is the future mentioned on the maps?"

Someone then blocked me from commenting on the PSD Facebook page when I attempted to explain that the maps were false.

In the end, the maps were used for the event. So much for the administration's concern about academic propaganda.

The next year, in the spring of 2016, the PSD hosted the anti-Israel film *The Zionist Story*. The film showed the same propaganda maps. In contrast, when MSNBC erroneously showed nearly the exact same four false maps, they later issued this statement: "The maps were not factually accurate, and we regret using them."[10] McGraw-Hill, a textbook publisher, also pulled textbooks that included them for the same reason.

Propaganda presented as academic material is very dangerous, in my opinion. Consider the story of Kasim Hafeez, the speaker whom PSD refused to sponsor. Hafeez was an anti-Israel activist in college who became radicalized. Planning a trip to a terrorist camp in Pakistan, he randomly came upon Alan Dershowitz's book *The Case for Israel*. Before he encountered the book, he said, "I thought I was an expert in the Middle East."[11] His first thoughts on reading were that "Dershowitz makes some absolutely ludicrous claims, he says the Jewish people have had a presence in the Holy Land for thousands of years," that "a Palestinian State has never existed." But, Hafeez thought, "no ... we all know there was a Palestinian State," because "we have all seen the maps, the Jews came from Europe ... and stole the land." After reading the book and researching the claims, he realized that he had been brainwashed.

Guess which maps Hafeez was referring to?

Hafeez was fed this propaganda by radical Muslims with a genocidal agenda. MU students are being fed this propaganda by their own academic departments.

In the beginning of this article, I stated that I did not grow up thinking of myself as Jewish. Often, I feel like I live in two realms. By orthodox Jewish law, I am considered Jewish; however, due to my upbringing, I have had to learn about the history of the Jewish people like an outsider. As I began to learn, I was haunted by the brutal history of Jew-hatred. To me, it is clear that PSD is simply continuing this hatred. Think about the outrageousness of the situation. PSD repeatedly promoted a map of Palestine as if it had once existed as a country, followed by an image of the Jewish people annihilating this country, which means that PSD has invented a false crime committed by the Jewish people, then hosted events to spread awareness of this false crime in order to encourage students to fight against this fictional injustice by destroying the Jewish State. Can anyone tell me the difference between this and spreading the classic antisemitic trope that Jews are thieves? Or the blood libel that Jewish people killed Christian children for their matzah? Can anyone tell me with a straight face that there is a difference between this lie and the murderous lies that have been told about the Jewish people for centuries?

In one sense I was lucky, because I had already graduated from MU when I took on the task of advocating for Israel, of advocating for truth, in a climate apparently hostile to both. Having graduated, I was less intimidated by the actors, was unaffected by the power of the grade, and had more self-confidence about being in the right. But I am very worried for the undergraduates at MU and other campuses. It takes real courage to stand up when the atmosphere around you is filled with hatred for you. Most will lack that courage. And when the very professors and departments are the source of the hatred and disseminate propaganda disguised as fact and offer speakers without credentials as if they are experts, what chance, really, does the next generation of students have of learning the truth about Israel?

DANIEL SWINDELL, University of Missouri 2010, majored in philosophy.

Notes

1. Jessica Karins, "Saree Makdisi's Lecture Incites Student Call for Action," Mizzou Global Communications, *The Missouri Atlas* (November 25, 2014), https://muglobalcommunications.wordpress.com/?s=Hanish+Shraideh (accessed November 6, 2017).

2. Letter to Editor, *Columbia Daily Tribune* (November 22, 2014), http://www.columbiatribune.com/99c23237-8257-5355-a59e-672c6aecf85b.html.

3. Ann Marion, "Canadian-Israeli Journalist Comments on Israeli-Palestinian Conflict," *The Maneater* (November 17, 2015), http://www.themaneater.com/stories/2015/11/17/canadian-raised-journalist-activist-and-israeli-ci/.

4. Ines Kagubare, "Talk About Racism, Discrimination in Israel Spurs Conversation at MU," *The Columbia Missourian* (November 10, 2015), https://www.columbiamissourian.com/news/higher_education/talk-about-racism-discrimination-in-israel-spurs-conversation-at-mu/article_01b882cc-87b5-11e5-a986-b31b6bb948e1.html.

5. Daniel Swindell, "Crude Joke at U of Missouri," *The Times of Israel* (April 19, 2015), http://blogs.timesofisrael.com/crude-joke-at-u-of-missouri/.

6. This and the next quotation are from Bruno Vernaschi, "MU Course on Zionism Canceled," *Columbia Daily Tribune* (June 24, 2015), http://www.columbiatribune.com/60d335b9-3ba8-57b6-ad57-6b6b86f3c778.html.

7. Letter to Editor, *Columbia Daily Tribune* (April 9, 2011), http://www.columbiatribune.com/6f373baf-1d04-5fbc-a50d-fd755e129fc0.html.

8. This and the next quotation are from Mayaan Jaffe, "Israel Crisis Averted in Missouri as Biology Professor's Anti-Zionist Course Nixed," *Jewish News Service* (June 11, 2015), http://www.jns.org/latest-articles/2015/6/11/israel-crisis-averted-in-missouri-as-biology-professors-anti-zionist-course-nixed.

9. "Debunking 'The Map that Lies,'" *Elder of Ziyon* (July 13, 2012), http://elderofziyon.blogspot.com/2012/07/debunking-map-that-lies.html.

10. "MSNBC Apologizes for Showing 'Not Factually Accurate' Maps of Israel," *Jewish Telegraphic Agency* (October 20, 2015), https://www.jta.org/2015/10/20/news-opinion/united-states/msnbc-apologizes-for-showing-not-factually-accurate-maps-of-israel.

11. This and the subsequent quotes are from "Kasim Hafeez: From Radical Islam to Pro-Israel Advocate," *Jewish Broadcast Service* (September 12, 2014), https://www.youtube.com/watch?v=rxnpoeVaS8Q&t=685s. Relevant portions are at minutes 27–29.

III. Concluding Thoughts

32 Inconclusive, Unscientific Postscript: On the Purpose of the University, and a Ray of Hope

Andrew Pessin

Andrew Pessin finds a ray of hope in a recent ruling by McGill University's Judicial Board, finding that BDS resolutions violate its student government's constitution. This ruling, reminiscent of the University of Chicago's famous *Kalven Report*, reminds us what the purpose of universities is and shows how BDS is in essence an attack on the norms of the university itself.

Firm conclusions are not yet possible because the battle is far from over. As we mentioned in our introduction to the volume, campus anti-Israelists are in it for the long haul. It remains unclear whether those who do *not* believe that Israel is an unqualified abomination will be able to stay in it for the long haul as well. It is a hard battle to fight, and the personal costs are great, as our volume has documented. It is easy to understand why so many Jewish students and faculty stay quiet. Their careers may even be at stake. But perhaps there is room for hope, for a remarkable event occurred at the end of May 2016 that just might signify that important change of campus momentum. It happened quietly, but it ought to be loudly disseminated across the Western world, for universities are at the heart of that world. In May 2016, a university's student government suddenly remembered what the overall purpose of student governments is—which itself ought to remind universities of what *their* overall purpose is.

We return to McGill University.

After three Boycott, Divestment, and Sanctions (BDS) failures in the previous couple of years, McGill anti-Israelists finally celebrated when their student government passed a BDS resolution in February 2016.[1] The celebrations were short-lived, however, for the student body as a whole failed to ratify that vote just a few days later.[2] That's when things got interesting. The anti-Israelists petitioned the university's Judicial Board, challenging the technical legality of the ratification process. At the same time, a McGill student, perhaps fed up with the relentless BDS assault on his student government, petitioned the Judicial Board to challenge the very *constitutionality* of that and any BDS resolution.

On May 31, 2016, the Judicial Board at McGill University ruled that student government resolutions affirming BDS against Israel violate the constitution and equity policy of its government, the Students' Society of McGill University (SSMU).[3] That meant that McGill, whose campus had spent several years embroiled in BDS debates, would finally be able to return full-time to its proper business: educating its students.

The reasoning in the decision was so clear that it was downright refreshing.

In the relevant university mandate documents quoted in their decision, the Judicial Board noted that SSMU's mission is to "facilitate communication and interaction between all students," to refrain from discrimination on the basis of "race, national or ethnic origin ... religion," and to create "an 'anti-oppressive' atmosphere where all of its membership feels included."

But, then, the Judicial Board asks, can the SSMU "take an authoritative, direct, and unambiguous stance" against a particular nation, as the recent BDS resolution demands that it do against Israel?

Unambiguously, no.

A university may well have students from both sides of any given conflict, and "by picking a side ... the government does not promote interactions ... but rather champions one's cause over another." Student governments must represent their members, but "it would be absurd for the government to claim that it is representing Israeli members as favorably as other nationals despite it supporting boycotts ... against Israel." Indeed, by "adopting official positions against certain nations ... SSMU would be placing members from those nations at a structural disadvantage within [the] community," failing to protect the rights of those minorities from "the tyranny of the majority," and in violating its "anti-oppression" mandate would be failing in "its obligations to its own members."

Or as they put it succinctly: "McGill is first and foremost a university, a place of knowledge and intellectual growth—a fact that is often forgotten.... [Our student government] cannot be the venue for a proxy war."

That all this is so obviously true—that anyone undertaking a neutral approach to designing student governments would concur—makes you wonder why (as the Judicial Board put it) it is so "often forgotten."

I have several hypotheses but will mention just one.

For any serious conflict, the *scholar* always recognizes that there are (at least) two sides. Any organization serving the scholarly mission of the university must always therefore ensure that all sides have equal opportunity to be heard.

The activist has no such constraint. The activist's goal is to win, to change the status quo, to defeat the other side, to overturn it, to silence it—by any means necessary, in fact, if the status quo is truly as evil as he or she claims it to be.[4]

Activism is surely wonderful and to be encouraged. I would even propose that activism as we today understand it has naturally grown out of scholarship, that as the Enlightenment led to intellectual liberty, it led to the recognition of the value of diversity in every sense—which in turn leads to the activism that admirably promotes that diversity.

But in our zeal for activism, we have forgotten that when a *student government* takes a side in a conflict, when it decides that there are *not* two sides after all, it thereby abandons its role in the scholarly mission of the institution *for* the activism. And as the Judicial Board noted, where a student government's objective should be to protect and promote the interests of minorities, including minority opinions, against the tyranny of the majority, when the government chooses one side, it *becomes* the tyrannical majority instead.

That is the moment when the activism begotten by scholarship *overthrows* the scholarship—the moment when the university launches its own destruction.

Indeed, the last time this was put so clearly was perhaps all the way back in 1967, when the University of Chicago's Kalven Committee produced its famous *Report on the University's Role in Political and Social Action*.[5]

It is worth some extended quotes:

> A university has a great and unique role to play in fostering the development of social and political values in a society. The role is defined by the distinctive mission of the university ... the discovery, improvement, and dissemination of knowledge.
>
> The instrument of dissent and criticism is the individual faculty member or ... student. The university is the home and sponsor of critics; it is not itself the critic.... To perform its mission in the society, a university must sustain an extraordinary environment of freedom of inquiry and maintain an independence from political fashions, passions, and pressures. A university, if it is to be true to its faith in intellectual inquiry, must embrace, be hospitable to, and encourage the widest diversity of views within its own community.... It is not a club, it is not a trade association, it is not a lobby.
>
> [It] is a community which cannot take collective action on the issues of the day without endangering the conditions for its existence and effectiveness. There is no mechanism by which it can reach a collective position without inhibiting that full freedom of dissent on which it thrives. It cannot insist that all of its members favor a given view of social policy; if it takes collective action, therefore, it does so at the price of censuring any minority who do not agree with the view adopted. In brief, it is a community which cannot resort to majority vote to reach positions on public issues.
>
> The neutrality of the university as an institution arises ... out of respect for free inquiry and the obligation to cherish a diversity of viewpoints.

Of *course*, one wants to say. Intellectual inquiry requires intellectual liberty and the freedom of speech. Don't we all agree on that? Doesn't every single fair-minded lover of knowledge, not seized by the hysteria of his or her own personal political agenda, agree with that?

But the instrument of that speech is the individual faculty member or student and the groups he or she may form to promote his or her viewpoint. Let him or her have at it, with maximal freedom of inquiry and speech ringing throughout the institution.

But that most noble goal of intellectual liberty and diversity can be achieved only when the organs of the institution itself—the university, the faculty governing body, graduate student unions, the student government—are above the fray. To maximize the freedom of inquiry and speech of their members, they must not be hijacked for the political agendas even of the majority of their members.

In our zeal for activism, for the clarity of one side (at the expense of the other), we have somehow failed to observe what could not be more obvious: that the BDS movement as it is manifest on our campuses does not merely target Israel and Israeli Jews. In its efforts to commandeer the organs of the university, it targets the fundamental goals and values of the university as a whole.

So let individual faculty and students criticize Israel all they want, as long as they obey the norms of intellectual inquiry (including respect for truth, of course). Let them form campus advocacy groups for Palestine, as long as they obey those same norms. But what they cannot do, what they must not be permitted to do, is to suppress the other side of the story, to pretend there is no other side, to silence those who see the other side. What they cannot be permitted to do—what no one should be permitted to do—is take over the organs of the university itself.

McGill's Judicial Board has done us all an immense service. Socrates, Hume, Mill—and ultimately all the many minority and disenfranchised voices themselves that have in recent years finally been getting their turn to be heard—should thank it.

And those who want to reclaim the university from the clutches of BDS should learn from it.

I close with an anecdote that perhaps perfectly expresses the current situation on our campuses, for those who do not hate Israel—and I think it too offers a ray of hope, in these dark times, for those who believe in the fundamental values of the university.

In the spring of 2014, Cornell Law School professor William Jacobson wrote several articles about the anti-Israel campus atmosphere at Vassar College.[6] The primary focus of these articles was the events surrounding a proposed study trip to Israel/Palestine, the subject of Jill Schneiderman's essay in the current volume. But the context for those events was the ongoing campus discussion over the BDS resolution approved several months earlier by the American Studies Association. After Vassar's president and dean of faculty had condemned that resolution, thirty-nine Vassar professors published an open letter in the school newspaper dissenting from that condemnation and endorsing BDS.[7] This, in turn, was followed by a letter from a Vassar alumni group calling itself "Fairness to Israel," complaining that "Vassar is no longer the open, innovative institution that transformed our lives, a college which stimulated—indeed compelled—independent and critical thinking. Rather, faculty and student supporters of the BDS movement against Israel have hijacked campus discourse and imposed an anti-intellectual atmosphere in which professors are ranting activists, not scholars, and students who disagree with the prevailing 'progressive' ideology are intimidated into a deafening silence."[8]

From outside, Jacobson noted that there didn't seem to be any Vassar faculty voices willing to make these points themselves, to stand up for Israel on campus. The head of Jewish studies at Vassar was himself an ardent BDS supporter and signatory to the pro-BDS letter. Even the campus Hillel was silent, perhaps because it had become an "Open Hillel"—meaning open to, or even dominated by, anti-Israel voices.

So Jacobson decided to do it himself.

He managed to get the Vassar Moderate Independent Conservative Alliance to sponsor him, and they put out an open invitation to the thirty-nine Vassar signatories to the BDS letter to publicly debate him. In announcing the event, he wrote: "Any or all of the 39 Vassar faculty members are welcome to debate me. All I insist on is equal time cumulatively. If none of the 39 Vassar faculty agree to debate, I will give a lecture on why the academic boycott of Israel should be opposed.... There will be a tendency to want someone to 'win' the debate. That's not the point. By simply hosting this challenge and debate, the Vassar campus wins."[9]

Not one—*not a single one*—of the thirty-nine faculty members accepted the challenge.

Not only that, but while the lecture he gave instead—"The Case for Israel and Academic Freedom"—filled the room to near capacity (158), the audience was comprised of "a significant local presence from surrounding area synagogues, alumni, [and only] a very small number of faculty, and students."[10]

One thing he learned was that "while most of the 39 professors did not respond to the debate invitation sent out by the student organizers, one of the professors who did respond said that I should be boycotted. Imagine that."[11]

Thirty-nine faculty members at a premier liberal arts college, including the head of the Jewish studies department, were bold enough to publicly endorse a BDS proposal against Israel—but not one was interested in honestly debating someone who actually knows something about the Middle East conflict.

And, apparently, not many of them, if any, even came to listen.

That silence, *their* silence, speaks volumes.[12]

ANDREW PESSIN is Professor of Philosophy at Connecticut College and Campus Bureau Editor of the *Algemeiner*. Author of many academic articles and books, a philosophy textbook, several philosophical books for the general reader, and two novels, his current research is focused on philosophical matters relevant both to Judaism and Israel.

Notes

1. Andrew Pessin, "BDS Motion Passes Easily at Canada's McGill University," *The Algemeiner* (February 23, 2016), http://www.algemeiner.com/2016/02/23/bds-motion -passes-easily-at-canadas-mcgill-university/.

2. Andrew Pessin, "McGill University's Student Body Rejects Student Government's BDS Vote," *The Algemeiner* (February 27, 2016), https://www.algemeiner.com/2016/02/27/mcgill -universitys-student-body-rejects-student-governments-bds-vote/.

3. Students' Society of McGill University Judicial Board, "Reference re Legality of the BDS Motion and Similar Motions" (May 31, 2016), http://ssmu.ca/wp-content/uploads /2012/01/Reference-Re-Legality-of-BDS-Motion-and-Similar-Motions.pdf?x26516 (accessed November 13, 2017).

4. Blogger Jon Haber puts it this way: "Ends always justify means when it comes to the BDSers getting a major institution on their side, with those means including use of truncated, distorted, or outright false information while shutting down member access to alternative points of view. Such a 'by any means necessary' approach also includes moral blackmail, stacking decision-making bodies with BDS supporters, colluding behind closed doors to get boycott and divestment measures passed before anyone knows they are even being discussed, or (when all else fails) fraudulently claiming support when none exists." See Jon Haber, "The BDS Playbook," *The Algemeiner* (July 10, 2016), http://www.algemeiner .com/2016/07/10/the-bds-playbook/.

5. "Kalven Committee: Report on the University's Role in Political and Social Action" (November 11, 1967), http://www-news.uchicago.edu/releases/07/pdf/kalverpt.pdf (accessed November 13, 2017).

6. William A. Jacobson, "Anti-Israel Academic Boycott Turns Ugly at Vassar," *Legal Insurrection* (March 27, 2014), https://legalinsurrection.com/2014/03/anti-israel-academic -boycott-turns-ugly-at-vassar/; William A. Jacobson, "The Anti-Israel Cultural Revolution at Vassar," *Legal Insurrection* (April 6, 2014), https://legalinsurrection.com/2014/04/the-anti -israel-cultural-revolution-at-vassar/; William A. Jacobson, "Anti-Israel 'Climate of Fear' at Vassar," *Legal Insurrection* (April 12, 2014), https://legalinsurrection.com/2014/04/anti-israel -climate-of-fear-at-vassar/.

7. Vassar Faculty, "Open Letter in Defense of Academic Freedom in Palestine/Israel and in the United States," *The Miscellany News* (March 1, 2014), http://miscellanynews .org/2014/03/01/opinions/open-letter-in-defense-of-academic-freedom-in-palestineisrael-and -in-the-united-states/.

8. Fairness to Israel, "Faculty Letter Squelches Campus Voices," *The Miscellany News* (March 26, 2014), http://miscellanynews.org/2014/03/26/opinions/faculty-letter-squelches -campus-voices/.

9. William A. Jacobson, "My Debate Challenge to Vassar Pro-Boycott Faculty," *Legal Insurrection* (April 21, 2014), https://legalinsurrection.com/2014/04/my-debate-challenge-to -vassar-pro-boycott-faculty/.

10. William A. Jacobson, "Vassar College Wins," *Legal Insurrection* (May 6, 2014), https://legalinsurrection.com/2014/05/vassar-college-wins/.

11. William A. Jacobson, "Vassar College Wins," *Legal Insurrection* (May 6, 2014), https://legalinsurrection.com/2014/05/vassar-college-wins/.

12. Part of this essay is adapted from my article, "McGill University and How Western Civilization May Have Just Saved Itself from Itself," *The Algemeiner* (June 6, 2016), https:// www.algemeiner.com/2016/06/06/mcgill-university-and-how-western-civilization-may-have -just-saved-itself-from-itself/. It is used here by permission.

Index

AAA (American Anthropological Association). *See* American Anthropological Association (AAA)

AAUP (American Association of University Professors), 194, 196–97, 205, 210n23, 282

Abdallah, Georges, 240, 242

AbuKhalil, As'ad, 208n1

Abunimah, Ali, 199, 201, 208n1

academic boycott/s: AAA and, 191, 193, 195, 282; academic disciplines and, 198; Australian academics and, 46, 47, 50, 55, 57n25, 173n15; by BDS, 45, 46, 47, 50, 52, 55; CPACS and, 44–46, 287; destruction of Israel and, 47, 49; Durban conference and, 8, 118n1; free speech and, 92, 194, 282; global academy and, 8, 15; identity politics and, 51; Israeli anthropologists and, 286–87; Jewish-Israeli academics and, 43, 50, 51; the Left/left and, 131; norms of scholarship and, 92; NWSA and, 129; Palestinian academics and, 9; pro-Israel support and, 194; SJP and, 13; South American academics and, 15; UCU and, 106, 108–9; in UK, 111n1; University of Toronto and, 145

academic career/s: harassment and bullying and, 72, 195–96; mock checkpoint event at CMC and, 276, 277, 278; pro-Israel support and, 1, 79, 130, 135, 139, 144, 194, 195, 388; tenure and, 87–88, 89; UCSC and, 299–300; water issues study trip to Israel/Palestine from Vassar and, 329–30

academic freedom: AAA and, 283, 285, 294, 295; ASA and, 231; BDS and, 230, 283, 285, 295; disruption of event at IIS, UT Austin and, 242; legal action against UCU and, 110; MSJC and, 214–15, 216, 217, 218; NWSA and, 129; PACBI and, 286; Rhodes University and, 137, 139–40; at UCSC,

301–2; University of Sydney and, 253; Vassar College and, 405; water issues study trip to Israel/Palestine from Vassar and, 324, 329; Weatherhead Center at Harvard and, 155, 157–59

Academic Friends of Israel, 106, 108

academic integrity: about, 346; AAA and, 295; administration's action/inaction and, 232; Australia and, 169; identity politics versus, 387; MSJC and, 213, 214, 215, 216, 219; MU and, 392, 393, 394–96, 397–98; UB and, 334, 338, 343–45; UCSD and, 92. *See also* norms of scholarship

academic organizations, 17. See also *specific organizations*

academics (scholarship). *See* Jewish-Israeli academics; scholarship (academics)

Academic Senate Executive Committee (SEC), UCSC, 301–2

the academy, 17. *See also* academic boycotts; global academy; politically correct academia; *specific organizations and universities*

Achcar, Gilbert, 185

ACLU (American Civil Liberties Union), 233, 305, 364

activism, 2, 132, 402–3, 404, 406n4. *See also* advocacy/advocacy groups

Adams, Roger, 136, 138, 140

ADL (Anti-Defamation League), 72, 74n17, 97, 100–101, 369

administration at university/ies action/ inaction: academic integrity and, 232; anti-Israelism and, 23–24; ASA resolution and, 231–32; BDS resolutions and, 18, 93, 95, 401–2, 403, 404; civility/anticivility and, 233; disruption event at University of Sydney and, 257–58, 260–64, 287; disruption of events at IIS, UT Austin

speech and, 192, 196; intersectionality and, 204; Nazism and, 193; political advocacy and, 192–93, 194, 198, 199–201, 199–202, 207; social media and, 204, 205, 210n21, 210n23; syllabi and, 192, 201, 204–5, 206, 207, 209nn14–15. *See also* curriculum
Curthoys, Ned, 167–68, 169, 170–71

Dalmar, Amal, 98, 99
Darshan-Leitner, Nitsana, 55
Darwish, Mahmoud, 371
Deek, Lamis, 380
defacements as hate crimes, 76, 77, 78, 277, 350, 381. *See also* visual evidence
defamation: disruption of event as IIS, UT Austin, 241, 244; double standards and, 88; Jewish/lesbian staff member and, 137; mock checkpoint event at CMC and, 268, 271, 272, 274, 277, 278; UCSC and, 298, 299, 300, 306, 307, 308, 309, 312–13; Weatherhead Center at Harvard and, 155
DeJulio, Tom, 68
De Klerk, Vivian, 137, 138, 139, 140
democracy/ies, 1, 48, 49, 51, 54
Derrida, Jacques, 291
Dershowitz, Alan, 7, 196, 397
Desai, Muhammed, 137
Despard, Edward, 242
destruction of Israel: academic boycotts and, 47, 49; Australia and, 164; BDS and, 10–11, 31n51–52, 31n57, 48, 50, 51, 208n1, 213, 215, 224, 284; Final Solution and, 284; free speech and, 111; Hezbollah and, 175; NWSA and, 127, 129; SJP and, 12; UCU and, 109, 116; UK anti-Israelism and, 175, 184–85, 186
Dheer, Ala Abu, 181
dialogue/s. *See* diversity of perspectives
Diaspora Jews. *See* Jewish community (Diaspora Jews); Jewish community (Diaspora Jews), and Israel relationship
die-in/vigil for Ferguson and Gaza, 380, 381
discrimination: Arab-Israeli-Palestinians, 49; Australia and, 54; Fordham University's allegations of religious discrimination, 68, 69; LGBTQ, 80–81, 132; McGill University and, 402; MSJC

and, 215, 222; Oberlin College and, 374; at Stanford University, 369; UC and, 312; UCLA and, 233, 365; UK and, 109, 114, 116, 117
disruption of event/s: about, 21; antisemitism and, 3–4; Brown University and, 384, 385; film screening at UCI and, 3, 26n13–14, 149, 150n2; Intifada/intifada chants and, 26n13, 149, 238, 239; Israeli academic speaker in Paris and, 350, 354n3; against Palestinians, 14, 33n73, 33n75; by SJP, 12–13, 19, 32n65; in UK, 3–4, 176. *See also* Institute for Israel Studies (IIS), UT Austin, and disruption of event
diversity of perspectives: balanced presentation versus, 131–32, 135; BDS and, 13, 49; calling-in model and, 132; coexistence and, 139; controversies and, 160–61; democracy and, 54; Jewish-Arab dialogue in Australia and, 165–66, 168; John Jay College and, 380, 381–83; NWSA and, 124, 129–31; pro-Israel support and, 131; Rhodes University and, 135–36, 139; SJP and, 12, 380, 383; UB and, 345; UCI and, 149; UK anti-Israelism documentation and, 182, 184–85; universities and, 131–32, 183, 192–98; University of Michigan and, 361–62n5; water issues study trip to Israel/Palestine from Vassar and, 328–29, 330; Weatherhead Center at Harvard and, 155, 160–61
divestment from Israel resolution/s, 98–101, 231, 308
Divine, Donna Robinson, 201
Dixon, Bruce, 204
Docker, John, 167–68, 173n15
Dorner, Dalia, 147, 148
double standard/s: activists' methods and, 132; anti-Israelism as antisemitism and, 139; defamation and, 88; human rights and, 139; for Israel, 89, 370, 375, 377, 379, 388; for Jews, 89, 115, 388
Douglas, Michael, 384, 385
dualistic thinking, 98, 101–2
Dubnow, Simon, 94, 95
Dugard, John, 178

by faculty against, 269, 277, 278; Campus Safety report and, 273; CMC investigation/report and, 268; confidentiality requirements violations by, 270, 273; faculty grievance against, 270, 271–73, 276, 278; personal attacks/verbal attacks, 276–77; Pitzer Code of Student Conduct and, 271–72; Segal as faculty advisor to, 268, 269–70; smear campaign against faculty, 268, 269, 276, 277, 278

Hammond, Keith, 109, 110

harassment and bullying: academic careers and, 72, 195–96; allegations against faculty and, 214, 215, 216, 217; anti-Israelism and, 2; ASA BDS resolution opposition and, 69, 70, 71; by BDS, 71; of Jewish students, 299; at MSJC, 213; Oberlin College and, 375; by politically correct academia, 72; Rhodes University and, 137, 138, 139; UCSC and, 298, 301, 302, 304, 305, 307. *See also* legal action for unlawful harassment by UCU

The Harvard Crimson (campus newspaper), 156, 159, 160–61, 388

Harvard University: administration's action/inaction and, 23, 152, 156, 157, 158; anti-Israelism and, 2; antisemitism and, 72, 157; BDS and, 8; neutrality policy and, 157, 158. *See also* Weatherhead Center for International Affairs, Harvard University

hate crime, and defacements, 76, 77, 78, 277, 350, 381. *See also* visual evidence

hate speech, 273, 345, 359, 381–82; anti-Israelism and, 2, 20, 76, 77, 78, 93, 192; antisemitism and, 2, 19, 37–38n124, 93, 119n6, 306; against Jews, 19, 37–38n124, 93; against Jews/Jewish students, 212, 359; MSJC and, 213, 215, 218; against Muslims, 306–7. *See also* free speech

Hebrew University, 44–45, 54, 287, 351

Hedley, Steve, 183–84

Hendler, Glenn, 67, 69–70, 73n7

Hennessy, John, 4

Herzl, Theodor, 199, 200

Herzliya Conference, 152–53, 160

Hessel, Stéphane, 178

Hezbollah, 175, 186, 311, 388

Higgens, Patrick, 237–38, 239, 241, 242, 243, 246

Hillel (campus organization): antinormalization and, 14, 33–34n77; BDS on campuses and, 96, 191, 195; Brown University and, 33–34n77, 384, 385, 386, 388–89; John Jay College and, 380, 381–82; Kesher Enoshi and, 96–97; Oberlin College and, 373, 374; Stanford University, 368; at UCI, 147; at University of Toronto, 145; Vassar College and, 405

Hillel (Talmudic sage), 97, 131

Hirsh, David, 107, 108, 120n21, 164, 196

Hiss, Yehuda, 340–41, 342, 343

historical continuity/collective memory, 229, 230

Hitler, Adolf, 58–59, 144, 154, 162n8, 174

Hofstader, Richard, 293

Holocaust: about, 344; antisemitic activities/discussions/evidence and, 2, 24–25n3, 63, 109, 110, 114; deniers of, 107, 177; Final Solution and destruction of Israel and, 284; genocide defined and, 154; post-Holocaust Jewish community and, 260, 263–64, 344. *See also* Nazism, and anti-Israelism; Nazism, and antisemitism

Holstun, James, 336, 341

homophobia, 71, 76, 77, 78, 81, 138, 140

homosexual rights, 80–82, 288, 385–86

Honest Reporting, 29–30n45

Horizon 2020, 288–89

Horton, Richard, 180

hostile environment. *See* harassment and bullying

human rights: BDS and, 7, 9, 11, 12, 14, 48, 52, 228, 229–30; double standards and, 139; for Palestinians, 12, 176, 178, 181, 384, 393, 395; SJP and, 11–12. *See also* justice

Hunt, Sally, 110, 114

IAW (Israeli Apartheid Week). *See* Israeli Apartheid Week (IAW)

identity politics: academic boycotts and, 51; academic integrity versus, 387; anti-Israelism and, 23, 384, 387, 388; dualistic thinking and, 98, 101–2;

SJP (Students for Justice in Palestine). *See* Students for Justice in Palestine (SJP)

smear campaign/s: about, 3, 5, 21, 23, 160; against director of IIS, UT Austin, 240, 241, 243, 244; against faculty member at CMC, 268, 269, 273–74, 275, 276; by intellectuals/elites, 71; against Israel, 8, 84, 86; Palestinian genocide allegations as, 154, 155, 156, 157, 158; UCLA and, 364–65. *See also* personal attacks

Smith, George, 394–96

Smith, Stephen, 148

Smith College, 132

Smuts, Izak, 139

SOAS (School of Oriental and African Studies), 14–15, 182, 183, 184, 185

SOCC (Students of Color Coalition), 367–68, 371

social media: anti-Israelism curriculum and, 204, 205, 210n21, 210n23; BDS and, 246–47; campaign against director of IIS on, 240, 242; cultural boycotts and, 13, 16; Nazism and anti-Israelism relationship in, 115; scholarly analysis of disruption of events at IIS, UT Austin and, 246–49; SJP presence on, 12

Sontag, Susan, 73n5

South Africa: BDS and, 8, 51–52, 137; Durban conference in, 8, 15, 28n33, 29n44, 39n153, 118n1; SAJBD in, 138; trade and labor unions in, 138; Zionist Federation in, 138. *See also* Rhodes University, and Jewish/lesbian staff member

South African Jewish Board of Deputies (SAJBD), 138

South American academics, and academic boycotts, 15

Spain, 16, 178

Sparrow, Jeff, 170, 171

Spellman, Mary, 268

SPME (Scholars for Peace in the Middle East), 92

SPUQ (Syndicat des Professeurs de l'Université du Québec), 63, 65n9

SSMU (Students' Society of McGill University), 402

staff members, university. *See* Rhodes University, and Jewish/lesbian staff member

StandWithUs, 138, 309, 379, 380

Stanford University: anti-Israelism as antisemitism and, 370; antisemitism at, 369–71; discrimination at, 369; Hillel and, 368; Jewish community support and, 370–71; Jewish global domination allegations and, 37–38n124, 370; Jewish students and, 366–67, 368, 369; J Street and, 369, 370; personal attacks/safety and, 369; senate representatives at, 366, 369, 370; silencing effect of anti-Israelism and, 373, 374; SOCC and, 367–68, 371

Stang, Fanny, 258

Statist Zionism, 94–95

Stern, Kenneth, 93

structural antisemitism, 84

Student Affirmative Action Committee (SAAC), 98

students, Israeli, 352. *See also* Jewish student/s

Students Allied for Freedom and Equality (SAFE), 357, 358–61, 361–62n5

Students for Justice in Palestine (SJP): academic boycotts and, 13; anti-Israelism and, 12, 373; anti-Israelism as antisemitism and, 24–25n3; antinormalization and, 13–14, 15, 374, 382; as BDS proxy, 225, 231; Brown University and, 14, 384–85, 387; California Legislature HR-35 and, 311; at Columbia University, 13; disruption of events by, 12–13, 19, 32n65; diversity of perspectives and, 12, 380, 383; Fordham University's prohibition of, 24n1, 72; free speech/Title VI antisemitism complaints and, 304–5, 306, 310; history of, 12, 31n61, 62n62; human rights and, 11–12; intersectionality and, 11, 14, 373–74, 380, 381, 385, 386; Jewish Student Campus Climate Report, 308, 311; justice and, 11–12; Kesher Enoshi and, 97; mock checkpoint event at CMC and, 268, 269, 270, 271, 275, 276; MSJC and, 215; Oberlin College and, 373–74; social media, 12; transgender black

CPSIA information can be obtained
at www.ICGtesting.com
Printed in the USA
FSHW01n1828020818
51109FS